Religion and Society

Fire and the Sword

Understanding the Many Facets of Organized Islamism

Volume 1

RELIGION AND SOCIETY

Additional books in this series can be found on Nova's website under the Series tab.

Additional e-books in this series can be found on Nova's website under the e-books tab.

RELIGION AND SOCIETY

FIRE AND THE SWORD

UNDERSTANDING THE MANY FACETS OF ORGANIZED ISLAMISM

VOLUME 1

CHRISTOPHER ANGLIM

Copyright © 2018 by Nova Science Publishers, Inc.

All rights reserved. No part of this book may be reproduced, stored in a retrieval system or transmitted in any form or by any means: electronic, electrostatic, magnetic, tape, mechanical photocopying, recording or otherwise without the written permission of the Publisher.

We have partnered with Copyright Clearance Center to make it easy for you to obtain permissions to reuse content from this publication. Simply navigate to this publication's page on Nova's website and locate the "Get Permission" button below the title description. This button is linked directly to the title's permission page on copyright.com. Alternatively, you can visit copyright.com and search by title, ISBN, or ISSN.

For further questions about using the service on copyright.com, please contact:
Copyright Clearance Center
Phone: +1-(978) 750-8400   Fax: +1-(978) 750-4470   E-mail: info@copyright.com.

NOTICE TO THE READER

The Publisher has taken reasonable care in the preparation of this book, but makes no expressed or implied warranty of any kind and assumes no responsibility for any errors or omissions. No liability is assumed for incidental or consequential damages in connection with or arising out of information contained in this book. The Publisher shall not be liable for any special, consequential, or exemplary damages resulting, in whole or in part, from the readers' use of, or reliance upon, this material. Any parts of this book based on government reports are so indicated and copyright is claimed for those parts to the extent applicable to compilations of such works.

Independent verification should be sought for any data, advice or recommendations contained in this book. In addition, no responsibility is assumed by the publisher for any injury and/or damage to persons or property arising from any methods, products, instructions, ideas or otherwise contained in this publication.

This publication is designed to provide accurate and authoritative information with regard to the subject matter covered herein. It is sold with the clear understanding that the Publisher is not engaged in rendering legal or any other professional services. If legal or any other expert assistance is required, the services of a competent person should be sought. FROM A DECLARATION OF PARTICIPANTS JOINTLY ADOPTED BY A COMMITTEE OF THE AMERICAN BAR ASSOCIATION AND A COMMITTEE OF PUBLISHERS.

Additional color graphics may be available in the e-book version of this book.

Library of Congress Cataloging-in-Publication Data

ISBN: 978-1-53613-715-6

Published by Nova Science Publishers, Inc. † New York

Contents

Preface		ix
Acronyms and Abbreviations		xi
Introduction		xvii
Chronology		lvii
Islamism in the Middle East		1
Chapter 1	The 1920 Revolution Brigades	3
Chapter 2	Abdullah Azzam Martyr Battalion (AAMB) (Katlbat Al-Shahld)	7
Chapter 3	The Abis Brigade/"al-Muqawama al-Islamiyya fi Bahrain"/ "The Islamic Resistance in Bahrain"/Liwa Abis	9
Chapter 4	Abu Hafs al-Masri Brigade (AHMB)	11
Chapter 5	Abu Bakr al-Siddiq Fundamentalist Brigades (ABSB)/ the Salafist Brigades of Abu Bakr/ Al-Siddiq/Abu Bakr al Seddiq Brigades	13
Chapter 6	Adalet ve Kalkınma Partisi (AKP) (Justice and Development Party)	17
Chapter 7	Aden-Abyan Islamic Army/ Islamic Army of Aden (AAIA)	29
Chapter 8	Al-Ahbash/Ja.'Wiyyat Al-Mashari' Al-Khalriyya Al-Islamiyya/ Association of Islamic Philanthropic Projects/ Islamic Charity Projects Association (AICP)	33
Chapter 9	Al-Asalah al-Islamiyah/Al-Aslah Islamic Society/ Islamic Purity Society	35
Chapter 10	Al-Aqsa Martyrs' Brigade (AAMB)	37
Chapter 11	Al Mahdi Army/Jaysh al-Mahdi	39
Chapter 12	Al-Qaeda (AQ)	43
Chapter 13	Al-Qaeda in Iraq (AQI)	57

Chapter 14	Al-Qaeda in the Arabian Pennisula (AQAP)	61
Chapter 15	Al-Takfir Wal Al-Higra/Apostasy and Immigration (ATWH)	67
Chapter 16	Al-Wefaq/National Islamic Society/ Islamic National Accord Association	75
Chapter 17	Amal Movement/Lebanese Resistance Detachments, Movement of Hope, Movement of the Deprived (Harakat al-Mahrumin), Afwaj al Muqawamah al Lubnaniyyah (AMAL), Battalions of the Lebanese Resistance	79
Chapter 18	Amal/Al-Amal-al Islami/ Islamic Action Party (Bahrain)	81
Chapter 19	Ansar al-Islam (AI)/Supporter of Islam	85
Chapter 20	Ansar Bayt al Maqdis (ABM)	89
Chapter 21	Asbat Al-Ansari/The League of Followers (AaA)	91
Chapter 22	Association of Muslim Scholars (Iraq)	93
Chapter 23	Benevolence International Foundation (BIF)	95
Chapter 24	The Center Party (Hizb al-Wasat) (Egypt)	99
Chapter 25	Charitable Society for Social Welfare (CSSW)	101
Chapter 26	Committee for Solidarity with Arab and Middle Eastern Political Prisoners/Comité de soutien avec les prisonniers politiques et arabes et du Moyen-Orient - (CSPPA)	105
Chapter 27	Dawa Groups	107
Chapter 28	Democratic Front for the Liberation of Palestine (DFLP)	111
Chapter 29	Developer's Coalition/Abadgaran/(Iran)	113
Chapter 30	Egyptian Islamic Jihad (EIJ)/Vanguards of Conquest/ Jihad Group/Al-Jihad Al-Islami/ Islamic Jihad/	115
Chapter 31	Egyptian Islamist Political Parties	119
Chapter 32	Egyptian Salafist Movement	125
Chapter 33	Emni (Division of ISIS)	129
Chapter 34	Fatah Al-Islam/Conquest of Islam	133
Chapter 35	Fighting Vanguards of the Mujahidin/ Al-Talap Al-Muqatlla	135
Chapter 36	Freedom and Justice Party (FJP) (Egypt)	139
Chapter 37	Great Eastern Islamic Raiders' Front (IBDA-C)/ Buyuk Dogu Anincilar Cephest/Islami/ Great Islamic Eastern Warriors Front	141
Chapter 38	Hamas	143

Chapter 39	Hamas Iraq Hamas in Iraq/Hamas (IRA)/ Islamic Resistance Movement Hamas, Iraq: Al Fatah Al Islamy Brigades	149
Chapter 40	Haq Movement for Liberty and Democracy	153
Chapter 41	Hayat Thahrir al-Sham (Liberation of al-Sham Commission) (HTS)	157
Chapter 42	Hezbollah in Lebanon	159
Chapter 43	Hirak/Southern Movement/ al-Hirak al-Janubi	165
Chapter 44	Houthis	169
Chapter 45	Iran, Islamist Political Parties	177
Chapter 46	Islamic Action Front (IAF) (Jabhat al-Almat al-Islami) (IAF) (Jordan)	181
Chapter 47	Islamic Revolutionary Guard Corps	185
Chapter 48	Islamic State of Iraq and Syria (ISIS)/ Islamic State (IS)/ the Islamic State of Iraq and the Levant (ISIL)/ISIS	189
Chapter 49	Islamic State in Yemen (Wilayah Yemen/Sanaa/ Al Beyda/Aden-Bayan/Shaba/Hadramout)	205
Chapter 50	Jabhat Fateh Al-Sham (the Front for the Conquest of the Levant) (JFS), Formerly Known, as the Jabhat al Nusra li Ahl al Sham (or Al Nusra Front)	207
Chapter 51	Jaish al-Fatah Coalition	211
Chapter 52	Jaysh Rijal al-Tariqa al-Naqshbandia (JRTN), also Known as the Naqshbandi Army	213
Chapter 53	Khorasan Group (KG)	221
Chapter 54	Militant Clerics Association/Ruhaniyun/ Majma-yi-Ruhaniyyun-i-Mobarez (Iran)	223
Chapter 55	Milli Nizam Partisi/Party for National Order (MNP)	227
Chapter 56	Mujahedeen-e-Khalq Organization (MEK)/Mujahedin-e Khalq Organization (MEK or MKO) National Liberation Army of Iran (NLA)/People's Mojahedin of Iran (PMOI)/ National Council of Resistance (NCR)/National Council of Resistance of Iran (NCRI)/Muslim Iranian Student's Society	229
Chapter 57	Mujahidin Shura Council in the Environs of Jerusalem (MSC)	235
Chapter 58	Muslim Brotherhood	237
Chapter 59	Muslim Brotherhood in Jordan/Jordanian Muslim Brotherhood	245
Chapter 60	Muslim Brotherhood in Syria	247
Chapter 61	National Turkish Student Union (MTTB)	251

Chapter 62	Palestinian Islamic Jihad (PIJ)/Harakat al-Jihad al-Islami fi Filastin/Islamic Jihad/Islamic Jihad Palestine (IJP)/Islamic Jihad – Palestine Faction and Islamic Holy War	253
Chapter 63	Popular Front for the Liberation of Palestine – General Command (PFLP-GC)	257
Chapter 64	State of Sinai/Sinai Province of the Islamic State/Wilayat Sinai	259
Chapter 65	Supreme Council for Islamic Revolution in Iraq	263
Chapter 66	Takfiri Groups	267
Chapter 67	Tawhid and Jihad/Monotheism and Jihad	271
Chapter 68	Turkish Islamic Jihad (TIJ)	273
Chapter 69	Waliy Al-Faqih/The Jurist's Guardian	277
Chapter 70	World Islamic Front for Jihad Against Jews and Crusaders	279
Chapter 71	Yemeni Association for Reform/Al-Tajammu' Al-Yemeni Li Al-Islah/Tajammu' al-Yamani li'l-Islah	281
Glossary		287
About the Author		301
Index		303

PREFACE

This guide assists its readers in understanding Islamist groups and the phenomenon of Islamism worldwide. While focusing on contemporary groups, this work includes the historical context needed to provide readers a better understanding of the formation and evolution of Islamist groups. The work provides a detailed explanation of selected groups in individual entries while providing cross-references to others. We have emphasized the most important Islamist groups, such as Al-Qaeda, Hezbollah, (ISIS (also known IS), Boko Haram, and the Muslim Brotherhood. While the guide includes smaller groups, they are not given extensive coverage. The work distinguishes between radical and moderate Islamist groups and explains their beliefs and actions, to provide a better understanding of their perspectives.

This guide covers: 1) the reasons, purposes, and development of Islamist groups; and, 2) the ideas and rhetoric that distinguish Islamist groups from the other Islamic groups.

The book lists the entries alphabetically and has transliterated them. The glossary provides access to the English forms of these and other terms. Theological and political concepts such as dar al-harb, jima, and jitra are presented in their transliterated forms. The chronology provides additional historical context.

The guide does not use a single, consistent phonetic transliteration of the names or words cited in this dictionary that were originally written in Arabic. Popular literature and media use familiarized users with inexact transliterations of Arabic and Persian words. This popular use has surpassed efforts by linguists to develop a consistent, universally observed practice of transliteration for these words. For instance, more readers are more acquainted with the Koran than with the more precise Quran, or with Hezbollah rather than Hezbollah. Therefore, to ensure that this reference volume is as accessible as possible to a wider readership, it uses current and more common spellings rather than more unfamiliar, alternative spellings. This work phonetically transliterates other Arabic and Persian names whenever a popular term was not already current.

Since the general public is more familiar with several Islamist groups with names given them by English language media outlets, rather than the language of the country or ethnic group in which they originated, this guide lists them under their most commonly used name as opposed to their formal, or the official name. To find such organizations, readers may search for the formal or official in the list of acronyms and abbreviations, where it is followed by the English name under which the organization may be found. Those acronyms, which are already in common use in news coverage of the group, are used whenever possible.

This guide lists the groups by their more popular names, as opposed to their English transliterations. For example, Hezbollah is listed rather than "Party of God". Groups, however, those are more commonly known by their French names, such as the Algerian group Front Islamique du Salut (Jue du Salut), will be found under "Islamic Salvation Front". Cross-references are included to help our readers. In addition to the cross-references, readers should use the list of acronyms and abbreviations which provides the group's name associated with the acronym.

References to the "Muslim Brotherhood" refer to the Egyptian Muslim Brotherhood unless otherwise mentioned.

Special thanks Professor Mohammad Al-Khawas of the University of the District of Columbia for his counsel and assistance.

ACRONYMS AND ABBREVIATIONS

This list includes all abbreviations found in this handbook. Whenever possible, this work uses acronyms based on the English versions of names. When, however, the organization has become well-known in its original language, this work uses the acronym based on that language.

AAMB	–	Al-Aqsa Martyrs' Brigade (al-Fatah Group) (Palestine)
ABIM	–	Jabhat al-Tahrir al-'Arabiyah Angkatan Belia Islam Malaysia/Movement of the Malaysian Youth
AI	–	Al-Irihad AI-Islami/Islamic Union Armed Islamic Group/Groupe Islamique Arme (GIA)(Algeria)
AIS	–	Arme Islamique du Salut/Islamic Salvation Anny Alliance for Justice and Democracy/Movement for Renewal (Algeria)
AKP	–	Adalet ve Kalkinma Partisi (Justice and Development Party) (Turkey)
ALF	–	Arab Liberation Front (group within the PLO) (Palestine)
Al-Aqsa	–	Al Aqsa Martyrs' Brigade (al-Fatah Group)
AML	–	Association of Muslim Lawyers (Great Britain)
ANO	–	Abu Nidal Organization (Palestine)
APHC	–	All-Parties Hurriyat Conference (Kashmir)
AQ	–	Al-Qaeda (International)
AQAP	–	Al-Qaeda in the Arabian Peninsula (Yemen, International)
AQI	–	Al-Qaeda in Iraq
AQIM	–	Al-Qaeda in the Islamic Maghreb, aka, the Salafist Group for Preaching and Combat (GSPC)
AS	–	Ansar al-Sunna (Iraq)
ASG	–	Abu Sayyaf Group (Philippines)
AW	–	As-Sunnah Wal-Janunah/Adherents of the Sunna and the Community (Somalia)
AUM	–	Al-Umar Mujahedeen/The Mujahedeen of Umar Benevolence International Foundation (International)
BIP	–	British Islamic Party
BKP	–	Badan Komuuikasi Pemuda Masjid Indonesia/Association for Communication between the Youth of Indonesian Mosques
BRN	–	Barisan Revolusi Nasional/Front of the National Revolution (Thailand)

BSO	–	Black September Organization (Palestine, International)
CAIR	–	Council on Islamic American Relations (United States)
CSAMPP	–	Committee for Solidarity with Arab and Middle Eastern Political Prisoners/Comite de soutien aux prisonniers politiques arabes et du Moyen-Orient (International)
CSSW	–	Charitable Society for Social Welfare (International)
Daesh	–	al-Dawla al-Islamiya al-Iraq al-Sham (also known as Islamic State, Islamic State of the Levant, or Islamic State of Iraq and Syria (International)
DDII	–	Dewan Dakwah Islamiyah Indonesia/Council of Predication for Indonesian Islam (Indonesia)
DeM	–	Dukhtaraan-e-Millati/Daughters of the Nation (Kashmir)
DFLP	–	Democratic Front for the Liberation of Palestine
DHDS	–	Dhamat Hourmet Daawa Salafia (Algeria)
EIJ	–	Egyptian Islamic Jihad
ETIM	–	East Turkestan Islamic Movement
FIS	–	From Islamique du Salut/Islamic Salvation Front (Algeria)
FIT	–	Front Islamique Tunisien/Tunisian Islamic Front (Tunisia)
FKAS	–	Forum Komunikasi Ahlu Sunnah wal-Jama'a/Forum of the Communication of the Faith of the Sunna and the Prophet (Indonesia)
FLN	–	Front de Liberation Nationale/National Liberation Front (Algeria)
FPL	–	Front Pembelam Islam/Front of the Defenders of Islam (Indonesia)
FRC	–	Fatah Revolutionary Council (Abu Nidal Organization) (Palestine)
FSA	–	Free Syrian Army
GeM	–	Gera Aceh Merdekal/Movement for the Independence of Aceh (Indonesia)
GIA	–	Group Islamique Arme/Armed Islamic Group (Algeria)
GICM	–	Group Islamique Combattant Morocain/Moroccan Islamic Combatant Group (also referred to as Moroccan Islamic Fighting Group
GMIP	–	Gerakan Mujahidin Islam Pattani/Movement of Holy Warriors of Islam Pattani (Thailand)
GMPR	–	Gabungan Melayu Patani Rayal/Association for a Large Malaysian Pattani Group Islamique Anne/Armed Islamic Group
GPII	–	Gemkan Pemuda Islam Indonesia/Movement of the Young Indonesian Muslims
GSPC	–	Groupe Salafiste pour la Predication et le Combat/Salafist Group for Preaching and Combat (Algeria)
Hamas	–	Ḥarakat al-Muqāwamah al-'Islāmiyyah/Islamic Resistance Movement (Palestine)
HeIG	–	Hizb-e-Islami Gulbuddin Hizb-ul-Mujahideen/Party of the Mujahedeen Barakat Al-Shabaab Al-Mujahideen\ Mujahideen Youth Movement (also referred to simply as al-Shabaab) (Somalia)
HM	–	Hizbul Mijahideen (Kashmir)
HT	–	Hizb al Thrir, aka, Tahrir al-Islami/Islamic Liberation Party (Tunisia, Indonesia)
HuA	–	Harakat-ul-Ansar/Movement of the Helpers (Kashmir)
HuJI	–	Harakat-ul-Jihad AI-Islamil/Islamic Struggle Movement (Lebanon)

HuJB	–	Harakat-ul-Jihad Al-Islami Bangladesh/Islamic Struggle Movement in Bangladesh
HuM	–	Harakat-ul-Mujahideen/Mujahedeen Movement (Pakistan, Kashmir)
HuMAA	–	Harakat-ul-Mujahideen Al-Alami/The Global Mujahedeen (International)
IAI	–	Islamic Army in Iraq
IAJCM	–	Islamic Afghanistan Justice and Charity Movement.
ICU	–	Islamic Courts Union (Sudan)
IF	–	Islamic Front (Syria)
IJU	–	Islamic Jihad Union (Uzbekistan)
ILO	–	Islamic Liberation Organization (Palestine)
IMU	–	Islamic Movement of Uzbekistan
IRP	–	Islamic Renaissance Party of Tajikistan International Security Assistance Force
IS	–	Islamic State (Iraq, Syria, International)
ISI	–	Inter-Services Intelligence (Pakistan's Intelligence Agency)
IMTIMU	–	Islamic Movement of Turkistan Islamic Movement of Uzbekistan
ISCI	–	Islamic Supreme Council of Iraq
ISE	–	Islamic Society of Engineers (Iran)
ISI	–	Inter-Services Intelligence (Pakistan)
ISI	–	Islamic State of Iraq (Iraq)
ISIL	–	Islamic State of Iraq and the Levant (Iraq, Syria, International)
IUP	–	Islamic Unity Party of Afghanistan/Hizb-e-Wahdat e-JaI Jamaat al-'adl wa al-Ihsan
JAT	–	Jamaat Al-Tawhid wa AI-Jihad/Group of Monotheism and Jihad/Jamaat-ul-Ulema-e-Islam/Assembly of the Islamic Clergy (Iraq, Jordan)
JeI	–	Jamaat-e-Islami/Islamic Party (Pakistan)
JeI	–	Jamaat-e-Islami/Jammu and Kashmir Islamic Party
JeM	–	Jaish-e-Muhammad/Army of Muhammad (Pakistan, Kashmir)
JI	–	Jemaah Islamiyah (Southeast Asia)
JKIF	–	Jammu and Kashmir Islamic Front Jammu and Kashmir
JRF	–	Jihad and Reform Front (Iraq)
JRTN	–	Jaysh Rijal al-Tariqah aJ-Naqshabandiai/Army of the Naqshabandi Sufists (Iraq)
JuM	–	Jamaat-ul-Mujahideen/Assembly of the Mujahedeen (Bangladesh)
JuMB	–	Jamaat-ul-Mujahideen in Bangladesh/Assembly of the Mujahedeen in Bangladesh
KAPAK	–	Komite Aksi Penanggulungan Akribat Krisis/Action Committee for a Crisis Solution
KG	–	Khorasan Group (Afghanistan)
KIuSDDI	–	Komite Indonesia untuk Solidal'itas dengan Dunia Islam/Indonesia Committee for Solidarity with the Muslim World
KRN	–	Karnpulan Revolusi Nasional/National Revolutionary Movement (Indonesia)
LDKD	–	Lembaga Dakwah Kampus/Dakwah Campus Centers Indonesia
LeJ	–	Lashkar-e-Jabbar/Army of the Mighty (Kashmir, South Asia)
LeJ	–	Laskar-e-Jhangvi/Army of Jhangvi (Pakistan)

LeT	–	Lashkar-e-Tayyibal/Army of the Pure (Pakistan)
LH	–	Lashkar Hizbullahi Group of the Party of God (Indonesia)
LIFG	–	Libyan Islamic Fighting Group (also referred to as Libyan Islamic Combatant Group)
MAB	–	Muslim Association of Britain
MB	–	Muslim Brotherhood (Egypt, International)
MBG	–	Misuari Breakaway Group (Philippines)
MeK	–	Mujahideen-e-Khalq/People's Mujahideen Organization of Iran
MIA	–	Movement of Islamic Action (Iraq)
MILF	–	Moro Islamic Liberation Front (Philippines)
MLF	–	Moro Liberation Front (Philippines)
MMeA	–	Muttallida Majlis-e-Amal/United Council of Action (Pakistan)
MMI	–	Majlis Mujahideen Indonesia/Council of Indonesia
MMS	–	Mujahideen Shura/Council (Iraq)
MSP	–	Movement for the Society of Peace (Algeria)
NDFB	–	National Democratic Front of Bodoland (Assam, India)
NIF	–	National Islamic Front (Afghanistan)
NII	–	Negara Islam Indonesia/Islamic State of Indonesia
NTC	–	National Transitional Council (Libya)
PDPA	–	People's Democratic Party of Afghanistan
PFLP	–	Popular Front for the Liberation of Palestine
PIJ	–	Palestinian Islamic Jihad
PISM	–	Parti Islam Se-Malaysia
PJD	–	Parti de la Justice et du Development/Justice and Development Party (in Arabic: Hizb AI-Adala wa AI-Tanniia)
PMIP	–	Pan-Malaysian Islamic Party
PLO	–	Palestinian Liberation Organization
PRMI	–	People's Resistance Movement of Iran/Jund Allah in Iran
PULO	–	Patani United Liberation Organization/United Organization for the Pattani Liberation (Thailand)
RaM	–	Rabitat al-Al am af-Islami/Muslim World League (Saudi Arabia, International)
RSM	–	Rajah Suleiman Movement (Philippines)
RSO	–	Rohingya Solidarity Organization (Burma)
SGPC	–	Salafi Group for Preaching and Combat (Algeria)
SIMI	–	Student Islamic Movement of India
SJ	–	Salafiya Jihadia (Morocco)
SSPA	–	Sipah-e-Sahaba Pakistan/Army of the Friends of Sahaba (Pakistan)
TCP	–	Tunisian Combatant Group
TII	–	Tentam Islam Indonesiai/Indonesian Islamic Army
TeJP	–	Tehrik-e-Jafaria Pakistan/Movement of the Pakistani Shiites
TJP	–	Tahrik-i-Jafaria (Pakistan)
TuM	–	Tehrik-ul-Mujahideen/Mujahedeen Movement
UDP	–	United Development Party (Indoensia)
UJC	–	United Jihad Council (Kashmir)
ULFA	–	United Front of Assam (India)

UMNO – United Malay National Organization (Malaysia)
UTO – United Tajik Opposition (Tajikistan)

INTRODUCTION

A. OVERVIEW

To place the people and organizations discussed in this guide to Islamism in context, this introduction discusses both Islamism and Islamic Fundamentalism. It discusses them as separate but often related phenomena, and proceeds to discuss their impact, significance, and role. The introduction provides essential background to the often confusing, controversial, but highly important topic of Islamism.

This work emphasizes the contemporary Islamic fundamentalist groups that emerged after the First World War (1914-1918) and through the present. The work also includes groups that existed before that conflict as necessary to provide historical context for the discussion of currently active groups. This work discusses the historical groups that have influenced or are referred to by contemporary events to provide historical and contemporary context.

In the section on Islamism, this part of the introduction discusses the struggle to describe the phenomenon that became known as Islamism as commonly understood today, the evolution of understanding Islamism as a concept, how Islamists have interpreted Islamism, the Issue of Defining Islamism, The distinction between Islam and Islamism, the meaning of Islamism, the various types of Islamism (such as Process Islamism and Revolutionary Islamism) and the distinction between them, the origins development of Modern Islamism, the Significance of the caliphate in Islamism, the different manifestations of Islamism, the goals of Islamism, and Islamism and terrorism,[1] and crucial contemporary issues such as whether Islamism and Democracy can be compatible or coexist?

In this discussion of Islamism, the reader should be aware that neither this author nor this guide condones or supports Islamophobia. Islamophobia is defined as an irrational fear, hatred, or prejudice against either Muslims or the religion of Islam. To the contrary, this work hopes to make a constructive contribution to the body of knowledge on Islamist groups, and to help dispel Islamophobia.

---

[1] Terrorism, in this Guide, refers to a systematic violent assault on innocent civilian populations (i.e.., those involved with or unable to affect the issues at dispute between the terrorist and their avowed enemies.

B. ISLAM

This section of the Introduction provides basic background on Islam as a religion, focusing on such issues as how Islam was created and developed. This work covers Islamist groups worldwide, including in nations where Muslims are in a minority, as long as these group claim to be motivated by an Islamic ideology.

1. The Rise and Growth of Islam

To understand Islamic Fundamentalism or Islamism, one must first understand the history of Islam. This being said, however, the reader should understand that within its mainstream traditions, Islam teaches piety, virtue, and tolerance. It should also be stressed that nothing in Islam advocates the radicalism, violence, and intolerance, of the few who have presented a perverted interpretation of that religion.

Muslims believe that the Prophet Mohammed, the founder of Islam, is Allah's last and most important prophet. A merchant and trader, Mohammed was born in Mecca, in present-day Saudi Arabia, in 570 AD. The Koran, Islam's Holy Book, emphasizes the five pillars of Islam (the declaration of faith, regular prayers, distribution of wealth, fasting, and pilgrimage).

Islam emerged among tribal people who lived in trading communities in the Arabian Peninsula during the seventh century. Islam spread throughout the Middle East facilitated by upheaval caused by querulous tribes in Mecca and Medina, the decline of the Persian and Byzantine empires, and the fact that Islam was adopted by Arab traders who traveled widely and brought the Koran to areas where Islam later flourished with the empires created by its adherents. Religious envoys and their armies came to several Arab nations. The Arab tribes eventually became united. In 622, Mohammad besieged Mecca with an army of 10,000 of his followers.

Tribal leaders emerged as powerful rulers, as Muslims increased their political prowess throughout the Arabian Peninsula. Doctrinal differences emerged related to power struggles that arose during the formation of ruling elites. These different religious doctrines eventually became the bases of various Islamic sects over the ensuing centuries. Millions of people converted to Islam during this time, as Arab armies created an empire that extended from Spain to South Asia.

While Western Europe developed slowly during the Medieval era, the Islamic world preserved the scientific knowledge of the ancient Greeks and Romans, and made significant progress in art and architecture, scientific innovations, and mathematics (including inventing algebra). This became known as the golden era of Muslim Civilization.

Beginning in the late fifteenth century, and following the European Renaissance, much of the Muslim world began to stagnate. In response, the ruling Muslim elites sought to consolidate their power, privileges, and prerogatives. In Europe, a modern industrial economy developed, which eventually lead to greater political dominance. From the 16th through the early 20th century, Britain and France colonized several majority Muslim nations.

2. Origins and Persistence of the Shia-Sunni Divide

While Islam is composed of several different sects, nearly 90 percent of the world's Muslim's are "Sunni". The name originates from the practices and teachings of Muhammad as recorded in his Sunnah (which literally means the path or way). Between 10 to 15 percent of the world's Muslims are Shia, who live primarily in Iran, Iraq, and Lebanon.

Sunni and Shia Muslims have peacefully co-existed for centuries worldwide and share many fundamental beliefs and practices. Sunnis and Shiites, however, have disagreed on certain religious and political issues very early in Islam's history. While there are few differences between Shias and Sunnis regarding belief and practice, the two branches differ significantly in doctrine, ritual, law, theology, and religious organization.

The Sunni and Shia branches of Islam have sharply diverged due to conflicts such as who should succeed Mohammed as Islam's leaders. Shias believed that the successor must be from the Prophet's family while Sunnis believed that the successor must be from the Prophet's tribe (the Quraysh).

The Shias, thus, supported Ali ibn Abi Talib, the Prophet's nephew and son in law, while other Muslims supported some of Mohammed's "companions". After being rejected three times, Ali became caliph in 656 CE. He was murdered in 661 CE.

Ali's supporters, referred to as the "Shiat Ali" (from which the name Shiite originates), beseeched Hussein, son of Hazrat Ali and grandson of the Prophet Muhammad, to seize control of the caliphate. The reigning caliph, Yazid, however, responded by sending Umayyad troops that killed Hussein in Karbala (in modern day Iraq) in 680 CE. Hussein's martyrdom became Shia's defining tragedy.

3. The Modern Shia-Sunni Divide

Iran is the world's leading Shiite nation. The Shah of Iran followed a policy of rapid modernization and Westernization, which exacerbated Iran's social crisis of the 1970's. In 1979, Ayatollah Ruhollah Khomeini (1902-1989) and his followers overthrew the Shah and installed a theocracy (a religiously-based state, governed by jurists or religious leaders) for the first time in Shiite history. Khomeini's major contribution to fundamentalist Islamist ideology was the concept that only Islamic jurists most knowledgeable in Islamic law should govern the nation. Khomeini preached for a revolution to replace existing governments with governance by Islamic jurists. In Khomeini's view, an Islamic State could be created violently if necessary.

Islamic fundamentalists worldwide began to view Iran's Islamic Revolution as a political success and a model for their own nations. They also believed that the Islamic Revolution was divinely ordained because the Iranian regime survived an expensive eight year war with Iraq, the freezing of its assets overseas, the destruction of its oil industry, and international sanctions. The Iranian government soon sought to expand its influence by creating jihadist organizations such as Hezbollah in Lebanon and agitating Shiites in Bahrain, Iraq, and Saudi Arabia's Eastern Province.

The Saudi monarchy responded to Iran's challenge of its religious leadership of the world's Muslims by spending heavily to build mosques and schools, establishing large organizations to promote Wahhabism, prostelyzing its puritanical interpretation of Sunni Islam, and publishing materials depicting Shiites as heretics, and Christians and Jews as subhuman. These Saudi initiatives, however, unintentionally and unexpectedly fostered the growth of extremist groups such as al-Qaeda and ISIS.

From 1990 through the present, sectarian tensions have oscillated in Saudi Arabia. After Ayatollah Khomeini's death, Iran's Islamist militancy has diminished, while the Saudi government had taken steps such as its first national dialog with its increasingly restive Shiite population in 2004.

Despite being a theocracy, Iranian government's national geopolitical interests, rather than Islamic ideology, are the driving force of Iranian foreign policy. Despite the Iranian regime's staunch anti-communist rhetoric, the Iranian government did not strongly object to the Soviet intervention in Afghanistan. It also supported Christian Armenia in its disputes with Shiite Azerbaijan. Iran did this, partly, to deter Azeri nationalism from spreading among Iran's substantial Azeri minority. It also cooperated with Russia to limit Turkish and Western influence in Central Asia in the post-Soviet era.

Iran has generally refrained from supporting Islamist groups in Central Asian nations apparently to avoid antagonizing Russia, its leading source of weapons and technology and an ally in support of Bashar Al-Assad, President of Syria.

C. Islamic Fundamentalism

1. Understanding Islamic Fundamentalism

Islamic fundamentalism (Arabic: usul, the "fundamentals") is a belief advocating adhering to Islam's fundamentals, especially the Koran and the Sunnah (traditions).

This section of the introduction provides a brief background on the semantics of fundamentalism, as the various fundamentalist groups claim to be faithful to Islam, and these groups claim to be motivated by the teachings of this religion, and how fundamentalists use Islamic Holy Writings (especially the Koran) to justify their beliefs and actions. This section then will consider issues such as the various approaches to Islamic fundamentalism, the scope of Islamic fundamentalism, the evolution of Islamic fundamentalism in one's individual life, political Islamic fundamentalism, and Jihadi Islamic Fundamentalism.

This section of the introduction presents both the historical context and the contemporary forces that motivate Islamic fundamentalism, to help promote a better understanding of Fundamentalist Islam's history and beliefs, including those on such controversial topics such as jihad, martyrdom, dress restrictions, and women's rights.

2. The Semantics of Fundamentalism

Fundamentalism entails the strict adherence to the basics of a religion. Fundamentalism is present in all religions and fundamentalism is not unique to Islam. Religious fundamentalism,

Introduction

whether moderate or radical, is a reaction to contemporary social and political phenomena. Thus, fundamentalism commonly describes the ultra-conservative belief systems of certain faith groups including those within Islam, Christianity, and Judaism.

In the Western world, fundamentalism historically has been based on a concept that emerged in the United States in the early twentieth century to describe a particular conservative type of evangelical Christianity, which stressed the absolute and uncompromising literalist interpretation of the Bible and that the world is in a state of spiritual decay. During the 1920s, due to the influence of many of the leading intellectuals of the time, Americans increasingly began to perceive that fundamentalism was a negative and largely uninformed reaction of relatively uneducated people who rejected the emerging new modernity of the time. Thus, many Americans associated fundamentalism with anti-intellectualism, and backward thinking. The term, fundamentalism, thus, initially was commonly used to describe certain Protestants who rejected various forms of social change (including changes in sexual behavior).

Until the late 1970s, Americans and Europeans primarilly used the term "fundamentalist" to refer to Protestant Christians who accepted the literal intepretation and irrerency of the Bible. A shift occurred in 1979 after Iran's "Islamic Revolution". Beginning at this time, some Muslims and Muslim groups began to be described as Muslim fundamentalists. The news media and other commentators used the term "Islamic Fundamentalism" by analogy to provide a context for Westerners to comprehend events that many found shocking and uncomprehensible. In the late 1990s, *The Concise Oxford Dictionary of Current English*, acknowledged how the usage had changed when it defined fundamentalism as the "strict maintenance of ancient or fundamental doctrines of any religion, especially Islam."[2]

Islamic fundamentalism is challenging to adequately and aaccurately define. Some commentators claim that Islamic religious doctrine requires all Muslims to be fundamentalists to some degree. Using the term "fundamentalism to discuss Islam, however also may confuse rather than clarify as Islam has a very different faith tradition and history than Christianity. The reader, then, understand the difficulties of using the term fundamentalist when applied to Islam. One should also be careful of the emotional connotations that accompany the term. This label like many other labels has been common throughout history to identify a dangerous "other" against which "our side" can unite against. In the contemporary world, many people fear what they perceive as "Islamic Fundamentalism", without fully understanding what the term means. Clearly, the terrorist events since September 11, 2001 make Americans concerned that Islamic Fundamentalists are attempting to destroy American society and its freedoms. While terrorism is a genuine threat to the United States and to Americans, and some of this terrorism is perpetrated by Jihadi extremists, who have misused and perverted Islam, the reader should avoid the misunderstanding that Islamic Fundamentalism is necessary equivalent to Jihadi extremism, or that all pious Muslims are covert terrorists. The reader must develop a sophisticated understanding of what Islamic Fundamentalism is and what it is not, the different aspects of Islamic Fundamentalism, and what motivates it.

One purpose of this guide, then, is to avoid the misunderstandings involved with Islam and Islamic Fundamentalism and build bridges of understanding between peoples of different

---

[2] Henry W. Fowler, *The Concise Oxford Dictionary of Current English* (Oxford: Clarendon Press, 1990).

faiths, cultures, and ideologies. In early 2018, with the world enmeshed in such incredible violence, upheaval, and fear, there has never been a need to build such bridges to help work for peace and understanding for all the diverse peoples of the world.

3. What Is the Meaning of "Islamic Fundamentalism"?

In addition to the lack of a consensus on how Islamic fundamentalism should be defined, there is controversy over whether the term "Islamic fundamentalism" should be used at all. Many scholars and commentators recommend using alternative terms term, such as "puritanical", "Islamic revivalism", or "Radical Islam". Other commentators, however, believe that the phrase, Islamic Fundamentalism, is now well-established, and, therefore, acceptable to use.

Muslim scholars including the contemporary Syrian philosopher Sadiq Jalal al-Azm accepts the term fundamentalism because the ideology of many of these Islamist groups demands an immediate return to Islamic 'basics' and 'fundamentals'. Thus, these groups can be reasonably described as "Fundamentalist".

"Fundamentalism", as previously mentioned, began being widely used as a term in the early 20th century to describe various Protestant denominations that taught the literal divine origin and inerrancy of the Bible. Those sects also rejected a liberal and modernist theology that presented a more critical and historical interpretation of the Bible. In terms of Islam, only a small number of Muslim theologians follow a liberal or modernist approach to the Koran. Muslims generally are fundamentalists in interpreting the Koran. Muslim fundamentalists, unlike other Muslims and how Christian fundamentalists approach the Bible, interpret the Koran in a scholastic and legalistic approach. Islamic Fundamentalists claim to derive their beliefs from the Koran, the traditions involving Mohammed, the Prophet, and several theological and legal works. Traditionalist fundamentalism views a sense of continuity between the founding texts of Islam and the commentators of those texts.

Some commentators believe term the Islamic Fundamentalism is misleading, because of its association with extremism, terrorism, and anti-Westernism. These commentators often recommend alternative terms such as "Islamic revivalism". Other commentators criticize use of the term, "Islamic Fundamentalism", because, many liberal, progressive, or moderate Muslims may describe themselves as "usulis" (fundamentalist) without fully understanding the negative associations the term has in the Western World. In the Islamic context, arguably, a more accurate description of the fanatical reductionism and narrow-minded literalism of extremist Islamist groups would be with a term such as "puritanical". This term, however, may invoke a particular historical paradigm for many westerners, and thus, may be misleading.

"Radical Islam" may better describe several Islamist groups that emerged since the 1920's, beginning with the rise of the Muslim Brotherhood, as these groups are associated with unprecedented extremist militancy, and, thus do not entail a reversion to the fundamentals of the past.

More than a solely religious issue, Islamic fundamentalism should also be considered a worldwide revolutionary one because this group pursues a combination of radical, social, religious and political objectives.

4. The Emergence of Modern Fundamentalist Islam

Wahhabism, one of the first major Islamic fundamentalist groups, emerged in the late 1700's. Muhammad bin Abd al-Wahhab, a Saudi theologian, called for what he believed was the removal of impure practices from Islam and a return to a fundamentalist interpretation of the Koran and Hadiths. Currently, Wahhabi Islam remains a powerful influence in Saudi Arabia, which has the strictest laws in the Muslim world.

The modern Islamic fundamentalist groups trace their origins to the late nineteenth century. These groups then grew in popularity and expanded from the nineteenth through the twenty-first centuries.

During the Cold War (1946-1990), the British and US governments facilitated the growth of fundamentalist Islamist groups in the Middle East and South Asia, by funding and arming them because they viewed these groups as potential allies against Communism. By the 1970's the Islamists were important supporters of several Middle Eastern governments, including those in Egypt, which had become an important U.S. ally.

Billions of dollars of Saudi oil wealth facilitated the spread of Wahhabism throughout the world since the 1970's. These funds helped financed Wahhabi-based schools, books, scholarships, and mosques. The Saudis were motivated to do this partly to contain Iranian Shiite influence, which grew after the Shah of Iran was overthrown and Ayatollah Khomeini's rose to power in 1979.

By the late 1970's, several fundamentalist groups were becoming increasingly militant and were growing more hostile to the Western-supported governments of many Muslim-majority nations. The Shah's downfall also represented dramatic changes in the political landscape of the Middle East. Subsequently fundamentalist militants initiated a civil war in Algeria, caused a near-civil war in Egypt, and fought in the Afghan-Soviet War (1979-1989).

The collaboration between militant Islamist groups and the United States government was closest during the Afghan-Soviet War. The United States, along with the Pakistani government, actively supported, financed, and provided military training to the Islamists (the mujahideen). These groups included al-Qaeda. The Saudis also supported and armed the Afghan militias against the Soviets in Afghanistan.

5. The Central Role of the Koran in Islamic Fundamentalism

The term, "Islamic Fundamentalism", lacks a universally accepted definition. In this work, Islamic fundamentalism refers to a belief system that requires an extremely strict adherence to the Koran and the Sunnah (Muslims are required to live their lives according to Muhammad's teachings). Islamic fundamentalists believe that the Koran is without error and God's literal word. They also believe that Muslims must strictly follow the practices and moral rules promulgated by the Koran. Islamic fundamentalism has two core principles: the belief that Islamic law (the sharia) is the only legitimate means to regulate human activity (whether individually, socially, and politically), and the belief an Islamic state or government is required to establish a genuine Muslim society. Islamic fundamentalists also believe that Islamic law is essential to establish a genuinely Islamic state and society. Islamic

Fundamentalists further reject any separation between religious and political affairs, a position that directly contradicts modern democratic principles, including the separation of religion and government and freedom of worship. The Koran, however, teaches that religious belief is both personal and a matter of free choice, and the Sharia states that each person may freely choose his or her religious belief.

Islamic fundamentalism stresses a return to the "fundamentals", in part, because fundamentalists believe that Westernization had corrupted the "sanctity" or "purity" of Islam. Islamic fundamentalists further argue that returning to Islam's roots will preserve the faith and provide for a morally just life for its believers. They stress the traditional Islam of the seventh century during the lives of Muhammad, his companions, and the four subsequent rulers (caliphs).

Although fundamentalists claim that adhering to "tradition" is a major part of their belief system, some commentators have criticized them for distorting or ignoring how Islam has historically been practiced.

Muslims perceive fundamentalism in very different ways. Many view fundamentalist beliefs and practices as the means to become a better Muslim. Other Muslims believe that being an observant Muslim must go beyond prayer or fasting, and must include forming a just, moral, Islam-based society. Many Muslims strongly distinguish between Islamic fundamentalists who are genuinely devout in following Islam as opposed to extremists, who misuse religion for radical political purposes.

Contemporary Islamic fundamentalist groups promote their various social and political goals worldwide. Islamic fundamentalism, however, is not synonymous with Islam as a religion. Extremists have grossly misused Islam by claiming that Islam sanctions violence. This violence has been fueled by a confluence of dysfunctional economic, political, and social conditions in many majority Muslim nations (including Egypt). Increasing populations, chronic underdevelopment, and declining standards of living, along with severe income inequality exacerbates conditions that give rise to fundamentalism. Also, radical extremists have grotesquely misinterpreted Islamic texts to provide religious justification for violence and extremism.

Islamic Fundamentalists believe that efforts to restore a pure Islam must be all-encompassing and that Islam is the sole means to resolve all human problems, whether they are matters of public policy or private conduct. Thus, Islamic Fundamentalists do not consider Islam to be solely a private matter of faith. They believe in a religion with an immutable faith, revealed by God, which governs every part of human life. They perceive their faith as a complete ideology that governs every aspect of life in the world. The law and ideology that fundamentalists promote may only be implemented by establishing pure Islamic governance. They view the quest to empower Islam as God's will and a sacred purpose and one that some Islamists believe can legitimately be accomplished done through coercion, deceit, or violence.

Many commentators of Muslim fundamentalist groups frequently express concern that Islamism poses a profound threat to the modern nation-state, secularism, peace, the global economy, and global domestic institutions. They argue that Islamism's view of religion and politics as one and inseparable is difficult to reconcile with Western ideas of pluralism and the separation of religion and state. Specifically, they express concerns with some some provisions of Islamic Law (the Sharia) that run contrary to modern ideas of human rights, including the limiting of women's rights and requiring stoning or amputations as penalties for crimes.

6. The Islamic Fundamentalists and Religious Texts

Islamic fundamentalists believe that Islam is based on the Koran, Hadith, and Sunnah. They consider the Koran as the inerrant and literal word of God, and that Muslims must strictly adhere to religious practices and moral codes prescribed in the Koran. Reformist fundamentalists oppose tradition, the commentaries, various types of popular religious practices (such as maraboutism, or, the cult of saints), deviations, and superstitions. As reformist fundamentalists, they accept and interpret the Koran as understood by the first three generations of Islam. During the Eighteenth Century, these beliefs were promoted by Shah Waliallah (1703-1762) in India and Muhammad ibn Abd-al-Wahhab (1703-1791) did the same in the Arabian Peninsula. Reformist fundamentalism is often associated with contemporary Salafism.

Salafi or Wahhabi clerics believe that reverence for shrines or saints is un-Islamic and that such practices are not genuinely Islamic religious practices. They believe that these devotions are polytheistic (the worship of multiple Gods). Thus, they demanded that the temples and tombs of Sufi saints or holy men be destroyed. Heretical innovations and superstitions, they believe, must be destroyed to purify Islam by every means necessary including violence and coercion. Salafis or Wahhabis call for a global jihad and strict literal interpretation of the Koran. They believe that because some leaders of contemporary Muslim societies who allegedly refuse to impose Sharia, are apostates, and should be killed.

7. The Evolution of Islamic Fundamentalism

Many fundamentalist Muslims adhere to a sharply dualistic ideology in which all people are either part of the group or against it. This belief then influences how Islamist fundamentalists interact with peoples of other faiths and beliefs, and the secular West. Islamic fundamentalists believe paganism (jahiliyyah) as encompassing all non-Islam thought.

Before the Soviet Union collapsed in 1991, Islamic fundamentalists viewed communists and all atheists as their primary enemies. Many Islamic fundamentalists became Arab soldiers (mujahedeen) who fought the Soviets in the Soviet-Afghan War (1979-1989). After the 1991 Gulf War and even more following the September 11, 2001, attacks, Islamic fundamentalists have perceived "Western culture" and "US imperialism" as evil and morally decadent. Islamic fundamentalists perceive that both the previous (the Communist) and current (the western world) enemies which have had or have a significant military presence in Muslim majority nations and sought to transform these nations to forsake Islam in favor of foreign values. While Islamists perceive Communists as atheists, they view Westerners as either Christian crusaders-invaders of Muslim nations or materialistic pagans. While Islamic fundamentalism is a major source of opposition to the West and secular modernism within the Muslim world, radical Islamic fundamentalists are only a minority of the total Muslim population. Many Muslims openly reject or resist the beliefs and actions of Islamist radicals.

8. Approaches to Islamic Fundamentalism: Internal, Comparative, Cultural, and Historical Considerations

A major challenge in defining "Fundamentalist Islam" is that the term often purports to describe a diverse variety of behavior and practices. For example, Fundamentalist Islam has been used to describe a new religiosity, which reaffirms faith in a transcendent God; a militant ideology, demanding immediate political action; a populist party that peacefully participates in elections, or a jihadi group that preaches death and destruction against those who don't believe as they do.

This guide provides the context of contemporary Islamist groups based on historical Islamic doctrines, and trends. While not a history of Islam, this work does analyze the many groups that adhere to various interpretations of Islam. General information on Islam can be found in any of the many general reference works on that subject. This work discusses topics such as ideological Islamism, i.e., using Islam for the social and political agendas of various groups. Fundamentalist Muslim groups are rather heterogeneous in religious, social, and political positions. Some fundamentalist groups promote an extremely conservative and narrow interpretation of Islam while others incorporate Marxist and other socialist ideological principles in their matrix of beliefs. It is important to clearly distinguish between Islam as a religion and Islamism as an ideology because these are two very different concepts.

9. The Rise of Modern Islamic Fundamentalism

Modern Islamic Fundamentalism emerged over a century ago when many Muslims worldwide became increasingly concerned that they were lagging far behind the West in terms of development and social progress. They were also marginalized and often colonized by Western nations.

Even in contemporary times, Islamic Fundamentalism attracts many Muslims because of the widespread social and religious sense of despair existing in many Muslim majority nations and because they perceive themselves as being socially marginalized and having no future.

Islamic revivalists attributed the decline of Muslim-majority nations to the abandonment of original Islamic values by the allegedly worldly-orientation Islam's great medieval empires. Renewal, thus, was viewed as only possible by returning to Islam's founding values. The degree to which such a revival should attempt to recreate a mythical past or incorporate modern technology was, and remains, controversial among differing Islamic fundamentalist groups.

Islamic fundamentalist groups have extensively also used advanced technology and media (Internet and social media) to reach a wider worldwide audience. Therefore, Islamic fundamentalism's growth into a global phenomenon.

From the late 19th through the early 21st centuries, Modernist Islamic Fundamentalists promoted an all-encompassing view of Islam. They argued that Islam is "dan wa dawla" (doctrine, life, and politics) and must be central to every aspect of the life of the individual and of the nation. Economics, government, law, politics, and theology, according to Modernist Islamists, should be under the purview of the all-inclusive and comprehensive Islamic system.

10. The First Phase of Modern Islamic Fundamentalism

Sayyid Jamal al-Din-al –Afghani (1838-1897), founder of the League of Afghans, a staunch anti-Imperialist and a leading modern Islamic fundamentalist, argued that Muslims could reject Western culture and philosophy, while adopting Western technology, which he claimed the West had appropriated from Muslims. Muslims, Afghani said, should reclaim their true accomplishments in science and technology, but totally reject other Western innovations (such as democracy). He also argued that the adoption of Western science and technology would strengthen Islam. While Afghani was strongly influenced by Western rationalist and ideological thought, he also had a traditionalist religiously-based hostility toward unbelievers. As a virulent anti-imperialist, he sought to use Islam as a means to repel European imperialism. Ever since that time, Islamic fundamentalists have both rejected and opposed Western culture and values. One of Afghani's contributions, however, is that he was the first individual to provide a sense of intellectual coherence for Islamism. Afghani was succeeded by Muhammad Abdu, as Islamic Fundamentalism's primary opponent of westernization and colonialism,

To overcome often dire social and political circumstances, Islamic fundamentalists taught that the true solution for all problems was to return to the teachings of Muhammad and his followers, emulating the lives they lived, and attempting to replicate the successes of early Islam. Early Islamic society was egalitarian, and people cared for each other at a time when pious, righteous rulers governed the Muslim world.

Islamic fundamentalism focuses on the fundamentals of Islam and reverting to the foundations of Islam. The term "foundation", in this context, refers to beliefs and practices that were adopted in Muhammad's lifetime and in the lifetimes of the "companions" that succeeded him, especially "the four well-guided caliphs" (al-khulf a' al-rashidun). Islamic fundamentalists seek to restore the doctrines and social norms that existed during Islam's formation in the seventh century, through a very austere interpretation of the Koran and the Hadith.

11. The Second Phase of Modern Islamic Fundamentalism

The second phase of Modern Islamic Fundamentalism occurred between World War I and World War II. Hasan al-Banna and the Muslim Brotherhood were the leading forces of this phase of fundamentalism. The Fundamentalists opposed the process of westernization occurring in predominantly Muslim nations that accompanied colonialism. In these Muslim nations, Westernization was manifested by an increased openness to Western culture and education.

12. The Third Phase of Modern Islamic Fundamentalism

The third phase of Modern Islamic Fundamentalism was a response to the secularization stimulated by the Egyptian revolution led by Gamal Nasser in 1952. It was particularly encouraged by the defeat of the Arab nations in the Six Day War with Israel in 1967. The third phase of Modern Islamic Fundamentalism began after that war and continued through September 11, 2001, as a response to the failures of socialism and capitalism, as well as the failure of society and government to meet the needs of their peoples.

After the oil embargo of the 1970s, many Muslims were convinced that God had blessed the Muslims with an abundance of oil revenue, which was then used to promote various schools of Islam. The Saudis, for example, financed the printing and distribution of Korans, built mosques worldwide, and sent Muslim missionaries abroad. During the 1970's and 1980's, Islamic religious revivalism spread throughout the Middle East that helped fuel Islamic fundamentalism.

13. Muslim Fundamentalists and Political Islamism

Many Muslims believed in the ideal of a pervasive religious hegemony over both private and public life. Islamic fundamentalists reject secularism because the separation of religion and politics contradicts Islam's claim to regulate all areas of human life.

Islamic Fundamentalists also seek to establish a caliphate (Islamic government) and strictly apply sharia (Islamic law) to both public and private life. The specific objectives and the degree of strictness in implementing these fundamentals, however, vary depending on the particular Islamic group. There is a broad range of Islamic Fundamentalism, with "Wahhabism" (or Salafiyya) being the strictest form of Islamic Fundamentalism.

The distinction between the concepts of Islamic Fundamentalism and Islamism remains an issue of some dispute. Some scholars believe that Islamic fundamentalism is neither completely synonymous nor antithetical to Islamism; with Islamism is the most conservative form of Islamic fundamentalism. Other commentators, however, see the terms Islamic fundamentalism and Islamism as virtually synonymous.

Islamic Fundamentalists are extremely legalistic and believe that Islamic Law (Sharia) is the most important part of Islam. Islamism is also political Islam within a broader fundamentalist revival.

Islamic fundamentalism includes several very different, diverse, heterogeneous groups -- some intolerant and exclusivist, some pluralistic; some favor relying on science, some oppose relying on science some primarily devotional and some primarily political; some democratic; some authoritarian; some peaceful, some violent. Mainstream Islamists and Fundamentalists are distinguished by the fact that fundamentalists are politically-oriented individuals seeking a "more original Islam," while Islamists pursue an overtly political agenda. Some commentators see the terms Islamic fundamentalism and Islamism as virtually synonymous.

Another factor that distinguishes fundamentalists from Islamists is that fundamentalists are much more adamantly opposed to the perceived "corrupting influence of the West". They eschew and condemn Western cultural practices such as clothing, neckties, laughter, Western forms of greetings, handshakes, and, applause.

14. Islamic Fundamentalism on Gender Roles and the Human Body

Among the Western values that Islamic fundamentalists strongly oppose is the increasing independence and freedom of women resulting from the greatly changed sex roles of contemporary secular society. Although women in the West are not completely equal to men, nevertheless, they have more rights than women in most Muslim majority nations.

Islamic fundamentalists believe in completely separate spheres for men and women in almost every activity. Men must strictly govern the religious side of their personal and family life, because, as recipients of Allah's will for the family, they are responsible for the salvation of all family members as well as their own individual salvation. The term, "Family", in this context includes extended relatives as well as immediate members. This concept of family is based on a centuries-old tribal system that persists in contemporary Islamic society. These regulations also dictate the daily life of men, including those on clothing, eating, prayer, grooming, and sexual behavior.

Islamic fundamentalists strictly regulate the lives and behavior of women. Islamic fundamentalists specifically define the role of women as mothers and wives. They also believe that motherhood is the highest status for any woman and require that great respect always be given toward mothers. The responsibilities and tension of the roles between mother and wife are directly related to the relationship that a woman has with a man, including son, husband, father, or, brother. Islamic fundamentalists believe that women must always be submissive to man's will, to comply with Islamic law.

The veil is a major issue in Islamic fundamentalism for women. There are three types of veils: the burka, the khimar, and the hijab. The degree of strictness of a particular Islamic fundamentalist group determines what type of veil a woman must wear and what parts of her body must be covered. The most radical fundamentalists believe that showing the entire face and body (including the hands) of a woman is sinful because they may distract men from worshipping Allah. These fundamentalists impose the use of the burka, which covers the whole body and the entire face. Some less extremist fundamentalist groups believe that the entire body and face of women are sinful except for the eyes only if the woman never looks directly at the man whom she is addressing. These groups require that women wear a khimar, which allows for only the eyes to be seen. More moderate Islamic fundamentalist groups believe the entire body is just as sinful except for the face only if the woman wears makeup. This group, therefore, requires the hijab, which reveals the woman's face only, covering her neck, ears, and hair.

Islamic fundamentalists also view the social interaction of unmarried men and women violate Islam, and thus, immoral.

15. Islamism and the Role of Women

Islamists generally favor educating women and allowing them to participate in social and political life. While Islamists generally believe that women may study and work, they are required to adhere to a strict dress code. Islamist groups include associations for women.

While fundamentalists preach that women should remain at home, many Islamists believe that men and women should be segregated from each other in public events.

16. Key Differences Among Different Types of Islamic Fundamentalists

Individual Islamic fundamentalist groups differ in their various attitudes toward rites and symbols, government, and international relations and foreigners. Islamic groups, thus, have often been categorized as popular Islamic fundamentalism, political Islamic fundamentalism, and jihadi Islamic fundamentalism.

Political Islam, unlike other types of Islamic fundamentalism, is willing to accommodate and selectively incorporate modernity into establishing an Islamist state. Fundamentalist Islam generally opposes all aspects of modernity. Groups that espouse violent jihad such as Al-Qaeda and ISIS are composed of fundamentalist Islamists, but they are referred to as Jihadi groups to distinguish them from other Islamic fundamentalists who do not advocate violence to achieve their goals.

There are three major contemporary Islamic fundamentalist groups—Islamism, Salafism, and Wahhabism. Significant political differences exist among and within these three main groups. There are moderate and radical brands of Islamism.

Salafism (includes puritanical Salafist and neo-Salafist), and Wahhabism (includes instructionist and Jihadist). Both Jihadist Wahhabism, and neo-Salafism are active Islamic groups that promote radical Islamism. Various Salafist and Wahhabis groups have engaged in terrorist or jihadist activities worldwide.

Radical and the moderate Islamic fundamentalist groups strongly differ with each other in strategies and rhetoric. There are significant differences between Islamic fundamentalists on the basis of: the active and the inactive, the jihadi and the nonviolent, the "takfiri" (a violent and intolerant Salafist group) and the tolerant, and the modern and the traditional.

Originating in the Middle East, Islamic fundamentalist groups expanded worldwide partly because several Western governments and conservative governments of Muslim majority nations helped disseminate the teachings of these groups for political reasons, including defeating Communism and other leftist groups.

17. Popular Islamic Fundamentalism

Most Muslims are "Popular Islamic Fundamentalists". When religious figures (such as Mohammad), for example, are criticized or satirized, many popular Islamic fundamentalists are much more likely to vent their anger against those who allegedly desecrate Islamic symbols than become involved in their nation's government, political system, or international relations. One example of this occurred after the French satirical magazine, *Charlie Hebdo*, published a cartoon of the prophet Mohammed. Mainstream Islam tradition forbids such depictions. To avenge the "insult against the prophet", a group of jihadists killed twelve people in Paris in January 2015. *Charlie Hebdo* published another cartoon of Mohammed in a subsequent issue of the magazine, which provoked many fundamentalists to protest and engage in violence because they believed that their prophet was insulted.

18. Political Islamic Fundamentalism

More Muslims generally regard their religion as a more pervasive presence in daily life and a more important source of civil law than contemporary Christians. Islam has a legal system governing all aspects of life, while Western governments tend to avoid intrusive governmental regulation of personal behavior. Fundamentalists who are political Islamists justify this pervasive presence of Islam on the belief that Islam provides the best possible social, religious, legal and political system in the world as they believe it is ordained by God (Khayru 'ummaten' unzilat linnas).

Fundamentalists, who are political Islamists, focus their energies on law, politics, and government. Along with religious objectives, they have socio-political religious ones. They use Islamic shibboleths to persuade Islamic fundamentalists to work within the legal and political system. It is a group composed of groups that seek political power, under the slogan " al-Islam huwa al-hall" (Islam is the solution). Political Islamic fundamentalist organizations encourages, sponsors, and/or approves of imposing religion on governmental and educational institutions. In addition to domestic issues, political Islamists may occasionally discuss international issues in relation to government policy.

Political Islamic fundamentalism emerged because of four factors: 1) socioeconomic issues (deterioriating economic conditions, joblessness, and poverty); 2) antipathy of many Muslims for the West (particularly related to those influences resulting from modernization and Westernization); 3) the dissolution of the Soviet Union; and, 4) continuing unrest in the Middle East (such as the Palestinian refugee crisis, the 1979 Iranian Revolution, and the assassination of Egypt's President Anwar Sadat in 1981).

Muslim Brotherhood has long been a guiding force of Political Islamism. Formed in 1928 by Hassan al-Banna in Egypt, the Brotherhood is the world's oldest and one of the most resilient Islamist organizations. Before World War II, the Muslim Brothers focused on social activism, and, mostly abstained from political involvement. After World War II, the group became more militant and relied on violence to achieve its goals. Brotherhood militancy led to increasing clashes between fundamentalists and the secular nationalist pan-Arab movement led by Gamal Nasser, Egypt's President from 1956 through 1970. While imprisoned in the late 1950's, many Brotherhood members increasingly believed that no secular government could ever peacefully be transformed into a genuinely Muslim one. They believed that secular government and society were so corrupt that their total elimination was necessary to lead to a genuinely Islamist government and society. To achieve such a total change, these fundamentalists believed that "jihad" was essential to remove and replace what they believed were corrupt un-Islamic regimes. They frequently analogized existing secular governments in Muslim nations to pre-Islamic idolatrous societies. The Brotherhood became a mass movement throughout the Middle East by the 1960s. In its continuing opposition to democratic values, the Brotherhood continues to condemn Western principles such as the separation of state and religion, in favor theocratic state.

All Islamic Fundamentalist groups oppose Western values and actions (including democracy and any foreign intervention). The more Islamic moderate groups re-interpret Western concepts of governance into Islamic concepts such as shura (consultation) for elections and (al-'odala, or, Justice) for equality.

Islamic fundamentalists strongly reject secular politics in Muslim majority nations, as sinful Western imports, with its alleged materialism, and supposedly un-Islamic philosophy. Islamic fundamentalists further claim that the malign legacy of Western colonialism include that leaders of many Muslim nations more often defer to Western political and economic interests, as much as or more than their own constituents. During the era of Western colonialization of majority Muslim nations, many Fundamentalist Muslims believe, Westerners controlled the economies to advance their interests over the interests of the subject peoples. Once many of these nations won independence, Muslim Fundamentalists believe that the successor governments were led by secular, Westernized elites developed by the former colonial powers and were associated with Christian business interests or were western-oriented military officers.

Rather than engage in the "marketplace of ideas", political Islamists are often ideologues, who primarily seek political power for themselves. Political Islamists believe that they must establish an Islamic state and an Islamic society based on the Sharia (Islamic Law). They believe, then that the purpose of government is to implement Islamist dogma as public policy, and that the government must enforce such policy.

Many Islamist organizations claim they seek to create governments based on those of the "Prophetic Era" (the lifetime of Muhammad, his immediate followers, and the first four caliphs). In other words, they advocate establishing a theocracy. The 1979 Iranian Islamic Revolution greatly inspired Islamic fundamentalists, who soon perceived both the revolution and its leader, Ayatollah Ruhollah al-Malawi Khomeini, as leading models of Islamic governance in the contemporary world. While the lives of ordinary Iranian farmers improved in the short-term vis-à-vis the Shah's reign, this progress has not been sustained. Iran's urban working class also endured increasing hardships, particularly under the sanctions regime. Iran's government has been unable to resolve many of the country's socio-economic problems and has pursued policies that have worsened them. While Iran could have become prosperous by investing its oil revenue for development, it instead, has financed a military expansion for the purpose of achieving dominance in the Middle East.

19. Concept of Governance Under Islamic Fundamentalism

Governance, according to Islamic Fundamentalists, should be based on the umma (the nation) in contrast to a secular civil society with a national identity. The Ulama (universal community of believers) is believed to transcend nation, territory, or ethnic group. The government (hukumiyya) must also be based completely on Allah's divine guidance. Muslim Fundamentalists view the ruler of the people (hakim) as the successor of the Prophet and the first four caliphs ("caliph" means successor). The "hakim" must govern in the same manner as the Prophet Muhammad and the first caliphs. The governed (mohkum) must then submit to the hukumiyya of Allah, and the nation should be governed by sharia (Islamic law) and fatwas (Islamic legal decrees). Since the governed must be submissive to Allah and his governance, the rulers must always govern according to Allah's will. Thus, the people must be confident that their ruler's decisions are based on Allah's will.

20. Sharia in Political Islamism

Sharia is law based on the Koran and other Islamic religious writings. Sharia governs both personal life (including food, personal hygiene, clothing, marriage and divorce, religious rituals, and financial matters) and public life (taxation, warfare, and, criminal punishment). Many commentators criticize Islamist applications of Sharia for denying women's rights, and the basic freedoms of speech and religion.

Fundamentalist Muslims, in contrast to Traditionalist Muslims and Secular Muslims, believe that the entire Sharia must be implemented and enforced as binding law. Fundamentalist Muslims believe that Islamic law provides political solutions for the problems of contemporary society. Acting with absolute certainty that they are following God's will, some Islamic fundamentalists are particularly hostile towards both Non-fundamentalist Muslims and non-Muslims. Some of these Fundamentalists will resort to violence. They are particularly hostile toward Western influence and practices, which they perceive as obstacles to implementing Sharia.

The context of political Islam must be considered. The political and economic environments in many nations with large Muslim populations, generate Islamist groups that extend beyond mere respect and reverence for Islam. Political Islamists use Islam as a political tool and claim to use Islamic principles to advocate for Islamically-based social and political reforms. Popular support for these fundamentalist approaches has increased in cases where other efforts at economic and political reform in various Muslim majority nations have failed. Political Islamists have been successful in many Muslim majority nations because they are very well organized, have an effective social base, and because many Muslims perceive them as legitimate. Other Muslims are attracted to Islamism because they perceive it as a plausible alternative to the secular nation-state, to a Western, non-indigenous, non-Islamic form of social organization and a man-made political system. Other Muslims oppose to transforming Islam into a political movement, arguing that this would be manipulating Islam to justify violence, and object to using Islam to justify extremism.

Many Western observers either view political Islam as reactionary and similar to fascism, or as a progressive movement of peoples long oppressed by colonialism and imperialism.

While the Muslim Brotherhood and similar groups seek to establish an Islamic state through the existing political and legislative systems, jihadist organizations such as Al-Qaeda and ISIS and reject this peaceful gradualist political approach. Osama Bin Laden (1957-2011) argued that this strategy would fail to establish a genuinely Islamic state, because it would require pragmatic political compromises that would form an un-Islamic government. This approach, Jihadists also believe, would also subject Muslim nations to U.S. influence. Jihadist groups such as Al-Qaeda believe that attacking the United States is the only way to eradicate US power and influence in the Middle East. Further, the group believes that such attacks would inspire the Muslim masses to revolt against the West. The ensuing conflict would then lead to an Islamic State (a Caliphate).

21. Jihadi Islamic Fundamentalism

Jihadi Islamic fundamentalists are a small but extremely dangerous minority of Muslims, who are motivated by a revolutionary and reactionary form of Islamism. These violent extremists have often successfully exploited the grievances of impoverished, disenfranchised, and marginalized people.

Jihadist Muslims only accept a government that: 1) has no parliamentary system, 2) strictly implements and enforces Islamic law (Sharia), 3) is hostile to the United States and the West, and 4) is committed to the destruction of Israel.

Jihadists are xenophobic and seek to completely eliminate any foreign presence within their nation as well as any foreign influence. Jihadists are more active when there is both a foreign military presence and the nation has a foreign policy that they view as Un-Islamic. Jihadi fundamentalists claim that their approach to foreign relations (or abstinence in this arena) would better ensure the development and perpetuation of an Islamic state.

Dysfunctional social, economic, and government conditions breed terrorism. Western nations should avoid actions deemed as supportive of the political, social, and economic structures responsible for these problems. However, Western support for democracy, economic justice, and non-violence in Muslim majority nations will significantly deter terrorism and prevent jihadism from taking hold.

22. Conflicts between the Fundamentalists and the Secular State

The efforts of Islamic fundamentalists to create an Islamic State based on Sharia conflicts with the ideals of the secular, democratic state, as promoted in the Universal Declaration of Human Rights. Western and Islamist concepts of government, the individual and society do not only diverge; they are often mutually exclusive. Fundamentalist Muslims reject such human rights as: gender equality, separation of religion and state, freedom of speech, freedom of expression, and, freedom of religion. Fundamentalist Muslims believe that Islam provides the only solutions for all of the world's problems and that liberal secularism contributes to these problems.

23. The Governing Principles of Islamic Fundamentalism

Fundamentalist principles largely govern both Saudi Arabia and Iran. The former, however, is more of a traditional Muslim government. Saudi Arabia has a government with separation of powers between "princes" (umarā) and "scholars" (ulama). In contrast, the ulamā (religious jurists) have the highest authority in Iran's Islamic Republic.

24. Efforts to Form a New Caliphate

Many Islamic fundamentalist groups seek an idealized unity and prosperity of Muslims in a caliphate, as a medieval-reactionary utopia, where all Muslims reside under a single government based exclusively on Islam. Both Sunni fundamentalist extremists such as Al-

Qaeda and the ISIS and the Shia fundamentalist extremists of Iran's Islamic Republic and Hezbollah in Lebanon continue to seek to establish this vision of governance and society derived from their interpretation of early Islamic history.

The last recognized caliphate ended when the Turkish Republic was declared in 1924. The Caliphate was a largely symbolic institution. It, nonetheless, symbolized the unity, solidarity, and strength of a Muslim empire governed by a single leader (or caliph), in what many Muslims perceive as Islam's great and glorious "golden age". Under the caliphs, the Islamic Empire expanded to include northern Africa, the Arabian Peninsula, eastern and southern Asia, and Indonesia. Fundamentalist Muslims have long dreamed of a restored caliphate, where all Muslims are together and live with dignity and social justice under Koranic teachings.

Over the decades, various groups attempted to form a caliphate. In 1952, the Muslim Brotherhood purchased land near Cairo to establish an Islamist utopia with 30,000 people living there. In 1954, however, Nasser thwarted the plan by confiscating the land. The group then attempted to establish a settlement in the desert, which subsequently failed

The Iranian Islamic Revolution in 1979 led many Islamic fundamentalists to believe that they could successfully re-establish a caliphate. The Arab Spring, which began in 2011, also encouraged many Muslims to believe that a caliphate could be restored. After ISIS seized territory in Syria and Iraq on June 29, 2014, Abu Bakr al-Baghdadi declared a caliphate, with himself as caliph and demanded the allegiance of all Muslims. Most Muslims and Muslim-majority nations rejected the legitimacy of the so-called "caliphate". By late 2017, the ISIS caliphate was defeated and had lost much of the territory it once controlled in Iraq and Syria.

25. Islamic Fundamentalism and International Relations

Jihad is a crucial concept in Islamic fundamentalism. Expected of all Muslims, Jihad means striving" or a "determined effort". Invoking the term, Jihad, to justify violence distorts the word's original religious meaning. The word describes two distinctly different actions. The greater jihad refers to the struggle to obey God, through the non-violent struggle to overcome evil desires and to live a life of virtue and morality. The second meaning of jihad is that it refers to fighting injustice and oppression, spreading and defending Islam, and creating a just society through preaching, teaching, and if necessary, armed struggle or holy war. The lesser Jihad, thus, can be used to describe the use of armed force to defend Islam from aggressors.

Based on the teachings of early Islam, Islamic fundamentalists perceive the world as being divided into two spheres: the dar al-Islam (land of Islam) and the dar-al-harb (land of war). The first is considered as territory (notwithstanding internationally recognized territorial boundaries) of an Islamic state. This state is viewed as sacred and pure and, therefore, must be preserved and remain unchanged. The Dar al-harb, however, is any territory not governed by Islamic law. Therefore, warfare or violence is permissible because that territory does not adhere to Allah's law.

Islamic fundamentalists do not recognize a long-term peace with any non-lslamic entity. They may only accept a temporary truce or armistice (hudna, or, cease-fire). Some medieval Islamic scholars wrote that Izudnas with a non-Muslim enemy should not be in force for longer than ten years. Since non-Islamic states do not adhere to Islamic law, Islamic fundamentalists deem any treaty or policy promulgated by them to be invalid. Islamic fundamentalists also argue that Islamic Law usually forbids Islamic nations to become allies with non-Islamic nations, particularly in opposition to other Islamic nations. They view it as acceptable to abrogate all agreements made with any non-Islamic government if that other state is not based on Islamic principles or because it is taking action against Muslims.

Islamic fundamentalists would permit the "dhimmi" (protected non-Muslim residents of Muslim-majority nations), to continue residing within an Islamic state. The dhimmi, however, would be denied all political rights. The dhimmi, for example, are forbidden to exercise judicial or political power over Muslims in an Islamic state. While they may not engage in any Muslim activity, they must adhere to the laws of the state. The dhimmi, for example, must pay taxes (jizya) to the Islamic state. The extent of restrictions and discrimination against non-Muslims depend on how extensively fundamentalist an Islamic state is. For example, while Islamic law allows the dhimmi to consume pork, they must do so privately.

26. Islamic Fundamentalism and Terrorism: Connections and Distinctions

Jihadist groups seek to replace secular governments with fundamentalist Islamic governments and are willing to use violent actions such as murder, bombings, hijackings, and kidnappings, to achieve their objectives.

Although jihadism is a form of religiously-motivated terrorism and although many terrorists are fundamentalist Muslims, not all fundamentalist Muslims are necessarily terrorists. These extremists are a marginal (but resilient) segment of Islamic fundamentalism. Terrorism is neither dependent on (nor does it necessarily result from) an Islamic fundamentalist belief system.

Although violent Islamic fundamentalists and violent Islamic fundamentalist groups exist, most Islamic fundamentalists and most Islamic fundamentalist groups reject terrorism. Islamic fundamentalism, like other social and fundamentalist religious groups, has both violent radical and peaceful adherents. Defining the terms "terrorism" and "terrorist" continues to be controversial, as one man's terrorist is another man's freedom fighter. The term, "terrorism", in this guide refers to violent acts against civilians just as frequently as security forces, for political purposes. The term ''terrorists'' refers to the militant extremists engaged in those acts.

Certain Islamic fundamentalist organizations, thus, may be defined as terrorist groups. Most internal terrorism within Muslim-minority nations is motivated by attempts to destroy a nation's social and economic infrastructure and replace it with an Islamic state. Some radical groups have emerged from moderate ones, and some terrorist groups defected from their parent groups often to follow a more extreme and violent strategy out of frustration with a lack of progress with more moderate strategies.

Islamic fundamentalist groups are often more focused on the smaller, regional issues in their tribes or communities. Relatively few Islamic fundamentalist groups have the resources necessary for large-scale or international attacks.

Some Islamic fundamentalist groups only accept individuals they designate as insiders as members, to maintain group cohesiveness and homogeneity. Other groups, however, recruit new members from many different backgrounds, to maintain or expand the size of their organizations.

Some Islamist terrorist groups have received government support, while others do not. Algerian and Egyptian terrorist groups are not state-sponsored, while Hezbollah in Lebanon, however, receives substantial support from Iran. Other terrorist Islamist groups accept foreign assistance, but remain operationally and ideologically autonomous from any type of government control.

27. Islamist Leaders

Leading Islamic fundamentalists, who are also considered Islamists, include Sayyid Qutb (1906-1966) (a leading Muslim Brotherhood ideologue and Salafist activist), Ruhollah Khomeini (1902-1989) (the first Supreme Leader of Iran), Mawlana Abul Ala Mawdudi (1903-1979) (founder of the Islamist Party, Jamaat-Islami, in India and Pakistan), and Israr Ahmad (1932-2010) (a leading Pakistani ideologue). While Qutb and Mawdudi were sometimes criticized for not being particularly deep philosophers, they did, however, develop a coherent ideology, based on a narrow reading of Islamic religious writings, which were reduced to slogans to justify Islamist extremism.

The Egyptian government executed Qutb in 1966 for allegedly inciting opposition to the Nasser regime. Qutb rejected democracy and nationalism as forms of Jahiliyah (paganism) and believed that pan-Arabism was an impediment to the formation of the umma (the universal community of believers). He argued it was permissible, indeed sometimes necessary, for Muslims to disobey the Koranic prohibition against overthrowing a Muslim leader by declaring that leader to be an infidel.

Believing that Islam was under siege and that redemption could not wait for a peaceful transformation, Qutb wrote that a vanguard should be organized, retreat from infidel society, denounce certain prominent Muslims as lax unbelievers, and forcibly overthrow the existing political order. Thus, he articulated an explicit rationale for an Islamic revolution.

Other Muslim leaders also promoted their various visions of Islam and Islamism. Pakistani President, General Zia ul-Haq (1924-1988) sought to Islamize Pakistani society, by establishing thousands of madrassas (religious schools), many of which taught Wahhabi Islam (an extremely intolerant version of Sunnism). Saudi Arabia and the Gulf states funded many of these madrassas. The students at these schools received a strictly religious curriculum, based on a highly puritanical version of fundamentalist Islam. Thus, these madrassas became a major breeding ground for violent Islamism in many majority-Muslim nations.

Other Middle Eastern authoritarian leaders manipulated Islamic fundamentalism to maintain power in their respective nations. In Shiite-majority Iraq, Saddam Hussein (1937 - 2006), the long-time President of Iraq, claimed to be the great defender of Sunni Islam, waging a war against Iran and oppressing Iraqi Shiites. Muamar Gadhafi (1942-2011), leader of Libya, presented himself as a devout Muslim who believed that Islam superseded sectarian lines. Bashar Assad (1965-), who succeeded his father to become President of Syria, both ruthlessly maintained Alawite dominance in Syria by repressing Syrian Sunnis, but also supported the Sunni-dominated Al-Qaeda in Iraq (AQI) by facilitating the transit of foreign fighters and arming them to fight Coalition troops and the Iraqi government in Iraq. AQI eventually transformed into ISIS, which fought against the Syrian government in the Syrian Civil War.

28. How Islamists Supplanted the Left in Majority Muslim Nations

From the end of World War II in 1945 until the 1970s, various Leftist movements were very influential in Muslim majority nations. Examples include: Gamel Nasser in Egypt, Ahmed Benn Bella (1916-2012) in Algeria, and Habib Bourguiba (1903-2000) in Tunisia. From the 1950s through the 1970s, left-wing military coups brought socialist regimes to power in Syria, South Yemen, Iraq, Somalia, Libya and Ethiopia.

In the mid-1960s, Indonesia had both one of the world's largest Communist party, which was officially atheistic, and the world's largest Muslim population. The Indonesian army destroyed the nation's Communist Party after 1965. The Islamist group, Sarekat-e-Islam, also participated in the coup against leftist President Sukarno (1901-1970). In the late 1950s and early 1960s, the national Communist party was the strongest political organization in Iraq, especially among the Shia in the south. Egyptian Abdel Gamal Nasser (1918-1970), imposed socialism in Egypt in 1961, was a practicing Muslim, however, Islamic fundamentalists strongly opposed him.

In Egypt and Syria, Islamist organizations such as the Muslim Brotherhood were used to destabilize left-wing governments. Anwar Sadat (1918-1981), President of Egypt, protected radical Islamists in the 1970s to help defeat leftist Nasserites and Communists, and later to recruit fighters against Russia in the Afghan-Soviet War. Jordan's King Hussein (1935-1999), a US ally, frequently relied on Islamist support to fight left wing opponents and Yemen's' President Abdallah Saleh (1942-2017) was supported by Islamist rebels in fighting Marxists in South Yemen. Sometime after being forced to resign as Yemen's president, he later joined forces with the Houthi rebels in Yemen against a coalition led by Saudi Arabia. In late 2017, he was killed by his former Houthi allies after switching sides and agreeing to support the coalition.

Islamic fundamentalism developed in most Muslim-majority nations to confront the Left. Eventually, the Fundamentalists eclipsed the Leftists in organizing protest groups against dysfunctional social and political conditions in those nations. Islamic fundamentalism exploited the failures of the Left in the late 1960s and 1970s. Beginning in the 1970s, following Egypt's defeat in the Six-Day War in 1967, and with the decline of radical middle class nationalism and Nasser's death in 1970, reactionary groups using Islam as an ideological shibboleth spread throughout most Muslim-majority nations, which accelerated the Left's decline. The Islamic Fundamentalists, and particularly the Islamists, have filled the void created by the decline of the left and eventually began to lead the opposition to the West.

29. The Islamic Fundamentalist View of Politics and Society

Frequently invoking the shibboleth of "revolution", Islamists argue that society will only be Islamized through social and political activism. Using their unique intepretation of the term "revolution", Islamists have strongly opposed modernity and Western political and economic beliefs. Islamic fundamentalists have little interest in associating with non-Muslims.

Political Islamists loudly denounce the failings and evils of current leaders and the existing political and social systems. In presenting their case, political Islamists present a largely mythical version of a glorious and imaginary distant past. Every version of Islamic fundamentalism invokes Islam as the answer to issues such as ending poverty and oppression. Islamism's political and social program – including its denunciations of injustice, corruption, and the tyranny of the government has gathered more of a popular following than its religious message, which is often viewed as reactionary, misogynist, and repressive. Thus, political Islamism emerged after it had transformed into a nationalist and anti-imperialist cause.

Islamism also gained significant popular support because of the failure of many governments in Muslim majority nations to provide even basic development in social welfare, public education, and other services. This failure worsened poverty in most Muslim-majority nations. Islamist organizations intervened and provided many of these services to the disenfranchised, through networks of welfare organizations and educational and health services. Through these services, political Islamists have asserted that they are the only hope of the Muslim masses.

30. An Inherent Incompatibility between Islamic Fundamentalism and Democracy?

In examining the various Islamist groups, this guide considers issues such as whether Islamic fundamentalism is compatible with democracy. Some scholars and commentators argue that basic characteristics of Islamic Fundamentalism directly contradict basic principles of liberal democracy. One argument is that Islamic fundamentalism and democracy are incompatible because fundamentalists believe in the concept of the Islamic State (caliphate). Islamic fundamentalists view the Islamic State as a divinely-ordained theocracy. A ruler of nation may impose policies or decisions, which are believed to be an interpretation of God's law. Thus, Islamic Fundamentalists perceive no need for legislation, legislative institutions, representatives in those institutions, or a process of choosing those representatives (elections).

Some scholars and other commentators believe that this incompatibility between fundamentalist Islam and democracy is because there are relatively few progressive Muslim intellectuals. Radical Fundamentalist Islam discourages intellectuals to question the status quo, when it is controlled by clerics or imams. This hinders the transformation and evolution of Islam, similar to what occurred with Christianity in the European Enlightenment. Throughout the world, including in Muslim majority nations, however, technology and globalization facilitate an unprecedented exchange of ideas, and this way, facilitate a genuine marketplace of ideas in Muslims communities worldwide, which could, in turn, facilitate a transformation in Islamic Law.

D. ISLAMISM

1. The Struggle to Describe the Phenomenon That Became Known as Islamism

In the wake of the Iranian Revolution that brought the Ayatollah Ruhollah Khomeini to power in in Iran 1979, public officials and the news media in the West began widely using a new vocabulary to describe a dramatically changed reality that had worldwide impact. These terms included: "Islamic Fundamentalism", "Radical Islam", "Islamic Revivalism", and

"Political Islam". Discussion of these terms became increasingly common in the ensuing decades. These concepts and their meanings have been discussed and debated in numerous books and articles.

Islamism is often used to define a particular ideology based on certain interpretations of Islam. Ideology is defined as a "set of ideas by which men explain and justify the ends and means of organized social action, with the aim of preserving or constructing a given reality."[3]

As the world grasped with a new phenomenon, these concepts both simultaneously clarified and muddied public understanding of Islamism. The discussion raised issues such as what relation Islamism had with Islam and what exactly Islamism entails or does not entail. Many commentators observed that Islamism had grown more political, often violent, often anti-Western, and hostile toward the established governments in majority Muslim nations. Since the 9/11 attacks in 2001, the term Islamism has been more widely used and scholars have increasingly debated the various aspects of this ideology and its affects worldwide.

2. The Evolution of Understanding Islamism as a Concept

Scholarly understanding of how Islamism or aspects of Islamism have also evolved. French scholars Olivier Roy and Giles Kepel, for example, who had once used both "political Islam" and fundamentalist Islam", increasingly relied on the term "Islamism" instead. Olivier Roy described political Islam as a failure, while also using the term, Islamism, to describe new forms of activist Islam.[4] Bruno Eitenne of the University of Aix-en-Provence defined "Radical Islamism" as an ideology that seeks to present a cure all for all the evils of modernity/modernization the return to political Islam's roots: the ideal State of the Rashidun (the "rightly guided four Caliphs: 632-661)".[5]

Representative examples of scholarly trends interpreting Islamism include: Malise Ruthven's treatise on *Fundamentalism,* which uses the term Islamism extensively. Other major scholars have used terms such as "Radical Islamism" (William E. Shepard), "Islamic Activism" (Quinan Wiktorwicz), or "Mobilizing Islam" (Carrie R. Wickham).[6]

Some Muslim-oriented and Western scholars have compared Islamism to totalitarian ideologies such as Nazism and Communism. Despite sectarian and other differences among the various Islamist groups, scholars observe that Islamist groups have similar objectives. They seek to restore an Islamist world order, whether one that actually existed or an idealized version of this order.

Different Islamist groups may articulate their ultimate goals differently and through different means. Generally, the leaders and ideologues of the Muslim Brotherhood, such as Hasan al-Banna and Sayyid Qutb, along with followers of Qutbian ideology such as Shukri Mustafa have explicitly articulated their theoretical interpretation of Islamism on various

---

[3] Zeen Sternhell, "Fascist Ideology," in Walter Laquer (ed.), *Fascism: A Reader's Guide* (London: Penguin Books, 1982), p. 329.
[4] Olivier Roy, *Globalized Islam: The Search for a New Ummah* (London: Hurst & Co., 2002); Gilles Kepel, Jihad: *The Trial of Political Islam* (London: I.B. Tauris, 2004); Giles Kepel, *The War for the Muslim Mind: Islam and the West* (Cambridge, MA: University Press, 2004).
[5] Bruno Etienne, *L'Islamisme radical* (Paris: Hachette, 1987).
[6] William E. Shepard, "Islam and Ideology: Towards a Typology," *International Journal of Middle East* 19/3 (August 1987), pp. 307-35; Carrie R. Wickham, *Mobilizing Islam* (New York: Columbia University Press, 2002); Quintan Wiktorwicz (ed.), *Islamic Activism* (Bloomington, IN: Indiana University Press, 2004).

issues, while other prominent Islamists, such as the Ayatollah Khomeini and Abul A'la Mawdudi focused on establishing Islamist governments in Iran and Pakistan respectively. Nonetheless, the ideal of forming an Islamic world government and world Umma constantly motivated their thoughts and action, although less theoretically than that pursued by al-Banna and Qutb.

3. How Islamists have Interpreted Islamism

Several prominent Muslim ideologues have invoked the concept of "Islamism" [Islamiyyun] in their writings. Hasan al-Turabi (1932-2016), for example, discusses the various types of Islamism in his treatise, *Al-Islam wal Hukm* [*Islam and Government*] (using the term "Islamiyyun" to describe "political Muslims for whom Islam is the solution, Islam is religion and government and Islam is the Constitution and the law"[7]), Slawa al-Sharafi[8], in *Al-Islamiyyun wal –Daimuqratitiyya* [*Islamists and Democracy*],[9] and Larbi Sadiki,[10] who critically analyzed Islamist rhetoric and ideology in his treatise, *The Search for Arab Democracy*.[11]

4. Issues in Defining Islamism

In terms of defining Islamism, Aziz al-Al-Ameh describes contemporary Islamist movements as a manifestation of "political Islamism" and avoided use of the terms "Islamic fundamentalism".[12] William Sheppard uses "Islamic totalism" to describe the tendency of adherents to perceive Islam beyond religious belief and action, such as "theological belief, prayer, and ritual worship, but as a total way of life with guidance for political, economic and social behavior".[13] Often, they argue that Muslims should reside in an Islamic state, where the government is based on Sharia law. This, then, forms a workable definition of Islamism for the purposes of this guide.

5. Islam and Islamism

The religious faith of Islam and the religionized politics of Islamism are not synonymous concepts. Islam is religion, with 1.4 billion followers, with a long history and different theological and juridical schools. The religion of Islam is neither an impediment to peace or a

---

[7] Hasan Al-Turabi, *Al-Islam wal-Hukm* (London: Al-Saqi, 2003), p. 49.
[8] Tunisian professor at the Institute of Press and Information Sciences and one of the founders of the Free Thought Association (an independent association formed by several of academics and intellectuals to defend freedoms in Tunisia) including academic freedom.
[9] Salwi al-Sharfi, *Al-Islamiyyun wal-Dimuquqratiyya* (Tunis: Manshurat Alamat, 2001).
[10] Tunisian author, political scientist and senior lecturer at the University of Exeter, in England.
[11] Larbi Sadiki, *The Search for Arab Democracy* (New York: Columbia University Press, 2004).
[12] Aziz al-Azmeh, *Islams and Modernities* (London.: Verso, 1993). For al-Azmeh, political Islam has little to do with traditional models of Islam.
[13] Henri Lauziere, *Making of Salafism: Islamic Reform in the Twentieth Century* 216 (New York: Columbia University Press, 2015).

threat to Non-Muslims. The Qur'an does not condone terrorism. Jihad does not necessary mean Holy war, but is most commonly used to describe the struggle to lead life according to God's will. Further, the Sirah (biography) of the Prophet Muhammad does not support an authoritarian dictatorial ideologization of Islam.

6. Examples of Islamism

Current manifestations of the wide scope of Islamism include the militant groups in Iraq and Lebanon, political parties in Tunisia and Egypt and the governments of Iran and Saudi Arabia.

Organizations referred to as Islamist groups vary greatly from each other. They use different tactics, appeal to different grievances, and have different political goals. This guide seeks to clarify and explain the differences between them.

In practical terms, only the first caliphates effectively controlled all territories where Muslims resided. There have been several attempts to restore caliphate since Kemal Atatürk abolished it in 1924 (with ISIS being the most notorious and best known example). Nonetheless, there has never been the Muslim consensus necessary to select the caliph, and ISIS has been no exception.

Self-proclaimed caliphs, such that of Abu Bakr al-Baghdadi, of the Islamic State (ISIS, ISIL, or Daesh), are invalid under Sunni traditions. The lack of a unifying leader is a major reason why Sunni Islamic authority is currently fragmented, with any number of individuals and organizations seeking to fill the void.

7. What Does Islamism Mean?

Islamism is an ideology that employs religious beliefs and symbols for political purposes. Not all commentators agree with this definition. Some Islamists believe that their version of Islamism is genuine Islam. Islamism, however, is a political interpretation of Islam rather than Islam itself. It is based not on the religious faith of Islam but on an ideological misuse of religion for political gain. Islamism, then, can be defined as a religiously-inspired ideology that assumes a holistic interpretation of Islam. Further, it seeks to eventually establish a world political order based on its interpretation of Islam. This holism is based on the Islamist concept of the absolute unity of Din [Religion], Duny [Way of Life], and Dawla [Government]

8. Islamism as a Political Movement

Often associated with terrorist organizations, the term Islamism refers to a political movement inspired by Islam. The current manifestations of political Islamism result from a surge of Islamist revivalism, which has been unprecedented since between the 11th and 14th centuries.

9. Goals of Islamism

The goals of Islamists include the Islamization of their societies, and ultimately a worldwide state based on Islamic principles.

10. The Three Main Types of Islamism

Islamism is not a monolithic movement. Despite the global aspirations of Islamists, Islamists do not have an overall pan-Islamist radical leadership and are heavily factionalized. Islamism is very divided, with different factions, within a diverse global movement that advocates different interpretations of what Islamism should represent.

The three major types of Islamism differ significantly in terms of religious doctrine, on the type of Islamist state to establish, and how to fulfill their objectives. For example, those who follow authoritarian Islamism believe that they have already accomplished the goal of creating an Islamic state. In contrast, the adherents of both revolutionary and process Islamism seek to replace governments currently in power and replace them with their versions of Islamist states.

11. How the Different Types of Islamism Differ from Each Other

Revolutionary and Process Islamism dramatically differ on the change they seek, and the nature and form of the Islamist government they aspire to create.

12. Origins of Modern Islamism

Modern Islamism originated after the Ottoman Empire collapsed. The three key events that influenced much of the early growth of modern Islamism were: 1) the abolition of caliphate in 1924 (which created a vacuum in Sunni political Islam)[14], the formation of the Muslim Brotherhood in 1928, and the establishment of Saudi Arabia in 1932.

13. Significance of the Caliphate

In theory, the caliphate is a sovereign government that united all Muslims under a single political and spiritual leader. Following the prophet Muhamad's death, the caliph (from the Arabic word for successor) was the political leader of Muslim community (umma), but did not have authority over issues of Islamic doctrine.

---

[14] The Islamic caliphate was one of the enduring political institutions in history. It was formed in 632 AD after Muhammad's death and exited until Mustafa Kemal abolished it in 1924.

14. The Caliph Succession and Shia/Sunni Divide

The divide between the Sunni and Shia branches of Muslim occurred over the issue of selecting the first caliph. Sunnis believed that Muhammad's successor should be elected; while Shiites believed the selection of the caliph should follow hereditary principles within the Prophet's family. Both branches developed different visions of political Islam, although they resemble each other.

Islamism, however, is divided into three main branches: Sunni, Shi'a, and Wahhabi. Wahhabi is a Sunni sect, but it differs significantly from other Sunni sub-sects. This may be considered as a separate entity in our consideration of Islamism. Sunnism is composed of four theological and juridical schools: Hanafi, Malaki, Shafi'i, and Hobnail. Wahhabism is derived from the Hanbali School and has a particularly dogmatic and strict interpretation of Islam.

15. The Muslim Brotherhood

Shortly after the Ottoman Empire collapsed, a school teacher, named Hassan al-Banna formed the Muslim Brotherhood in Egypt. The society had three objectives that have remained constant throughout its history: 1) social renewal based on Islamic values, 2) long-term implementation of traditional Islamic law, and 3) ending colonization (chiefly by Great Britain). Al-Banna's vision envisioned gradual Islamization. He advocated re-Islamization through charity and indoctrination, and emerged as the founder of the Sunni branch of Process Islamism.

16. Revolutionary Islamism

Sayyid Qutb, an Egyptian civil servant, helped form the ideology of Sunni revolutionary Islamism. Qutb rejected al-Banna's gradualist approach and believed that only the violent overthrow of existing governments (all of which he considered to be "un-Islamic") would lead to the establishment of a genuinely Islamic state. Qutb's advocacy of Revolutionary Islam led the Egyptian government to arrest and execute him in 1966.

Both al-Banna and Qutb were Muslim Brothers and represent the two factions that have dominated the Islamist movement since the 1950s (the gradualist/process activism versus the revolutionary/terrorist activism).

17. Formation of Saudi Arabia and Islamism

Formed in 1932, Saudi Arabia was the first Arab nation to be explicitly formed on Islam. It also provided sanctuary for Islamists, who were repressed in other Muslim nations. Saudi Arabia's stature as the region's ideological power was greatly enhanced with oil production, The Saudi oil wealth allowed that nation to widely disseminate its own version of Sunni Islam (whether Salafism or Wahhabism) beginning in the 1960s.

18. Ideological Differences among Islamism

Every form of current political Islamism claims to have Salafist influence. There is, however, no consensus among the various Islamist groups as to what genuine Salafism means. Upon attaining independence, several nations including Egypt, Tunisia, and Morocco repressed the existing institutional Islamic clergy. Salafism, therefore, spread in several Muslim majority nations both because Saudi Arabia supported proselytism and because of the religious vacuum resulting from government repression.

19. The Salafist Movement and Islamism

Salafism, as a movement, is not necessarily a militant one. It is an ideology advocating the return to the purest form of Islam as practiced by Muhammad's "companions". The term, "Salaf", means "ancestors or predecessors". Currently, Salafism is practiced mainly in Saudi Arabia, the United Arab Emirates, and Qatar. It is strongly influenced by the belief that obedience to authority (including to the political sovereign) is crucial part of the believer's religious life.

Revolutionary Islamists (who claim to be the genuine Salafis) rejected the idea of blind obedience to the sovereign, and believe that all almost existing governments in Muslim-majority nations are un-Islamic and therefore, can be legitimately attacked.

20. How Revolutionary and Process Islamists Differ

While Process Islamists, such as the Muslim Brothers) sympathize with Salafism's rhetoric of Islamic renewal, their gradualist strategy has, in a practical sense, entailed compromise on issues such as gender equality and political pluralism. Most hardline Salafist ideologues reject such arrangements claiming that they violate Islamic principles. One clear example of this is Ayman al-Zawahiri's (al-Qaeda's current leader) condemnation of the Muslim Brotherhood for its allegedly tacit cooperation with Egypt's leadership since the Brotherhood was organized 1928. More recently, Al-Zawahiri's offered contradictory support for the Muslim Brotherhood following the forced removal of Egyptian President Muhammad Morsi. Many commentators viewed this as a mere tactical move by Al-Zawahiri rather than any effort toward rapprochement.

21. Effect of the Shiites and Ideological Divides on Islamism

Shiite Islamism lacks the ideological divisions of Sunni Islam. Shiite Muslims do not challenge the revolutionary-turned-authoritarianism Islamism of Iran. It does, however, have both revolutionary and electoral branches.

22. Islamist Extremism

Extreme Islamism is often divisive. Beyond denouncing "Jews and crusaders" as the enemy, Radical Islamists also attack various non-Muslims worldwide, including the Hindus and Jamir and Malaysia, Buddhists and Confucians in China and South east Asia, vs African animists faiths in Sudan.

Islamists denounce all non-Islam's as kuffar (infidels) and thus, "enemies of Islam'. Islamists also attack Liberal Muslims and thus, generates severe conflict within the Islamic community. In its jihad against Islam's enemies", Islamists often seek to excommunicate liberal Muslims from the Umma (the worldwide Muslim community).

Some scholars argue that for contemporary Islamism to have a constructive role, it must both 1) be committed to democracy, and 2) must be able to communicate its concerns, values, principles and beliefs to connect to non-Muslims.

Islamist jihadists heavily employ religious rhetoric in their propaganda, they wear Islamic garments, its attackers recite and quote the Qur'an. Suicide bombers are promised paradise in the afterlife, complete with several virgins.

23. The Islamist View of a Perfect Society

Islamists reject western social, economic, and political model both because of what they view as the injustice of Western powers. They also condemns what they view as "dissolute" Western social norms that Islamists believe could corrupt the Muslim majority nations.

Islamists have clear and definite views of a better society should be like, and it would recreate the community of the prophet Mohammad. In addition, Islamists have selectively adopted Western technologies, including channels of mass communication and weapons of mass destruction. Islamism, thus, differs from previous types of Islamic traditional movements and presents itself as modern movement despites its anti-modern ideology.

24. Different Manifestations of Islamism

Islamism is manifested differently throughout the world, including in majority Muslim nations. Islamists passionately advocate for a role of religious law (the Sharia) for peoples in public and private life in nations such as Egypt, Iran, and Turkey. Some Islamists are involved in Islamist movements seek to destabilize regimes, and even the international order because they perceive these institutions are hostile or corrupt. Their political positions are based on particular interpretations of Islam. There are other groups and individuals, less well known than the Islamist extremists that derive from Islam an inspiration to struggle for democracy and peaceful relations with other nations, peoples, and cultures.

25. The Goal of Unity of All Muslims

Islamists rely on Islam and its supporters to realize the dream of a unity of all believers within one single umma (community) and (theoretically) under a single state or government. Muslims worldwide, however, live in diverse circumstances. There are four major large and geographically and culturally distinct Islamic regions: Middle Eastern[15], Indian, Malay and African. The Middle East is the most complicated of these regions because of the collective identities, political issues, and ethnic-religious conflicts involved.

Although Islamists seek Muslim unity, Islamism is not a monolithic movement. It differs significantly from country to country, and from one historical period to the next. Further, most Islamists do not advocate violence.

Whether peaceful or jihadist, Islamism has generally increased in numbers and power in Muslim majority nations over the past three decades.

The world especially took notice of Revolutionary Islamism first became widely acknowledged in the 1970s in nations such as Egypt and Syria, and particularly, with Iran's Shia Islamic revolution in 1979, and with the first hostage takings and suicide bombings in Lebanon in the 1980s.

Since the 1980s, Islamism has continued to expand and it has grown increasingly extreme. During the 1990s, there was a sharp rise of jihadist attacks worldwide from Nigeria to Indonesia. The Islamists have also increasingly targeted the West. In responding to the threat, some Western policies have been criticized for enabling increasing Islamist jihadist violence.

26. The Response of Muslims to Living under Non-Islamist Governance

Beginning in the 19th century, Muslims living under what they perceive as un-Islamic governance evolved over time: traditionalist, reformist, proto-fundamentalist, and modernist.

1) Traditionalist: Conservative Sufis and ulamma who argued against substantial change either acquiesced to British governance or similar to Sayyid Ahmad Barelwi – rejected coexistence. Barelwi and his followers advocated for Muslim withdrawal to areas not under that they viewed as "infidel control", and then prepare for jihad (struggle) to regain lost territory that they believed was under a House of War status.
2) Reformists and protofundamentalists interpreted Muslim policies losses as resulting from a failure to obey Islam, which brought God's wrath on them. Although many followed the 18th century conservative Islamist ideologue, Shah Waliallah, they also included pantheists and Sufis. They sought to purify Islam from what they viewed as superstitions (including the veneration of tombs of saints and other practices supposedly originating in Hinduism. They stressed the ideal of an ulama-led religious community.
3) Modernists eventually emerged as the most significant branch of Islamism. Muslim aristocrats and civil servants attempted to regain the lost influence and prestige of Muslims through accommodation. This, however, presupposed both Anglicization and modernizing Islam, which emphasized education. While the British were opening schools for (mainly) Hindu young people to develop an indigenous English-speaking Indian elite – the joint socializing of youth from throughout India facilitated

---

[15] This work uses the term "Middle East", a commonly used phrase that describes a region of Western Asia and Northern Africa where 400 million Muslims live. The term is somewhat controversial because officials with the British Empire developed the term and it reflected their Eurocentric worldview.

a modernizing intellectual atmosphere that was key to developing a new pan-Indian mindset. The leading Muslim intellectual, Sayid Ahmad Kahn, established an alternative Aligarth School in 1875, to provide both Islamic religious instruction and Western scientific education. Khan believed that Islam and modernity were compatible and sought to develop a new generation of an influential Muslim elite in a new India.

27. Islamists Invoking Islam

Islamism can take the form of national liberation movements. This often occurs where Muslims perceive themselves as an oppressed community, and use Islamic shibboleths to mobilize the Indian community. One tactic name was to invoke religious feeling in naming a group such as Lashkar-e-Taiba (Army of the faithful), a Pakistani jihadist group that seeks Kashmir's annexation to Pakistan.

- *Moral Islamism* – Encourages Muslims to live a more pious or orthodox lifestyle.
- *Process Islamism* – involves Islamism campaigning on a political program to gain political power within a Muslim-majority nation and ensuring that its government and legal policies conform to Sharia.
- *Revolutionary (or Jihadist) Islamism* – often relies on violence and terrorism to effect change with the goal of creating an Islamist state. Revolutionary Islamism is not synonymous with all Islamism, certainly not Islam, or Muslim fundamentalism.

28. Emergence of Revolutionary Islamism

The concept that an Islamic revival would be triggered by revolution gained in popularity during the 1970s. Israel's victory over the Arab powers in the Six-day War in 1967 discredited Islamism's main political rival, pan-Arabism. The Ayatollah Khomeini preached a political Islam and in 1979 established the first Revolutionary Islamist government in the 20th century when Khomeini also claimed Iran's primacy over all Muslims (this despite the fact that only 10% of Muslims are Shia and 90% are Sunni) and agitated for the overthrow of the Arab monarchies bordering Persian Gulf.

29. Influence of the Islamic Revolution on the Sunni Revolutionary Movements

Sunni revolutionary Islamism, despite its doctrinal differences with the Shia, was inspired by Iran's Islamic Revolution, and occasionally some Sunni Revolutionaries have been funded by Iran as well.

29.1. Iran Seeks to Depose the Arab Monarchies

While Iran's rhetoric deeply concerned its neighbors in the Middle East, anxiety increased when actual attempts to overthrow these governments occurred, including, against the Saudi government in 1979 and then the Bahraini government in 1981. To leaders of established governments in the Middle East, this was confirmation that revolutionary Islamism (whether Sunni or Shia) posed a genuine, serious, and present threat. The Egyptian Islamic Jihad assassinated Egypt's President, Anwar Sadat, during a military parade in 1981. Similar jihadist groups arose in Algeria, Palestine and Lebanon, and all sought to overthrow their governments.

Arab governments adopted a strategy involving three broad approaches to oppose revolutionary Islamism: 1) control the civilian population (including repressive measures in some cases), 2) engage in sectarian rhetorical confrontations with Iran, 3) coopt certain Islamist organizations considered to be moderate, and 4) during the Afghan-Soviet War (1979-1988), actively recruit young men who were attracted to revolutionary Islamism to fight against the Communist occupation of a Muslim-majority nation.

29.2. Growth of Revolutionary Islam

Neither the concept of revolutionary Islam nor its leaders such as Osama Bin Laden dissipated over time. The Soviet defeat in 1988 galvanized Revolutionary Islamism, which would seek to expand its jihadist mission. US forces arrived in the Arabian Peninsula to repel Iraq's invasion of Kuwait in 1990 which angered jihadists who opposed foreigner troops in Muslim lands and the Palestinian Liberation (PLO's) renounced violence which led to the rise of Hamas in 1987, veterans of the Afghan-Soviet War began to train in bases in places such as Somalia, Sudan, and Yemen. They established a database of the would-be fighters who attended. Hence, US intelligence agencies began referring to this jihadist organization by the name, al-Qaeda (Arabic for "the base).

30. Globalization of Revolutionary Islam

Revolutionary Islamist terrorist attacks, involving suicide bombings became globalized beginning in 1998. Groups such as al-Qaeda, Islamic State, Beit al-Maqdis, Ansar al-Sharia routinely engaged in terrorist acts to destabilize existing governments and encourage Muslims to resist these governments. They used different strategies and tactics against different targets. While al-Qaeda sought to attack the "far enemy" (the United States and the West), other jihadist groups such as Islamic State focused on fighting the "near enemy" including secular Arab governments and adherents of different faiths. These tactical choices were made more by feasibility rather than ideology.

31. Failures of Revolutionary Islam

Sunni revolutionary Islamist groups have yet to provoke the widespread popular uprising they were hoping for. In nations such as Algeria, Iraq, Bosnia, or Saudi Arabia, Sunni revolutionary Islamism never received the large-scale and enduring support. This sharply contrasts to the Iranian Revolution, which was a mass uprising that did receive widespread popular support among the Iranian people.

32. The Process Islamists

The Process Islamists are groups that chose to follow Hassan al-Banna's tactics of a gradual and incremental Islamization of society. They became increasingly political influential beginning in the late 1970s. Examples include the election of National Islamic Front (NIF) members to Sudan's parliament in 1979 and later with the formation of the Islamic Salvation Front (ISF) in Algeria in 1988. Hezbollah, a Shiite militia created in 1984 with Iran's support, has competed in Lebanon's elections since 1992. The Muslim Brotherhood, although formally prohibited from nominating individual candidates for political office in Egypt from 1984 to the present, nonetheless sponsored successful candidates who ran as "independents". Its Palestinian counterpart, Hamas, won in Palestinian elections in 2006, while Turkey's AKP (formed in 2001), won a majority in 2002 and has governed Turkey ever since. In Iraq, several Islamist parties, both Shia and Sunni, have been politically dominant in Iraq since Saddam Hussein was removed from power in 2003.

33. Growth of Islamist Political Parties

The overthrow of governments in Tunisia and Egypt provided Sunni Islamist parties with the necessary momentum to gain power. In Tunisia, Ennahda (the Tunisian Muslim Brotherhood party), received 37% of votes cast in Tunisia's first free elections; in Egypt, six Islamist parties participated in the 2011 elections, with the Muslim Brotherhood's Freedom and Justice party receiving 34.9% and the Salafist party, Nour, receiving 25% of the vote respectively. The Muslim Brotherhood's candidate, Muhammad Morsi, then became president in 2012 with 51.73% of the vote. Morsi was overthrown on July 3, 2013.

34. Characteristics of the Differing Islamist Political Parties

Although these parties share some broad political goals, they nevertheless disagree over specific policies and strategies. In Egypt, Nour joined the anti-Muslim Brotherhood alliance despite their common Islamist ideology, because they claimed that the Brotherhood is too lenient on issues such as allowing women and Christians to serve in political office, and too lenient towards Iran.

Following the doctrine articulated by Hassan al-Banna, the Egyptian Muslim Brotherhood has not sought the immediate establishment of an Islamist state. Although al-Banna called for an Islamist state, he nevertheless accepted Egypt's existence as a secular nation.

35. Skeptics of Process Islam

Some commentators and government officials have distrusted Process Islamism because some of its adherents and leaders had former connections with revolutionary movements (such as Hamas in the Palestinian territories, Dawa in Iraq, and Hezbollah in Lebanon, or reverted to violence's as the Algerian Islamic Front).

36. Process Islamists in Political Power

When Process Islamists win power, the results have been very different among individual nations. The Sudanese National Islamic Front (NIF) supported both an authoritarian government and a strict implementation of Sharia law, Dawa had played a divisive role in Iraq, and the Tunisian Ennahda successfully embraced politically pluralism.

President Morsi's constitutional decree of 2012, which granted him near absolute powers, generated concerns that he would establish an undemocratic Islamist regime in Egypt. This undermined the Brotherhood's claims that it sought a pluralistic and democratic society.

37. Islamist Governments and Their Legitimacy

Only a very few nations have genuinely become Islamic states. Along with Saudi Arabia and Iran, Islamist governments have had power in Afghanistan (1996-2001) and Iraq and Syria under ISIS (2014-2017), and somewhat in Sudan (1989 to the present).

Both Saudi Arabia and Iran assert that the legitimacy of their governments is based on certain forms of Islamism, however, both are essentially, authoritarian regimes. Saudi Arabia forbids jihad on its territory and argues that its political system perfectly adheres with Islamic doctrine, and thus, there is no need for elections or political pluralism. Iran's political system is based on the primacy of the Shiite clergy.

38. The Key Differences between Saudi Arabia and Iran

The differences between Saudi Arabia and Iran is that while Iran's revolutionary-oriented political organizations, such as Hezbollah, accept its authoritarianism, Sunni revolutionary and political Islamism challenge the Saudi government either through violence or through presenting political alternatives. Although ideologically distinct from Iran, the Sunni political and revolutionary branches nevertheless seem to reflect Iran's rhetoric of radical change – which fosters the Saudi government's concerns of a possible alliance between Sunni forces demanding change and Iran. Some commentators, however, argue that such an alliance is unlikely considering the different political goals of Sunni and Shia revolutionary Islam in Syria, Iraq, Palestine, and Lebanon.

39. The Saudi Approach to Islamism

Seeking to defeat both revolutionary and process Islamism, Saudi Arabia has adopted hard line positions in recent years. It declared both Hezbollah and the Muslim Brotherhood to be terrorist organizations, although the exiled Brotherhood has operated exiled in Saudi Arabia for decades. Although the Saudis had once supported Islamist groups in Syria fighting the Assad government, it joined the air campaign against ISIS. Saudi Arabia also sent troops to Bahrain in 2011 to defeat a Shia uprising. The Saudis have also financially supported the Egyptian government to ensure stability in a nation that has historically been a leading center of political Islamism. Since 2015, the Saudis have been leading a coalition to defeat Houthi rebels, supported by Iran, in Yemen.

40. The Struggle within Islamism

Although they frequently invoke doctrinal and sectarian rhetoric, the ongoing struggle among the three manifestations of Islamism basically revolves the acquisition and maintenance of political power.

40.1. The Development of Islamism Since 9/11
Following the 9/11 attacks, the subjects of Islamism and Islam became even more increasingly controversial and even more emotional. Tensions in Muslim-majority nations have been exacerbated and some ill-conceived Western (especially U.S.) policies made contributed to these problems.

Certain very Conservative groups and their spokespeople in the United States and Europe have promoted the concept of conflict between Islam and the West as a "clash of civilizations". To avoid perpetuating narrative, the Obama administration abandoned use of the terms Islamization and jihadism.

41. Criticisms of Islamism

Critics of Islamism have criticized it as a regressive ideology that is oriented towards a romanticized version of the past (salaf). Its ideal is the Medina model under the Prophet Muhammad as well as the caliphate of the first four caliphs (Khulafa al-Rashudan). This is articulated in Sayyid Qutb's argument that, "if Islam is again to play the role of the leader of mankind, then it is necessary that the Muslim community be restored to its original form."[16]

42. The Vision of the Caliphate After the Fall of ISIS

One issue that remains relevant is why the ISIS vision of the Caliphate appealed to so many Muslims throughout the world, and why the vision of the caliphate still appeals to so

---

[16] Sayyid Qutb, *Ma'alim fi al-Tariq* [*Milestones*] (1964), Chapter 4.

many Muslims today. During the Arab Spring, many people in the Middle East had hoped that the Arab nations would pursue meaningful reform to be responsive to their citizens' aspirations for effective governance, decent living standards and the rule of law. The results were widely disappointing and included failed states, deepening conflicts, or worsened repression.

As the first attempts at a modern Islamist state failed with the fall of ISIS in Syria and Iraq in 2017 and 2018, some observers deliberated over the broader context, including that many young Muslims were born and raised in environments of nationalism, ethnocentrism, racism and harsh police states, and how these factors contributed to their support for some type of caliphate. Many of these people were lured to the self-proclaimed caliphate, a supposed Islamic state that proclaimed itself to be a paragon of justice and equality but was in actuality a place of unfettered brutality and violence, with several tiny colonialistic enclaves. Despite the failure of the ISIS caliphate, the appeal of some form of an idealistic caliphate still exists for Muslims world-wide.

Despite the fall of ISIS, the vision of an Islamist caliphate may have been revitalized by ISIS' failures, among a large number of young, disenfranchised professionals and activists in the Arab world to European Muslims, middle-class and marginalized alike, who feel increasingly alienated by societies in their home countries.

When Al-Baghdadi announced the ISIS caliphate, he stressed that Islam did not recognized the concept of the nation-state. These statements and their significance, however, were often overlooked, in the context of ISIS' wanton violence and Baghdadi's apocalyptic visions.

One result of the discussion of the caliphate has been an emerging mainstream acceptance of a collective Muslim identity that is worldwide and openly political. The dream of a claiphate continues to encourage young Muslims to view themselves as a collective community, for whom a caliphate would ameliorate the adverse conditions they currently face. Many were attracted by the vision of an idealized future Islamist caliphate with both its spiritual and practical aspects: a place of employment, opportunity, justice, and no pressure to secularize.

Throughout the Middle East, young Muslims reside in nations where it is difficult to find employment, many are unable to marry before age 40 because they cannot afford to, official corruption is common, and the government actively represses Islamist- activism. As a result of these factors, along with many others, many young people claim to be "citizens of Islam", as opposed to a particular political nation.

Supporters of a caliphate include activists who participated in the Arab Spring to Twitter caliphate supporters. These may include hard-core Islamists to the nostalgic, who are attracted by the grace and security that perceived caliphate rule once provided. Some idealistic Islamists argue that such a state would provide enlightened and ethical governance that would grant Muslims "social harmony", which could include "a polity with an elevated culture based on the Arabic language and a neo-Ummayad frontier military ideal.

The emotional commitment to a caliphate remains strong among those who became a part of ISIS, only to see it fail. Some of those who traveled to the caliphate found that ISIS was a group of violent and vicious men seeking to steal and hoard material goods and women.

Intellectuals who support a version of caliphate generally opposed ISIS. They, however, had very different visions of what an eventual caliphate might be. The options include 1) a conventional nation, which is governed by Sharia, 2) a federation of Muslim-majority nations united under Islam, similar to the European Union, 3) a caliphate based on the classical, form, which they perceive as a divinely-ordained empire, or 4) a sectarian state.

ISIS held itself out to be a caliphate. The idea of a caliphate retains a strong appeal despite the failure of ISIS. The vast majority of Muslims who wish to seek an Islamic state are not jihadist-oriented and oppose violence. These Islamists, however, are angered that the government prohibits the public expression of their viewpoints throughout the Arab Middle East; being banned from civil society or mainstream media platforms. For the reasons mentioned above, Islamism and the dream of the caliphate will remain crucial issues well into the foreseeable future.

E. Islamic Alternatives to Islamism

Some of the voices advocating for change in Muslim majority nations can be seen in the work of the Muslim Reform Movement. The group opposes Islamism and advocates a progressive view of Islam. It stresses the need for global Islamic reflection, and focusing on tolerance, and a more secular version of Islam. It also recognizes the threat posed by global jihadist groups and political Islamism. Similar organizations include: the American Islamic Forum for Democracy, the Council for Muslims Facing Tomorrow, and the Coalition of Canadian Muslim Organizations. On December 4, 2015, Muslim reformers from Europe, Canada and the United States announced the establishment of the Muslim Reform Movement, and released its Declaration of Reform.

These reformers announced their opposition to violent Islamist ideologies, social injustice and political Islam, and instead articulated a vision for an Islam of peace, human rights and secular governance.

The group announced their support for the following principles:

Peace: We reject interpretations of Islam that call for any violence, social injustice and politicized Islam. We invite our fellow Muslims and neighbors to join us.

Human Rights: We reject bigotry, oppression and violence against all people based on any prejudice, including ethnicity, gender, language, belief, religion, sexual orientation and gender expression.

Secular Governance: We are for secular governance, democracy and liberty. Every individual has the right to publicly express criticism of Islam. Ideas do not have rights. Human beings have rights.

Further Reading

Aboul-Enein, Youssef H. *Militant Islamist ideology: understanding the global threat.* Annapolis, MD: U.S. Naval Institute, 2013.

Abu-Rabi', Ibrahim M. *Contemporary Arab Thought: Studies in Post-1967 Arab Intellectual History.* London: Pluto Press, 2004.

Abuza, Zachary. *Political Islam and Violence in Indonesia.* New York: Routledge, 2007.

Akbarzadeh, Shahram. *Uzbekistan and the United States: Authoritarianism, Islamism and Washington's Security Agenda.* London: Zed Books, 2005.

Almdaires, Falah Abdullah. *Islamic Extremism in Kuwait: from the Muslim Brotherhood to al-Qaeda and Other Islamist Political Groups*. Abingdon, Oxon: Routledge, 2010.

Almond, Gabriel, & Appleby, R. Scott. *Strong Religion: The Rise of Fundamentalisms Around the World*. Chicago: University of Chicago Press, 2003.

Calvert, John. *Islamism: a Documentary and Reference Guide*. Westport, CT: Greenwood Press, 2008.

Calvert, John. *Sayyid Qutb and the Origins of Radical Islamism*. Oxford: Oxford University Press, 2013.

Casaca, Paulo, and Siegfried O. Wolf. *Terrorism Revisited: Islamism, Political Violence and State-Sponsorship*. Cham, Switzerland: Springer, 2017.

Desai, Meghnad. *Rethinking Islamism: the Ideology of the New Terror*. London: I.B. Tauris, 2007.

Donohue, John J., and John L. Esposito. *Islam in Transition: Muslim Perspectives*. New York: Oxford University Press, 2007.

Fakhry, Majid. *A History of Islamic Philosophy*. New York: Columbia University Press, 1970.

Fuller, Graham E. *The Future of Political Islam*. New York: Palgrave Macmillan, 2004.

Griffin, Michael. *Islamic State: Rewriting History*. London: Pluto Press, 2016.

Hale, William M., and Ergun Özbudun. *Islamism, Democracy and Liberalism in Turkey: the Case of the AKP*. Abingdon: Routledge, 2010.

Hamzeh, Ahmad Nizar. *In the Path of Hizbullah*. Syracuse, NY: Syracuse Univ. Press, 2006.

Hansen, Stig Jarle. *Al-Shabaab in Somalia: The History and Ideology of a Militant Islamist Group*. Oxford: Oxford University Press, 2016.

Heywood, Andrew. *Political Ideologies: an Introduction*. London: Palgrave Macmillan, 2017.

Høigilt, Jacob. *Islamist rhetoric: Language and Culture in Contemporary Egypt*. London: Routledge, 2013.

Karam, Azza M. *Transnational Political Islam: Religion, Ideology, and Power*. London: Pluto Press, 2004.

Litvak, Meir. *Constructing Nationalism in Iran: from the Qajars to the Islamic Republic*. London: Routledge, Taylor & Francis Group, 2017.

Martin, Richard C., and Abbas Barzegar. *Islamism Contested Perspectives on Political Islam*. Stanford, CA: Stanford University Press, 2010.

Marty, Martin E. *Fundamentalisms Observed*. Chicago: University of Chicago Press, 1991.

Marty, Martin E. *Fundamentalisms and Society: Reclaiming the Sciences, the Family, and Education*. Chicago: University of Chicago Press, 1993.

Marty, Martin E. *Fundamentalisms and the State: Remaking Polities, Economies, and Militance*. Chicago: University of Chicago Press, 1993.

Marty, Martin E. *Accounting for Fundamentalisms: The Dynamic Character of Groups*. Chicago: University of Chicago Press, 1994.

McCants, William F. *The ISIS Apocalypse: the History, Strategy, and Doomsday Vision of the Islamic State*. New York: St. Martin's Press, 2015.

Mecham, Quinn, and Julie Chernov-Hwang. *Islamist Parties and Political Normalization in the Muslim World*. Philadelphia: University of Pennsylvania Press, 2014.

Moaddel, Mansoor. *Islamic Modernism, Nationalism, and Fundamentalism: Episode and Discourse*. Chicago, IL: University of Chicago Press, 2005.

Montclos, Marc-Antoine Pérouse de. *Boko Haram: Islamism, Politics, Security, and the State in Nigeria*. Los Angeles (Calif.): Tsehai Publishers, 2015.

Munhanif, Ali. *Different Routes to Islamism: History, Institutions, and the Politics of Islamic State in Egypt and Indonesia*. Montreal: McGill University, 2011.

Nafī, Bashīr M., and Sayyid Qāsim Ẕākirī. *Islām'garāyān*. Tihrān: Idārah-i Nashr-i Vizārat-i Umūr-i Khārijah, 1391.

Osman, Tarek. *Islamism: What It Means to the Middle East and the World*. New Haven, CT: Yale University, 2016.

Pande, B. M. *Qutb Minar and its Monuments*. New Delhi: Oxford University Press, 2006.

Quṭb, Sayyid. *Milestones*. New Delhi: Islamic Book Service, 2016.

Roy, Olivier. *Islam and Resistance in Afghanistan*. Cambridge: Cambridge University Press, 1990.

Roy, Olivier. *The Failure of political Islam*. Cambridge, MA: Harvard University Press, 1996.

Rubin, Barry M. *The Iranian Revolution and the Resurgence of Islam*. Philadelphia: Mason Crest Publishers, 2007.

Salih, Mohamed Abdel Rahim M. *Interpreting Islamic Political Parties*. New York: Palgrave Macmillan, 2009.

Shahibzadeh, Yadullah. *Islamism and Post-Islamism in Iran: an Intellectual History*. New York: Palgrave Macmillan, 2016.

Sharīf, Wilyam. *Islamism: Religion & Ideology*. Tranent, Scotland: Jerusalem Academic Publications, 2009.

Surūsh, Ab al-Karim. *Reason, Freedom, & Democracy in Islam Essential Writings of 'Abdolkarim Soroush*. New York, N.Y.: Oxford University Press, 2000.

Tibi, Bassam. *The Challenge of Fundamentalism Political Islam and the New World Disorder*. Berkeley: University of California Press, 1998.

Tibi, Bassam. *Islam between Culture and Politics*. Houndmills, Basingstoke, Hampshire: Palgrave, 2001.

Tibi, Bassam. *Islamism and Islam*. New Haven: Yale University Press, 2012.

Tibi, Bassam. *Political Islam, World Politics and Europe: From Jihadist to Institutional Islamism*. Abingdon, Oxford: Routledge, 2014.

Tohamy, Ahmed. *Youth Activism in Egypt: Islamism, Political Protest and Revolution*. London: I.B. Tauris, 2016.

Volpi, Frédéric. *Political Islam: a Critical Reader*. London: Routledge, 2011.

Willis, Michael J. *The Islamist Challenge in Algeria: a Political History*. Washington Square, NY: New York University Press, 1997.

CHRONOLOGY

610:	The Prophet Muhammad received his first revelation from God. Muhammad established Islam in Mecca.
622:	Muhammad and his followers fled to Medina, where Islam began to flourish.
630:	The Prophet Muhammad captured Mecca.
632:	The Prophet Muhammad died. Abu Bakr, an early convert to Islam and trusted advisor and close friend of Muhammad, became the first caliph (successor of Muhammad).
680:	The Shi'ite Millenarian Rebellion.
691:	The Dome of the Rock (Al Asqa), one of Islam's holiest sites, was constructed in Jerusalem.
1090-1256:	The Isma'ili Fedayeen cult of "assassins" launched a terror campaign against the Abbasid Islamic empire until Mongol invaders vanquished the group.
1098-1270:	The Crusades occurred.
1258:	**January:** The Mongols led by Hulagu Khan (grandson of Genghis Khan) invaded Baghdad, ending the rule of the Abbasid Caliphate. February: The Mongols began their rule over present-day Iran and Iraq.
1263:	**January:** Ahmad ibn Taymiyya (d. 1328) was born. Historians and commentators often view him as the founder of Islamic fundamentalism. He was an adherent of the school founded by Ahmad ibn Hanbal. Many subsequent Islamic scholars, such as Ibn Abd al-Wahhab and Abu Alaa al-Maududi, extensively relied on Taymiyya's writings. Taymiyya's works continue to influence much of Fundamentalist Islam in contemporary times.
1266:	Death of Berek Khan, a Mongol leader and Muslim convert.
1270:	The Eighth Crusade. King Louis IX led the Crusader invasion of Tunisia, which later failed.
1281:	Osman I began his reign and established the Ottoman Empire. He died in 1324.
1299:	The Mongols invaded Syria, and the Marinids attacked the Ziyyanid capital of Demcen in present-day Algeria.
1393:	The Ottoman army invaded Bulgaria.
1400s-1500s:	The Ottoman Empire is at the height of its power and influence.
1448:	**October:** The Turks defeated the Serbs in the Second Battle of Kosovo. Turkey annexed Serbia and made Bosnia a territorial vassal.

April 6 1453:	Mehmed II conquered Constantinople, which he ruled until 1481. The Byzantine Empire collapsed and the Ottoman Empire is united.
1492:	The united kingdoms of Aragon and Castile captured Granada. King Ferdinand and Queen Isabella expelled all Muslims, Jews, and other non-Catholics from Spain.
1501 (1487-1524):	The founder of the Safavi Empire became shah (king) of Iran. Shi'ism became the official religion of Persia.
1516:	The Ottoman Empire conquered Egypt and Syria.
1517:	The Ottoman Empire assumed control over Mecca and Medina, Islam's two most sacred places.
1520:	Suleiman the Magnificent became Emperor of the Ottoman Empire, which reached its power and influence during his reign. The Ottomans conquered Hungary and the Mediterranean coastal areas of Algeria and Tunisia during Suleiman's reign.
1556:	Akbar the Great (1542-1605) established the Mughal dynasty in northern India.
1625:	The Islamic Mataram Sultanate seized control of Java.
1703:	Birth of Ibn Abd al-Wahhab, whose extensive reform of Islam would be eventually referred to as Wahhabism. His theology is based on the teachings of Taymiyya (and an austere interpretation of traditional Islam, derived from a literal interpretation of the Koran). Wahhabism became a leading Islamic religious school and highly influential in the Gulf States.
1740:	Muhammad ibn Saud, founder of the first Saudi state and the Saudi dynasty, and the Islamic scholar, Ibn Abd al-Wahhab, pledge to collaborate to establish a true Islamic state. Wahhabism remained Saudi Arabia's principal form of Islam.
1790:	The Whabbaban Alliance controlled most of the Arabian Peninsula and often raided Medina, Syria, and Iraq.
1794:	The Qajar dynasty ousted the Afghans from Persia (modern-day Iran). The Qajar dynasty ruled Persia from 1795 to 1925.
1798:	Napoleon invaded Egypt.
1800s:	European nations began to establish colonies in former Ottoman territories.
1801:	The Whababan Alliance attacked Karbala, in present day Iraq.
1803:	Abdul Aziz entered Mecca. Abd al-Wahhab's forces destroyed historical monuments, tombs, and shrines.
1804:	The Mughal Empire officially ended after Shah Alam II accepted the protection of the British East India Company.
1805:	Egypt became independent of the Ottoman Empire. It then assumed control of western Arabia and extended its boundaries to the Sudan.
1813:	The Egyptian army captured Mecca and Taifa, which forced the Saudi Arabs from the Hijaz.
1815:	The Egyptians, fighting under the Ottoman Empire, defeated the Wahhabi forces.

1818:	**September:** The Saudi army surrenders, which ended the Saudi-Ottoman War. The Ottomans captured and destroyed the Wahhabi capital of Dariyah, thus ending the first Saudi state.
1828:	The Russo-Turkish War began.
1829:	**September 14:** Treaty of Adrianople formally ended the Russo-Turkish War.
1830:	The French military entered Algiers, which ends Ottoman rule in Algeria.
1832:	The French recognized Prince Abd al-Qadir as Algeria's emir.
	December 21: Egyptian forces defeated the Turkish army in the Battle of Konya.
1839:	The Tanzimat ("reorganization") era began in the Ottoman Empire, which involved a comprehensive program of modernization in government, the judiciary, and medicine.
1840:	Egypt withdrew its military from Syria under European pressure.
1847:	**December 21:** Abd al-Qadir of Algeria surrendered to the French army after he was refused entry into Morocco.
1849:	Reformist Egyptian ruler Muhammad Ali Pasha died.
1850:	In Constantinople, non-Muslim citizens are declared legally equal to practicing Muslims throughout the Ottoman Empire.
1857:	**May 10:** The Indian Rebellion (the Sepoy Uprising) led to the last Mughal ruler in India, Bahadur Shah Zafar, being ousted from power. The British then seize control of India. The British destroyed Muslim holy sites in Delhi.
1871:	Jamal al-Din al-Afghani relocated to Egypt after being exiled from Afghanistan for his puritanical Islamic views.
1876:	**August 31:** The reign of Abd al-Hamid II began. This reign was one of the most religiously conservative periods in Ottoman history.
1878:	**June 13- July 31:** Congress of Berlin recognized the independence of the Balkan states that the Ottomans once controlled. Thus, Turkey lost most of its European territory.
1879:	Egypt expelled Jamal al-Din al-Afghani for his Islamist socio-political views.
1881:	**May 12:** Under the Treaty of Bardo, the French army occupied Tunisia. French rule in Tunisia lasted until 1956.
1881:	**June 29:** Muhammad Ahmad declared himself to be the Mahdi of Sudan.
1882:	**April:** The British occupied Egypt.
1884:	Muhammad Abdu joined Jamal al-Din al-Afghani in Paris. They collaborated in publishing the influential Islamist journal -- *al-Urwa al-Wurhqa*.
1885:	Muhammad Ahmad declared that Sudan will enforce sharia law.
1886:	Abdullah Suhrawardy established the *Anjuman-e-Islam* in Loudon, which was later called the Pan-Islamic Society of London.
1899:	Great Britain began to officially govern Sudan. Muhammad Abdu became the mufti of Egypt.
1902:	Ibn Saud captured Riyadh, the future capital of Saudi Arabia.
1906:	**April 7:** After the Conference of Algeciras, Morocco became a joint French and Spanish protectorate.

1906:	**August 5:** The Persian Constitutional Revolution led to the promulgation of the Persian Constitution.
1912:	The Muhammadiyya, an Indonesian reform movement, was established. The Islamic Union, a movement in Southeast Asia to modernize Islam in that region, was established.
1914:	**November 2:** The Ottoman Empire, one of the Central Powers (along with Germany and Austro-Hungary), declared war on the Allied Powers (United Kingdom, France, and Russia).
1916:	**May 16:** The Sykes-Picot Agreement divided much of the Middle East between the British and the French governments.
1916:	**June:** The Arab began revolting against the Ottoman rule. Abd-al-Aziz united the fractious Bedouin tribes and launched the Saudi "Ikhwan" (Brotherhood).
1917:	**November 2:** The British government issued the Balfour Declaration to support the establishment of a Jewish homeland in Palestine.
1918:	**October 30:** Under the Armistice of Mudros, the Ottoman Empire lost much of its territory in the Middle East.
1918:	**November 11:** World War I ended after the belligerents signed an armistice.
1920:	**April 25:** The British Mandate for Palestine and the French Mandate for Syria and Lebanon were established.
1921:	**April 1:** Abdullah I became king of Jordan.
1921:	**August 23:** Faisal I became the king of Iraq. Both were sons of the former Sharif of Mecca.
1922:	Great Britain granted independence to Egypt.
1924:	**March 3:** The Republic of Turkey, then governed by Kemal Atatürk, officially abolished the Islamic caliphate after dismissing the Emperor Abdul Majid II.
1925:	**December 15:** Reza Shah Pahlavi overthrew the Qajar dynasty in Persia (present day Iran) and established the Pahlavi dynasty.
1926:	The Tablighi Jamaat (TJ) Islamic reform movement was formed in northern India.
1926:	**January 10:** King Abdul-Aziz of Saudi Arabia declared himself king of Mecca and the Hijaz.
1928:	Hassan al-Banna established the Muslim Brotherhood in Egypt, which sought to restore the caliphate (the Muslim Empire). The group adopted the motto, "Allah is our purpose, the Prophet, our leader, the Koran is our constitution, jihad our way and dying for Allah our supreme objective."
1932:	**October 3:** Great Britain granted independence to Iraq, which later entered the League of Nations.
1935:	Reza Shah Pahlavi renamed "Persia" as "Iran".
	Abd al-Rahman al-Banna established the Muslim Brotherhood in Palestine. He was the brother of Hasan al-Banna, the movement's founder.
1939:	**September 3:** World War II began.
1941:	**August 26:** Deobandi-trained Sayyid Abu'l A'la Mawdudi formed the Jamaat-e-Islami (Islamic Party) in Lahore, India.
1942:	A Muslim Brotherhood group was established in Jordan.

1943:	**November 22:** France granted independence to Lebanon.
1945:	A Muslim Brotherhood group is established in Syria.
	Thousands of Holocaust survivors emigrate to British-controlled Palestine.
	August: World War II ended.
	August 17: Indonesia proclaims itself as an independent republic.
1946:	**March 11:** The Fedayeen-i-Islam, an Iranian Islamic fundamentalist group, began a ten year assassination campaign against westernized Iranian intellectuals by murdering Ahmad Kasravi, a prominent anti-Shi'ite secularist and historian.
	April 17: France granted independence to Syria.
	May 25: Great Britain granted independence to Jordan.
1947:	**August 14:** Pakistan, partitioned from India, became an independent nation, and held itself out as having an Islamic government.
1948:	Spring: Relations deteriorated between the Arab nations and the growing Jewish community.
	May 14: The State of Israel was created.
	November: The United Nations partitioned the British Mandate of Palestine. Palestinians referred to the event as the nakba (catastrophic).
	Muslim Brotherhood operatives assassinated Egypt's prime minister.
1949:	**February 12:** Hasan al-Banna, the Leader of the Muslim Brotherhood, was assassinated in Egypt.
1951:	Italy granted independence to Libya.
1952:	**July 23:** During the Egyptian Revolution of 1952, Gamal Abd al-Nasser led a military coup, which forced King Faruq to abdicate.
1953:	Taqiy al-Din al-Nabhani established Hizb at-Tahrir al-Islami (HTI) in Jerusalem.
	August: Iranian Prime Minister Muhammad Mossadegh is overthrown in a coup d'état.
	November 9: King Abd al-Aziz of Saudi Arabia died.
1954:	**October 26:** Following the attempted assassination of Egyptian President Nasser, that country's government imprisoned hundreds of Muslim Brotherhood members. The Egyptian government subsequently prohibited the group from operating in Egypt.
1956:	Jam'iyyat af 'Ulama' al-Muslimin (JUMM) disbanded in Algeria.
	March 20: France granted Tunisia independence.
	April 7: France granted Morocco independence.
1957:	A Pan-Islamic Congress met in Lahore.
	August 31: Great Britain granted independence to Malaya, which then declared Islam to be the national religion.
1958:	**July 14:** Iraq is declared a republic after Brigadier General Abd al-Karim Qasim conducted a successful coup d état against King Faisal II.
1960:	France granted independence to Mali, Niger, and other former French colonies in Africa.
	April 26: The Iraqi Islamic Party was established from the remnants of the Iraqi Muslim Brotherhood. Iraqi Prime Minister Abd al·Karim Qasim prohibited the Iraqi Islamic Party for one year.

1962:	**March 19:** France granted independence to Algeria, ending the Algerian War for Independence. This conflict had begun on November 1, 1954.
1964:	Fathi Yakan establishes the Al-Jama'a al-lslamiyya (AJI) in Lebanon.
	The Islamic religious scholar Hasan al-Turabi (1932-) became the secretary-general, the leader of the Islamic Charter Front in Sudan, which was the political appendage of the Sudanese Muslim Brotherhood.
	The Egyptian government dissolved the Muslim Women's Association.
1965:	Mujahideen-e-Khalq (MeK) was founded in Iran.
1966:	**August 29:** The influential Egyptian Muslim Brotherhood leader and theologian Sayyid Qutb is executed for allegedly seeking to overthrow the government.
1967:	**June 10:** Israel defeated the Egyptian, Jordanian, and Syrian armies during the Six-Day War. Israel then occupied East Jerusalem, the West Bank, Gaza, the Golan Heights, and the Sinai Peninsula.
	The late 1960s. Sheikh Abdel Tahman developed and led Al-Jihad.
1968:	The International Islamic Union for Student Organizations was established during a pilgrimage to Mecca.
	Shukri Mustapha created the group, al-Takfir was al-HiJra (ATAH), in Egypt.
1969:	**September 1:** Colonel Muammar Gadhafi led a successful coup de etat that deposed King Idris of Libya. Gadhafi would become leader of Libya.
1970:	Abd al-Azziz al-Na'mani established Morocco's Mujahideen movement.
	Anwar al-Sadat became President of Egypt.
	October 26: Necmettm Erbakan Milli formed Turkey's Nizam Partj.
1971:	Egyptian President Anwar al-Sadat released the influential female Islamist Zaynab al-Ghazali from prison.
	Egypt formally recognized Sharia as a source of law.
1972:	**October:** The Milli Nizam Partisi was dissolved in Turkey and was reorganized into Milli Selamat Parfisi.
1973:	**July 17:** Afghani King Zahir Shah was overthrown.
	October 6: The Yom Kippur War began between the Arab nations and Israel.
	October 25: Israel was victorious in the Yom Kippur War.
1975:	The An-wi movement was formed in Lebanon.
	Civil War began in Lebanon.
1976:	**November:** The Egyptian government executed Salih Sirriyya, leader of Tanzim al-Fanniyya al-'Askariyya (Organization of the Military Techniques).
1977:	Egyptian President, Anwar Sadat, entered into peace negotiations with Israel, which was the first time that an Arab government negotiated with Israeli government.
	December 20: Taqiy ad-Din al-Nabhani, founder of Hab al-Tahrir al-Islami (HTI), died in Beirut.
1978:	Israel invaded Lebanon to target Palestinian militants bases in that country.
	Harakat Al-Islah (HaA), a Muslim Brotherhood branch, was formed in Somalia.

	August: Musa al-Sadr, a Shiite leader in Lebanon, disappeared while visiting Libya. **September 17:** Prime Minister Menachem Begin, for Israel, and President Anwar Sadat, for Egypt, signed the Camp David Accords, following secret negotiations.
1979:	The National Islamic Front (NIF) became increasingly influential within the Sudanese government. **February 11:** Ayatollah Ruhollah al-Musawi Khomeini led the Iranian Islamic Revolution, which overthrew the Pahlavi dynasty in Iran and installed the world's first modern Islamist theocracy. **March 26:** Egypt and Israel signed the Camp David peace accords. **November 20:** Islamic fundamentalists seized control of the al-Masjid al-Haram of Mecca (the "Grand Mosque"). They were able to hold off Saudi security forces for two weeks. More than 200 people were killed in this incident. **December:** The Soviet Union invaded Afghanistan.
1980:	Egypt recognizes Sharia as the main source of legislation. Abdullah Yusuf Azzam and Osama bin Laden begin to organize the mujahedeen to fight the Soviet Army in Afghanistan. **April 9:** The Iraqi government executed Muhammad Baqir al-Sadr, the Hizh al-Da 'wa al lslamyya spiritual guide, and his sister, Amina Sadr bin al-Huda. **September 22:** The Iran-Iraq War began. It ended on August 20, 1988. Late September: Muhammad Abd al-Salam Faraj's and Karam Zuhdi's Egyptian groups merged to form Tanzim al-Jihad (TaJ).
1981:	**June 6:** Harakat al-Itfijah al-Islami (the subsequent Harakat al-Nahda - lslamiyya) was formed. **September:** Egyptian President Anwar al-Sadat assumed direct government control of all mosques and arrested thousands of militants. **October 6:** Khalid Islambouli led a group of militant extremists affiliated with Egyptian al-Jihad (EAJ), which assassinated Egyptian President Anwar al-Sadat during a military parade in Cairo.
1982:	Hezbollah in Lebanon is formed in Lebanon **February:** Syrian forces suppressed an Islamist rebellion, resulting in thousands of deaths. It what became known as the Hama massacre. **February 2:** Syrian President Hafiz al-Assad ordered the destruction of Hama. Muslim Brotherhood militants occupied the city, seeking to overthrow the Syrian regime. **June 6:** The Israel military entered southern Lebanon, beginning the First Lebanon War. September 16-18: Lebanese Phalangists killed several Palestinians at the Sabra and Shatila refugee camps in Beirut to avenge the killing of Bashir Gemayel, the newly elected Lebanese President and Phalangist leader, by militants associated with the pro-Palestinian Syrian Social Nationalist Party.
1983:	The Second Sudanese Civil War began.

April 18: An Islamic Jihad (IJ) suicide truck bomber partially destroyed the US embassy in Lebanon, killed 49 people, and forced the US to relocate its embassy from West Beirut.

October 23: An Islamic Jihad (IJ) suicide truck bomber destroyed the US Marines' temporary barracks at the Beirut airport, which killed 241 Marines.

1984: **March 16:** Islamic Jihad kidnapped William Buckley, a CIA station chief in Beirut, as part of its hostage-taking campaign against Westerners in Lebanon. Buckley was later murdered, and his remains were returned in December 1991.

December 12: Suicide truck bombers of al Da'wa, a pro-Iranian Islamic fundamentalist group, attacked the US and French embassies in Kuwait City.

1985: **June 14:** Shiite extremists, affiliated with Hezbollah, hijacked Trans-World Airlines Flight 847, which was flying from Athens to Rome. The militants forced the plane to land in Beirut, where they held the crew and 145 passengers for 17 days. The hijackers killed a U.S. Navy sailor. The impasse ended after the Israeli government released 435 Lebanese and Palestinian prisoners.

1987: **November 7:** General Zine al-Abidine Ben Ali overthrew Tunisian President Habib Bourguiba.

1988: August 20: The Iran-Iraq War ended.

1989: Al-Qaeda began to form.

February 14: Ayatollah Khomeini issued a fatwa demanding the killing of Salman Rushdie, author of The *Satanic Verses*.

February 18: Abbassi Madani established the Islamic Salvation Front (ISF) in Algeria.

June: Sudanese Militants associated with the National Islamic Front (NIF), led by General Omar al-Bashir and Hassan al-Turabi, overthrow Sudan's government in a non-violent coup d'état, and the NIF came to power.

1990: **August:** Saddam Hussein invaded and annexed Kuwait as the nineteenth province of Iraq. US troops entered Saudi Arabia.

1991: The Islamic Salvation Front (FIS) won in elections held in Algeria. That country's military, however, cancelled national elections as the FIS was expected to prevail.

The Armed Islamic Group (GIA) was formed a Islamist jihadist group in Algeria.

February 28: The Gulf War ended, and the Iraqi troops were forced to leave Kuwait.

April 25-28: Hasan al-Turabi established the first and only International Islamic Congress in Khartoum, Sudan.

December: The Algerian Civil War began. This conflict would cost the lives of between 100,000 to 150,000 people.

1992: Militants formed the Hizb Jabhat al-'Amal al-Islami (Islamic Action Front) in Jordan.

February: Israeli forces killed Sheikh 'Abbas al-Musav', the leader of Hezbollah in Lebanon.

	August 28: Rashed al-Ghannoll Shi, the Tunisian Ennahda leader, was sentenced to death in Tunisia but escaped to England.
1993:	Al-Jihad operatives attempted to assassinate two high-ranking Egyptian government officials.
	February 26: Ramzi Yousef and other Al-Qaeda militants placed explosives in the parking lot basement of the North Tower of the World Trade Center in New York City.
	March 18: Professor Hamid Nasr Abu Zayd is charged with apostasy in Egypt.
1994:	GIA operatives hijacked Air France Flight 7969, intending to crash it into the Eiffel Tower. September: The Taliban army was formed in Afghanistan.
	October 26: Israel and Jordan signed peace accords, resulting in Islamic insurgencies against Jordanian King Hussein.
	Hamas continued to conduct terrorist operations against Israel.
1995:	**Summer:** The Algerian Armed Islamic Group (AIG) attacked the French public transportation system.
	Al-Qaeda is implicated in the bombing of US barracks in Saudi Arabia.
	June: Al-Gama al-Islamiyah (AGI) failed in an attempted assassination of Egyptian President Hosni Mubarak while he was visiting Addis Ababa, Ethiopia.
	October 26: Fathi Shaqaqi, a co-founder of the Palestinian Islamic Jihad (PIJ), was killed in Malta.
	November 4: Yitzhak Rabin, the Israeli Prime Minister, was assassinated in Tel Aviv.
1996:	The Taliban establish a regime in Afghanistan.
	Bin Laden and al-Qaeda relocated from Sudan to Afghanistan, where they received Taliban support.
	January 5: The Israeli military killed explosives expert Yahya Abd-al-Latif 'Ayyash in Gaza forces, which inspired certain Palestinian jihadists to create the Yahya 'Ayyash Brigades (AAB) in Palestine.
	June 25: Al-Qaeda is believed to have carried out the bombing of the Khobar Towers in Riyadh, Saudi Arabia.
	June 28: Necmettin Erbakan was elected the first Islamist prime minister of Turkey.
1997:	The Islamic Salvation Army (AIS) agreed to a cease-fire with the Algerian government.
	Abd al-Fatrah Abu Ghudda, a former Syrian Muslim Brotherhood leader, died in exile.
	September 25: Hamas leader, Ahmad Yassin, was released from an Israeli jail.
	November 17: The Egyptian Islamic Group (EIG) killed sixty-five tourists in Luxor, Egypt.
1998:	The Salafist Group for Preaching and Combat (GSPC) intensified its terrorist activities in Algeria.
	February 23: Osama bin Laden requested that all Muslims join a worldwide jihad against all Westerners and Jews through various terrorist actions

	August 7: Al-Qaeda-linked terrorists bombed the United States embassies in Nairobi, Kenya, and Dar-es-Salaam, Tanzania, which killed 263 people and injured more than 5,000 others.
2000:	**October 12:** Terrorists connected with Al-Qaeda connected to "The USS Cole" while it is docked in Aden, Yemen. This attack killed 17 sailors and wounded 39 others.
2001:	**March 2:** The Taliban destroyed the sixth-century Bamiyan Buddha statues in Afghanistan.
	September 11: Al-Qaeda-linked terrorists highjacked four American commercial airliners and crashed them into the Pentagon in Washington, D.C.; a field in rural Shanksville Pennsylvania; and New York City's World Trade Center (which completely destroyed the twin towers). The "9-11 attacks" killed 2,973 people. Responding to these terrorist acts, the US attacked the Taliban and al-Qaeda in Afghanistan. The US government also launched its global "War on Terror".
2002:	Al-Qaeda militants bombed the Limburg, a French ship off the Yemeni coast. Bombers reportedly connected to al-Qaeda attacked nightclubs in Bali.
	March 1: The United States invaded Afghanistan to fight the Taliban army and Al-Qaeda.
	Hamid Karzai became the interim president of Afghanistan. The Taliban continued to fight the Afghan Government and Coalition forces near the Afghan-Pakistan border.
2003:	**February:** The Darfur conflict began in Sudan.
	March 19: The United States invaded Iraq and overthrew Saddam Hussein and his Baathist regime. Hussein was eventually captured and later executed. Following the invasion, the jihadist presence in Iraq worsened. Anti-Western hostility and terrorism increased in Iraq.
	April 14: The Association of Muslim Scholars, a Sunni organization, was formed in Iraq.
	May 16: The Salafia Jihadia (S.J.) group, directed by Al-Qaeda, conducted the Casablanca suicide bombings, in Morocco, that killed over 30 people and injured over 100.
	August: Zarqawi ordered the bombing of the Jordanian Embassy, UN headquarters, and the Imam Ali Shrine.
2004:	Afghanistan ratified a new constitution that established Afghanistan as an Islamic state and granted the president strong executive powers. Karzai subsequently won Afghanistan's first presidential election.
	March 11: Islamic militants conducted several bombings in Madrid, killing 191 and injuring 1,824 injured.
	October: Abu Musab al-Zarqawi established and leads Al-Qaeda in Iraq (AQI). Unrest occurs in the Middle Eastern nations of Bahrain, Iraq, Jordan, Kuwait, Lebanon, and Libya. Morocco, Oman, and Syria.
	January: Egypt's Muslim Brotherhood announced that Abdel Moneim Abul Fotouh would be its candidate in upcoming legislative elections; other Islamist leaders campaign for the presidency. May 2: U.S. Navy SEALs

killed Osama bin Laden as they attempted to apprehend him in Abbottabad, Pakistan.

June 12: The Turkish Islamic Party (TIP) won in national elections that would dramatically change Turkey's foreign policy.

September 30: Anwar al-Awlaki, the American-born al-Qaeda recruiter, was killed in Yemen. October 18: Israel exchanged 1,024 Hamas prisoners for an abducted Israeli soldier, Gilad Shalit. October 23: Ennahda (Renaissance Party) won the first free elections in Tunisia.

November 26: The Morocco Islamist Party, Justice and Development (Adalet ve Kalkmma Partisi), won in new elections.

November: AQ-I bombed hotels in Amman Jordan.

November 30: The Egyptian Muslim Brotherhood Party won the Egyptian elections. The Salafi party al-Nour placed second with 25 percent of the votes. Many al-Nour members had previously supported jihadism, and some were imprisoned for their activities.

2006: **January:** Al Qaeda in Iraq (AQ-I) and its supporters formed the Mujahideen Shura Council to oppose those it considers "polytheists", "infidels", and "secularists".

In the UAE's first-ever national elections, a small number of hand-picked voters chose half of the members of the Federal National Council - an advisory body.

February: AQ-I attacks the Shiite Golden Mosque in Samara, Iraq.

June: a US airstrike kills Abu Musab al Zarqawi. Zarqawi is succeeded by Abu Ayub al Masri as leader of AQ-I.

October: Al Masri announced the formation of the Islamic State of Iraq (ISI). He appointed Abu Umar (Abdallah Rashid) al Baghdadi as leader of the group. Al Masri apparently retained operational control of the group.

2007: The US-supported Iraqi Security Forces and Sunni Awakening/Sahwa Movement helped to weaken ISI.

2008: **October:** The US Forces military attacked ISI's foreign fighter network in Abu Kamal, Syria.

2009: **February:** President Obama ordered 17,000 additional troops to Afghanistan.

August: Afghan President Karzai won re-election in a vote tainted by fraud.

December: President Obama ordered 30,000 troops to Afghanistan in 2010, which brought the total US military force to nearly 100,000.

August-December: ISI gained increasing support among Iraqis. High profile ISIS attacks indicates that the group had rejuvenated itself.

2010: **April 18:** Abu Bakr al-Baghdadi became the leader of ISI, after ISI's two highest-ranking leaders, Abu Omar al-Baghdadi and Abu Ayyub al-Masri, were killed in a joint US-Iraqi airstrike in Tikrit.

May: Abu Bakr al-Baghdadi was appointed as the emir of ISI.

2011: **March 2011 to March 2013:** Pro-Democracy demonstrations in Syria turned into a revolution and then into a protracted civil war. Islamist organizations such as Al-Qaeda's Nusra Front entered the conflict. ISIS militants entered Syria exploiting the chaos to seize territory. ISI also began a bombing campaign in Iraq.

March: The Syrian uprising began.

March 2, 2011: The jihadist, Arid Uka, killed two U.S. airmen and injured two others at Frankfurt airport after apparently being inspired by a false internet video that claimed to prove US military atrocities in Afghanistan.

November 2, 2011: The offices of Charlie Hebdo in Paris were firebombed after the satirical magazine ran a cover featuring a caricature of the Islamic prophet Muhammad. There were no injuries.

2012:

January: Jabhat al Nusra (JN) was formed. JN was led by Abu Mohammed al Jawlani.

January 21: Boko Haram killed almost 200 civilians in the Nigerian town of Kana. The group was increasingly better trained and armed, due to possible support from al-Qaeda in the Islamic Maghreb (AQIM).

January 30: The Taliban and the United States announce peace talks that were to take place in Qatar.

February: ISI's Abu Mohammad Adnani calls for regional sectarian war in the Middle East.

March: A gunman claiming to be connected to Al-Qaeda killed three Jewish schoolchildren, a rabbi and three paratroopers in Toulouse, southern France.

July: ISI Leader, Abu Bakr al Baghdadi supports the revolt in Syria and calls for an Islamic state in the Middle East.

September: The Syrian Islamic Liberation Front (SLIF) was formed.

December: The Syrian Islamic Front (SIF) was formed.

2013:

The Egyptian military overthrew Egypt's Muslim Brotherhood-led government.

March: ISI and the Nusra Front fighters enter the northeastern city of Raqqa.

April: Baghdadi claimed that ISI has absorbed the Nusra Front to form what they called the Islamic State of Iraq and the Levant (ISIL) or ISIS, which operated across Iraq and Syria. The Nusra Front denied it accepted the merger, resulting in an internal leadership dispute within al-Qaeda that was played out in open.

March 13: Syrian warplanes and helicopters fire rockets into northern Lebanon, days after Damascus warns Beirut to stop militants crossing the border to fight Syrian government forces.

May: At least ten people are killed in sectarian fighting in Tripoli, Lebanon, between supporters and opponents of the Syrian regime.

May 22: Two Al Qaeda-inspired extremists ran down British soldier Lee Rigby in a London street, then stabbed and hacked him to death.

June: Several people are killed in clashes between Hezbollah gunmen and Syrian rebels within Lebanon. At least 17 Lebanese soldiers are killed in clashes with Sunni militants in the port city of Sidon.

July: European Union designates the military wing of Hezbollah as a terrorist organization, making it illegal for Hezbollah supporters in Europe to send the group money, and allowed the group's assets to be frozen in Europe.

July: Jesuit priest Paolo Dall'Oglio was reported missing in Raqqa after seeking the release of hostages and arranging a truce between ISIS and Kurdish rebels. Shortly thereafter, jihadists seize control of the city, seize two Christian churches, and replace the crosses on the steeples with their flags.

August: A large number of people were killed in bomb attacks at two mosques in Tripoli, Lebanon. The twin attacks, are associated with tensions over the Syrian conflict. The attacks caused the most casualties in Lebanon since the civil war ended in 1990.

September: The United Nations refugee agency reported there are at least 700,000 Syrian refugees in Lebanon.

Autumn: Images of ISIS's brutal rule are widely disseminated over the Internet worldwide.

November: Double suicide bombing outside Iranian embassy in Beirut Lebanon killed at least 22 people. It is one of the worst attacks in Shia southern Beirut since the conflict in Syria began.

December: The shooting of a tribal leader at a military checkpoint in the eastern province of Hadramawt, in Yemen, sparked mass protests in the provincial capital Mukalla.

December: Hezbollah leader Hassan Nasrallah claimed the Saudi intelligence services were responsible for the bombings outside the Iranian embassy in Beirut, Lebanon.

December: Mauritania's President Ould Abdel Aziz's Union for the Republic party won a majority of seats in the first parliamentary polls since 2006. Most opposition refused to participate in the election.

2014: Boko Har kidnapped nearly 240 schoolgirls in Chibok, Nigeria.
ISIS headed two American journalists and one British aid worker. ISIS seized Fallujah in Iraq.

January: ISIS captured Fallujah in Iraq and much of Ramadi, the capital of Anbar's province, in Iraq. Over 13,000 families fled that region. In Syria, ISIS began fighting rival rebel groups over contested territory.

National Dialogue Conference in Yemen reached an agreement that would lead to the creation of a new constitution for the country.

January 14: ISIS seized the city of Raqqa in northern Syria after intense fighting with competing insurgent groups. Raqqa became the first Syrian provincial capital completely lost by the Syrian government in the Syrian conflict. The city would later become an ISIS stronghold and capital of the group's caliphate.

February: A Presidential panel approved a plan for Yemen to become a federation of six regions as part of a political transition plan.

Nigeria rescheduled its presidential from February 2015 because of Boko Haram-related unrest.

April: The first round of the Afghan presidential election were inconclusive. It went on to a second round between Abdullah Abdullah and Ashraf Ghani.

UN announced that number of Syrian refugees registered in Lebanon now exceeded one million. The growing number indicated that nearly 25% of the people living in Lebanon was a refugee from the Syrian conflict.

May 24: A former French fighter connected to ISIS in Syria shot and killed four people were killed at the Jewish Museum in Brussels.

June: Mauritania President Ould Abdel Aziz won another five-year term in elections that the opposition boycotted.

June: Afghanistan held its second round of the presidential election. Over 50 Afghanis were reported killed in various attacks related to the election.

June 9: ISIS began a surprise blitzkrieg in northwestern Iraq.

June 10: ISIS militants seized Mosul. The group captured local government, police and military headquarters, and seized a significant amount of US-supplied military equipment.

June 11: ISIS captured most of Nineveh province and Tikrit. The group seized 500 billion Iraqi dinars ($429 million) from Mosul's central bank.

June 16-18: Mass kidnappings and executions were reported from Iraq and Syria. Tens of thousands of Christians and Yazidis fled before the ISIS advance.

June 29: ISIS announced that it had formed a "caliphate" and renamed itself the Islamic State.

July: Afghan election officials conducted a recount of all votes cast in Afghanistan's presidential run-off, to resolve conflicts between candidates over alleged widespread fraud.

Nigeria and neighboring nations agreed to form a joint military force to confront the growing regional threat posed by Boko Haram.

Houthi Tribesmen destroy Yemen's largest oil pipeline, disrupting supplies from the interior to a Red Sea export terminal.

France announced the establishment of a long-term military operation to prevent jihadist fighters from finding sanctuary in the Sahel, which included nations such as Mauritania, Chad, and Niger.

July 5: Baghdadi delivered a sermon at Al-Nouri Mosque in Mosul and demanded that Muslims swear allegiance to him and join the caliphate. ISIS's conflicts with al-Qaeda worsen.

August: Yemeni President Mansour Hadi dismissed his cabinet and cancelled a fuel price increase after prolonged anti-government protests in which Houthi rebels participate.

Boko Haram declared an Islamic state (or Caliphate) over territory under its control in northeastern Nigeria.

Syrian rebels overrun border town of Arsal. They withdraw after being challenged by the military but take 30 soldiers and police captive.

Syrian rebels seized control of border town of Arsal. They withdrew after being confronted by reinforcements from the Lebanese military. The rebels, however, captured 30 soldiers and police officers.

ISIS seized control of several Kurdish-held towns. US war planes supported Kurdish Peshmerga forces by striking jihadist positions. ISIS repelled defending Kurdish Peshmerga forces defending town of Sinjar. Yazidis sect fled from Sinjar. US, Iraqi government supply Peshmerga fighters with weapons to assist them battle Islamists.

Iraqi Prime Minister Nuri al-Maliki, who had been perceived as increasingly divisive personality, who alienated the Sunnis and the Kurds - is replaced by Haider al-Abadi.

August 5: ISIS attacked the Iraqi district of Sinjar, largely populated by Yazidi Kurds, a religious minority considered by radical Sunnis to be heretical. Thousands fled, with hundreds are killed, kidnaped, and women held as sex slaves.

August 8: The US launched air strikes against ISIS targets in northern Iraq, at the request of the Iraqi government.

August 21: Three Americans became involved in foiling an attempted mass shooting in Paris, France. They helped to overpower an armed gunman who began shooting on a train from Amsterdam to Paris. European counterterrorism agencies were monitoring the attacker and appeared to be sympathetic to ISIS.

September: Prime Minister Salam appeals to the UN to assist Lebanon face a "terrorist onslaught" and the flood of refugees from Syria.

Houthi rebels seize control of Sanaa, the capital of Yemen. The UN negotiated a peace agreement in which Houthi fighters agreed to withdraw from urban areas they had captured after a new national unity government takes control.

Five Arab nations began participation in US-led air strikes on ISIS fighters in Syria.

Afghan presidential candidates, Ashraf Ghani and Abdullah Abdullah, agreed to a power-sharing arrangement, after an investigation of the disputed election results was conducted. Ghani became new president of Afghanistan.

Lebanese Prime Minister Salam asked the global community at the UN to assist Lebanon repel a "terrorist onslaught" and assist with a growing number of Syrian refugees.

September 5: President Obama vowed to create an international coalition to defeat ISIS.

September 23: The US and its Arab allies launched air strikes against ISIS in Syria.

October: Intense fighting in Tripoli Lebanon broke out between the Lebanese military and Islamist fighters. This fighting was an expansion of violence from the Syrian conflict.

The United States and Britain formally concluded combat operations in Afghanistan. Afghan opium poppy cultivation in Afghanistan reached a record high.

The Nigerian government announced a ceasefire with Boko Haram and that the abducted Chibok schoolgirls would be freed. Boko Haram responded by denying that it has entered into a ceasefire and claimed that it had married off the girls. Nigerian President Goodluck Jonathan announced that he will seek reelection.

November: ISIS announced it would seek to expand its caliphate into Yemen, which led to the first open conflict between AQAP and ISIS.
Boko Haram launched attacks in northeastern Nigeria. Boko Haram militants seized several towns near Lake Chad and conducted raids in Chad and Cameroon in early 2015. Hundreds of people in the north-east were killed and thousands more displaced.
November-December: Al-Shabab conducted a mass killing in northeast Kenya, including passengers on a bus and laborers at a quarry.
November: Amnesty International accused UAE of carrying out an unprecedented clampdown on dissent since 2011. The UAE published its list of terrorist organizations', including Islamist groups and charities.
December: NATO's ISAF formally concluded its combat mission in Afghanistan, transferring this role to the Afghan National Army. Fighting continued through much of Afghanistan.
A Mauritanian blogger, Mohamed Cheikh Ould Mohamed, received a death sentence for allegedly blaspheming the Muslim prophet, Muhammad. Mauritania's Supreme Court heard the appeal.
December 2, 2015: A married couple shot and killed 14 people in San Bernardino, Cal. The FBI is investigating the shooting as an act of terrorism inspired by ISIS.

2015: Nigeria conducted Presidential elections. Incumbent President Goodluck Jonathan is defeated.
Ramadi, Capital of Iraq's Anbar province, falls to ISIS. Palmyra, Syria, falls to ISIS.
January: The NATO-led mission "Resolute Support" begins, with some 12,000 troops involved in providing training and support for Afghan security forces.
January 7: Jihadist militants launched an attack against the French satirical magazine, Charlie Hebdo in Paris, which killed twelve people. AQAP later claimed responsibility for the attack, however this was not independently confirmed.
January: Boko Harm made significant advances in Nigeria.
The Houthis rejected the draft of a new constitution proposed by the Yemeni government. They seized state TV and clash with troops in the capital, in what the government describes as a coup attempt.
Yemeni President Hadi and his government resigned in protest at the takeover of the capital by Houthi rebels. He later rescinded his resignation.
Three activists, including former presidential candidate Biram Ould Abeid, were sentenced to two years in prison for their part in anti-slavery protests in Mauritania.
Israel launches air strikes on Syrian side of the Golan, killing Hezbollah fighters and an Iranian general. Several clashes ensue across Israeli-Lebanese border.
New restrictions on Syrians entering Lebanon take effect, further reducing the number of refugees from the war in Syria.

January: Israel launched air strikes on Syrian side of the Golan, killing Hezbollah fighters and an Iranian general. Several clashes ensue across Israeli-Lebanese border.

January 19: ISIS fighters shoot at Canadian special forces accompanying Iraq military forces. The Canadians responded in self-defense. This was the first time that ISIS and western ground troops clashed.

ISIS kidnapped two Japanese contractors and demanded a $ 200 million ransom. February: Houthi rebels claimed that they were seizing power in Yemen and that a transitional five-member Yemeni presidential council would replace President Hadi. UN Security Council denounced the Houthi move, and demanded they negotiate a power-sharing agreement under the Gulf Cooperation Council framework. Yemeni President Hadi flees house arrest in Sanaa, escapes to Aden.

February 15: A Danish national who was inspired by ISIS went through Copenhagen, killing two and wounding five police officers.

March: President Obama announced that the US would delay its troop withdrawal from Afghanistan, after meeting with Afghan President Ghani.

Hard-line Afghan clerics are condemned after the a Christian woman was killed after falsely accused of burning a Koran in Kabul. Police were accused of not doing enough to save her. The incident led to widespread protests against the treatment of women in Afghanistan. **February-March:** Nigeria, Chad, Cameroon and Niger formed a united military effort to fight Boko Haram. They reported successes against the militants. The Nigerian army seized Gwoza, believed to be Boko Haram's main base, in late March, which left the Jihadist militants controlling only two towns.

March: two attackers shot tourists and other civilians at the National Bardo Museum in Tunis. Twenty-two people were killed in this attack. In a third attack, a bomb destroyed Kuwait's oldest Shiite mosques during Friday prayers. Twenty-seven people were killed in this attack, which was the first major terrorist attack in Kuwait in more than twenty years. ISIS claimed responsibility for the attack. ISIS claimed responsibility for the attack.

ISIS conducted major attacks in Yemen, including two suicide bombings against Shia mosques in Sanaa that killed 137 people. Houthi rebels began advancing towards southern Yemen. Yemeni President Hadi leaves Aden. A Saudi-led coalition of Arab nations began air attacks against the Houthis and imposed a sea blockade. The Iranian government denounced the Saudi-led action. Amid a rapidly increasing civilian death toll, the UN reported that Yemen is near "total collapse".

Muhammadu Buhari won the presidential election in Nigeria, becoming the first opposition candidate to so in Nigerian history.

March 2: Iraqi government forces and Shiite militias began a campaign to force ISIS out of Tikrit, which ISIS had seized in May 2014.

March 20: The ISIS affiliate in Yemen claimed responsibility for several suicide bombings that killed 137 people and wounded 345.

March 31: The Iraqi government announced that Tikrit had been liberated from ISIS. Fighting between government forces and ISIS fighters, however, continue for several days afterwards.

April: Boko Haram reportedly used children as human bombs and forced women into sexual slavery in Nigeria.

Al-Shabab claimed responsibility for killing 148 people, mainly Christian students, at Garissa in Somalia.

April 18: Afghan President Ghani said that ISIS was responsible for a suicide bombing in Afghanistan. At least 35 people were killed, and 125 were wounded in the attack.

May: John Kerry, then US Secretary of State, briefly visited Mogadishu, Somalia, the first US cabinet member to do so. This visit occurred shortly after an Al-Shabab attack on the government quarter of the city that killed 17 people.

A Taliban delegation and Afghan government representatives began informal peace negotiations in Qatar. Both sides agreed to continue negotiations, although the Taliban vowed that it would continue fighting until foreign military intervention ends in Afghanistan. Four men were sentenced to death after killing a woman they believed had burned a Koran.

The Vatican formally recognized Palestinian statehood.

May 15: ISIS captured the ancient city of Palmyra in central Syria. Eventually, the group destroyed the pre-Islamic World Heritage site. ISIS also seized the last border crossing to Iraq. Jaish al-Fatah seized control of Idlib Province, thus, pressuring the Syrian government's coastal stronghold of Latakia.

May 22: A suicide bomber attacked a Shiite mosque in eastern Saudi Arabia as a group gathered to celebrate the birthday of a saint. The attack killed 21 people and wounded several more. The attack occurred in the eastern Qatif region, home too many of Saudi Arabia's Shiite Muslims. It was the deadliest terrorist attack in Saudi Arabia in over ten years. ISIS assumed responsibility for the attack.

May 29: A suicide bomber impersonating a woman blew himself up in the parking lot of the only Shiite mosque in the Saudi city of Dammam. Four people were killed in the attack. ISIS claimed responsibility for the attack.

June: ISIS and Kurdish militants intensified fighting between Raqqa and the Turkish border. The Kurds seized Ain Issa and the frontier town of Tal Abyad. ISIS attacked Kobane and captured part of Hassakeh, the principal city in north-eastern Syria.

Nigeria assumed command of a regional military force to counter Boku Haram, to include troops from Chad, Cameroon, Niger, and Benin.

Sunni extremist conducted a suicide attack on a Shia mosque in Kuwait. The attack killed 27 worshippers and injured more than 200. Seven people are sentenced to death in connection with the attack.

A US drone strike kills Nasser al-Wuhayshi, the leader of AQAP, in Yemen.

June 3: Boko Haram intensified its attacks in northeast Nigeria, killing several people in assaults and suicide bombings. Nigeria's President Muhammadu Buhari promised to destroy the group.

June 4: Amnesty International report accuses the Nigerian military of atrocities in fighting Boko Haram. The report concluded that these abuses are war crimes and possible crimes against humanity. The report also named several senior officers that are allegedly responsible for these acts.

Amnesty International accused the Nigerian military of using torture, mass shootings and starvation in fighting Boko Haram. The group characterized these abuses as war crimes and possible crimes against humanity. The report also named the senior military leadeers it believed to responsible for the alleged abuses.

June 12: Several Boko Haram night-time raids on six remote villages kill at least 37 people in Northeastern Nigeria.

June 16: Suicide bombings reportedly conducted by Boko Haram jihadists killed 24 people and wounded more than 100. This was the first such attacks in Chad's capital N'Djamena. The attacks targeted the police headquarters and a police academy.

June 17: Chad began prohibiting women from wearing the full-face veil, following two suicide bomb attacks.

June 19: Boko Haram militants burned several homes in Niger, killing at least 40 people.

June: A US drone strike killed Nasser al-Wuhayshi, the leader of Al-Qaeda in the Arabian Peninsula (AQAP) in Yemen.

June 22: Two teenaged female suicide bombers killed thirty people at a mosque in Maiduguri. Boko Haram said this was to commemorate the beginning of Ramadan because the group believed the victims were showed insufficiently devoted to "the Prophet". The second teenager reportedly ran from the scene. She also blew herself up away from the scene and killed only herself.

June 26: A gunman killed 38 tourists, mostly British citizens, in the coastal resort of Sousse, Tunisia. ISIS claimed responsibility for the attack.

June: Negotiations on Yemeni conflict began in Geneva, Swtizerland.

June 26: In separate attacks, terrorists attacked an American owned gas plant near Grenoble, France; killed 28 tourists in an attack on a beach resort in Tunisia, and bombed a Shiite mosque in Kuwait.

June 27: Nigerian President Muhammadu Buhari dissolved the board of the Nigerian National Petroleum Corporation, the state oil company where billions of dollars could not be accounted for. Buhari subsequently named a cabinet.

July 7: Boko Haram militant group attacked the central Nigerian city of Jos, and killed at least 44 people.

July 10: The Afghan government stated that by Mullah Akhtar Muhammad Mansour, the Taliban's deputy leader, had authorized negotiations with the Taliban in Pakistan. The Taliban leadership was reportedly divided over whether to negotiate peace.

July 13: A Suicide car bomb attack killed 25 people and injured 15 outside Camp Chapman, the United States military base in southeastern Afghanistan. The Taliban asserted responsibility for the attack. This was the same base was the site of a suicide bombing in 2009 that killed seven Central Intelligence Agency operatives.

July 14: Nigerian President Muhammadu Buhari replaced Nigeria's top military officers, who were blamed for poor performance in fighting Boko Haram.

July 16: US military expanded airstrikes in Afghanistan, including a new campaign against ISIS. The coalition also intensified attacks by drones and airstrikes against ISIS targets.

ISIS controlled area in Syria and Iraq contracted by 9.4% in the first six months of 2015. ISIS now controls approximately 32,000 square miles.

July 1-2: Boko Haram militants attacked several mosques. Forty-eight men and boys were killed on July 1 at a mosque in Kukawa. Seventeen were wounded in the attack. Ninety-seven others, mostly men, were killed in several mosques on July 2nd. Also, several women and young girls were killed in their homes. Also, an unknown number were wounded.

July 1: ISIS launched several attacks on five Egyptian military checkpoints.

July 4: The Syrian Observatory for Human Rights received a video depicting ISIS militants executing 25 prisoners in Palmyra, Syria.

July 5: A suicide bomber struck a church in the Potiskum area of Nigeria's Yobe State. Five people were killed in the attack.

July 6: Boko Haram struck the central Nigerian city of Jos. The attack killed at least 44 people. Boko Haram was responsible for more than 200 people being killed in one week.

July 17: Boko Haram reportedly conducted two bombings in Nigeria that killed about 50 people.

In an Eid al-Fitr celebration (which marks the end of the fast for Ramadan) ISIS militants detonated a truck bomb in a crowded marketplace. At least 120 people were killed and at least 160 were wounded.

July 21: President Obama met with Nigerian President Muhammadu Buhari at the White House. Obama congratulated Buhari on his democratic election and applauded his continued fights against corruption and Boko Haram.

July 24: Nigerian President Buhari criticized the US Government for refusing to sell Nigeria weapons to fight Boko Haram.

July 28: Saudi Arabia agreed to suspend its military offensive against Houthi rebels in Yemen for five days to allow for shipment of humanitarian aid. The violence, however, does not cease. Nearly half of Yemen country has dangerous food shortages and nearly six million of Yemen's people are in danger of starvation.

August: ISIS destroyed antiquities in Palmyra Syria, including the nearly 2,000-year-old Temple of Baalshami. The U.N.'s cultural organization UNESCO condemned the destruction of the temple as a "war crime".

The Pro-Yemeni Government coalition supplemented its air power with hundreds of ground troops. By mid-August, the Yemeni government forces had retaken Southern Yemen, however, confront a growing threat from ISIS and Al-Qaeda-linked fighters.

August 5: The Cameroon government expelled over 3,000 Nigerians in fighting against Boko Haram, which had been conducting cross-border attacks. The clampdown included the arrest of suspected extremists in a camp in northern Cameroon.

August 6: A suicide bomber attacked a mosque in a police compound in western Saudi Arabia. The attack killed 15 people in the most lethal attack on the kingdom's security forces in several years. Eleven of the victims were a part of an elite counterterrorism group, which helped protect pilgrims attending hajj. ISIS claimed responsibility for the attack.

August 11: Rebels advanced into Alawite strongholds by seizing much of the Sahl al-Ghab plain in northwestern Syria.

The Nigerian government blamed Boko Haram for an explosion at a market in the village of Sabon Gari in which at least 24 people were killed, and for a separate attack of a town in Cameroon by hundreds of militants.

August 16: A suicide bomber killed at least three people near a market in the Nigerian state of Borno. The attack was similar to Boko Haram attacks, although no group claimed responsibility.

August 22: At least 50 people - mainly women and children - were killed when the Syrian government attacked Douma town in an opposition-controlled suburb of Damascus with barrel bombs. Several buildings were destroyed by the attacks. Nearly 100 people were injured.

August 27: The Saudi Arabian government arrested Ahmed al-Mughassil, who allegedly organized the 1996 bombing of the Khobar Towers building complex. Nineteen US air force personnel were killed and 400 people were wounded. Mughassil led the Iranian-supported Saudi militant group Hezbollah al-Hijaz. His arrest underscored tensions between US and Iran even as two sought to reach an agreement on Iran's nuclear weapons.

August 30: ISIS militants attacked Qadam and Asali south of Damascus from Al-Hajar al-Aswad. They clashed with Jaysh al-Islam militants in Qadam and those of Ajnad al-Sham in Asali.

August 31: At least 13 civilians were killed at a water plant in Mukalla, Yemen, in Saudi-led airstrikes. The Saudis appear to target certain strategic civilian facilities.

September: Russia conducted first air strikes in Syria, targets ISIS. The West and Syrian opposition say it overwhelmingly targets anti-Assad rebels instead.

September: President Hadi returns to Aden after Saudi-backed government forces recapture the port city from Houthi forces and launch advance on Aden.

September 1: "Levant Front" clandestine security conducted an undercover raid into ISIS-controlled northern Aleppo. Three foreign ISIS fighters are killed in this raid.

September 2: Reports indicate a possible Russian bombing campaign in Syria, mostly against ISIS and other Islamist targets.

US Air Force commander Lt General Thomas McInerney asserted that Iran is the world's 'leading radical Islamic group'. He also asserted that Saudi Arabia's exclusive support of Salafist Islam and suppression of religious pluralism is a more destabilizing influence to the Middle East than Iran.

September 3: 24 people are killed in attacks on two villages by gunmen on horses. Boko Haram conducted similar raids, with guns and explosives. Nobody claimed responsibility for attacks near Biu, in northeastern Nigeria.

September 4: Fighting occurred Marea town north of Aleppo, where Levant Front rebel soldiers killed seven ISIS militants and seized several hostages, besides destroying three ISIS vehicles. The Shamiya Front also seized weapons from the ISIS militants, as many withdrew from the area after suffering significant losses. Other rebel forces attacked the ISIS-held villages of Harbal, Sandaf, Kafrah and Harjal near Aleppo.

September 5: Anti-government riots erupted in Sweida, Syria, where many members of the Druze sect live. This followed the killing of Druze leader Sheikh Wahid Al-Balous, a leading cleric in explosions that occurred on the day before. At least 25 were killed. The rioters believed that the government responsible for the cleric's death destroyed the statue of late President Hafez Al-Assad and attacked several security offices.

September 11: Russian troops were reportedly fighting in Syria. Jaysh al-Islam attacked Adra Prison, seizing two buildings.

September 12: An explosion occurred at the Yolo refugee camp. This was the largest camp for those displaced by Boko Haram attacks. At least seven people were killed, including five children. Boko Haram was believed to the attack.

September 15: The Levant Front shot down a Syrian government M6 jet near the Nairab military airport in Aleppo province. Assad forces also seized control of much of Hamdaniyah district after fighting against pro-Assad militias, killing at least fifteen government soldiers. The Front also attacked a Syrian government security headquarters in the Salahaddin neighborhood. The government forces retaliated by dropping more than six barrel bombs on the rebel-held areas of Dahiya and Shekhan in Aleppo. These attacks killed over ten civilians.

Taliban fighters attacked Ghazni prison and freed 351 of 436 prisoners, including 148 Taliban terrorists charged with national security crimes. The early morning jail break, began with a car bomb explosion that killed four guards and wounded seven others in subsequent shootout.

September 16: Nearly 15 civilians (at least six children and nine women) were killed and dozens wounded after pro-Assad military jets attacked residential structures in the rebel-held al-Maadi area in Aleppo city. More than 25 injured were injured in the attacks.

September 17: A video is released depicting Free Syria Army (FSA) soldiers in Idlib installing sensor wires on a missile defense system for areas they control to protect civilians. They said they would install such systems in other areas.

Syrian Government helicopters drop barrel bombs on a crowded market place, where many were purchasing back to school supplies in the FSA-held Bosra. The attacks killed between 17 and 24 people. Many others were wounded, some severely.

At least 47 people were killed in Syrian government air strikes against rebel-held areas of Aleppo. Syrian warplanes conducted several airstrikes against ISIS targets in Raqqa.

September 18: US Defense Secretary Ashton B. Carter held talks on Syria with Russian Defense Minister, Sergei K. Shoigu, to ensure that US and Russian forces avoid air clashes with each other in Syria.

The "Islam Army" posted a video depicting its members launching several rockets at the Bassel airport, where Russian troops operated.

500,000 children were reportedly displaced over the previous five months because Boko Haram. This raised concerns over Nigerian prime minister Muhammadu Buhari's claims that progress was being made against Boko Haram's rampage of violence and kidnapping.

September 21: Pro-Assad forces targeted the al-Shaar neighborhood in eastern Aleppo city with surface-to-surface missiles, which struck a crowded public market, killing more than 30 civilians and dozens wounded.

September 22: The Syrian army recaptured the towns in the Hama suburbs. Several bombings occurred in the northern Nigerian town of Maiduguri. They were blamed on Boko Haram. Over 100 people are killed in these attacks. The militants used Muslim holiday celebrations to inflict as many casualties as possible, and generate doubt as to the government's claims that Islamist extremist group is being defeated.

September 24: The Nigerian military prohibits all moving vehicles, including animals used for transportation, in northeastern state of Borno during the Muslim holiday to deter Islamic extremists attacks such as the bombings in Maiduguri and Monguno, in which over 100 people were killed.

September 26: The U.S military reports that US-trained Syrian rebels surrendered their vehicles and ammunition to militants connected to al-Qaeda, apparently to gain safe passage.

September 27: British Prime Minister David Cameron indicated that Assad could conceivably be part of a Syrian transition government, but added that Assad could not have a role in Syria's government in the long term. France conducted its first airstrikes in Syria, which targeted ISIS training camps. Russian President Putin condemned U.S. support for rebel forces in Syria as illegal under the UN charter and ineffective. Putin further claimed that U.S.-trained rebels were joining ISIS with weapons supplied by the US.

September 28: Saudi Arabia denied that its military helicopters killed 30 civilians in the Yemeni town of Bani Zela in Hajjah Province. The Houthis claimed that 28 civilians were killed in the attacks and 17 others were wounded.

September 29: The Pentagon reportedly suspended the "train and equip" program for Syrian Rebels referred to as the New Syrian Forces (NSF).

Taliban seized the northern Afghan provincial capital of Kunduz after a prolonged siege. Government forces retreated to city's airport. This is a significant military and political victory for the Taliban and demoralizing defeat for the government. The Afghan government said that they would launch a counterattack.

Kunduz was the first Afghan city captured by the Taliban since 2001. This raised concerns regarding US withdrawal plans and the combat preparedness of Afghan troops.

September 30: Russia began a bombing campaign in Syria. Russian airstrikes hit areas where ISIS had not been known to be present, contradicting Russia's claim that it would only attack ISIS extremists. The airstrike in Hamas Province on US-supported rebels raised concerns that Assad was using the Russian military to destroy all opposition and that moderates may ally themselves with the extremists.

The Saudi led coalition airstrikes against Houthi rebels in Yemen killed nearly 81 people at a village wedding.

October 1: Seven US service members were killed in supporting operation against ISIS militants.

The massive migration of Syrian refugees into Europe, along with concerns that ISIS militants may travel across Europe's open borders, lead world leaders to request to meet with Antonio Guterres, UN high commissioner for refugees. Guterres had pleaded Syrian refugee cause to world community since 2011. Four million refugees had arrived in Europe from Syria since 2011. Guterres argued that the new found attention arose because ISIS is now impacting wealthy nations.

The Nigerian capital, Abuja, was struck by explosions. Boko Haram is largely believed to be responsible.

October 2: Russian warplanes targeted the Syrian rebel coalition, the "Army of Conquest" (or Jaish al-Fatah), instead of ISIS, despite Russian denials. The US government, who prioritized the defeat of ISIS, objected to the attacks and believed that Russia joined the conflict primarily to maintain Bashar al-Assad in power.

October 4: Egyptian President Abdel Fattah el-Sisi announced his support for the Russian military intervention in Syria.

US airstrikes struck a hospital operated by Doctors Without Borders in Kunduz, Afghanistan. The US military was targeting militants near the hospital and acknowledged that it caused the fatalities. The incident sparked new complaints that the US military was not doing enough to prevent civilian casualties.

October 5: "Doctors Without Borders" announced it would leave Kunduz in northern Afghanistan after its hospital is hit by an airstrike that killed 22 people (twelve were staff members). The group's hospital was the only no-cost trauma hospital in northern Afghanistan. The hospital functioned even after Taliban seized the city.

October 6: Russia announced that it would send ground troops to fight in Syria against ISIS. NATO warned Russia after a Russian jet came into

Turkey's airspace. Tensions increased between Russia and the US as the Russians prepared a ground offensive against Syrian rebels, not affiliated with ISIS, who oppose Assad.

ISIS militants destroyed second-century Roman triumphal arches in Palmyra, Syria. Residents also endured government airstrikes aimed at terrorists, and were having difficulty in safely fleeing the city.

Suicide car bombings targeted exiled Yemeni officials and the Saudi and Emirati troops supported efforts to regain Yemen killed at least 15 people in Aden. A new ISIS affiliate claimed responsibility for the assault, which officials earlier blamed on Yemen's Shiite rebels.

General John F Campbell, US commander in Afghanistan, reported that Afghan forces asked for the airstrike against the Taliban in Kunduz.

October 7: The "Fourth Hama Offensive" began with Iranian and Russian support. The FSA repelled an attack by Assad forces in a rural area near Hama.

ISIS insurgents reportedly used chemical weapons. ISIS has reportedly developed, and deployed a small-scale chemical weapons program

ISIS assumed responsibility for several bombings in Yemen's two largest cities. These actions killed at least 25 people. ISIS also targeted the military headquarters in Arden.

October 8: FSA rebels claim to have shot down two Syrian government helicopters that were accompanying Russian warplanes in an attack on the village of al-Mugheer. The Syrian Army captured a significant amount of territory in northern Hama.

US officials denied they were coordinating attacks on ISIS in Syria with the Russians, who were supporting Assad and targeting any opposition group, Islamist or not.

Three suicide bomb attacks killed 18 people in northeastern Nigeria, while Nigerian troops killed 100 members of Boko Haram after the insurgents attacked the military.

Saudi-led coalition airstrikes against insurgents in Yemen killed 23 people at a wedding in Dhamar Province. From April through October, 2015, the coalition's military actions had killed over 1,100 civilians in Yemen.

October 9: President Obama's advisors believed that that the US had very limited immediate options US options to help resolve with the Syrian conflict. They included an the increase in Russian military involvement or defeating ISIS. Obama reportedly believed that Russia would become unsuccessful in achieving its goals and entangled in Syria's civil war and tribal conflicts.

October 10: The Syrian Army reportedly seized the strategic villages of Asthana and Om Harte in. The Army was intending to advance to seize Khan Shayk Hun in southern Idlib province. Senior Hezbollah leader Hassan Hussein al-Haj was killed in the fighting.

Two suicide bombings killed over 100 people at a peace rally in Ankara, Turkey. Although ISIS denied it carried out the attack, Turkish officials believed that ISIS agents had conducted the attack.

October: Militants believed associated with Boko Haram launch suicide bombings at a market and refugee camp in Chad. The attack killed 36 people.

October 12: The Taliban reportedly controlled more Afghan territory than at any time since the US incursion in 2001. This report contradicted the congressional testimony of US commander Gen John F Campbell, who testified that the Taliban controlled much less territory.

President Obama deployed 300 US troops to Cameroon to fight Boko Haram.

Iraqi Shiites supported Russian intervention in Syria to oppose ISIS fighters. Many Shiites believed that Assad's government helped effectively controlled Sunni militants.

October 13: Russian agents arrested terrorists allegedly carrying a bomb. The Russians claimed that several of those detained had trained with ISIS in Syria.

October 14: ISIS made significant territorial advances in fighting local Taliban fighters in Afghanistan. The conflict between the two groups worsened living conditions for civilians. ISIS exercised brutal control, often executing those connected to the Afghan government or the Taliban.

The Taliban announced it would withdraw its forces from Kunduz and end their seizure of the city. The insurgents had controlled the city for over two weeks before Afghan government forces ousted them.

October 15: ISIS released a video of two Canadians, one Norwegian and one Filipino who were kidnapped by ISIS sympathizers on Mindanao Island, Philippines. In the video, the hostages pled for their lives, with militants and ISIS flags in the background.

Turkish government officials expressed concerns about the US and Russian governments providing military aid to Syrian Kurds. The Turkish government blamed Kurds, its main opposition group, for violence and insurrections. The US government supported the Kurdish militants who were a part of the multi-national fight against ISIS in Syria.

The Taliban seizure of Kunduz, Afghanistan, forced many women to flee the city as militants terrorized those who participated in women's groups or education. The Taliban also destroyed buildings used by these organizations, and abrogated much of the progress in women's rights in a city long known for its violence against women.

October 16: The Malaysian government arrested Ardis Ferizi, who allegedly operated an Internet hacking group in Kosovo. This group transferred stolen personal data of over 1,300 American military personnel to ISIS. The US government sought to have Ferizi extradited and charged with providing material support to ISIS.

October 19: The Taliban threatened employees of Afghanistan's major television stations. Prior to this time, the Taliban had not attacked or threatened those associated with the media. The Taliban did so because it was angered by reports that Taliban fighters raped women after they seized Kunduz.

October 20: US and Russian military leaders agreed on steps to avoid possible conflicts in Syria airspace. Canadians Prime Minister-elect, Justin Trudeau said that Canada would end its involvement in air attacks against ISIS in Syria and Iraq.

October 21: Joint Chiefs of Staff chairman Gen Joseph F Dunford Jr visited Iraq to evaluate the accomplishments and capabilities of the Iraqi military and the American-led coalition in fighting ISIS. The Syrian government military and their allies sought to take Aleppo assisted by Russian warplanes and helicopters. This campaign indicated the significant extent that Russian support has helped Syrian forces combat ISIS.

Investigators reported that unfamiliarity with the area and lack of experience working together led to the US and Afghan attack on Doctors without Borders hospital in Kunduz in northern Afghanistan. The attack may have been a consequence of the gradual withdrawal of US troops in Afghanistan and an expedited relocation of forces.

Taliban militants in Ghormach in Northwest Afghanistan killed almost two dozen police officers and captured the police chief.

October 22: Large numbers of migrants from Syria and Iraq continue to arrive in Europe. Some observers express concerns that such massive migration could lead to an increase in crime, unrest and militancy. Intelligence authorities in Germany and neighboring countries assert that European governments should not focus on the small possibility that jihadists are entering with the migrants but on helping the refugees integrate into European society. They argue that a relatively smooth transition will make migrants less likely to be subjected to manipulation by extremists.

October 23: Master Sgt Joshua L Wheeler, of the US Army's Delta Force, is killed seeking to free hostages being held by ISIS in Iraq. Wheeler is first American solder to be killed in action in Iraq in four years.

October 24: Boko Haram militants are forced to retreat back into Nigeria by the Cameroonian military, after the militants attack a village in northern Cameroon and killed eight people.

October 27: The Bangladeshi government arrested four suspects in the murder of an Italian aid worker in Dhaka. The investigators denied reports from social media that ISIS killed the victim, stating that the crime was intended to spark political unrest.

October 28- Prisoners are rescued in an American- and Kurd-led raid on the ISIS prison in Hawija, Iraq. They related stories of torture and execution threats during their captivity. Many of the prisoners were incarcerated because of suspected involvement with American or Kurd forces.

Turkey reported that it struck positions in Syria held by the Kurdish military over past year. This contributed to strains to government efforts to combat ISIS in Syria, because the Kurds are US allies.

October 29: Over 200 ISIS fighters from Chechnya and other central Asian countries were killed for attempting to defect from ISIS to join Jabhat al-Nusra (now known as Jabhat Fateh Al-Sham). Iran accepted an invitation to join in negotiations on ending the Syrian conflict. Iran joined nations such as the United States and Saudi Arabia, who previously had sought to prevent Iran from attending any parleys to discuss Syria's future. The invitation came following a landmark nuclear agreement. This was the first time the United States had diplomatically engaged Iran on the Syria crisis. Iran's inclusion in the talks pointed to both changing dynamic of the Syrian war and Iran's emergence from political marginalization.

The Nigerian military announced that it had freed more than 300 people who had been kidnapped by Boko Haram. Most of these captives were women and children. At least 30 Boko Haram fighters were killed in the skirmish.

October 31: A bomb destroyed a Russian airliner shortly after leaving a popular Red Sea resort of Sharm el-Sheikh in Egypt for St. Petersburg, Russia. The plane crashed in the Sinai Peninsula, where a ISIS affiliate operates. All 224 people on the plane, mostly Russian tourists, died in this attack. ISIS claimed responsibility for the attack, saying it was in retaliation for the Russian intervention in Syria. The crash suggested a possible security breach. The attack raised serious issues about how safe Sharm el-Sheikh is from jihadist violence;

November 3: Efforts supported by the US government to train and arm Syrian rebels to fight ISIS encountered serious difficulties. The force largely consisted of Kurdish militias that largely lacked experience, equipment, and organization. The US effort to develop a military force of Arabs and Kurds to fight ISIS continued to deal with major political and logistical barriers.

Iran sent hints that it is contemplating withdrawal from the Syria peace talks because of disagreements with Saudi Arabia.

November 12: The US Defense Department announced that the Islamist militant Mohammed Emwazi (aka "Jihadi John") was struck and killed in a US drone strike, while Emwazi was traveling in his vehicle in Raqqa, Syria. The US military later confirmed that Emwai was killed in the air strike.

Two suicide bombs struck the Bourj al-Barajneh district of southern Beirut (a Shiite neighborhood), killing 43 people and wounding 200 others. ISIS claimed responsibility for the attack.

November 13: To inflict financial damage on ISIS, the US began increasing airstrikes on the oil fields ISIS controls in eastern Syria.

After two days of fighting, the Peshmerga Iraqi Kurdish military force seized the Iraqi town of Sinjar from ISIS. U.S.-led coalition air power supported the fighters.

Kurdish and Yazidi forces collaborated in launching an offensive against ISIS militants in northern Iraq. At first, they seized a strategic main highway that jihadists used as a supply line. They proceeded toward Sinjar, assisted by heavy airstrikes that pummeled ISIS.

Three groups of ISIS suicide bombers attacked six areas in and around Paris. At least 129 people were killed, and over 350 hundred others were wounded in these attacks. Most of the casualties occurred at the Bataclan concert hall, while several other casualties occurred at upscale restaurants, and near the French national stadium, the Stad de France. ISIS claimed responsibility for the attack, which was the worst in Paris' history, which it said was in retaliation for the French role in the U.S.-led airstrikes against ISIS targets in both Iraq and Syria.

November 14: ISIS claimed responsibility for bombings in Baghdad that targeted Shiites and killed 26 people.

November 16: French war jets attacked Raqqa, Syria, and destroy at least two major targets. This action, coordinated with the US military, was intended as retaliation for the Paris attacks.

President Obama provided tactical support for the French operation. Obama, however, reiterated his opposition to committing US ground troops to Syria. Obama administration officials argued that airstrikes, raids, and supporting local allies were more effective long-term strategies than deploying US ground forces.

Increasing evidence indicated that the Paris terror attacks were planned in the Molenbeek area of Brussels. The investigation then focused on three brothers who resided in the neighborhood. Ibrahim Abdeslam was identified as one of suicide bombers, his brother Mohamed was arrested, and third brother Salah was still being sought. He was believed to have participated in the attack but fled Paris. Ismael Omar Mostefai, another suicide bomber, was believed to have visited Syria.

The Nigerian government claimed that it has made significant progress in destroying Boko Haram, despite the fact that the group continued to conduct lethal terrorist attacks. President Buhari coordinated efforts between Nigeria and its neighbors to help destroy the group.

November 17: ISIS announced that it killed the Norwegian and Chinese hostages it had captured. ISIS also indicated that it would continue kidnapping and killing hostages within the territory it holds in Iraq and Syria.

French President Francois Hollande issued a call to arms, explaining to the French Parliament 'France is at war' and requested expeditious action to destroy ISIS. Security forces pursued Belgian suspect Abdelhamid Abaaoud, a radical jihadist that reportedly led the Paris terrorist attacks.

American air strikes destroyed 116 ISIS oil-smuggling trucks in eastern Syria to constrict the group's revenues. This mission was planned before the Paris terrorist attacks.

President Obama claimed that the strategy of airstrikes and assisting local forces has been effective and has been weakening ISIS. This is true despite the terrorist attacks in Paris. Obama also defended his decision not to deploy ground troops to Iraq or Syria or act under political pressure. His critics, however, especially Congressional Republicans, accused him of naiveté, and not fully understanding the seriousness of the ISIS threat.

November 18: Between January and mid-November, 2015, ISIS had executed or inspired attacks worldwide that killed more than 800 people. ISIS killed thousands of Syrians and Iraqis in 2015 in mass executions, bombings, and various other lethal attacks.

Several nations worldwide agreed that ISIS must be defeated. However, there remains considerable debate on how to accomplish this goal, and what the potential consequences might be. Some of the major issues include the future of President Bashar al-Assad and the place of Islam in the new Syria.

Russia said that its military would collaborate with the French military against ISIS. Through this statement, the Russian government first acknowledged that the jet was bombed and also seemed to signal that it wished to improve relations with the United States.

An explosion in the Nigerian city of Yola killed 32 people at a marketplace and wounded another 80 individuals. The Nigerian government believed that Boko Haram conducted the attack.

November 24: ISIS militants attacked a hotel in the northern Sinai Peninsula, killing at least seven people.

November 26: ISIS claimed responsibility for an attack on a Shiite mosque during evening prayers in which gunmen attacked worshipers with machine guns, killing one man and injuring three others.

December 2: a married couple shot and killed 14 people in San Bernardino, California. The attack is considered an ISIS-inspired terrorist act.

December 7: ISIS claimed responsibility for a car bomb that killed a provincial governor and eight of his body guards.

December 29: Iraqi troops retake most of western city of Ramadi, ending seven-month occupation by Islamic State; soldiers encounter fierce resistance by extremist fighters.

2016: The IAEA, the UN's nuclear monitoring agency, lifted International economic sanctions from Iran after confirms that Tehran had complied with commitments to reduce its nuclear activities.

January 3: Saudi Arabia executes Shiite cleric Sheikh Nimr al-Nimr, an outspoken critic of Sunni-dominated nation's treatment of Shiites, sparking regional condemnation and leading Iranian protesters to ransack Saudi Embassy in Tehran. Nimr is executed on terrorism charges along with 47 other prisoners. The government action was interpreted as a warning to domestic dissidents. Several commentators feared execution would exacerbate sectarian tensions across Middle East and further embolden ISIS.

January 4: ISIS militants attempted to capture an oil port along Libya's coast, in fighting that left at least seven people dead.

Saudi Arabia severed diplomatic relations with Iran and instructed Iranian diplomats to leave kingdom in 48 hours; following the harsh criticism Iranian officials made of Saudi execution of Shiite cleric Sheikh Nimr al-Nimr, which led protestors to attack the Saudi Embassy in Tehran.

January 6: The United Nations reported that at least 81 Yemeni civilians were killed airstrikes by Saudi-led coalition, despite cease-fire called on and agreed to by both sides.

January 7: ISIS claimed responsibility for an attack on a hotel in Cairo Egypt near the Giza Pyramids. There were no injuries.

A man shot and wounded a Philadelphia police officer sitting in a patrol car in the name of ISIS.

January 8: Armed assailants reportedly carrying a ISIS flag attacked at a Red Sea resort, in Egypt, injuring at least two tourists.

Iran's claim that Saudi Arabian airstrike hit its embassy in Yemen is contradicted by reports of near-miss by embassy guards and eyewitnesses; civil war in Yemen between Saudi-led coalition and rebels allied with Iran escalated after execution of Shiite cleric by Saudi Arabia, which inflamed sectarian tensions across region.

January 11: A teenager attacked a Jewish teacher with a machete in Marseille France. He later claimed that he conducted the attack in the name of ISIS.

January 12: In Turkey, a Syrian suicide bomber attacked the historic central district of Istanbul, killing ten people and wounding at least 15 others. The Turkish government blamed ISIS for the attack.

January 14: ISIS claimed responsibility for explosions and gunfire in central Jakarta, Indonesia that killed at least two civilians.

January 19: Iraqi security officials suggest that three missing American contractors working at Baghdad airport were abducted. This was the first kidnapping of Americans in several years in Iraq.

January 20: The United Nations reported that nearly 19,000 people in Iraq have were killed and more than three million displaced from January 2014, when ISIS first began seizing territory, through October 2015.

Islamic extremists conducted several attacks that apparently targeted victims at random and killed several people in Iraq, Burkina Faso, Indonesia and Turkey. These apparently uncoordinated attacks were believed to be a part of international terror campaign, promoted by both Al Qaeda and ISIS.

January 21: ISIS destroyed St Elijah's monastery in Mosul, Iraq. ISIS's destruction of the 1,400-year-old structure, one of oldest Christian sites in Iraq, was part of the group's efforts to eliminate other religious faiths from the Middle East.

US airstrikes in Iraq, beginning in the summer of 2015, have targeted storage facilities with ISIS cash reserves. The US military argues that the tactic significantly incapacitated ISIS's fighting capacity, while some observers believed that the structure of ISIS's revenue streams hinders efforts to disrupt the group's finances.

Iran's supreme leader Ayatollah Ali Khamenei condemns the attack on Saudi Arabian embassy in Tehran following Saudi Arabia's execution of dissident Shiite cleric. Khamenei made these remarks prior to a meeting between regional leaders also expressed support for committee that disqualified reformist parliamentary candidates in upcoming elections.

January 23: The US Defense Department reported that commanders were considering whether to put in place US forces at Iraqi military bases and outposts north of Baghdad prior to forthcoming battle against ISIS militants in Mosul.

January 25: ISIS released a video showing suspects of the November 2015 Paris attacks conducting executions in Syria and Iraq. The video appears to have substantiated reports that the perpetrators were a core members of ISIS. The video also threatened attacks on Britain.

January 29: The US Defense Department believed that additional trainers, commandos and advisers from United States and its allies were necessary in both Iraq and Syria to fight and defeat ISIS. US military officials report to President Obama's national security advisers that significant progress has been achieved against ISIS, however, is required to defeat the group.

February: Boko Haram fighters attacked two villages in northeast Nigeria, killing at least 30 people. In a second attack, two female suicide bombers killed 58 people at a Nigerian refugee camp for villagers seeking to flee from terrorist violence. A suspect in the assault on the camp said that Boko Haram had sent her and the two suicide bombers to conduct the attack.

The Saudi government claims that the Yemeni government controlled more than seventy-five percent of Yemen's territory, however, government forces encounter difficulties moving forward in Taiz, a southwestern province and Marib in the center of the country.

February 5: Russian air support allowed the Syrian government forces to encircle rebels holding Aleppo, a crucial commercial city. Saudi Arabia suggests it would deploy ground forces along with US troops fighting ISIS in Syria. The conflict had become a proxy war among regional powers. This led the United Nations to suspend peace talks.

February 7: The Leader of Iran's Revolutionary Guards Corps ridiculed Saudi Arabia's assertion that it could send ground forces to assist Syrian rebels. Maj Gen Mohammad Ali Jafari argues Saudi Arabia lacks both the capability and courage to become involved in conflict as complicated as the Syrian civil war.

February 9: Iraqi forces recaptured the Sunni town of Ramadi, capital of the Iraqi province of Anbar. The jihadists had captured Ramadi in May 2015.

February 12: The Syrian Center for Policy Research reported that 470,000 people had died in Syria's war and caused $255 billion in economic damage to the country.

US Defense Secretary Ashton B. Carter reported that he had received pledges from 90 percent of the 40 countries participating in efforts to defeat ISIS.

February 14: US Secretary of State John Kerry warned Russia that its military efforts in Syria to support President Bashar al-Assad would fail.

February 15: Human Rights Watch report suggested Saudi Arabia may have launched US-made cluster munitions in civilian areas of Yemen. The use of such weapons is prohibited by international treaty and may also violate law.

February 14: Syrian government forces and their allies besieged the rebel-held section of Aleppo, Syria to starve the rebels into submission.

March 22: In two suicide bombings, one at Brussels Airport and the other in the city's subway system, 32 people were killed. The ISIS cell that claimed responsibility for the Brussels attack was also linked to those involved in the November 13, 2015 terror attacks in Paris.

April: UN-sponsored negotiations began between the Yemeni government and the Houthis and former Yemeni President Saleh's General People's Congress.

April 14: Captors of the teenage girls abducted from Chibok send videos to negotiators to prove that they were alive.

May-June: ISIS claimed responsibility for several attacks, including a suicide car bombing that killed at least 40 army recruits in Aden.

May 17: Amina Ali Nekei, one of more than 200 Chibok schoolgirls that Boko Haram had abducted, became the first to be released after two years of being held captive. The Nigerian army reported that its forces had rescued her. This was contradicted by reports that the girl had left the Sambisa Forest in Northeastern Nigeria on her own with her infant and a man.

June: Suicide bombings in Al-Qaa, allegedly by Syrian nationals, aggravate already strained relations between Lebanese and more than 1 million Syrian refugees in Lebanon.

June 12: Omar Mateen attacked the Pulse gay nightclub in Orlando, Fla. He killed 50 people. Mateen pledged allegiance to ISIS on a 911 call, in one of the worst mass shootings in U.S. history, and the worst terrorist attack on U.S. soil since 9/11. ISIS later claimed responsibility for the attack.

June 26: Iraqi forces recaptured Fallujah. Jihadist fighters had captured Fallujah in early 2014, and made the city into an ISIS stronghold.

July: ISIS is believed responsible for several bombings in Saudi Arabia, including one near the Prophet's Mosque in Medina - the second most sacred site in Islam.

July 14: Seventy-seven people were killed in Nice, France, when a truck drove through a crowd on Bastille Day. ISIS claimed responsibility for the attack.

July 26: Two Jihadists took five people hostage during a Mass at a church in Normandy and murdered an elderly priest by stabbing him in the chest and slitting his throat. The hostages were freed later, and the two suspects were arrested. The suspects claimed to have conducted the attack in the name of ISIS.

August 3: *Al-Naba*, an ISIS publication, claimed that Sheikh Abu Musab al-Barnawi is Boko Haram's new leader. Some Boko Haram members confirmed that al-Barnawi, son of the group's founder, who Nigerian security forces killed in 2009, was Boko Haram's new leader.

August 6: The Syrian Democratic Forces coalition of Arab and Kurdish fighters supported by US air power retook Manbji in Northern Syria, after a two month fight with ISIS.

August 9: After three months of UN-sponsored peace talks in Kuwait collapse in a stalemate, coalition aircraft supporting the Yemeni government resume their attacks on Sana'a.

August 14: Boko Haram released a video of some of the girls kidnapped in April 2014 and demanded the release of Boko Haram fighters in exchange for the girls.

August: A UN-appointed panel accused the Bahrain government of carrying out a systematic campaign of harassment against Bahraini Shias.

September: Libyan National Army (LNA) of General Khalifa Haftar seized major oil export terminals in eastern Libya.

October: A Saudi-led coalition air strike struck a large funeral in Sanaa, and killed 140 mourners and injured another 500.

The parties to the conflict were accused of allegedly violating an UN-sponsored 72-hour ceasefire declared during the ongoing peace talks.

Syrian rebels retook Dabiq, Syria, from ISIS. This was a serious symbolic blow to ISIS because Dabiq is where ISIS had vowed an apocalyptic war would occur between the jihadists and the West.

October 13: Boko Haram militants transferred 21 Chibok schoolgirls to authorities after several negotiations with the Nigerian government. This was the first mass release of any of the more than 200 girls and women kidnapped from their school in April 2014.

October: A "lone wolf" attacker launched a knife attack in Hamburg, Germany and killed one teenager.

November 5: The Nigerian military found one of the Chibok schoolgirls along with her ten-month infant.

November: Several people were injured after Abdul Razak Ali Artan, a student, plowed his car into a group of pedestrians at Ohio State University and began stabbing people with a butcher knife, before a police officer shot him to death. ISIS claimed responsibility for the attack and called Artan a "soldier" for ISIS.

December 19: A large truck was used as a weapon in a Christmas market in central Berlin. Twelve people were killed and 48 others were injured in this attack. ISIS claimed responsibility for the attack and said the attacker was "a soldier of the Islamic State".

2017:

January: An American led raid killed several suspected Al-Qaeda fighters and civilians in the first American military strike in Yemen during the administration of President Donald Trump.

Five UAE diplomats were killed in a bomb attack in Afghanistan.

In its first execution since 2011, Bahrain executed three Shia activists convicted of killing three policemen in a bomb attack in 2014.

January 5: The Nigerian military reports that it found and retrieved a missing Chibok girl and her baby during raids against suspected Boko Haram terrorists.

January 7: Pro Yemeni government troops supported by coalition planes and ships launch operation "Golden Spear" around the strategic Bab al-Mandab Strait between the Red Sea and Aden.

January 17: Several people were killed when a Nigerian fighter jet mistakenly bombs a camp for the internally displaced during an operation in Rann against Boko Haram militants, according to Nigerian officials and the Red Cross. The Nigerian government issues no official death toll.

January 29: A US raid killed several suspected Al-Qaeda militants and civilians in the first US military action in Yemen under President Donald Trump.

February: The Somali Parliament elected former Prime Minister Mohmed Abdullahi Mohamed (commonly known as Farmajo) as President. Al-Shabab threatened to attack any individual collaborating with him.

Rumors about a possible Al-Qaeda – ISIS network.

February 1: Leaders of the Saudi-led military force fighting the Houthi uprising in Yemen announced it would create an independent war crimes investigation committee.

February 3: A machete-wielding man yelling "Allahu Akbar" attacked soldiers in a shopping mall near the Louvre in Paris. The soldiers shot and wounded the attacker.

February 6: AQAP retook part of the Yemeni Province of Abyan and execute some of President Haidi's guards.

February 9: Al-Qaeda reportedly resumed activities in Afghanistan.

March: Pirates seized a tanker off the coast of Puntland in Somalia in the first hijacking of a large vessel in Horn of Africa region since 2012.

March 22: A man drove a car into pedestrians on the Westminster Bridge in London and then stabbed a police officer to death before being fatally shot by police on the Parliament's grounds. Five people, including a London police officer who was stabbed and the perpetrator, were killed in a terror attack. More than 40 people were injured outside the Parliament building. ISIS claimed that the attacker was a "soldier of the Islamic State".

April 3: A suicide bombing on the subway in St. Petersburg city killed and injured several passengers.

April 7: Five people were killed when a truck driven by a man drove into a pedestrian shopping street and department store in Stockholm, Sweden, wounding over a dozen others. The suspect claimed to be an ISIS member.

April 20: On Champs Elysees attack in Paris, an attacker exited a car and fired an automatic weapon at a parked police van, killing the officer inside, before shooting at others standing on the nearby sidewalk, injuring two before the police shot and killed him. President of France denounced the attack as "terrorist in nature" and vowed "utmost vigilance". ISIS said it was responsible for the attack.

May: Somali Mohamed at a London conference asked that the arms embargo on Somalia be ended to help the Somali government defeat Al-Shabab. Antonio Guterres, the U.N. Secretary General, argued that the conditions exist for the Somali government to be successful.

A Bahrain court convicted Isa Qassim, a major Shia cleric, of illegal fundraising and money laundering. The Court then granted him a suspended sentence.

Houthis continued launching missiles into Saudi Arabia territory, and claimed to have launched one toward the Saudi capital, Riyadh.

Egyptian military forces launched several airstrikes against reputed jihadist training camps in Derna, Libya, after ISIS assumed responsibility for attacking and killing Christians on a bus.

May 6, 2017: Boko Haram released some of the Chibok schoolgirls following negotiations between Boko Haram and the Nigerian government.

Spring: The Jihadist organization Ansar al-Sharia, which allegedly participated in the attack on the US consulate in Benghazi in 2012, announced it was dissolving itself.

May 22: A suicide bomber with apparent connections to an organized terror network detonated a bomb at the end of the singer Ariana Grande's concert in Manchester. Twenty-two people were killed and dozens more injured by the explosion.

May 26-27: The UN reported that ISIS fighters killed more than 200 civilians in Mosul.

June-November: A cholera epidemic killed 2,100 and infected nearly 900,000 others in Yemen, largely due to the conflict in that nation.

June: A militia group in Zintan, Libya freed Saif al-Islam Gaddafi, son of Libyan President, Moammar Gaddafi.

Saudi Arabia initiated an air, land and sea blockade by several Arab countries, to force Qatar to end its alleged ties to terrorism and distance itself from Iran.

June 3: Three attackers kill seven people were killed and injured by three attackers who drove through pedestrians on the London Bridge and stabbed several others in Borough Market.

July 10: Iraqi Prime Minister Haider al-Abadi declared that Iraqi forces had recaptured Mosul from ISIS.

July 26: Al-Qaeda reportedly increased its presence in Idlib province, in Syria.

August: Bahraini human rights groups accused Bahrain's National Security Agency of torturing detainees.

Jordan and Iraq reopened their main border crossing for the first time in two years after sections of the main highway to Baghdad was under jihadist control.

August-October, 2017: Houthi rebels in Yemen conduct rocket attacks into Saudi Arabia as Saudi-led coalition increase bombing of rebel-held territory in Yemen.

August 1: Hamza bin-Laden, son of Osama bin Laden, criticized Saudi Arabia in video message, as Hamza sought to lead an Al-Qaeda revival.

August 17: A van attack killed 14 people in Barcelona, while another person was stabbed to death by the attacker as he fled. Another attack in nearby Cambrils on August 18 killed another individual. ISIS claimed responsibility.

September: Kurdish voters overwhelmingly supported an independent Kurdistan in a referendum. Those opposed to Kurdish independence boycotted the referendum.

September 15: At least 22 people were hurt when an apparent bucket bomb exploded on a London subway, causing panic and flash burns.

October: Hamas allowed the Ramallah-based unity government to seize public institutions in Gaza as part of a reconciliation process between the two rival administrations.

US special forces in Libya captured a suspect in the attack on the US diplomatic compound in Benghazi in 2012.

October 17: ISIS lost control of its self-declared capital, Raqqa, in Syria. Major military operations had ended, although there was still some resistance in the city.

October 31: Sayfullo Saipov, an Immigrant from Uzbekistan, drove a rented truck into a crowd of pedestrians and cyclists on a bike path near the World Trade Center in Manhattan. An immigrant from Uzbekistan drove a truck through pedestrians and bicyclists on a path in New York City, killing eight people and wounding twelve others. The driver claimed he conducted the attack in the name of the ISIS.

November: The Saudi heir to the throne purges leading political and business leaders in an apparent effort to consolidate power.

The Iraqi military, assisted by their Shia and Kurdish allies, force ISIS out from all but a few of its hideouts. Later, an Iraqi military offensive forces Kurdish fighters to retreat. The Iraqi government launched this military campaign to prevent the Kurdish regional government from creating an independent Kurdistan.

November 21: A suicide bomber kills 50 people in Nigeria at a mosque.

November 25: Islamist militants, believed to be inspired or linked to ISIS, kill 325 Sufi Muslims attending Friday prayers at a mosque in Sinai. This was the worst terrorist attack in Egyptian history.

December: UN sought to evacuate thousands of African migrants after reports surfaced that slave markets were operating in Libya.

US President Donald Trump recognized Jerusalem as Israel's capital, against the expressed wishes of Arab nations and several Western nations.

Houthi fighters killed former president Ali Abdullah Saleh fighting in Sanaa, the capital of Yemen.

December 5: President Trump announced that the United States officially recognized Jerusalem as the capital of Israel. The announcement resulted in protests in the Middle East and was opposed by Egypt, the Palestinian Authority, Saudi Arabia, France, Germany, Great Britain, China, and Russia. Islamist groups such as Hezbollah called for protests against this decision.

December 6: the British Government announced that it had disrupted an Islamist conspiracy to assassinate British Prime Minister Theresa May.

December 9: The Iraqi military asserts that it has completed liberated all of Iraq's territory of "ISIS terrorist gangs" and regained complete control of the Iraqi-Syrian border. By this point, eradicate the self-styled "Islamic State" had taken over three years and almost 25,000 coalition air attacks.

December 11: An immigrant from Bangladesh, attempted to set off a pipe bomb in a failed attack on the New York City subway system, injuring four people. The suspect claimed to be inspired by ISIS.
Official Iraqi Celebration of ISIS defeat in Iraq.
December 15: US Ambassador to the United Nations, Nikki Haley criticized Iran for supplying missiles to Houthi rebels in Yemen.
December 22: Australia halts anti-ISIS airstrikes.
December 26: ISIS claims responsibility for a suicide bombing attack on the Afghan Intelligence Agency, in which six civilians were killed.
December 28: ISIS operative launch multiple explosives at a cultural center used by Shia Muslims. While 40 people are killed, eighty people are injured.
The United States sells twelve fighter jets to Nigeria.
December 31: At least 10,000 Afghan civilians were killed in 2017 in terrorist-related incidents.

2018:
January 2: Nearly 200 people held captives by Hoko Haram on several islands in Lake Chad escaped their captors and arrived in Borno state, in Nigeria.
January 19: Four Nigerian soldiers were killed and eight wounded in Niger in a suspected Boko Haram attack on a village near Lake Chad. The jihadists also took military vehicles.
January 24: ISIS claims responsibility for an attack on the offices of Save the Children office in Jalabad. Four people were killed in this attack.
January 25: The Afghan Taliban killed Four Americans in an attack on the Kabul Intercontinental Hotel.
January 28: Yemen's President Abrel Mansour al-Hadi requested that the Saudi Coalition enter Aden, which was being attacked by separatists.
January 27: A suicide car bombing in Kabul killed 103 people and injured 235 others.
January 29: ISIS attacks the Kabul Military Academy, in Kabul Afghanistan, killing 11 Afghan soldiers and wounding 11 others.
Saudi Arabia accused the United Nations of favoritism of the Houthis after the UN issued a report critical of Saudi Arabia's actions in Yemen.
January 31: Yemeni separatists captured most of the Southern Yemeni city of Aden, currently where the recognized government was housed.
February 2: Large-scale protests are held in Kabul with the protestors demanding more government protection for the Afghan people from terrorism.
February 12: Several Afghan officers were killed in an insider attack.
Early February: ISIS reportedly returned to Northwestern Syria (where it was forced out in 2016) to fight against the Assad government
February 14: Military leaders from central Asian nations, Pakistan, the US and NATO allies meet to discuss ways to defeat terrorism and drug trafficking in Afghanistan.

February 15: The Afghan Taliban issues an open letter to the American people and US Congress calling for dialogue and an end to the fighting in Afghanistan.
NATO agrees to expand the Iraqi training mission.
February 19: Boko Haram kidnapped 76 school girls. They are freed two days later by the Nigerian military.
February 20: Over 200 Boko haram suspects were convicted in Nigeria on charges relating to involvement with a terrorist organization.
February 24: Afghan Taliban attacks throughout Afghanistan killed at least 20 soldiers.
February 25: ISIS claimed responsibility for a suicide car bombing and gun attack on a Yemeni counterterrorist unit in Aden that killed 14 and injured 40 other people.
February 26: Boko Haram seizes 110 female students after a Boko Haram attack at a girl's college in the town of Dapchi, Nigeria. Dapchi is in Northeastern state of Yobe. Two bodies were recovered and 13 girls were still missing.
February 27: Afghan Taliban asked for Direct Dialogue with the United States for peace in Afghanistan.
February 28: Afghan President Ashraf Ghani called for the Afghan Taliban to be recognized as a political group, offered the Taliban a ceasefire and proposed the release, with no preconditions, and that the Taliban must recognize the Afghan government as legitimate.
Early March: ISIS reportedly making a comeback in some of its old strongholds in Syria.
March 1: The Afghan Taliban rejected President Ghani's offer to recognize the Afghan government as legitimate in discussions for a peace talk between the government and the Taliban.
March 9: ISIS claimed responsibility for a suicide bombing in Kabul targeting the Shiite community, killing ten people. The Afghan Taliban on local police station in Northern Takshar Province killed at least 20 people. Six security forces were killed throughout Afghanistan.
March 13: US Secretary of State, James Matthis, in Afghanistan, supported President Ghani's calls for the Afghan Taliban to become a political party.
March 15: US Defense Secretary, James Matthis, asked Congress to support Saudi airstrikes in Yemen.
April 7: A van drove into a crowd in a city square Munster, Germany, killing seven people and injuring 20 others. ISIS claimed responsibility.
April 22: ISIS suicide bombing at voting registration center in Kabul Afghanistan killed 57 people. Afghans were registering to vote in upcoming parliamentary elections. Six other people are killed in a bombing of a voter registration station in the northern province of Baghlan.
April 23: Taliban attacks in Western Afghanistan killed 18 soldiers and police officers.

Human Rights Watch accuses the Egyptian government of human rights abuses in its counter-terrorism campaign in the Sinai Peninsula.

April 23: The US Air Force established its first armed drone base in Niger to assist West African nations fight against jihadist groups affiliated with either ISIS or Al-Qaeda.

Boko Haram attacks killed 21 people in Northeast Nigeria.

April-May: Thousands of Palestinians, many organized by HAMAS, launch weeks of protests against Israel, with some Palestinians seeking to enter that nation to reclaim land they argued that Israel had taken from them.

May 9: Mohamad Mahathir led the Pakatan Harapon (Alliance of Hope) to an upset victory over the Barisan Nasional (BM) (led by the United Malays National Organization, UMNO). The BN had led Malaysia since that nation's independence in 1957. Prime Minister Najib Rezak, whom Mahathir accused of corruption, resigned as leader of UMNO.

May 13: The Marching Toward Reform Alliance led by populist Shia cleric, Moqtada Al-Sadr, finishes as the leading vote-getter in the first parliamentary election in Iraq since ISIS was defeated in that nation. Al-Sadr opposes both United States and Iranian influence in Iraq.

May 14: The United States officially relocated its embassy from Tel Aviv to Jerusalem, which exacerbates tension in the Middle East, and places the Peace Process at risk. Turkey responds by recalling its envoys from the Untied States and Israel.

Islamism in the Middle East

Chapter 1

THE 1920 REVOLUTION BRIGADES

As the military branch of the National Islamic Resistance in Iraq, this Iraqi Sunni militia group composed of members from Sadaam Hussein's army that was disbanded by the Iraqi Provisional Government after the Iraq War in 2003. To distinguish themselves from "Salafist jihadists" (such as ISIS, Ansar al-Sunna, or the Islamic Army), the 1920 Revolution Brigade asserted that they were operating under the mantle of "moderate Islam" (such as the Mujahideen Army). Claiming to act in the name of jihad, the Brigades used improvised explosive devices (IEDs) to attack American and coalition personnel. In 2004, the group claimed responsibility for attacking employees of the al-Arabiya a television network, which it claimed was "treacherous network" that used allegedly used US spies who spoke Arabic. The group also used indiscriminate car bombings against Shiite civilians. The Brigades sought to establish an independent Islamic Iraqi state that was free from foreign occupation. The group's name alludes to the Iraqi insurrection against British rule in 1920.

Because Al-Qaeda in Iraq (AQI) was seizing property of and launching suicide bombings against members of the 1920 Brigades and their mosques, and 15 Brigade members that AQI had captured, the Brigades began to cooperate with the Iraqi Government. This led to the arrest and expulsion of Al-Qaeda fighters and the establishment of new Allied bases in Diyala Province in Iraq.

In March 2007, some of the members of the group defected to form "Hamas of Iraq". Other former Brigade members joined the "Sons of Iraq" (aka, the "Awakening Councils"), which tribal leaders had formed to fight Al-Qaeda in Iraq (AQI). The 1920 Revolution Brigades actively fought in Baghdad, Fallujah, and Buhriz. During the ISIS offensive in 2014, the Brigades fought against ISIS while also fighting the Iraqi military. Nouri al-Maliki was Iraq's prime minister at the time and his government was dominated by Shiites. The Sunni-oriented Brigades greatly distrusted the new government largely for this reason.

Kataib Thawrat al-Eshreen is the current leader of the 1920 Revolutionary Brigades. Composed of radicalized, extremist Sunni Arab Iraqis organized around a core of the Iraqi Muslim Brotherhood, they collaborated with Abu Massub Zarqawi's AQI. It was led by anti-American cleric Harith al-Dhari, who orchestrated several terrorist campaigns before the surge of American troops, which included kidnappings, bombings, torture, and the use of rockets and mortars against security forces.

Al Qaeda in Iraq (the Islamic State of Iraq) boasted that the Islamic Army in Iraq and the 1920s Revolution Brigades were integral parts of its organization. While Al Qaeda, through its campaign of intimidation and assassinations, did co-opt some elements of the domestic Sunni insurgent groups, and six of the 31 major tribes in Anbar province. The full contingents of domestic insurgent groups such as the 1920s Revolution Brigades did not join AQI, but opposed it.

AQI launched a successful suicide bombing in Habbaniyah that attacked Sunni religious and insurgent leaders who opposed AQI. Several senior commanders of the 1920 Revolution Brigades were killed in the attack. Mohammed Al-Mar'awi, the imam of the mosque, had denounced AQI for targeting US soldiers in civilian areas.

Elements of the 1920 Revolution Brigades and other elements of the Sunni insurgency began fighting Al Qaeda in Anbar Province, and are fighting with government forces. AQI retaliated by killing many of the leaders of the Sunni opposition.

The AQI bombing of the Habbaniyah mosque, the assassination attempt against Abdul Sattar Abu Risha, leader of the Anbar Salvation Council, and the attack in Amiriya were facets of the AQI campaign to kill the most important leaders of the Sunni opposition in Iraq.

See also: Al-Qaeda (volume 1); Al-Qaeda in Iraq (AQI) (volume 1); ISIS (volume 1).

FURTHER READING

"A Widening Sectarian Rift Pushes Iraq to the Brink of Civil War; Al-Qaeda is Now Actively Pitting Sunnis Against Shiites, Fueling Civil Violence." *The Christian Science Monitor* Jul. 25, 2006.

"Are Any of Them Ready to Talk? Iraq's Insurgency (Iraq's Varied and Violent Opposition)." *The Economist,* December 3, 2006, 65.

Carpenter, Ami C. *Community Resilience to Sectarian Violence in Baghdad.* New York: Springer-Verlag, 2016.

Dagher, S. "In Iraq, Sunni Insurgents Still Aim to Oust U.S., Shiites." *The Christian Science Monitor,* (April 10, 2008): 1.

Hashim, Ahmed. *Iraq's Sunni Insurgency.* New York: Routledge, 2017.

Kadhim, Abbas. *Reclaiming Iraq.* Austin: University of Texas Press 2014.

Katzman, Kenneth. *Iraq: Post-Saddam Governance and Security.* Washington, D.C.: Congressional Research Service, Library of Congress, 2009.

Munson, Peter J. and Steven Metz. *Iraq in Transition: The Legacy of Dictatorship and the Prospects for Democracy.* Washington, D.C.: Potomac Books, 2009.

Prados, John. "Blind in Baghdad: How Much Harm Has Been Done by an Administration that Refuses to Abandon Wishful Thinking About the Conflict in Iraq?"(Opinion). *Bulletin of the Atomic Scientists,* 61, no. 1 (2005): 18-20.

Serena, Chad C. *It Takes More Than a Network.* Stanford, California: Stanford University Press, 2014.

Shehata, Samer Said. *Islamist Politics in the Middle East: Movements and Change.* London; New York, NY: Routledge, 2012.

Siegel, P. "Iraq Equals Israel?" *Foreign Policy in Focus,* July 1, 2007.

Springer, Devin, James L Regens; and David N Edger. *Islamic Radicalism and Global Jihad,* Washington, D.C.: Georgetown University Press, 2009.

"Sunni Muslim Sheikhs Join US in Fighting Al-Qaeda." *The Christian Science Monitor* (May 3, 2007): 1.

Trendle, G. "Young Radicals on the Rise: Within the Shi'a Community, Clerics Are Filling the Power Vacuum Created in the Wake of Saddam Hussein's Downfall. the Moderates Are Increasingly Finding Their Voices Drowned out by Firebrand Speeches from a Younger, More Radical Forces." *The Middle East*, 341 (January, 2004): 28.

Chapter 2

ABDULLAH AZZAM MARTYR BATTALION (AAMB) (KATLBAT AL-SHAHLD)

Abdullah Azzam Martyr Battalion (AAMB) is anti-western Sunni Islamist jihadist group affiliated with Al-Qaeda. It is a global jihadist movement, which opposed to Western-aligned governments and other non-Muslim entities. Formed by Saudi Saleh al-Qaraawi, the group operates in several countries, such as Egypt, Iraq, Syria, Jordan, and Lebanon.

Abdullah Azzam was a prominent founder of the contemporary jihad movement. Originally a member of the Palestine Liberation Organization (PLO) Azzam became disaffected with the PLO's secularist orientation. Azzam became a radical Wahhabi Islamist, who believed that only jihad would resolve the Palestinian crisis. Azzam said, "Jihad and the rifle alone: no negotiations, no conferences, no dialogs" (McGregor, 92). Azzam was a professor of Islamic Law at a Saudi Arabia university, where he taught and mentored Osama bin Laden.

After the Soviet invasion of Afghanistan in 1979, Azzam was one of the first Arabs to come to Pakistan to fight with the mujahidin. After arriving in the border town of Peshawar, he declared that all Muslims, not only Afghans, had a religious duty to oppose the Soviet invasion. In 1984, he formed the Maktab al-Khadamat (Services Bureau), which trained Muslims from throughout the world to fight with the Afghan resistance. By 1989, Azzam's organization had trained between 16,000 and 20,000 fighters.

Azzam went to Iraq in 2003 to aid the insurgency against coalition-led forces. While seeking to enter Iraq, he was detained. Azzam said, "If I find the way, I would go today to fight jihad in Iraq because it is compulsory for me as a Muslim. But it can only take place inside the borders of Iraq, you cannot bring it outside."

The Abdullah Azzam Martyr's Battalion (AAMB) was specifically formed to oppose the Egyptian government of former president Hosni Mubarak (in office 1981-2011). Other unrelated groups have adopted Azzam's as a name of convenience in several countries.

Like many Islamist groups, the AAMB attacks tourists in Egypt, which threatens one of that country's largest sources of income. Thus, terrorism continues to perpetuate the cycle of poverty and oppression through which the group recruits its supporters. The AAMB attacked Sinai resorts in Taba, Ra's Al-Sultan, and Nuwayba killing 34 people, mostly Egyptian and Israeli nationals. In 2005, AAMB was blamed for several car bombings in the Egyptian seaside city of Sharm el-Sheikh, which killed 88 and wounded 200.

In October 2009, AAMB launched rockets from Lebanon to Israel. On August 2010, a suicide bomber attacked a Japanese oil tanker sailing through the Strait of Hormuz, and in May 2011, AAMB bombed several NATO fuel vehicles in Pakistan.

In 2010, Qaraawi claimed that the Lebanese Army, Hezbollah, and the United Nations Interim Forces in Lebanon (UNIFIL) were serving Jewish interests. In discussing Lebanon, he also claimed that after the assassination of Prime Minister Rafik Hariri, Lebanese leaders were divided into two coalitions. According to Qaraawi, the disagreements between the two groups on domestic issues was a pretext, and that the crisis "was really an international conflict that used the opposition as a tool to kill its rivals' leaders" (Zaatari, 2010).

Qaraawi further asserted that Lebanese Sunnis was oppressed "because the Lebanese Army was killing Sunnis and imprisoning them while it was not laying a hand on any Shiites " (Zaatari, 2010). He also accused Lebanese Shiite factions of controlling the Lebanese intelligence services and of not defending the Sunnis during the Nahr al-Bared war in 2007. Some argued that Qaraawi was angered after the Lebanese Army defeated Fatah al-Islam, a militant group connected to Al-Qaeda, in the battle in Nahr al-Bared.

After being badly injured during drone strikes in Pakistan, al-Qaraawi was captured and returned to Saudi Arabia by the Saudi government. Majid-al-Majid assumed the AAMB leadership. Majid was a Saudi, who was affiliated with Faten al Islam and al-Qaeda. Al-Majid became the AAMB's emir in June 2013. The Lebanese government captured him on December 27, 2013, and died of kidney failure on January 4, 2014.

See also: Al-Qaeda (volume 1); Fatah al-Islam (volume 1); Hezbollah (volume 1).

FURTHER READING

Azzām, Abdullah. "Brigades Alive and Well, Despite Key Arrests." *The Daily Star* (Beirut, Lebanon), Feb. 20, 2014.

Azzām, Abdullah. *Join the Caravan*. London: Azzam Publications, 1996.

Azzām, Abdullah. *Defence of the Muslim Lands*. London: Azzam Publications, 2002.

Jaeger, David A. *Israel, the Palestinian Factions, and the Cycle of Violence*. London: Centre for Economic Policy Research, 2006.

Schnelle, S. "Abdullah Azzam, Ideologue of Jihad: Freedom Fighter or Terrorist?" *Journal of Church and State*, 54 no. 4 (2012): 625-47,

"What is the Abdullah Azzam Brigades?." *The Daily Star* (Beirut, Lebanon), Nov. 20, 2013. .

Winter, L. "The Abdullah Azzam Brigades." *Studies in Conflict & Terrorism*, 34, no. 11 (2011): 883-95.

Zaatari, Mohammed. "Al-Qaeda says Hizbullah, LAF hindering terror." *The Daily Star (Beirut, Lebanon)* April 6, 2010.

Chapter 3

The Abis Brigade/"al-Muqawama al-Islamiyya fi Bahrain"/"The Islamic Resistance in Bahrain"/Liwa Abis

Formed in 2014, the Abis Brigade (Liwa Abis) is an Islamic extremist group engaged in a "jihad and resistance" against who it regards as the "oppressors", which includes the Bahraini Government. This violent anti-government jihadist group also denounces Bahrain's internal security forces as "mercenaries". The rhetoric and imagery that the group uses seem to indicate connections with Iran.

The Abis Brigade claimed to have conducted an attack on Sitra, Bahrain. Although the group did not assume responsibility for kidnapping British journalist James Brandon in Iraq in 2004, it demanded that the British military withdraw from Najaf, Iraq for freeing him. Moqtada al Sadr's radical Shiite Mahdi Army in Iraq negotiated Brandon's release and Brandon was released after one day in captivity.

Bahraini jihadist groups focus many of their attacks on Bahrain's infrastructure and economy. Saraya al-Mukhtar, another Bahraini jihadist group, has attacked Automatic Teller Machines (ATMs) from January through March 2014. Because of these attacks, the U.S. government cautioned Americans in Bahrain to be careful in using ATMs. Liwa Abis continued its violent campaign in April 2014 under what referred to as the "Symptoms of the Intifada".

Liwa Abis attacks economic targets that it claims buttresses Saudi control of the country. In the Spring of 2014, a the group attacked a manufacturing facility because the plant flew the flag of the "Saudi occupation" and because a government supporter owned the building. Liwa Abis also said that the "Rijal Allah" or "Men of God" of "Saraya 'Abis" (the Brigades of Abis) launched the attack. "Rijal Allah" is the name also used by a group of Shiite fighters in Syria that are supported by the Iranian government.

Youths have been attacking Bahraini police facilities in Sitra beginning in 2012. Militants in that city have also attacked Bahraini security personnel with improvised explosive device (IEDs). On April 11, 2014, Liwa Abis attacked a police facility in Sitra to avenge the government's exile of Hasan Mushaima. Mushaima, a leading Bahraini Shia leader of the Haqq Movement, strongly opposes Bahrain's current government and had been imprisoned.

The name, "Liwa 'Abis" alludes to 'Abis bin Abi Shabib, loyal, military leader and companion of Imam Hussein who fought in the Battle of Karbala (680 CE), a major event in Shiite history and tradition. The group's logo has two green swords crossing each other and a red background and a display of a fist. The fist resembles the fist that appears on Saraya al-Mukhtar's logo. These images are framed in a circular shaped combination of lines and words. Bahraini jihadists use the circle to represent a pearl, a traditional symbol of Bahrain.

The flag also cites 32:22 from the Koran: "And who is more unjust than one who is reminded of the verses of his Lord; then he turns away from them? Indeed we, from the criminals, will take retribution." This invocation by Bahraini jihadists, especially belonging to Saraya al-Mukhar, is intended to: 1) express that the group seeks revenge for the deaths of protesters killed by Bahrain's military; 2) denounce the Khalifa royal family and their supporters to be infidels; and 3) reject Bahraini government claims that the militants are terrorists, and 4) denounce the government as criminal, corrupt, and unjust. Liwa Abis continues to be an active group.

See also: Al-Mahdi Army.

FURTHER READING

Al-Mdaires, Falah. "Shiism and Political Protest in Bahrain." *Digest of Middle East Studies* 11, no. 1 (2002): 20-44.
"Backward steps; Bahrain's Pre-Election Jitters (Bahraini jitters before an election)." *The Economist,* Oct. 16, 2010, 62.
Katzman, Kenneth. *Bahrain Reform, Security, and U.S. Policy.* Washington, D.C.: Congressional Research Service, 2012.
Kingdom of Bahrain Financial System Stability Assessment, including Reports on the Observance of Standards and Codes on the Following Topics: Banking Supervision, Insurance Supervision, Securities Regulation, and Anti Money Laundering... Washington, D.C.: International Monetary Fund, 2006.
Kingdom of Bahrain: Detailed Assessment of Anti-Money Laundering and Combating the Financing of Terrorism. Washington, D.C.: International Monetary Fund, Legal Dept., 2007.
Knickerbocker, B. "US Faces Difficult Situation in Bahrain, Home to US Fifth Fleet (USA)." *The Christian Science Monitor,* February 19, 2011, 1.
"White House Readies a Push for Middle East Reforms; At Upcoming Meetings, the US Will Advocate Building on Local Advancements such as Judicial Reforms in Bahrain." *The Christian Science Monitor*, Feb. 23, 2004.

Chapter 4

ABU HAFS AL-MASRI BRIGADE (AHMB)

Abu Hafs al-Masri Brigade (AHMB) was named after a former police officer, Mohammad Atef (a.k.a. Abu Hals al-Masri), an Al-Qaeda leader closely connected to Osama bin Laden in Afghanistan. He died during US air strikes in Afghanistan in November 2001. Al-Masri was a fighter with Islamic Jihad, then led by Ayman al-Zawahiri (the current leader of Al-Qaeda). Al-Masri's daughter married a son of Osama bin Laden.

This jihadist group was formed around 2003. It is unclear whether it is still active. Very little is known about AHMB, except its claimed association with Al-Qaeda. The group had made several claims of responsibility for terrorist attacks, usually through email. AHMB said it conducted the high-profile subway bombings in Madrid in 2004 and London in 2005, UN Headquarters bombing in Baghdad in 2003, and the hotel bombings in Istanbul in 2004. AHMB further claimed that it carried out the 2003 blackouts in North America, which it referred to as "Operation Quick Lightning in the Land of the Tyrant of This Generation." American officials dismissed this claim and attributed the outage to domestic technical problems. AHMB's dubious claims have led commentators to believe that the group is most likely a fictitious organization, composed of a small number of jihadists who conducted very few actual attacks. These exaggerated claims has caused AHMB to lose credibility. AHMB echoed al-Qaeda's rhetoric, by publicly repeating the statements of Osama bin Laden and Ayman al-Zawahiri, such as blaming West for jihadist attacks on civilians solely because they are democracies. AHMB claims to attack westerners for their alleged complicity in alleged committed by Western governments against Muslims worldwide.

Commentators AHMB often describe as an al-Qaeda copy-cat "wannabe" with jihadist ambitions. Its size and membership are unknown, as are what access it might have to Al-Qaeda resources and its network. Mustafa Setmariam Nasar, a reputed AHMB leader, formerly lived in London, but relocated to Iraq. Nasar was reputedly an Al-Qaeda member, who operated training centers for that group in Afghanistan. He then restructured Al-Qaeda after the 9-11 attacks. He later led Al-Qaeda's operations in Europe and allegedly helped plan the 7/7 bombings in London. Nasar is now imprisoned by US government.

In February 2006, AHMB posted online threats of jihad against Denmark, to retaliate for cartoons of Muhammad that were published in the Danish newspaper *Jyllands-Posten*.

See also: Al-Qaeda; Egyptian Islamic Jihad.

FURTHER READING

"7/7: The War on Britain: Get Out of Iraq threat." *Daily Mirror*, Jul. 20, 2005.

"Al Qaeda Claims Attacks in Turkey; Statements Sent to Arabic News Media." *The Washington Post,* Nov. 17, 2003.

"Egyptian Roots: Abu Hafs al-Masri Brigades: Fact or Fiction?" *Crime and Justice International* 21, no. 88 (2006): 37.

Parry, R. "Group Threatens London." *The Times*, Mar. 19, 2004.

Torres-Soriano, Manuel. "The Abu Hafs al-Masri Brigades and al-Qaeda: Facts and Conjecture." *Media, War & Conflict* 8, no. 2 (2015): 181-98.

Chapter 5

ABU BAKR AL-SIDDIQ FUNDAMENTALIST BRIGADES (ABSB)/THE SALAFIST BRIGADES OF ABU BAKR/ AL-SIDDIQ/ABU BAKR AL SEDDIQ BRIGADES

A currently inactive Salafist terrorist group, Abu Bakr al-Siddiq Fundamentalist Brigades (ABSB) was named after one of the prophet Muhammed's companion at Muhammad's Basin (hawd) and in the Cave and who was considered Muhammad's, greatest supporter, and, closest confidant. Abu Bakr al-Siddiq was also Muhammad's father in law and governed the Rashidun Caliphate between 632 and 634. He also became the first Muslim after Muhammed had passed away.

Following the US occupation of Iraq in April 2003, much of Iraq was in anarchy. This allowed for the rampant kidnapping of several targets from diplomats to foreign laborers. Iraq, at the time, had almost no security and law enforcement infrastructure to protect either its citizens or foreign nationals on its territory.

ABSB was one of several Iraqi jihadist groups that kidnapped foreigners in Iraq. ABSB, in September 2004, claimed it had kidnaped and murdered a Turkish citizen and an Iraqi whom ABSB said had collaborated with the Israeli government. ABSB released a video indicating that it would kill the Turkish hostages it held, mostly truck drivers, if their company did not close operations in Iraq within three days. The Turkish construction company, Vinsan, complied and ceased operations in Iraq to obtain the safe return of ten kidnaped employees. The Turkish goods transfer company, Atahan, followed suit.

In October 2004, ABSB kidnaped and held hostage a Polish woman, Teresa Borcz-Khalifa. Khalifa was an Iraqi-Polish national who resided in Iraq with her husband, Abdul Hussein. She had worked for the Polish embassy, while Hussein was a translator for an American food contractor that served coalition troops. ABSB claimed that Borcz-Khalifa worked with the American military in Iraq. The group demanded that Poland withdraw its military and that the US Government free all women incarcerated in Abu Gharib Prison in Iraq. Poland strongly supported the United States during the war and its fight against the ensuing insurgency. At the time, Poland commanded 6,000 troops from 15 different countries, including nearly 2400 from Poland. Poland had the fifth largest number of troops deployed in Iraq following the United States, Great Britain, Italy, and Australia. Khalifa, in a videotape, asked the Polish government to comply with the kidnapper's demands. Poland, however, refused to negotiate with the group and did not comply with their demands. Khalifa was safely released on November 19, 2004.

At the time of her abduction, there were nearly 160 non-Iraqis being held hostage in Iraq, with the first incident being in April 2004, with the kidnapping of Matthew K. Maupin, an American soldier. While Iraqis were being kidnapped almost always for ransom, foreign nationals were most often kidnapped pursuant to some of political demand. Despite the motive, the kidnappers demonstrated no reluctance to kill their hostages, particularly if the hostage came from a Western nation.

ABSB has not asserted responsibility for any attack since the October 2004 kidnapping. There also have been no reports of arrests or detentions of any ABSB members, however many of its fighters most likely continued to actively participate in the Iraqi insurgency. There are other organizations, however, with similar names including the Abu-Bakr al-Siddiq Brigade, which was active in Syria ca. 2012. This latter group has no connections with ABSB.

Abductions in Iraq declined during the second term of Prime Minister Nouri al-Maliki (2010-2014). Kidnappings, however, dramatically increased after ISIS seized control of much of Iraq in June 2014.

Many of these recent abductions are politically motivated. In a kidnapping in September 2015, for example, eighteen Turkish workers in Baghdad were abducted while working on constructing a sports facility east of the Iraqi capital. A group known as the "Death Squad" claimed responsibility. The group demanded that Turkish President Recep Tayyip Erdogan end Turkish attacks on two Shiite villages in northern Syria. The "Death Squad" was a previously unknown a Shiite group.

See also: Al-Qaeda (volume 1); Al-Qaeda in Iraq (AQI) (volume 1).

FURTHER READING

Alford, P. "Hostage Murder Turns Up Heat on Koizumi." *The Australian*, Nov. 1, 2004.
"Another Day, Another Wave of Executions, Kidnapping: 11 Iraqi Guardsmen Slaughtered on Video." *Edmonton Journal*, Oct. 29, 2004.
Briggs, B. "War Blamed for 100,000 Increase in Civilian Death Toll." *The Herald*, Oct. 29, 2004.
Beckett, Ian F. *Insurgency in Iraq: An Historical Perspective*. Carlisle Barracks, PA: Strategic Studies Institute, U.S. Army War College, 2005.
Chehab, Zaki. *Iraq Ablaze: Inside the Insurgency*. London: I.B. Tauris, 2006.
Hashim, Ahmed. *Insurgency and Counter-Insurgency in Iraq*. Ithaca: Cornell University Press, 2006.
Hashim, Ahmed. *Iraq's Sunni Insurgency*. Abingdon, U.K.: Routledge for the International Institute for Strategic Studies, 2009.
Hoffman, Bruce. *Insurgency and Counterinsurgency in Iraq*. Santa Monica, CA: Rand, National Security Research Division, 2004.

Morin, M. and T. Perry. "Car Bombing Kills 9 Marines in Iraq." *St. Louis Post-Dispatch*, October 31, 2004, 1.

Pelletiere, Stephen C. *Losing Iraq: Insurgency and politics*. Westport, CT: Praeger Security International, 2007.

Youssef, N. "CARE Pulls Plug on Iraq Aid Work." *National Post*, Oct. 29, 2004.

Chapter 6

ADALET VE KALKINMA PARTISI (AKP)
(JUSTICE AND DEVELOPMENT PARTY)

OVERVIEW

Currently, Turkey's governing political party. The Adalet ve Kalkınma Partisi (AKP) had its ideological origins in the Turkish-Islamist political movement that emerged in reaction to the modern Turkish state that was formed after Ottoman Empire collapsed in World War I.

Mustafa Kemal Atatürk formed the Turkish Republic in 1923 as a nationalist and secular state, which was governed under one party rule by the People Republican Party (Cumhuriyet Halk Partisi) (CHP) until 1950. The CHP articulated the principles of "Kemalism", i.e., nationalism, statism, and secularism. Political Islamism was effectively barred from the governance of Turkey during this era.

The Kemalists imposed their version of modernization on Turkey. Their reforms included abolishing the caliphate which had ruled the Ottoman Empire since 1299, the Arabic alphabet, Islamic-oriented education, and the Tariqas (Sufi brotherhoods), which historically had an influential role in Turkey's religion and culture. Kemalist Turkey also adopted a variation of legal codes from Western Europe, the Western alphabet and the Gregorian calendar, Western holidays, and Western fashion. The government also significantly revised Turkey's official history and language. The new education system elevated pre-Islamic Turkish civilizations over the history of the Ottoman Empire. Many Arabic and Persian terms were not longer permitted for official use. The new government further required that the "azan" (the call to worship) be said in the modern Turkish language as opposed to the original Arabic (which many devout Muslims objected to).

Despite significant and ambitious reforms, the reach of secular Kemalism did not extend to much of the nation. The rural and highly religious peoples of Anatolia were largely unaffected by the initiatives of the central government. The military, the bureaucracy, and the urban middle class, however, adopted or adapted to the Kemalist Westernism. The Republic viewed religion a strictly private matter and perceived political Islamism as a threat to Turkey's modernization efforts and the secular nature of the Republic.

Religious conservatives and ethnic Kurds strenuously objected to Kemalist plans for a Westernized and secular Turkey. Between 1923 and 1938, the Kurds and Islamist launched several failed uprisings.

THE RISE OF POLITICAL ISLAMISM IN TURKEY

Turkish politics transformed significantly in the post-World War II era. As the Cold War began, Turkey aligned with the United States and Western Europe, and became a part of the North Atlantic Treaty Organization (NATO). The nation was also transformed into a multiparty democracy. Left wing and right wing political parties emerged. Many Kurds became socialists, while political Islamists aligned themselves with anti-communist right wing parties.

In 1950, the Democrat Party, led by Adnan Menderes, came to power and was more tolerant of public Islamism. Despite the emergence of multi-party democracy, the military retained tight political control. The military intervened in the government in 1960, 1971, and 1980 to "safeguard the secular republic" against what it perceived as dangerous political extremists.

After 1970, political Islamist parties became increasingly active. The National Order Party (Milli Nizam Partisi) (MNP), was the first of these parties. The Turkish Constitutional Court, dominated by the secular-oriented military, outlawed the MNP in 1971. The Islamist National Salvation Party (Milli Selamet Partisi) (MSP) was formed in 1972. The MSP joined the secular People's Republic Party to form a coalition government in 1974. The military intervened in 1980 and subsequently outlawed the MSP. In 1980, the Islamists formed the Welfare Party (Refah Partisi) (RP).

When Turgut Özal, of the right of center Motherland Party, served as Prime Minister Turkey from 1983 through 1989, Turkey's capitalism thrived and an entrepreneurial Muslim business class emerged. This group also became more politically engaged. This business class sought the creation of a business-friendly environment, that would ensure access to the world's currency exchanges and a stable government, as opposed to imposing theocracy based on Islamic law (Sharia). The Turkish business community, however, increasingly supported political Islamism.

TURKISH POLITICAL ISLAM IN A NEW ENVIRONMENT

With the end of both European Communism and the "Cold War" in 1991, many of Turkey's underlying identity issues became more pronounced, especially those involving the Kurds and Islamists. Turkish politics became polarized between 1) Turkish and Kurdish identity, and 2) Islamic and secular identity. During the 1990s, Turkey experienced increased conflict involving Kurdish separatism, disputes over what religion's place should be in society, socio-economic upheaval, and weak governance by differing political coalitions. Also during the 1990s, political Islamist parties such as AKP became more powerful and political Islamism seemed to moderate.

In 1995, the Welfare Party joined a governing coalition with a party known as the "True Path Party" (Doğru Yol Partisi) (DYP). Pressured by Turkey's secular elite, this coalition dissolved in 1997. The Constitutional Court outlawed the Welfare Party in 1998, which Political Islamists argued was a military coup against the RP led Coalition government. After the Turkish government had outlawed the Welfare Party, the Virtue Party (Fazilet Partisi) was formed in 1997 and was outlawed by the Court in 2001. The Government prohibited it from political involvement. The Felicity Party (Saadet Partisi) (SP) then emerged as Turkey's Islamist political party.

In 1994, the Islamist Welfare Party (RP) won unexpected victories local elections throughout Turkey and gained control of Ankara and Istanbul. The RP's leader, Necmettin Erbakan, had close connections with the Egyptian Muslim Brotherhood. After nearly 70 years of political dominance, Turkish secularism's political power was eroding. In 1995, the Welfare Party won the most seats in Parliament, leading to an Islamist-led coalition to govern the nation.

Necmettin Erbakan, Turkey's prime minister from 1996 through 1997, helped developed several of the Islamist parties. All of these parties based their ideology on Milli Görüş, (the "National View"), which is based on Islamism, nationalism and antipathy toward Western values. Erbakan's followers largely followed the "National View", which they claimed best represented Turkish and Muslim identity. Both the AKP and Recep Tayyip Erdoğan's political belief systems had their origins with the National View.

The new government did not last long. Concerned that the Islamists had become too powerful and would suppress the secularists, the military intervened. The military also expressed concern that the government was willing to allow Islamic clothing in universities, and that the party would abandon the country's Western political and military alliances. The Welfare Party, however, maintained moderate political policies. The secularist, however, remained concern that the government would impose strict Islamism on the country.

On February 28, 1997, the Turkish military, supported by several secular groups, nonviolently ousted the government. Turkey's Islamists then implemented new strategies, some of which were controversial movement for ideological reasons.

The RP's pragmatic younger leaders, including Recep Tayyip Erdoğan and Abdullah Gül, knew what limits Turkish secularism would tolerate and sought to remain within them. In 1999, Erdoğan, then Istanbul's mayor, was incarcerated for four months for a speech that included poetry with Islamist allusions.

THE CREATION AND THE RISE OF THE AKP

In 2001, the political Islamists created AKP, an Islamist political party, with the same political ideology as the previously outlawed Welfare and Virtue Parties. Erdoğan described the party as "conservative democratic" as opposed to Islamist.

The AKP is the latest of five key transformations of the major Turkish Islamist political parties. It was also a party that presented a political vision calculated to attract a sufficient number of voters and win a grudging acceptance of the secular military.

After more than three decades of democratic political involvement, Turkey's Islamists moderated to broaden their appeal. By the late 1990s, many observers believed that political Islamism had become a part of Turkey's mainstream politics.

Each of Turkey's successive Islamist parties have reemerged, more moderate and pragmatic, and each time their predecessor party was outlawed. Authoritarian secular governments in many Muslim majority nations that prohibit religious parties, frequently find themselves dealing with violent covert groups that seek to overthrow the government and destroy the existing society. Despite being repeatedly outlawed, Turkish Islamist politicians generally eschewed violence, accepted democracy, and became more mainstream.

The evolution of Turkish political Islamism seemed to exemplify a productive interaction of democracy and democratic institutions with a moderate form of political Islamism. Legitimate elections and the Turkish practice of capitalism led Islamist parties to operate within the country's existing legal framework. Turkey's militarily coerced secularism tended to moderate the extremist religious rhetoric that had previously ensnared previous Islamic politicians, resulting in some being imprisoned.

Despite its Islamist origins, the AKP began holding itself out as a center-right party to avoid being outlawed and gain broader acceptance, partly due to the fact that Turkey's electorate have been focused on economic matters, as opposed to ideological issues.

ERDOGAN'S POLITICAL PROGRAM

Initially, Erdoğan stressed political moderation to broaden the AKP's appeal. He prioritized democratic reforms to prepare Turkey to join the European Union (EU), which gained support from Turkey's business interests, liberal intellectuals, and middle class Turks. He also won increasing support from the military, as closer ties with Europe was a major goal of Turkish secularists. By prioritizing social services, the AKP increased its appeal to the poor. Erdoğan successes resulted in the party winning the most seats in Turkey's parliamentary elections in November 2002.

From 2002 through 2006, the AKP government reformed the country's human rights practices, the relationship between civilian and military authorities, and the judiciary to comply with European standards. The party also increased access to health care, housing assistance, food assistance, student aid, and made significant improvements in impoverished urban areas. The party also expanded the rights of ethnic minorities such as Kurds and non-Muslims. Many observers also credited the AKP Turkey's economic recovery from a severe economic recession of 2001 by complying with International Monetary Fund (IMF) rules.

From 2002 through 2011, Turkey's economy grew at an average rate of 7.5 percent a year. Declines in inflation and interest rates contributed to large increases in consumer spending. Turkey was also attracting increased foreign direct investment, because of the government's privatization efforts.

ERDOGAN AND THE AKP-SKEPTICS

While the AKP appeared to become more liberal, secularists still believed that the party had a covert Islamic agenda and that the AKP was pursuing EU membership as a ruse to reduce the political role of Turkey's military.

Efforts to build a country that would eventually meet standards of democratic systems of governance made significant progress under the AKP government in the 2000s. Turkey had "sufficiently" complied with the EU's "Copenhagen political criteria"—including respect for freedom of expression and minority rights, as well as transparent and accountable government answerable to the rule of law. This led to accession negotiations in 2005 for Turkey to become an EU member. When Turkey-EU relations worsened in 2006 and resistance to Turkey's proposed membership was increasing among some major EU member countries, then-Prime Minister Erdoğan reiterated his commitment to the standards. The EU hesitancy in admitting Turkey and the European economic crisis persuaded the AKP to exert its influence in other Middle Eastern countries, Africa, Russia, and Central Asia and use soft power.

Turkey became increasingly polarized politically from 2006 through 2008. The AKP was pursuing efforts to eliminate prohibitions against wearing Islamic clothing— (such as headscarves) in higher education and ending negative practices against Islamic high school graduates, including different standards for higher education placement tests. Many Turks supported the AKP in both initiatives. At the time, more than 50 percent of Turkish women wore headscarves.

AKP leaders preferred reform through political consensus as opposed to confronting the skeptical secularist establishment that highlighted Erdogan's actions such as briefly seeking to make adultery a penal offense in 2004, appointing Islamists to key government positions, and hindering the sale of alcoholic beverages.

Differences between the military and the AKP dramatically increased after Erdogan's nomination of Abdullah Gül, then foreign minister, as president (a largely ceremonial position). The military and political opposition both objected, because they perceived this as a further step toward creating an Islamist state (a caliphate).

On April 27, 2007, the military warned that it would intervene to defend secularism. Some observers interpreted the message as a warning of a pending military coup. Erdoğan, however, defied the armed forces by scheduling early elections. The AKP won the 2007 elections by carrying nearly 47 percent of the votes (it had won only 34 percent of the vote in the election in 2002).

The parliament then elected Gül to the presidency. The powerful and disapproving presence of the military, however, remained. Leading military leaders boycotted the inauguration. In 2008, the chief prosecutor of Turkey, sought to outlaw AKP alleging that the party was engaged in Islamist conspiracy to destroy the secular government. The court, however, voted against prohibiting the party by one vote.

Between 2008 and 2011, the AKP was growing more politically powerful. Despite political and economic crises, Turkey successfully endured the global financial crisis of 2008. The economy grew substantially in 2009. By 2012, Turkey had very low unemployment and a very low budget deficit.

ERDOGAN'S GOVERNMENT IS RE-ELECTED

In June 2011, voters chose political stability and returned Prime Minister Erdoğan's government to power. Turkey was enjoying increased prosperity and better social services, especially in the housing and health sectors. When the AKP won in 2011, it was one of only a very few times since 1946, when Turkey became multiparty democratic system, that a party was victorious in three straight elections. The AKP was also the first Turkish party to increase its vote share three straight times: from 34.3 percent in 2002, to 46.6 percent in 2007, and 49.9 percent in 2011.

Erdoğan continued his consistent denials that the AKP is an Islamist party, asserting that it is a "conservative democratic party". His critics argued that the supposed transformation from political Islam to "conservative democracy" was merely an act of political expediency and to pay empty deference to Turkish secular political secular tradition.

ERDOGAN CONSOLIDATES POWER

In June 2011, the AKP won nearly a majority of the vote. Turkey and its democratic government was well-regarded throughout the world. As the Arab Spring expanded, political reformers throughout the Middle East viewed AKP-governed Turkey as a model to consider adopting.

When the AKP gained control of Turkey's military, it represented the first time that the military was under civilian leadership in the history of the Turkish Republic. This occurred after the military chief of staff resigned in July 2011 after clashing with Erdoğan on promotions in the military. This was immediately followed by requests from leaders of the various branches of Turkey's armed forces asked for early retirement. In early 2012, several military officers were imprisoned for allegedly conspiring against the AKP-run government. This was a remarkable reversal for a nation with a long history of military interventions in national politics.

The AKP justified its actions with claims that it was promoting democratic governance and many of its more senior politicians had been in electoral politics for over two decades. Turkey, however, remains a divided nation. The political opposition parties grow increasingly concerned about Erdoğan's authoritarian behavior and that some version of an Islamist state will be instituted. Erdoğan's critics denounce the AKP government as an incremental dictatorship and claims that the party manipulates the judiciary to suppress the armed forces, the opposition press, and the political opposition.

Kurdish efforts for greater autonomy are largely prevented by legal and political barriers imposed after the military-drafted 1982 constitution went into force. In spite of the AKP's stated intentions that it would redress Kurdish grievances, Erdoğan has failed to grant additional political rights for the minority ethnic groups. He may have reverted to the historical Turkish argument that the democratization process cannot proceed when the country threatened by terrorism. Thus, unrest has continued to spread in Turkish Kurdistan.

BACKTRACKING ON DEMOCRACY?

Currently, Turkey is not a truly liberal democracy under AKP governance, despite regular multiparty elections. The nation's democracy, however, has shown signs of continuing development with these elections, as well as civil society, with several different parties, and the media all having increased power and influence. Also, under AKP leadership, the government is genuinely under civilian control. The military, which once dominated the nation's politics, is no longer able to intervene or in position to make threats to intervene.

By 2012, however, the AKP was backtracking on its commitment to democracy and political freedom. It increasingly began suppressing its critics, such as those in the media.

Erdoğan also had not implemented promised reforms on major issues such as Kurdish autonomy and human rights. Due to increased Kurdish militancy, growing economic problems, and ISIS terrorism, Erdoğan seemed to be increasingly authoritarian, and less willing to implement promised reforms despite his increased political power.

In 2015, violent clashes broke out throughout Turkey. The Kurdistan Worker's Party (PKK) killed military and police officers, much of the nation was placed under curfew, and the Turkish Air Force raided PKK sanctuaries. Fighting between young Kurds and military became common in Turkish Kurdistan, as the PKK continued to seek self-rule. There were growing concern that this violence may get out of control, even to the point of civil war between Kurds and Turks.

In the June 2015 general elections, the governing AKP was unable to win the necessary parliamentary seats to form a government on its own. Thus, the AKP was unable to adopt a new constitution to grant the president expanded executive power.

Erdoğan had sought to resolve the Kurdish issue to gain Kurdish support for the AKP. The AKP also introduced several reforms to recognize Kurdish cultural rights during the 2000s. Erdoğan also initiated a dialogue with the imprisoned leader of the PKK Abdullah Öcalan in 2012. These efforts were somewhat successful. In the 2007 and 2011 general elections, the AKP garnered 26 out of the 38 seats in provinces with a large Kurdish presence.

When ISIS besieged the Kurdish town of Kobani on the Syrian-Turkish border in October 2014, the Turkish government reluctantly chose to support the Kurds. This along with allegations that Turkey was supporting ISIS to prevent Kurds from gaining control of parts of northern Syria, added to Kurdish resentment of the Turkish government. Erdoğan did not assist in the defense of Kobani believing that ISIS would seize control of the city. In the context of Kobani's destruction and the flight of more than 200,000 Syrian Kurds to Turkey, trust and cooperation completely dissipated between the Turkish government and the Kurds. Assistance from Kurds in Turkey and Iraq, as well as from the United States, prevented Kobani from falling to ISIS.

THE TWO ELECTIONS OF 2015

After the AKP experienced significant losses in the June 2015 parliamentary elections, many observers interpreted the results in June 2015 as indicating that voters favored limits on Erdoğan aspirations for greater power. The results initially indicated that a coalition government, was necessary.

Erdoğan, however, averted the need to form such a coalition, by calling for a new election in November 2015. This call occurred when violence throughout Turkey was escalating and the economy was in a downturn. Erdoğan called the election assuming that the increase in violence would make the AKP particularly attractive to nationalist and conservative votes. Further, he depicted the HDP and its leaders as allied with the PKK, and partly responsible for the nation's instability.

The November 7, 2015 election results surprised many political observers, as the AKP won nearly 50 percent of the popular vote, allowing it to form a single-party government. The AKP, however, was still denied the supermajority necessary to amend the Turkish constitution that would grant Erdoğan the additional powers he sought.

Before the June 7, 2015, election, Erdoğan and the AKP supported a Kurdish peace process, seeking to win Kurdish votes. Not only did the AKP did not win additional Kurdish votes, but support for the Nationalist Action Party (MHP)—a far-right Turkish nationalist party—greatly increased, apparently because nationalist Turks were angered with the AKP-led peace talks with the Kurds.

For political reasons, Erdoğan and the AKP allowed peace talks to collapse while the Syrian civil war generated rapidly increasing instability in Turkey. Instability along with opposition to the MHP leaders' perceived refusal to form a coalition government, motivated nearly two million MHP voters to vote for the AKP instead. The AKP benefitted from the failure of peace negotiations, along with a worsening refugee crisis, ISIS attacks, and a serious economic downturn.

Seeking security and stability, Turkish voters chose the AKP in the November elections, which they believed could deliver. Erdoğan's strategy, which consisted of several political maneuvers working together, was successful, with nearly one million conservative Kurdish voters choosing the AKP.

Critics, however, accused the AKP government of generating the instability that caused this profound voter anxiety. Other parties accused the government media of allowing the government to manipulate the election results. The elections may have been free in that Turkish voters could vote for the candidates of their choice. These elections, however, were widely criticized as unfair because of factors such as alleged media manipulation and because of the government's obstruction of the political opposition to freely disseminate its message. Because the government maintained control over traditional and social media, opposition voices were largely not heard. The government, for example, prevented Selahattin Demirtaş, leader of the pro-Kurdish Peoples' Democratic Party (HDP), from broadcasting his appeals on television during the campaign.

The HDP again received, at least, ten percent of the vote and maintained representation in parliament. The HDP in Parliament may help alleviate some of the political polarization within the country, and facilitate a resumption of the Kurdish peace process.

Currently, the AKP does not have the supermajority in Parliament to redraft the Constitution to transform Turkey's government structure into a presidential system, although it may gain extra momentum to pursue these efforts. The adoption of a presidential system would also require support from the opposition and popular support through a referendum. To prevail, Erdoğan and the AKP would likely need to show improvements in the economy, national security, the Kurdish issues, Syrian refugees, and national stability. Instability in Turkey, particularly with new outbreaks of violence in the Kurdish region, will deter investment and worsen the national economic situation.

With its new majority, the AKP was able to negotiate with the HDP on Kurdish issues. The refugee crisis granted the AKP additional leverage in working with the EU. If the AKP uses its new mandate to reach positive developments on those fronts, it would greatly benefit Turkey.

Turkey's progress towards a more democratic society became recognized as a model for the Middle Eastern and Muslim nations worldwide. This process, however, began to deteriorate after the AKP's 2011 election victory. Erdoğan became increasingly authoritarian, especially in how he has treated the opposition. He frequently blamed Turkey's increasing internal and external problems on various alleged conspirators. His government continued to jettison the main tenets of democracy (including the rule of law, an independent judiciary, freedom of speech, and accountability). Regional leaders such as Tunisia's Rached Ghannouchi, ceased referring to Turkey as a model. Instead, Erdoğan's governance increasingly was resembling Vladimir Putin's government in Russia.

In November 2015, Turkish President Recep Tayyip Erdoğan's party received almost 50 percent of the popular vote, as opposed to the 41 percent it received in the June 7, 2015, elections. AKP won 317 seats in parliament, which allow it to form a one-party government. Turkey's main opposition party, the Republican People's Party (CHP), did slightly better than it did in the June election (winning nearly 25 percent of the vote). Both the Turkish and Kurdish nationalist parties, the Nationalist Action Party (MHP) and the Peoples' Democratic Party (HDP), lost vote share: from 16 percent to 14 percent and from 13 percent to 11 percent, respectively. The AKP supposedly received more than two million disaffected votes from the MHP and over one million conservative Kurdish voters from the HDP.

Erdoğan's AKP reportedly won in November 2015 because he was able to manipulate a domestic environment characterized by violence and economic problems, which would motivate voters to support the AKP, as the party would be considered a stabilizing force.

AKP supporters argued that the government under current Prime Minister Ahmet Davutoğlu's leadership, with a strong majority, would decisively address Turkey's economic, ethnic, social, and foreign policy challenges.

AKP critics, however, asserted that the repression of free expression and the overall climate of fear before the election inhibited free and fair elections. These critics add that the results would further deepen existing divisions between the supporters of AKP and its opponents.

Davutoğlu, perhaps recognizing how polarized Turkey was, adopted a conciliatory tone. He promised a government that would represent all of Turkey's people, not only AKP supporters. He also promised to ensure security, freedom, and prosperity.

Many Turks remain concerned about polarization in Turkey and the increasingly authoritarian tendencies of the AKP government. Turkey's political future appears problematic, as Turkey appears to be departing from the principles and policies that had been moving it toward a fully democratic system.

Erdoğan's authoritarianism worries many Turks as members of the world community. The November 2015 election results may to strengthen AKP and the prime minister and the president in their efforts in constitutional reform to impose a presidential system in the country. Davutoğlu argued that the results constituted a mandate for a Turkey required a new system of government.

Without checks and balances necessary to a democratic presidential system, many observers voiced concerned that Turkey may eventually become an authoritarian nation. While Davutoğlu has discussed inclusiveness and democracy, he has not discussed the importance of the institutions or consensus politics needed for advanced democratic governments.

Turkey's failure to become an advanced democracy seems likely lead to additional polarization, chaos, and instability. Many commentators argue that the most productive path forward is for the AKP to return to its reformist, democratic, and inclusive roots.

On November 24, 2015, the Turkish military shot down a Russian warplane involved in the Syrian civil war, igniting a crisis and strained relations between Turkey and Russia. The Russian infringement seemed very minor, apparently lasting only 17 seconds. Further airspace infringements occur regularly. Russia applied sanctions on Turkey, even though both were each other's largest trading partners, and at a time when Turkish economy is going through an economic slowdown. The crisis has lasted through August 2016, when Russian President Vladimir Putin and Erdoğan resumed diplomatic relations and trading with each other. Facing a collapsing economy, Erdoğan initiated the rapprochement to restore economic and trade relations with Russian, and Russian tourists to return to Turkish resorts.

THE COUP AND ITS AFTERMATH

On July 15, 2016, elements of Turkey's military staged a failed coup against the Turkish government. The government reported that the coup failed because huge numbers of Erdogan supporters took to the streets to defy the military. The government reported that 239 people died in that coup attempt, and another 2200 were injured. Following the coup, President Erdogan and other Turkish leaders blamed Fethullah Gulen, a Muslim cleric who has lived in self-imposed exile in Pennsylvania since 1999. Gulen has denied any involvement in the attempted coup. Turkey has issued a warrant for Gulen on August 3, 2016.

Gulen, a now estranged Erdogan ally, was never a part of Turkey's old secular elite, Gulen currently leads a rival Islamist movement. Erdogan has called for Gulen's extradition since 2013 when he accused Gulen's followers, who were judges, or conducting a corruption inquiry that implicated Erdogan's closest advisers. Turkey also issued an arrest warrant for Gulen in 2014, accusing him of leading a terrorist organization that engaged in eavesdropping on the Turkish president and prime minister.

Since the failed coup, the Turkish government has dismissed tens of thousands of people in the police, judiciary military, and education sectors that it claimed were connected to Gulen's movement.

Currently, Gulen is legally able to reside in the United States, and that the Justice Department would have to follow a rigorous process before extraditing him, especially to a nation where due process is increasingly unlikely and torture is reportedly used against detainees.

Erdogan complained that Western nations had not condemned the coup firmly enough. He apparently believed that those governments were alarmed over his reaction to the crisis to remove nearly 66,000 individuals from their positions in the military, government ministries, schools and universities. Government critics charged that this was too excessive to be justified and would radically compromise the character and competency of those institutions. With so many army officers forced from their positions or incarcerated, Turkey's army is in disarray.

The large numbers of dismissals and mass arrests made in the wake of the coup have confirmed for many some of their worst fears about Erdogan's government, as it pursues a vision of a "New Turkey", a modern nation that emphasizes Islamism and abandons secularism. Prior to coup, the Turkish government had harshly repressed the press and civil society, supported extremist militants in Syria, suspended a promising peace process with the Kurds, and sought to amend the Turkish constitution to permit him to rule in a more authoritarian manner. The Turkish government's clampdown against enemies real and imagined, presents a serious threat to NATO, relations with the United States and Turkey's long-term stability. The United States and NATO need to deal with a crucial ally that appears to be reversing is progress in adopting democratic norms. The West may find it difficult to perceive Turkey as a trusted ally if it embraces principles and practices so contrary with the West, or how Turkey can ensure its own continued development and security without NATO support. Currently, Turkey is pursuing a path toward international isolation, and perhaps even economic crisis and civil war.

Further, many commentators believe that Turkey under Erdogan is abandoning its role as the world's leading Muslim democracy. It is a nation where a free press and the rule of law largely no longer exist. Erdogan has also indicated that he favors reintroducing the death penalty into law if parliament approves it. Such a move would likely terminate Turkey's candidacy for membership into the European Union. The government, for its part, marked the failed coup with statues and monuments, and to make the first anniversary of the failed coup a national holiday and Turkey's second war of independence in what Erdogan supporters claim was an Islamist defense of democracy.

See also: Islamic State of Iraq and Syria (volume 1); Muslim Brotherhood (volume 1); Milli Nizam Partisi (volume 1).

FURTHER READING

Baran, Zeyno. *Torn Country Turkey Between Secularism and Islamism*. Stanford, Calif.: Hoover Institution Press, Stanford University, 2010.
Hale, William and Ergun Zbudun. *Islamism, Democracy and Liberalism in Turkey: The Case of the AKP*. Abingdon: Routledge, 2010.
Inal, Kemal and Guliz Akkaymakiz. *Neoliberal Transformation of Education in Turkey Political and Ideological Analysis of Educational Reforms in the Age of the AKP*. New York: Palgrave Macmillan, 2012.
Kieser, Hans-Lukas. *Turkey Beyond Nationalism Towards Post-Nationalist Identities*. London: I.B. Tauris, 2013.
Kuru, Ahmet T and Alfred C. Stepan. *Democracy, Islam, and Secularism in Turkey*. New York: Columbia University Press, 2012.
Rabasa, Angela and F. Stephen Larrabee. *The Rise of Political Islam in Turkey*. Santa Monica: RAND, 2008.
Yavuz, M. Hakan. *Islamic Political Identity in Turkey*. Oxford: Oxford University Press, 2003.
Yesilada, Birol and Barry Rubin. *Islamization of Turkey Under the AKP Rule*. London: Routledge, 2011.
Zdemir, Gamze and Simten Cosa. *Silent Violence: Neoliberalism, Islamist Politics and the AKP Years in Turkey*. Ottawa: Red Quill Books, 2012.

Chapter 7

ADEN-ABYAN ISLAMIC ARMY/ ISLAMIC ARMY OF ADEN (AAIA)

Aden-Abyan Islamic Army (AAIA) is an Islamic Jihadist group in Southern Yemen that conducted violent attacks, to advance its objective to "hoist the banner of al-Jihad, and fight secularism in Yemen and the Arab countries." As an Al-Qaeda Yemeni affiliate, the AAIA is a local organization that assisted the larger jihadi network in launching attacks against Western targets. AAIA's name was apparently chosen to appeal to right wing Yemenis, including deposed aristocrats, mujahideen, and religious conservatives. It appeared to reflect the fustrations of Yemenis from Aden, Abyan, and other parts of the former South Yemen. The term Islamic Army" seems to invoke an appeal to jihad and a populism.

During the mid-1990s, AAIA was a small and loosely-organized group of fighters, whose ranks included both mujahdeen from Soviet-Afghan war and jihadists from several nations. Usually, AAIA jihadists engaged in small-scale attacks such as bombings, kidnappings, and small arm skirmishes. Over time, AAIA became a key group in the Al-Qaeda network.

From 1996 through 2003, AAIA militants abducted several foreign nationals particularly in northern Yemen. Among their demands, the kidnappers sought the construction of schools, new roads, jobs, and the release of imprisoned militants.

In 1998, the group emerged publicly and issued several political demands. It expressed support for Osama bin Laden, demanded the overthrow of Yemen's government, and called for attacks against Western targets in that nation. Also AAIA abducted sixteen Western tourists in Abyan in Southern Yemen in December 1998. AAIA conducted the kidnapping apparently in retaliation for the Allied strikes on Iraq. Four of the hostages were killed and another 13 hostages were released after Yemeni security forces conducted a rescue operation at the site where the hostages were being held. Two militants were also killed.

A Yemeni court sentenced AAIA's leader, Zein al-Abideen al-Mehdar (Abu El-Hassan El-Mohader), to death for the group's involvement in the kidnapping. In addition to al-Mehdar, the court sentenced two other defendants to death for their role in abductions. All three of the accused were also charged with sabotage and forming the AAIA.

Abu Hassan and the AIAA have repeatedly threatened the Yemeni government and Westerners following the capital sentence. In March 1999, the AAIA ordered the U.S. and British ambassadors in Yemen to leave the country immediately. Leaders of both Yemen's government and the AAIA entered into an agreement that would provide government jobs for

AAIA members in exchange for the group's agreeing to refrain from violence and terrorism. Yemeni extremists, however, rejected the deal. The AIAA then captured Al Jawf governate in northern Yemen as its headquarters after the government expelled them from Abyan and Shebewa. On October 17, 1999, Yemen's President Saleh approved Abu Hassan's execution, which was then carried out immediately.

In a shift in strategy, The AAIA began attacking high profile American targets The group, along with local Al-Qaeda militants, attacked the U S Cole, a US destroyer, off the coast of Aden in October 2000 by using a powerful boat bomb while the destroyer refueled at Aden harbor. Seventeen American sailors were killed in the attack. AAIA reportedly collaborated with al-Qaeda in the Arabian Peninsula (AQAP) in its attacks. In September 2004, a Yemeni court sentenced two men to death and sentenced four other defendants to prison for their role in the attack.

AAIA jihadists also threw a grenade into the British embassy compound in Sanaa, Yemen's capital, in October 2000. In 2001, the Yemeni Government held an AAIA member, and three accomplices liable for that attack.

AAIA also asserted it conducted a suicide boat attack on the French oil tanker MV Limburg off the Yemeni coast near Hadramout, an AAIA stronghold in October 2002. AIAA militants also collaborated with Al-Qaeda in the attempted attack on the USS Sullivan's. That attack failed when the small boat to be used in the attack sank under the weight of the explosives placed into it.

AAIA was also believed to have conducted an attack on a medical convoy in June 2003 in the Abyan Governate. Yemeni authorities responded with a raid on a suspected AAIA facility that killed several jihadists and arrested others, including Khalid al-Nabi al-Yazidi, the group's leader at the time. Al-Yazidi was released from prison in October 2003.

In addition to Islamists, Yemen has long had many other political dissident movements that protested poor economic conditions and the arbitrary actions of the Yemeni security forces. A pro-democracy movement also emerged in Yemen. In several of Yemen's large cities, jurists and intellectuals criticized the constitutional amendments supported by the ruling General Congress Party led by President Abdullah Saleh to increase presidential powers and diminish the authority of the elected parliament. Many Yemenis are concerned by their country's long term economic stagnation, unrealized aspirations for a democratic government, and then, civil war.

See also: Al-Qaeda (volume 1); Al-Qaeda in the Arabian Peninsula (AQAP) (volume 1).

FURTHER READING

Cook, David. *Paradigmatic Jihadi Movements*. Ft. Belvoir: Defense Technical Information Center, 2006.

Lippold, Kirk. *Front Burner: Al Qaeda's Attack on the USS Cole*. New York: Public Affairs, 2012.

"No Quick Fixes; Yemen's Local and Global Terrorism." *The Economist,* Nov. 6, 2010.

Quin, Mary. *Kidnapped in Yemen: One Woman's Amazing Escape from Terrorist Captivity*. Edinburgh: Mainstream, 2005.

West, Deborah L. *Combating Terrorism in the Horn of Africa and Yemen.* Cambridge, Mass.: World Peace Foundation, Program on Intrastate Conflict and Conflict Resolution, Belfer Center for Science and International Affairs, John F. Kennedy School of Government, Harvard University, 2005.

Willems, P. "Yemen: The Stakes Are Higher; in the Last Few Months Instability in Yemen Has Increased, Reaching the Highest Levels since the Civil War in 1994." *The Middle East,* Mar. 1, 2003.

"Yemen Tries to Salvage Image: Twenty Yemenis Have Been Arrested in a Crackdown Since the Sept. 11 Attacks on the US." *The Christian Science Monitor,* Sep. 25, 2001.

Chapter 8

AL-AHBASH/JA.'WIYYAT AL-MASHARI' AL-KHALRIYYA AL-ISLAMIYYA/ASSOCIATION OF ISLAMIC PHILANTHROPIC PROJECTS/ISLAMIC CHARITY PROJECTS ASSOCIATION (AICP)

Al-Ahbash (AICP) is a conservative Sunni Islamist and a pro-Syrian political organization. AICP is also unique and one of the most controversial Muslim groups. Its origins are particularly unique and it has eclectic theological origins, which define the group's separate identity from mainstream Sunni thought.

Al-Ahbash is currently based in Beirut. Ahmad al-Ajuz formed the AICP in the 1930s. The group was established in Lebanon in the 1950s and led by Sheikh'Abd Allah al-Habashi, an Ethiopian cleric who settled in Beirut. He became known as "Habashi", or "the African". Their theology was a combination of Sunni and Shia beliefs and Sufi spiritualism. The group came to adhere to the religious doctrines of the Ethiopian theologian Abdullah al-Harari, who began leading the group in the 1980s. By the late 1980s, the group had become one of Lebanon's largest Islamist movements. The group is regarded as an activist type of Lebanese Sufism. While the group's religious doctrine comports to traditional Sunni religious doctrines, other Sunni groups have condemned Al-Ahbash as takfir (heretical) for its adherence to the Shafi school and Ash'ari theology. The Sufi part of Al-Ahbash is derived from the Rifa'iyya and Qadiriyyah orders. Al-Abhash also rejects the doctrines of Islamist Jihadist ideologues such as Ibn Taymiyyah, Muhammad ibn Abd al-Wahhab, and Sayyid Qutb, and advocates an ideology of Islamic moderation and toleration, that emphasizes the idea that Islam supports pluralism, and that Islam opposes violence against the existing government.

The Ahbash and the Wahhabis have frequently clashed over religious issues. Part of this is due to the different historical contexts in which the two groups evolved. The Ahbash represent a moderate interpretation of Islam that developed in nations where Muslims had long had significant interaction with Christians. The Wahhabis developed their puritanical ideology in an isolated desert environment and later joined with the Muslim Brotherhood to assert themselves as leaders and guardians of international Islamism.

During the 1990s, particularly because of Syrian government support and funding, Al-Ahbash grew from being a small minority organization to the largest Sunni religious organization in Lebanon. The group also cultivated close connections with Syria's intelligence services. The Syrian government supported AICP to control and limit the influence of Lebanon's radical and fundamentalist Sunni movements. Al-Ahbash made its debut in Lebanese when the party offered candidates to stand for the parliamentary election of 1992.

Ahbash offers many educational and extracurricular programs, to win popularity among ordinary Lebanese. Among its teachings, Al-Ahbash preaches that modern Islamists who ignore the Prophet Muhammad's teachings are guilty of nonbelief (kafr).

Al-Ahbash has long had rivalries with many of Lebanon's other Sunni groups, including former Prime Minister's Sa'd al-Hariri's Future Movement and the hardline Al-Jamaa al-Islamiya. Al-Ahbash and the Shiite militant group, Hezbollah, and also have a long contentious history, even though both are Syrian government allies. Al-Ahbash, viewed Hezbollah with considerable suspicion, especially after the Shiite group began to expand into territory near areas under AICP control in Beirut during Lebanon's Civil War (1975-1990).

A UN inquiry implicated al-Ahbash in the bombing murder of Lebanese Prime Minister Rafik Hariri in 2005 (both al-Ahbash and Hezbollah opposed the Special Tribunal for Lebanon charged with investigating al-Hariri's assassination in 2005). Al-Abhash was accused of several other killings in Lebanon, including several imams and the Mufti of Lebanon, Sheik Hassan Khaled. These killings were supposedly done in order to extend AICP's influence. Leaders of al-Ahbash have denied those allegations.

FURTHER READING

Barnett, N. "The Plot Thickens." *The Middle East,* Jan. 1, 2002, 18.

Blanche, E. "Syria Plays the Palestinian Card in Lebanon." *The Middle East,* Jan. 1, 2006, 24-28.

Kabha, Mustafa and Haggai Erlich. "Al-Ahbash and Wahhabiyya: Interpretations of Islam." *International Journal of Middle East Studies,* 38 no. 4 (November 25, 2006): 519-538.

"Pressure Builds on Syrian regime; Another UN Report this Week Could Further Push for Sanctions." *The Christian Science Monitor,* Oct. 24, 2005.

Rougier, Bernard. *Everyday Jihad: the Rise of Militant Islam Among Palestinians in Lebanon.* Cambridge, Mass.: Harvard University Press, 2007.

Shalmil, 'Abd Allāh Muḥammad. *A Warning and Refutation of the Heretical Group known as the Habashis [al-Ahlbal]: translated excerpts from Abdullah Muhammad al-Shami's [al-Radd Eala Eabd Allah al-Hibabashil] "the Refutation of Abdullah al-Habashi": Islamic Theological Studies.* Warminster, Pa.: AlgebraTan Pub., 1994.

Chapter 9

AL-ASALAH AL-ISLAMIYAH/AL-ASLAH ISLAMIC SOCIETY/ISLAMIC PURITY SOCIETY

The dominant Salafi Islamist political party in Bahrain, al-Asalah, is also a branch of the Islamic Educational Society in that nation. Al-Asalah was established on June 6, 2002 under Bahrain's 2005 Political Societies Act, which legalized political societies, but not political parties. Ghanim al-Buaneen, the Asalah Party Chair since 2005, is the party's leader. Al Tarbiya Al Islamiya (Islamic Education Charity Society) finances the party's activities and operations.

Asalah participated in the parliamentary and municipal elections in 2002 and 2006. Asalah members currently serve both in Bahrain's Council of Representatives and its National Council.

Al-Asalah has close connections with Saudi Arabia. It also promotes a Salafi type of strict Islamism that is against most of Bahrain's modernization efforts. The party has four representatives in Bahrain's parliament and has one cabinet position in the current government. During its decade-long involvement in partisan politics, Al-Asalah has cooperated with the Bahraini government. This group adheres to the traditional Salafi model of swearing absolute obedience to the leader and prohibiting all types of political activism. Despite this prohibition, political activities are allowed based on the religious doctrine of allowing one type of evil to occur to prevent a greater evil. In addition to giving Absolute obedience to the ruler, Al-Asalah also unequivocally opposes al-Qaeda and jihadist Salafist philosophy.

In addition to emphasizing Bahraini Islamic identity, Al-Asalah offers a political program that seeks to increase living standards; increase political, social and economic stability; and strengthen financial and administrative oversight of both the public and private sector.

Al-Asalah, which is a religiously conservative party, receives most of its support from Sunni enclaves such as Muhrraq and Riffa areas (two of the three largest cities in Bahrain). Its members oppose modernity within Bahrain and adhere to an austere version of Islam. Al-Asalah strongly opposes women's rights, veneration of icons, and divination. Although they oppose Shiite theology, most al-Asalah followers agree with the Shiite adherence to strict religious conservatism.

Asalah usually supports the government in the Bahraini Parliament. The party usually aligns with the Minbar Al Islami Party (a Sunni association that seeks to promote Sharia, but is more open to Aslah to some aspects of modernization such as allowing women to participate in government) which usually allows it to prevail over the Wifaq party.

Although Asalah has historically maintained loyalty to the ruling family (the Al-Khalifa family) and has not become involved in international movements, some observers believe that the party may be turning its interests to regional issues. One example was Abdelhalim Murad, an Asalah member of parliament organized Bahraini jihadists' travel to Syria and met with Suqur al-Sham and Liwa Dawud, both hardline Islamist militias operating in that nation.

FURTHER READING

"Al-Wefaq Wins Big in Bahrain Elections." *Arab News (Jeddah, Saudi Arabia)*, Oct. 25, 2010.

"Bahrain Parliamentary Elections Results Confirmed." *Bahrain News Agency*, Nov. 1, 2010.

"Bahrainis Excited Ahead of Saturday's Poll." *Arab News (Jeddah, Saudi Arabia),* Oct. 21, 2010.

Byman, Daniel L. and Green, Jerrold D. *Political Violence and Stability in the States of the Northern Persian Gulf.* Santa Monica, CA: Rand, 1999.

Ehteshami, Anoushiravan and Wright, Steven M. *Reform in the Middle East oil monarchies.* Reading, Berkshire, UK: Ithaca Press, 2008.

Gresh, Geoffrey F. *Gulf Security and the U.S. Military: Regime Survival and the Politics of Basing.* Stanford, California: Stanford University Press, 2015.

"HRH Premier receives Al Asalah Islamic Society board members." *Bahrain News Agency*, (June 1, 2011): 1.

Kaye, Dalia Dassa. *More Freedom, Less Terror?: Liberalization and Political Violence in the Arab World.* Santa Monica, CA: RAND, 2008.

"Peaceful voting in Bahrain." *Arab News (Jeddah, Saudi Arabia)*, Oct. 23, 2010).

Pollack, K. M. *The Arab Awakening: America and the Transformation of the Middle East.* Washington, DC: Brookings Institution, 2011.

"Shi'ite Group Wins 18 Seats in Bahrain polls." *Kippreport,* Oct. 25, 2010.

Wright, R. B. *Sacred rage: The wrath of militant Islam: Updated with new chapters.* New York: Simon & Schuster, 2001.

Chapter 10

AL-AQSA MARTYRS' BRIGADE (AAMB)

Known as Al-Aqsa or Kata'ib Shuhada' al-Aqsa, a Palestinian nationalist group, named after Al-Aqsa Mosque on the in Jerusalem's Temple Mount, one of the holiest sites in Islam. Its name in Arabic means "the farthest place". Muslims believe that the Prophet Muhammad ascended to heaven from the location of the al-Aqsa Mosque. Likud Party leader Ariel Sharon visited that site in September 2000, which ignited a conflict that Palestinians call the "al-Aqsa intifada". The individual militias that comprise AAMB are often named after recently killed Palestinian militants.

The AAMB is allegedly associated with Al-Fatah, Hamas, and the Islamic Jihad of Palestine. It has conducted several assassinations, suicide bombings, and other types of attacks on Israeli both military and civilian Israeli nationals.

The AAMB is composed of local, autonomous units that united under a joint alliance to Fatah. Because of its decentralized power structure, the US government has had difficulty identifying the group's leaders.

In 2000, the brigade began after defecting from Fatah, a secular Palestinian nationalist movement then led by Arafat. Fatah is the Palestine Liberation Organization's (PLO) largest faction. When Israel and the PLO entered into a peace agreement in 1993, Arafat explicitly denounced terrorism and formed a new, Palestinian government in the West Bank and Gaza Strip. The AAMB conducts suicide bombings often connected with such Muslim fundamentalist organizations as Hamas and Palestinian Islamic Jihad. The group, however, is a secular Palestinian nationalist group and does not promote political Islam.

The AAMB is a network of West Bank militias affiliated with former Palestinian leader Yasir Arafat's Fatah and was a leader in the "Second" or "Al-Aqsa Intifada". AAMB, at first, said it would attack only the Israeli military and Jewish settlers in the West Bank and Gaza Strip. In early 2002 AAMB collaborated with Hamas and Palestinian Islamic Jihad in several terrorist attacks against Israeli civilians in urban areas. In March 2002, following a particularly gruesome AAMB suicide bombing in Jerusalem, the US government designated the group as a foreign terrorist organization. The US also stopped viewing Arafat as a credible partner in efforts to the Middle Eastern peace process.

In 2004, the AAMB entered into a ceasefire with Israel. The group then renewed its attacks following Hamas victories in the Palestinian elections in 2006. AAMB continues to participate in Palestinian on Palestinian violence, which adds to insecurity and instability in the area. While the AAMB operates primarily in the West Bank, it also conducts attacks in the Gaza Strip and Israel.

The Israeli-Palestinian Secular brigade members often clash with Hamas members in Gaza. Although the brigade agreed to a unilateral ceasefire in 2004, it resumed attacks on Hamas after Hamas emerged victorious the 2006 parliamentary elections. The conflict that began as intermittent street conflicts with assassinations of leaders on both sides became a civil war after the failure of power-sharing agreements. Eventually, Palestinian territory was governed by two different Palestinian groups: a Hamas-controlled Gaza and Fatah-controlled West Bank. AAMB cells in the West Bank and Gaza are only nominally affiliated with each other. The two groups apparently do not coordinate on targets or plans.

FURTHER READING

"Arafat Faces Generational Crisis; A Palestinian Power Struggle Is Epitomized By The Young Man Who Runs Jenin." *The Christian Science Monitor*, Jul. 21, 2004.

Blanche, E. "The Human Bombs: The Palestinian Suicide Bomber Has Become a 21st Century Political Phenomenon, Which Divides Public Opinion in the Arab World and beyond. Are These Bombers Martyrs to the Cause or Murderers of Innocent Civilian Targets?" *The Middle East*, Nov. 1, 2002.

Jasper, W. F. "A Bad Investment: U.S. Support for So-Called "Moderate" Terrorists as the Alternative to Worse Terrorists, as We Have Given in Palestine, is a Recipe for Disaster." *The New American*, Apr. 28, 2008.

"Militant Rampage Raises Questions about Abbas's Control; Palestinian Fugitives Went on a Shooting Spree Late Wednesday in Ramallah." *The Christian Science Monitor*, Apr. 1, 2005.

"Palestinians need Hanna Sahrawi," *The Christian Science Monitor*, Jun. 7, 2002.

"The Gazafication of the West Bank; The Palestinian Territories (The chaos of the Gaza Strip is spreading to the West Bank)," *The Economist*, Feb. 3, 2007.

"Why a Palestinian Girl Now Wants to be a Suicide Bomber: On Friday, a Suicide Bomber Killed Herself and Two Israelis, Joining Two Other Female 'Martyrs,' "*The Christian Science Monitor*, Apr. 1, 2002.

Chapter 11

AL MAHDI ARMY/JAYSH AL-MAHDI

OVERVIEW

Jaysh al-Mahdi (or the Mahdi Army) is the armed wing of the Office of the Martyr Sadr in Iraq. They were led by the Shiite rebel leader, Moqtada al-Sadr (1973–), son of the late, respected Grand Ayatollah Sayyid Muhammad Baqr al-Sadr (1935 – 1980). Barred from participation in the new Iraqi political system, Moqtada Al-Sadr believed that the only way he could gain influence was through an armed insurgency. Thus, he and his followers created the Mahdi Army.

MAJOR ATTACKS

Iran provided covert support for the Mahdi army soon after the coalition invaded Iraq in 2003. Iran began supporting al-Sadr after Sadr visited Tehran in June 2003. He was also receiving funding from Iranian Grand Ayatollah Kazem al_Haeri (1938 -) until October 2003, when al-Haeri began to curtail ties to Sadr. In Teheran, the group met with Iran's Supreme Leader Ayatollah Ali Khamenei (1939 -), former President Ali Akbar Hashemi Rafsanjani (1934-2017), and Ayatollah Mahmoud Hashemi Shahroudi (1948 -). The clerical leaders in Najaf Iran disapproved of Sadr's visit.

Hezbollah in Lebanon, a jihadist group supported by Iran, also has had connections with Sadr since August 2003. Hezbollah sent several of its fighters in Najaf to support Sadr's Shia militant activities. Hezbollah began recruiting and training Sadr's fighters supplied weapons such as rocket-propelled grenades (RPGs), and anti-tank missiles for Sadr's fighters.

In March 2004, the Mahdi Army forced the residents of Qawliya Iraq from their homes, claiming that the village was a hub of prostitution and later bulldozed the houses in the town. The group also has been charged with frequently flinging acid in the faces of women failing to wear Muslim garb and threaten those who sought to operate women's centers. By late April 2004, the Mahdi Army had controlled major religious shrines in Najaf, Kufa, and Karbala, in addition to Sadr City in Baghdad.

Later in 2004, the Mahdi army began clashing with the US military in Najaf and Sadr City. The Mahdi Army and other Iraqi jihadist groups sought to wear down US forces in Iraq through attrition and to keep the American military engaged in Iraq.

In October 2004, Iran supplied explosive devices for the Mahdi army. The shipments were made to Iranian operatives or Hezbollah from Iran. In 2005, the Iranian government permitted Hezbollah to train Iraqi jihadists in Iran. In the summer of 2007, the three small camps were being used to train fighters from the Mahdi army.

The Shia gained control of the Iraqi government. On April 21, 2006, the Iraqi parliament select Nouri al-Maliki (1950–), leader of the Islamic Dawa Party, as Iraq's Prime Minister. On May 20, 2006, Maliki's cabinet took office. The Iranians and Hezbollah shifted their strategy and set up a network similar to Hezbollah to assist the Iraqi government survive and enhance Iranian control and influence over operations in Iraq.

On November 29, 2006, the Sadrists boycotted the Iraqi Parliament. On January 21, 2007, the Sadrists rejoined the Iraqi government.

Al-Sadr departed for an extended stay in Iran in late January 2007. Sadr's absence eroded the leadership structure of the Mahdi Army. In May 2007, the Golden Mahdi Army, based in Najaf and claimed to be following Sadr's order, sought to purge the Mahdi Army of rogue elements not responsive to Najaf. This group was opposed by local groups named the Noble Mahdi Army, based in Hurriyah in Baghdad to oppose the efforts of the Golden Mahdi Army.

The secret cells function allowed for Iranian support for the Mahdi Army. Sadr City remained the support base for these cells, the Mahdi Army and many rogue Mahdi Army operate within Baghdad.

In 2007, The Mahdi Army worked with secret cells and other militias (these groups have overlapping members. Some may have had some association with the Mahdi Army and had broken away. In the Spring of 2007, the Mahdi Army fractured. Sadr ordered his militias not to fight Iraqi Security Forces as they enforce an effort known as Fardh al-Qanoon (Enforcing the Law, or, the Baghdad Security Plan. The Maliki Government then deemed all militia organizations the fought the Iraqi Security Forces were "rogue groups, "and thereby legitimate targets for military attack. The ISF and rogue militia groups fought in Diwanyah in March and Amarah in June 2007.

Sadr declared a ceasefire in August 2007. A-Mahdi Army fighters began a gun battle at the holy shrine in Karbala that skilled several hundred people. The Shiite community condemned the Mahdi Army for the attack.

Because the surge was successful in lessening the threat to Shiite areas, the Mahdi Army was no longer need as a security force. Sadr, deferring top public pressure, ordered his forces to stop fighting. Violence sharply declined.

In the Spring of 2008, Prime Minister Maliki decided to break the Al-Mahdi army's control of Basra. He initiated Operation "Charge of the Knights" in Basra, which the Coalition supported. The operation successfully ousted the militias from the city. The Mahdi Army responded by firing rockets from Sadr City into the Green Zone.

In March 2008, the US army conducted operations within Sadr City to defeat the Mahdi Army threat. This was in response to The Mahdi Army's use of that area to fire several rockets in the "Green Zone". As part of the effort, the US military built a three mile concrete barrier to create a buffer between the insurgents and other parts of Sadr City. The barrier restricted the range of rocket attacks, restricted the insurgents' freedom of movement, and enable reconstruction efforts outside the wall. Facing overwhelming firepower, Moqtadr Al-

Sadr was forced to end hostilities against Coalition Forces. Iraqi Security Forces occupied Sadr City beginning on May 2008.

JIHADIST GROUP AS SERVICE PROVIDER

These Iraqi militias have had a dual nature in Iraq. On one hand, they created death squads and played as major role in sectarian cleansing. They also joined government departments, with Mahdi Army members having a significant presence in the Ministry of Health and the Ministry of the Interior.

At the same time, the Mahdi Army had a very important role in filling governance gaps in Iraq, extending beyond security gaps, but also filling in the various service gaps. The Mahdi Army definitely fulfilled this role with its base in impoverished areas in Baghdad and Basra. The problem is that the service provision of the Mahdi Army was not politically neutral and alternative service providers were hard to implement in the chaos of post-Sadaam Iraq.

See also: Hezbollah (volume 1); Iranian Revolutionary Guard (IRGC) (volume 1).

FURTHER READING

Cerny, Jakub. *Death Squad Operations in Iraq*. Camberley, Surrey: Defence Academy of the United Kingdom, Conflict Studies Research Centre. 2006.

Crytzer, Kurt S. *Mahdi and the Iranian Nuclear Threat*. Carlisle Barracks, PA: U.S. Army War College, 2007.

Johnson, David E., Markel, M. Wade, and Shannon, David E; *The 2008 Battle of Sadr City*. Santa Monica CA: RAND, 2013.

Krohley, Nicholas. *The Death of the Mehdi Army: The Rise, Fall, and Revival of Iraq's Most Powerful Militia*. New York, NY: Oxford University Press, 2015.

Møller, Pia Kramer. *The Development of the Sadrist Movement and its Mahdi Army, 2003-2009*. København, 2011 (thesis).

Chapter 12

AL-QAEDA (AQ)

aka The Base, Islamic Army for the Liberation of the Holy Places, Islamic Salvation Foundation, Osama bin Laden Network, World Islamic Front for Jihad Against Jews and Crusaders, Qa'idat al-Jihad, Maktab al-Khidamat, International Islamic Front for Jihad Against Jews and Christians, Islamic Army for the Liberation of Holy Shrines, Islamic Sal, Al-Jabhah al-Islamiyyah al-'Alamiyyah li-Qital al-Yahud wal-Salibiyyan.

OVERVIEW

Al-Qaeda (Arabic term meaning "The Base", AQ) is a jihadist group that pursuant to its view of Islam, conducts terrorist attacks on Western targets both completely on its own initiative with its own resources and also as an umbrella group. As an "umbrella group", AQ coordinates and facilitates with various jihadist organizations in conducting various types of attacks by providing logistical and training assistance for these other groups. Claiming itself to be the "vanguard" of radical militant Salafism worldwide, AQ collaborates closely with several similar jihadist organizations.

Ayam Zawahiri (1951-), AQ's current leader, explained that the group provides a "base for indoctrination, training, and incitement that gathered the capabilities of the ummah (the worldwide community of Muslims), trained them, raised their consciousness, improved their abilities, and gave them confidence in their religion and themselves." AQ, Zawahiri further explained, required "large amounts of participation in jihad, bearing the worries of the ummah, and seizing the initiative in the most urgent calamities confronting the ummah." Thus, AQ asserts itself to be the Islamist "vanguard" to defend what it perceives as Muslim interests worldwide.

In terms of its religiosity, AQ does not adhere to mainstream Islamic theological thought. Instead, it purports to apply Islamic principles to achieve its agenda of radical social and political change, through militant and revolutionary action.

AL-QAEDA'S OBJECTIVES

AQ affiliates and similar jihadist organizations share many of the same objectives, which generally focus on seeking to eradicating Western influence from traditionally or majority.

Islamic nations and eventually forming an Islamic state (a caliphate) governed by Islamic law (Sharia).

Al-Qaeda, to achieve its goals, requires the following:

Radical Salafist Islamist Reform

to enforce an extremely harsh version of Sharia, although the AQ leadership have not firmly determined how fast impose Sharia on populations either the group or its affilaites controls.

Defensive Jihad

AQ members must oppose all types of Western influence, are instructed to use violent means to oppose what the groups considers to be aggression by western powers, including the deployment of the US military in areas that they claim as Muslim territory.

Attacks Directed Against the "Far Enemy"

AQ has conducted several major attacks against various high-profile targets, including the 9-11 attacks against the United States and the later assaults in London, UK; Madrid, Spain; and Istanbul, Turkey. AQ argues that these attacks are necessary and justified to eradicate Western presence in Muslim majority nations. AQ views America as Islam's main opponent because it claims that the US government pursues an oppressive and imperialistic foreign policy against Muslims. The group also argues that America is the most significant factor preventing the establishment of a worldwide Islamist government. AQ, therefore, believes that the United States must be destroyed.

Attacks Directed Against Israel ("The Near Enemy")

Because AQ views the State of Israel as a foreign entity governed by who it considers are "unbelievers" located on sacred Muslim territory, AQ believes that Israel must be destroyed and replaced with an Islamist Palestinian state. While AQ leaders often threaten severe violence in their anti-Israel rhetoric, AQ has launched conducted few if any attacks against Israel or Israeli targets.

The Destruction of "Apostate Regimes"

AQ's jihadi Salafi ideology demands that its members overthrow "apostate governments", i.e., regimes not based on its harsh puritanical interpretation of Sharia. AQ views such governments as empowering human rulers and elevating human government over God's law. Under AQ ideology, democracy as un-Islamic and apostasy, and punishable by death. AQ also demands the destruction of Islamic governments of several Middle East nations that do not adhere to its interpretation of Islamism (such as the government of Saudi Arabia) because they are immoral and heretical regimes specifically because they have not imposed AQ's version of Sharia. The Saudi monarchy particularly arouses AQ's ire, as it rules the country where Islam's holiest places are located. Among Osama Bin Laden's (1957-2011) long list of grievances against the Saudi ruling class was that they permitted the American military to operate from there during the First Gulf War in 1991 to help liberate Kuwait.

Economic Jihad Against the West

AQ leaders instruct their members to weaken both Western nations and various Middle Eastern governments that it views as apostate by launching assaults on various economically-related targets, including petroleum facilities to curtail oil supplies from the Middle East to various Western nations.

Jihad Against Non-Radical Sunni Muslim Religious Groups

Al-Qaeda considers Non-Sunni Muslim sects such as Shia Muslims to be apostates and deviants from true Islam. Some AQ leaders have called for attacks against Shias and Shia targets. Other AQ leaders oppose such actions concerned that they could cause a backlash within the broader Muslim community.

THE LEADERSHIP OF AL-QAEDA

The small number of men who lead Al-Qaeda comprise the majlis al-shura (or consultative council). The Shura renders all major decisions for AQ, including approving attacks and the making what they term as "fatwas" (or Islamic decrees). AQ different committees for matters dealing with various issues under the categories of military, business, public relations, and religion. Very few of the elite AQ members may communicate with the group's executive leaders. The relevant fighters are activated immediately before the planned attack without any forewarning. Thus, Western intelligence agencies have had considerable difficulty infiltrating the network.

OSAMA BIN LADEN AND THE CREATION OF AL QAEDA

Al-Qaeda's origins and development are strongly associated with the biography of its founder, Osama bin Laden (1957-2011). Bin Laden's father was a highly successful contractor and a Saudi Arabia multi-millionaire. Osama Bin Laden inherited between $270 and $300 million from his family.

Believing that the Afghan-Soviet War (1979-1989) to be a jihad and a holy war between Islam and the atheistic Soviets, bin Laden travelled to Afghanistan to assist and fight with the mujahideen in 1979.

The Afghans, at the time, did not have the resources necessary for a prolonged conflict. Bin Laden allied himself with Abdullah Azzam (1941-1989), a militant leader with the Palestinian Muslim Brotherhood, to form the Maktab al-Khidamat (Afghan Services Bureau or MAK), which would recruit thousands of Islamist fighters worldwide for the war in Afghanistan. Bin Laden financed their transportation to Afghanistan and trained them in guerrilla warfare and terrorist tactics. Local Afghan leaders, in return, provided the land and other resources.

Between 175,000 and 250,000 mujahideen fought the Soviets each year in Afghanistan. Few of them, however, were ethnic Afghans. About half of AQ's fighters were from Saudi Arabia. In addition, about 3,000 were from Algeria, and about 2,000 were from Egypt. Many thousands more came from nations such as Pakistan, Yemen, and Sudan. Many of these militants became AQ's core fighters

In 1988, bin Laden, believing that Azzam's goals were too restricted, split with the latter to form AQ, which was dedicated to a worldwide jihad. In 1989, Azzam was killed when his car was firebombed by his Afghan enemies.

Receiving funded and training by the Central Intelligence Agency (CIA), the mujahideen defeated the Soviets. The Soviets withdrew from Afghanistan on February 15, 1989. Despite the victory, Bin Laden sought to continue and expand the jihad throughout the world. He formed Al-Qaeda for this express purpose.

Through a network of thousands of jihadist fighters, bin Laden dispatched militant Islamists to their nations of origin to create militant cells and fight guerrilla warfare to overthrow what he claimed to be "heretical regimes". He sent mujahideen to fight in Somalia, the Balkans, and Chechnya. AQ also sought to unite Islamist groups worldwide as part of global jihad.

Bin Laden came back to Saudi Arabia to prepare for war against the Saudi government, which he believed had become apostate. From 1989 through 1991, conspired against the Saudi Royal Family arguing that the Saudi King failed to follow Islam in rule of the kingdom.

During the 1991 Gulf War, Bin Laden strongly objected to stationing US troops in Saudi Arabia. Outraged by American military deployment in Saudi Arabia during the First Gulf War, bin Laden became increasingly virulent in opposing the Saudi government. His recorded speeches that strongly denounced the Saudi and the US diatribes were widely disseminated throughout Saudi Arabia.

Because of bin Laden posed a threat to the monarchy, Saudi intelligence monitored his activities. Eventually, the Saudi government banished him from Saudi Arabia and revoked his citizenship for behavior the government viewed as seditious and treasonous. Bin Laden, his family, and nearly 300 to 480 AQ jihadists relocated to Sudan, a country governed by the radical Islamist, Omar al-Bashir (1944-), in 1989. Al-Bashir had close connections with the Muslim Brotherhood

Bin Laden was able to establish a new venue for AQ operations in Khartoum through collaborating with Hassan al-Turabi (1932-2016), Sudan's leading radical Islamist ideologue and leader of the National Islamic Front (NIP). Sudan granted asylum for AQ militants, sites for new training camps, and false travel documents allowing AQ members to travel overseas under false names. Bin Laden, for his part, financed badly needed infrastructure in Sudan. Facilitated by Sudanese authorities, AQ formed connections with the Iranian regime and Hezbollah, which Iran strongly supports. AQ continued to expand in size and influence.

EARLY HIGH PROFILE AL-QAEDA ATTACKS

In its first attack, Al-Qaeda's bombed hotels in the Yemeni port city of Aden on December 1992. The attack injured several tourists, but was targeted at US troops assigned to carry out the relief mission, "Operation Restore Hope" in Somalia. Western intelligence, reportedly, had not found that the relatively new AQ conducted the attack until sometime later.

On February 26, 1993, AQ also attacked the World Trade Center (the "Twin Towers") in New York City. Six people were and near a thousand more suffered injuries. Egyptian Gama'a al-Islamiyya (GAI), which collaborated closely with AQ, was also involved in the attacks. The bomb-maker in the attack, Ramzi Ahmed Yousef (1963-), operated in an AQ facility in Pakistan, both prior to and after the attack. Yousef was captured and convicted in a US court in 1998 for his involvement in the attack. Yousef admitted that he was a terrorist and that he was proud of it.

AQ then attacked American marines in Somalia's capital of Mogadishu, in October 19, 1993. AQ-trained militants disrupted US attempts to capture a radical Islamist warlord. The militants downed two military helicopters and forced another crash land. Eighteen US troops died and 78 suffered injuries in that attack.

In 1994, several governments worldwide effectively thwarted several AQ conspiracies, including attempts to assassinate Pope John Paul II and to destroy 11 passenger jets in mid-air.

In April 1994, motivated by his antipathy to the Saudi government, bin Laden formed the AQ Committee for Advice and Reform Committee, which publicly denounced the Saudi government as heretical and apostate.

While in Sudan, AQ orchestrated attacks on American troops based in Saudi Arabia. The first, occurred in Riyadh in November 1995, killed five Americans and two Indians in a truck bomb explosion near a US Government-operated Saudi National Guard base. The group also attacked the Khobar Towers, which housed US soldiers in Dhahran, in June 1996. The large truck bomb explosion killed nineteen Americans and injured 500 others.

AQ also conducted two other attacks in 1995. On June 26th, AQ conducted a failed assassination attempt of Egyptian President Hosni Mubarak, in Ethiopia's capital of Addis Ababa. On November 19th, AQ was responsbile for a car bombing at the Egyptian embassy in Pakistan. Fifteen Egyptians and Pakistanis died in the attack, with 80 others suffering injuries.

Following the attacks on US personnel in Saudi Arabia, the United States government sanctioned the Sudanese government for providing sanctuary to AQ and bin Laden. Due to both improving US-Sudan relations and in answer to repeated U.S. requests, Sudanese authorities asked bin Laden and his AQ followers to leave country on May 1996. Bin Laden and his followers went to Afghanistan, where the Taliban had seized control of most of that nation during fighting between various militant groups. Bin Laden developed connections with the Taliban movement. These ties helped him develop training camps and a terrorist network.

BIN LADEN ANNOUNCES A WORLDWIDE JIHAD

Soon after arriving in Afghanistan, on August 23, 1996, bin Laden delivered what he described as a "declaration of war" against the US Government, in announcing "Jihad on the Americans Occupying the Country of the Two Sacred Places" [Saudi Arabia].

In February 23, 1998, bin Laden announced the creation of a group called the World Islamic Front for Jihad Against Jews and Crusaders and said that Muslims should kill Americans, including civilians, anywhere and under any circumstances. In declaring this jihad, bin Laden invoked allusions to struggles between Muslims and European Crusaders in the Middle Ages, depicting his foes as "the alliance of Jews, Christians, and their agents." He further blamed these groups for the killings of Muslims in "Tajikistan, Burma, Kashmir, Assam, the Fatani, Ogaden, Somalia, Chechnya, and Bosnia-Hercegovina."

Bin Laden's second fatwa in 1998 stated:

The ruling to kill the Americans and their allies – civilians and military – is an individual duty for every Muslim who can do it any country in which its is possible to do it, in order to liberate Al-Asqa Mosque and the holy mosques from their grip, and in order for their armies to move out of all the lands of Island, defeated, and unable to threaten any Muslim. This is in accordance to the words of Almighty God, "and fight the pagans all together as they fight you all together," and "fight them until there is no more tumult or oppression, and there prevails justice and faith in God.

On May 28, 1998, bin Laden formed a coordinating group: the International Islamic Front for Jihad Against the United States and Israel. This organization clearly demonstrated the depth and breadth of the AQ network. The Front included the Egyptian Al Jihad (EIJ), the Egyptian Armed Group, the Pakistan Scholars Society, the Partisans Movement in Kashmir, the Jihad Movement in Bangladesh, and the Afghan military branch of the Advice and Reform Committee. In "declaring war" on America and Israel, bin Laden argued that the United States could be vanquished in battle and that it was permissible and justifiable to target US non-combatants in jihad.

On August 7, 1998, AQ bombed the US embassies in Kenya, and Tanzania. These attacks killed 224 and injured thousands of others. bin Laden justified the Kenyan attack because he claimed that it was the largest spy network in the Middle East. The bombings occurred on the seventh anniversary of when the US military was deployed to Saudi Arabia in the First Gulf War in 1991 to liberate Kuwait from occupation by Saddam Hussein's Iraq.

Following these attacks, U.S. intelligence had a significant breakthrough. On August 15, 1998, Mohammed Odeh (1970 -) was arrested at a Pakistani airport. Odeh, an AQ member, while being interrogated, described AQ's operations, his role in the two embassy attacks in 1993, and bin Laden's role in the network. Odeh's testimony also provided U.S. intelligence with valuable information to significantly improve monitoring of AQ.

After connecting AQ to the two embassy attacks, the US government retaliated against the group. On August 20, 1998, the US launched cruise missiles against several AQ training camps in Afghanistan and a drug factory in Sudan. US intelligence believed that the drug factory was manufacturing the ingredient EMPTA, which is used as nerve gas. The United States killed at least six AQ jihadists in attacks in Afghanistan, however, on the factory in the Sudan was based on erroneous intelligence.

On September 28, 1998, an Egyptian, Ali Mohamed (1952–), was apprehended in the United States as a suspected AQ member. Mohamed taught at a military training facility at Fort Bragg, North Carolina. While there, he gathered a significant amount of intelligence on the US army. This incident illustrates how AQ "sleepers," could successfully operate within the United States. Despite the fact that he was a fighter in Afghanistan and often engaged in AQ missions in the Middle East, Mohamed was able to infiltrate into the U.S. Army.

In June 1999, the FBI named bin Laden to its "most wanted" list. In July 1999, the US government sanctioned Afghanistan's Taliban government for providing a refuge for bin Laden. Later in 1999, two AQ militants were apprehended in Turkey upon arriving from Iran. One suspect confessed that that he had ties to AQ and warned that the group was attempting to attack a meeting on European Cooperation and Security (ECS).

In December 1999, Jordanian authorities transferred over to the US government a large terror manual used to train AQ jihadists. It was seized when AQ members were apprehended in Jordan for attempting to launch terrorist operations in the forthcoming millennium celebrations. AQ militants were apprhended in the US and several nations in Europe and the Middle East in connection with this conspiracy. By this time, national governments worldwide had become increasingly concerned with the AQ threat to national security.

In 1999, the Saudi government uncovered a conspiracy that was sending nearly $50 million dollars to AQ, from funds donated as "zakat" (alms). Supporters from the United Arab Emirates (UAE) also reportedly generously funded AQ.

In early 2000, the US government announced it had documents describing AQ functions, including weapons purchases, fundraising, and the counterfeiting of documents. U.S. intelligence, thus, appeared to be making significant progress in controlling the threat from AQ. On June 30, 2000, a Lebanese military court convicted eight alleged AQ militants on charges including conspiracy on a variety of crimes including terrorism and forgery. In the fall of 2000, Jordan convicted several AQ-affiliated suspects in the so-called "millennium plot", to attack various celebrations marking the new century. In December 2000, a US District Court indicted five AQ-affiliated suspects for conspiracy in the East African embassy attacks.

AQ continued to attack targets worldwide. In April 2000, the Abu Sayyaf Group (ASG), an Al- Qaeda affiliate in the Philippines, abducted 50 people, and demanded the release of Ramzi Ahmed Yousef, the AQ jihadist who conducted the 1993 World Trade Center bombing, and imprisoned in the United States.

On October 12, 2000, AQ-linked jihadists attacked the U.S.S. Cole, during refueling in the Yemeni port city of Aden. The attack killed seventeen US Navy personnel, and another 39 sailors suffered injuries. The bombing also cost $25 million dollars in damage. AQ planned and directed the attack.

AL-QAEDA AND CONFLICTS IN AFGHANISTAN AND IRAQ

On September 11, 2001, nineteen hijackers connected to AQ, and supported by several sleeper cells within the United States, seized four airplanes. The hijackers deliberately crashed two of the planes into the World Trade Center (WTC) in New York City, which destroyed both of the iconic "Twin Towers". The hijackers deliberately crashed a third plane into the Pentagon, in Washington, D.C.. A fourth plane, was highjacked while flying to Washington, D.C., before the passengers rose up against the highjackers, and the plane crashed in Shanksville in western Pennsylvania. Nearly 3,000 Americans perished in the 9/11 attacks, the largest number of Americans killed in the United States on one day.

On October 7, 2001, the US government, under President George W. Bush, initiated "Operation Enduring Freedom", in Afghanistan in response to the AQ attacks. The US military overthrew the Taliban regime in Afghanistan within two months and captured nearly half of AQ's senior leaders. Many fighters connected with AQ and the Taliban fled to the remote frontier regions Afghanistan and Pakistan as the conflict escalated.

AQ continued to use modern technology to coordinate its international network of Islamist extremists. The group was forced to transform itself from a centrally-directed and controlled organization to a much more decentralized group united more by its terrorist mission than by the desire to occupy territory. The group included various indigenous groups connected to AQ and supported by its financial resources and technical advice.

Despite the success of the 9-11 attacks, AQ failed to attract large numbers of Muslim recruits. The group's credibility suffered when bin Laden, to appease the Taliban, initially denied that AQ was involved in the attacks. When the US government attacked AQ in Afghanistan, it denied giving AQ the type of clear enemy -- a large-scale "Crusader" army -- the jihadists had anticipated. The US military presence remained relatively small presence, but included significant airpower. The US also used special operations personnel and CIA operatives to collaborate with friendly local peoples to overthrow the Taliban government and attack AQ bases.

Despite several major attacks, the international media did not report on AQ as much as it did the subsequent Iraq War. Many Muslims worldwide condemned the US incursion in Iraq, which began in 2003. Jihadists claimed this conflict as the clear "war between cultures" they sought. Bin Laden and Zawahiri (1951-) depicted the clash as a massive conflict between the United States and Islamists that would attract large numbers of Muslims to AQ and, be extraordinarilly costly to the US and its allies. In late 2004, bin Laden referred to the Iraqi War as AQ's "war of attrition" on the US.

AQ sought to create Iraq as its caliphate (Islamic state), which would support AQ operations in in place of the deposed Taliban-ruled Afghanistan. Zawahiri. AQ's second-in-command, in 2005, claimed that victory will arrive when "a Muslim state is established in the manner of the Prophet in the heart of the Islamic world. …The center would be in the Levant and Egypt." Zawahiri believed that the jihadists must have "popular support from the Muslim masses in Iraq, and nearby Muslim countries" to defeat the United States and establish an Islamic state. Zawahiri believed that gaining such support would be facilitated by the continuing US military presence in Iraq. To retain their influence after the U.S. troop withdrawal, however, Zawahiri said, AQ jihadists must alienate ordinary Muslims with sectarian or excessive violence. These militants needed to collaborate with different Muslims of various ideological and religious viewpoints so long as they favored imposing a government based on Sharia. Zawahiri told Zarqawi that declaring an "Islamic State" before AQ had developed a strong coalition of Islamist militant organizations and this state had widespread support among the Iraqis, any type of Islamic State would not succeed and would be defeated by their enemies.

Zarqawi's followers chose to ignore Zawahiri. AQ in Iraq (AQI) declared a caliphate (Islamic State) shortly after Zarqawi's death in a coalition aerial strike in 2006. Zawahiri's warnings were soon borne out as true. AQI alienated many moderate Sunni Muslims with its harsh interpretation of Sharia and its continuing attacks on Iraqi Shiite Muslims. Many AQI supporters who once supported the insurgency abandoned AQI as when he demanded complete unquestioned obedience and attacked them and civilians if they did not comply. Because AQI's "Islamic State", initially, controlled very little territory, most Sunni militants in Iraq and elsewhere, at first, largely ignored it.

AL-QAEDA AFTER BIN LADEN

In 2011, the U.S. military located and killed Bin Laden in Abbottabad, Pakistan. Ayman al-Zawahiri, Bin Laden's second in command, then became AQ's leader. An arduous and persistent US-led anti-terrorism campaign against AQ since 2001 has greatly degraded the group's capacity to stage attacks.

Zawahiri has had difficulty retaining the legitimacy and popular support among AQ jihadists and other Salafists that Bin Laden had. Zawahiri does not have Bin's Laden's personal appeal and younger jihadists do not seem to fully recognize his authority.

While Bin Laden occasionally had difficulty controlling some affiliates, Zawahiri encountered greater resistance, including consistent noncompliance to his orders intended to prevent internal disputes and collateral damage. In 2013, Zawahiri reportedly ordered ISIS to deploy its fighters only in Iraq and cease its Syrian operations. Abu Bakr al-Baghdadi (1971–), ISIS's leader, openly and adamantly refused to comply with Zawahiri's order, which he claimed opposed "Almighty God's command".

Following the 9-11 attacks, the number of Islamist groups supporting AQ's jihadist cause grew dramatically, particularly in the Middle East and Africa. While some of these organizations allied themselves to Ayman al-Zawahiri, AQ's leader, others did not. Even among those groups that are formally allied with AQ, there are differences over how operationally integrated they should be with "AQ Central". Some of these organizations, despite the formal alliances, emerged from local disputes and to sustain themselves. In 2014, Zawahiri, in admitting AQ's decentralization, said that "AQ is a message before it is an organization."

After bin Laden was killed, Leon Panetta, former Secretary for the US Defense Department asserted that the US was close to a strategic victory over AQ, while President Barack Obama claimed, that the United States was making significant progress in defeating the terrorist group. The group, however, remains as a threat to global peace and security as its affiliates continue to engage in violent attacks both in the Middle East and North Africa.

The "Arab Spring" also gave AQ new opportunities to extend its activities in the Middle East, after authoritarian secular leaders in Egypt, Tunisia, and Libya were deposed, which allowed jihadists to form new Islamist spaces. During the Arab Spring, Islamists in Egypt, Libya, and Tunisia, Islamists, however, did not pursue AQ's vision of an autocratic government through harsh Sharia (Islamic Law). They instead became involved in the political system. They were political Islamists. Even many adherents of the same theological beliefs as AQ, such as the ultraconservative Salafis, chose to engage in the democratic process and formed political parties. Egyptians who supported AQ deliberated over whether to maintain strict adherence to that organization's authoritarian concepts of government, or support Salafist religious leaders, who advocated participation in the political system. Some commentators on Jihadi Internet sites that supported AQ and denounced the evil of partisan politics, however, viewed such participation as better than Mubarak's rule.

After the deaths of bin Laden and many of his leading associates in Afghanistan and Pakistan, AQ refocused its attention from Central and South Asia to Somalia and Yemen. In Somalia, al-Shabaab, continuing its long struggle to seize control of the country, formally joined AQ in February 2011 to regroup from its military losses. In Yemen, Ansar al-Sharia (an affiliate of AQ) took advantage of the chaos in that country to seize areas in the southern part of that country. Ansar al-Sharia provided essential services to residents of areas that it had seized and documented its activities for propaganda purposes.

The Arab Spring also provided AQ new opportunities in Syria, after its president, Bashar al-Assad (1965–), refused to cede power. Many AQ supporters traveled to Syria to fight the Assad regime.

AQ introduced its "General Guidelines for Jihad in September 2013, which was widely circulated among jihadist circles and stressed restrained tactics. Al-Qaeda's Shura Council approved the document along the leaders of Al-Qaeda franchises and then signed by Ayman al-Zawahiri, the leader of Al-Qaeda. The document said that Al- Qaeda to embed itself in the local community and refrain from attacking noncombatants. The group continued to devote its primary focus on the United States and Israel along with their allies, with a secondary emphasis on local partners. These guidelines manifested successfully in the activities of groups such as al Qaeda in the Arabian Peninsula, helping make al Qaeda look restrained and reasonable compared with the Islamic State.

President Barack Obama, in May 2014 declared that, "Today's principal threat no longer comes from a centralized AQ leadership. Instead, it comes from decentralized AQ affiliates and extremists, many with agendas focused in the countries where they operate." While these Islamist organizations attack mostly local targets, the U.S. government believes they remain credible threat to America, its allies, and American interests in the Middle East and Africa.

Thousands of AQ members belong to these groups worldwide. The continued efforts to attack Western targets indicates the network's continued reach worldwide and its resilience.

Possessing considerable resources, contemporary technology, and motivated by an unquenchable hatred toward the West, AQ continues to plan and prepare for future attacks. AQ began as a hierarchical organization. The group became decentralized after the United States and its allies invaded Afghanistan to remove the Taliban from power. As a result, AQ was denied Afghanistan as a safe haven. AQ has several affiliated groups, several of them pre-dated the 9/11 attacks. Having no formal connections to other groups, the affiliates soon began to align themselves formally with AQ. Despite these connections, most of the other groups retained their locally-oriented focus and ignored AQ's call to an anti-Western jihad as the first goal. Although Bin Laden once described the conflict between the West and the jihadists as a "Third World War," Al Qaeda affiliates continue to focus largely on issues important to their own nations have conducted at least two failed attacks on U.S. territory, appears to be an exception. Most AQAP attacks, however, continue to against Yemeni military and security forces.

AQ affiliates, or organizations allied to AQ leadership and had officially been regarded as affiliates include: Al-Qaeda in the Islamic Maghreb (AQIM), Al-Qaeda in the Arabian Peninsula (AQAP), the Nusrah Front, and Al Shabaab. Jihadi groups that are not AQ affiliates but may have organizational connections or may be ideologically similar with AQ or its affiliates and represent a credible threat to the United States or U.S. interests include:

ISIS: The Islamic State (Also Known As ISIL or Daesh)

ISIS is the successor organization to Al-Qaeda in Iraq (AQI), which attacked U.S.-led coalition forces. The leaders of AQ Central, in February 2014, denounced the organization because of its brutality, conflicts with other Sunni organizations, and prolonged disputes over its appropriate areas of operation.

Al Murabitoun

Al Murabitoun, which publicly allied itself with AQ in 2014. The US government views it as the greatest threat to American interests in the Sahel. AQ's leaders have not yet accepted Al Murabitoun as an AQ affiliate.

Some jihadist groups are known as "affiliates of affiliates," such as Ansar Bayt al Maqdis, Ansar al-Sharia, and Boko Haram. At least some of these affiliates have some operational connections to AQ affiliates. Ansar al-Sharia has conducted various attacks on American diplomatic interests in the Middle East.

AQ is distinguished from the Muslim Brotherhood because AQ claims that is mission and vision transcend geography, culture, ethnicity, and personalities. The Muslim Brotherhood politically pragmatic and follows a reformist strategy in the nations where it is active. It is willing to participate in the democratic process and does not prohibit its operatives from participating in elections. While claiming to adhere to its central purpose of creating an Islamic state, the Muslim Brotherhood is willing to engage in the peaceful competition of political power.

RECENT AL-QAEDA ACTIVITIES

Currently, Al-Qaeda remains an active transnational jihadist organization, which is able to conduct large-scale terrorist attacks. Bin Laden's onetime chief lieutenant, Ayman al-Zawahiri, remains nominally in charge of the group. He is presumed to be hiding in Pakistan. In 2014, he formed a new branch of the group known as Al-Qaeda in the Indian Subcontinent (AQIS), which has attracted a large number of followers in impoverished areas of Karachi, Pakistan.

Al-Qaeda had gained a small advantage by maintaining a low profile, portraying itself as a moderate jihadist alternative to ISIS and portraying its struggle as an insurgent effort in the "long war". Al Qaeda has made inroads with militants at the local and regional level in 2016 and 2017. Al Qaeda continues to conduct jihadist attacks worldwide. Al-Qaeda militants continue to fight in Afghanistan. There are currently 300 Al-Qaeda fighters active in that nation.

Al-Qaeda captured and held a major city in Yemen for several months in 2016 and had some major successes in that civil war. The US military continues to use drones to attack targets connected to the Al-Qaeda in the Arabian Peninsula (AQAP).

Al-Qaeda has launched several recent attacks in Africa. In 2015, it launched attacks in Burkina Faso, the Ivory Coast, and Mali.

The Al-Qaeda franchise in Syria, formerly known as Al-Nusra, remains an active jihadist group in Syria under the name of Jabhat Fateh Al-Sham. It may be seeking to establish a base on Syrian territory to conduct attacks outside the Middle East.

Taking advantage of the chaos generated by the Syrian Civil War, Al-Qaeda has also developed a major presence in Syria. Al-Qaeda seeks to exploit discontent among the local Sunnis to recruit new jihadists. With ISIS losing control of the territory it claimed for its caliphate and becoming less attractive to disenchanted would-be jihadists, Al-Qaeda and its affiliates remain viable alternatives.

AL-QAEDA'S FUTURE

While the world community has focused on ISIS, Al-Qaeda has quietly sought to rejuvenate itself while largely ignored. The US and allied military response to 9/11, as well as beefing-up of homeland security and intelligence capabilities, were devastating for al-Qaeda. Allowing ISIS to distract the world while it quietly rebuilt itself was just about the best thing that could have happened to al-Qaeda. In recent years Al-Qaeda has sought to rebuild itself, leading some commentators to believe that it may be becoming as strong or even stronger, as it was before 9/11.

According to one school of thought, Al-Qaeda continues to decline because it lacks sufficient popular support, counterterrorism efforts by the United States and other nations have been effective, and because Al-Qaeda has engaged in a large-scale killing of Muslim noncombatants. Commentators holding to this viewpoint believe that Al-Qaeda's decline is genuine and could be permanent.

Other commentators believe that Al-Qaeda is transforming itself from a small-scale jihadist organization with struggling affiliates to a powerful transnational network of branches that has greatly increased numbers and fighting capacity that is active in Middle East, Africa, and Asia. The group, thus, has been growing stronger due to a strategy of deliberate and low-key growth. Al-Qaeda's strength has varied due to factors such as the fall of governments in nations such as Iraq, Libya, Syria, and Yemen.

In recent history, Al-Qaeda has attempted to recruit quality jihadists instead of mass sign-ups. It relies on a social network of mosques and financiers to select jihadists instead of slick ISIS internet content.

Before 9/11, Al-Qaeda's active membership was in the thousands worldwide. Currently, its quasi-affiliate in Syria has an estimated 30,000 fighters. There are also thousands more jihadists fighting for Al-Qaeda-affiliate in nations such as Somalia, Yemen, Afghanistan, and North Africa.

Currently, the Al-Qaeda-connected Syrian group, Hayat Tahrir al-Sham (HTS), commands between 20,000 to 30,000 fighters, is the strongest fighting force in the rebel-held province of Idlib in northwest Syria and has been one of the most effective fighting forces in the Syrian civil war.

There appears to be a new generation of Al-Qaeda that may be poised to assume control of the organization and provide it with future direction. Osama bin Laden had preparing his son, Hamza, for years, prior to his death. In August 2015, Hamza called for lone-wolf attacks in the West. His focus on continuing to incite attacks by Muslims in the West, along with criticisms of the Saudi Kingdom, seem to indicate Hamza is seeking to perpetuate his father's legacy.

See also: Al-Qaeda in the Arabian Peninsula (AQAP) (volume 1); Al-Qaeda in the Indian Subcontinent (AQIS) (volume 2); Al-Qaeda in the Islamic Maghreb (AQIM (volume 2); Al-Shabaab (volume 2); Ansar al-Sharia (volume 2); Ansar Bayt al Maqdis (volume 1); Boko Haram (volume 2); Islamic State of Iraq and Syria (volume 1); Jabhat Fateh Al-Sham (volume 1); Muslim Brotherhood (volume 1); Tawhid wa'l jihad (volume 1).

FURTHER READING

Atwan, Abdel Bari. *The Secret History of Al-Qaeda*. Berkeley: University of California Press, 2006.

Bergen, Peter L. *Holy War, Inc.: Inside the Secret World of Osama bin Laden*. New York: Free Press, 2001.

Eggen, Dan, and Bob Woodward. "U.S. Develops Clearer Picture of Plot: Hijackers Spent $500,000; at Least Four Trained in Afghan Camps." *Washington Post*, September 29, 2001.

Greenberg, Karen J. *Al-Qaeda Now: Understanding Today's Terrorists*. New York, NY: Cambridge University Press, 2005.

Gunaratna, Rohan and Merv Smith *Inside Al-Qaeda Global Network of Terror*. New York: Columbia University Press, 2002.

Jenkins, Brian Michael. *Countering Al-Qaeda an Appreciation of the Situation and Suggestions for Strategy*. Santa Monica, Calif.: RAND, 2002.

MacFarquhar, Neil. "Word for Word/Jihad Lit; Beware of Hidden Enemies and Their Wolves and Foxes." *New York Times,* Dec. 9, 2001.

Riedel, Bruce O. *The Search for Al-Qaeda its Leadership, Ideology, and Future*. Washington, D.C.: Brookings Institution Press, 2010.

Ungoed-Thomas, J. "Egypt Used Torture to Crack Network." *The Times,* Nov. 25, 2001.

Wright, Lawrence. *The Looming Tower: Al-Qaeda and the Road to 9/11*. New York: Knopf, 2006.

Yonah, Alexander and M. Swetman. *Osama bin Laden's al-Qaida: Profile of a Terrorist Network*. New York: Transnational, 2001.

Zernike, K., and D. Van Natta, Jr. "Hijackers' Meticulous Strategy of Brains,' Muscle and Practice." *New York Times*, Nov. 4, 2001.

Chapter 13

AL-QAEDA IN IRAQ (AQI)

OVERVIEW

The Predecessor to ISIS, this jihadist Sunni network was formed in 2004 by the merger of Tawhid wa-I-jihad and al-Qaeda. Abu Musab al-Zarqawi (1966-2006), who formed Tawhid wa-I-jihad, a jihadist organization in Iraq, after being released from prison in 1999. In 2004, the group merged with al-Qaeda to form al-Qaeda in Iraq (AQI). AQI evolved into ISIS, which emerged as a separate an autonomous organization in 2013 and it became independent of Al-Qaeda and a rival of the older group.

EVOLUTION OF AQI

Following the U.S. incursion into Iraq in 2003, the Jordanian jihadist Abu Musab al-Zarqawi presided the merger of his jihadist organization, Jama'at al-Tawhid w'al-Jihad, with al-Qaeda, to form al-Qaeda in Iraq (AQI).

Zarqawi's AQI focused on attacking US forces, their international allies, and local collaborators. AQI intended to bait the United States into a sectarian civil war. AQI also attacked Shias and their holy sites to provoke them to retaliate against Sunni civilians.

U.S. air strike killed Zarqawi in 2006. U.S.-supported "Awakening Councils", or "Sons of Iraq", also began to oppose AQI as Sunni tribesmen reached an amicable understanding with Iraqi Prime Minister Nouri al-Maliki's government. Zarqawi's successors renamed AQI as the Islamic State of Iraq (IQI), and later, the Islamic State of Iraq and al-Sham (ISIS). The name refers to a geographical area that encompasses the Levant, or eastern Mediterranean, which indicates the group's greater ambitions after an uprising in Syria began in 2011.

AQI benefitted from intense Sunni unhappiness with their situation in both Iraq and Syria. In Iraq, the Sunni minority was effectively prevented from meaningful participation in Iraqi national politics after 2003, first by the leaders of the U.S.-led Coalition Provisional Authority and then by the public officials who represented Iraq's Shia majority. Prime Minister Maliki (1937-) further concentrated his own power as the U.S. increasingly withdrew its military from Iraq in 2010. Maliki did so by largely excluding Sunni political leaders from the process and by granting Shia Iraqis a disproportionate amount of the public largesse. The Awakening Councils ceased to exist after Maliki failed to carry out his promises to integrate many Sunni militiamen into the Iraqi national security forces. Maliki also ordered the arrest some of several key Sunni leaders. In 2013, Iraqi security forces suppressed protests that focused on a wide range of grievances including improved governance, and resolving issues involving the alleged persecution of Sunnis.

Maliki removed military officers that he perceived as potential rivals. This purge, along with desertion and corruption, led to the Iraqi army's catastrophic defeat as Islamic State jihadists captured Mosul, Iraq's second-largest city, in June 2014.

In Syria, the civil war that emerged from a broad-based popular uprising against President Bashar al-Assad in 2011, pitted the ruling minority Alawis, a heterodox Shia sect, against the Sunni majority. This uprising, granted AQI new opportunities to expand. Its early militant successes attracted militant Sunni jihadists from across the region to fight the Assad government. As extremists increasingly captured territory in Syria's north and east, Assad claimed the ISIS threat supported his argument that only his government could launch an effective campaign against "terrorists"—a term he has used to describe all his opposition.

THE SCHISM BETWEEN AQI AND AL-QAEDA

AQI became an al-Qaeda franchise by 2004, but later defected from the organization founded by Osama bin Laden (1957-2011) and become its ardent rival. The division between the two jihadist groups reflected their strategic and ideological differences. Al-Qaeda focused on attacking the United States and its Western allies, whom it held responsible for bolstering Arab governments it considered apostate, including those ruling Saudi Arabia and Egypt, rather than capturing territory and establishing a state. Bin Laden, like Abu Bakr al-Baghdadi (1971-), the leader of ISIS, sought to establish a caliphate, but he considered it a goal that generations of the future would need to accomplish.

In 2005, bin Laden deputy Ayman al-Zawahiri (1951-) condemned AQI's Zarqawi for indiscriminately attacking civilians, particularly Shia Muslims. Zawahiri believed that such violence would alienate Sunnism from the jihadist crusade. That was indeed what occurred, as many Sunnis chose to ally themselves with the government during the Awakening movement and refused to support AQI.

A complete break between the two jihadist groups came after the start of Syria's uprising. Zawahiri, who succeeded bin Laden as al-Qaeda's chief in 2011, ordered that the relatively new Syrian Al-Qaeda affiliate, Jabhat al-Nusra, remain independent from Baghdadi's ISI. Baghdadi publicly denounced the decision. Since 2016, the Al-Qaeda group has been known as Jabhat Fateh Al-Sham.

See also: Al-Qaeda (volume 1); Islamic State of Iraq and Syria (volume 1); Jabhat Fateh Al-Sham (volume 1); Muslim Brotherhood (volume 1); Tawhid wa'l jihad (volume 1).

FURTHER READING

Fishman, Brian. "After Zarqawi: The Dilemmas and Future of Al Qaeda in Iraq." *The Washington Quarterly* 29, no. 4 (2006): 19-32.

Gerges, Fawaz A. "The Rise of Al-Qaeda." *The Rise and Fall of Al-Qaeda*, 2011, 29-68.

Kraner, Timothy A. *Al Qaeda in Iraq: demobilizing the threat*. Monterey, CA: Naval Postgraduate School, 2005.

Naylor, David H. *Al Qaeda in Iraq*. Nova Science Publishers Incorporated, 2009.

Shayan, Fatemeh. "Regional Rise of the Al Qaeda Threat Following the Iraq War." *Security in the Persian Gulf Region*, 2017, 149-73.

Chapter 14

AL-QAEDA IN THE ARABIAN PENNISULA (AQAP)

OVERVIEW

Operating from its base in Yemen, Al-Qaeda in the Arabian Pennisula (AQAP) has launched several attacks on the "far enemy" (the United States), captured much of Yemen from the government of Yemen ("the near enemy") and attacked targets in Saudi Arabia. Beginning in 2011, AQAP has conducted a Jihadist insurgency in Southern Yemen as an armed group under the name of "Ansar al Sharia" (Partisans of Sharia).

AQAP'S LEADERSHIP

Nasser al Washsayshi (1976-2015), AQAP's first leader, once served as secretary to Osama bin Laden (1957-2011). Al Wushayshi's connection to bin Laden apparently enhanced his credibility with AQAP members. After Taliban rule collapsed in Afghanistan in 2001, he escaped to Iran, He was apprehended in that country and imprisoned. In 2003, Washsayshi was deported to Yemen, where he was later apprehended, convicted, and imprisoned. Along with 22 other militants, he escaped confinement. Washsayshi led the Al-Qaeda branch in Yemen prior to leading the Al-Qaeda branch in Saudi Arabia. Washsayshi led one of AQAP's predecessor groups, before becoming head of AQAP in January 2009. In 2013, Ayman al-Zawahiri (1951-) encouraged al Wuhayshi to conduct major terrorist attacks against US targets. Wuhaysi, in agreeing to do so, vowed to launch spectacular large-scale attacks.

THE AQAP INSURGENCY IN YEMEN

AQAP started making successful advances in the Spring of 2011 during the Arab Spring. when Yemeni government infighting and indecision in Saana, Yemen's capital, hindered the national government from stopping AQAP from capturing key areas of southern Yemen. At the time, AQAP's leaders such as Nasser al-Wahishi perceived the collapse of the regime of

Ali Abdulah Saleh as the space to create an Islamic emirate in Yemen. At this time, AQAP developed a group of insurgent fighters, Ansar al-Sharia (AAS), which did not owe allegiance to AQAP, gave AQAP the ability to build its forces and collaborate with many fighters who might not have otherwise collaborated with an Al-Qaeda affiliated group. AAS were then able to gain control over most of Abyan and Shabwa governates in Southern Yemen from 2011 through 2012. AQAP, at the time, sought to position itself as a more formal government.

Abdu Rabu Mansour Hadi was elected as Yemen's President in February 2012. The new Hadi government was able to achieve some military successes against AQAP, regained urban areas that AQAP had seized earlier. These successes proved to be short-lived. AQAP continued to launch attacks in Hadramawt province. The Yemeni military sought to collaborate with local tribal leaders to remove AAS influence from Abyan and Shawa governates in Southern Yemen in the early Summer of 2012. The military, however,

Hadi began to face intensified challenges from both the Houthi Rebels and ISIS activity in Yemen. ISIS began exercising active presence in Yemen beginning in 2014. Although AQAP was unable to prevent ISIS from growing within Yemen, ISIS efforts to force its ideology on a Yemeni population not willing to accept it adversely affected the group's appeal. In contrast, AQAP's approach to functioning in Yemen along with its reputation helped it withstand attacks from both the Yemeni government and ISIS.

Currently, the Yemeni national government does not have control over much of Southern part of the nation. Generally, the serious political, social, and economic issues especially in the provinces of Abyan, Aden Hadramawt, and Shabwa (all part of the former South Yemen) generate the grievances that fuel the AQAP insurgency. There is also a great deal of discontent because of under-investment in that area.

The War between the Yemeni government, supported by its Gulf allies and the Houthi rebels, supported by Iran, has had the perverse effect of benefitting AQAP. The tenuous position of the Yemeni government led the global community to focus on efforts to restore order and bolster the recognized Hadi government. The War against the Houthis also greatly impacted the effectiveness of the Yemeni military in fighting AQAP. The Iran-Saudi conflict involved in the Houthi conflict also exacerbated sectarian conflict within Yemen. AQAP was then able to capitalize on this sectarianism in its propaganda.

AQAP AND YEMENI POLITICS

Internal Yemeni politics is complicated because the most powerful stakeholders: the tribes, Hirak secessionists, local authorities, and AQAP jihadists agree on certain issues, while clashing on other issues. Yemeni Extremists who had fought in Afghanistan, Iraq, and Syria blend in with the local population and attempt to recruit young men especially in areas where tribal authority has deteriorated. Although the Yemeni government has had occasional successes in persuading the local people to oppose the AQAP, it is likely that the challenges posed by AQAP will persist well into the future. Although AQAP has not been able to seize territory as it had in the past, it continues to clash with groups loyal to either the government or the tribes, by attacking with car bombings, abductions, and killings.

AQAP Attacks Against the United States

AQAP is the Al-Qaeda affiliate most likely to attack the United States. In 2010, the US government designated AQAP as a terrorist group. On several occasions, AQAP has attempted to bomb U.S. commercial airplanes and train homegrown jihadi militants. AQAP launched several attacks against US targets including: 1) a failed bombing of Northwest Airlines flight bound to Detroit on December 25, 2009; 2) a failed attempt (which was disrupted by Saudi authorities) to send mail bombs to Jewish targets in Chicago in October 2010; and 3) a failed attempted bombing, in which an AQAP jihadi gave a concealed bomb to a Saudi national who then gave the device to the government.

The US government prosecuted a Nigerian citizen, Lawal Olaniyi Babafemi (1980-) for assisting AQAP. He appeared to have no Boko Haram connections. After the Nigerian government extradited Babafemi from Nigeria, he pled guilty to being involved in the group's propaganda and recruitment efforts targeted at recruiting Anglophone Nigerians.

In January 2012, a U.S. appeals court upheld the conviction and life sentence of the Nigerian AQAP operative, Umar Farouk Abdulmutallab (1986-), who pled guilty in 2011 to the failed "Christmas Day" bombing of a passenger jet in 2009.

The Continuing Challenge Posed by AQAP

Yemen's people face a large number of extremely challenging terrorism challenges. The recognized Yemeni government is weak and AQAP is now both an international terror organization and insurgent group at home.

AQAP claimed responsibility for an attack on the French satirical leftist magazine, *Charlie Hebdo* in Paris, France, in January 2015, which killed twelve people. AQAP said that the attack was in retaliation for the magazine publishing a cartoon of the prophet Muhammad. Islamic Fundamentalists forbid any depiction of the prophet, which they view as offensive. Some commentators believe AQAP assumed responsibility for the attack to prove its continued relevance in the wake of being significantly eclipsed by the rise of ISIS.

ISIS has successfully recruited former AQAP fighters who became alienated with the group, which had suffered significant losses in its leadership due to a continuing American-led commando and air campaign. Three key AQAP leaders died in US air attacks on November 2 and Nov 20, 2017. US Central Command oversees US military operations in the region that includes Yemen.

As previously mentioned, AQAP is believed to be the most direct threat to the West of all the Al-Qaeda franchises. AQAP had planned three attacks on US targets between 2009 and 2012, and is home to master bombmaker Ibrahim Hassan Tali al-Asiri.

The Current Status of AQAP

AQAP remains one of al-Qaeda's most important affiliates. AQAP's strength grew from 2015 fighters to 4,000 in 2016 fighters. AQAP has been particularly strong in the South of

Yemen. Since Yemen's civil war began in 2015, AQAP is one of the most effective fighting groups in Yemen.

In January 2017, US President Donald Trump approved a major special operations raid on AQAP in Yemen. This was a controversial on-the-ground confrontation. The U.S. military officials reportedly learned much about AQAP's tactics in that raid and may plan more such attacks.

Throughout 2017, AQAP has conducted suicide attacks and car bombings on progovernment military targets. Although the US targets AQAP in Yemen with drones and has offered a five million dollar reward for the capture of AQAP leader, Qasim al-Raimi, the group continues to operate and employs several different tactics to recruit and spread its jihadist ideology. The Yemeni civil war has also become a conflict characterized by proxy warfare and geopolitical considerations, since Iran supports the Houthis fighting the Yemeni Government, supported by Saudi Arabia. Both Iran and Saudi Arabia are rivals for regional influence. This combination of factors has allowed AQAP the space and territory to rebuild itself.

AQAP continues in its attempts to position itself as a more moderate organization than ISIS. It seeks to portray foreign forces are invaders of Muslim lands, AQAP, which mainly targets government installations and military over civilian targets, uses this to recruit. ISIS, which has had only a minimal presence in Yemen, but has killed civilians, has been much more extreme than AQAP, although both organizations have many of the same long-term objectives including creating a government based on Sharia (Islamic law).

AQAP's long-term presence in Yemen has long threatened that nation's security. Al-Raimi asserted in May 2017 that it was fighting with all Muslims in Yemen, including the Muslim Brotherhood and Sunni tribes. AQAP uses Sectarian tension as an effective recruiting tool. The success of the Houthis in northern Yemen has allowed AQAP to claim that it is fighting and stopping the spread of that particular Shia movement. By exploiting this division, and in the relative absence of worldwide attention, AQAP has enhanced al-Qaeda's reputation and grown. AQAP's pragmatism has allowed it to adapt into Yemen's political life and collaborate with relative moderate Sunni Islamists. This helped AQAP gain respect and legitimacy among Yemen's influential tribal leaders and local politicians and some Yemeni people.

See also: Al-Qaeda (volume 1); Islamic State of Iraq and Syria (volume 1); Muslim Brotherhood (volume 1).

FURTHER READING

"AQAP Tries Again; International Terrorism (al-Qaeda in the Arabian Peninsula)." *The Economist,* May 12, 2012.

Byrne, Anthony. *Review of the Listing of AQAP and the Re-listing of six terrorist organisations*. Canberra, A.C.T.: Commonwealth of Australia, 2011.

Difo, Germain. *Yemen and U.S. Security Assessing and Managing the Challenge of Al-Qaeda in the Arabian Peninsula (AQAP)*. Washington, D.C.: American Security Project, 2010.

Gabr, Ben Gabr and R. Nicholas Palarino. *Terrorism in Yemen: Challenges and United States Foreign Policy*. Washington, DC Georgetown University 2013.

Harris, Alistair. *Exploiting Grievances Al-Qaeda in the Arabian Peninsula.* Washington, DC: Carnegie Endowment for International Peace, 2010.

Koehler-Derrick, Gabriel. *A False Foundation?: AQAP, Tribes and Ungoverned Spaces in Yemen*. West Point, NY: Combating Terrorism Center at West Point, 2011.

Stier, Eric. "Is Anwar al-Awlaki's Importance to Al-Qaeda Overstated?" *The Christian Science Monitor. May 10, 2011.*

West, Eleanor T. Yemen: Hearts, Minds and Al-Qaida. *World Policy Journal.* 28 no. 2 (2011):122-23.

Chapter 15

AL-TAKFIR WAL AL-HIGRA/APOSTASY AND IMMIGRATION (ATWH)

OVERVIEW

Takfir wal-Hijra, also known as Martyrs for Morocco, Rejection of Sins and Exodus, al-Takfir wa al-Hijra (Excommunication and Holy Flight), Fight from Sin and Atonement, al-Takfir and al-Hijra, Takfir wal-Hijra, Excommunication and Exodus, Anathematization and Exile. The Non-Aligned Mujahedeen is an active group formed c. 1970.

The radical Islamist movement *Al-Takfir Wal-Hijra* (ATWH) was formed in Egypt in 1969 as a splinter group of the Muslim Brotherhood. Believing that much of the world is heretical, the movement's members adhere to a strict Salafi interpretation of Islam, and seeks ultimately to return to what they consider to be a true Islamic society—the Islamic Caliphate.

THE IDEOLOGY OF TAKFIR WAL-HIJRA

Some commentators argue that currently Takfir Wal-Hijra is less of a jihadist organization than a radical Islamist ideology. ATWH is a network of Islamist militants worldwide connected only by their beliefs. Takfir is principally an ideology that organized jihadist groups adhere more or less loosely to its founding principles. ATWH, thus, has emerged as a generic brand name. Some commentators refer to it as a type of "Islamist fascism". As an ideology, Takfir Wal-Hijra currently has no overall, coherent, centralized structure. There is no one agreed upon leader of the movement. Over time, ATWH developed an aura of mysticism and is now considered transnational. Its members reside in most Muslim countries, Europe and North America. Apart from Al-Qaeda, ISIS, and to a lesser extent Hezbollah, no other Islamist movement or ideology has had the same international significance as ATWH.

As a group, ATWH originally officially referred to itself as the "Jama'at al-Muslimeen" (Society of Muslims), although, some group members, preferred the name "Takfir Wal-Hijra". Takfir means to declare a person a kufr (an infidel), or, to excommunicate an individual. The term, hijra, refers to the journey of Muhammad and his jama'at (community) from Mecca to Yathrib (Medina) in 622 AD. Both the Egyptian media and the Egyptian security forces, also refer to the group as al-Takfir wa al-Hijra (ATWH).

ATWH members believe that they have the duty to eradicate all infidels from the world. ATWH violently attacks those it perceives as *kufar* (heretics), including those Arabs and Muslims whom Takfiris believe do not live a genuinely Islamic lifestyle. Takfiris must also obey fatwas given by influential radical clerics, such as the "blind sheik," Omar Abdel Rahman.

Prisoners developed much of what became Takfiri doctrine while imprisoned in Egyptian jails following the mass arrests of Muslim Brotherhood members in the mid-1960s where many of its members were tortured and/or executed. Many of these Brotherhood members joined Jama'at al-Muslimeen (Society of Muslims), which adhered to a radical interpretation of Egyptian writer Sayyed Qutb's (1906-1966) work *Ma'alim fi'l-Tariq* (*Milestones on the Road*). Cutb's writings is believed to have inspired the extremism of many prisoners who later became members of ATWH.

One of prisoners, the sheikh of Egypt's al-Azhar mosque, Ali Ismael, argued that not only were Egyptian President Gamel Nasser (1918-1970) and his followers apostates, but so was the entire Egyptian society because it failed to oppose the Egyptian government and had thus accepted Non-Muslim Rule.

ATWH ideology was a radical interpretation of the concept of takfir (to excommunicate), first articulated by Sheik Ibn Taymiyyah (1263-1328) and further developed by Sayyid Cutb, both of whom are considered instrumental in developing jihadist ideology.

After Sheik Ismael reversed himself and denounced takfiri ideology, many of supporters followers supported Shukri Ahmed Mustafa (1944-1978), a charismatic young agronomist (agricultural engineer), who joined Jama'at al-Muslimeen while in prison. Mustafa became the founder and spiritual leader of ATWH in 1969 and was released from prison in 1971. Mustafa believed that all present societies are un-Islamic and that only ATWH members were true Muslims. It believes that an Islamic state (or Caliphate) cannot be peacefully achieved and can only be established by violence. The group also views that all those outside the group are infidels (kofir), un-Islamic, and jihad may be used against them. Anyone seeking to leave the movement was declared an enemy of God and threatened with death for apostasy and desertion. The group claimed that the classical system of Islamic law must be rejected because it is not the word of God but only the work of man. ATWH also claimed to rely solely on the Quran.

ATWH members would exile themselves (al-Hijra) in the desert practicing complete isolation (al-Uzla) from excommunicated (al-Takfir) Muslim societies. Mustafa said that the group would progress in two phases: Al-isitid'af (weakening, to make weak) and al-tamkin (enabling). In the first stage of al-isitid'af, the group leaves Egypt and retreats into the desert to regroup. Then, in al-tamkin, the group is strengthened and returns to " jahili" society to overthrow it and govern.

Jihad has been the constant imperative throughout the ATWH's history. Mustafa initially believed that an imminent world war between the superpowers would allow the jihadists, then still weak, to seize power.

Arguing that Egyptian man-made laws were illegitimate, ATWH taught that theft, kidnapping, forced marriages and even the assassination of anyone not a part of the group (such as apostates) were all justified in the name of jihad. Takfir groups continue to believe in these precepts. ATWH also rejects any type of consultation or governance, relying instead on jihad.

Part of the cover of Takfiris is that they act as non-observant Muslims. Takfiris justify this behavior in the name of conducting Jihad. ATWH doctrine promotes "jihad without rules", which allows its members engage in non-Muslim practices such as consuming alcohol and drug trafficking as a cover for extremist activities. The group aspires to subjugate the whole planet under a global caliphate ruled exclusively by Islamic Sharia law. Its targets civilians, media, mosques, journalists, political leaders, military, and Jews with assassination, armed assault, and bombings.

Many ATWH members believed Mustafa to be the Mahdi, who, according to Islamic tradition, would be the faithful at the end of time.

The Egyptian government repressed the ATWH during the clampdown of Islamic extremism in the 1970s. In Cairo, ATWH members abducted and assassinated Sheik Muhammad Husayn al-Dhahabi (1915-1977), the Egyptian minister of waqf (religious endowments) and Azhar affairs, in July 1977. The government captured Mustafa and executed him in 1978. After Mustafa's execution, surviving ATWH members along with its ideology, was dispersed across several Muslim majority nations. Several Takfiri groups, not connected to one another, emerged and engaged in violent acts worldwide.

The Takfiri name periodically re-emerged in the late 1990s and early 2000s. Several Takfiris traveled to nations including Afghanistan or Bosnia where they assisted in providing logistical support for the foreign mujahideen. ATWH members fought with Osama bin Laden's (1957-2011) mujahedeen in the Soviet-Afghan War. Bin Laden also had allegedly financed the group. After the Taliban established a "true" Islamist state in Afghanistan in 1996, many Takfiris migrated to that country.

Beginning in 1999, ATWH announced its support for Al-Qaeda's strategy and sought to attack the West. ATWH has been frequently associated with Al-Qaeda, although the nature of their relationship is unclear. While many Al-Qaeda members are Takfiri, ATWH is not an affiliate of Al-Qaeda and operates independently. Takfiri, nonetheless, have been suspected in several terrorist plots attributed to Al-Qaeda-connected groups.

A group operating under the name ATWH, targeted both the Syrian government and non-observant Muslims. It also claimed responsibility for shelling Christian civilians in Dinnieh Lebanon.

During the early-1990s Algeria, "Takfir" was the major inspiration for the decade-long, killings of "excommunicated" Muslim civilians following the cancellation of elections that the Islamic Salvation Front (FIS) appeared to win. GIA (Groupe Islamique Arme) groups adopted Takfir ideology throughout Algeria until the GIA's ideology became effectively indistinguishable from the Takfir's. This "merger," the first for ATWH, would continue to shape the ideology of many contemporary Takfir groups. They would adhere to a less exclusionary interpretation of jihad. While initially Takfir members attacked fellow Muslims and were primarily concerned with Muslim societies, beginning in the mid-1990s, ATWH transformed itself in several ways: some of its branches—beginning with the North African branch that had bonded with the GIA—began to work with jihadi support networks in Europe.

In the 1990s, the ATWH name was invoked in the context of attacks both on mosques in the Sudan and Sudanese government facilities. Abbas Al-Bakr Abbas led these attacks, with group members who formerly fought with Ansar Al-Sunna Al-Mohamadiya.

In Sudan, ATWH conducted at least five attacks on worshippers since 1994, resulting in several deaths and hundreds of injuries. Takfiri members, however, are also believed to have attempted the assassination of Osama bin Laden, who lived in Sudan in 1996.

On December 31, 2000, hundreds of ATWH members suddenly attacked in Northern Lebanon, killing civilians and fighting with the Lebanese army in its largest operation since that country's civil war.

The September 11, 2001 attacks revealed large ATWH networks throughout Europe specialized in logistical support to terrorist groups. While law enforcement had previously encountered the group, many were surprised at the extent and reach of its presence. Once considered as merely an Egyptian fringe group, its ideology has evolved, with Takfir groups charged in terrorist attacks, criminal activities and cooperating with Al-Qaeda in its jihadist mission.

Ayman Al-Zawahiri (1951-), Al-Qaeda's lieutenant, and Mohammed Atta, the lead suicide hijacker in the 9/11 attacks, are two among several international terrorists also with connections to ATWH. Some commentators believed that Abu Musab al-Zarqawi, Ramzi Yousef, Khalid Shaikh Mohammed, Ali Mohammed (of the U.S. Special Forces) and Mahmoud Abouhalima are/were Takfiri as well.

Takfiris are perceived as so extreme that even many radical Islamists such as Abu Hamza (1958 -), the imam of London's Finsbury Park Mosque, who supported the 9/11 attacks, disavow them. Hamza described Takfiris as "nothing but a bunch of extremists... [they] create nothing and destroy everything. It is not right to be as harsh as they are. These people want to be judges and executioners."[17] Hamza now serves a life sentence in the "Supermax prison in Florence, Colorado.

In November 2002 Takfiris clashed with Jordanian security forces. The group may also have been involved in the murder of U.S. diplomat Laurence Foley in that country.

In Morocco, several Takfir cells have been active since 2000, culminating with the attacks on Casablanca in 2003.

ATWH members may have been involved in the March 11, 2004, train bombings in Madrid.

In 2005, Syrian security forces clashed with Takfiris suspected of preparing terrorist strikes.

In Egypt, the group, or rather the ideology has periodically re-emerged. The ATWH was implicated in a plot that killed four people to destroy al-Aznar University in Egypt in 2005.

In Africa, Kenyan security services warned of an al-Zarqawi-connected ATWH group in the country. Reportedly, there were reports of ATWH cells in Somalia where the group is believed to have a training camp.

While there have been arrests and executions of Takfiris in Saudi Arabia, it is unclear whether these were true Takfiris since the media uses this term interchangeably for those who only believe the house of Saud, and no other Muslims, apostates.

In Iraq, ATWH is reportedly involved in some of the violence, particularly targeting police and government officials. There were groups with very similar ideologies that do not adopt the name of the original group; for example, Morocco's Salafiyya Jihadiya and Assirat al-Mustakim are virtually identical to ATWH in doctrine.

---

[17] Nicholas Hellen. "If you think Bin Laden is extreme - these men want to kill him because he's soft," *The Sunday Times* (U.K.), October 20, 2001.

The rise of the Taliban, the Algerian civil war and the Western diaspora resulted in significant changes in Takfiri methods. Instead of separating themselves from what they consider "infidel society", the neo-Takfiris sought to infiltrate it. They have since provided logistical support of jihad in the West, maintaining their own networks in nations such as Belgium, the Netherlands, France and Germany. Beginning in 1994, ATWH members have been arrested in Europe, where various governments have uncovered Takfiri involvement in supporting terrorism: smuggling weapons, trafficking drugs and sheltering and transporting fighters from various conflicts. Further arrests were made in Switzerland and France in 1998 when Takfir members Tesnim Aiman and Ressous Houari were arrested. In Paris, a ten-man Takfiri cell specialized in raising funds through counterfeit clothing was uncovered in 2003. In North America, the leader of the Lebanese Takfir, Bassam Ahmad Kanj, and one of his lieutenants, Kassem Daher, would eventually lead a logistical support network in Canada and the United States, financed by drug trafficking and charity front organizations. Kassem Daher also had connections to several jihadi groups and individuals, including Jose Padilla.

In addition to fundraising and logistics, ATWH members had launched several failed plots, including significant operations such as targeting Algerian interests in Marseilles, the U.S. Embassy in Paris, NATO headquarters in Brussels and a failed 2002 attack on the St. Denis football stadium in France. The European ATWH appears better organized than its Middle Eastern counterpart; a 2002 report produced by France's intelligence service, cites the Takfir group (along with the GSPC) as a group most likely to launch terrorist attacks in Europe. In Spain, home to a large and structured Takfir network, the group participated in the Madrid attacks, while in Barcelona Takfiris were involved in a conspiracy to obtain materials for a "dirty bomb" in 2005. Takfiri doctrine inspired several attacks, including the murder of Theo Van Gogh in the Netherlands.

Neo-Takfiris have adapted Mustafa's doctrine. While Mustafa opposed modernity and intellectualism, neo-Takfiris use technology and modernity as weapons against their targets. Where Mustafa preached withdrawal from infidel society, neo-Takfiris remain within in it, utilizing secrecy and assimilation as major tactic. While the first Takfir (and its surviving affiliates) excommunicates other jihadi groups, the neo-Takfiris no longer focus on excommunicating fellow Muslims. Instead, neo-Takfiris seek to cooperation with other jihadist. Al-Qaeda's role in the worldwide jihad appeared to shape a new direction for the Takfiris. For Al-Qaeda, working with the Takfir comports with Al-Qaeda's work to subsume doctrinal differences between Muslim extremists, federating and uniting all jihadist efforts to oppose the West. While some commentators have viewed Al-Qaeda is a Takfiri group, Al-Qaeda apparently has not excommunicated Muslim societies other than their governments and its supporters, even if, Al-Qaeda believes that Muslims who do not support them are wrong.

Unlike the various Al-Qaeda groups, Takfiris are not an organized, structured entity, are formally a part of Al-Qaeda or have not sworn allegiance to bin Laden. Takfiris have been considered semi-aligned "free agents" who collaborate with other jihadi groups on an "ad hoc basis", working toward the same final goals. Most cells consist of ten to fifteen people and are usually formed from individual initiatives.

Unlike Salafi-Jihadists, the Takfiris are not led by a recognized religious scholar and an elaborate ideology because Mustafa lacked an advanced religious education. Because of its lack of theological credentials, the Takfiri doctrine has several "deviancies" from mainstream Islamic thought. Without a central leadership, the group's extreme ideology, evolves through self-appointed idealogues who also lead the various cells. Thus, Takfir legitimizes criminal activities, justifying these activities on the theory of the fay'e (the licit) by appropriating the goods and property of infidels and apostates. Criminal activities such as theft and drug trafficking are thus encouraged if twenty percent of the proceeds are used to fund jihad. In several Muslim countries, Takfiris stole from both private homes and mosques. In 2000, Mohammed Chalabi led a Jordanian cell that was was involved in robbery and drug trafficking in Maan. In 2000, a Takfir logistical support network based in France and Italy engaged in theft, trafficking, and forging documents.

As sleeper cells, Takfiris have "theologically" authorized themselves to violate any and every Islamic rule to comport with Western society. They do not attend mosques and often consume illegal drugs and alcohol. The Takfir in Algeria used several drugs while many Takfiris involved in the Madrid attacks were drug users. The Takfiris operate outside the restrictions imposed by Islam, they claim, to better defend it, recognizing Jihad as their only law, through their doctrine of "sinless sin". Group members include the disenfranchised, juvenile delinquents and convicted criminals. They are often recruited because of their fundraising abilities. The Takfiris are engaged in what essentially a lawless jihad that allows for any and all activities that Muslims normally consider as sinful—including bizarre and macabre rituals involving dismembering victims. The group conducted several mutilations when it entered Lebanon in 2000. In Morocco, the group mutilated corpses in Casablanca where the Takfiris ritually murdered 166 civilians in 166 in 2002. In Madrid, Takfiris reportedly have exhumed and dismembered the body of the GEO sub-inspector who died in the anti-terrorist operation in Leganes Spain following the March 11, 2004 train bombings.

The secrecy and dissimulation of Takfiris make them particularly difficult to monitor or infiltrate. They are also highly unpredictable as attacks may be sporadic and improvised. The dissemination of the Takfir doctrine through the internet, its reliance on criminal activities and the atomization of small, secretive autonomous cells seriously challenge to counter-terrorism efforts. Takfiri activities require recruitment in prisons and high-crime areas and strengthen the connections between criminal behavior and terrorism.

See also: Al-Qaeda (volume 1); Muslim Brotherhood (volume 1); Salafist Group for Call and Combat (GSPC) (volume 2); Takfiri Groups (volume 1).

FURTHER READING

"A Constitution and Bombs." *Dar Al Hayat, International Ed. (Beirut, Lebanon),* Nov. 5. 2012.

Aboul- Enein, Youssef H. "Al-Ikhwan Al-Muslimeen: The Muslim Brotherhood." *Military Review* 83, Part 4 (2003): 26-31.

Cozzens, Jeffrey. "Al-Takfir wa'l Hijra: Unpacking an Enigma." *Studies in Conflict & Terrorism* 32, no. 6 (2009): 489-510.

Darwish, A. "Lebanon's Millennium Fireworks." *The Middle East,* Feb 2000, 15.

Gleis, Joshua L. *National Security Implications of Al-Takfir Wal-Hijra.* Al Nakhlah, 2005.

Harris, Ian Charles. *Longman Guide to Living Religions*. New York, N.Y.: Stockton, 1994. (In section 2 Strict Sects, Terror Suspects Find Inspiration).

"Indictment Links Madrid Train Bombings to Sept. 11 Attacks." *Chicago Tribune, Apr. 28, 2004.*

"Jordanian attack on Militants Reveals a National Rift; For the First Time Since 1970, Jordan has Resorted to Using the Armed Forces to Quell Domestic Instability." *The Christian Science Monitor,* Nov. 15, 2002.

Khashan, Hilal and Lina Kreidie. "The Social and Economic Correlates of Islamic Religiosity." *World Affairs* 164, No. 2, (2001): 83-96.

Mattar, A. "Four Killed, Dozens Arrested in Southern Jordan as Authorities Crack Down on Armed Muslim fundamentalists." *AP Worldstream,* Nov. 11, 2002.

Timani, Hussam S. *The Khawarij in Modern Islamic Historiography (Ph-D – dissertation).* Ann Arbor, MI: UMI Dissertation Services, 2002.

Chapter 16

AL-WEFAQ/NATIONAL ISLAMIC SOCIETY/ISLAMIC NATIONAL ACCORD ASSOCIATION

OVERVIEW

Prior to being outlawed, Al-Wefaq was the largest and most powerful Islamic political party in Bahrain, Al-Wefaq (Bloc of Believers) was a Shiite political party led by Ali Salman, its Secretary-General. In Sunni ruled Bahrain (which has a Shiite majority population), Al-Wefaq was the country's main Shia opposition group. Claiming to have thousands of members, the group also was connected with the Islamic Scholars Council.

King Hamad bin Isa al-Khalifa formed the Al-Wefaq soon after becoming Bahrain's king on February 14, 2002. After ascending the throne, he initiated reform under the National Charter. While Al-Wefaq supported the legislation when it was first introduced.

Al-Wefaq boycotted the 2002 elections when the proposed constitution provided that a chamber of the parliament (the king selected all the members) would share power with the popularly elected chamber. Members, however, still ran in the municipal elections in 2002 and slowly reemerged as a political party. Al-Wefaq members once led the Manama and the Muharraq City Councils (two of the largest cities within the kingdom) and have collaborated with the "Salafi al-Asalah Islamic society" on several issues. On religious issues, al-Wefaq has adamantly supported theocratic governance, asserting that secular legislators may not pass Islamic-oriented legislation because only religious leaders, knowledgeable in Islamic doctrine, have the legitimate authority to do so. The group also addressed issues such as electoral scandals and fraud committed by members of the parliament.

AL-WEFAQ, THE 2010 ELECTIONS AND THE ARAB SPRING

The relationship between Al-Wefaq and the Shia-oriented Islamic Scholars Council helped the party win 17 of the 18 seats out of 40 seats in Parliament that its candidates competed for (62 percent of the voters chose that party) in the 2010 elections.

On February 27, 2011, all of Al-Wefaq's Parliamentarians resigned their positions in protest of the government's use of force against Bahraini reform demonstrators who took to the streets in large numbers during the "Arab Spring" protests. The Shia opposition led this uprising which they characterized as a large-scale popular and pro-democracy protest movement. Bahrain continues to bans protests and gatherings not licensed by the government.

Sporadic protests and small-scale clashes, however, persist. Since the authorities street protests in 2011, demonstrators have clashed frequently with security forces, which have been targeted by several bomb attacks. The Bahraini government asserts that the protesters are supported and influenced by Iran, however, the protestors claim they are fighting for political freedom and human rights.

A NEW BOILING POINT?

In the summer of 2016, the government began to increasingly clamp down on the opposition leadership. In late May 2016, a Bahraini court sentenced Al-Wefaq's political leader, Ali Salman, to nine years after convicting him of seeking to overthrow the regime and inciting sectarian hatred. An appeals court in May 2016 more than doubled a prison sentence against the group's secretary general, Ali Salman, following his conviction on charges that included incitement and insulting the interior ministry. Bahraini officials accuse him of creating a sectarian atmosphere and of forming groups that "follow foreign religious ideologies and political entities". The Court was making reference to Iran, which Bahrain and allies view as a destabilizing entity that seeks to generate unrest in Bahrain. Iran denies it is interfering in Bahraini affairs, but adamantly denounced the actions taken against Qassim.

In June 2016, Bahrain's government revoked the citizenship of Ayatollah Isa Qassim (1937 -), Bahrain's leading Shia religious figure and Al-Wefaq's spiritual leader. The government also announced it would prosecute him for alleged illegal fund raising and money laundering. These actions angered his supporters who staged a sit-in outside his home in a village near Manama, Bahrain's capital out of concern that their leader would be either imprisoned or deported.

In addition to individual leaders, the government began taking action against opposition political parties. In June 2016, amidst a Bahraini court Al-Wefaq to suspend its activities after finding the party responsible for engendering "an environment for terrorism, extremism and violence as well as a call for foreign interference in internal national affairs." The Bahraini justice ministry justified the suspension as part of the efforts to combat extremism and protect society.

In late July 2016, the court dissolved Al-Wefaq allegedly for fostering violence and "terrorism" in the kingdom, and further accused the party of undermining the state, spreading sectarianism, and having connections to "terrorist" activities. The court further found that Al-Wefaq had attacked the "respect for the rule of law and the foundations of citizenship based on coexistence, tolerance and respect for others; provided an atmosphere for the incubation of terrorism, extremism and violence and for foreign interference in national affairs". With this ruling, the state treasury then seized Wefaq's funds.

In response to the Bahraini clampdown, the UN human rights office requested release of Bahraini political prisoners. UN Secretary General, Ban Ki-Moon, expressed its concern over restrictions on the opposition and efforts against human rights activists. He specifically objected to the dissolution of Al-Wefaq, and asked that an all-inclusive national dialogue for peace and stability in Bahrain be resumed. He declared that Al-Wefaq's dissolution to be "the latest in a series of restrictions of the rights to peaceful assembly, freedom of association, and freedom of expression in Bahrain." Ban stressed that the dissolution of Al-Wefaq, and other actions such stripping Sheikh Issa Qassem and others of citizenship, a travel ban on human rights defenders, and the increased sentence for Salman risked escalating an already tense situation in the country.

Many Bahraini human rights observers also denounced the court's action. Brian Dooley, director for human rights defenders at the Washington-based Human Rights First, described the court ruling as the Bahrain "government's single most repressive act" since the Arab Spring Protests. He added that the action left no genuine avenue "for peaceful grievance left in Bahrain" and that the government was essentially telling its people that "not only are you not allowed rights, you're not allowed to complain about it."

Responding to the situation in Bahrain, several US senators expressed their concerns to US Secretary of State, John Kerry the Bahraini government's targeting of peaceful political opponents and civil society activists, saying the situation could destabilize the nation, prompt further violence and encourage Iranian interference. The State Department had also reported that Bahrain had so far not implemented political and human rights reforms recommended by an independent commission following the disturbances in 2011.

See also: Al-Asalah (volume 1).

FURTHER READING

"Backward Steps; Bahrain's Pre-Election Jitters (Bahraini jitters before an election)." *The Economist,* Oct. 16, 2010.

Belfer, Mitchell. *Small State, Dangerous Region a Strategic Assessment of Bahrain.* Frankfurt: Peter Lang GmbH, Internationaler Verlag der Wissenschaften, 2014.

Chick, Kristen. "Bahrain Backs Off Plan to Ban Opposition After US Criticism." *The Christian Science Monitor,* Apr. 15, 2011.

Chick, Kristen. "Bahrain Rights Activist's Wife Details Torture, Unfair Trial. (Abdulhadi al-Khawaja)." *The Christian Science Monitor,* May 16, 2011.

Chick, Kristen. "Bahrain Opposition on Verge of Pulling Out of Government Talks." *The Christian Science Monitor,* Jul. 15, 2011.

"Not So Sunny for Shias; Bahrain. (Bahrain's awkward sectarian division)." *The Economist* Dec 1, 2008.

Seymour, Richard. "Bahrain Rings the Changes." *The Middle East,* Jan. 2011.

"Shoot First, Then Talk; Bahrain's Crisis. (Talks in Bahrain got off to a rocky start)." *The Economist,* Jul. 9, 2011.

Slosberg, Karen E. *The Sensationalized Media Coverage of Bahrain's Arab Spring*. Paris: American University of Paris, 2012.

Chapter 17

AMAL MOVEMENT/LEBANESE RESISTANCE DETACHMENTS, MOVEMENT OF HOPE, MOVEMENT OF THE DEPRIVED (HARAKAT AL-MAHRUMIN), AFWAJ AL MUQAWAMAH AL LUBNANIYYAH (AMAL), BATTALIONS OF THE LEBANESE RESISTANCE

A political Islamic fundamentalist group comprised of Lebanese Shia Muslims. Amal's name is derived from the Arabic word for "hope". It is also the acronym of Ajwaj al Muqawama al Lubnaniya (Lebanese Resistance Detachments). The Iranian-born Shia Imam (cleric) Musa Sadr (1978-?) established Amal as a militia in 1975. Sadr had earlier formed the "Movement of the Deprived" in 1974, to confront the existing power structure and alleviating the socio-economic hardships of the poor and then-marginalized Shiite community,

Amal was a prominent Shia Muslim militia during Lebanon's Civil War. Syrian assistance and connections were and are important to maintaining Amal's effectiveness. Due to clashes between Israel and radical Palestinian groups in the early 1980s, nearly 300,000 Shia fled from southern Lebanon to become internal refugees. This refugee crisis fueled the growth of Amal. The group claims that its goals include obtaining greater influence and rights for Lebanon's Shia population. Amal also seeks obtain a greater allocation of resources for largely Shia Muslim populated southern Lebanon.

Iran supported Amal financially especially after the Iranian Islamic Revolution of 1979. After Hezbollah assumed a position of power in Lebanon in 1982, Iran steadily reduced its support of Amal, before totally withdrawing it. Amal then sought support from the Syrian government. While Amal sought to increase Shiite control over Lebanon, it did not intend to impose an Iranian-style Islamist theocracy. This lack of willingness both to pursue an Islamic state and emphasize jihadism led the more extreme Amal members to defect and form the Islamic Amal Movement, while others joined Hezbollah in Lebanon. Nevertheless, the Lebanese Shiite community generally supported Amal since the group sought to protect and secure the position of Lebanese Shiites. On August 31, 1978, Musa Sadr vanished with two of his colleagues while on an official visit to Libya, leading many Amal members to suspect

Moammar Gadhafi (1942- 2011) as being involved, which further deteriorated Amal's relationship with Iran.

Sadr was succeeded by Hussein Husseini (1937-), who later became speaker of the Lebanese Parliament. Nabih Berri (1939-) succeeded Husseini as Amal's leader in 1980, and became particularly popular among Lebanon's Shia after Israel's invasion of Lebanon in 1982. In that conflict, Berri and Walid Jumblatt (1949-) (the socialist leader of the Druze Party) fought against the government of Armine Gemayel (1942), leader of the leader of Kataib Party and a Christian political leader.

Hezbollah and Amal have opposed each other almost since the former was founded in the early 1980s. Much of Amal's membership was coopted by Hezbollah, and there was often a mistaken connection between the two, resulting in Amal being accused of many of the attacks that Hezbollah had actually conducted. Furthermore after the 1985 TWA Flight 847 attack, Hezbollah and Amal clashed openly with each other, resulting in Amal seeking financial support from Syria.

After the Lebanese Civil War ended in 1990, the two groups reconciled and cooperated with the southern Lebanese to fight the Israeli army. Nabih Berri helped rebuild the relationship between Amal and Iran. Amal continued to support Syria and have political influence in Lebanon, winning 14 of the 128 sears in the Lebanese parliamentary elections in 2005. The alliance between Amal and Hezbollah remains tenuous, even though Amal was a Hezbollah ally in the 2006 Israeli-Hezbollah war.

Berri supports the abolishment of political sectarianism in Lebanon and the sectarian system governing that country. He favors establishing a national committee to do under the Taif Accord of 1989 and supports establishing a national committee to do so. He called for party members to join demonstrations calling for non-sectarianism in Lebanon's political life.

Amal fighters reportedly are fighting for the Assad regime in Syria in that nation's civil war. Currently, the Lebanese Amal Movement is led by Lebanese Parliament speaker Nabith Berri. Hezbollah and Amal are the two largest Shia Parties and represent that sect in Parliament and the cabinet. They are considered to be political allies. Normally, differences over internal issues between the two groups are not made public. The leadership of both parties also stress their agreement on political issues, resisting Israel, and Hezbollah's involvement in Syria. There have been recent violent clashes that have periodically occurred between the supporters of both groups that began with partisans of both groups allegedly destroying posters or banners of the other. So far, the leadership of both parties have intervened so as to prevent the clashes from escalating.

FURTHER READING

"Iran: Amal's Relationship with Iran." *Info-Prod Research*, Nov. 16, 1999.

Norton, Augustus Richard. *Amal and the Shia: Struggle for the Soul of Lebanon*. Austin: University of Texas Press, 1987.

Saad-Ghorayeb, Amal. *Hizbullah Politics and Religion*. London: Pluto Press, 2002.

"Shiite Factions Clash in Beirut Suburb; Iranian-Backed Hezbollah Ousts Amal Militia from 2 Key Positions," *The Washington Post,* May 7, 1988.

Chapter 18

AMAL/AL-AMAL-AL ISLAMI/ ISLAMIC ACTION PARTY (BAHRAIN)

OVERVIEW

A predominantly Shiite Islamist "political society", AMAL or (the "Islamic Action Society," jam'iyyat ai-Amal ai-lslami. Bahrainis often refer to the group as "the Shirazi faction"). The other predominantly Shiite party is the Islamic National Accord (Al-Wefaq) Society.

VOICE OF BAHRAINI SHIITES

It continues to be illegal to from or belong to any political party in Bahrain. Licensed political societies have many of the same roles and functions of political parties, particularly in mobilizing popular support for candidates of the election to the Chamber of Representatives (Majlis al-Nuwaab) and negotiating coalitions among representatives during debates in parliament. Organized political societies are licensed by the Ministry of Justice and Islamic Affairs under the Political Societies Law enacted in 2005.

Amal is the non-violent successor to the former Islamic Front for the Liberation of Bahrain, which launched a failed insurrection in 1981 inspired by Iran's Islamic revolution. The King, Hamad bin Isa al-Khalifa, succeeded in ending a large-scale popular uprising that raged between 1994 and 1999 by announcing plans for a comprehensive reform plan that included restoring the constitution and creation of the National Assembly (al-Majlis-al-Watani).

AMAL CONTESTS IN PARLIAMENTARY RACES

Amal refused to register as a "legal" political society before the 2002 parliamentary election in Bahrain, a year in which all of major political societies boycotted the poll. Amal only registered when it became clear that the government was planning to outlaw any association that did not willingly comply with the new regulations on the grounds that refusing to register amounted to violating the country's 2002 constitution.

Amal also failed to win any seats in the 2006 election. Al-Wefaq, the other largely Shiite political society, won 17 of the 40 seats. The Islamist political societies, overall, did well and captured 30 of the 40 seats. The election, however, was tarnished by alleged government interference and widespread irregularities.

Amal decided not to participate in the 2010 election. Amal's Secretary General, Sheikh Mohammed al-Mahfouz, justified this decision by stressing his group's objections to Bahrain's political system as being undemocratic, unjust, and discriminatory against the Kingdom's Shia majority.

AFTERMATH OF THE ARAB SPRING

In February 2011, as part of the Arab Spring protests, anti-government protestors began holding demonstrations across Bahrain demanding that the ruling family relinquish power. The Al-Khalifah royal family responded by clamping down on dissent. In March 2011, troops from Saudi Arabia and the United Arab Emirates intervened in the Bahrain crisis. Large numbers of people were killed and injured or arrested in the ensuing unrest. Human rights groups, such as the Bahrain Center for Human Rights, condemned Bahrain's government for allegedly handing down excessively long sentences to anti-regime activists.

Bahrain's government has considered Amal a sufficient enough of a threat to outlaw the group in 2012. Bahrain's minister of justice brought a complaint against Amal accusing the party of inciting unrest. In 2011, Mahfouz, the society's general secretary, was sentenced to ten years in prison upon being convicted of those charges. In November 2012, a court of appeals voted to reduce his sentence to five years. He has recently been released.

LIMITS OF THE SECTARIAN APPEAL

Since the 1979 Iranian Revolution, the main Shiite political factions in Bahrain have either called for reforms while maintaining and working within the framework of its Bahraini national identity; the other is more revolutionary, being inspired by the Iranian Revolution of 1979, viewing Bahrain as an extension of Iran, and calling for fundamental change. Shiite revolutionaries coalesced in 1979 under the name of the "Popular Front for the Liberation of Bahrain."

One key factor hindering the adoption of the Iranian political position is that the Bahraini popular movement Shiites self-identify as Arab, which is exemplified in the 1970 "UN-supervised" referendum when the Shiites voted for an independent Arab Bahrain. Even in terms of ethnicity, which is a highly salient factor in the political culture of Gulf States, the large majority of Bahraini Shiites are ethnic Arab. The Shiites of Bahrain are genuinely ethnic Arab Bahraini, not migrants from Iran or anywhere else. It is notable in this context that many of the most prominent leaders of leftist and pan-Arabist movements in the Gulf were Bahraini Shiites.

The Significance of Ongoing Discrimination and Alleged Oppression

Over the years, the political appeal of Shiite opposition in Bahrain has been largely generated by government discrimination against its Shiite citizens and the lack of the concept of equal citizenship between Sunnis and Shiites in Bahrain. Shiites, for example, who constitute a majority (60-70%) of the population, are found in only 17% of high-ranking government positions. Socio-economic indicators, such as unusually high unemployment rates (19%) while Bahrain was enjoying tremendous economic growth also helped in elevating social tensions that lead to sectarian violence.

See also: Al-Wefaq (volume 1)

Further Reading

Al-Hassan, Omar. *Ten years Under King Hamad: Rights, Freedoms and Development in Bahrain*. London: Gulf Centre for Strategic Studies, 2009.

Haddad, Bassam. *The Dawn of the Arab uprisings: End of an old order?* London: Pluto Press, 2012.

Hunter, Shireen. *The Politics of Islamic Revivalism: Diversity and Unity*. Bloomington: Indiana University Press, 1988.

Khalīfah, Shaikh Abdullah bin Khalid, & Rice, Michael. *Bahrain through the Ages: the History*. London: Kegan Paul International, 1993; London: Routledge, 2014.

Chapter 19

ANSAR AL-ISLAM (AI)/SUPPORTER OF ISLAM

An extremist Salafi Sunni Muslim Islamic group that promotes radical Islam and Islamic law (sharia) in Kurdish areas of Iraq. AI conducts attacks only within Iraq. Formerly known as Ansar al-Sunna (AS), the group originated in the Northeastern region of Halabja, Iraq, near Iran. In this area, AI operated military training camps in the villages of Btyara and Tawela. AI was created as a result of a merger between the Jund al-Islam (Soldiers of Islam) and a faction of the Kurdish Islamic Movement (KIM) in September 2001. Mullah Krekar (1961-), the former leader of KIM became AI's leader. Most AI fighters engaged in the Afghan-Soviet War (1979-1989) as mujahideen and oppose the Patriotic Union of Kurdistan (PUK). Ansar al-Islam has conducted several attacks, mostly suicide bombings (istishhad) and assassinations. AI has also kidnaped hostages and had killed several of them. AI allied itself with Jamaat Ansar al-Surma (JAS) (Group of the Followers of the Sunna) and the Kurdistan Islamic Group (KIG). AI has collaborated with Al-Qaeda, received support from that group, and promotes itself as an affiliate of that larger group. AI also has collaborated with the Taliban in Afghanistan.

In early 2001, AI granted sanctuary to Abu Musab al-Zarqawi (1966-2006), the founder of Al-Qaeda in Iraq (AQI) in AI's enclave in northern Iraq. During the Iraq War in 2003, Kurdish and Allied Coalition forces assaulted AI positions, forcing the group's fighters to abandon their bases and scatter throughout Iraq and also Kurdish-held territory in northwestern Iran. Seeking to become Iraq's preeminent Sunni Islamist militant group, AI rebranded itself as Ansar al-Sunna (AS). It asserted itself to be the major coordinating group for Iraqi and Arab jihadists opposing Coalition forces in Iraq. During the same time, AQI under Abu Musab al-Zarqawi conducted the earliest major terrorist attacks in the conflict. In August 2003, the group launched suicide bombings against Jordan's Embassy in Baghdad, the UN Headquarters in Baghdad, and the Shia Imam Ali Mosque in Najaf. AQI's ascent as Iraq's strongest jihadist organization undermined the credibility of Ansar Al Sunna's claims of being the major coordinating organization of jihadist groups in Iraq, as it was apparently not the most effective conduit for funds, militants, and other resources streaming to Iraq from outside jihadi supporters.

In 2003, Abu Abdallah al-Shafi'i (a.k.a. Warba Holiri al-Kurdi) had reportedly succeeded Krekar as AS's leader after a Norwegian Court had sentenced the latter to house arrest. Iraqi security forces captured al-Shafi'i on May 3, 2010. He remains imprisoned by the Iraqi government. Reportedly, AS had approximately several hundred to 1,000 members.

In November of 2007, Abdullah al-Shafii renamed the group Ansar Al-Islam. Earlier in 2007, the group was appearing to splinter. AAS's legal council condemned AQI for killing certain AAS fighters and for collaborating with a group that AS members believed deviated significantly from Islamic Law (Sharia). Acting against the advice of its legal council, AAS announced its support for many of ISIS's most notorious terrorist activities and its support for joint actions with ISIS. To remedy the discrepancy, AS merely renamed itself, Ansar Al Islam (AI), its former name. After the name change, AI continued to cooperate with ISIS and ISIS's increasing brutality against opposing insurgents and politically involved Sunnis.

AI receives financial support from several different sources including expatriate remittances worldwide. Its associations with Al-Qaeda benefits AI financially, strategically, and ideologically. Al-Qaeda provides AI funding, training, equipment and military support.

See also: Al-Qaeda (volume 1); Al-Qaeda in Iraq (AQI) (volume 1); Islamic State of Iraq and Syria (volume 1); Taliban (volume 2).

FURTHER READING

Fam, Miriam. "Ansar al-Islam's Stronghold Provides Grim Example of Militant Rule." *AP Worldstream*, March 8, 2004.

Fam, Miriam. "Ansar Al-Islam Prisoner Shows Techniques." *AP Online*, March 16, 2004.

Guenther, Christoph. "Al-Qaida in Iraq beyond Rhetoric." *Sociology of Islam 3*, no. 1-2 (2015): 30-48.

"Iraq: Iran Turns Its Back On Ansar Al-Islam." (Claims no links with extremist group). *Info-Prod Research,* Apr. 2, 2003.

"Iraq's New Terrorist Threat: Ansar Al Sunnah." *The Middle East,* Feb. 2005, 24-25.

"Iraqi Funds, Training Fuel Islamic Terror Group: Two Iraqi Arabs Held in a Kurdish Prison Tell of Contacts Among Ansar al- Islam, Al-Qaeda, and Aides to the Iraqi President." *The Christian Science Monitor,* Apr. 2, 2002.

Nance, Malcolm W." Jihad Is the Only Way…" Iraqi Islamic Extremists—Ansar al-Islam, Ansar al-Sunnah: The Islamic Army in Iraq and Others," in, *The Terrorists of Iraq: Inside the Strategy and Tactics of the Iraq Insurgency 2003-2014, 2nd ed.,* Boca Raton, FL CRC Press, 2014, at 173-204.

Schanzer, Jonathan. "Ansar al-Islam: Back in Iraq." *Middle East Quarterly 11, no. 1 (2004):* 41.

Sennott, G. S. "Kurds Say Other Enemy Is Ansar Al Islam." *Boston Globe,* Mar. 19, 2003.

Tehan, Dan. *Review of the Re-listing of Ansar al-Islam, Islamic Movement of Uzbekistan, Lashkar-e Jhangvi and Jaish-e-Mohammad.* Canberra: Commonwealth of Australia, 2015.

"The Rise and Fall of Ansar al-Islam; Former members of Ansar al-Islam Talk to the Monitor about the Militant Group's Ties to Al-Qaeda, the Foreign Fighters that Joined its Ranks, and its Eventual Destruction." *The Christian Science Monitor,* Oct. 16, 2003.

Zenko, Micah. "Foregoing Limited Force: The George W. Bush Administration's Decision Not to Attack Ansar Al-Islam." *Journal of Strategic Studies*, *32* no. 4 (2009): 615-49.

Chapter 20

ANSAR BAYT AL MAQDIS (ABM)

Ansar Bayt al Maqdis (ABM) formed in the Egyptian Sinai Peninsula after Egyptian President Hosni Mubarak fell from power in January 2011. ABM claims that it seeks to form an Islamic state (caliphate) and impose sharia (Islamic Law) in Egypt. The group primarily conducts attacks against the Egyptian government and targets that nation's economy by attacking its gas pipelines and the tourism industry. ABM has also apparently killed Israelis in cross-border attacks (particularly on Israeli patrols and social gatherings) and foreign tourists. ABM is focused on Egyptian and Israeli targets.

ABM was originally a Palestinian organization that clashed with Hamas. It fled to the Sinai Peninsula with about 150 to 200 Palestinians at the time. It allied itself with some local jihadists already in the Sinai and focused on attacking Israeli targets. The group then allied itself with the Egyptian Al-Tawhid Wa al-Jihad (ATWH) organization, which had conducted the bombing attacks of Taba and Sharm al-Shaykh between 2004 and 2005. That group resumed and escalated its activities after the January 2011 Revolution because of the breakdown of order and subsequent lawlessness in the region. The ABM, unlike the ATWH, is not a takfiri group (which denounce Muslims not adhering to its beliefs as infidels). Instead, ABM is a part of the Jihadi Salafist movement led by Al-Qaeda. Thus, Al-Qaeda reportedly operates in the Sinai Peninsula and operates training camps there to prepare its fighters to engage in the Syrian Civil War.

While ABM operates mostly in the Sinai Peninsula, it has also conducted attacks in Cairo and against Israel. The ABM's most high-profile attacks on the Sinai include a suicide bombing against South Sinai Security officials in October 2013, shooting down an Egyptian helicopter with a shoulder-fired missile in January 2014, and bombing a tour bus in Taba in the Sinai in February 2014 (which killed four people, including three South Korean tourists). ABM has allegedly conducted or has been involved in several cross-border attacks since August 2011. In August 2012, ABM reportedly attacked the southern Israeli city of Eilat with grad missiles in retaliation for a film that it claimed insulted the Prophet. ABM attempted unsuccessfully to assassinate the Egyptian Interior Minister using booby trapped vehicles in September 2013. This attack was described as one in keeping with Al-Qaeda practice and ideology.

The new Egyptian government has declared that the nation is engaged in a war against terrorism shortly after former President Mohammed Morsi was removed as the nation's president and imprisoned. Egypt's security forces intensified anti-terrorism activities in the

North Sinai in response to repeated jihadist attacks against army and police officers, attacks that increased greatly since Morsi's removal. The Egypt foreign affairs ministry reported that 971 people have died in terrorist attacks between January 2011, including 664 security personnel.

In May 2014, Egyptian security officials claimed to have killed the emir of ABM, Shadi El-Menai. The group, however, denied both the claim that El-Menai was killed and that he was the group's emir.

The ABM has not yet attacked U.S. personnel or facilities. The group, however, has vowed a harsh response if the US military threatened to engage ISIS. Observers speculated that ABM leaders use existing smuggling networks in the Sinai to finance its operations. ABM swore allegiance to ISIS in December 2014, at a time when the group was suffering significant attrition at the hands of the Egyptian military. After ABM swore its allegiance, ABM adopted propaganda and battlefield tactics that more closely resembled ISIS in Iraq and Syria. This included attacking certain international targets such as: the bombing of a Russian airliner taking off from Sharm el-Sheikh, the beheading of a Croatian expatriate, and an attack on the Italian consulate in Cairo. Most ABM actions, however, are hit and run tactics against Egyptian military targets.

The ABM is recognized as a terrorist group by the United States, Great Britain, and Egypt. While the Egyptian government argues that the Muslim Brotherhood is connected to groups such as ABM, the US Department of State has said that it has not seen sufficient evidence to make such a connection.

See also: Al-Qaeda (volume 1); HAMAS (volume 1); Islamic State of Iraq and Syria (volume 1); Muslim Brotherhood (volume 1); Takfiri Groups (volume 1); Tawhid and Jihad (volume 1).

FURTHER READING

Aftandilian, Gregory L. *Assessing Egyptian Public Support for Security Crackdowns in the Sinai*. Carlisle, PA: Strategic Studies Institute and U.S. Army War College Press, 2015.

Forest, James J.F. *Countering Terrorism and Insurgency in the 21st century: International Perspectives*. Westport, CT: Praeger Security International, 2007.

Germani, L Sergio & Kaarthikeyan, D. R. *Pathways Out of Terrorism and Insurgency: The Dynamics of Terrorist Violence and Peace Processes*. Elgin, IL: New Dawn Press, 2005.

Mansour, M., McGregor, A., Gold, Z. & Basinsky, K. *Terrorism in Post-Morsi Egypt: A Militant Leadership Monitor Special Report*.

Rougier, Bernard, Lacroix, Stéphane & Schoch, Cynthia. *Egypt's Revolutions: Politics, Religion, and Social Movements*. Houndmills, Basingstoke, Hampshire; New York City: Palgrave Macmillan, 2016.

Stork, Joe, *Mass Arrests and Torture in Sinai*. New York: Human Rights Watch, 2005.

Chapter 21

ASBAT AL-ANSARI/THE LEAGUE OF FOLLOWERS (AAA)

A Salafi Islamic fundamentalist group (aka, the "Partisans' League") favors imposing Islamic Law (Sharia) in Lebanon and opposes Western secularist influence. Connected to Al-Qaeda and similar Sunni jihadist organizations, AaA has conducted several assassinations and bombings against civilian targets throughout the 2000s. Ahmad Abdulkarim as-Sa'idi (a.k.a. Abu Mahjin), the group's leader, received a death sentence in absentia. He worked with Abu Musab al-Zarqawi until 2006. Most AaA militants are refugees from Palestinian, who live in the Ayn al-Hilwah refugee camp in the south of Lebanon.

While Hamas, Hezbollah, and al-Fatah generally control Palestinian refugee camps in Syria and Lebanon, small extremist organizations, such as AaA also operate there. They attract members who have been disaffected with the larger organizations. AaA advocates an extremist and jihadist version of Salafism. The group strongly opposes the existence of the state of Israel, Western influence and power, and other religious faiths practicing their beliefs in Lebanon including the Shia, Christians, and Druze. The group seeks to make Lebanon into Islamist state (a Caliphate).

Hisham Shreidi, an itinerant Islamic preacher and Palestinian refugee, formed AAA in the late 1980s or the early 1990s. al-Fatah operatives killed Shreidi was killed in 1991. Soon after he died the Asbat al-Ansar (AaA) (Band of Followers) splintered into three distinct groups: Jund as-Sham (Soldiers of the Levant), Asbat al-Nour (Band of Light), and Jama'at al-Nur (Assembly of Light). Hisham's eldest son Abdullah reportedly formed Asbat al-Nour because of a leadership struggle with Ahmad Abd al-Karim al-Saadi (a.k.a. Abu Mohjen). Abu Mohjen was Sheik Hisham Shreidi's second in command and his successor. al-Fatah militants assassinated Abdullah in 2003 and, then killed his brother, Mohammed in 2004. Mohammed was also one of the leaders of the faction. Asbat al-Nour has resumed its affiliation with AaA. The Jund as-Sham subsequently became a part of the "Tawhid and Jihad network formed by Abu Musab al-Zarqawi (the founder of Al Qaeda in Iraq, the predecessor organization of ISIS. Jund as-Sham has clashed with the other AaA factions. Al-Zarqawi reportedly appointed Abu Mohjen as a leading deputy in Iraq. Whatever the disputes are between the three AaA factions, they are believed to be relatively inconsequential. The Lebanese government has issued capital sentences against Abu Mohjen, after trying him in absentia in multiple occasions. Today, Mohjen is reportedly active in Iraq or Lebanon.

AaA has attacked various "soft targets" such as nightclubs, taverns, and cinemas. AaA also has attacked opposing jihadist and sectarian leaders, such as Sunnis who AaA accused of being overly moderate or not "pure" enough. During the late 1990s, with apparent Al-Qaeda financial support, AAA shifted its tactics and attacked "hard targets" perceived to have greater significance. After reportedly assasinating four members of the Lebanese judiciary in 1999, the AaA used rockets to attack the Embassy of Russia in Lebanon in January 2000 (believed to support jihadists from Chechnya), multiple failed attempts to kill the US Ambassador, and a failed attempts to assault the Embassy of Italy, the Consulate General of the Ukraine, and offices of the Lebanese Government in 2004. The AaA also staged a fail coup in 2000 conducted by its close ally, Tafkir wa Hijra (TWH), a regional Sunni jihadist organization. The failed plot killed several people, including both Lebanese soldiers and civilians. Later, AaA bombed fast food restaurants in Lebanon, and clashed with Fatah over who should control Ayn al-Hilwah, Lebanon's the largest Palestinian refugee camp.

AaA is connected with Al-Qaeda and its affiliated groups. AaA seeks to transform Laebanon into an Islamist state (or caliphate). AaA has also adopted Al-Qaeda's pan-Islamic ideals, and seeks to conduct terrorist operations in Syria, Israel and Iraq. While AaA remains small in terms of membership, the group nonetheless, continues to be quite dangerous and continues to pose a threat to Lebanon.

AaA, which had long been allied to the Al-Nusra Front (Now known as Jabhat Fateh Al-Sham and is affiliated to Al-Qaeda), recently shifted its loyalties to ISIS. Among the latest incidents involving AaA is that the group abducted two Orthodox Christian bishops in Syria in April 2013.

FURTHER READING

Dawisha, Adeed. *The Second Arab Awakening: Revolution, Democracy, and the Islamist Challenge from Tunis to Damascus*. New York: W.W. Norton & Company, 2013.

Dingel, Eva. *Islamist Politics in Egypt and Lebanon: The Struggle for Power of Hizbullah and the Muslim Brotherhood*. I B Tauris & Co., 2016.

Malthaner, Stefan. *Mobilizing the Faithful: Militant Islamist Groups and their Constituencies*. Frankfurt: Campus Verlag, 2011.

Rougier, Bernard. *Everyday Jihad: The Rise of Militant Islam among Palestinians in Lebanon*. Cambridge, MA: Harvard University Press, 2007.

Rubin, Barry M. *Lebanon: Liberation, Conflict, and Crisis*. New York City, NY: Palgrave-Macmillan, 2009.

Wiegand, Krista E. *Bombs and Ballots: Governance by Islamist Terrorist and Guerrilla Groups*. Farnham, Surrey, England: Ashgate Pub., 2010.

Yadav, Stacey Philbrick. *Islamists and the State: Legitimacy and Institutions in Yemen and Lebanon*. London: I B Tauris. 2013.

Chapter 22

ASSOCIATION OF MUSLIM SCHOLARS (IRAQ)

The Association of Muslim Scholars (AMS) claims that it seeks to unify scholarly religious opinion in Iraq and provide guidance on interacting with Shiite and Coalition forces to end sectarian violence and divisions in post-Saddam Iraq.

After the occupation, the AMS assumed the responsibilities of the Iraq Awqaf Ministry, including caring for mosques and serving the needs of mosque imams and preachers. The Council conducted social activities seeking to assist those who lost their sources of income. The Council also cared for the Iraqi families of insurgents.

The AMS, in its weekly newspaper, "Al-Bashir" on October 14, 2004, asked Iraqi police and military forces to refrain from supporting US coalition forces. The statement requested these forces to disobey any orders issued by their superiors that failed to comply with the AMS interpretation of Sharia (Islamic law) and Iraq's unity. The statement also stated that, "the duty of the army is to protect the borders and defend values, holy places, and properties. Under Sharia, the army is prohibited from participating in actions leading to the imposition of foreign control of the country." The AMS in Iraq further requested "the Iraqi police and national guard personnel to adhere to their original duties and carry out their work in compliance with the Sharia."

On October 22, 2004, US forces in Iraq arrested several AMS members after they participated in a conference calling to boycott the Iraqi elections.

The AMS resisted the US military presence in Iraq. Its relations with other groups in Iraq reflected its continuing opposition to that presence. The AMS also did not recognize the shift in power from the US to the Shi'a and Kurdish parties and the creation of the Iraqi transitional government. Thus, the AMS was largely unsuccessful in attempts to recruit Shia Iraqis as allies. An alliance between AMS and Moqtada Sadr developed only during negotiations over the draft constitution when Sadr organized mass demonstrations against federalism. Sadr closely cooperated with AMS leaders and even Baathists from Saddam's regime. In Ramadi and other "Sunni triangle" towns in Iraq, Iraqi demonstrators paraded with pictures of both Sadr and Saddam Hussein. Sadr also supported AMS when the latter accused the Badr Brigades, operating under the pretense of providing security, of launching attacks against Sunni clerics, particularly AMS members. From when the Iraqi incursion began in 2003 until the end of September 2005, the AMS claims, 107 ulama were assassinated and 163 arrested, and 663 Sunni mosques have been destroyed or seized. Harith al-Dhari and Bashar al-Faydhi, both AMS leaders, were killed also during this time.

The AMS focus on the most radical Shia groups and with the occupation and armed resistance not only alienated the Islamic Supreme Council of Iraq (SCIRI) and Dawa, but also the more moderate leaders such as Grand Ayatollah Sayyid Ali Husaini Sistani. Meanwhile, Sunni organizations that were beginning to function as political parties, such as the Iraqi Islamic Party, began to extend beyond their Sunni Arab minority base. Although AMS demand for a deadline for a US troop withdrawal was popular with many Iraqis, AMS' inflexibility on this and other issues precluded its acceptance as the Sunni version of the marja'iyya (Shia religious establishment).

The AMS initially characterized the ISIS offensive in Iraq in June 2014 as a genuine revolution against what they perceived as Iraqi Prime Minister Nouri Al-Maliki's unjust treatment of Iraq's Sunni Muslims. AMS claimed that four major forces comprised the "Iraqi revolution". The first were the tribal militias who resented the alleged injustices of the Maliki government and alleged violations of tribal rights. They, therefore, claimed they supported ISIS for self-defense. The second "revolutionary group" initially supporting ISIS were Sunni resistance groups, such as the "Rashideen Army", the "Tab'een Army", "Al-Ishreen revolutionaries", and "Mohamed the Conqueror Army", which fought Coalition forces. They fought the new Iraqi government because they believed that Al-Maliki was a puppet of the United States and Iran. The third group initially supporting ISIS was the Iraqi revolutionaries' military council, which emerged from Iraq's Anbar province, and conducted attacks throughout Iraq. Many former Iraqi Baathist soldiers were a part of this council and fought for ISIS.

See also: Al-Qaeda in Iraq (AQI) (volume 1); Islamic State of Iraq and Syria (volume 1).

FURTHER READING

Filali-Ansary, Abdou & Sikeena Karmali Ahmed. *The Challenge of Pluralism: Paradigms from Muslim Contexts*. Edinburgh: Edinburgh University Press in association with the AGA Khan University, Institute for the Study of Muslim Civilisations, 2009.

Khanbaghi, Aptin. *Interpretations of Law and Ethics in Muslim Contexts*. Edinburgh: Edinburgh University Press, 2012.

"Muslim Scholars Stress Ethics, Nonviolence." *Washington Post,* Nov. 2, 2002.

Sajoo, Amyn B. *Muslim Modernities: Expressions of the Civil Imagination*. London: I.B. Taurus, 2008.

Thuli, Muḥammad b Muḥammad & Badakhchani, Sayyed Jalal. *Contemplation and Action: the Spiritual Autobiography of a Muslim Scholar* (New edition.). London: I.B. Taurus in association with The Institute of Islamic Studies, 1998.

Chapter 23

BENEVOLENCE INTERNATIONAL FOUNDATION (BIF)

The Benevolence International Foundation (BIF) claims to be a nonprofit charitable trust based in Saudi Arabia. Adel bin Abdul-Jalil Batterjee of Jeddah formed the BIF in 1988. Batterjee also formed the Islamic Benevolence Committee in both Jeddah, Saudi Arabia, and Peshawar, Pakistan. The group openly supported the mujahideen fighters during the Afghan-Soviet War (1979-1989).

Another alleged BIF founder, Mohammed Jamal Khalifa of Jeddah, was the brother in law of Osama bin Laden (1957-2011), the leader of Al-Qaeda. Asserting that it assists the victims of wars, BIF claimed that it provided emergency food distribution, and longer term assistance providing education and training to the children, widowed, refugees, and the wounded.

BIF has operated in several nations, including Afghanistan, Azerbaijan, Bangladesh, Bosnia and Herzegovina, Canada, China, Croatia, Georgia, Great Britain, the Netherlands, Pakistan, the Palestinian Territories, Russia, Saudi Arabia, Sudan, Tajikistan, the United Kingdom, the United States, and Yemen.

In 1988, BIF claimed to be an "import-export" company. It was later alleged to be a front for the Abu Sayyaf Group (ASG), a Filipino jihadist group. In 1992, BIF ceased operating openly in the Philippines and the Islamic Benevolence Committee renamed itself as the Benevolence International Foundation (BIF). ASG would eventually focus on attacking U.S. interests in the Philippines. Khalid Sheik Mohammed reportedly led the group's other functions.

The BIF relocated to the United States and named Enaam Arnaout as its first director and first operated in Plantation, Florida. Arnaout married an American national and received US citizenship. In 1993, BIF relocated its base of operations to Chicago.

In 1994, US Ambassador Melissa Wells, then a United Nations official, visited the BIF office on behalf of US President Bill Clinton. She met with Ma'moun Muhammad al-Hasan Bilou and praised BIF and its humanitarian relief work.

In late 1994, Mohammed Jamal Khalifa traveled to the United States to meet with Mohamed Loay Bayazid, BIF's president. US Federal agents arrested Khalifa and Bayazid in California in December 1994. The Filipino government had informed the FBI that Khalifa had funded "Operation Bojinka", a failed terrorist conspiracy. The Immigration and Naturalization Service (INS) had deported Khalifa to Jordan in May 1995. A Jordanian court acquitted Khalifa. Until his death, he resided in Saudi Arabia. Bayazid was also released. His location remains unknown.

The U.S. Government alleged that BIF sent funds and communications to Osama bin Laden (1957-2011), purchased arms for Al-Qaeda members in Chechnya, Afghanistan, and Pakistan, and redirected funds intended for charity purposes to fund terrorism. The U.S. government alleged that BIF facilitated the travel of terrorists, such as Khalifa, Bayazid, and Al-Qaeda co-founder Mamdouh Salim. The government further alleged that the group was assisting BIF members in escaping from Bosnian law enforcement authorities.

In a hearing on August 2003, U.S. District Judge Suzanne Conlon found that there was a lack of evidence that Arnaout had aided and abetted terrorism. The federal government withdrew these charges as part of a plea bargain in February 2003, in which Arnaout pleaded guilty to racketeering charges. In return, Arnaout was to provide information to prosecutors. He publicly denies any connections to Al-Qaeda.

Because it allegedly operated as a "front" for Al-Qaeda, BIF is currently outlawed worldwide by the United Nations Security Council Committee Resolution 1267. The US Department of the Treasury has also outlawed BIF. The UN has personally sanctioned Batterjee in U.S. Federal Court and Arnaout began serving a ten-year sentence for racketeering in 2003.

FURTHER READING

Abowd, M. "Arabs Still Reeling from 9/11 backlash." *The Chicago Reporter,* Dec. 1, 2002.
Crimm, Nina J. "The Government's War on the Financing of Terrorism and Its Implications for Donors, Domestic Charitable Organizations, and Global Philanthropy." *William and Mary Law Review* 45 no. 4 *(2004):* 1341-1451.
Emerson, Steven. *Jihad Incorporated: a Guide to Militant Islam in the US*. Amherst, N.Y.: Prometheus Books, 2006.
"Few Convictions on Terror Since 9/11: Most Arrested Not Linked to Extremists." *Washington Post*, June 12, 2005.
"Follow the Money; Terrorist Finance (Cutting Off Terrorists' Financing) (International Effort is Partially Successful)" *The Economist,* June 1, 2002.
Garver, Rob. "In Brief: Two Nonprofits Added to Terrorism List." *American Banker,* Dec. 18, 2001.
Goodman, B. These are Difficult Times for Islamic Organizations: Unaware Assume the Worst about Groups. *The Non Profit Times,* Dec. 1, 2001.
Matthew Levitt's Testimony before the Senate Judiciary Subcommittee on Terrorism, Technology, and Homeland Security, Sep. 10, 2003.
Müller, Sebastian R. *Hawala: An Informal Payment System and Its Use to Finance Terrorism*, Saarbrucken: VDM Verlag Dr. Müller, 2006.
Pope, T. "Islamic Charities Struggle from Terrorism Fallout." *The Non Profit Times,* Sep. 1, 2006.
"The Iceberg Beneath the Charity; Terrorist finance (Charities as sources of terrorist finance)." *The Economist*, Mar. 15, 2003.

"U.S.-Based Muslim Charities Face Scrutiny for Terrorism Links." *Church & State* 55, no. 2 (2002): 18-19.

"US Muslims in a Quandary over Charities." *The Christian Science Monitor,* Nov. 17, 2004.

Williamson, R. S. "Islamic charities under spotlight's red glare: Feds are seizing assets." *The Non Profit Times,* Jan. 2001.

Chapter 24

THE CENTER PARTY (HIZB AL-WASAT) (EGYPT)

Formed by several young and respected members of the Muslim Brotherhood, The Egyptian Center Party was led by Abdu-Ila Madi, who also officially founded the party. He was joined by leading Brotherhood defectors, Salah Abd al-Karim and Essam Sultan and other fairly high ranking members of the Brotherhood. The party seemed to offer new energy and new perspectives into Egypt's political system. The young reformers within the Center Party were accessible, skilled in the use of all media, and well-prepared political activists.

The party's religious ideology is based on Wasatiyya (centrist) ideology, a liberal interpretive tradition in Islamist thought based in Islamic law, which seeks to interpret its principles consistent with the values of a liberal democratic government.

Both the government of Hosni Mubarak and the Muslim Brotherhood criticized the Center Party. The Mubarak government asserted that the party was a merely a thinly-veiled facade for the outlawed Muslim Brotherhood, while the Muslim Brotherhood leadership expelled all of its members who became Center Party members.

The Center Party existed at the time of the January 25, 2011 revolution that overthrew the Mubarak government and was officially recognized as a legitimate Egyptian political party in February 2011. Despite its lack of legal status up through 2011, the Center Party still sought to cooperate with other parties and organizations in efforts to achieve political reform.

On the key political issues of the day, the Party claimed it favored: 1) Guaranteeing equal citizen rights to all Egyptians, regardless of religion, sex, race, status, or wealth, all emergency laws and special courts, and limiting the scope of such laws to bona-fide disasters; 2) imposing term limits on the presidency, and reducing the powers of the executive branch; 3) supporting free elections and allowing a peaceful transfer of power; 4) ensuring the right to form political parties, associations, and all civil society institutions, and 5) promoting transparency and accountability in government.

On socio-economic issues, the Center Party supported: 1) alleviating hardships for the impoverished and for middle class Egyptians; 2) achieving greater and balanced growth rates in all economic sectors to satisfy the basic needs of Egypt's people; 3) supporting investment in the private sector; 4) encouraging communities to fight poverty through local development projects and zakat (alms) institutions; 5) Reaffirming the social and moral characteristics of Arab-Islamic civilization; 6) Introducing comprehensive educational reforms and combatting illiteracy; and 7) providing universal health insurance to all Egyptians and improving the quality of public hospitals.

In foreign policy, the Center Party favored: 1) improving relationships with Sudan and other Nile Basin nations; 2) Supporting efforts to resolve the Palestinian issue; and 3) encouraging cooperation between Arab nations in military, political, economic and cultural affairs.

In terms of how it approached religion and politics, the Center Party believed that prayers alone were insufficient. Assuming an idealized vision of the umma (Islamic Community), the Party believed that Islamic activism was necessary to transform their slogans into prayers and must shift from their role in defending the umma to a role in awakening the umma.

The Center Party also viewed that the government should be subservient to the community. The Party interpreted modern Egyptian history as being shaped by factors such as the government bureaucracy and technology. They argued that because Egypt had authoritarian institutions that superseded the law and formal legal institutions, there was little room for meaningful political participation.

Center Party candidates campaigned for Parliament in 2011-2012 as independents and won nine seats in the Assembly. Both Madi and a leading party official, Essam Sultan, were arrested in July 2013 for criticizing the military coup that ousted President Mohamed Morsi and for inciting violence. The two men continue to be detained by Egyptian authorities.

FURTHER READING

Acemoglu, Daron, Tarek A. Hassan and Ahmed Tahoun. *The Power of the Street: Evidence from Egypt's Arab Spring*. London: Centre for Economic Policy Research, 2014.

Aswānī, Alā & Jonathan Wright. *On the State of Egypt: What Made the Revolution Inevitable*. New York: Vintage Books, a division of Random House, 2011.

Bubalo, A., G. Fealy and W. Mason. *Zealous Democrats: Islamism and Democracy in Egypt, Indonesia and Turkey*. Double Bay, N.S.W.: Longueville Books, 2008.

Danahar, P. *The New Middle East: The World After the Arab Spring*, London: Bloomsbury, 2015.

Haerens, M. and L. M. Zott. *The Arab Spring*. Detroit: Greenhaven Press, 2013.

Thompson, Elizabeth. *Justice interrupted: The struggle for constitutional government in the Middle East*. Cambridge, Massachusetts: Harvard University Press, 2013.

Chapter 25

Charitable Society for Social Welfare (CSSW)

Overview

Formed by Sheikh Abd al-Majid Zandani in March 1990, the Charitable Society for Social Welfare (CSSW) held itself out a group of volunteers and philanthropists seeking to provide charity work, community social work, caring for vulnerable individuals, and working on sustainable development projects.

CSSW and Possible Al-Qaeda Connections

Critics charged that CSSW was established as a fundraising organization that was financed by Al-Qaeda. Zindani fought in the Afghan-Soviet War and the subsequent Afghan civil war. He worked with Osama bin Laden (1957-2011) in Afghanistan and later became Al-Qaeda's secretary-general. Another prominent Islamist extremist, Anwar al-Awlaki, a Yemeni-American cleric, was CSSW's vice president from 1998 to 1999. Al-Awlaki raised significant financial contributions for CSSW, because of his prominent role with Al-Qaeda in the Arabian Peninsula (AQAP).

In 2009, the U.S. Department of Labor awarded a large grant to a joint venture that included CSSW as a recipient. The Labor Department's Office of Child Labor, Forced Labor, and Human Trafficking (OCFT) made a grant of at least $3.5 million to fund a three-year partnership between CSSW and CHF International (a Maryland-based foundation organized to fight child labor and child trafficking) beginning in the fiscal year 2008.

In 2009, CSSW spokesperson, Jamal Al-Haddi, denied that CSSW was connected to the Yemeni CSSW and denied that Awlaki was employed by the Yemen branch of the organization.

The US government alleged that the Yemeni government considered the Al Iman University, operated by Zindani, exported and propagated terrorism. Awlaki taught at the University.

Al-Haddi also denied that either Awlaki or Zindani had any role in CSSW, whether as founders, members of Managerial Boards, employees, consultants volunteers or any position in CSSW.

The CSSW website, however, apparently contradicted Al-Haddi's statement. CSSW's website had articles on the 2009 "Orphan's Festival" event referring to Zindani as a speaker. The CSSW's newsletter also mentioned Zindani in its article on the event. In response, Al-Haddi claimed that Zindani was a mere attendee at the 2009 festival, because of his position in the Yemeni government at the time.

RECENT CSSW ACTIVITIES

The CSSW claims to be a leading NGO in Yemen seeking to prevent early marriage and the practice of exchanging wives by increasing educational enrollment for girls and reducing poverty in rural areas practicing early marriage and exchange marriage.

Pursuant to its stated mission, the CSSW claims to have developed significant humanitarian work in development and poverty reduction in Europe through partnerships with local and international organizations. The European Union has supported some of CSSW's initiative "stop early marriage and exchange marriage", which CSSW argues increases legal protections and employs Islamic values to protect women's rights.

The CSSW project also grants women from disadvantaged households the opportunity to form income-generating business by granting them micro-credit loans, along with business training, and a business monitoring service from loan officers. Using their skills and business training, they are more likely to secure a source of income, making them less vulnerable and more independent.

The project also appeals to professionals such as lawyers such as lawyers, judges, imams, public speakers, journalists, and teachers, by involving them in awareness raising activities of the rights of men and children, including the native consequences of early and exchange marriage.

CSSW PROVIDES SPECIAL OPPORTUNITIES FOR WOMEN

CSSW initiatives have been credited for providing important opportunities for Yemeni women. Prior to Yemen's unification, women worked with men in every economic sector in Marxist-governed South Yemen (the People's Democratic Republic of Yemen). After Yemen was unified, Yemen's Islamists challenged the free and open movement of women in society. Efforts to sequester women in their homes, however, was thwarted somewhat by the emergence of CSSW female activists who donated their time and effort to help the needy and oppose political corruption. While the activists (both paid and unpaid) are mostly middle-class women, and the beneficiaries, the needy, consist of the poor, the outcome of activities benefits the actors and the beneficiaries differently. Most of the activists are university students, university graduates, or students in secondary schools planning to attend universities. These women have the time and opportunity to engage in welfare activities because of child care support in extended families and a steady income. These middle class women gain mainly non-material personal benefits such as friendships and networks, as well as emotionally a strong sense of worth and self-satisfaction.

In Aden, however, the leading female activists of Islah-Aden were neither students nor middle class. They often originated from modest social backgrounds or from the former political elected, and worked as full-time non-aid activities in leading positions not only in the political party and in the charity. These women adopted aspects of the Adeni women's liberation movement. In their social work, these women sought to remedy the negative political and economic conditions in the town. They also believed they were opposing corruption and mismanagement in local politics. These women believe they are acting according to Islamic beliefs and values as morally righteous persons and as devoted Muslims.

FURTHER READING

Clark, J. A. *Islam, Charity, and Activism Middle-class Networks and Social Welfare in Egypt, Jordan, and Yemen*. Bloomington, Ind.: Indiana University Press, 2004.

Glenn, C. L. *The Ambiguous Embrace Government and Faith-based Schools and Social Agencies*. Princeton, N.J.: Princeton University Press, 2000.

"Hamas Charities Thrive Despite U.S.-Led Fund Freeze; Foreign Donations Smuggled to Social-Welfare Wing." *Washington Times,* October 20, 2006.

McConkey, D. and P. A. Lawler. *Faith, Morality, and Civil Society*. Lanham, MD: Lexington Books, 2003.

Chapter 26

COMMITTEE FOR SOLIDARITY WITH ARAB AND MIDDLE EASTERN POLITICAL PRISONERS/COMITÉ DE SOUTIEN AVEC LES PRISONNIERS POLITIQUES ET ARABES ET DU MOYEN-ORIENT - (CSPPA)

Paris-based Shiite Muslims closely connected to Hezbollah and the Iranian government that sought to compel the French government to release Georges Ibrahim Abdallah (leader of the Lebanese Armed Revolution faction) from incarceration. The French government arrested Abdallah in 1984 in France on charges of terrorist activities against Israeli and U.S. diplomats in France.

From 1985 through 1986, CSPPA bombed several public places in Paris that killed 13 and injured over 300 others. The bombing campaign was part of Iran's attempt to force the French government to adopt a more amenable foreign policy towards Iran and its allies. The Iranian government, for example, sought to expedite negotiations over a one billion dollar financial claim against the French government, force the French government to cease providing arms to the Saddam Hussein government in Iraq, and force the French government to release several suspected Hezbollah and Iranian government agents. CSPPA claimed responsibility for the bombing. The group further demanded that the French government release several convicted terrorists including Anis Naccache. Naccache participated in a conspiracy to assassinate Shahpur Bakhtiar, Iran's Prime Minister, in 1980. Georges Ibrahim Abdallah, a citizen of Lebanon, was charged with a conspiracy to assassinate an American military attaché and an Israeli diplomat; and an Armenian, Waroujian Garabedjian, was convicted of involvement of a bombing at a Turkish Airlines counter at Orly Airport, in Paris, in July 1983.

Initially, the French government believed the Lebanese Armed Revolutionary Faction (LARF) conducted the attacks. In early 1987, however, French officials were informed that the attacks were conducted by a group of Shiite Muslims associated with an Islamic school near Paris, led by Fouad Ben Ali Saleh. Acting on information supplied by wiretaps, investigators began to suspect Wahid Gordji, a translator at Iran's embassy, of aiding the attacks. In June, the French government subpoenaed Gordji, who fled to the embassy leading to a six-month confrontation in which French police surrounded the Embassy. In response, the Iranian police surrounded the French Embassy in Tehran. Both France and Iran severed diplomatic relations in July. Hezbollah, during this time, kidnaped several French citizens. The confrontation ended in November 1987 when the French government briefly interviewed Gordji before he returned to Iran. Hezbollah released the French hostages in Lebanon after Gordji's release. France and Iram restored full diplomatic relations in June 1988.

Iran's government claimed that France facilitated the repayment of loans made by Iran, suppressed anti-Iranian regime activity in France and paid a substantial ransom to the hostage-takers. French Prime Minister Jacques Chirac, however, denied that any such arrangements were agreed to or carried out.

Chirac reportedly agreed to release Abdallah or impose a light sentence if he was convicted. Abdallah still received a life sentence. Before the trial, it was publicized that Iran supported CSAPPA.

Eight suspects were charged with conspiracy and with illegal possession of automatic weapons, ammunition, and liquid explosives. The suspects apparently had planned to kill several French officials, including President Francois Mitterrand and Prime Minister Chirac. CSPPA's leader, Fouad Ben Ali Saleh, was arrested and sentenced to life imprisonment in 1992 for his role in the bombings. Two accomplices were given life sentences, and a third received a 20-year sentence. Six of the suspects were identified as Tunisians. Several Lebanese citizens received trials in absentia because they had fled France. These sentences further expediting the group's demise. CSPPA activity has apparently remained inactive since the mid-1980s.

FURTHER READING

"Abdallah Supporters Prepare for Welcome." *The Daily Star (Beirut, Lebanon),* Jan. 1 4, 2013.
"Activists Protest Procrastination in Abdallah Case." *The Daily Star (Beirut, Lebanon),* Mar. 18, 2013.
"Democracies on Trial." *Boston Globe,* Mar. 1, 1987.
"France's Judiciary Further Delays Abdallah's Release." *The Daily Star (Beirut, Lebanon),* Apr. 5, 2013.
"France-Iran Diplomacy Shattered; Translator's Drama Ends Rapprochement." *Washington Post,* Jul. 19, 1987.
"French Pols Back War on Terror. Disagree Over the Identity of the Enemy." *Chicago Sun-Times,* Sep. 20, 1986.
"Light Sentence Sought For Alleged Terrorist; France Fears Extremist Vengeance." *Washington Post,* Feb. 28, 1987.
"Official Says Abdallah Is Not Terrorist Chief." *Boston Globe,* Feb. 2 6, 1987.
"Terror Group Says It Shot Renault Chief;Statement Disclaims Two Other Attacks" *The Washington Post,* Feb. 12, 1987.
"Terrorist Suspect Told to Stand Trial;French Court Rules Against Lebanese in Killing of U.S. Officer," *Washington Post,* Jan. 29, 1987.
Timmerman, Kenneth R. "Chirac's Hostage Dilemma." *The Nation,* Nov. 29, 1986.
"Two Blows Against Terrorism; Arrests and Sentence in France Surrounded by Controversy" *The Washington Post,* March 2, 1987.

Chapter 27

DAWA GROUPS

Individual Dawa groups spread their version of radical-Islamist thought by missionary activity, or, by violent jihad, while some Dawa groups engage in both. While a certain Dawa group may be conducting its work nonviolently, it does not follow that the specific organization has completely eschewed violence achieve its aims. Often they forego violent jihad for strictly practical reasons, including cases where jihad is counterproductive or not feasible because of the adversary's much greater strength, or, for religious reasons, i.e., jihad against non-believers is only possible when all Muslims have returned to "pure" Islam.

VIOLENT DAWA GROUPS

One example of where a Dawa group engaged in political violence after invoking jihad was when it conducted attacks against French targets in retaliation for the French government actions of granting asylum in 1981 to Abolhassan Bani-Sadr (1933 -), the former President of Iran, despite the objections of the Iranian government.

Furthermore, Dawa-oriented groups often make ambiguous statements on whether armed jihad is justified in areas where they believe Muslims are oppressed and persecuted (examples include: Kashmir, Chechnya, or Iraq). Supported by prominent Mullahs, some Dawa groups often implicitly approve of some form of armed jihad, although they avoid explicitly inciting people to it or to be associated with recruitment.

Radical-Dawa-Salafist groups may focus on they deem as "re-Islamization" of Muslim minorities in the West. These organizations include missionary, socio-cultural and finance organizations that claim to be apolitical and peaceful, but whose activities are often viewed upon extreme puritan, intolerant, and strongly anti-Western beliefs. They urge Muslims living in Western nations to reject the values associated with the West. They seek an extreme isolationism from Western society and propagate "exclusivism" and parallelism. Sometimes, they advocate the creation of fully Islamist districts in large cities in the West or even pursue parallel social structures in autonomous Sharia "enclaves" in anticipation of the "Umma" (the entire community of Muslims who are united by their religion). The Umma seek to expand throughout the entire world, including the West.

IRAQ'S DAWA PARTY

Hizb al-Da, wah al-Islamiyyah, a Shia Islamist political party, was formed in Iraq in 1957 to disseminate Islamist values, promote political activism, and oppose secularism. It evolved into a revolutionary movement to oppose Saddam Hussein's government. The regime responded by assassinating its spiritual leader, Muhammad Baqir al-Sadir (1935-1980), forcing many Dawa Party members into exile during the Iran-Iraq War (1981-1988).

After regaining its sovereign status following its governance under the Coalition Provisional Authority (CPA) in 2004, a largely Shia-run government has governed Iraq. An estimated 60% of the Iraqi population is Shia, it is not surprising that the Shiite parties did well in the nation's elections. In 2005, Iraq's two largest Shiite Muslim parties, the Supreme Council for the Islamic Revolution and the Islamic Dawa Party, formed a strong coalition known as the United Iraqi Alliance (UIA), formed the Iraqi government. Iraq's Grand Ayatollah, Ali-al Sistani (1930-), the senior Shiite cleric in the nation, supported the UIA in that election. Both former Prime Ministers Nouri al-Maliki (1950-) and his successor, Iraq's current Prime Minister Haider al-Abadi (1952-) are members of the Dawa Party. Abadi has been Iraq's Prime Minister since 2014.

LEBANON'S DAWA PARTY

Lebanon's Islamic Dawa Party in Lebanon (Ḥizb al Daʿwa al-Islāmiyya) was formerly the leading Shia party in that country and was connected with the larger Islamic Dawa Party of Iraq. The Lebanese Dawa Party was formed by Najaf-educated Shia clerics, who returned to Lebanon. Shiekh Sayyed Mohammad Hussein Fadlallah (1935-) is the spiritual guide of the Dawa party.

Similar to the Iraqi Dawa Party, the Lebanese Dawa Party operates covertly and secretly to comply with Shia approach to protect the community from persecution.

After Iran's Islamic Revolution in 1979, many of Lebanon's hardline Shia clergy, with Iran's blessings, abandoned the Dawa Party claiming that its clandestine quality undermined its ability to function as a political party.

By 1982, Hezbollah, a radical but a more public Shia movement, had largely coopted Dawa. By the end of 1984 the Dawa had combined with several other Lebanese militant organizations, such as the Hussein Suicide Squad, Islamic Students Union, Dawa, Jundallah (Soldiers of God) and Islamic Amal. Lebanon's al-Da'wa party continues to be influential in shaping various aspects of Hezbollah, including its ideology.

See also: Al-Qaeda (volume 1); Amal (volume 1); Hezbollah (volume 1); Jundallah (volume 2).

FURTHER READING

Levitt, Matthew. *Hamas: Politics, Charity, and Terrorism in the Service of Jihad.* New Haven: Yale University Press, 2006.

Sakai, K. "Modernity and Tradition in the Islamic Movements in Iraq: Continuity and Discontinuity in the Role of the Ulama." *Arab Studies Quarterly* (Winter 2001): 37-54.

Shanahan, Rodger. Shi a Political Development in Iraq: the Case of the Islamic Da'wa Party. *Third World Quarterly* 25 no. 4 (2004): 943-54.

Sikand, Y. "Peace, Dialogue and Dawai: an Analysis of the Writings of Maulana Wahiduddin Khan." *Islam and Christian-Muslim Relations 14 no.* 1 (2003): 33-49.

Stenhouse, Paul. "Ignoring Signposts on the Road: Da'wa: Jihad with a Velvet Glove." *Quadrant* 51 no. 6 (2007): 40-46.

Yasmeen, Samina. "Islamisation and Activism of a Muslim NGO in Pakistan: Jama'at-Ud-Da'wa as a Case Study." *Australian Journal of Social Issues* 47 no. 3 (2012): 407-24.

Chapter 28

DEMOCRATIC FRONT FOR THE LIBERATION OF PALESTINE (DFLP)

An affiliate of the Palestinian Liberation Organization (PLO), the Democratic Front for the Liberation of Palestine (DFLP) seeks to form a free and independent nation of Palestine in the Gaza Strip and West Bank. Formerly known as the Popular Democratic Front for the Liberation of Palestine (PDFLP) (which was formed in 1969), the group renamed itself to the DFLP in August 1974. The DFLP emerged along with other Palestinian nationalist groups, such as Fata and the Popular Front for the Liberation of Palestine (PFLP), after the 1967 Arab-Israeli War, in which both Gamel Nasser (1918-1970) lost and the hopes of a pan-Arabist state were lost. The DFLP argued for the primacy of class analysis and struggle.

The DFLP seeks an armed struggle led by the working classes to supplant what it considers an imperialist-capitalist economy with an Islamic economy. Consistent with its socialist economic ideology, however, DFLP rejects pan-Islamism. Currently, this group receives only internal financial support. Regimes in Syria, Libya, and South Yemen formerly supported the group. The DFLP advocates violence, but only within Israel and the disputed territories.

During the 1970s, DFLP's engaged in bombing and kidnapping attacks against Israeli civilians. On May 15, 1974, three DFLP members attacked a school in Ma'alot, Israel, taking 90 schoolchildren hostage. In exchange for the children, the attackers demanded that 23 Arab prisoners be released. After negotiations had failed, the Israeli security forces attempted to seize the school. However, the DFLP members killed 21 children and seven adults and injured over 70 more hostages.

The DFLP was most active during the 1970s. In the early 1980s, it once had between 1000 to 2000 members. Currently, the group may have nearly 500 members. Because of its lack of activity and a sharp decline in membership, many nations have removed the DFLP from their terrorist watch lists. The group, however, is still monitored, and its financial assets remain frozen.

Some commentators argued that the DFLP had an instrumental role in placing the idea of a democratic Palestinian state (the two-state solution) with equal rights on the political agenda of the PLO. Although the DFLP has frequently adopted a pragmatic approach on issues, such as advocating dialogue with the Israeli "left", the front continues to oppose the Oslo peace process. The DFLP designated a foreign terrorist organization beginning with the first list in

October 1997. Because of some reconciliation with Yasir Arafat (1929-2004) and its apparent acceptance of eventual peace with Israel, the Front began to be excluded from the list beginning in October 1999).

The DFLP had suffered some significant recent political defeats, including, in the 2005 Palestinian Authority (PA) presidential elections when its candidate won only 3.5 percent of the votes. In 2006, the DFLP conducted several attacks from June to August 2006. Some commentators believe that the DFLP was seeking to remain relevant in Palestinian politics, while groups such as Hamas were growing in power and popularity.

See also: Hamas (volume 1).

FURTHER READING

Alexander, Yonah. *Palestinian Secular Terrorism: Profiles of Fatah, Popular Front for the Liberation of Palestine, Popular Front for the Liberation of Palestine-General Command and the Democratic Front for the Liberation of Palestine.* Ardsley, NY: Transnational Publishers, 2003.

"Camelot, Hamas-style; Palestine (Hamas forms its first government)." *The Economist,* April 1, 2006.

Democratic Popular Front for the Liberation of Palestine. Manchester: Committees for Solidarity with the Palestinian Revolution, 1969.

"From the Circus Ring to the Tightrope; Palestine's Election (Palestine's Presidential Election)." *The Economist*, January 8, 2005.

Historical Development of the Palestinian Struggle. S.l.: DPFLP Foreign Languages Press, 1971.

"Palestine's War Against Itself. (Includes related article on Arab-Israeli peace talks)." *The Economist,* April 18, 1992, 1.

"Palestinian Refugees: Losers, Always. (Israeli president says they cannot come back). *The Economist,* August 28, 1997.

Towards a Democratic Solution to the Palestinian Question. Quebec: Presses Solidaires, 1970.

Chapter 29

DEVELOPER'S COALITION/ABADGARAN/(IRAN)

A reactionary political faction in Iran, Abadgaran was an Iranian conservative political federation or "umbrella group" of parties and organizations. The main groups within the alliance were Front of Followers of the Line of the Imam and the Leader members and Society of Devotees of the Islamic Revolution. The Coalition's name emphasizes the concept of "development" in contrast to the economic policies of the reform government, and specifically to draw a distinction to the "Executives of Construction", to connote a group more responsive to the people, particularly poor people. The party's informal name, Abadi means "village" in Farsi, which alludes to rural roots and values.

Abadgaran was formed in 2003 and was mostly composed of individuals younger than fifty and non-clerics. At first, the group was largely composed of Basij (a volunteer paramilitary organization that answered to the Islamic Revolutionary Guards). They were veterans who had been to mid- and senior-level positions, however, were being increasingly ignored by Iranian President Akbar Hashemi Rafsanjani's (1934-2017) reformist government. In addition, conservatives felt threatened by ideas of "regime change" in Iran promoted by US President, George W. Bush (1946-).

The Developer's Coalition was frequently viewed as "neo-conservative" because of its expressed dedication to the Islamic revolution, its Islamist cultural perspectives, and aggressive, anti-Western foreign and national security policies.

Former Iranian President, Mahmoud Ahmadinejad (1956 -) was a member of the Coalition, which gained considerable power after The Developer's Coalition, mostly active in Iran's capital of Tehran, won the Iranian Local Council elections, in 2003 and made almost a clean sweep of the seats representing the cities of Tehran, Rey, Shemiranat and Eslamshahr in the Iranian Majlis (Parliamentary) election of 2004. The Abadgaran–led Tehran City Council chose Mahmoud Ahmadinejad as Tehran's mayor. Ahmadinejad became Iran's President in 2005.

By the time he was elected chosen as mayor, Ahmadinejad was on a political ascent in the Developers Coalition. In, 2005, the Abadgaran–dominated Tehran City Council strongly supported Ahmadinejad in the country's presidential election. Many conservatives had hoped that Ahmadinejad's victory would end the protracted political infighting between conservatives and reformists in Iran that followed the death of Ayatollah Khomeini (1902-1989), the founder of the Islamic Republic, in 1989.

Promoting a perspective of "social justice" that sought recreate the utopian "original revolutionary spirit", develop a "renewed and truly revolutionary Islamic Republic", and "guarding the revolution and the independence of" Iran, the Coalition sought to marginalize the reformers politically. To accomplish this, they first reduced the power of incumbent President Mohammad Khatami (1943-). Khatami served as Iran's President from 1997 through 2005.

With a majority in parliament, the conservatives enacted statutes both to hinder foreign investment and the Khatami administration's negotiations with international business firms.

These laws made foreign investment more difficult, hampered the government's ability to negotiate deals with foreign companies and curtailed privatization plans. These steps were done in the name of preserving what they considered an egalitarian and government-owned economic policy.

In pursuit of a messianic foreign policy, these hardliners also rejected the "Additional Protocol" that Hassan Rouhani (1948 -) (Iran's current President, who has held that office since 2013) had negotiated. The Coalition also sought to withdraw from the Non-Proliferation Treaty, a step rejected by Ayatollah Ali Khamenei (1939-), Iran's current Supreme Leader (who has held that position since 1989).

Abadgaran and other Iranian conservative parties were victorious in the 2003, 2004, and 2005 elections because they turned out their base of 25% of the electorate, recruited military veterans, attracted independents on issue of national security, hardliners within the political and security establishments, and many religiously-oriented voters from Iran's lower and middle classes. The conservative victory was due mostly to the fact that women, college students, and the salaried middle class who composed the reformists base of support did not vote in sufficiently large enough numbers. For example, voter participation in the 2004 Majlis election declined by 51%. The conservatives, in other words, had only limited political support. It was voter apathy that played the largest role in allowing them to make a comeback.

See also: Islamic Revolutionary Guards (IRGC) (volume 1).

FURTHER READING

Faris, David M. *Social Media in Iran: Politics and Society after 2009*. Albany: State Univ of New York Pr, 2016.

Groot, Joanna De. *Religion, Culture and Politics in Iran from the Qajars to Khomeini*. London: I.B. Tauris, 2007.

Kazemzadeh, Masoud. *Islamic Fundamentalism, Feminism, and Gender Inequality in Iran Under Khomeini*. Lanham, MD: University Press of America, 2002.

Menashri, David. *Post-revolutionary Politics in Iran: Religion, Society, and Power*. London: Routledge, 2007.

Rieffer-Flanagan, Barbara Ann J. *Evolving Iran: an Introduction to Politics and Problems in the Islamic Republic*. Washington, DC: Georgetown University Press, 2013.

Tezcür, Güneş Murat. *Muslim Reformers in Iran and Turkey: the Paradox of Moderation*. Austin: University of Texas Press, 2010.

Chapter 30

EGYPTIAN ISLAMIC JIHAD (EIJ)/VANGUARDS OF CONQUEST/JIHAD GROUP/AL-JIHAD AL-ISLAMI/ ISLAMIC JIHAD/

The Egyptian Islamic Jihad (EIJ) was established in 1979 by Karam Zuhdi (leader of the Saidi Jamaa llanllya), Abd al-Salam Faraj (1954-1982) (ideological leader of an Islamic cell in Cairo), and Ayman al-Zawahiri (1951-)(who became the leader of Al-Qaeda after Osama bin Laden [1957-2011] was killed in 2011). Many EIJ members defected from the more established Muslim Brotherhood, because they believed that the Brotherhood had lost much of its militancy and jihadism. Some EIJ members were veterans of the Afghan-Soviet War (1979-1989).

Originally the EIJ sought to violently depose the Egyptian regime and form an Islamist state (a caliphate). Later, it also began targeting American and Israeli interests in Egypt and other nations. Currently, EIJ seeks both to form an Islamic caliphate in Egypt and to attack Israeli and Western military forces.

EIJ conducted several high-profile assassinations and bombings. On April 6, 1981, EIJ militants assassinated Egyptian President Anwar al-Sadat (1918-1981). After Sadat's murder, EIJ members and leaders, including Faraj and Zuhdi, were imprisoned (Zuhdi until 2003) and some executed (Faraj on April 15, 1982). The imprisoned Abud al-Zumur (1948 -) and Sayyedtimam al-Sharif (aka, Dr. Fadl) (1950-) soon became EIJ leaders. Al-Zawahiri, especially remained influential, grew more powerful, and in 1991 became EIJ's sole leader. The EIJ also assassinated Rifaat al-Mahgoub (1926-1990), Speaker of the People's Assembly of Egypt in October 1990.

In addition to assassinating Sadat and Al-Alfi, the EIJ also attempted but failed to assassinate Atef Sedky (1930-2005), Egypt's Prime Minister, and Hassan al-Alfi, the country's Interior Minister, in 1993; the bombing of the Egyptian embassy in Islamabad, Pakistan in 1995; the attempted assassination of Hosni Mubarak (1928 -), President of Egypt, in Addis Ababa, Ethiopia in 1995; and, also attempt to bomb the US Embassy in Albania in 1998. The EIJ has also allegedly conducted the 1998 attacks against American interests in Nairobi, Kenya, and Dar es Salaam, Tanzania.

During the early 1980s, Egyptian President Hosni Mubarak harshly repressed EIJ. A schism soon developed within the group. Abbud al-Zumar, who was still incarcerated, sought for peaceful negotiation. Zumar's group, however, failed to win significant support. Ayman al-Zawahiri led a faction that was increasingly violent. In 1987, and under government pressure, EIJ transferred its base of operation to Afghanistan. This faction also shifted its strategy from focusing on only targets in Egypt to one based on Osama bin Laden's idea of directly attacking US interests. In 1998, EIJ became a part of the organization al-Zawahiri was beginning to lead Al-Qaeda's "Worldwide Front for Jihad Against Jews and Crusaders". EIJ members, then, collaborated in the bombings of the US embassies in Nairobi, Kenya and Dar es Salaam, Tanzania, on August 7, 1998. EIJ was also reportedly involved in the 2000 bombing of the USS Cole docked in Aden, Yemen, and the September 11, 2001, attacks on the World Trade Center and Pentagon.

Becoming increasingly violent, EIJ killed people it considered apostates and infidels. The group also used suicide bombings, similar to Hezbollah's tactics in Lebanon. EIJ militants are skilled in weapons training and strategic military planning, which made Al-Qaeda particularly interested in recruiting them. Al-Qaeda helped finance EIJ in 1998. The two groups merged in June 2001 to form Jamaat Qaeda al-Jihad, led by al-Zawahiri.

Despite the Egyptian government's strict security measures and their harsh implementation, EIJ's merger with Al-Qaeda ensured the group's survival. EIJ's attacks in Egypt declined beginning in the 1990s because the Egyptian government had either killed or detained a large number of EIJ members.

EIJ continues its terrorist activities particularly targeting foreign embassies. It also extended its operations to nations such as Sudan. Despite its small size, Jamaat Qaeda Al-Jihad has become almost synonymous with Al-Qaeda. Most members of Al-Qaeda's shura (consultation) council originally were EIJ members.

Atef and Zawahiri, who were incarcerated in Egypt for their participation in President Sadat's 1981 assassination, were widely suspected of organizing the Al-Qaeda attacks on US embassies in East Africa in 1998, and then the attacks on the World Trade Center in New York City and the Pentagon in Washington, DC in 2001. Atef was reportedly killed in an American attack in Afghanistan in 2001.

See also: Al-Qaeda (volume 1); Hezbollah (volume 1); Muslim Brotherhood (volume 1); Worldwide Front for Jihad Against Jews and Crusaders (volume 1).

FURTHER READING

Bas, Natana J. *Wahhabi Islam: From Revival and Reform to Global Jihad*. Oxford: Oxford University Press, 2004.

Faris, D. M. "Why Egypt's Muslim Brotherhood isn't the Islamic Bogeyman." *The Christian Science Monitor*, Feb. 14, 2011.

"Islam's new Egyptian face. (Egypt's tighter control over Islamic extremists)." *The Economist*, (February 3, 1996).

Knapp, Michael G. *The Concept and Practice of Jihad in Islam*. Ft. Belvoir: Defense Technical Information Center, 2003.

Lia, Brynjar. *Architect of Global Jihad: the Life of al-Qaida Strategist Abu Musab al-Suri*. New York: Columbia University Press, 2008.

Murphy, D. "Ayman al-Zawahiri: How Will He Shape Al-Qaeda?" *The Christian Science Monitor, May 5, 2011.*

Orr, Tamra. *Egyptian Islamic Jihad*. New York, NY: Rosen Pub. Group, 2003.

"Special briefing: How Radical Islamists See the World?" *The Christian Science Monitor,* Aug. 2, 2005.

Spencer, Robert. *The Myth of Islamic Tolerance: How Islamic Law Treats Non-Muslims*. Amherst, NY: Prometheus Books, 2005.

Stephan, Maria J. *Civilian Jihad: Nonviolent Struggle, Democratization, and Governance in the Middle East*. New York: Palgrave Macmillan, 2009.

Zayyalt, Muntaṣir Zayyāt; Sara Nimis, Ahmed Fekry & Ibrahim M Abu-Rabi' Rabi, I. M. *The Road to Al-Qaeda the Story of Bin Laden's Right-hand man*. London: Pluto Press, 2004.

Chapter 31

EGYPTIAN ISLAMIST POLITICAL PARTIES

THE RISE OF THE ISLAMIST PARTIES AFTER THE ARAB SPRING

Hosni Mubarak (1928-) was deposed as Egypt's President in the popular revolution that occurred in January 25, 2011, one of the major events of the "Arab Spring". Egypt's 1971 constitution prohibited the formation of religiously-based parties. In the wake of the January 25th Revolution, Egypt adopted a new constitution in 2012 that abolished these restrictions and several Islamist parties were formed. These included parties such as the Freedom and Justice Party (FJP), the political branch of the Muslim Brotherhood.

Egypt's first fair and free Parliamentary elections were held in from November 2011 through January 2012. In this voting, Islamist parties won a majority. In Egypt's first fair and free Presidential elections in May 2012, Mohammad Morsi (1951-), the Muslim Brotherhood candidate was elected in the second round of voting.

In these parliamentary elections, a small number of Islamist parties received 70% of the seats in Egypt's first post-revolutionary parliament when their votes were combined. Morsi's Freedom and Justice Party, the political branch of the well-organized Egyptian Muslim Brotherhood received 218 of the 498 elected seats, or approximately 43.7%. The Nour Party, affiliated with Egypt's Salafist movement won about 108 seats, or 21.7%. Al Nour, Freedom and Justice and the liberal Al Wafd Party were the only political parties that won more than 5% of the seats in the People's Assembly (Egypt's lower house of parliament), which was the minimum threshold to win seats in that body. Commentators generally expressed surprise at the success of hardline Salafi parties, and by the anemic showing of political parties connected to members of former President Hosni Mubarak's government.

Despite their overwhelming performance in the Parliamentary elections, many commentators believed that the Islamist parties would not vote as a single cohesive bloc. For its part, the Muslim Brotherhood's Freedom and Justice Party denied that it would form a coalition with the Salafi parties.

Despite receiving a popular majority in Parliamentary elections, the Muslim Brotherhood government faced considerable challenges. The party faced many difficult issues such as citizenship, rule of law, freedom of the press and media, inequalities in income distribution. It was also unable to form alliances with the liberal secularists and political support for the implementation of a moderate Islamist form of governance.

Morsi's failure in development effective democratic governance and that was inclusive, empowered women, productively employed the revolutionary energies of young Egyptians, and protected the rights of members of religious and ethnic minority groups resulted in growing instability toward the end of Morsi's tenure.

By mid-2013, Egyptian Army General Fateh al-Sisi (1954-) began rallying popular support to remove President Morsi. Sisi successfully encouraged thousands of Egyptians to participate in street demonstrations against Morsi's government. The Muslim Brotherhood government, in some cases, used violence to dispel the peaceful protestors. These tactics resulted in generating popular uprising against the government.

EFFORTS TO OUTLAW THE ISLAMIST PARTIES

After Morsi was removed from power, Sisi assumed the duties of governing Egypt. Early on, he began the process of drafting a new constitution to replace the 2012 Constitution. In 2013, a Constitutional Amendment Commission proposed several amendments to the suspended constitution of 2012, which recommended an amendment to prohibit religiously oriented political parties. When enacted, it effectively outlawed 15 Islamist Egyptian parties. By that time, the government had already began prosecuting the FJP, Al-Witan Party, Nour Party, Al-Asala Party, Al-Wasat Party, Egyptian Reform Party, the Virtue Party and People's Democratic Party.

The Islamist parties responded to the government crackdown by seeking to remove overt Islamist characteristics from their parties and policy positions. Many of these parties either renounced or denied any Islamist characteristics to avoid being outlawed under this constitutional prohibition. These included the Nour Party, which claimed to be inclusive and referred to religiously-oriented parties in other nations to argue that they were not a threat to democracy. Al-Asala Party said that its Islamism complied with Article 2 of the constitution, which was not amended and requires that Sharia (Islamic Law) be the basis for all Egyptian law.

The effects of such revision became a matter of considerable debate. Some commentators argued that the revision would not affect parties such as the FJP and Nour because their bylaws do not prohibit individuals from other faiths being party members. Other commentators argued that no secular party programs or secular activities should be based on religious belief.

EGYPT'S ISLAMIST PARTIES

Most, if not all, of the Islamist political parties are currently prohibited from political involvement under Egypt's current constitutional provisions that outlaw religiously-based political parties.

AL-ASALA

Al-Asala is a Salafi party established following the Egyptian revolution by Adel Abdel Maqsoud Afifi (1945-), the older brother of influential Salafi preacher, Muhammad Abdel Maqsoud Afifi. This ultra-conservative party that seeks to establish an Islamic state and implement Sharia as Egypt's main source of law. The Party says that it seeks to ensure justice and equality through a contemporary interpretation of original Islamic principles.

AL-NOUR

The Nour Party was formed by al-Da`wa al-Salafiyya ("The Salafi Call") in the aftermath of the Egyptian Revolution. The ultraconservative Nour Party seeks to from an Islamic state and impose Sharia s as Egypt's primary legal source. It seeks gradual reform views the principles of Islam as a comprehensive framework for religion and government. Prior to the 2011 parliamentary elections, al-Nour was a part of the "Islamist Bloc", which was an alliance of Egyptian political parties consisting of Al-Nour, the Authenticity Party, and the Building and Development Party, the political affiliate of the Islamic Group (al-Gama`a al-Islamiyya). Al-Nour won 111 of the 127 seats won by the Islamist Bloc in the 2011 Egyptian parliamentary elections.

AL-WASAT

Formed in 1996 by a several former Muslim Brotherhood members. The Egyptian Political Parties Committee refused to grant the party a license. This Commission was led by the governing National Democratic Party and explained that its refusal was based on Al-Wasat's alleged connections with the Muslim Brotherhood. Al-Wasat's founding members had defected from the Brotherhood because they opposed what they considered to be the overly centralized nature of decision-making in that group. Al-Wasat also presented a more moderate Islamist ideology than the Brotherhood. Based on the Wasatiyya (centrist) ideology, the combine Sharia legal principles with an acceptance of a liberal democracy. After they applied for legal status in 1996 and 1999, major Wasat Party leaders received permission from Egypt's Ministry of Social Affairs to form the Egyptian Association for Culture and Dialogue, a non-governmental organization through which Wasat leaders could conduct many of their social programs and outreach activities. Opposed to the Mubarak regime, Wasat leaders were among the early opposition leaders to the Egyptian government and participated in the 2004 formation and subsequent activities of the Kefaya movement (the first political organization that sought for Mubarak's resignation). Al-Wasat was the first political party to apply for and receive a license following the January 25, 2012 revolution.

AL-WATAN

The Watan Party was formed after a schism within the Salafi Nour Party. In December 2012 Nour Party chair Emad Abdel Ghafour (1960 -) resigned and said that he would form the Watan Party. Abdel Ghafour was opposed to the Nour Party's oversight by Salafi clerics, al-Dawa`an al-Salafiyya (the Salafi Call), and he wanted greater freedom to form alliances with other parties such as the Freedom and Justice Party. Abdel Ghafour said that Al-Watan was representative of the aspirations of ordinary Egyptian, while the Nour Party had become politically detached.

ALLIANCE (TAHALUF)

An opposition party that first emerged for the 1987 elections by the Socialist Labor Party, the Muslim Brotherhood and the Socialist Liberal Party. It became known as the SLP list, since the Muslim Brotherhood, as a religious group, could not legally participate in elections at the time.

BUILDING AND DEVELOPMENT

The Building and Development Party is the official political party of the Islamist organization al-Gama`a al-Islamiya. Once committed to overthrowing the Egyptian government, al-Gama`a al-Islamiya's imprisoned leaders renounced violence in 2003. Formed by leading Islamists, including Tarek al-Zumar (1959 -), this right wing groups claims that it seeks to form a democracy with principles based on Sharia. Party leaders assert that the party accepts the principles of political pluralism and equality. In March 2011, Zumar was freed from prison after serving a 30 year sentence for his role in planning President Anwar al-Sadat's assassination in 1981.

FREEDOM AND JUSTICE

The Freedom and Justice Party (FJP) was formed shortly after the 2011 Egyptian revolution, as the political branch of the Muslim Brotherhood. Currently, the FJP is the leading Islamist party in Egypt. The FJP was led by President Mohamed Morsi, who won Egypt's first post-Mubarak presidential election in June 2012. The Brotherhood at first said it would run a presidential candidate. The group later backtracked on that decision. Earlier, in the 2011-2012 parliamentary elections, FJP candidates won nearly 40 percent of the vote, the largest percentage of seats held by a single party in the assembly, which the subsequent military government dissolved. The Muslim Brotherhood's success was largely attributed to the social services that it had long provided for impoverished Egyptians, in addition to their effective organization, which permitted FJP candidates to run effective campaigns throughout Egypt.

Officially outlawed for decades by the Egyptian government, the Muslim Brotherhood had never participated formally as a political party in previous Egyptian elections. After the FJP was created, it was difficult for members and commentators alike to delineate between the Brotherhood and the FJP. FJP leaders claimed that the two groups are separate entities but share the same Islamic ideals. The FJP is also not directly a part of the Muslim Brotherhood infrastructure. FJP leaders also resigned their positions within the Brotherhood's guidance bureau prior to assuming a political role. Yet the two organizations remain tightly connected, with the Brotherhood explicitly demanding that Brotherhood members join only the FJP as their political party.

The Muslim Brotherhood is an Islamic revivalist movement, formed in 1928 and outlawed by the Egyptian government in both 1948 and 1954. President Anwar Sadat freed imprisoned Brethren and made it legal for the group to conduct its activities. The Brotherhood seeks Sharia (Islamic law) as the sole basis of Egyptian law. While not a political party, the Brotherhood has engaged in the political process through the New Wafd Party (1984), and the Alliance (1987). Jihadist groups such as the Hizb al-Tahrir al-Islami (Islamic Liberation Party) argue that the Brothers' willingness to engage in the political process signifies its willingness to compromise its commitment and loyalty to Islam.

STRONG EGYPT

Former presidential candidate and moderate Islamist Abdel Moneim Aboul Fotouh (1951-) formed the Strong Egypt Party as an economically progressive and socially moderate political party. Aboul Fotouh has urged political parties to engage in the political process to prevent any one party from accumulating excessive political or governmental power. This Islamist-oriented party was first formed prior to the 1984 elections, but remains very small.

See also: Dawa (volume 1); Muslim Brotherhood (volume 1).

FURTHER READING

Arjomand, Said Amir and Nathan J. Brown. *The Rule of Law, Islam, and Constitutional Politics in Egypt and Iran*. Albany, NY: State University of New York Press, 2013.

Armajani, Jon. *Modern Islamist Movements: History, Religion, and Politics*. Chichester, West Sussex, UK: Wiley-Blackwell, 2012.

Ismail, Salwa. *Rethinking Islamist Politics: Culture, the State and Islamism*. London: I.B. Tauris, 2003.

Zuhur, Sherifa. *Egypt: Security, Political, and Islamist Challenges*. Carlisle, PA: Strategic Studies Institute, U.S. Army War College, 2007.

Chapter 32

EGYPTIAN SALAFIST MOVEMENT

Many young Egyptians have adopted Salafism, and some of these individuals become radical Islamists. Throughout the majority Muslim nations of northern Africa, intense poverty, lack of opportunities, and oppressive political systems, have fueled the attractiveness of Salafism. Since Salafism doctrine teaches that Muslims may attain a life of purity only through complete adherence to the Koran and the Hadiths, this simple and straightforward theology appeals to many desperate and dispossessed Egyptians.

Salafism emerged during the 1970s when young militants rejected the Muslim Brotherhood's political strategy. The Salafists either abandoned the Brotherhood disappointed with its lack of Jihadist militancy or created a new type of radical Islam. They were also bolder in confronting President Hosni Mubarak's (1928 -) government, sometimes through violence.

As the Salafists began taking stronger action, the government became increasingly repressive. The key events in this conflict include: President Anwar Sadat's (1918-1981) assassination in 1981 and major civil unrest in the 1990s when Egyptian authorities actively repressed a Salafi insurgency.

While the Salafists concurred with the Muslim Brotherhood on goals, they disagreed over how these goals should be attained. The Brotherhood advocated caution, believing that the government would destroy any and all militant actions. Egypt's Islamists–especially the al-Jihad and the Islamic Group (which had been a part of the Jam'iyat Movement, or, al-Jama'a al-Islamiyya) clashed with the government throughout the 1990s. These Jihadi groups were increasingly active from 1990 through 1995 and became less active after that point. The government successfully suppressed these insurgents because of: 1) relatively strong government's institutions and the firm loyalty of the security forces; 2) the militants did not have sufficient support among the people; and 3) because of the internal division among insurgents.

The Salafists continued to be weak, because of their internal divisions, with many factions and leadership struggles. The most significant difference between those who emerged from the Jam'iyat organizations (Islamists engaged in community service) and the al-Jihad (a group exclusively devoted to violent jihad). Upwards to nearly 700 al-Jihad militants were veterans of the Afghan-Soviet War, which equipped them to attempt to launch an insurgency in Egypt.

Jam'iyat militants left the violent jihad, after concluding that such fighting would be futile. Some in al-Jihad, however, wanted to renounce violence by the late 1990s. Other group members were dedicated to fighting against Egypt's government and agreed with Osama bin Laden (1957-2011) that the United States was the main enemy. As Islamist fighters during the 1970s and 1980s died, were incarcerated, or abandoned terrorism, they were replaced by militants who were younger and less educated.

Extremist Salafis in Egypt increased their terrorist attacks on Coptic Christians. For example, in January 2010, Salafi militants randomly killed several Coptic Christians leaving church services in Naga Hammadi, in Upper Egypt. Salafis target Christians, whom they view as apostates. Salafi militants also target security forces, Sufi Muslims (adherents of a mystical interpretation of Islam), and Western tourists. To suppress the extremist Salafis, the Egyptian government prosecuted any suspected members of Salafist organizations, disseminating their message, and those involved in anti-government activities and assert claims of apostasy.

The Egyptian uprising that deposed the Mubarak government in 2011, however, originated not from Salafist actions, but from the Arab Spring uprising, a rejuvenated Muslim Brotherhood and Egypt's military. Following the overthrow of the Mubarak government, elections were called, and the Salafists no longer believed that violent jihad was necessary. Instead, they believed that they could achieve their goals through the political process and social intimidation.

The Salafi groups did not confront Egypt's military, which governed the nation, from 2011 through 2012, out of the belief that the military would prevent them from forming a government based on Islamic law (Sharia). The Salafists avoided violent confrontations with the military government, the Brotherhood, or the Morsi regime because they believed that they were making satisfactory progress to achieve their goals.

Deep divisions caused by political competition among leaders and often trivial theological disputes hampered Salafist efforts, as they lacked the Muslim Brotherhood's cohesiveness and discipline. The Salafists garnered nearly a quarter of all votes cast in the first round in the Parliamentary elections. The Salafist "al-Nour Party" seemed to be in a favorable position to promulgate Sharia law through the political process. While seeking to position themselves as a more genuine Islamist alternative as compared to the Muslim Brotherhood, many Salafists favored the actions the governing party was taking. Others sought greater progress and implemented them more expeditiously. Internal divisions among the Salafists hampered their influence, as perhaps did an agreement that made them the junior partner of the Brotherhood.

The Nour Party, which is affiliated with the Islamist organization, Dawa Salafiyya, became Egypt's second largest Islamist faction. Nour was established after Mubarak was ousted in February 2011. The party came in second to the Brotherhood in Egypt's 2011 parliamentary elections. Nour supported a new military-drafted constitution passed in a referendum in 2014. The Nour Party also provided some Islamist support for the military's actions since it removed Morsi from the presidency in the wake of mass protests against his government. Nour, however, was sharply criticized by many Islamists for supporting the army's decision to depose Morsi.

See also: Egyptian al-Jihad (volume 1); Egyptian Salafist Movement (volume 1); Muslim Brotherhood (volume 1).

FURTHER READING

Chick, K. "Egyptian Cabinet Reshuffle Fails to Satisfy Protesters." *The Christian Science Monitor,* Jul. 18, 2011.

DeAtkine, N. "Al-Qaeda's Emir Calls on Egyptian Salafi Leader to Continue Revolution." *American Diplomacy*, Jan. 16, 2013.

Saadany, Salah. *Egypt and Libya from Inside, 1969-1976: the Qaddafi revolution and the Eventual Break in Relations, by the Former Egyptian Ambassador to Libya*. Jefferson, N.C.: McFarland, 1994.

Chapter 33

EMNI (DIVISION OF ISIS)

OVERVIEW

The Emni, an intelligence branch of ISIS, which was both an internal police force and an external operations branch, which conducted terrorist attacks in areas outside of ISIS control. Emni, for example, conducted attacks in Paris France on November 13, 2015. Emni began sending jihadist fighters to various nations in 2014.

The Emni was a multilevel network commanded by ISIS's most senior Syrian operative, spokesman and propaganda director, Abu Muhammad Al-Adnani (1977-), who was born in Binnish in northern Syria. Al-Adnani also commands IS's special forces and supervises lieutenants who plan and execute attacks worldwide. Adnani issued the global call in 2016 for Muslims to attack unbelievers wherever they are. Adnani was authorized to approve attacks and delegating his subordinates to handle the details. The organization is divided geographically by its European, Asian, and Arab operations.

THE EXTERNAL OPERATIONS BRANCH

The Emni has directed or coordinated at least ten deadly attacks against Western targets. More than 30 Emni operatives have been arrested before they could conduct these attacks.

The Emni is a major part of ISIS operations and is completely free to recruit and reassign fighters from all the component parts of ISIS from new arrivals to veteran militants, and from the group's special forces and its elite commando units. Emni operatives are chosen by national origin and organized by language and assigned to small, discrete units whose members sometimes only meet one another only shortly before they are sent on their attacks.

HOW EMNI CONDUCTS ITS OPERATIONS

The Emni had a crucial role in ISIS terrorism operations. Its trainees led the Paris attacks and made the suitcase bombs used in the attacks on the Brussels airport terminal and subway station. The group has also sent its jihadists on Emni missions to nations such as Austria, Germany, Spain, Lebanon, Tunisia, Bangladesh, Indonesia and Malaysia. It is believed that nearly 30 Emni recruits were successfully deployed outside of ISIS controlled areas, and launched both successful attacks and attempted attacks that failed. Some of the militants formed sleeper cells.

Emni's European operatives use new converts to Islam as an intermediaries to connect individuals interested in conducting attacks with jihadists who convey instructions on several different matters including how to make a suicide vest to how to credit their violent actions to the ISIS.

ISIS recruits first go to a dormitory in Syria, near the Turkish border. In the bureaucratic intake process, the recruits interviewed, fingerprinted and undergo a physical examination. In the interview, the recruits provide their name, name of parents, where there parents are originally from, educational attainment, and future plans.

Originally, the Emni is responsible for ensuring internal security within the ISIS Dawla (state) and oversees "external security" by sending abroad people they recruited. The Emni also policed ISIS members, including conducting interrogations and rooting out spies. Beginning in 2014, the Emni coordinated terrorist attacks outside ISIS controlled territory, including the attack on the Bardo Museum in Tunis, Tunisia, and the shooter responsible for the attacks on a beach in Sousse, Tunisia, in June, 2015.

In terms of Asian recruits, the Emni focuses its recruitment efforts on jihadists who were veterans of Al-Qaeda's network in that area, especially in areas such as Bangladesh, Malaysia and Indonesia. Many Al-Qaeda members from these areas have become ISIS fighters.

The Emni keeps many of its operatives underground in Europe. They act as nodes that can remotely activate potential suicide attackers who have attracted by propaganda. Linking them are new converts to Islam with no established connections to radical groups. These people are not in direct contact with individuals who are conducting the attacks, because they know if these people start talking, they will get caught. They mostly use new converts to Islam, who contact with ISIS agents, and act as couriers. In the case of some videotaped pledges of allegiance to ISIS, the intermediary sends the video on to European handlers, who uploads it for use by ISIS for propaganda.

The Emni uses Europeans to assist in planning attacks. Several French and Belgian citizens were assigned "managing roles" in conducting the attacks. They are often given autonomy in determining tactics and strategy, even if the operation must receive approval from ISIS leaders.

Emni is also in charge of ISIS' "quwat khas" (special forces). The unit only admits single men who agreed not to marry during their training. In addition to providing the offensive force to infiltrate cities during battles, it was one of several elite units that became a recruiting pool for the external operations branch.

See also: Al-Qaeda (volume 1); Al-Qaeda in the Islamic Maghreb (volume 2); Islamic State of Iraq and Syria (volume 1).

Further Reading

Glass, Charles. *Syria Burning: ISIS and the Death of the Arab Spring.* New York: OR Books, 2015.

Hall, Benjamin. *Inside ISIS: The Brutal Rise of a Terrorist Army*. New York: Center Street, 2015.

Israeli, Raphael. *The Internationalization of ISIS: The Muslim State in Iraq and Syria*. New York: Routledge, 2017.

McCants, William F. *The ISIS Apocalypse: The History, Strategy, and Doomsday Vision of the Islamic State*. New York: Picador/St. Martin's Press, 2016.

Nance, Malcolm W. *The Terrorists of Iraq: Inside the Strategy and Tactics of the Iraq Insurgency 2003-2014*. Boca Raton, FL CRC Press, 2015.

Sekulow, Jay. *The Rise of ISIS: A Threat We Can't Ignore*. New York: Howard Books, 2015.

Stern, Jessica Stern and J.M. Berger. *ISIS: The State of Terror*. London: William Collins: HarperCollins, 2016.

Warrick, Joby. *Black Flags: The Rise of ISIS*. London: Gorgias Press, 2016.

Worth, Robert Forsyth. *A Rage for Order: The Middle East in Turmoil, from Tahrir Square to ISIS*. New York: Farrar, Straus and Giroux, 2017.

Chapter 34

FATAH AL-ISLAM/CONQUEST OF ISLAM

Established in November 2006 and once led by Shakir al-Abssi (1955-2008), Fatah al-Islam is a Sunni Islamist jihadist organization. This group is not affiliated with Al-Fatah or the Fatah Revolutionary Council (FRC). It was established by former members of Palestinian Fatah-Intifada, who had defected from the Palestinian Fatah (Palestinian National Liberation Movement).

Abssi had long supported or has been directly engaged in terrorist activities. Convicted in absentia, he received a capital sentence for conspiracy to assassinate Laurence Foley, a US diplomat in Jordan, in 2002. In 2003, al-Abssi began to attack the U.S. military in Iraq and collaborated with Al-Qaeda for over a decade. Al-Abssi, however, claimed that he had no connections with that terrorist group. Abssi reportedly collaborated with Abu Musab al-Zarqawi (1966-2006), Al-Qaeda in Iraq's (AQI) founder and one-time leader, who was killed in Iraq. Shortly after it was formed, Fatah al-Islam seized control of Nahr al-Bared, a northern Lebanon camp, from Fatah al-Intifada. The group reportedly had training camps in Jordan and Syria. Its membership reportedly is in the low hundreds and is largely composed of Lebanese, Palestinian, and Syrian Sunni extremists. Jihadist who fought against the United States and Coalition forces in Iraq also joined the Fatah al-Islam.

Fatah al-Islam seeks to: 1) destroy Israel, 2) remove all Western influence in the Middle East, 3) institute Sharia (Islamic law) throughout Lebanon, Syria, and Palestine, and, 4) to disseminate Islamist beliefs among Palestinians in Lebanon.

Constantly fighting with the Lebanese army, the group has attacked several civilian and political targets. On May 20, 2007, over 40 people were killed in fighting between Fatah al-Islam and Lebanese troops. This conflict was Lebanon's worst outbreak of violence since that country's civil war ended in 1990. The clashes ignited when Lebanese security forces investigating a bank robbery raided a residence near Tripoli. Fighters associated with Fatah al-Islam retaliated by seizing military positions at the Nahr al-Bared refugee camp. The Lebanese army then retaliated by sending in tanks against the militants.

On September 2, 2007, the Lebanese army captured the Fatah al-Islam camp at Nahr al-Bared after three months of conflict. These clashes killed 222 militants and several civilians. The group's actions also led to conflict and turmoil between other local groups and had led to further unrest in Lebanon and the Palestine territories. Al-Abssi fell from power as the leader of Fatah-al-Islam after the group lost its camp.

Syria allegedly financially supported Fatah al-Islam. After Abd al-Rahman had succeeded Al-Abssi, Saudi Arabia became the main sponsor of the group. In August 2010, al-Rahman died in a clash with the Lebanese military. This clash effectively destroyed Fatah al-Islam. Because of group's relative inactivity, several nations have delisted it from their terrorist watch lists by the fall of 2010.

The Lebanese government believed that Fatah al-Islam was connected with the Syrian intelligence services. Both the Syrian government and Fatah al-Islam denied any such association or collaboration.

See also: Al-Qaeda (volume 1); Al-Qaeda in Iraq (AQI) (volume 1).

FURTHER READING

Deeb, Marius. *Syria, Iran, and Hezbollah: the Unholy Alliance and Its War on Lebanon.* Stanford, California: Hoover Institution Press, 2013.

Frisch, Hillel. "Has the Israeli-Palestinian Conflict Become Islamic? Fatah, Islam, and the Al-Aqsa Martyrs' Brigades." *Terrorism and Political Violence* 17 no. 3 (2005): 391-406.

Haddad, Simon. "Fatah al-Islam in Lebanon: Anatomy of a Terrorist Organization." *Studies in Conflict & Terrorism* 33 no. 6 (2010): 548-69.

Sultan, Cathy. *Tragedy in South Lebanon the Israeli-Hezbollah War of 2006.* Minneapolis: Scarletta Press, 2008.

The Battle for Nahr al-Bared: Lebanon Takes on Fatah al-Islam. Coulsdon: Jane's Information Group, 2007.

Chapter 35

FIGHTING VANGUARDS OF THE MUJAHIDIN/ AL-TALAP AL-MUQATLLA

The Fighting Vanguards of the Mujahidin were a small number of jihadist members of the Syrian Muslim Brotherhood led by Marwan Hadid (1934-1970) during the late 1960s. Following Egypt's jihadists as a model, Hadid had joined militant Palestinians to overthrow King Hussein bin Talal (King Hussein of Jordan) (1934-1999) in the Jordanian civil war (September 1970 to June 1971, which jihadists refer to as "Black September"). The "Fighting Vanguards" are more extreme than the Brotherhood as the Vanguards as they perceive violence as the only way to achieve an Islamic state (caliphate).

The Vanguards were inspired by the writings of Sayyid Cutb (1906-1966), including Cutb's argument that the Muslim Brotherhood would eventually fail if it did not engage in jihad. While small, the Fighting Vanguards participated in several significant anti-Baathist attacks. Said Hawwa (1935-1999), the leading ideologue of the Muslim Brotherhood of Syria, supported the Vanguards. The group sponsored several anti-Baathist insurrections throughout the 1970s. Hadid ordered the assassinations of leading Baath authorities. The Baath government, in turn, blamed the Muslim Brotherhood for all the attacks conducted by the Vanguards. The Vanguards killed over 80 Alawi students at a military academy in Aleppo, Syria in 1979, leading the Syrian government to begin brutally suppressing the Brotherhood. Under intense pressure, the Brotherhood eventually supported the Vanguard-led uprising in Hama, a decision that proved to be a disaster for the Brotherhood and their near total eradication in Syria.

Hadid was captured in 1976 and died while incarcerated. The Vanguards continued its terrorist activities. In 1980, the fighting finally reached its height after a brief but brutal civil war in the north-central cities of Syria.

The conflict ended in a three-week siege in Hama in February 1982 during which government forces killed thousands of people and forced many Brotherhood supporters into exile. This clash essentially represented the end of the Muslim Brotherhood's presence in Syria. This also is why the Muslim Brotherhood has so little influence in the Syrian Civil War of 2013-present. The Syrian Muslim Brotherhood, unlike their Egyptian counterparts, had always lacked organization and structure. Most surviving Brotherhood leaders have not been in Syria for decades.

After the Hama Rising in 1982, Syrian security forces destroyed most of the Fighting Vanguard forces, then led by the charismatic ideologue, Adnall Uqla (1951-1982). The surviving Vanguard fighters became part of the National Islamic Front. Eventually, many of the Fighting Vanguards surrendered after accepting a general amnesty presented by the Syrian government.

Many Vanguard survivors of the 1982 Hama massacre relocated to Afghanistan, where the jihadists accepted and valued them for their fighting experience. One leading Vanguard member, Abu Mus'ab al-Suri (1958-) helped establish Al-Qaeda and later produced much of its propaganda.

Motivated by economic and political grievances, widespread corruption and a belief that contemporary Syrian society offers no hope or opportunity, many young Syrian Sunnis resorted to Islamism and jihadism. Aware that Islamism had a significant attraction, Bashar Assad (1965 -), who succeeded his father, Hafez Assad (1930-2000) in 2000, first attempted to co-opt and control Syrian Islamism. He devoted significant time and effort in mentoring religious leaders, controlling mosques, and ensuring that the growing number of Islamists complied with the regime's wishes. The younger Assad also financed religious institutions, created Islamic banks and reduced government regulations on public piety, including the wearing of headscarves in public buildings and prayer in the military. Bashar's conciliatory attitude towards Islam was a dramatic departure from the Baath Party's long-standing view that religion was politically deviant and that Islam is reactionary, as the Baath Party follows a Pan-Arab Socialist and secular political ideology.

As the current Syrian Civil War continues, global jihadists, radicalized by the failure of Hama uprising and continued government repression, returned to Syria for vengeance and to continue the battle began by the Vanguard to overthrow the Ba'ath party. The Ba'ath government had granted safe passage to many of these Jihadists through Syria to fight the US-led coalition forces in Iraq after 2003. The two Assad regimes fueled the rise of Syria's jihadist movement, which now threatens to destroy the current Assad government in the Syrian Civil War.

See also: Al-Qaeda (volume 1); Muslim Brotherhood (volume 1); Muslim Brotherhood in Jordan (volume 1); Muslim Brotherhood in Syria (volume 1).

FURTHER READING

Dam, Nikolaos. *The Struggle for Power in Syria Politics and Society under Assad and the Ba'th Party.* London: I.B. Tauris, 2011.

Khatib, Line, Raphaël Lefèvre and Jawad Qureshi. *State and Islam in Baathist Syria: confrontation or co-optation?*. Fife, Scotland: University of St Andrews Centre for Syrian Studies, 2012.

Krummrich, Seth. *Shaping Jihadism How Syria Molded the Muslim Brotherhood.* Fort Belvoir, VA: Defense Technical Information Center, 2007.

Lefervre, Raphaël. *Ashes of Hama: the Muslim Brotherhood in Syria.* New York, NY: Oxford University Press, 2013.

Lefervre, Raphaël. *The Muslim Brotherhood Prepares for a Comeback in Syria.* Washington, D.C.: Carnegie Endowment for International Peace, 2013.

Lund, Aron. *Struggling to Adapt: the Muslim Brotherhood in a New Syria.* Washington, D.C.: Carnegie Endowment for International Peace, 2013.

Pargeter, A. *The Muslim Brotherhood: From Opposition to Power* (New ed.). London: Saqi, 2013.

Chapter 36

FREEDOM AND JUSTICE PARTY (FJP) (EGYPT)

After Egyptian President Hosni Mubarak (1928-) fell from power in 2011 during the Arab Spring uprising in Egypt, several groups applied for and legal recognition as political parties, which allowed them to compete in elections. One of these groups was the Freedom and Justice Party (Hizb a/Horriya W'Aiaadald), the political branch of the Egyptian Muslim Brotherhood. The FJP stressed its commitment to good governance so as to allay public fears of political Islamism. As the largest and best organized of Egypt's political parties, the FJP converted its organizational strength into political success during the parliamentary elections in 2011-2012. Campaigning as the oldest and most established member of the "Democratic Alliance" of parties competing in the elections, the FJP won more than 43 percent of the Assembly's seats contested in that election, and over 58 percent of the contested seats in the Shura Council. FJP member Mohammed Saad Tawfik al·Katani (1952 -) was elected speaker of the Assembly, and FJP member Ahmed Fahmy became Shura Council speaker. In February 2012, the FJP nominated Muslim Brotherhood strategist Mohammad Khalrat al-Shater (1950-) as its candidate for the May 2012 presidential elections. Egypt's military government, however, rejected al-Shater's candidacy, compelling the FJP to name its chair Mohammed Morsi (1951-) to be its presidential candidate In early 2013 Saad Al-Katani was elected party chair. On August 9, 2014, Egypt's highest court dissolved the FJP and confiscated its assets.

Considering the Muslim Brotherhood's Islamist ideology, it was not surprising that the FJP supported the full implementation of Sharia Law (Islamic Law) as the foundation of national legislation. This would include impact economy and social freedoms. FJP party officials clearly stated that political freedom must comply with Sharia. The FJP's conservative positions on issues such as women's rights were one of many controversial stances.

The FJP, through its public statements and programs, sought to create a more tolerant public image of the party. In many of their statements, FJP officials often stated that the party sought to create a "civil state" that would allow freedom of religion. The FJP also claimed that they did not want either the military or Islamic clerics to run the government, but added that they would seek guidance in governance from the "objectives" of Sharia.

The FJP was advantaged by its connections to the Muslim Brotherhood, as the Brotherhood had been in existence for nearly a century and has a well-established network through which the FJP interfaces with the public. The Brotherhood under the Mubarak era was a fixture in society and attracted support as a populist alternative to the Egyptian government. The Brotherhood received much popular support as it provided many social services in Egypt, and had performed these functions since the 1930s.

When the FJP won the majority of seats in parliament and the presidential election it proceeded to draft a constitution. Critics charged that the new constitution was "undemocratic and too Islamist", and that it could allow clerics to intervene in the lawmaking process and leave minority groups without appropriate legal protection. This dispute stemmed from several new constitutional provisions on Islamic law. Similar to the existing 1971 constitution, the 2012 draft included Article 2, which states that Islamic principles are the main source for legislation. The draft, however, added Article 219, which provided that "The principles of Islamic Sharia include general evidence, foundational rules, rules of jurisprudence, and credible sources accepted in Sunni doctrines and by the larger community."

The FJP's insistence on implementing Sharia Law and its efforts to prohibit former New Democratic Party (NDP) members (supporters of the Mubarak government) to participate in politics contributed to a polarized and radicalized political system in Egypt. The ideological gulf between the FJP and the secular opposition parties continues to be vast. This grew worse by President Mohamed Morsi's ouster on July 3, 2013 and a proposed constitution that sought to make Islam the fundamental arbiter of all aspects of Egyptian society. For these reasons, many commentators blamed the FJP for the failure of Egypt's brief democratic experiment.

See also: Egyptian Salafist Movement (volume 1); Minor Egyptian Political Parties (volume 1); Muslim Brotherhood (volume 1).

FURTHER READING

Amin, Ğalāl Ahmad. *Egypt in the Era of Hosni Mubarak: 1981-2011*. Cairo, Egypt: American University in Cairo Press, 2011.

Arafāt, Alā' al-Dīn. *The Mubarak Leadership and Future of Democracy in Egypt*. New York: Palgrave Macmillan, 2009.

Arafāt, Alā' al-Dīn. *Hosni Mubarak and the Future of Democracy in Egypt*. New York: Palgrave Macmillan, 2011.

Deeb, Marius. *Party Politics in Egypt: The Wafd & its Rivals, 1919-1939*. London: Ithaca Press for the Middle East Centre, St Antony's College, Oxford, 1979.

Osman, Tarek. *Egypt on the Brink: From Nasser to Mubarak*. New Haven: Yale University Press, 2010.

Quraishi, Zaheer Masood. *Liberal Nationalism in Egypt: Rise and Fall of the Wafd party*. Allahabad: Kitab Mahal, 1967.

Rutherford, Bruce K. *Egypt After Mubarak: Liberalism, Islam, and Democracy in the Arab World*. Princeton: Princeton University Press, 2008.

Tadros, Mariz. *The Muslim Brotherhood in Contemporary Egypt: Democracy Defined or Confined?* London: Routledge, 2012.

Wickham, Carrie Rosefsky. *The Muslim Brotherhood: Evolution of an Islamist Movement*. Princeton: Princeton University Press, 2015.

Chapter 37

GREAT EASTERN ISLAMIC RAIDERS' FRONT (IBDA-C)/BUYUK DOGU ANINCILAR CEPHEST/ISLAMI/GREAT ISLAMIC EASTERN WARRIORS FRONT

A Sunni Salafist group, the Great Eastern Islamic Raiders' Front (IBDA-C) was a large radical Turkish Islamist extremist group that became formally organized in 1985. It was particularly active in and around Istanbul, where it attacked bars, discos, and churches.

The IBDA-C seeks to supplant the secular Turkish Republic with a caliphate that would govern Turkey according to Islamic Law and end what they considered the oppression of Muslims. Turkey became a secular republic with the election of Kemal Ataturk (1881-1938) as President in 1923. Turkey's Islamist political parties greatly grew in influence during the 1980s and 1990s. In 1994, The Islamist Welfare Party, became a part of Turkey's coalition government.

The IBDA-C became particularly well-known after conducting widespread demonstrations in Istanbul in 1989. In addition, IBDA-C had several bookstores, websites, and publishing houses.

The IBDA-C became increasingly violent at the beginning of the 1990s. Attacking secularist targets in Turkey, IBDA-C militants assassinated several journalists, politicians, and professors. The IBDA-C specifically attacked leftist, secular, and western targets. Virulently anti-Jewish and anti-Christian, it attacked churches and Jewish temples. The group also publicized a "hit list" of several Jews it was targetting. The group killed a well-known movie reviewer, and threatened a Turkish television reporter that the jihadist group believed was opposed to Islam. Other IBDA-C targets included discos, financial institutions, brothels, and bars, as well as symbols of Turkish historical secularism such as statues of Kemal Ataturk, the first president of the Turkish Republic. The group also bombed the Ecumenical Patriarchate Cathedral in Istanbul in 1997. The group also assassinated Ahmet Taner Kislali (1939 -1999) in 1999. Kislali was a former minister, professor, and journalist, who strongly criticized Islamic fundamentalism.

Group members organized independently within the IBDA-C framework. Group followers would form a team and conduct attacks without a centralized command and control system. Often, they work as teams of four or five people.

Turkey's secular government has long prosecuted and arrested IBDA-C militants. With the successful resolution of several terrorist cases, the Turkish government began to reduce the threat that the group poses.

Salih Izzet Erdis (Salih Mirzabeyoglu) (1950-), was the commander and leader of IBDA-C. Erdis was arrested on December 29, 1998 and later incarcerated. He stood trial for seeking to overthrow Turkey's secular government and replace it with Islamic law (Sharia). In 2002, Erdis received a death sentence for "the armed attempt to overthrow the constitutional order." Two of Erdis's codefendants received 18 year prison sentences. After Turkey abolished the death penalty, Erdis' sentence was commuted to life imprisonment.

After the convictions of these high-profile leaders, IBDCA-C still launched small-scale operations prior to becoming temporarily inactive.

In late November 2003, four attacks rocked Istanbul Turkey. There were suicide blasts at two synagogues that killed 25 people. Less than a week later, the main offices of HSBC were damaged when a truck loaded with explosives blew up. Shortly thereafter, another explosion occurred at the British consulate. At least 27 people died and another 400 were wounded in those attacks. The IBDCA-C, along with Al-Qaeda, announced they were responsible and vowed to continue additional attacks against the United States and its allies.

The group has since been revived, but does not appear to be as prominent as it once was. In 2015, one person was killed and three people were injured when a blast occurred at the offices of a magazine, *Adimlar (Steps)*, linked to the IBDCA-C. Both the United States and the European Union designate the IBDCA-C as a terrorist organization.

See also: Al-Qaeda (volume 1).

FURTHER READING

Kurkucu, Ertugrul. "The Crisis of the Turkish State." *Middle East Report* (April-June 1996): 2-7. Lapidot, Anat (Vol. 3, 1997). Islamic Activism in Turkey since the 1980 Military Takeover. *Terrorism and Political Violence*, 64 [Special Issue, Religious Radicalism in the Greater Middle East, ed. by Bruce Maddy-Weitzman and Efraim Inbar, 62-74].

Toprak, Binnaz. Religion as State Ideology in a Secular Setting: The Turkish-Islamic Synthesis, in, *Aspects of Religion in Secular Turkey*. Ed. Malcolm Wagstaff. Occasional Paper Series No. 40. Durham, UK: University of Durham, Center for Middle Eastern and Islamic Studies, 10, 1990.

Zubaida, Sami. "Turkish Islam and National Identity." *Middle East Report,* April-June 1996, 11.

Chapter 38

HAMAS

OVERVIEW

Hamas is an abbreviation for the formal name of the group, which is, *Harakat al-Muqawam al-Islamiyah* (the Islamic Resistance Movement). Hamas is also an Arab term for "zeal." This Palestinian Sunni Islamist movement was established shortly after the first Intifada began in December 1987. Led by Sheik Ahmed Yassin (1937-2004), the unrest began when seven Egyptian-based Muslim Brotherhood members organized regular protests against Israeli control of Palestinian territory.

GOALS OF HAMAS

Hamas opposes what it perceives as the secularization and Westernization of Arab society. It also seeks to become the sole internationally recognized representative of the Palestinian peoples. The Palestinian Liberation Organization (PLO) has held this status since it was conferred on PLO by Arab League in 1974.

Hamas seeks to end the Israeli occupation, destroy the nation of Israel (which Hamas describes as the "Zionist entity"), and replace it with an Islamist state in Palestine. To achieve these objectives, Hamas encourages and supports Palestinian jihadist efforts and believes that Palestinian self-determination is only achievable through violent jihad. Hamas adopted the principles of the PLO's National Charter of 1968, which asserts that relinquishing any part of Palestinian territory amounts to relinquishing a part of Islam.

In Article 8 of its charter, Hamas stresses that violent jihad is fundamentally crucial and religiously justified as resistance against Islam's enemies: "Allah is the target, the Prophet is its model, the Koran its constitution: Jihad is its path and death for the sake of Allah is the loftiest of its wishes."

To achieve its goals, Hamas pursues the following strategy: (1) social welfare work to generate popular support, (2) political activism within Palestinian political institutions, and (3) terrorist attacks against the Israeli military and civilians.

Hamas relies on grass-roots activism. Its guiding publications are the Hamas Charter, political memoranda, and communiqués. Hamas published several influential Islamist leaflets since the first Intifada began in 1987. The "Bayanat", two-page leaflets, popular among many Palestinians, advocate both martyrdom and jihad. These leaflets instruct Palestinians on violent protest, suicide bombings, and how to respond to Israeli attacks. While the Israeli Defense Force may easily destroy television and radio stations, Hamas has circumvented this problem by printing its messages and disseminating these massages by hand.

RISE OF HAMAS

Hamas justifies its existence because the PLO announced that it would accept a peace settlement with Israel beginning in the 1970s. During Iraq-Iran War (1980-1988), the Palestinians complained that both Arab and the international community were ignoring Palestinian grievances. Hamas also opposed the US-Israeli strategic cooperation agreement (agreed to in 1981), and various Israeli actions in the 1980s, including annexing the Golan Heights, Israel's destruction of an Iraqi nuclear reactor, and its invasion of Lebanon in 1982. Hamas argued that the Islamist movement in Palestine confronted two major challenges. The first was prioritizing the Palestinian cause among the most important of Arab concerns. Second, Hamas argued that the PLO's shift from armed struggle (jihad) to accepting a settlement that Islamists opposed was unacceptable and ineffective. Thus, Hamas argued, Palestinian militancy (jihad) was necessary. The first such Palestinian uprising was the Usrat al-Jihad in 1981, which Sheikh Ahmad Yassin modeled the uprising he led in 1983.

Ahmad Yassin both directed and controlled Hamas's Intifada attacks. Before he was assassinated, Yassin also authored much of the group's propaganda. Under one interpretation of events, Hamas is said to perceive the Palestinian conflict as a narrow religious struggle between Judaism and Islam. Hamas's role in the Israeli-Palestinian conflict, however, is more complicated. Hamas uses Islamic rhetoric to agitate the Palestinians and to oppose official Palestinian and Arab organizations for either negotiating or supporting negotiations with Israel. Over time, however, Hamas has went through a political evolution and no longer justifies its movement in purely ideological-religious terms, e.g., a struggle between Muslims and Jews (or Christians).

Hamas' political position on Israel has also evolved somewhat. Currently, Hamas distinguishes between the religion of Judaism and the movement of "Zionism". Hamas, however, continues to assert that Israeli state is a major foe of all Arabs and Muslims, as well as all Palestinians.

AHMED YASSIN AND THE FOUNDING OF HAMAS

Hamas was originally an adjunct of the Muslim Brotherhood. In 1972, Israel allowed the Brotherhood to create an Islamic charitable organization in Israeli-controlled areas. Later in 1972, Ahmed Yassin was elected to lead the group in the disputed territories. Yassin was injured at age 16 in a sporting accident and later was reportedly wounded in a bomb explosion. Confined to a wheelchair, he was employed as a teacher before the Israeli government terminated him for anti-government activities. He then raised farm animals to support his wife and 11 children.

Yassin was arrested in 1983 for allegedly forming an armed militia within the Muslim Brotherhood and convicted of maintaining a large cache of weapons in his home. His 13-year sentence was reduced and he was freed in a 1985 exchange of prisoners. In October 1991, Yassin received a life sentence for approving the killing of several Palestinians suspected of collaborating with Israel. Charges that he planned and carried out the kidnapping and murder of two Israeli soldiers were withdrawn in a plea bargain. Under Yassin and his colleagues, Hamas grew rapidly throughout the disputed territories.

THE HAMAS CHARTER

The Hamas charter (issued on August 18, 1988) demanded "the liberation of Palestine in its entirety, from the (Mediterranean) sea to the (Jordan) river." In a leaflet distributed in October 1990, Hamas said that "every Jew is a settler, and it is our obligation to kill him."

In addition to its political objectives, Hamas advocates social policies requiring strict adherence to Sharia (Islamic law). It opposes the use of drugs, alcohol, corruption, bribery, and prostitution. Hamas claims that it favors Christians, Jews and Muslim peacefully co-existing within an Islamic state. Christians and Jews, however. would be required to abide by Sharia.

FUNDING HAMAS

Hamas is funded mainly from the "zaka," which is a 2.5 percent tax on its follower's income. Critics allege that Hamas uses physical intimidation to force businesses and employees to pay the tax, whether or not they are Hamas supporters. Hamas is also funded through religious donations from Islamist sympathizers in the Persian Gulf states and Saudi Arabia. Saudi Arabia also provides significant financial assistance to Hamas and ideologically influences the group. In addition to purchasing weapons and paying its "enforcers," Hamas uses its funds to help the poor, and establishing special charities, medical clinics, mosques and orphanages.

HAMAS SUPPORTERS

While Hamas fighters are usually jobless young men, Hamas leaders are professionals such as doctors, lawyers, professors, and, engineers. They are also knowledgeable about the Quran and Muslim religious practices. Hamas also receives significant political support from Palestinian professional associations, business associations, and labor organizations.

Al-Qassam, Hamas' military wing, controls the people under its sway through terror by killing suspected Palestinian collaborators, prostitutes, and drug dealers. Formally known as the Martyr Sheikh Al Ezz-Edin al-Qassam military unit, it often attacks Israelis and Israeli government targets. Al-Qassam targets and kills Jewish civilians as well as those serving in the Israeli military.

THE HAMAS CHARTER

The Hamas Charter discusses interactions with Palestine jihadist groups, focusing more in moral rather than, political terms. The Hamas Charter asserts that Hamas and all Palestinian movements mutually respect each other, so as long as they do not ally themselves either with the "Communist East" or the "Crusading West," or cooperate with the Israeli government in the disputed territories. Hamas initially expressed some reservations in its Charter in recognizing the PLO. Because the PLO agreed to both the Oslo and Cairo Agreements, Hamas accused the PLO of capitulating and further asserted that the PLO no longer truly represented the Palestinian people or their aspirations. Hamas claimed that its attacks were directed at the PLO's corrupt and imperialist leadership, rather than against its members or the movement.

Although the Hamas Charter described the PLO membership as being "as close as it could be to the Islamic Resistance Movement, Hamas denounced the PLO's "secularist approach," while also attempting to leave room for some future reconciliation. "The day that the PLO shall adopt Islam as a way of life, we shall be its soldiers and fodder for the flame with which it shall consume the enemy."

HAMAS AND THE POLITICAL NATIONAL COUNCIL

From the mid-to-late 1990s, some degree of representative democracy began to emerge in the Palestinian territories after the PLO established the Palestinian National Council (PNC). The Hamas leadership sought to adapt to changed circumstances to retain political power and influence. Hamas, thus, demanded four conditions before it would consider participating in the PNC including that: the PLO had to cease making concessions; that the "Zionist" presence in any part of Palestine be deemed as illegitimate; that Palestinian organizations be given seats commensurate with the size of their membership; and that their version of "genuine democracy" be implemented.

RELATIONS BETWEEN HAMAS AND THE PLO

Hamas and the PLO adhere to very different ideologies. While the PLO is a secular organization, Hamas ideology integrates Islamist religiosity and Palestinian nationalism. Hamas also seeks to form a caliphate (i.e., a government formed under the strict interpretation of Sharia or Islamic Law). Many Palestinians believe that Hamas functions more efficiently and effectively than the bureaucratized and structured PLO. Also, the PLO leadership is widely perceived as corrupt. Hamas, like the Egyptian Muslim Brotherhood, has a leadership that many Palestinians perceive as being effective, "pure", and honest.

See also: Muslim Brotherhood (volume 1).

FURTHER READING

Ahmad, Hisham. *Hamas – From Religious Salvation to Political Transformation: The Rise of Hamas in Palestinian Society*. Jerusalem: PASSIA, 1994.

Azza, Abdullah Abu. *The Islamic Movements in the Arab Counties*. Kuwait: Al-Qalam Publishing House, 1992.

Barguthi, Iyad. *The Islamization and Politics of the Palestinian Occupied Lands.* Jerusalem: Markaz al-Zahra' lil-Dirasat wal-Abhath, 1990.

Beinin, Joel and Lisa Hajjar. Palestine, Israel and Arab-Israeli Conflict: A Primer." *Middle East Research & Information Project* 2009, 9-12.

Da'na, Seif. "Islamic Resistance in Palestine: Hamas, the Gaza War and the Future of Political Islam." *Holy Land Studies* 8 no. 2 (2009): 211-28.

El-Awaisi and Abd al-Fattah. *The Muslim Brotherhood's Conception of the Palestine Question*. Cairo: Islamic House of Publishing and Distribution, 1989.

El Husseini, Rola. "Hezbollah and the Axis of Refusal: Hamas, Iran, and Syria." *Third World Quarterly* 31, no. 5 (2010): 803-15.

Frisch, Hillel. "The Evolution of Palestinian Nationalist Islamic Doctrine: Territorializing a Universal Religion." *Canadian Review in Nationalism,* 21, no. 1-2 (1994): 51-53.

Getler, Michael. "The Language of Terrorism." *Washington Post,* Sep. 21, 2003.

Jad, Isiah. "Islamist Women of Hamas: Between Feminism and Nationalism." *Inter-Asia Cultural Studies* 12, no. 2 (2011): 176-201.

Kjorlien, M.I. "Hamas in Theory and Practice." *Arab Studies Quarterly,* 1 and 2 (1993): 4-7.

Litvak, Meir. "The Islamization of Palestinian Identity: The Case of Hamas." *Middle Eastern Studies* 34, no. 1 (1998): 148-63.

McVittie, Chris; Andy McKinlay and Rahul Sambaraju. "Social Psychology, Religion, and Inter-Group Relations: Hamas Leaders' Media Talk About Their Vision for the Future." *Journal of Community & Applied Social Psychology* 21, no. 6 (2011): 515-27.

Pascovich, Eyal. "Social-Civilian Apparatuses of Hamas, Hizballah, and Other Activist Islamic Organizations." *Digest of Middle East Studies* 21, no. 1 (2012): 126-48.

Pelletiere, Stephen C. *Hamas and Hezbollah: The Radical Challenges to Israel in the Occupied Territories*. Carlisle, PA: U.S. Army War College: Strategic Studies Institute, 1994.

Rowley, Charles K. and Jennis Taylor. "The Israel and Palestine Land Settlement Problem, 1948-2005: An Analytical History." *Public Choice* (2006): 78-81.

Sahliyeh, Emile. *In Search of Leadership: West Bank Politics Since 1967*. Washington, DC: Brookings, 1988.

Satloff, Robert. "Islam in the Palestinian Uprising." *Policy Focus, The Washington Institute for Near East Policy, No. 7.* Washington, D.C.: Washington Institute for Near East Policy, 1988.

Sayigh, The. "The Armed Struggle and Palestinian Nationalism," 23-25, in Avraham Sela and Moshe Ma'oz, *The PLO and Israel: From Armed Conflict to Political Solution, 1964-1994*. New York: St. Martin's Press, 1997.

Schiff, Ze'ev and Ehud Ta'ariu. *Intifada: The Palestinian Uprising – Israel's Third Front*. New York: Simon and Schuster, 1989.

Sivan, Emmanuel. *Radical Islam.* New Haven, Conn.: Yale University Press, 1985.

Steinberg, Matti. The PLO and Palestinian Islamic Fundamentalism, *Jerusalem Quarterly* 52 (1989): 37-54.

Taleghani, Mahmud. *Society and Economics in Islam*. Berkeley: Mizan Press, 1982.

Chapter 39

HAMAS IRAQ HAMAS IN IRAQ/HAMAS (IRA)/ISLAMIC RESISTANCE MOVEMENT HAMAS, IRAQ: AL FATAH AL ISLAMY BRIGADES

OVERVIEW

Hamas Iraq is a Nationalist Sunni Jihadist group based in Iraq, which defected from the 1920 Revolution Brigade in 2007. The group is vehemently anti-American and is strongly opposed to the United States. Hamas Iraq is relatively inclusive in its Islamist ideology. For example, it believed that Sunni Jihadists must collaborate with Shiite organizations to ensure the eradication of foreign influence in Iraq. Thus, Hamas has opposed either indiscriminate violence or violent attacks against civilians based on their ethnic or sectarian affiliations.

Hamas Iraq is unaffiliated with Hamas in either Palestine or Kurdistan. Hamas Iraq, however, claims to have been influenced by jihadist movements in Palestine, particularly Hamas. Hamas Iraq modeled from Hamas Movement in Palestine: its jihadist tactics, how it frames and implements its political agenda, avoids unnecessary conflicts, and resolves internal disagreements.

EMERGENCE OF HAMAS

In 2007. Hamas joined a political council of other Islamist jihadist organizations seeking the removal of the foreign military forces assisting the Iraq government. Hamas' defected from the 1920 Revolutionary Brigade after the killing of Harith Fhar al-Dari (1941-2015), spiritual leader of that group. Al-Qaeda in Iraq (AQI) militants reportedly killed Dari in an ambush.

Approximately at the same time of Dari's death, AQI conducted a chorine gas attack in the vicinity of Fallujah. Hamas joined the Brigade in denouncing the attack. Following Dari's death and the chlorine attack, two factions arose and splintered the Brigade, as they had clashing visions for group's future. While one faction sought to fight AQI directly and possibly cooperate with the US supported Sons of Iraq. The rival faction wanted to continue to fight against the US military and take a more passive, rhetorical approach to opposing AQI.

The second faction defected from the Revolutionary Brigade in March 2007 and renamed itself Hamas Iraq (also known as Hamas in Iraq or Iraqi Hamas). The Brigade then asserted that Hamas Iraq was assisting US troops in their military operations in Diyala Province against AQI.

On July 2, 2007, Hamas Iraq joined with the Islamic Front for the Iraq Resistance and Reformation and Jihad Front (RJF), a coordinating body composed of Ansar al Sunnah Sharia, the Mujahedeen Army, and the Islamic Army in Iraq, to form a new coordinating body known as the Political Council for the Iraqi Resistance (PCIR).

The PCIR presented a political agenda that included freeing Iraq of any foreign military presence, rejecting cooperation with those involved in the political institutions established during the US administration of Iraq, and the abrogation of all agreements and laws entered into by such institutions. Furthermore, the PCIR sought to work with other Shia and Sunni rejectionist groups to establish an ad-hoc technocratic government that would assume power after a US military withdrawal. The PCIR, however, never appeared entered to enter into negotiations with any of the rejectionist groups.

Although the PCIR did not negotiate with the US government, Hamas Iraq appeared to have cooperated with the US government in its offensive in the Diyala Province against AQI and 1920 Revolutionary Brigade both accused Hama Iraq of collaborating with US military forces in Diyala. Hamas Iraq denied all allegations of cooperating with the occupiers vowed that it would never do so.

Hamas Iraq largely diminished in importance between 2009 and 2013, with many of its members apparently joining the Sunwa Movement, a US supported tribal force fighting AQI beginning in 2008.

Although Hamas Iraq has purportedly increased its activities since the Sunni insurgency began in 2013, little is known about the group's current status or activities. Nonetheless, it remains an active organization.

TARGETS AND TACTICS

From 2007 through 2009, Hamas Iraq primarily targeted US forces in Iraq. Since 2013, the group appears to have mostly targeted the Iraqi government, although some have speculated that Hamas actually cooperated with the Iraqi Army to confront ISIS. Although Hamas Iraq denounced sectarian violence on several occasions and criticized AQI for targeting Shiite civilians, the group has often targeted Shiite militias, based on claims that they were legitimate targets because of their cooperation with the US-supported Iraqi government.

RESOURCES

Hamas Iraq claims that it is the only contemporary jihadist group unassisted by any government. Its leadership also claim they rejected offers of assistance from the Iranian government for funding and arms.

POLITICAL ACTIVITIES

Hamas Iraq relations with the Iraqi Islamic Party (IIP), the largest Sunni political party in Iraq, has been a contentious issue. While some commentators claimed that Hamas Iraq is an armed branch of the IIP, other commentators have claim that the two groups merely cooperate with each other, while still others assert that there is no connection between the two organizations.

See also: 1920 Revolutionary Brigade (volume 1); Al-Qaeda (volume 1); Al Qaeda in Iraq (volume 1); Islamic State of Iraq and Syria (volume 1).

FURTHER READING

Atwan, Abdel Bari. *The Secret History of Al-Qaeda*. London: Saqi, 2012.
Bonner, Michael David. *Jihad in Islamic History: Doctrines and Practice*. Princeton: Princeton University Press, 2006.
Drake, Laura. *Hegemony and its Discontents: United States Policy Toward Iraq, Iran, Hamas, the Hezbollah and Their Responses*. Annandale, VA: United Association for Studies and Research, 1997.
Dunning, Tristan. *Hamas: Jihad and Popular Legitimacy: Reinterpreting Resistance in Palestine*. Taylor and Francis, 2016.
Hokayem, Emile. *Syria's Uprising and the Fracturing of the Levant*. Abingdon: Routledge for the International Institute for Strategic Studies, 2017.
Levitt, Matthew. *Hamas: Politics, Charity, and Terrorism in the Service of Jihad*. New Haven: Yale University Press, 2007.
Naylor, David H. *Al- Qaeda in Iraq*. New York: Nova Science, 2009.
Roy, Olivier *The Politics of Chaos in the Middle East*. New York: Columbia University Press, 2009.

Chapter 40

HAQ MOVEMENT FOR LIBERTY AND DEMOCRACY

Shia Arabs represent a majority of Bahrain's population. Since the 1990s, there have been several outburst of violence against alleged discrimination against the Shias by Bahrain's Sunni ruling family. During the 1990s, Shia protests shook the nation and forty people died in the unrest.

Formed in 2005, the Haq Movement presents itself as a movement that seeks "awareness, nationalism, sovereignty, independence, and legitimacy" (As-Safir, 2013). Haq is a Bahraini Shia opposition group currently led by Shia Cleric Hasan Mushaima. Mushaima received a life sentence for attempting to depose the Bahraini government.

Many Haq members formerly belonged to the Al-Wefaq Nation Islamic Society and the National Democratic Action Society. Hasan has served as its secretary-general of Haq since it was created. Sheikh Jalil al-Singace, a prominent Sunni cleric, also became influential in the movement. Haq was formed after several radical leaders who defected from the Al-Wefaq party. Wefaq boycotted Bahrain's first election in 2002 to protest the parliament's limited powers but participated in the 2006 elections. Wefaq, like Haq, has strong support from Iran.

Rejecting Al-Wefaq's approach of working through the nation's parliamentary political process. Haq claims that Al-Wefaq policies legitimize the Bahraini government. Haq, thus, instead focuses on organizing riots and mass protests. Haq claims that its main goal is to achieve a more democratic Bahraini state. In so doing so, it rejects Al-Wefaq's more sectarian strategy. Some Bahraini and US government sources, however, dismiss these criticisms and claim that Haq merely is the representative of Iranian political interests in Bahrain.

Haq disputed the legitimacy of the king's reform process and opposed the 2002 Bahraini constitution because King Hamad ibn Isa al-Khali-fa abused and exceeded his power in creating it. In 2001, voters approved a referendum approving Bahrain's structure of government. Over 98 percent of the voters approved the reforms proposed in the National Action Charter.

On November 15, 2006, Haq complained to the United Nations that secret government committees were organized specifically to manipulate both municipal and parliamentary elections in Bahrain. Haq requested a formal inquiry into the allegations. Salah al-Bandar alleged that the granting of citizenship had become a highly selective process intended to manipulate Bahrain's demographics.

In December 2007, Shia youths fought with security forces in response to the death of a man at an earlier demonstration. Four people were injured in that violence. Ali Jassem was killed after inhaling tear gas and attacking a police officer. At Jassem's wake, riot police confronted 1500 mourners. The government said that the security forces only acted after demonstrators when they began destroying public and private property. The protestors claimed that security forces were firing indiscriminately with rubber bullets and tear gas.

Four years, Some Haq Movement leaders were targeted in a security clampdown in August 2011. The Bahraini government claimed that it had discovered a conspiracy involving those who sought to forcefully overthrow the government. Also in 2011, the Haq Movement joined the "Coalition for a Republic" that sought to end the monarchy. Many commentators blame the Coalition for causing the government to suppress dissent in 2011 and damaging chances for a political solution to Bahrain's crisis.

Some observers believe that the Leaders of the Haq Movement have long-standing connections with Iran, either to its government or to its clerical leadership. They also claim that Iran had influence unrest in the nation.

See also: Al-Wefaq (volume 1); Muslim Brotherhood (volume 1).

FURTHER READING

Afza, Talat & Rashid, Muhammad Amir. Marginalized Women Social Well-being Enterprise Development: A Glimpse of Remote Women Status in Pakistan. *Journal of Chinese Entrepreneurship, 1*(3), (2009): 248-267.
"Bahrain Arrests Four More Shiite Activists as Elections Near." *The Daily Star (Beirut, Lebanon)*, Aug. 19, 2010.
"Bahrain Charges 23 with Bid to Oust Government." *Times of Oman (Muscat, Oman)*, Sep. 5, 2010.
"Bahrain Presses Terror Charges Against Opposition Leaders." *Daily News Egypt*, Sep. 5, 2010.
"Bahraini Protesters Move to Parliament Building." *Kippreport*, Feb. 28, 2011.
"Bahrain Says Shi'ite Figures Plotted Overthrow." *Kippreport*, Sep. 5, 2010.
"Exiled Bahraini Opposition Leader Home after Beirut Arrest." *The Daily Star (Beirut, Lebanon)*, Sep. 5, 2010.
Gengler, Justin. *Group Conflict and Political Mobilization in Bahrain and the Arab Gulf: Rethinking the Rentier State,* Bloomington, Ind.: Indiana Univ. Press, 2015.
Gresh, Geoffrey F. "A Light Footprint in Bahrain," in, *Gulf Security and the U.S. Military Regime Survival and the Politics of Basing."* Stanford, California: Stanford University Press, 2015, 91-116.
Hunter, Shireen. *The Politics of Islamic Revivalism: Diversity and Unity.* Bloomington: Indiana University Press, 1988.
Is Bahrain Next? (2013). Retrieved July 25, 2017, from http://www.al-monitor.com/pulse/politics/2013/07/bahrain-opposition-tamarrud-protests-august-14.html.
Lour, Laurence. "The Political Impact of Labor Migration in Bahrain," *City & Society 20, no. 1* (2008): 32-53.
Matthiesen, Toby. *Sectarian gulf: Bahrain, Saudi Arabia, and the Arab Spring That Wasn't.* Stanford, Calif.: Stanford Briefs, an imprint of Stanford University Press, 2013.

Nuruzzaman, Mohammed. "Politics, Economics and Saudi Military Intervention in Bahrain." *Journal of Contemporary Asia 43, no.* 2 (2013): 363-378.

Pandya, Sophia. *Muslim Women and Islamic Resurgence: Religion, Education, and Identity Politics in Bahrain*. London; New York: I.B. Tauris, 2012.

"Sectarian Bad Blood; Iraq, Bahrain and the Region (Sunnites and Shiites)," *The Economist*, Apr. 2, 2011.

"Shiite Groups in Bahrain Call for Setting Up of a Republic." *The Daily Star (Beirut, Lebanon),* Mar. 9, 2011.

Chapter 41

Hayat Thahrir al-Sham (Liberation of al-Sham Commission) (HTS)

On January 28, 2017, Hayat Thahrir al-Sham (HTS) was initially formed by five rebel factions in Syria's Civil War: JFS, Harkat Nour al-Din al Zinki, Liwa al-Haq, Liwa Ansar al-Din, and Jaish al-Sunna. HTS is not like Jaish al-Fatah in that the factions that comprise HTS do not retain a nominal separate identity. To the contrary, the organizations that comprise HTS officially dissolved, and became a part of the new group. In early 2017, HTS had tens of thousands of fighters. Some estimates at the time placed the figure at approximately 31,000. After HTS was created, it and Ahrar al-Sham became the two major Sunni rebel groups in Syria, with the exception of ISIS. A large number of Ahrar al-Sham fighters also defected to HTS.

The emergence HTS presented several advantages for Al-Qaeda. Al Qaeda now had a larger coalition with tens of thousands of fighters who were indoctrinated to its ideology and outlook

When Hayat Thahrir al-Sham (HTS) collaborated with Harakat Nour al-Zinki, a faction in Aleppo that was reputed to be particularly efficient, and maintained an authoritarian management of the life of civilians.

HTS established a dar al-qada [court] that was once active and "authoritative in Northwestern Syrian. In all of the HTS areas, including its stronghold, the group was never able to administer activities by itself. The HTS was never like ISIS in that it never sought to or was able to set up an all-encompassing totalitarian society, so governance of territory was shared with other groups in territory under its control. In areas where HTS was active, its efforts had been most complementary to parallel to other opposition civilian organizations. The result was often an imperfect division of responsibilities, in which HTS operates the courts and law enforcement, and mostly leave local councils, political civil society organizations, and charitable organizations to serve civilian population to keep these areas livable. HTS was even forced to discontinue efforts to impose its will on towns in rural western Aleppo because relief groups decline to collaborate with urban areas connected with the "Public Services Administration." The relief groups stressed they would only work with civilian local councils, because they were the accepted local partner and implementer.

In areas such as rural Western Idlib, where HTS had more control, and marginalized other opposition groups, foreign relief largely sustained the civilian population. HTS was forced to

HTS was depended on Idlib and its vicinity. Generally, HTS's dependence on this small geographic area primarily meant that the group's viability was to be determined by Idlib and the ability or inability of the regime to gain more territory within the province.

Within the region, HTS retains a strong place in the opposition to Assad, which make. HTS dominated and consumed the rest of the opposition in in Northwestern Syria is problematic because if HTS is viewed as the only form of opposition governance in Idlib, civilian relief and stabilization could be endangered.

In the end, HTS lacked the resources and the capacity to sustain the rebel-held Northwestern Syria, centered on Idlib, unilaterally, either militarily or in the governance or humanitarian terms.

Chapter 42

HEZBOLLAH IN LEBANON

Hezbollah (or "Party of God") is a Shiite Muslim political party and jihadist group. The group seeks to capture Jerusalem, destroy Israel, and establish an Islamic state in Lebanon. Hezbollah is officially listed as a terrorist group by the Gulf Arab nations, Israel, the European Union, and the United States because it is deemed to threaten stability in the Middle East. Hezbollah bases its ideology on martyrdom and jihad.

Iran provides Hezbollah with significant funding, ideological inspiration, and logistical assistance. With its ideology formed in the Shia Islamist revival of the 1960s and 1970s, Lebanese Shiite clerics formed Hezbollah after Israel invaded Lebanon in 1982 during the Civil War in Lebanon (1975 and 1990). While Israel had sought to destroy the Palestinian insurgency in southern Lebanon, the conflict instead inspired many other disaffected Shiites to seek an Iranian-style theocracy through force. US Marine and Israeli military presence in Lebanon during the early 1980s also reportedly increased Hezbollah's popularity.

Hezbollah primarily operates in Shiite-majority areas, such as the southern outskirts of Beirut, the Bekka Valley, and the south of Lebanon. It later formed small groups worldwide. Strongly supported by the Iranian and Syrian governments, Hezbollah operates like an independent government within Lebanon. The group has its own military, political, and social service networks within that nation. Hezbollah's major foreign policy objectives are to oppose Israel and Western power and influence in the Middle East. The group represents Iranian interests and won support from some non-Shiites as well (at least until the Syrian Civil War).

For much of Lebanon's history, Shiite Muslims have historically been that country's least influential religious group. During the 1970s, Amal had represented Lebanese Shiites. Amal was considered more secular and moderate than Hezbollah. After the Islamic revolution in Iran in 1979, and the Israeli incursion into Lebanon in 1982, several Lebanese Shiite clerics established Hezbollah to force Israel to retreat from Lebanon and to establish an Islamic state. Many of Amal's more alienated, younger, and radical members joined Hezbollah.

Hezbollah became the major source of terrorism against the West and particularly against the United States during the 1980s. Ahmad Qasir, the first suicide bomber affiliated with Hezbollah, killed himself and 76 Israeli officers in the Israeli military headquarters in Tyre on November 11, 1982. Hezbollah commemorates this day as "Martyrdom Day" in Qasir's honor.

Hezbollah's role as the leading Shiite militant resistance group was greatly enhanced by the group's suicide attacks of the US embassy and US Marine barracks in Beirut in October 1983. Almost 260 American military personnel were lost in that attack. After these attacks, President Ronald Reagan, withdrew the Marines who had served with the UN peacekeeping mission in Lebanon. Hezbollah hijacked TWA Flight 847 in 1985, kidnapped 18 Americans in Lebanon during the 1980s and 1990s, and the bombing of an Argentine-Jewish corporation in Buenos Aires in July 1994. Hezbollah also conducted a bombing that killed US personnel in Torrejon, Spain in April 1984. During the war in Southern Lebanon between 1985 and 2000, Hezbollah conducted countless rocket attacks against Israeli civilians, which killed or injured many of them.

During the 1980s, Hezbollah repeatedly attacked Israel and fought Amal in the Lebanon civil war. Hezbollah also has often used terrorist tactics such as kidnappings and car bombings, most often directed against Western interests.

Hezbollah issued its first manifesto in 1985, which swore Hezbollah's loyalty to Iran's supreme leader, Ayatollah Ruhollah Khomeini; urged the establishment of an Islamic state; and called for the expulsion of the United States, France, and Israel from Lebanese territory, and for the destruction of the Israeli state. The manifesto further states:

> "Our primary assumption in our fight against Israel states that the Zionist entity is aggressive from its inception and built on lands wrested from their owners, at the expense of the rights of the Muslim people. Therefore, our struggle will end only when this entity is obliterated. We recognize no treaty with it, no cease-fire, and no peace agreements, whether separate or consolidated." (Rabinovich and Reinharz, 2007)

In declaring that it sought an Islamic state based on Sharia law, Hezbollah expressed its opposition to the existing Lebanese government. From 1988 through 1990, Hezbollah and the Amal Party fought each other. The former enjoyed both military and political successes in its attempts to overthrow the Lebanese government and implement Sharia.

The 1989 Taif Accord, which ended Lebanon's civil war, called for disarming the militias. Hezbollah renamed its military wing as an "Islamic Resistance" force dedicated to ending Israel's occupation, which allowed it to retain its weapons.

Hezbollah preaches a strong adherence to the Quran and uses Quranic concepts and justifications in its political propaganda. Hezbollah differentiates between those who adhere to tawhid (oneness of Allah), Sharia (Islamic law), and the divine governance of Allah (hakilni-yu) as opposed to those who do not (Hizb-al-Shaytan) (Party of Satan). Those considered belonging to the "Hizb-al-Shaytan" hold beliefs supposedly consistent with (unbelief), the laws of human governance, and paganism.

Many fundamentalists argue that many Muslims belonging to "Hizb-al-Shaytan" because they believe in a society based on man's law and do not adhere to Sharia. Since members of "Hizb-al-Shaytan" live an un-Islamic lifestyle, are considered to be in state of dar al-harb (abode of war), and thus, a jihad is justified against them.

Only a small group of Islamic scholars (umla) who are considered to be the most learned men of Islam may issue Quranic interpretations. This practice follows Shiite tradition in which average Muslims may not interpret the Quran. Hezbollah members believe that the ulama framework will glorify Islam. An umla (a leading scholar) leads the ulama and then directs the people. The means by which an act is performed, however, is delegated to the people's discretion.

The Majlis-al-Shura (the Consultative Council), consisting of seven members, leads Hezbollah. The council is chaired by Hezbollah's top commander, Hasan Nasrallah. Muhammad Hillsayn Failjallah is Hezbollah's spiritual leader.

Nasrallah has been Hezbollah's general secretary since 1992. He succeeded one of Hezbollah's founders, Abbas al-Musawi. Nasrallah was a former member of al-Dawa al-Islamiya (The "Islamic Call"), a jihadist organization that followed Mohammed Baqir al-Sadr, the leading Iraqi cleric. Dawa was also considered an ideological predecessor of Hezbollah. Major Hezbollah leaders also include Naim Qassem, a top lieutenant, and Hussein al-Khalil, Nasrallah's political advisor.

Nasrallah oversees five sub-councils: 1) the political assembly, 2) the jihad assembly, 3) the parliamentary assembly, 4) the executive assembly, and 5) the judicial assembly. Hezbollah also has committees on: ideology, information, finance, judicial affairs, military affairs, political affairs, and social affairs.

Hezbollah believes that al-jihad al-akhar (the greater struggle) provides a greater service to Islam. With beliefs based on orthodox Shiite traditions. Hezbollah members believe that peace and unity will arrive with the return of the twelfth -Imam, the Mahdi. This event would then lead to a revolution of the Islamic order.

For more than two decades, Imad Fayez Mugniyah was believed to be Hezbollah's chief architect of global terrorist operations. Mugniyah joined the group early in its history and rapidly became a senior leader. He was killed in a car bombing in Damascus in February 2008, which Hezbollah officials blamed on Israel. The Israeli government denied involvement in the attack.

After the Syrian military intervened in Lebanon in 1990, Hezbollah continued terrorist operations in South Lebanon. It also became actively involved in Lebanese politics. In 1992, Hezbollah participated in national elections for the first time.

After Israeli forces withdrew from Lebanon in 2000, Hezbollah was credited for that withdrawal. The group refused to disarm, which it justified based on Israel's continuing presence in disputed areas. Instead of disarming, Hezbollah continued to strengthen its military arm. Its military capabilities eventually exceeded those of the Lebanese army in some areas.

Hezbollah demonstrated its military capabilities against Israel in the 2006 war. On July 12, 2006, Hezbollah, attempting to pressure Israel into releasing three Lebanese terrorists jailed in Israeli prisons, attacked Israel, killed several Israeli soldiers and abducted two. These developments led Israel to begin a major military action against Hezbollah. In the 34-day conflict between Hezbollah and Israel, more than 1,000 Lebanese were killed, and more than a million others were made homeless. Because they fought the Israeli army to a stalemate, which no other Arab militia had previously accomplished—Hezbollah and its leader, Hassan Nasrallah, became heroes to many Arabs. This war also emboldened Hezbollah. Although it has significantly upgraded and expanded its military arsenal and recruited many new fighters, there has been no major new conflicts along the Israeli-Lebanese border. This border is patrolled by UN peacekeepers and the Lebanese army.

Following the 2006 war, Hezbollah has sought to use its political power to topple Lebanon's government after its demands for more cabinet seats were rejected. Representatives from both Hezbollah and Amal resigned from the cabinet. The opposition then declared that the existing cabinet was illegitimate and demanded the formation of a new government, in which Hezbollah and its opposition allies had veto power.

Late in 2007, the ongoing power struggle between the Hezbollah-led opposition and the Western-supported government prevented the National Assembly from selecting a new Lebanese President, following Émile Lahoud's nine-year term, which ended in November 2007. The opposition boycotted the process to seek for the veto power, which prevented the assembly from obtaining the two-thirds vote required to form a government. Thus, Lebanon had no president as the factions failed to reach a consensus on a candidate and composition of a new government.

In May 2008, Hezbollah and government supporters clashed in Beirut because of government initiatives that included plans to end Hezbollah's private telecommunications network and remove Beirut airport's security director over its connections with Hezbollah. Nasrallah denounced the government actions by declaring war and mobilizing Hezbollah forces, which seized much of Beirut. The Lebanese government then rescinded the decisions, however, the violence continued. Both factions met in Qatar and agreed to grant veto power to the Hezbollah-led opposition.

In July 2008 Hezbollah and Israel agreed to exchange several Lebanese prisoners and the remains of Lebanese and Palestinian fighters in return for the remains of Israeli soldiers. The exchange included the remains of two soldiers whose capture by Hezbollah led to the war in 2006.

In 2009, Nasrallah articulated the group's "political vision". It did not reiterate the demand for an Islamic state that appeared in the 1985 manifesto. It, however, retained its hostile rhetoric toward and the United States and Israel. Hezbollah's also reiterated its refusal to surrender its weapons.

In November 2009, after prolonged talks after National Assembly elections, Hezbollah and its allies announced that they would enter into a unity government with Prime Minister Saad al-Hariri's "March 14" bloc. Tensions increased in 2010 when UN Special Tribunal for Lebanon, examining the killing of Rafiq al-Hariri, a former Prime Minister, was preparing indictments against senior Hezbollah officials. Nasrallah claimed that the tribunal was politically biased, and its investigation was based on forged evidence. He demanded that the Lebanese government cease its cooperation with the tribunal. The March 14 bloc supported the tribunal's work, leading to a confrontation between the March 14 bloc and Hezbollah. After Syria and Saudi Arabia had failed in their attempts to mediate between the two sides, Hezbollah's two ministers and nine ministers from Hezbollah allies resigned from their cabinet posts, which led to the collapse of the unity government. In January 2011, Hezbollah and its parliamentary allies supported Najib Mikati, a wealthy Sunni businessman, to serve as prime minister. Mikati's appointment represented Hezbollah's increasing political influence. These events led to protests by supporters of the March 14 bloc, who were concerned about the new government's close connections with Iran and Syria, Hezbollah's most significant supporters. In June 2011, after prolonged deliberations, Mikati formed a new 30-member cabinet, with Hezbollah allies in 18 of the positions. Members of the March 14 bloc received no positions.

In June 2011, the UN Special Tribunal for Lebanon issued arrest warrants for four suspects in Rafiq al-Hariri's murder, who were identified as Hezbollah commanders and operatives. Nasrallah, however, denounced the tribunal and refused to surrender the four suspects.

The "Arab Spring" uprisings that spread throughout the Middle East in early 2011 presented a serious quandary for Hezbollah. After actively supporting revolutionary movements in Tunisia, Egypt, Libya, and Bahrain, the group perceived that its interests threatened by a similar movement directed against its major ally, Syrian President Bashar al-Assad. As protests spread throughout Syria, and more civilians were killed, Nasrallah announced that he supported Assad and reiterated Assad's denunciations of the Syrian opposition as a mere extension of a foreign conspiracy. The conflict deteriorated into a civil war. By late 2012, Hezbollah fighters were covertly fighting in Syria with the Syrian army. In May 2013, Nasrallah confirmed Hezbollah's involvement and vowed to fight until the Syrian rebels had been defeated.

Hezbollah expanded the scope of its mission during the Syrian Civil War, beyond fighting Israel to supporting its allies and Shiite co-religionists throughout the Middle East, used resources that had been exclusively devoted to fighting Israel, exacerbated sectarian tensions in the Middle East, and alienated many Lebanese Sunnis who had once supported Hezbollah.

Hezbollah continues to be fighting in Syria for the long-term. Within Lebanon, Hezbollah's critics argue the group's involvement in Syria places Lebanon at risk of renewed conflict. Others accuse Hezbollah of diverting its resources from its original mission of fighting Israel. Due to Hezbollah's growing military support of the Assad regime in the Syrian civil war in support of the Assad regime, supporters of the predominantly Sunni Muslim Syrian rebels have responded with violent deadly reprisals in Beirut.

Several Middle Eastern nations including Saudi Arabia have expressed displeasure with Hezbollah's resilience and its involvement in Syria's civil war. Iran and Saudi Arabia have long been regional rivals and Iran is Hezbollah's most important supporter, which pays Hezbollah nearly $200 million a year, which is an especially substantial amount for the nation, considering the economic burden that international sanctions imposed on Iran (the sanctions were largely lifted in January 2016). The Syrian civil war has become a proxy sectarian conflict between Saudi Arabia, a major supporter of the largely Sunni-led revolt in Syria, and Shiite-led Iran, an ally of Syria's government.

FURTHER READING

Aliboni, Roberto. "Diplomatic Opportunities After the Israeli-Hezbollah Conflict," *The International Spectator 41,* no. 4 (2006): 101-107.

Allāh, Ḥasan Naṣr, Nicholas Noe, Nicholas Blanford & Ellen Khouri. *Voice of Hezbollah: The Statements of Sayyed Hassan Nasrallah,*. London; New York: Verso, cop. 2007.

Avon, Dominique & Khatchadourian, Anaïs-Trissa. *Hezbollah: a History of the Party of God.* Cambridge, Mass.: Harvard University Press, 2012. .

Azani, Eitan. *Hezbollah: the Story of the Party of God: from Revolution to Institutionalization.* New York: Palgrave Macmillan, 2009.

Childs, Steven. "From Identity to Militancy: The Shia of Hezbollah." *Comparative Strategy 30,* no. 4 (2011): 363-372.

Gleis, Joshua L & Berti, Benedetta. *Hezbollah and Hamas: a Comparative Study.* Baltimore: Johns Hopkins University Press, 2012.

Goodheart, Eugene. "The London Review of Hezbollah." *Dissent 54, no.* 1 (2007):57-60.

Habshi, Pierre. "Re-examining Hezbollah." *SAIS Review 27 no.* 2 (2007): 211-214.

Harb, Zahera. *Channels of Resistance in Lebanon Liberation Propaganda, Hezbollah and the Media*. London: I.B. Tauris, 2011.

Harik, Judith P. *Hezbollah: the Changing Face of Terrorism*. London: I.B. Tauris, 2004.

Jaber, Hala. *Hezbollah: Born with a Vengeance*. New York: Columbia University Press, 1997.

Jaber, Hala. *Hezbollah*. London: Fourth Estate, 1998. .

Lambeth, Benjamin S. *Air Operations in Israel's War Against Hezbollah Learning from Lebanon and Getting It Right In Gaza*. Santa Monica, CA: RAND, 2011.

Norton, Augustus R. *Hezbollah: a Short History*. Princeton: Princeton University Press, 2007.

Norton, Augustus R. "The Role of Hezbollah in Lebanese Domestic Politics." *The International Spectator 42, no.* 4 (2007): 475-491.

Rabinovich, Itamar & Reinharz, Jehuda. *Israel in the Middle East: Documents and Readings on Society, Politics, and Foreign Relations, 1948-Present,* New York: Oxford University Press, 2007, 427.

Salamey, Imad & Pearson, Frederic. "Hezbollah: A Proletarian Party with an Islamic Manifesto - A Sociopolitical Analysis of Islamist Populism in Lebanon and the Middle East." *Small Wars & Insurgencies 18 no.* 3 (2007):416-438.

Salamey, Imad & Copeland, Gary. "How exceptional are Islamists? Comparing support for Hezbollah and the Lebanese Forces." *Journal of Balkan and Near Eastern Studies 13 no.* 2 (2011): 157-175.

Talbot, Brent J & Harriman, Heidi. "Disarming Hezbollah." *Mediterranean Quarterly 19, no.* 4 (2008):29-53.

Chapter 43

HIRAK/SOUTHERN MOVEMENT/ AL-HIRAK AL-JANUBI

The Republic of Yemen is one of the weakest nations in the world and the nation is becoming a failed state. The government has extreme economic, political and security challenges. The government's control is challenged by the Houthi Movement in the North, tribal leaders in the East, and Al Qaeda in the Arab Peninsula

Hirak claims to represent the southern provinces of present-day Yemen, which were a part of the former socialist People's Republic of Yemen. The People's Republic merged with the northern Yemen Arab Republic (YAR) in 1990 to form the Republic of Yemen.

Hirak is motivated in the current conflict by a combination of historical grievance which have achieved a new sense of salience because of the civil war now occurring in that country.

Hirak contends that after the Yemeni Civil War in 1994 that the entirety of Southern Yemeni society was politically, socially, and economically excluded to benefit the northern part of the nation. Southern Yemenis, thus, believe that they have been denied respect, equal treatment, and equal treatment with Northern Yemenis.

FROM THE MID-2000S FORWARD

After Hirik was formed, it lacked a clearly recognizable leadership. The movement was mostly composed of relatively unknown younger South Yemen activists, older politicians who held prominent positions during the socialist era, but are mostly in exile today, and military officers who were forced to retire after the civil war in 1994. This left the movement without a clear direction or representation in the various political processes that began after President Saleh was removed in 2011, including the implementation of Yemen's transition. To a more democratic and accountable political system.

This lack of cohesion was well demonstrated during the national Dialogue Conference (NDC) which ran from March 2013 through January 2014. The NDC attempted the address Yemen's major political, social, and economic crises.

Mainly because of Yemen's inability to implement confidence-building measures for Southern Yemen and the southern working group's failure to arrive a tangible solutions for the region, most Hirak activities in the South rejected the NDC's proposals, although nearly half the delegates at the conference were representatives for Southern Yemen or were of Southern Yemeni background.

For much of its existence, al-Hirak had been engaged in a cycle of public protests and expressions of civil disobedience with little practical effect. The milliunyahyahs (million people demonstrations) were among al-Hirak's most notable protest events, during which southern identity and commonality have been performed and reaffirmed both for Yemen and the wider world. However, these protest that have occurred on anniversaries of key historical events for the South have not had long-term political impact.

To some extent, however, there were changes after former President Saleh and the Houthi forces advance on southern Yemen in the Spring of 2015.

In February and March 2015, Saleh loyalist and Houthi forces began to expand from Saana to the southern part of Yemen. Although they were ostensibly pursuing President Hadi who had fled to Aden with his cabinet on February 21, 2015, their objective was to seize as much territory as possible to enhance their legitimacy as Yemen's de facto political authority and enjoy a stronger position in future negotiations.

The Saleh/Houthi forces attacked Aden with such ruthlessness as to suggest plans to punish the city and its residents in ways similar to what occurred during the 1994 civil war.

Led mostly by Saleh-loyalist, the assault devastated the city. The advance promoted the concept of an oppressive and tyrannical northern regime that was intent on subjugating the South, and highlighted the untenable nature of Yemeni unity.

The Saleh/Houthi offensive in the Spring of 2015, along with the sack of Aden between April and June of 2015 brought the Southern Movement to the forefront of political and military developments in the region. In response to the northern attacks, Hirak activities in western part of south Yemen, which was attacked from Saleh. Houthi forces organized themselves into what they called the Southern resistance Army.

With former PDRY military officers providing training and commanding units, fresh recruits defended Aden and eventually repelled the Saleh/Houthi forces from city, with assistance from the United Arab Emirates (UAE).

Once the Saleh/Houthi forces advanced beyond Saana in February 2015 and Prescient Hadi escaped to Aden, southern Yemen became contested territory in the nation's civil war.

The Southern Resistance fought under the former PDRY flag be and although it opposed the Saleh. Houthi alliance, it had different long term objectives from the Saudi coalition on the future of an independent South. In addition to rejecting the NDC;s proposal that Yemen be divided into federal entities, the Southern Movement (Hirak) and Resistance clearly demanded southern self-determination and rejected any one attempt t0 to revive the Full Cooptation Council's transitional process, which had brought the Hadi government to power.

IDEOLOGY

There is not a significant or single ideology uniting the Southern movement and providing it with public support. Al-Hirak activists realized the importance of religion and ideology at the beginning of their struggle. They believe that the movement needs an ideology that defines the country and defeats the Al-Islah ideology. Hirak has realized how important religion is in attracting support and recruited religious leaders to mobilize the people of the South and legitimize the call for separation. Attacks on the A.

See also: Al-Qaeda in the Arabian Peninsula (volume 1); Houthis (volume 1).

Chapter 44

HOUTHIS

The Houthis are a followers of a branch of Shia Islam known as Zaidism. They live in northern Yemen and believe they descended from the Prophet Muhammad. Commonly used, the term "Houthis," refers to a Zaidi fundamentalist political and rebel movement fighting in northern Yemen. The rebel group calls itself "Ansar Allah" (Partisans of God). The group's name is derived from Hussein Badr al-Din al-Houthi, a dissident Shi'a cleric who led the Houthi's first uprising in 2004 to obtain greater autonomy for their part of Saada province, and to defend their religious and cultural traditions from perceived Sunni Muslim encroachment.

The Houthis are a regional militant separatist movement that rebelled against Yemen's government, and also fought against the northern tribes and Al-Qaeda in the Arabian Peninsula (AQAP). The Houthis claim that they are fighting to rectify what they perceive as historical injustices committed against the Zaidis. They also seek to expand their political influence both in the province of Saada and throughout Yemen. Further, they oppose the influence of Saudi Arabian "Wahhabi" or "Salafi" in Yemen, including Saudi-supported proselytizing in Saada. The Houthis believe that both the Zaidis and Zaidi Shiism had lost influence in Yemen because of the government's failure to resolve various problems in the Saada governorate and continuing Saudi-supported religious activities in Saada.

One-third of Yemen's population is Zaidi, named after their fifth Imam, Zayd ibn Ali. He was the grandson of Husayn. Zayd, who fought against the Ummayad Caliphate in 740 CE, which he claimed, was corrupt. Zaidis believe that their imam (ruler) should be both descended from Ali (the cousin and son-in-law of the Prophet Muhammad) and a person who assumes a religious obligation to oppose unjust rulers and corruption. Yemeni tribes established a Zaidi state (or "Imamate") in northern Yemen in 893. Yemen's twentieth-century imams governed an isolated area in the Yemeni highlands, which required foreigners to receive the ruler's permission before entering the kingdom. This imamate existed in various forms until Yemen's republican revolution of 1962. The Houthis emerged in reaction to that revolution.

Despite the fact that Zaidism is a branch of Shia Islam, the sect's legal traditions, and religious practices resemble Sunni Islam. Its doctrine also significantly differs from the "Twelver Shiism" (as found in Iran).

The Houthis have fought Yemen's government and the Saudi Arabia military in Sa'ada for well over a decade. The Saudi military intervened after Houthi militants began attacking southern Saudi Arabia.

After the Yemeni military killed Houthi in late 2004, Houthi's brother Abel Malek al-Houthi, became the rebel leader. Both the government and the Houthis agreed to a cease-fire. The two sides began fighting again in 2007, beginning a conflict that lasted until 2010. Houthi led several other uprisings before agreeing to a ceasefire with the government in 2010. In 2011, the Houthis participated in protests against President Ali Abdullah Saleh and took advantage of the chaos to increase the areas they controlled in Sa'ada and the adjacent Amran province. Eventually, they became a de facto government in parts of Yemen.

The Houthis seek to increase their power by receiving greater autonomy and a redistricting of Yemen's regions to formally give them access to the Red Sea and/or access to the nation's oil resources, and retaining their own militia.

The situation is made more complicated because AQAP is a dangerous Al-Qaeda regional affiliate operating in Yemen. The US government has sought to defeat AQAP through a hybrid strategy of drone strikes, local counter-terrorism operations, and security assistance to the Yemeni government.

Recent violence in Yemen had largely resulted from conflicts over power and resources. These include: continued clashes between the Yemeni government and the Houthis in Northern Yemen; Hirak violence in Southern Yemen; AQAP terrorism; infighting within tribal and military groups; and the Saleh government's repression of protests by young people and pro-democracy protestors that led him to eventually resign. Although Yemen has much oil reserves, its oil revenue, however, has not benefitted most of the nation's people. Yemen remains one of the most impoverished Arab nations, with over half of its people living in poverty. A sharp increase in Yemen's population has increased the stress on the country's natural resources, especially water and public services. Instability in Yemen has resulted in displacing a large number of people, in addition to problems such as poor governance, corruption, the depletion of essential resources, and inadequate infrastructure. These conditions have all greatly impeded Yemen's development. Joblessness, the high cost of goods, and lack of social services continue to be major social problems. These conditions have also caused significant food insecurity in the country. Further, high unemployment has forced many Yemenis to engage in highway robberies and smuggling.

The Houthis believe that Yemen's government cooperates too closely with the United States. The US government has provided supply and training assistance to Yemen's military to fight terrorism. The Houthis sought to depose the Pro-Western government and install a Shia theocracy instead. Yemen's government accused the Houthi rebels of attempting to overthrow democratic government and install theocratic rule.

While the Houthi slogan is "God is great. Death to America, death to Israel," they have neither harmed Americans nor Israelis. While AQAP has kidnapped and sometimes killed, foreigners, the Houthis have not. The Houthis and the U.S. government also both seek to destroy AQAP.

Yemen's military underwent an often-delayed restructuring effort intended to remove corruption and end the "cult of commander" that commentators often viewed as more important than loyalty to the government. The U.S. sought many of these changes in 2011 and 2012, however; it became less focused as the government has struggled.

Abdrabbuh Mansour Hadi succeeded Saleh and became Yemen's President in February 2012, in an agreement in which Saleh resigned in exchange for immunity. While in office, Hadi had strong relations with the United States, although many commentators believe that he did not have a particularly strong domestic power base. Nonetheless, Haidi was widely considered an important US ally against AQAP.

Hadi's new government called Yemen's political groups to meet in a National Dialogue Conference (NDC) to arrive at an agreement to govern the country. The Houthis were one of many groups that attended the NDC. In February 2014, President Hadi issued proposals make Yemen into a federation of six regions. The GCC convened the NDC to draft a plan to allocate powers between the central government and the provinces. In the fall of 2013, the NDC also presented its recommendations to establish a new constitutional framework. When the NDC concluded in early 2014, Yemen's political transformation was still very incomplete, as a constitution had not been written, so a referendum to approve was not held, and subsequent presidential and parliamentary elections remained to be called. Because the transition moved so slowly, many observers were concerned that Hadi would lose momentum to the opponents of the internationally supported transition process, including former President Saleh and his Houthi allies.

The Houthis opposed Hadi's proposal to divide Yemen into six federal regions, in which Sa'ada would be part of a region that included the nation's capital. The Houthis also claimed that the Yemenis were disenchanted with a transitional government managed by officials connected with the old regime, such as the Saleh and Ahmar clans, and the Islah (Reform) Party, Yemen's leading Sunni Islamist party. Houthi supporters protested and demanded reductions in fuel prices and a new government.

Shortly after the NDC adjourned, the Houthis who had been sporadically fighting the government since 2004, began a new attack against Hadi's various tribal allies. In July 2014, the Houthis defeated various tribes and militias in Amran province that were affiliated with the Islah Party. Following military successes in northern Yemen, Houthi leader Abdul Malik al-Houthi demanded in mid-August 2014 that Hadi reinstate subsidies (that were abolished which adversely affected the poor) and that he would replace the existing government with a government more representative of the various factions in Yemen. A massive number of Shia and Sunni Houthi protestors participated in sit-ins at public facilities in Sanaa and prevented highway access to the capital's airport.

In the summer of 2014, the Houthis seized control of Sana'a and other parts of Yemen. On September 2, 2014, Hadi proposed to reorganize the government and promised to reduce gasoline prices by nearly 30 percent to arrive at a consensus and to restore order. The Houthis, responded by rejecting the proposals as insufficient. The crisis worsened when the Yemeni military shot several Houthi protestors in Sanaa, killing several of them.

In September, Houthi militants eventually seized Sanaa and demanded political concessions from Hadi. In mid-September, Houthis and Yemeni soldiers clashed for several days in the capital. The rebels seized government buildings and captured the base of a military unit that followed Brigadier General Ali Mohsen al-Ahmar, a Sunni Islamist who fought against the Houthis in northern Yemen between 2004 and 2010. His family members included many prominent Islah leaders.

On September 20, the Yemeni government entered into an agreement with the Houthis. Prime Minister Mohammed Basindwa resigned, shortly thereafter. Islah members feared Houthi persecution and that the Houthis would reinstall the Zaidi imamate.

The factions agreed to a peace agreement on September 21, in which the Houthis would withdraw from Sanaa and the government would meeting the following demands: 1) restore fuel subsidies; 2) form a new "technocratic national government"; 3) appoint advisers affiliated with either the Houthis and the Hiraak al-Janoubi ("Southern Movement"), which favored the secession of southern Yemen from the rest of the nation; and implement NDC-approved policies. The Houthis refused to agree to a "security appendix" that would require them to withdraw from Sanaa and other cities in the north and surrender their arms to the government in 45 days.

Individuals living in Sanaa wanted the rebel fighters to evacuate the city. The Houthis, however, dismissed government administrators and demanded oversight of government agencies to "purify" what they deemed as political corruption.

In 2014 and early 2015, the Houthi rebellion was both impeding the ongoing political transition and it was intensifying the country's internal conflicts. Former President Saleh and his tribal allies assisted the Houthis. The Houthis eventually seized Sanaa and compelled the national government to agree to a cease-fire agreement granting the Houthis control over selecting cabinet ministers. The Houthi rebels entered into the predominantly Sunni central and western parts of Yemen, resulting in clashes with AQAP militants. Houthi military actions led to internal uprisings throughout Yemen. Southern Yemenis demanded independence and sought to secede. AQAP recruited additional Sunni Arabs to launch jihad against the Houthis, referring to them as "Shia heretics."

On January 2015, Houthi militants and government troops clashed near the presidential palace. Despite the ceasefire, the rebels seized the presidential palace and shelled Hadi's house. Al-Houthi claimed that the government had failed to implement their political agreements. He also demanded changes in the commission drafting a new constitution that would increase Houthi influence.

On January 17, 2015, the Houthis kidnaped Ahmed Awad bin Mubarak, Hadi's chief of staff. The group complained of "irregularities" in both the language of the agreement and the government's implementation of it.

The Houthis virtually kept Hadi under house arrest. The fragile agreement collapsed after the Houthis seized the presidential palace and made additional demands on Hadi, who then resigned. The ensuing chaos plunged Yemen into uncertainty. Nearly 10,000 people marched from Sana'a University towards Hadi's home to protest his forced resignation. Protesters asked Hadi to use the government's power and authority to confront the Houthis. Hadi's resignation did not become effective until the Yemeni parliament approved it. Hadi blamed Houthi control of Sana'a for ending his attempt to stabilize Yemen.

After parliament had approved Hadi's resignation, Speaker Yahya al-Ra'i, of the General People's Congress party (GPC) became interim president while new elections are held. Former President Saleh was also a GPC member.

Hadi accused President Saleh of attempting to obstruct Yemen's political transition. During his presidency from 2012 through 2015, Haidi sought to reduce Saleh's influence by ousting Saleh loyalists who were still senior leaders in the government and military.

The US government and the UN Security Council also claimed that Saleh helped the Houthis seize control of Sana'a to destroy the national government's legitimacy, generate chaos, and eventually overthrow the government.

In November 2014, the United Nations Security Council sanctioned Saleh and two key Houthi leaders for endangering Yemen's peace and stability and disrupting political functions. Saleh partisans then suggested that Ahmed, his oldest son, compete in elections that would replace Hadi as president.

While the Houthis claimed that they sought a smooth, democratic transfer of power, the UN Security Council and Yemen's Gulf neighbors supported retaining Hadi. France condemned the "forced resignation" of Hadi and demanded that Houthi fighters immediately withdraw from Sanaa.

Growing violence continued to plague Yemen. Gunmen on a motorbike killed two intelligence agents. Large demonstrations occurred in the southern cities of Taiz and Ibb. Houthi gunmen reportedly shot and wounded four people at a protest at the Red Sea port of Hodei.

Secessionist militants in southern Yemen, affiliated with the Southern Movement, seized police checkpoints in Ataq, the capital of Shabwa province without resistance. Several southern cities and provinces declared their allegiance to a Houthi dominated government.

Many world governments are concerned that instability in Yemen could further destabilize the Middle East. The US and Gulf Arab governments are concerned with Yemen's instability because of that nation's strategic location next to Saudi Arabia, the world's exporter of oil, and transit routes in the Gulf of Aden. Western governments also remain concerned that chaos in Yemen could facilitate jihadists, just as similar conditions helped jihadist groups in Syria and Iraq.

The Houthi could also worsen religious and political conflicts throughout the Middle East. Saudi Arabia, the leading regional Sunni nation, argues that Iran provides Iran with political, military, and financial assistance. Both Iran and the Houthis, however, deny these charges.

Many observers believe that the crisis in Yemen will most likely help Iran's government. Yemeni government officials have long charged that Iran involves itself in Yemeni affairs by assisting secessionist movements opposed to Saudi Arabia.

Iran continues to increase its presence in Yemen. In January 2013, an American Navy vessel carrying a Yemeni Coast Guard crew aboard went into Yemeni seas, to assist that government intercept and inspect a vessel suspected of smuggling illegal goods into Yemen. A joint U.S./Yemeni force found various weapons and explosives, apparently shipped from Iran and concealed in the vessel. The Yemeni Coast Guard then assumed control of the ship.

Despite Houthi control over much of Yemen, they are likely to clash with their partner, former President Saleh, Sunni tribes in the oil-producing province of Marib, Saudi Arabia, and the AQAP. The status and loyalties of the many Yemeni military units throughout the nation are opaque. Some of these units could fighting the Houthis or remain neutral.

The US government became concerned with the safety of American personnel in Yemen. These concerns were particularly expressed after Houthi militants shot several times at a US Embassy armored vehicle in Sanaa on January 19, 2015. There were no casualties or serious injuries in that incident. Anticipating further domestic unrest, the US, and other western nations closed their embassies.

Hadi's ouster complicated US government policy on Yemen. Since all strategic military bases in Sana'a fell at least partly to Houthi control, the future for US sponsored military operations remains unclear.

The United States and the world community have largely not formally recognized Houthi self-proclaimed government, asserting that Hadi continues to be the legitimate president of Yemen. The US government insisted that all parties adhere to existing international agreements, including the 2011 Gulf Cooperation Council (GCC) transition plan and the September 2014 Peace and National Partnership Agreement.

The United States continued its drone campaign against AQAP following Hadi's resignation. The US Defense Department has stated that it is continuing its counterterrorism cooperation, and U.S. Special Operations forces remain in Yemen. The country's political instability, however, has hindered overall U.S. counterterrorism operations.

Yemen presents formidable counterterrorism challenges to the US Government. Yemen's national government has deteriorated, and AQAP has emerged as both an international terror organization and an insurgent group at home. To contend with the situation, the US government expanded its covert activities in Yemen, from merely pursuing high value targets to a larger counterinsurgency mission. The American airstrikes in Yemen greatly increased since the conflict began in Yemen 2011, and when AQAP formed the Jihadist Ansar al-Sharia (AAS) militia.

Despite the Houthi military successes, the international community, including the United States, maintains some leverage over the Houthis. International aid, including grants from Saudi Arabia, had funded the national government, including paying Yemeni public employees. Saudi Arabia curtailed payments to Yemen's government. If the Houthis seek to rule without including other factions, they may find it difficult finance the government. If Yemen's economy collapses because the government failed, however, the US and other western governments would most likely continue their humanitarian aid to Yemen.

Both the Houthis and the US government oppose the AQAP. While defeating terrorism is important to Yemen's people, they are more concerned about ending corruption in government, job creation, providing an effective education system, and ensuring nation's water supply. Most Yemenis also see AQAP as more of a concern to the US government. They also perceive the U.S. government as committed to defeat AQAP, but not necessarily as committed to helping to resolve Yemen's problems.

In February 2015, the Houthis dissolved Yemen's parliament and created a "presidential council". President Hadi escaped Saana and went to the southern port city of Aden. He reclaimed the presidency, setting up a government there supported by Gulf nations that have rejected the Houthi takeover as a coup. Along with Hadi, General Mahmoud al-Subaihi, Yemen's Defense Minister, also left Saana to regroup in Aden. On March 16, 2015, the Houthis freed Khaled Bahah, Yemen's Prime Minister and members of his cabinet, who were placed under house arrest in January 2015. The Houthis said this was intended as a goodwill gesture to facilitate negotiations in Yemen's political transition. The Houthis were reportedly under pressure from different militias and political groups to release the prime minister.

The United Nations sponsored negotiations to help remedy Yemen's political divisions and end its civil war. The UN warned that the crisis in Yemen could be a crisis very similar to Syria, Libya or Iraq if Yemen's factions are not able to reach an agreement. The Houthis continue to be in indirect negotiations with Saudi Arabia. Tensions had increased between the two parties after a civil aviation agreement suspected to have Iranian connections and Houthi military drills on the Saudi border. Iran had also agreed to help the Yemenis develop their harbor facilities, construct energy plants, and supply them with petroleum.

Yemen's civil war has its roots in a continuing long-standing conflict between the Yemeni government and marginalized tribes in northern Yemen, which escalated due to a decline in the legitimacy and competence of Yemen's central government. Saudi Arabia intervened not as much to oppose Iranian expansionism but to protect its southern border against the Houthi threat.

The Houthis entered into an alliance with their former foe, President Saleh. Saleh viewed the Houthis as competent fighters but incompetent in governance. Saleh allied himself with the Houthis to avenge those who forced him out in 2011, and may have sought a way to return to power. The combined strength of the Houthis and Saleh military loyalists alarmed the Saudi government. In March 2015, Saudi Arabia and the United Arab Emirates, assisted by the United States and Great Britain, conducted an air and, ground attacks against the Houthi-Saleh alliance.

Due to the war, Yemen currently suffers from one of the worst humanitarian crises in the modern era. Seven million Yemenis reside in areas that are suffering famine, nearly two million children are suffering from acute malnutrition, and an outbreak of cholera has infected over 600,000 people. More than 8,600 people have been killed and 49,000 injured in fighting that has occurred between March 2015 and December 2017, many of them in air strikes by the Saudi-led multinational coalition that supports Hadi. The conflict and a blockade imposed by the coalition have also left 20 million people requiring humanitarian assistance and created the world's largest food security emergency. Apparently the Houthi is showing signs of strain, which could offer space for negotiations to an end to the war.

See also: Al-Qaeda in the Arabian Peninsula (volume 1); Hirak (volume 1).

FURTHER READING

Boucek, Christopher. *War in Saada from Local Insurrection to National Challenge.* Washington, DC: Carnegie Endowment for International Peace, 2010.

Dumm, Andrew. *Understanding the Houthi Conflict in Northern Yemen: A Social Movement Approach.* S.l.: Bibliobazaar, 2011.

Freeman, Jack. "The Al Houthi Insurgency in the North of Yemen: An Analysis of the Shabab al Moumineen." *Studies in Conflict & Terrorism 32, no. 11* (2009): 1008-1019.

Gillam, Jarrod J H, & Moran, James E. *The United States and Yemen Coin in the Absence of a Legitimate Government.* Monterey, California: Naval Postgraduate School, 2011.

Hedberg, Nicholas J. *The Exploitation of a Weak State: Al-Qaeda in the Arabian Peninsula in Yemen.* Monterey, California: Naval Postgraduate School, 2010.

"Held Hostage; Instability in Yemen," *The Economist,* Jan. 24, 2015.

Horton, M. "Fresh fighting in Yemen ignites refugee crisis; Refugees in northern Yemen say that their villages were bombed in an escalating conflict with Houthi rebels. The population of the largest refugee camps doubled in the past month, prompting UNHCR. *The Christian Science Monitor,* Dec. 22, 2009.

"Houthis Take Over; Yemen's Violent Politics," *The Economist,* Sep 27, 2014.

LaFranchi, H. "Yemen Chaos Puts Uncertainty into Obama Terror Fight - or Does It?" *The Christian Science Monitor,* Jan. 22, 2015.

Phillips, Sarah. *Yemen and the Politics of Permanent Crisis.* Abingdon, Oxon.: Routledge for the International Institute for Strategic Studies, 2011.

Phillips, Sarah. *Yemen and the Politics of Permanent Crisis.* Taylor and Francis 2017.

Terrill, W Andrew. *The Conflicts in Yemen and U.S. National Security*. Carlisle, PA: Strategic Studies Institute, U.S. Army War College, 2011.
"Who's Houthi?" *The Economist,* Sep. 13, 2014.

Chapter 45

IRAN, ISLAMIST POLITICAL PARTIES

Article 26 of the Islamic Republic of Iran's 1979 constitution allows the formation of political parties. A party's law went into effect in 1981. There became more than 100 of them. Parties in the sense of entities with mass membership have been slow to take hold in Iran. Some Iranian observers were critical of them.

Some critics have criticized the fact that strong or powerful political parties had not developed. Instead of a situation where candidates are chosen by established powerful and popular political parties that have a good deal of credibility. Iran's politics have tended to be transient and spontaneous.

ISLAMIC COALITION SOCIETY (JAMEYAT-E-MOTALEFE-YE-ESLAMI) (JME)

A coordinating body of Iranian hardline conservative clerics and business people that were connected to the late Ayatollah Ruhollah Khomeini (1902-1989), the Islamic Coalition Society (JME) has an influential position in Iran's judicial system as well as the quasi-charitable groups that were established to assist war victims and the poor, and which currently control much of Iran's non-economic sector. There was both significant opposition to political liberalization in Iran and significant resistance to economic reform measures, including those with business support.

The JME views itself as "the arm of the order and guardianship of the supreme jurisprudence" which takes actions according to "its organizational articles of association to support the principles of the order and the state" (BBC, 2006). Hamid Reza Tariqqi, the leader of the Party's political center, stressed that political parties in Iran have the duty to fulfil religious democracy in the country. He said that "strengthening religious belief and the intense combination of religion and politics are important factors which will cause society to accept political parties" (BBC, 2006).

In the 2005 presidential elections, the JME initially supported Ali Larijauni but subsequently switched its support to the eventual winner, Mahmoud Ahmadinejad, candidate of the principleists, reportedly on the request of Iran's supreme leader, the Ayatollah Ali Khamenei.

In the 2006 Iranian Assembly of Experts, the JME supported candidates of the Society of Combatant Clergy. Before the 2009 parliamentary elections the JME supported United Fundamentalist Front (UFF) candidates.

In the 2009 Iranian presidential election, the JME supported Mahmoud Ahmadinejad. In 2010 JME party secretary general Mouhammad Nabi Habibi supported proposals to allow political parties in Iran, however, adding that political groups should become parties only when they have articulated a specific political program. The JME supported Ahmadinejad in the 2012 parliamentary elections. Al Akbar Velayati, the 2013 JME's presidential candidate, received 6.3 percent of the vote. In 2014, JME Party official Hamid Reza Taraqqi criticized a proposed law that would create a more formal party system for Iran.

The JME has regularly had good relations with the Chinese Communist Party, particularly the Sichuan Provincial Party (Sichuan borders Iran). This was part of the cultivation of friendly relations between China and Iran, as it was seen in the interest of both nations to promote bilateral cooperation, particularly in areas of peace and development.

ISLAMIC IRAN DEVELOPMENT AND JUSTICE PARTY (IIDJP)

After a two year gestation, the Islamic Iran Development and Justice Party (IIDJP), a "principlist" party (a Iranian political party that supports the principles of the Iranian Revolution of 1979), held its first congress on December 12, 2007. This party stated that its purpose is to increase public participation in Iranian politics and thus lead to better governance. Some IIDJP leaders said that they sought to create a party in which "culture" would take precedence over politics. Claiming to eschew partisanship, the party also expressed the hope of creating a coalition government (including both Principlists and Reformists) that would implement and carry forth the ideals of Iran's Islamic Revolution, govern by consensus, and avoid damaging extremism.

Widespread concerns about unemployment, inflation and social problems in Iran during the administration of President Mahmoud Ahmadinejad led to the formation of IIDJP, which recruited candidates to compete in the 2008 parliamentary election. IIDJP leaders expressed their support for Ali Lanarijani, who competed in the June 12, 2009 presidential election. Larijani is a longtime strategist for the government and national-security adviser to the Supreme Leader, Ayatollah Ali Khamenei. He eventually became speaker of parliament. The party also supported the presidential candidacy of the independent conservative Mohsen Rezai, an Iranian politician, economist, military commander with the Islamic Revolutionary Guard Corps (IRGC) and secretary of the Expediency Discernment Council. In 2015, Rezai withdrew from politics to return to the IRGC.

See also: Islamic Revolutionary Guard Corps (IRGC) (volume 1).

FURTHER READING

Abrahamian, Ervand *A History of Modern Iran*. Cambridge, U.K.: Cambridge University Press, 2008, 2017.

Ansari, Ali M. *Iran, Islam and Democracy: The Politics of Managing Change*. London: Royal Institute of International Affairs, 2000.

Ghods, M. Reza. *Iran in the Twentieth Century: A Political History*. Boulder: L. Rienner, 1989.

Kamrava, Mehran. *The Political History of Modern Iran: From Tribalism to Theocracy*. Westport, CT: Praeger, 1992.

Keddie, Nikki R & Richard, Y. *Roots of Revolution: An Interpretive History of Modern Iran*. New Haven: Yale University Press, 1981.

Mirsepassi, Ali. *Democracy in Modern Iran: Islam, Culture, and Political Change*. New York: New York University Press, 2010.

Moslem, Mehdi *Factional Politics in Post-Khomeini Iran*. Syracuse: Syracuse University Press, 2002.

Mottahedeh, Roy P. *The Mantle of the Prophet: Religion and Politics in Iran*. New York: Simon and Schuster, 1985.

Nasr, Seyyed Vali. *The Shia Revival: How Conflicts within Islam will Shape the Future*. New York: Norton, 2006.

Schirazi, Asghar. *The Constitution of Iran: Politics and the State in the Islamic Republic*. London: I.B. Tauris, 1997.

Chapter 46

ISLAMIC ACTION FRONT (IAF) (JABHAT AL-ALMAT AL-ISLAMI) (IAF) (JORDAN)

The Islamic Action Front (IAF) was formed in late 1992 in Jordan by the Muslim Brotherhood and other Islamists, some of whom later withdrew because the Brotherhood dominated the new party. Like the Muslim Brotherhood, the IAF promotes the establishment of a Sharia-based Islamic state and retaining the monarchy. Although the IAF is often viewed as opposing Israeli- PLO and Jordanian-Israeli peace talks, a significant minority wing exists within IAF that favors such negotiations.

IAF leaders opposed to election law changes introduced in mid-1993. It further accused the government of interfering with IAF political activities before the November house elections. After threatening to boycott the election, however, the IAF ran 36 candidates, 16 of whom were elected. IAF candidates did not perform as well as anticipated in the July 1995 municipal elections. Potential support apparently went instead to tribally based parties. Subsequently, IAF and Muslim Brotherhood leaders suggested that King Hussein was attempting to restore authoritarianism to Jordan. No IAF members became part of the new government that came to power in February 1996. The IAF also boycotted the 1997 legislative election. After party member, Abd al·Rahim Akour accepted a position in the new cabinet of June 2000, the IAF suspended him.

After winning 17 seats in the 2003 parliamentary elections, the IAF became the leading opposition party in Jordan's legislature. Following the suicide bombing attacks on hotels in Amman in 2005, which the IAF denounced, the IAF urged the government to consider individual freedoms as it began writing new anti-terrorism legislation.

Following the victory of Hamas in the Palestinian elections in 2006, the IAF elected Zaki Said Bani·Irshayd, a Hamas supporter, as its new secretary general. When the Jordanian government began to clamp down on Islamists, including dismissing two deputies from the lower house of parliament, tensions grew between the government and the IAF. This resulted in the IAF deputies walking out of Parliament for several weeks. In early 2007, the IAF sought to eliminate the one- person, one-vote system, which it claimed was unfair in multiple candidate districts. The IAF also opposed a new law approved by the parliament in 2007, which required political parties to have a minimum of 500 members (instead of 50) to be officially recognized. Defying the government, several groups joined the IAF to protest the political parties law, which they denounced as detrimental to the progress of democracy in

Jordan. The IAF also strongly criticized the government's failure to enact promised political reforms, including changing the "Press Law" that permitted journalists to be imprisoned for stories they wrote crticial of the government. The legislature later repealed this law.

In 2007 the IAF elected the first Christian, Aziz Masa'ada, to its administrative board, but he resigned within a week. Following its boycott of municipal elections In July 2007, the IAF decided to participate in parliamentary elections in November of that year. It secured only six seats, a significant decline for what had been the leading opposition group in the lower chamber. The lack of support for the IAF was attributed to its inability to achieve socio-economic changes and to divisions within the party between hawks and doves, the hawks opposing the doves' decision to participate in polling, which the hawks believed would not be fair and transparent. Also, the hawks were said to be angered by the way the JAF candidates were chosen without consultation with the full membership. Some observers believed that the party was facing a major crisis furthered by Hamas's decision to form a Palestinian Muslim Brotherhood, resulting in divisions in the IAF between pro- Jordanian and pro-Hamas factions. In June the two factions resolved the contentious issue of whether Zaki Said Bani-lrshayd should retain his post as secretary general. He had been blamed by some for allegedly undermining the position of the group's parliamentary candidates in the 2007 elections, leading to a loss of IAF seats. Ultimately, Banl-lrshayd was allowed to retain his post, and four members who had resigned in protest returned.

In March 2009 the IAF criticized Egypt for denying entry at the Rafa border crossing to 17 parliamentarians, including IAF members, who were on a mission to express solidarity with the people of Gaza. The IAF was also highly critical of Arab leaders who failed to accept an invitation to an emergency summit in Qatar to consider measures against Israel following the Gaza attacks.

In June 2010 Hamza Mansur, leader of the moderate faction of the IAF, was elected secretary general in a close election by the Shura Council. He defeated the "hawk" candidate, Mohammad Zyod, who favored closer ties with Hamas, on a vote of 62 to 55. The IAF announced in August that it would boycott the 2010 legislative elections. The IAF expelled five members who violated the boycott and ran in the assembly elections. One dissident, Ahmed Qudah won election to the assembly.

In May 2011 the IAF joined other opposition parties to form the opposition group the National Front for Reform. The party boycotted the 2013 elections. In 2013 the IAF condemned government plans to close the border with Syria to stem the flow of refugees into Jordan. As violence in Syria and Iraq escalated in 2014, IAF officials denounced alleged harassment of Islamists resulting in long delays at border crossings.

See also: Hamas (volume 1); Muslim Brotherhood (volume 1).

FURTHER READING

Brown, Nathan J. *Jordan and its Islamic Movement: The Limits of Inclusion?* Washington, D.C.: Carnegie Endowment for International Peace, 2006.
Davis, Joyce. *Between Jihad and Salaam: Profiles in Islam.* New York: St. Martin's Press, 1997.

Fondren, Billy R. *The Muslim Brotherhood in Egypt, Jordan and Syria a Comparison.* Monterey, CA: Naval Postgraduate School, 2009.

Hassani, Kawtar B., et al. *Rising but Not Winning?: The Cases of the Moroccan Party of Justice and Development and the Jordanian Islamic Action Front.* Ifrane: Al Akhawayn University Press, 2008.

Schwedler, Jillian. *Faith in Moderation: Islamist Parties in Jordan and Yemen.* Cambridge: Cambridge University Press, 2007.

Wakeman, Raffaela Lisette. *Containing the Opposition: Selective Representation in Jordan and Turkey,* 2009 (thesis).

Chapter 47

ISLAMIC REVOLUTIONARY GUARD CORPS

Also Known As: Islamic Revolutionary Guards, Pasdaran ("Guards"), Revolutionary Guards. Sepah ("Corps"), Sepah-e Pasdaran-e Enghelab-e Eslami ("Islamic Revolutionary Guard Corps").

OVERVIEW

The Islamic Revolutionary Guards Corps (IRGC) is responsible for protecting the Islamic Republic of Iran and the asserted ideals of the 1979 Iranian Revolution. The IRGC conducts traditional military missions against what it perceives as its enemies within Iran. The IRGC is Iran's primary force for spreading the ideology of the Islamic Revolution worldwide. It swears complete allegiance to Iran's clerical establishment. The IRGC is Iran's main connection to its jihadist proxies, which Iran's government uses to support its influence worldwide.

IRGC is comprised of units such as the Basij militia and the Quds Force (IRGC-QF). The Basij (which means "mobilization") is a paramilitary group responsible for generating popular support for the government. The Basij became well –known for recruiting volunteers, many of them teenagers, for "human wave attacks" in the Iran-Iraq war, from 1981-1988 . Currently the Basij has two key formal responsibilities: 1) to provide defensive military training to protect the government against the threat of invasion by foreign powers, and 2) to suppress domestic anti-government activity through instigating street violence and intimidating potential anti-government targets . After the highly contentious Iranian presidential elections in 2009, for example, the Basij harshly suppressed protests and attacked student residence halls.

In its activities abroad, the IRGC's Quds Force provided training, funding and weapons to jihadist groups, including Iraqi insurgents, Hezbollah, and Hamas. The Quds Force also allegedly participated in the 1994 suicide attack of a Jewish community center, which killed more than 80 and injuring about 300. Since that time, the Quds Force has armed anti-government jihadists in Bahrain, and materially aided an assassination attempt on Saudi Arabia's ambassador to the United States in 2011. The Quds Force continues to have a crucial role in supporting Syrian government forces in Syria's civil war.

IGRC Ideology

The IRGC is an Iranian government organization responsible for defending the Iranian government against internal and external threats. Espousing a radical jihadist ideology and a paranoid outlook, the IRGC relentlessly suppresses those who it views as its enemies within Iran, and employs terrorist tactics against its enemies throughout the world.

Legal Status and Role of the Islamic Revolutionary Guard Corps

Under Iranian law, the IRGC as "an institution commanded by the Supreme Leader whose purpose is to protect the Islamic Revolution of Iran and its accomplishments, while striving continuously ... to spread the sovereignty of God's law."

In the aftermath of the 1979 Iranian revolution, prior to its formal legal recognition, the IRGC functioned as a network of jihadist activists who owed their loyalty to Ayatollah Ruhollah Khomeini, the leader of the Iranian Revolution. In conducting their activities, the IRGC sought to suppress dissident voices within the revolutionary movement in the name of defending the "Islamic republic", as created by Khomeini, and faithfully carrying out the will of Supreme Leader Ali Khamenei, who succeeded Khomeini after the latter's death in 1989.

While the IRGC is a powerful government agency, it also is able to generate the zeal and fanaticism of an ideologically motivated terrorist group. The IRGC's mission combines traditional military roles with relentless focus on pursuing supposed domestic enemies. The Iranian Ministry of Defense defines the role of the IRGC as to "protect [Iran's] independence, territorial integrity, and national and revolutionary ideals, under the shadow of the orders given by the Commander in Chief, the Grand Ayatollah Imam Khamenei." Political opinions deemd to contradict "revolutionary ideals" are considered to be military threats that will be dealt with military means. Ali Jafair, the IRGC commander Jafari once stated: "today's war is not fought on land or sea, it is fought at the level of belief, and the enemy is investing efforts to gain influence inside the Islamic Republican system."

The IRGC's doctrine demands strict loyalty to Iran's clerical establishment along with much paranoia pertaining to the world outside Iran. IRGC media depicts Iran as being perpetually threatened by US and "Zionist" conspiracies, which Iran's government claims are able to able significantly influential within Iran. Allegations of foreign involvement in Iran provide the justification for terrorism abroad, generating high-profile international conflicts that provide the basis for ever harsher crackdowns on internal dissent.

Domestic repression overshadowed traditional military missions, as the IRGC's influence began to influence every aspect activity of Iranian life. In 2007, after the Basij militia was formally incorporated into the IRGC, the IRGC Commander Mohammad Ali Jafari proclaimed that, "The new strategic guidelines of the IRGC have been changed by the directives of the Leader of the Revolution [i.e., the Supreme Leader Ali Khamenei]. The main mission of the IRGC from now on is to deal with the threats from the internal enemies." The second priority of the corps was to "assist the military in case of foreign threats."

The IRGC stresses that its loyalty to Supreme Leader Ali Khamenei a religious obligation. At times, the organization's devotion to Khamenei slips into hero-worship: deputy

IRGC commander Mohammad Hejazi credited Khamenei with rejecting the objections of scientific experts to direct research towards increased accuracy in ballistic missiles.

THE ORGANIZATION OF THE IRGC

Under Iranian law, the Supreme Leader has the power to appoint and remove the IRGC commander. The Supreme Leader also appoints clerical representatives to the various units of the IRGC whose guidance and instructions are binding on commanders. Iranian law makes "belief and practical obedience to the principle of clerical rule" a condition of IRGC membership, further emphasizing absolute loyalty to Supreme Leader Ali Khamenei as the IRGC's guiding principle.

The IRGC is under the command under the Joint Armed Forces General Staff, of the Ministry of Defense. These levels of oversight, however, fail to give Iran's nominally elected civilian authorities genuine or substantive control over the IRGC, because Iran's entire military remains is under the control of the Supreme National Security Council, which is responsible to the Supreme Leader Ali Khamenei.

In the IGRC, individuals carry greater importance than institutions in national security decision-making. Thus, certain key personal networks, often predicated on connections of family, friendship, or service in the 1980-1988 Iran-Iraq War as major factors in IRGC leadership. The opacity of the IRGC's real command structure contribute to make Iran an erratic and therefore especially dangerous actor in Middle Eastern affairs.

Basij

The Basij militia (the name refers to "mobilization") holds itself out as a popular volunteer association, despite the fact that it is a state-run entity. There are more than ten million members who Basij who are unpaid volunteers acting out of ideological zeal or hopes of advancement. The exact number of "active Basij members remains unknown. They receive salaries and work full time to organize volunteer members. The Basij has been nominally subordinate to the IRGC beginning in the early 1980s, and more recent organizational reforms have increased the IRGC's direct control over the Basij, reportedly better coordinate the repression of internal dissent between the two groups.

Quds Force

The Quds Force (IRGC-QF) is a special division of the IRGC responsible for special missions the IRGC conducts outside of Iran's borders. The IRGC-QF has had an active role in providing training and arms to jihadist organizations including Iraqi insurgents, Lebanese Hezbollah, and other similar groups. Major General Qasem Soleimani is the commander of Quds Force. In addition to overseeing the group's violent attacks, Soleimani also serves as an emissary of Supreme Leader Ali Khamenei. Apparently uses both violent actions and bribery to exercise great influence over Iraqi politics. He is also believed to coordinate much of Iran's support for the Ba'ath regime in the Syrian civil war. Soleimani has also occasionally clashed with IRGC commanders over the boundaries of his authority.

IRGC Recruitment

The IRGC is consistently the third-wealthiest entity in Iran following the National Iranian Oil Company and the Imam Reza Endowment. Because of its great wealth, the IRGC is able to successfully recruit because it has the means to pay those who join the group a fairly attractively salary. The Basij and Quds Force operate under the IRGC aegis and are responsible for most of the IRGC recruitment. Both Basij and Quds Force have organized procedures for recruiting and training interested individuals. Both groups station recruiters near holy sites, mosques, schools, and community centers to attract volunteers. The IRGC also trains jihadists from organizations such as Hezbollah and Hamas.

See also: Iranian Minor Islamist Political Parties (volume 1).

FURTHER READING

Bodansky, Yossef. *Target America & the West: Terrorism Today*. New York: S.P.I. Books, 1993.
Cordesman, Anthony H. *Iran's Developing Military Capabilities*. Washington, D.C.: CSIS Press, 2005.
Iran's Islamic Revolutionary Guard Corps: Fueling Middle East turmoil: Hearing before the Committee on Foreign Affairs, House of Representatives, One Hundred Fourteenth Congress, first session, December 2, 2015. Washington: GPO, 2015.
Lustick, Ian S. Yerushalayim and al-Quds: Political Catechism and Political Realities. *Journal of Palestine Studies* 30, no. 1 (2000): 5-21.
O'Hern, Steven K. *Iran's Revolutionary Guard: The Threat that Grows While America sleeps*. Washington, D.C.: Potomac Books, 2012.

Chapter 48

ISLAMIC STATE OF IRAQ AND SYRIA (ISIS)/ ISLAMIC STATE (IS)/THE ISLAMIC STATE OF IRAQ AND THE LEVANT (ISIL)/ISIS

THE MANY NAMES OF ISIS

ISIS, sometimes spelled DAIISH or Da'esh, is an acronym for Dawlat al-Islamiyah f'al-Iraq wa al-Sham (or Al-Dawla Al-Islamiya fi al-Iraq wa al-Sham). The first three terms refer to the ISIS of Iraq and "al-Sham" refers to Syria and adjacent territory. The term, Daesh, is a transliteration of the Arabic acronym which means the Islamic State of Iraq and Syria in English.

ISIS is also referred to as the Islamic State (IS), or the Islamic State of Iraq and the Levant (ISIL), or Islamic State in Iraq and Syria (ISIS). ISIS is mostly a multi-national Sunni Islamist insurgent and terrorist organization that seeks to overthrow the governments of Iraq and Syria to establish a caliphate (one transnational Islamic state) based on Islamic Law (Sharia).

ISIS has been known by several names over its history. Abu Musab al-Zarqawi (1966-2006) formed and led the group that became in Iraq from 2002 through 2006 under the name of the Tawhid wal Jihad (Monotheism and Jihad) (TWJ) and Al-Qaeda in the Land of the Two Rivers (aka Al-Qaeda in Iraq, or AQ-I).

Under the name, Al-Qaeda in Iraq (AQI), the group waged guerilla warfare in the name of jihad during the sectarian insurgency following Saddam Hussein's (1937- 2006) ouster from power in Iraq in 2003 and against the Iraqi government and US-led coalition forces. ISIS adopted the name of AQI after allying itself to Osama bin-Laden (1957-2011) in October 2004. Abu Bakr al-Baghdadi (1971-), who became the group's leader, declared that its official name was the Islamic State in Iraq (ISI) in 2006. In 2013, Baghdadi added the phrase "and al-Sham" to the group's name that created the acronym "ISIS" in 2012, for the Islamic State of Iraq and Syria (ISIS) or the Islamic State of Iraq and the Levant (ISIL). ISIS did this to publicize its increased ambitions as its fighters joined the Syrian Civil War to oppose both the Assad-led government and Syrian secular and rival Islamist groups.

In June 2014, al-Baghdadi proclaimed himself "caliph" (ruler) of what he called "Islamic State (IS)" ISIS omitted the last two letters of the acronym, and demanded that the group be called the "Islamic State" to recognize their self-declared caliphate. The large majority of Muslim leaders and organizations responded by rejecting the use of this term to avoid legitimizing a terrorist group. They further assert that ISIS is an un-Islamic perversion of Islam to justify violence, and that the group is not a "State" or government, but a terrorist organization. The group, they argue further, should be rejected both by faithful Muslims and the global community (the umma).

Both the US and British governments generally use the acronym ISIL, while American and British media most often use the term "ISIS." The French government refers to the group as ISIS instead of the previous name, EIIL (L'Etat islamique en Irak et en Syrie). The US Defense Department also increasingly uses Daesh to refer to the group.

The term, Levant (an archaic French term for the "lands of the rising sun"), has long referred to a vaguely defined region including and surrounding Syria. This is the area that comprises modern-day Syria, Lebanon, Israel, Palestine, and Jordan.

The Obama administration used the acronym ISIL as the term "Levant" is considered a better translation of the Arabic term. The French government uses the name "ISIL" to identify the terror group, because the other names obscure the significant distinctions among Islam, Muslims, and Islamists, and because it also obscures the fact that the group is a terrorist group and not a state or government.

The Genesis of ISIS

Abu Musab al-Zarqawi, a Jordanian Arab, led Islamist jihadists in Herat, Afghanistan, before fleeing to the north of Iraq in 2001. While in Iraq, Zarqawi began collaborating with Ansar al-Islam (Partisans of Islam) (AaI), a group of extremist Kurdish separatist fighters. He led Arab jihadists associated with that group. Zarqawi reportedly trained terrorists and conducted numerous bombings and beheadings in Iraq.

Before the Iraq War began in 2003, the U.S. government reported to the United Nations Security Council, that ISIS was connected with Al-Qaeda (Zarqawi formally allied himself to Al-Qaeda in October 2004). The U.S. government listed AQI as a terrorist group also in October 2004. Al-Qaeda benefitted by the affiliation with ISIS because Al-Qaeda was able to remain relevant even after the destruction or displacement of its core forces in Afghanistan.

The Coalition Provisional Authority (CPA), which the United States and its coalition allies formed as Iraq's transitional government, issued two orders after Saddam Hussein was overthrown that may have inadvertently fueled the insurgency: 1) The CPA prohibited Ba'ath party members from Iraqi government service ("de-Baathification"); and, 2) The CPA disbanded Iraqi's army and security services, which resulted in thousands of individuals hostile to the new government, including many well-armed Sunnis, who were not answerable to the CPA.

Zarqawi sought to defeat the coalition by: 1) isolating U.S. forces by attacking its allies; 2) intimidating the Iraqis from involvement with the new government by targeting government infrastructure and personnel; 3) impeding reconstruction projects by attacking civilian contractors and aid workers; and 4) forcing the U.S. military into a Sunni-Shiite civil war by its attacks on Shiites.

ISIS fighters were first recruited from Zarqawi's allies in Pakistan and Afghanistan. The group later recruited fighters from Syria, Iraq, and other neighboring countries. By 2006, most of AQI's member were Iraqi. AQI membership grew significantly in 2006 and 2007, and then considered the most violent part of Iraq's sectarian civil war. A US counterterrorism campaign, including U.S. Special Operations Forces and the U.S.-supported Sahwa, or Sunni Awakening movement, also seriously weakened ISIS.

ISIS's relationship to the leaders of Al-Qaeda Central between 2006 and 2013 was both murky and fraught. Osama bin Laden and Ayman al-Zawahiri (1951-), Al-Qaeda's two most prominent leaders, argued that AQI's killings of other Muslims would encourage Muslims to reject Al-Qaeda in the Middle East and worldwide. In July 2005, the two Al-Qaeda leaders denounced Zarqawi's brutal tactics. AQI and Al-Qaeda ceased cooperating with each other after Zarqawi refused to comply with Al-Qaeda orders to cease attacking Shiite religious sites.

After Zarqawi's death in June 2006, the U.S. and Iraqi governments made significant gains against AQI. Both U.S. counterterrorism efforts and the Sunni "Tribal Awakening," which maintained local security had largely repelled AQI advances. AQI violence, thus, significantly decreased.

Zarqawi was succeeded as AQI's leader, by Abu Ayyub al-Masri (1968-2010), who was born in Egypt an expert in using explosives, and a close associate of Zawahiri. In October 2006, Masri and other AQI leaders officially renamed ISIS as the "Islamic State of Iraq (ISI)" to attract greater local support, which had declined and to assert its territorial goals. While ISI was signficantly weakened, it was not destroyed.

Two major Islamic State of Iraq (ISI) leaders died in 2010, including Masri. He was succeeded by Ibrahim Awad Ibrahim al-Badri al Samarra'i (commonly referred to as Abu Bakr al-Baghdadi) the current leader of ISIS. He is based and had operated in Raqqa Syria, which had been the capital of Baghdadi's caliphate. Under al-Baghdadi's leadership, ISIS rejuvenated itself. After the US began its military withdrawal from Iraq in late 2011, ISIS intensified its attacks mostly against Shiites to reignite conflict between Iraq's Sunni minority and Prime Minister Nouri al-Maliki's (1950 -) Shiite-led government. Sunni Iraqis, who believed that Iraq's Maliki government had marginalized them, began demanding reforms in Anbar province in December 2012. Prominent Shiite clerics including the Grand Ayatollah Ali Sistani (1930 -) and Moqtada al-Sadr (1973-) believed that some Sunni grievances had merit and needed to be resolved. The Government, however, appeared to largely ignore Sunni concerns.

In 2012, ISI changed its name to ISIS or ISIL, to emphasize its expanded ambitions in the worsening Syrian Civil War. This conflict created new opportunities to exploit. ISIS leader Abu Bakr al-Baghdadi assigned Muhammad al Jawlani (1974-2017) to establish the Al-Nusrah Front (ANF) (now known as Jabhat Fateh Al-Sham) in Syria to fight the Bashar al-Assad government. ISIS provided Jawlani with funding, personnel, and leadership, although ANF did not publicly reveal its connections to Al-Qaeda.

By early 2013, ISIS was conducting several deadly attacks a month within Iraq. Nearly eight thousand civilians died in 2013, the most killed since 2008. Also, in 2013, ISIS seized large areas of northwestern Iraq and northeastern Syria, presenting a grave threat to the security of both countries and stability in the entire Middle East.

THE SPLIT BETWEEN ISIS AND AL-QAEDA

In April 2013, al-Baghdadi, ISIS's leader, unilaterally announced that ISIS forces in Iraq and Syria would merge with the ANF to create the "Islamic State of Iraq and the Levant (ISIL)". Al-Nusra was an Al-Qaeda affiliate with greater local connections in Syria than ISIS. The leaders of both al Nusra and Al-Qaeda, however, rejected the merger and ordered it to be rescinded.

After rejecting the merger, Zawahiri, bin Laden's successor and leader of "core Al-Qaeda," demanded that ISIS confine its attacks only to Iraq. Baghdadi rejected Zawahiri's orders and challenged his authority, despite the fact that ISIS had sworn obedience to Al-Qaeda. ISIS leaders later claimed that their organization had never been a part of Al-Qaeda and asserted their claim to be a sovereign state and that they had merely given Al-Qaeda's leaders deference as opposed to obedience. Several Islamist militant organizations opposed to ISIS merged in late 2013 to form the "Mujahedeen Army" to defeat ISIS in Syria.

In February 2014, Zawahiri publicly severed all Al-Qaeda's connections with ISIS, because of ISIS's brutal tactics, infighting with other Sunni groups, and refusal to relinquish Syrian operations to ANF.

ISIS' BATTLE IN SYRIA

In June 2014, the Syrian air force was bombing ISIS-controlled territory in Raqqah and Hasakah provinces, with assistance from the Iraqi military. Syria later attacked positions near the Iraq-Syrian border and continued the air assault on ISIS. From late July through early August 2014, ISIS increasingly attacked Syrian regime military positions in the northeast of Syria. The militants seized several bases, large supplies of arms, and killed a large number of Syrian army prisoners of war.

Most ISIS fighters in Syria belong to tribes in either Syria or Iraq. Similar to other opponents of the Assad regime, these tribesmen were largely unwilling to the regime's military outside their own territories.

Since 2013, ISIS fighters have conducted ground attacks against targets in Iraq from bases in Syria. Early in 2014, ISIS regained much of Raqqah province and retook areas in Dayr az Zawr, an oil and gas producing province next to the Anbar region of Iraq.

In late 2013, the ISIS gained control of several oil fields in Dayr az Zawr and were paid for oil sales by the Assad regime. This revenue made ISIS became operationally independent of Al-Qaeda. ISIS was also able to pay its fighters relatively well. ISIS raised funds by taxing inhabitants under its rule and diverting humanitarian relief for its own purposes

Most ISIS fighters in northeastern Syria refrain from engaging regime forces in Syria's major cities in the west of the country. In early August 2014, however, Syrian rebels allied with ISIS fought with the Lebanese military for control of Arsal Lebanon, which is a small town near the Syrian border. Reportedly, the local group had not pre-arranged the attack with ISIS leaders.

ISIS focused its attacks on the provinical capital of Dayr az Zawr to strengthen its supply line to Abu Kamal, a strategic town near the border of Iraq and Syria. In July, ISIS subdued most of Dayr az Zawr, although fighting continued in areas of the city. After ISIS had declared itself a caliphate, a large number of local militiamen and tribal fighters in that area pledged their loyalty to the terrorist group. ISIS, however, continued to face resistance from Syrian government troops southwest of Raqqah and several armed Syrian rebel groups near Aleppo.

The Islamist opposition to the Assad regime in Syria remains very divided. While Al-Qaeda-affiliated groups in Syria fought with the secular opposition, the Free Syrian Army (FSA) entered into a truce with ISIS in September 2014, which was perceived as acknowledging ISIS's continuing military strength.

THE CALIPHATE AND ITS CRITICS

In June 2014, Baghdadi declared the establishment of an Islamic caliphate (or Islamic State) and demanded the allegiance of all Muslims worldwide, and ultimately world domination.

ISIS had some of the normal characteristics of a sovereign nation, including having a military force (the ISIS militia), some services (albeit, limited services) and social control (although through ultraconservative and violent methods).

ISIS supporters (including private individuals in Jordan, Syria, and Saudi Arabia) largely funded the group and its predecessor organizations in the past. The Iranian government had also financed AQI, despite sectarian differences, as Iran sought to defeat the Coalition and the US-supported Iraqi Government.

ISIS earned most of its revenue from enterprises such as smuggling, and extortion. ISIS then shifted to relying on financing and personnel from with the areas it occupied in Iraq and Syria. Even before ISIS captured Mosul, Iraq, in June 2014, the group regularly extorted funds from local businesses.

ISIS overtly seeks war with governments it perceives as apostate (religious deviants), including those of Iraq, Syria, and the United States. ISIS's public statements articulate an uncompromising, exclusionary worldview along with unlimited ambition. Al-Baghdadi, ISIS's leader, and ISIS spokesperson, Abu Mohammed al Adnani (1977-2016), issued sectarian oriented appeals for violent jihad. He denounced Shiites as non-Muslims and unsupportive Sunnis as enemies who must be destroyed in ISIS's efforts to establish a caliphate.

ISIS describes Iraqi Shiites as "rejectionists" and "polytheists" and describes the Iraqi government as a "vassal state" of Iran. Similarly, ISIS similarly criticizes Syrian Alawites and the Assad government. ISIS and its predecessor groups, however, received financial and security assistance from the Syrian regime from 2003-2011, when US maintained a particularly large presence in Iraq.

THE ISIS OFFENSIVE IN IRAQ

Throughout 2012, ISIS attacks in several cities killed several Iraqis. In four days, ISIS coordinated attacks killed more than a hundred Iraqis.

In April 2013, Iraqi security forces (ISF) attacked a Sunni protest camp at Al-Hawijah, which inflamed Sunni militancy. Car bombings and suicide attacks dramatically increased throughout Iraq, with coordinated ISIS attacks directed against Shiite markets, cafes, and mosques. In 2013, 7,818 civilians (including police officers) were killed in terrorist attacks, more than twice the death toll in 2012. Nearly 18,000 people were injured, which made 2013 Iraq's most violent year since 2008. In late 2013, the ISF attempted to close a protest camp in Ramadi. This resulted in a major uprising, forcing ISF to abandon the city and nearby Fallujah. ISIS, then, seized those areas.

Thousands of Sunni jihadists flocked to Syria to fight Bashar al-Assad's regime. The minority Alawite sect, a Shiite faction, is the most powerful and most loyal part of Assad's government.

With relative ease, ISIS captured northwestern Iraq and northeastern Syria, where a large number Sunni tribespeople lived who were alienated with their governments. This include included Syria's remote eastern provinces, which would bear the brunt of devastation from the forthcoming devastation.

The ISIS led an insurgency that had formed alliances with non-jihadi Sunnis, including fighters supported by Sunni Arab tribes and Baathists once loyal to Saddam Hussein. These Sunnis were involved despite the fact that many were weary of ISIS's extreme brutality and plans to impose a harsh version of Sharia (Islamic Law).

The ISF had halted an earlier ISIS-led insurrection in Anbar Province in January 2014. In early 2014, Iran's government offered military assistance to the Iraqi government to fight Sunni Jihadists in Anbar. By June 2014, ISIS defeated the ISF in Fallujah and seized control of the area.

ISIS also attacked areas in Hasakah Province north of Dayr az Zawr, which placed ISIS forces near Nineveh Province in Iraq. This helped ISIS to eventually attack and seize Mosul.

ISIS military successes in Iraq allowed it to open new supply lines to facilitate the movement of arms and jihadists into Syria's eastern frontier.

In the Spring of 2014, ISIS jihadists proceeded along the Tigris and Euphrates rivers, capturing several cities and towns in that area. On June 10, 2014, ISIS captured Mosul, Iraq's second largest city. The largely Shiite army, weakened by desertions and corruption, quickly disintegrated ISF troops surrendered en masse. In addition, nearly 60 of 243 Iraqi army combat battalions remained unaccounted for in that battle. After the ISF defeat in Mosul, the insurgents freed more than one thousand prisoners, captured large amounts of arms, equipment, and supplies that the United States Government had provided to the ISF, and looted banks, which would further expanded ISIS's capacity and reach. ISIS had become the wealthiest terrorist organization in the world.

After capturing Mosul, ISIS led fighters then advanced to Saddam Hussein's hometown of Tikrit and other cities, and into Diyala Province, whose population is divided nearly equally between Sunnis and Shiites.

ISIS-led fighters captured the city of Tal Afar west of Mosul on June 16 and came close to Baqubah, capital of Diyala, about 38 miles northeast of Baghdad, by June 17. ISIS-led insurgents in Anbar, supported by its tribal allies, seized additional cities along the Euphrates River.

ISIS AND ITS CRIMES AGAINST HUMANITY

ISIS controlled its captured territory with extreme brutality and intimidation, and often enforced its control assisted by local militias. The ISIS advances in Iraq also resulted in a humanitarian crisis that impacted thousands of Iraqi Christians and Yezidis, who were some of the religious and ethnic minorities that ISIS planned to eliminate. The Yazidis are mostly Kurdish-speaking and follow several different ancient religions, including Zoroastrianism, which was Iran's major religion before Iran converted to Islam. In mid-July 2014, ISIS in Mosul ordered the city's remaining Christians there to leave the city, which most apparently did.

Allegations of human rights violations committed by ISIS militants emerged, including murder, kidnappings, forced conversions, and physical and sexual assault. In capturing territory, ISIS jihadists engaged in the widespread killing of hundreds of civilians (many being from various ethnic or minority religious groups) that they viewed as infidels.

CONFRONTING INTENSE ISIS BOMBARDMENT, THE RELATIVELY LIGHTLY ARMED KURDISH FORCES

Were forced from several towns where mostly Christians and other Iraqi minorities, particularly the Yazidis, resided. Concerned about ISIS threats of genocide unless they converted to Islam, nearly 35,000–50,000 Yazidis fled to Sinjar Mountain. In early August 2014, the YPG established security corridors close to the Iraq border, allowing refugees fleeing from ISIS-controlled Iraq to enter Syrian territory controlled by the YPG.

In early 2016, the United Nations reported that ISIS enslaved about 3,500 people, mostly Iraqi children and women, with the majority of these are Yezidi. There were many other from a large number of other minority ethnic and religious groups. The UN further reported that many of ISIS's widespread and horrific abuses could war crimes, crimes against humanity, and possibly even genocide. Despite the outcry from the international community, ISIS continued to unlawfully kill civilians through shootings, beheadings, bulldozings, burning them live and throwing them from buildings. The group also abducted hundreds of children from their families to force them to take up arms as ISIS fighters.

THE ISIS OFFENSIVE AGAINST THE KURDS

After Mosul fell to ISIS, Prime Minister Maliki asked the Kurdish security forces (the Peshmerga) also to join with the government in fighting ISIS. After maintaining a relatively quiet front line with territory controlled by the Kurdistan Regional Government (KRG) and its Peshmerga militia fighters, ISIS-led fighters attacked Kurdish-controlled territory in early August 2014. ISIS military advances in northern Iraq forced the Peshmerga to retreat.

ISIS-led jihadist attacks on the KRG's main oil refinery at Baiji led to gasoline shortages in northern Iraq, including in the KRG. The fighting had only limited effect on Iraq's overall oil production and exports because 75 percent of Iraq's oil is produced and exported from southern Iraq, where far fewer Sunni insurgents operated.

After the ISF collapsed in northern Iraq, the Kurdish militia (the Peshmerga) seized Kirkuk and large nearby oil fields that the ISF had abandoned. The Kurds had long sought control of that oil-producing area (which they assert is historically Kurdish territory) and to annex the province with their autonomous region under KRG control. On July 11, the Peshmerga reportedly seized control of two major oil fields near Kirkuk from the Iraq government

By August 8, ISIS-led fighters had advanced to within about 40 miles of the KRG capital of Irbil, causing residents to flee from the city, and increasing U.S. concern for the safety and security of U.S. diplomatic and military personnel located there.

ISIS-led forces also seized Iraq's largest dam, the Mosul Dam, which could have been damaged or used by ISIS to flood much of northern and central Iraq.

THE ISIS BATTLE AGAINST THE SHIITE MILITIAS

In addition Kurdish assistance, Prime Minister Maliki also mobilized Shiite militias accused of sectarian killings and Iraqi forces that were accused of indiscriminate airstrikes against civilians. Maliki principally enlisted Shiite militias to assist the ISF in protecting Baghdad from ISIS (a city where 80 percent of its residents are Shiites). Grand Ayatollah Ali al-Sistani (1930-), Iraq's leading Shiite cleric, also issued a call for Shiites to join the militias. This militia assistance enabled ISF to regroup in order to fight ISIS.

ISIS jihadists failed to seize Baghdad International Airport in southwest Baghdad. ISF and allied forces also began counterattacking Tikrit and its vicinity in Anbar Province. Aided by Iranian and US air strikes, the ISF recaptured Tikrit in March 2015.

THE WEST CONFRONTS THE ISIS CHALLENGE

In July 2012, al-Baghdadi said, "the mujahidin have set out to chase the affiliates of your armies that have fled... . You will see them in your own country, God willing. The war with you has just begun." In January 2014, Al-Baghdadi also denounced the United States, "Know, O defender of the Cross, that a proxy war will not help you in the Levant, just as it will not help you in Iraq. Soon, you will be in direct conflict—God permitting—against your will." (Blanchard, Humud, and Nitkin, 2013).

ISIS English language propaganda of the executions of two U.S. journalists James Foley and Stephen Sotloff in August 2014 indicated that ISIS seeks to depict itself as fighting U.S. aggression, a tactic used by its predecessor organizations and Al-Qaeda.

Hillary Clinton, a former US Secretary of State, asserted that ISIS is a greater threat to the United States than Al-Qaeda. Secretary Clinton added that President Barack Obama was correct and justified in launching a military offensive against ISIS in Syria and Iraq. "It is a serious threat because this is the best-funded, most professional, expansionist jihadist military force that we have ever seen...This is far more advanced and far richer than Al-Qaeda ever was" (Gearan, 2014).

Clinton added that ISIS would continue to attack targets in the West if opportunities present themselves. Former Defense Secretary Leon Panetta criticized the Obama administration for failure to follow his and Clinton's advice to arm Syrian rebels in 2012 to deter the growing power of the jihadist group. In August 2014, Clinton seeming criticized the administration enabling the jihadists to seize much of Iraq. She added that Obama had facilitated the emergence of ISIS by failing to develop a "credible" military strategy. "The failure to help build up a credible fighting force of the people who were the originators of the protests against [Syrian leader Bashar] Assad — there were Islamists, there were secularists, there was everything in the middle — the failure to do that left a large vacuum, which the jihadists have now filled." (Goldberg, 2014).

In September 2014, Clinton clarified her earlier comments, explaining that she supported Obama's strategy in arming the Syrian rebels and conducting airstrikes. "Whatever the debates might have been before, this is a threat to the region and beyond," Clinton said, "the situation now is demanding a response and we are seeing a very robust response" (Mercia, 2014).

Growing threats to the West include those presented by jihadists with Western connection. Approximately 12,000 foreign fighters traveled to Syria, including more than 1,000 Europeans, and more than 100 U.S. citizens.

These fighters from more than 50 countries include Al-Qaeda-affiliated veterans of previous conflicts. The U.S. government became increasingly concerned that ISIS-sympathizers, perhaps encouraged or motivated by ISIS propaganda, would conduct limited, self-directed attacks (or "lone-wolf attacks") within the United States with no prior warning. US government officials, however, continued to believe that domestic threats from such extremists are likely to be limited in scope and scale.

The US government has long been concerned that ISIS controlled areas in the Middle East may become sanctuaries for anti-Western jihadists. The US government responded to the ISIS threat by increasing support for the Iraqi government, including greater assistance to Iraq's counterterrorism units and providing missiles and surveillance drones. While some commentators disagree as to what extent ISIS represents a direct terrorist threat to U.S. territory, or to U.S. facilities and personnel in the Middle East, most agreed that ISIS poses a direct and significant threat to the West, as well as to Iraq and Syria.

The international community has also strongly condemned ISIS and its tactics. The US government has increased monitoring of Iraq's political challenges and Syria's civil war. At a NATO meeting in Wales in September 2014, President Obama presented a strategy to defeat ISIS using military action, support for allied forces in Iraq and Syria, diplomacy, intelligence sharing, and financial actions to progressively reduce the geographic and political space, as well as the personnel, and financial resources available to ISIS. The US and its allies also agreed to refrain from deploying ground troops to either Iraq or Syria.

The Obama administration also sought to obtain Sunni support in both Syria and Iraq to defeat ISIS. Critics were skeptical that the strategy of the Obama administration would significantly impact ISIS's operations because local anti-ISIS fighters do not have the combat support of U.S. or other Western forces.

THE ISIS CRISIS AND THE IRAQI GOVERNMENT

The ISIS crisis caused a major upheaval in Iraq's government. In response to concerns that Maliki's policies had alienated Sunni Arabs, elections for the Iraqi Council of Representatives (COR) were conducted on April 30, 2014. This election led to the formation of a new government. By informal agreement, A Sunni Arab is speaker of the COR; a Kurd is the president (a largely ceremonial position), and a Shiite Arab is the Prime Minister (a powerful executive position). Several Iraqi factions, as well as some within Maliki's coalition, opposed giving Maliki a third term despite the strong performance of Maliki's "State of Law" coalition in the election. U.S. Secretary of State John Kerry asked the Iraqis to choose leaders who would both be inclusive and willing to share power.

In July 2014, the COR selected Salim al Jabburi (1971-) (a Sunni) as Speaker, and two deputies, and Kurdish leader Fouad Masoum (1938 -) as Iraq's President. The President has the constitutional duty to request the candidate of the largest bloc in the COR to form a government. On August 11, President Masoum formally requested Haydar al-Abbadi (1952-), from Maliki's Da'wa Party, to become the next Prime Minister. Both the U.S. government and several Iranian political leaders supported al-Abbadi's selection, which contributed to the failure of Maliki's challenge to that appointment. The Prime Minister-designate worked to form and win parliamentary confirmation for a new cabinet. The COR approved his program and almost all of his ministerial nominations on September 8, and al-Abbadi became prime minister. Permanent ministers for the two powerful security posts of Interior and Defense Minister, however, remained unfilled at the time. Al-Abbadi sought to have Sunnis serve to a newly-created "national guard" force to help protect Sunni territory recaptured from ISIS.

IRAN'S ROLE IN THE ISIS CRISIS

Both US and Iranian interests in Iraq seemingly converged during the ISIS Crisis. After ISIS had captured Mosul, Secretary of State John Kerry announced the willingness of the US government to discuss Iraq-related issues with Iran.

Many observers expressed skepticism that that the United States could or should substantially cooperate with Iran in Iraq. Iran assisted in forming many of the Shiite militias that fought the United States from 2003 through 2011. Iran also sent Islamic Revolutionary Guard-Quds Force (IRGC-QF) personnel into Iraq to advise the Shiite militias fighting the ISF. Militia involvement exacerbated tensions with Iraq's Sunnis, including residents of mostly Shiite-inhabited Baghdad and in provinces such as Diyala, which have mixed populations. Some Shiite militia fighters have reportedly conducted reprisals against Sunnis whom the militias accuse of being ISIS supporters. Some Shiite militia members who are fighting in Iraq had returned from Syria, where they had been fighting to keep President Assad in power against Sunni-led militants.

Through an extended military campaign against both governments and opposition forces, ISIS eventually gained control over a roughly contiguous area along the Tigris and Euphrates rivers that extended for hundreds of miles. ISIS has between 20,000-32,000 fighters.

Beginning in April 2015, ISIS mobilized in Syria to bolster its forces in Anbar and Salah ad-Din provinces. It also recruits for suicide bombers and commandoes. The Assad regime has lost towns in the Homs desert to ISIS, as well as peripheral areas in southern Syria on and near the Jordanian border, and in the northern Syria in Idlib province to several Syrian rebel forces.

HOW ISIS GOVERNED ITS "TERRITORIES"

From its de-facto capital in Raqqah, until ISIS lost most of its territories in Iraq and Syria in 2017, ISIS ruled the territory it captured in northeastern Syria and northwestern Iraq.

In certain respects, ISIS fiananced its operations in a manner similar to a conventional government in that it assessed taxes and fees for schools, garbage collection, and telephone service. The organization also had a diverse income stream that include oil and gas infrastructure and antiquities smuggling. Despite Coalition airstrikes, was also able to sustain itself for a period of time by increasing taxes.

ISIS developed a fairly efficient local government administration. that collected taxes and conducted ordinary government services such as garbage collection, handled marriage licenses. Although ISIS was never not recognized as a nation-state, it acted like one. ISIS built its administration on the foundation of the previous one, incorporating the administrative knowledge and skill of government workers in the territory it occupied. One of the reasons why ISIS had the success it did in administering its territory was its diverse sources of revenue. ISIS received its income from so many parts of the economy that airstrikes by themselves were insufficient to destroy it.

The jihadist derived income from several source of sources, including agricultural products such as what, milk, and fruits at the markets it controlled. Thus, ISIS was self-financed and was not reliant on donors from outside the area. Also, taxes on ordinary daily commerce and agriculture, not petroleum, drove the caliphate's economy. Black-market oil sales at one point brought in an estimated $2 million per week, however the ratio of money earned from taxes versus oil stood at 6:1. ISIS raised funds throughout the supply chain: Prior to a sowing of seed of grain, ISIS collected rent for the fields it had confiscated. Then, when the crops were ready for harvest, it collected a harvest tax.

ISIS reorganized local governments agencies using the term "diwan", which was first used in the seventh-century rule of one of the earliest caliphs. These included well-known ones for education and health, but also ones for "Hisba",the morality police.

THE ISIS PROVINCES

Despite losing control of territories in Syria and Iraq, ISIS claims to operate official "provinces" (wilaya) in Sinai, Nigeria, Libya, Algeria, Yemen, Saudi Arabia, and the Caucasus regions. In Africa, for example, ISIS recognizes the caliphate province of Alkinaana (which includes Chad, Egypt, and Sudan), Habasha (which includes Eritrea, Ethiopia, Somalia, Kenya, and Uganda), and Maghreb (which includes Algeria, Libya, Mauritania, Morocco, Niger, Nigeria, and Tunisia).

In areas outside of Iraq and Syria, ISIS, however, lacks the same depth of organic roots and financial resources that it once had in either Syria and Iraq. ISIS has also perpetuated or inspired several massacres in Iraq, Syria, Sinai, Kuwait, and Tunisia. The group remains an international terrorist threat.

Within ISIS strongholds (such as Mosul and Raqqa), the group had very little effective local opposition that could effectively challenge ISIS control. ISIS, in fact, had the governmental and bureaucratic power necessary to imposes its will. Also, ISIS's internal security and intelligence gathering organization were able to brutally and effectively suppress opposition against them and divide its opponents against each other.

END OF THE CALIPHATE

When ISIS proclaimed its caliphate in 2014, it promised to achieve justice through a strict and harsh interpretation of Sharia, along with providing such public services as utilities, agricultural loans, and assistance to impoverished people. ISIS also began disseminating propaganda promoting its version of an Islamic utopia to jihadists worldwide. By early 2016, ISIS had proven itself to be no utopia of any type. The group operated as a criminal syndicate attempting to function as a government. ISIS's claims to be based on Sharia (Islamic law) and "Islamic values" was increasingly viewed as empty propaganda. Widespread Public disillusionment in ISIS-occupied territories with the group's conduct and performance increased as the group continued to fail to provide "Ideal Islamic governance" that would fully and always provide equality, justice, and competent and honest governance. Many critics in the Middle East even began analogizing ISIS rule to that of Bashar Assad (1965 -).

Instead of bringing about any genuine semblance of social equality, ISIS cultivated a new elite, jihadi fighters, who were granted preference both in society and in the ISIS courts. The Jihadists often dismissed non-Jihadists, who they despise as "commoners". They also regularly disregarded the counsel of their own clerics.

In territory that ISIS once controlled, the group permitted or engaged in systematic injustice. In ISIS courts, judges were openly biased in favor of ISIS members. The judges justified this inequality by misinterpreting or misapplying Koran passages, including "God prefers those who fight in jihad over those who sit" (an-Nisa 4:95).

ISIS became increasingly unable to provide public services to the population it controlled largely because of the accumulation of military defeats had inflicted genuine financial damage on the group. For most of people living territory that ISIS controlled, water and electricity became scarce, while energy costs soared.

Also, the air campaigns of both the United States and Russia destroyed much of ISIS's ability to produce oil, which had provided much of ISIS's revenue. From 2015 through 2016, ISIS lost nearly 40 percent of the territory it once controlled in Iraq and Syria. January 2017, there were nearly 35,000 ISIS fighters in Iraq and Syria controlling more than 17,000 square miles. In December 2017, between 1,000 and 3,000 jihadists controlled less than 2,000 square miles. Most of these fighters were in the rural desert region d Dayr Az Zawr in Syria, Southeast of Raqqa, and Anbar province in Iraq. Nearly 8 million people lived under ISIS control when the "caliphate" was at the peak of its power. Five million were freed from ISIS control in 2017 and 2.7 million Iraqis returned to their homes in that year (Shinkman, 2017).

ISIS once was able to recruit is fighters in areas it controlled because its members received benefits that other individuals living in those areas did not receive. Young men often joined ISIS to escape poverty or protect themselves or their families from ISIS brutality. After it became increasingly difficult to recruit volunteers, ISIS used conscription to fill its ranks of fighters. According to most sources, ISIS was effectively defeated as a fighting force in 2017.

WHY DID THE CALIPHATE COLLAPSE?

ISIS had its origins in the longstanding collective dream to restore the military, political and technological superiority over western nations that Muslim majority nations had centuries ago or the strong belief that that the end of the world was near. This vision failed to come to fruition with the ISIS caliphate. There three key reasons why the caliphate failed. First, ISIS required continuous successful conquests because this was viewed as a sign that ISIS had Allah's blessings. Such Expansion would yield new recruits to replace wounded and killed fighters, more arms and supplies, archaeological item to sell, property to loot, food to distribute and new communities and resources, such as oil wells and refineries, to confiscate. After ISIS seized Sunni-dominated territories, the caliphate could no longer expand. It was too weak to seize control of Turkey, Israel and Jordan.

Second, the violent intolerance of dissent and brutality by ISIS towards the communities it seized A key reason for ISIS rapid expansion was that Sunni tribal leaders and other political leaders in Iraq and Syria perceived key advantages in ISIS control. ISIS rule brought relative security, a rude form of justice, and defend against perceived Shia injustice and perceptions of a corrupt Iraqi government.

By 2015, a weakened and wounded ISIS clearly could no longer provide anything other than violence and misery. Defections began and began to rapidly cascade. With the end coming near, it was foreign fighters who defended the hospital and stadium in Raqqa, because the Syrian militants had surrendered days earlier.

Third, ISIS sought to confront western nations, which responded. The combination of western combat technology and funding for local military and security forces reportedly successfully made the difference for the West in nations such as Pakistan, Nigeria, Somalia, Libya, and Mali. The military targets attacked by western nations were usually forced at the least to forego attempts at conquering additional territory, particularly in urban areas.

"ISIS 2.0"

Although ISIS no longer controls significant amounts of territory in Iraq and Syria, and is no longer a physical caliphate, the group still exists as a transnational jihadist terrorist organization and still operates throughout the world. It continues to inspire and radicalize marginalized individuals to carry out "lone wolf" attacks via the Internet and social media (especially through its weekly digital magazine *Al-Naba*) as "soldiers of the caliphate. The fact that the group is still able to strike without warning in major cities worldwide continues to be a major serious security concern for the nations that oppose the jihadists. In 2017, ISIS took responsibility for attacks such as the one at an Arianna Grande concert in Manchester England, a driver who drove pedestrians on Halloween day in New York City, and bombings in Baghdad, Iraq. ISIS claims to have conducted 38 operations conducted by 60 jihadists in

19 countries in 2017. These attacks reportedly occurred in Australia, Bangladesh, Belgium, Egypt, France, Germany, Great Britain, Indonesia, Iran, Italy, Jordan, Kenya, Palestine, Russia, Spain, Sweden, Tunisia, Turkey, and the United States. The group claimed that 24 percent of the attacks involved attackers who used bombs and grenades, 21 percent involved attackers who used stabbing, 19 percent used firearms, 18 percent used suicide missions, 13 percent used vehicle ramming and 5 used involved fire (O'Connor, 2017).

The ISIS presence has also been increasing Yemen, which has been devastated by ongoing conflict. While the ISIS is still small, it has greatly increased in 2017, as ISIS fighters and leaders fled the collapsing caliphate in Iraq and Syria. ISIS has particularly gained a foothold in areas that fell into anarchy due to continuing conflict between Houthi insurgents supported by Iran and military forces supporting the Yemeni government in exile in Saudi Arabia. ISIS also has recruited fighters who defected from Al-Qaeda in the Arabian Peninsula (AQAP), which had been weakened by severe losses in leadership due to a continuing U.S.-led commando and air campaign. Between 300 and 500 Islamic State group fighters currently operate in Yemen, chiefly in territory that had been historically ungoverned or where government has failed to function due to the continuing conflict between Houthi insurgents supported by Iran and forces loyal to the government in exile in Saudi Arabia.

See also: Al-Qaeda (volume 1); Al-Qaeda in Iraq (volume 1); Al-Qaeda in Arabian Peninsula (volume 1); Islamic State of Iraq and Syria -- Libya (volume 2); Khorasan Group (volume 1).

FURTHER READING

Bennis, Phyllis. *ISIS and Syria: the new global war on terror*. Toronto: Between the Lines, 2017.
Blanchard, Christopher M., Humud, Carla & Nitkin, Mary Beth. "Armed Conflict in Syria: Overview and US Response." *Current Politics & Economics of the Middle East 6, no. 2* (2015): 325.
Byman, Daniel. *Al Qaeda, the Islamic State, and the Global Jihadist Movement: What Everyone Needs to Know*. New York, NY: Oxford University Press, 2015.
Covarrubias, Jack, Tom Lansford and Robert J. Pauly. *The New Islamic State: Ideology, Religion and Violent Extremism in the 21st Century*. Abingdon, Oxon: Ashgate Publishing, 2016.
Enayat, Hamid. "The Concept of the Islamic State." *Modern Islamic Political Thought*, 1982, 69-110.
Flibbert, Andrew. "The Consequences of Forced State Failure in Iraq." *Political Science Quarterly* 128, no. 1 (2013): 67-96.
Fradkin, Hillel Gideon, Ḥusain Ḥaqqānī, Eric Brown and Hassan Mneimneh. *Current trends in Islamist ideology*. Washington, D.C.: Hudson Institute, Center on Islam, Democracy, and the Future of the Muslim World, 2015.
Griffin, Michael. *Islamic State: Rewriting History*. London: Pluto Press, 2016.
Inside the Mind of ISIS: Understanding Its Goals and Ideology to Better Protect the Homeland: Hearing Before the Committee On Homeland Security and Governmental

Affairs, United States Senate, One Hundred Fourteenth Congress, Second Session, January 20, 2016. Washington: U.S. Government Publishing Office, 2017.

Isakhan, Benjamin. *The Legacy of Iraq: From the 2003 War to the "Islamic State"*. Edinburgh: Edinburgh University Press, 2015.

Malkasian, Carter. *Illusions of Victory: the Anbar Awakening and the Rise of the Islamic State*. New York, NY: Oxford University Press, 2017.

Manne, Robert. *The Mind of the Islamic State: ISIS and the Ideology of the Caliphate*. Amherst, NY: Prometheus Books, 2017.

Micallef, Joseph V and Joseph V. Micallef. *Islamic State: Its History, Ideology and Challenge*. Vancouver, Portland: Antioch Downs Press, 2015.

Moubayed, Sami M. *Under the Black Flag: at the Frontier of the New Jihad*. London: I.B. Tauris & Co. Ltd., 2015.

Murad, Nadia and Jenna Krajeski. *The Last Girl: My Story of captivity and My Fight Against the Islamic State*. London: Virago Press Ltd, 2017.

Nance, Malcolm W. *Defeating ISIS: Who They Are, How They Fight, What They Believe*. New York: Skyhorse Publishing, 2016.

O'Connor, Tom. "What Did ISIS Do In 2017? Islamic State Reveals Its Favorite Terror Attacks and Calls for More." *Newsweek.* Nov. 18, 2017.

Ogu, Emmanuel C., Michael I. Ogu and Chiemela Ogu. "Insights from Terrorism Intelligence and Eradication Efforts - Al-Qaeda, ISIS, Boko Haram - for More Pragmatic Botnet Countermeasures." *International Journal of Collaborative Intelligence* 1, no. 4 (2016): 258.

Oxnevad, Ian. "The Master Plan: ISIS, Al-Qaeda, and the Jihadi Strategy for Final Victory." *Politics, Religion & Ideology* 18, no. 3 (2017): 353-55.

Shinkman, Paul D. "ISIS by the Numbers." *U.S. News and World Report.*" Dec. 27, 2017.

Turner, John A. "The Islamic State." *Religious Ideology and the Roots of the Global Jihad*, 2014, 45-61.

The Counterterrorism Strategy Against the Islamic State Of Iraq and the Levant: Are We on the Right Path?: Hearing Before the Subcommittee on Emerging Threats And Capabilities of the Committee on Armed Services, House of Representatives, One Hundred Fourteenth Congress, First Session, Hearing held June 24, 2015. Washington: U.S. Government Publishing Office, 2016.

The Ideology of ISIS: Hearing Before the Committee on Homeland Security and Governmental Affairs, United States Senate, One Hundred Fourteenth Congress, second session, June 21, 2016. Washington: U.S. Government Publishing Office, 2017.

The Islamic State of Iraq and Syria: the history of ISIS/ISIL. Cambridge, MA: Charles River Editors, 2014.

The Tribal Factor in Syria's Rebellion: A Survey of Armed Tribal Groups in Syria. The Jamestown Foundation, (June 27, 2013).

UNAMI, Public Information Office. "UN Gravely Concerned about Situation in Northern Iraq; Calls for Urgent Response" (August 7, 2014).

UNOCHA. *Iraq: OCHA Flash Update: Iraq Crisis – Significant Displacement from Sinjar*, No. 2 (August 4, 2014).

Weiss, Michael and Hassan Hassan. *ISIS: Inside the Army of Terror*. New York: Regan Arts, 2016.

Chapter 49

Islamic State in Yemen (Wilayah Yemen/Sanaa/Al Beyda/ Aden-Bayan/Shaba/Hadramout)

Yemeni jihadists claiming to be allied to ISIS have sought to capitalize on continuing fighting in Yemen to repeatedly attack targets associated with Zaydi Muslims, including their mosques. Zaydism is a sub-sect of Shia Islam (but with legal traditions and religious observances similar to those of Sunni Muslims). ISIS jihadists have also attacked supporters of the Houthi Movement, which is predominantly Zaydi militia and political party that currently controls much of northern Yemen. The Zaydis seek to restore the "Inmate or Zaydi-led monarchy that had governed northern Yemen for most of the period from 893 through 1962. The Houthis are engaged in fighting a coalition of predominantly Sunni Arab nations led by Saudi Arabia. ISIS may be seeking to use conflict to generate increased religious enmity in Yemen between the Shia and Sunni. Although devastated by prolonged warfare, Yemen has historically not suffered much of the same sectarian conflict as other Arab nations such as Iraq and Lebanon. Internal leadership and other organizational infighting may have impeded the growth of the Islamic State of Yemen, as has opposition from opposing jihadist groups, especially the larger and established Al-Qaeda in the Arabian Peninsula (AQAP).

In October 2017, the US launched airstrikes against Islamic State in Yemen targets in Yakla and Al-Abl in Southern Al-Bayda Province, which were strongholds of the group. Many of the ISIS fighters affiliated with Islamic State in Yemen were originally affiliated with Al Qaeda in the Arabian Peninsula (AQAP), who were deployed to the Yemeni affiliate in Yemen to fight the Houthi rebels.

See also: Al-Qaeda in the Arabian Peninsula (AQAP) (volume 1); Hirak (volume 1); Houthis (volume 1).

Further Reading

Bonnefoy, Laurent. "Violence in Contemporary Yemen: State, Society and Salafis." *The Muslim World* 101, no. 2 (2011): 324-46.

Clausen, Maria-Louise. "Islamic State in Yemen – A Rival to al-Qaeda?" *Connections: The Quarterly Journal* 16, no. 1 (2017): 51-63.

Eleftheriadou, Marina. "Elements of 'Armed Non-State Actors' Power: the Case of Al-Qaeda in Yemen." *Small Wars & Insurgencies* 25, no. 2 (2014): 404-27.

Holbrook, Donald. "Al-Qaeda and the Rise of ISIS." *Survival* 57, no. 2 (2015): 93-104.

Kendall, Elisabeth. "Al-Qaeda and Islamic State in Yemen." *Oxford Scholarship Online*, 2017.

Mendelsohn, Barak. *The Al-Qaeda Franchise: the Expansion of Al-Qaeda and its Consequences*. Oxford: Oxford University Press, 2016.

Phillips, Sarah. "Al-Qaeda and the Struggle for Yemen." *Survival* 53, no. 1 (2011): 95-120.

Terrill, W Andrew. *The Struggle for Yemen and the Challenge of Al-Qaeda in the Arabian Peninsula*. Carlisle Barracks, PA: Strategic Studies Institute, 2013.

Chapter 50

JABHAT FATEH AL-SHAM (THE FRONT FOR THE CONQUEST OF THE LEVANT) (JFS), FORMERLY KNOWN, AS THE JABHAT AL NUSRA LI AHL AL SHAM (OR AL NUSRA FRONT)

Jabhat Fateh Al-Sham (the Front for the Conquest of the Levant) (JFS), once known as Jabhat al-Nusra (JAN), is one of the largest jihadist groups operating in Syria. JAN disguised its connections with Al-Qaeda and discontinued portraying itself as an Al-Qaeda affiliate. The group did this to allow it to operate as part of a broader rebel coalition in Syria. The connection between Al-Qaeda and JAN was revealed when Abu Bakr Al-Baghdadi, the leader of ISIS insisted that JAN was subservient to him. In response, JAN's emir, Abu Muhammad al-Julani acknowledged that JAN was an Al-Qaeda affiliate. He then appealed to the Al-Qaeda Ayman al-Zawahiri to resolve the dispute with Baghdadi. In 2013, Zawahiri supported Julani, while also criticizing him for revealing JAN's connections with Al-Qaeda without informing Al-Qaeda central.

In early August 2016, JN adopted its new name followed its announced disassociation from Al Qaeda on July 28, 2016. JFS announced that this action was intended to unify the various rebel factions fighting the Assad regime under JFS leadership. Critics of JFS, however, asserted that JFS took this action merely for publicity and a means to repackage itself to win over additional supporters. JFS currently claims that it is completely independent of Al-Qaeda and that the group is not subservient to or funded by any outside organization.

JFS was formerly known as Jabhat al Nusra li Ahl al Sham (the "Support Front for the People of Syria," Nusra Front A Salafi-jihadist militia, Jabhat al Nusra li Ahl al Sham (the "Support Front for the People of Syria," known as Jabhat al Nusra or the Nusra Front) emerged in Syria in late 2011 and has claimed that it conducted several major suicide bombing attacks against government security forces and carried out summary executions of captured Syrian government soldiers. The JFS distinguished itself from other jihadi groups not only with the lethality and efficiency of its operations, but with its highly religiously inspired rhetoric and objectives.

The JAN/JFS ideology, message, and tactics are very similar to other Al-Qaeda affiliates in the Middle East, Africa, and South Asia. JFS also conducts organized relief work and service efforts to win the loyalty of local people. JFS has also cooperated with other secular and Islamist organizations. It also fights ISIS in Syria. The prospect for future conflicts between the JFS and its previous partners persists, as Nusra's Front's uncompromising views on implementing Sharia is likely to lead to clashes with Sunni Arabs, Kurds, and various religious minorities in Syria.

JFS militants became active throughout Syria. In northern and eastern Syria, the group's battles with ISIS weakened JFS's control on areas it currently or formerly held. JFS continues to cooperate with other Syrian opposition groups. In southern Syria, the JFS continues to fight Assad's military in Dara'a province and parts of the Golan Heights bordering Israel. It is estimated that the JFS may have approximately 6,000 fighters in Syria.

Abu Muhammad al-Julani is the current leader (emir) of JFS. His family apparently came from the Golan Heights. Jawlani is believed to have fought against Coalition forces in Iraq before returning to Syria after the Syrian uprising began in 2011 to form an Al-Qaeda affiliate in that country. ISIS leader and emir, Abu Bakr al Baghdadi, initially supported Jaulani. Baghdadi wanted JAN's leaders in Syria to serve as ISIS's vanguard in in the battle against Syria's Assad government. The two men, however, clashed after Baghdadi sought to place the JFS under his command in April 2013, a move which Jaulani rejected. The rupture between the two groups surprised and divided jihadists worldwide. Various jihadi-oriented clerics, militant leaders, and individual supporters all voiced their own opinions on the conflict. Generally, other Syrian opposition forces believe that JFS is more pragmatic and cooperative than ISIS, including those that reject JFS's ideology.

In July 2014, Julani's emirate plan was revealed which sought to establish an emirate in the Levant and implement Sharia in areas under JAN control. To achieve this goal, JAN would have needed to unite the disparate al-Qaeda units in Syria, defeat ISIS, and properly arm its allies.

In September 2014, U.S. military forces attacked the "Khorasan Group" in Syria (Al Qaeda's external operations group), which is believed to be affiliated with the JFS, as there were reports that members of this group were collaborating with Al Qaeda-affiliated bomb makers in Yemen and Syria-based Western foreign fighters to place explosives aboard commercial aircraft. The United States Government responded by enhancing aviation security measures.

JFS attacks were intended to deter attacks against the United States and other western nations. The JFS has not directly attacked the United States, however, many sources believe that the group seeks to attack US interests in the Middle East and even the US homeland. In the Syrian Civil War, JFS fighters fight with other members of the Syrian opposition against the Assad regime (along with moderates and other Islamists), adding to the difficulty for Western nations to assist Anti-Assad Non-Islamist forces.

See also: Al-Qaeda (volume 1); Islamic State of Iraq and Syria (volume 1).

FURTHER READING

Byman, D. *Al Qaeda, the Islamic State, and the Global Jihadist Movement: What Everyone Needs to Know*. Oxford; New York (N.Y.); Auckland: Oxford University Press, 2015.

Cooper, Tom. *Syrian Conflagration: The Civil War,* 2011-13. Solihull, West Midlands, England: Helion & Company Limited, 2015

From al-Shabaab to al-Nusra: How Westerners Joining Terror Groups Overseas Affect the Homeland: Hearing Before the Committee on Homeland Security, House of Representatives, One Hundred Thirteenth Congress, First session, October 9, 2013. Washington, DC: Government Printing Office, 2013.

Lesch, David W. *Syria: The Fall of the House of Assad.* New Haven, CT: Yale University Press, 2012.

Lister, Charles R. *The Syrian Jihad: Al-Qaeda, the Islamic State and the Evolution of an Insurgency,* New Delhi: Pentagon Press*, 2017*

Steenkamp, Christina. *Violent Societies: Networks of Violence in Civil War and Peace.* Houndmills, Basingstoke, Hampshire: Palgrave Macmillan, 2014.

White, Jonathan R. *Terrorism and Homeland Security.* Belmont: Wadsworth, 2017.

Chapter 51

JAISH AL-FATAH COALITION

Through its Syrian affiliate Jabhat Al-Nusra (JN) (now known as Jabhat Fateh Al-Sham), Al-Qaeda formed the Jaish Al-Fatah (JF) Coalition in March 2015 to help establish an Islamist emirate in Syria. JF was a loosely-organized alliance, rather than a unified armed force, because its constituent groups shared resources and coordinated their efforts in fighting, but were autonomous, and had no one military commander to direct all actions. JF mostly consisted of Islamist factions, including both JN and the most influential Sunni-rebel rival to Hayat Tahrir al-Sham (HTS), Ahrar al-Sham.

JF arose as a result of reasons including plans developed by and actions of Al-Qaeda. From April through July 2014, ISIS had seized control of the governate of Deir al-Zour from Al-Qaeda and other rebel groups. The defeat of JN meant that a new strategy had to be developed. This led to the creation of JF. JF enjoyed significant successes soon after being created, capturing the provincial capital of Idlib, Syria. This proved to be an unprecedented success for JN and the coalition created a signficant safe haven for jihadists connected to Al-Qaeda.

See also: Al-Qaeda (volume 1); Islamic State of Iraq and Syria (volume 1); Jabhat Fateh Al-Sham (volume 1).

FURTHER READING

Dam, Nikolaos Van. *Destroying a Nation: The Civil War in Syria*. I.B. Tauris, 2017.
Dicker, Katie. *The Syrian Civil War*. Cavendish Square, 2018.
Glass, Charles, Patrick Cockburn and Armen Mazloumian. *Syria Burning a Short History of a Catastrophe*. Verso, 2016.
McHugo, John. *Syria: From the Great War to Civil War*. London: Saqi, 2014.
Postel, Danny and Nader Hashemi. *The Syria Dilemma*. Massachusetts Institute of Technology Press, 2013.

Chapter 52

JAYSH RIJAL AL-TARIQA AL-NAQSHBANDIA (JRTN), ALSO KNOWN AS THE NAQSHBANDI ARMY

OVERVIEW

The Jaysh Rijal al-Tariqa al-Naqshbandia (JRTN), also known as the Naqshbandi Army, was formed in December 30, 2006, and remains an active organization. JRTN derives its name from the Naqshbandi Sufi movement, a mystical branch of Sunna Islam that emphasizes spiritual connection with God and forsaking worldly desires.

However, by the mid-twentieth century the Naqshbandi Order in Iraq transformed itself into more of a political and business patronage network than a religious or devotional group. In the late 1970s, Naqshbandi Order members named Izzat Ibrahim al-Douri, Saddam Hussein's second in command, as their leader. Douri was ordained as a Naqshbandi Sheik and used his influence in the Hussein regime to develop an alliance between the Ba'ath party and the Naqshbandi Order.

After the execution of Saddam Hussein in December of 2006, many of the remaining Ba'athists and Naqshbandi Order members in Iraq relied on Douri for leadership as the most senior remaining Ba'athist in the country. They united behind him January 2006 to form the JRTN. Although the group chose a name that emphasized its Sufi roots, the group itself has always been vehemently secular in its ideology.

Douri established the group with the explicit aim of expelling the US-led coalition partners in Iraq and replacing the government formed under Coalition guidance with a Ba'athist state. To this end, the JRTN repeatedly attacked coalition forces, utilizing a network of high-quality fighters and an arsenal that included mortars, Rocket Propelled Grenades (RPGs), road bombs, and rockets.

In response, U.S. coalition forces targeted the JRTN; the most notable instance of which was when the U.S. captured several JRTN minor leaders in a raid on December 12, 2009.

While the JRTN carried out its own attacks, it more commonly coordinated other organizations' attacks on coalition forces. In particular, they helped finance, organize, and provide intelligence for attacks carried out by the 1920s Revolutionary Brigades, Ansar al-Islam, and Al Qaeda in Iraq (AQI), among other groups. Although it occasionally worked with AQI, the predecessor organization to ISIS, the JRTN also often condemned AQI for using tactics that resulted in the deaths of Iraqi civilians. In stark contrast, the JRTN chose to limit its own attacks to "the unbeliever-occupier" and denounced any groups that targeted civilians based on their ethnic or sectarian association.

After the US Coalition's military withdrawal from Iraq in 2011, the JRTN revised its objectives and now sought to depose Prime Minister Maliki's Shia dominated government. The JTRN directed its resources towards suppressing the Kurdish independence movement which it viewed as incompatible with its Arab Nationalist agenda. The JRTN also formed the Intifada Ahrar al-Iraq (IAAI), which served the public relations needs for the group. It would often issue press releases and videos depicting JRTN attacks.

In 2013, the JRTN was active in the General Military Council for Iraq's Revolutionaries (GMCIR). The GMCIR leadership largely made up of ex- Ba'athist army officers of ethnic Arab and tribal descent and its fighters are largely Arab Sunni tribesmen, many of whom fought in the 2007 Anbar Awakening. The group, whose most prominent member, the 1920's Revolutionary Brigades, coordinates the actions, attacks, and resources of its component groups, which are often local tribal militias. Although the JRTN is not technically a member group, it continues to help advise and direct the GMCIR. Like the JRTN, the GMCIR is vehemently anti-Iranian, anti-Maliki, and seeks to overthrow the recognized Iraqi government

ISIS and the JRTN are ideological rivals with the JRTN seeking to form a secular Ba'athist state within the internationally recognized borders of Iraq and is aiming to establish a Salafist caliphate stretching across the Middle East, North Africa, and parts of Europe, there have been several instances of cooperation between the two groups in recent years.

Both groups hatred of for the United States and Iraqi government made them unlikely allies. The JRTN was instrumental in the ISIS conquest of Fallujah in January 2014 and was responsible for the seizure of five vital bridges in Mosul when ISIS captured that city on June 10, 2014.

Yet within days of the fall of Mosul the two groups began to clash, including in Hawija where a firefight that killed 17 ISIS and JRTN fighters. There are conflicting reports as to the cause of the skirmish; some sources attribute the fighting to a dispute over two oil tankers, while others allege that it begun after JRTN fighters refused to acknowledge al-Baghdadi as their caliph. After additional skirmishes between JRTN and ISIS forces in May 2015, Douri declared that no alliance could or ever would exist between the two groups.

Douri also condemned ISIS tactics, namely its expulsion of Christians from Mosul and massacre of the Yazidis, implicitly comparing these atrocities to JRTN's policy of not targeting civilians. For a time, JRTN was largely viewed as the second most powerful insurgent group operating in Iraq after ISIS.

JRTN's Leadership

Azhar al-Obeidi (Unknown to Present): Obeidi, former Ba'athist army general who became a JRTN leader. After Mosul fell to ISIS on June 10, 2014, ISIS named Obeidi as the governor of Mosul in appreciation to its JRTN allies. Obeidi replaced as Mosul's governor and his fate remains unknown.

Wathiq Alwan al Amiri (Unknown to December 12, 2009): Amiri, was a JRTN media representative before Iraqi and US forces captured him in Tikrit Iraq in December 12, 2009.

Abd al Majid Hadithi (Unknown to December 12, 2009): Hadithi was the JRTN's media manager and propaganda disseminator before Iraqi and US forces arrested him in Tikrit Iraq in December 12, 2009.

Izzat Ibrahim al-Duri (December 30, 2006 to April 17, 2015): Following Saddam Hussein's execution in December 2006, Douri became the de facto leader of the remaining Ba'athists in Iraq and one of key founders of the JRTN. On April 17, 2015, Iraqi state-run television reported that Iraqi security forces and Shiite militia fighters had killed Douri in a mountainous region between Kirkuk and Tikrit. The Governor of the Salah al-Din province (where the alleged assassination occurred) corroborated the report. Photos were released of what was claimed to be Douri's corpse. However, the JRTN said these claims were false and in May 2015 released an audio recording of Douri discussing events that occurred after he had reportedly died.

THE IDEOLOGY AND GOALS OF THE JRTN

The JRTN is a Ba'athist, Nationalist, Sufi, and Sunni group. As a Sufi organization, the JRTN derives its name from the Naqshbandi Order of Sufism, which was formed in the Fourteenth century and is characterized by its peaceful, apolitical ideology. Under Saddam Hussein's government, however, the Order began functioning as more of a political and business network than a religious organization. During this time, however, the Order began recruiting major Ba'athist officials, especially Izzat Ibrahim al-Douri. Thus, when al-Douri founded the JRTN in 2006, he emphasized the group's Ba'athist rather than Sufi ideology. Indeed the group is regarded as tolerant of the major religious faiths of the area—Shiism, Sunnism, Sufism, Judaism, and Christianity. It also condemned Islamic State's targeted killings of civilians because their religious beliefs. JTRN seeks to reunify Iraq, including all its religious and ethnic groups, under a secular (Ba'athist) government similar to that of Saddam Hussein. To this end, the JRTN employs vehemently nationalistic rhetoric, resembling the Arab Nationalist appeals Egypt's Gamal abd al-Nasser promulgated in the 1950s and 1960s. To reach this goal of a reunified Iraq, the JRTN has ordered most of its attacks against coalition forces (prior to 2011), the Maliki government, Iran, and Iraq's Kurdish separatist groups.

THE SIZE OF JRTN

In 2009, the group had 1,500-2,000 members. In June 2014, the group was estimated to have between 1,500-5,000 members

TERRORIST GROUP DESIGNATION

Despite primarily targeting American and Coalition forces, the JRTN has not been officially designated as a foreign terrorist organization by the United States, UN, or EU. However, the Department of the Treasury listed JTRN pursuant to E.O. 13438: Blocking

Property of Certain Persons Who Threaten Stabilization Efforts in Iraq. E.O. 13438 requires specific actions intended to disrupt international financing of listed organizations and individuals.

FINANCIAL AND HUMAN RESOURCES OF THE JRTN

The JRTN relies heavily on large-scale contract and small business level extortion as well as donations from tribal leaders for revenue. Exiled Ba'ath Party members, particularly former Republican Guard officers, who found refuge in Jordan, Yemen, and Syria also appear to be a key source of funding for the JRTN.

EXTERNAL INFLUENCES

Beginning in early 2015, the JRTN began cultivating a relationship with Saudi Arabia, Jordan, and other Arab states, making public statements praising the late Saudi king, eulogizing the Jordanian pilot burned alive by IS, congratulating Saudi Arabia's new King Salman, and extolling the Saudi air campaign in Yemen. The main assistance these states provide to the JRTN appears to be safe havens for the group's leaders, such as al-Douri, who purportedly ran JRTN operations from Qatar for a period of time after being taken there for emergency medical treatment.

GEOGRAPHICAL LOCATIONS

Although there are scattered cells of JRTN fighters across Iraq, the JRTN ISIS concentrated in Salah al-Din, Ninawa, Tikrit and Kirkuk. It has been particularly active in and around Mosul, Hawija, and the "occupied territories" in the north of the country where Kurdish forces have seized control and asserted their autonomy.

TARGETS AND TACTICS

The JRTN often hires other groups to carry out attacks on the targets it chooses and helps coordinate the finances, logistics, and intelligence collection of these groups in return. It remains unclear exactly why the JRTN utilizes this strategy. One possibility is that the group does not want to risk being associated with attacks in which citizens are accidentally harmed. The group has made clear its policy of only targeting government and coalition fighters and protecting Iraqi citizens regardless of their religion or ethnicity. To be seen as going back on this policy would harm to the group's relationships with the communities in which it operates.

Although the JRTN often hires other groups to carry out its attacks, it also has its own well trained and organized, if small, military branch. Immediately after the JRTN's formation in 2006, local cells consisting of around 7-10 JRTN fighters, each lead by an Emir, were established in almost every province. The JRTN quickly became known for its military-like structure and precision in its attacks; forward deployed cells were organized into brigades, platoons, battalions, and companies. However, despite the video propaganda it has released praising the group, the actual structure of JRTN's army is likely more ad hoc than the semantics may suggest.

Regardless, there is evidence that the JRTN utilizes an intricate and sophisticated system for planning and executing attacks, which is at least partially responsible for the noticeably high quality of their fighters and the precision of their attacks. When an attack is first planned, the initial step in the preparation process is the collection of personal recommendations concerning cells' reliability. Then, JRTN leaders personally visit and evaluate the chosen cell, after which trainers, who are usually former Revolutionary Guard elites, are sent in to prepare the cell tactically. This is usually includes an extended 90-day course during which fighters are physically and mentally pushed to their limits. Reports suggest that the JRTN uses this process for both its own cells and cells from other insurgent groups that it subcontracts for individual attacks.

The JRTN chooses its targets very carefully. It only targets fighters who operate in the name of the Maliki government, Iran, coalition forces, or insurgents groups that oppose the creation of a Ba'athist state in Iraq. The JRTN has explicitly forbidden its fighters from killing Iraqi citizens, regardless of their sectarian or ethnic affiliation.

In carrying out its attacks, the JRTN has used light and medium rifles, IEDs, anti-tank RPG-7s, RKG-3 grenades, and unspecified missiles.

THE JTRN'S MAJOR ATTACKS

Although the JRTN was known to be carrying out attacks prior to 2009, none were verifiably documented. This may be in part due to the JRTN's strategy of subcontracting other militant organizations to carry out the attacks that it organizes and finances.

2009: A child recruited by JRNT threw an RKG-3, an anti-vehicle grenade, at a passing US convoy in the Kirkuk province. The attack was taped and circulated on the Internet. (Casualties unknown).

February 2009: Hamas Iraq troops used Rocket Propelled Grenades to attack US forces in Baqouba, the provincial capital of Diyala. It was not until the Hamas Iraq cell was apprehended that the U.S. discovered that the cell had been subcontracted by the JRTN, which was responsible for planning, financing, and facilitating the attack. (Casualties unknown).

August 31, 2010: The JRTN claimed responsibility shooting and killing a US soldier in the city of Tikrit in Iraq's Salah ad Din province. (1 killed, 0 wounded).

October 4, 2010: The JRTN made a statement on Al Jazeera claiming responsibility for attacking a US soldier in Baghdad on an unspecified date. However, the claim could not be independently verified. (0 killed, unknown wounded).

February 18, 2011: Senior commander of JRNT accused of being involved in an IED attack in a car showroom in the town of Muqdadiyah. (7 killed, unknown wounded).

June 10, 2014: The JRTN played a critical role in IS's capture of Mosul and was responsible for seizing control of the five bridges that connect the western and eastern sections of the city.

June 21, 2014: JRTN soldiers clashed with ISIS fighters in the city of Hawija near Kirkuk. Reports differ as to whether the skirmish occurred because there was disagreement over which group would assume control of several captured oil tankers or because the JRTN fighters refused to lay down their weapons and swear fealty to al-Baghdadi. (17 killed, unknown wounded).

January 3, 2015: The JRTN used a RKG-3 to target an Iraqi Army convey west of Mosul. (0 killed, 3 wounded).

June 6, 2015: According to the JRTN's official website, the group was responsible for launching several rockets into the city of Hawija near Kirkuk. (Casualties unknown).

The groups launched its first attack on February 2009: Hamas Iraq troops used Rocket Propelled Grenades to attack US forces in Baqouba, the provincial capital of Diyala. It was not until the Hamas Iraq cell was apprehended that the U.S. discovered that the cell had been subcontracted by the JRTN, which was responsible for planning, financing, and facilitating the attack. The Casualties unknown).

Last Attack June 6, 2015: According to the JRTN's official website, the group was responsible for launching several rockets into the city of Hawija near Kirkuk (Casualties unknown).

JRTN's Connections to Other Groups

One of the central messages promulgated by the JRTN is the need for cooperation and unity among Iraq's Sunni insurgent organizations. The JRTN cooperated with Hamas Iraq, the 1920s Revolution Brigades, Ansar al-Sunna, the Islamic Army, and Al-Qaeda in Iraq (AQI) before it became IS, often hiring them to carry out attacks on its chosen targets. There is also evidence that the JRTN has assisted in managing the finances, intelligence collection, and other logistics of these groups in exchange for video recordings of their attacks, which JRTN then posts on its own online media outlets. In the summer of 2013, the JRTN formalized several of these cooperative relationships when it helped to create the General Military Council for Iraq's Revolutionaries (GMCIR), an umbrella organization comprised of several moderate Sunni militant groups including the 1920s Revolution Brigades. The JRTN also belongs to the Supreme Command for Jihad and Liberation (SCJL), another umbrella organization in which the JRTN ISIS the largest militant group.

The alliance of convenience between the JRTN and ISIS has become increasingly strained as cooperation born out of common interest has given way to ideological rivalry. Whereas ISIS seeks to establish a global caliphate, the JRTN seeks the resurrection of a secular Ba'athist state within the internationally recognized borders of Iraq. Despite these differences, however, the two groups initially cooperated in an effort to overthrow their mutual enemy, the Maliki government. However, as early as June 16th, reports surfaced of skirmishes between ISIS and JRTN fighters over the proliferation of Saddam Hussein banners in Mosul. Then on June 21st, 17 JRTN and ISIS fighters were killed when the two groups clashed in Hawija. Reports vary on whether this clash was the result of the JRTN fighter's refusal to swear allegiance to Baghdadi or if it was simply a skirmish over control of two oil tankers. Yet despite these clashes, on July 13th, Douri publically praised ISIS for its leadership in taking Mosul and expressed "the love and pride" he felt for the group. It was not until April of 2015 that the JRTN directly denounced IS, when Douri stated that "the bitterest enemies" of the Arab nation are those that subscribe to "Takfiri ideas." Takfiri ideas are those that brand Muslims of different sects as infidels and call for their deaths—an ideology that ISIS subscribes to. As an Arab Nationalist group that claims to represent the Arab Nation, the JRTN was making clear its opposition to IS's ideology. As this tension between the JRTN's secular, Arab Nationalist goals and IS's vision of a Salafist caliphate heightened, the groups' alliance of convenience dissolved. After additional clashes between JRTN and ISIS forces in May 2015, Douri released another statement stating definitively that no alliance existed between the two groups. However, neither group has openly declared war on the other.

COMMUNITY RELATIONSHIPS

The JRTN works hard to foster positive relations with the communities in which it operates. By virtue of its Ba'athist roots, the organization has strong relations with many tribes across Kirkuk, Rashad, northern Diyala, Salah al-Din and Hawija. Mimicking an old Hussein regime strategy, the JRTN typically cultivates alliances with a wide range of sub-tribes rather than attempting to negotiate with the preeminent tribes, which are more prone to ideological interagency that could destabilize a larger alliance network. From 2007-2011, JRTN tailored its rhetoric to match the specific dispositions of local populations, particularly playing on Sunni fears of an Iranian sponsored Shiite rebellion and framing the Coalition as the "unbeliever-occupier." After the Coalition's withdrawal in 2011, the JRTN turned its focus to the growing anti-Maliki sentiments among Iraq's Sunni population, capitalizing on such events as Maliki's arrest of Sunni MP Ahmed al-Awani or the Iraqi Security Force's (ISF) brutal crackdown on a protest in Hawija in April 2013 to bolster recruitment.

Additionally, the JRTN publishes a local monthly magazine that promotes group ideology, reports recent military accomplishments, requests donations, and even has a question and answer section where readers can write in to ask theological questions that are then answered in the next addition by prominent Naqshbandi sheiks. The group also posts videos detailing its military endeavors as well as speeches by prominent Baathist and Sufi leaders on its official website and YouTube channel. The JRTN uses all of these platforms—its magazine, website, and YouTube channel—to put out propaganda and recruit new members.

Another important aspect of the JRTN's public relations campaign is its repeated promises not to kill Iraqi citizens, regardless of their religious affiliation or ethnicity, as long as they are not cooperating with the al-Maliki government. The group makes a point to target the "occupiers" and "oppressors," perpetuating their reputation as an "Iraqi first" group. Where many other militant organizations in Iraq have large foreign components, the JRTN is almost entirely comprised of Iraqis—a fact that lends it credibility in the public's eyes.

See also: Al-Qaeda (volume 1); Islamic State of Iraq and Syria (volume 1).

Further Reading

Dahnhardt, Thomas Wolfgang Peter. *Change and Continuity in Naqshbandi Sufism: A Mujaddidi Branch and its Hindu Environment*. University of London, 1999 (diss.)

DeJong, Frederick & Radtke, Bernd. *Islamic Mysticism Contested: Thirteen Centuries of Controversies and Polemics*. Leiden, Netherlands: Brill, 1999.

Khan, Ali Khan & Ram, S. *Sufism and Naqshbandi Order*. New Delhi: Anmol Publications, 2003.

Mardini, Ramzy. *Volatile Landscape: Iraq and its Insurgent Movements*. Washington, DC: The Jamestown Foundation, 2010.

Naqshbandī, Muḥammad Ḥasan, Ansari, Ishrat Husain & Qureshi, H.A. *Sufis of Naqshbandia Mujaddidya Order: English Translation of Maulvi Muhammad Hasan Naqshbandi Mujaddadi's Urdu Book Masha, ikh Naqshbandia Mujaddidya*. Delhi: Idarah-i Adabiyat-i Delli, 2010.

Chapter 53

KHORASAN GROUP (KG)

The Khorasan Group (KG) is a cell of Afghan and Pakistani jihadists within the Al-Nusra Front (now known as Jabhat Fateh Al-Sham), which is affiliated with Al-Qaeda in Syria. The group emerged in June 2014, resulting from an alliance between Al-Qaeda jihadists in Syria and militants affiliated with Al-Qaeda in the Arabian Peninsula (AQAP). AQAP, based in Yemen, has several members who are skilled in constructing bombs and using explosives. The KG is a stand-alone organization, but is believed to be network inside a network, which conducts certain types of terrorist operations.

As a relatively small Al-Qaeda franchise, Khorasan Group (KG) is composed of nearly 50 hard-core fighters from various Jihadist groups. These experienced and Al-Qaeda veterans include several senior-ranking operatives. In conjunction with Al-Nusra Front (Jabhat Fateh al-Sham), KG fights ISIS in Syria. Some KG members also were a part of an elite sniper group of Al-Nusra referred to as the "Wolf Group". In addition to fighting ISIS, another one of KG's primary purposes is to attack western targets using weapons such as bombs composed of clothing soaked with explosives.

"Khorasan" is an historic Islamic geographical term denoting the eastern boundaries of what Islamists claim as the "Muslim world." The term has religious significance in the context of jihad and regional groups use the term in several different ways. Al-Qaeda uses the term Khorasan to include Afghanistan, Pakistan, Iran, parts of Central Asia and China's Xinjiang province.

Muhsin al-Fadhli (1981-2015), jihadist from Kuwait, emerged as KG's de-facto leader. Once based in Iran, he operated as a leading Al-Qaeda facilitator and financier. He was a close adviser to Osama bin Laden (1957-2011) and was one of a few Al-Qaeda leaders who had advance knowledge of the planned 9/11 attacks. Al Fadhli was an Al-Qaeda and Taliban fighter in Afghanistan and later obtained financial and material support for Al-Qaeda in Iraq (AQI), the group that became ISIS. Al-Fadhli conducted several terrorist attacks, including on the French ship MV Limburg with a suicide boat and against U.S. Marines on Kuwait's Faylaka Island, both in October 2002. He traveled to Syria in April 2013 to fight with the Al-Nusra Front. Eventually, he left Al-Nusra.

The key differences between ISIS and the Khorasan group (KG) is that, while ISIS seeks to retain and expand its caliphate, KG, as an Al-Qaeda affiliate, primarilly seeks to launch large-scale attacks against Western targets. Reportedly, the group has been planning imminent attacks against various Western targets, including those in the United States. While jihadist organizations including ISIS and Al-Nusra (now known as Jabhat Fateh Al-Sham) confine most of their attacks within Syria and Iraq, the KG appears to focus on planning attacks against western targets.

In September 2014, United States Central Command conducted an air campaign against KG bases and facilities near Aleppo, Syria. The mission was largely unsuccessful, largely because group members had received advance warning.

On November 6, 2014, the coalition forces attacked targets in the Syrian provinces of Idlib and Aleppo. Despite US military statements claiming that only the KG was targeted, there were reports that targets associated with both Ahrar ash-Sham and the Al-Nusra Front were also struck. The KG's chief bomb maker David Drugeon (1991-2015), a French national, was severely wounded in those attacks. He died in a subsequent attacks.

On November 18, the Syrian Army attacked KG targets rural Latakia Province. Eleven KG militants were killed, and another 13 were wounded or captured. The Kazakh and Chechen KG field commanders, along with Burmese and Saudi jihadists, and Al-Nusra fighters were killed.

On March 24, 2015, US airstrikes killed 17 KG fighters. In September 2015, the US military forces conducted operations against KG in view of reports that KG was seeking to conduct imminent large-scale attacks.

On July 8, 2015, al Fadhli was killed in a targeted strike, while traveling near Sarmada, Syria. The US Defense Department claimed that his death will degrade and disrupt ongoing Al-Qaeda efforts against the United States and its allies.

See also: Al-Qaeda (volume 1); Al-Qaeda in Iraq (AQI) (volume 1). Al-Qaeda in the Arabian Peninsula (AQAP) (volume 1); Islamic State of Iraq and Syria (volume 1); Jabhat Fateh Al-Sham (volume 1); Taliban (volume 2).

FURTHER READING

Coon, C. "ISIS and Khorasan: A Humanist Perspective." *The Humanist,* November 2014.

Mulrine, A. "Is Khorasan a Real Threat - or a Way to Avoid a Vote on US Military Action?," *The Christian Science Monitor,* Sep. 29, 2014.

Phillips, James. *The Rise of Al-Qaeda's Khorasan Group: What It means for U.S. National Security*. Washington, D.C.: Heritage Foundation, 2014.

Weed, Matthew C. *A New Authorization for Use of Military Force Against the Islamic State: Comparison of Current Proposals in Brief*. Washington, D.C.: Congressional Research Service, 2014.

Chapter 54

MILITANT CLERICS ASSOCIATION/RUHANIYUN/MAJMA-YI-RUHANIYYUN-I-MOBAREZ (IRAN)

In Iran, the majority of ruling clerics became a part of two organizations, the Combatant Clerics Association and the Militant Clerics Association (MCA). The Combatant Clerics represented the right wing and the MCA the left wing of the clerical establishment. The conservatives used a type of electoral gerrymandering to exclude the leftwing from the Assembly of Experts in elections held in 1990 and from the Majilis in the elections held in 1992. The MCA staged a comeback to play a major role in the 1997 elections.

The Militant Clerics Association (also known as the Militant Clerics Society) was formed in 1987, when two dozen Shiite clerics broke away from the older and more conservative Association of Militant Clergy accusing the latter of failing to follow the radical policies advocated by Ayatollah Khomeini. At the time, MCA was critical of the conservative clerics in the combatant Clergy Society for their economic policies and were much more skeptical about the value of détente with the United States. The major figures in the breakaway group included Mohammad Khatami and Mehdi Karrbi. Khatami became President of Iran in 1997. Karrubi eventually became Speaker of Iran's parliament.

In early August 2005, the MCA elected former President Hojatoleslami Mohammad Khatami as its secretary-general, but he declined the position citing time constraints. On August 28, 2005, Hojatoleslami Mohammad Moussavi Khoeiniha was elected unanimously by the MCA as its secretary-general. Khoeinha was a firebrand cleric who was the leader of the group, "Students Following the Line of Imam", and also a leader of the group radical Islamist students who seized the US embassy in Tehran in 1979. This group held 52 Americans as hostages for 444 days. Khoeinha gave the approval for the approval for the storming of the US embassy.

After losing an internal power struggle within the clerical leadership, Khoeiniha turned away from firebrand politics and like many of members of the MCA became self-styled moderates, as the term is understood in Iranian politics.

Khoeniha served as Iran's state prosecutor and led the subsequently outlawed "Salam" newspaper. This occurred after Iran's Special Court for the Clergy found Khoeniha himself guilty of spreading fabrications, disturbing public opinion, and publishing classified documents in 1999. He previous revolutionary credentials led court to suspending the sentence of 2.5 years in jail a public flogging. He, instead, was fined. He was also prohibited from publishing for three years and the newspaper was outlawed for five years.

The MCA, who originated in the Revolution in 1979, similar to a several other clerical organizations were initial supporters of Iran's right-wing. They underwent a shift only in the 1990s.

Formal parties in Iran in the traditional sense of the term had been outlawed in 1987 and were legalized again in the 1990s. Once this occurred, groups such as the MCA were again able to formally enter the political arena. By that time, the MCA had largely abandoned their radical domestic and anti-Western politics, and had even called for détente with the United States and the introduction of political and economic reforms. The MCA and the National Trust Party, formed by former member Medi Karrubi, both appeared to have concerns what they perceived as extreme and racial reformists that seek to undermine the nature of Iran in favor or a more secular government.

The NTP refused to form coalitions with other reformist groups, The MCA, however, has shown an interest in forming coalitions. In the 2004 Mallis elections and the 2005 Presidential elections, the MCA allied itself with reformist parties under the banner of the 2nd Khordad Front. The MCA candidate in the 2005 elections, Medhi Karrubi, however, failed to win the support of the majority of the members of the MCA and defected following the election to form the National Trust Party (NTP)

Many of Iran's conservative clerics are affiliated with the Militant Clerics Association (MCA), which includes the Supreme Leader Ayatollah Ali Khamenei, Ayatollah Ali Meshkini (until his death in July 2007), the former speaker of the Iranian Parliament, Ali Akbar Nateq Nouri, and former "Reformist" President Mohammad Khatami. The Militant Clerics Association is a conservative group that claims to support Ayatollah Ruhollah Khomeini's (1902-1989) legacy, but is also a "Reformist Group," the main political opponents of the more conservative "Principists." Iranian Reformists have generally promised some relief from Iran's stifling political atmosphere that emerged after the success of the Islamic Revolution in 1979. The MCA, for example, favors free enterprise, privatization, and a cautious foreign policy that will not imperil the stability of the Iranian political system. Much of MCA's support comes from financially powerful merchants. The conservative MCA is thus distinguished from the Association of Militant Clerics, which is left-wing and supports state-run economy and trade.

Since the Assembly of Experts began holding elections, the main rivalry has been between the MCA and the Qom Seminary Scholars Association (QSSA) and some independents. The most important role of the Assembly of Experts in Iran is that it elects Iran's Supreme leader. The MCA, like the other Reformist Parties, have frequently had their candidates prohibited from running for office by hardline conservatives who control the unelected Guardians Council and the Expediency Council.

See also: Iranian Minor Islamist Political Parties (volume 1); Islamic Revolutionary Guard Corps (IRGC) (volume 1).

FURTHER READING

Abdo, Geneive & Lyons, Jonathan. *Answering Only to God: Faith and Freedom in Twenty-first-Century Iran*. New York: Henry Holt and Co., 2003.

Bakhash, Shaul. *The Reign of the Ayatollahs: Iran and the Islamic Revolution*. New York: Basic Books, 1984.

Dabashi, Hamid. *Theology of Discontent: the Ideological Foundations of the Islamic Revolution in Iran*. New York: New York University Press, 1993.

Louër, Laurence & King, John. *Shiism and Politics in the Middle East*. New York: Columbia University Press, 2012.

Mohammadi, Mağīd. *Political Islam in Post-Revolutionary Iran: Shi'i Ideologies in Islamist Discourse*. London: I.B. Tauris, 2015.

Chapter 55

MILLI NIZAM PARTISI/PARTY FOR NATIONAL ORDER (MNP)

Established by Necmettin Erbakall, an engineering professor at Istanbul Technical University, in January 1970. Milli Nizam Partisi (MNP) became Turkey's first legally-recognized Islamist political party, and one which adopted the "National View" (Milli Gorus) ideology. When it was established, the MNP stressed that was it was formed to represent the Turkish Nation, which Allah had chosen "to enjoin the right and forbid the wrong" (Erken, 2013).

The MNP opposed secularism and what it considered false doctrinal interpretations. It advocated what it claimed was the moral basis of social justice to guarantee a peaceful social order in Turkey. Although the MNP could not promote the imposition of Islamic beliefs, it did advocate religious programs in Turkey's education system.

The party, however, was dissolved in 1971 after the Turkish Constitutional Court held that the MNP was exploiting Islam for political purposes. After this decision, several party members created the Milli Selamel Partisi (National Salvation Party) (MSP), which became a part of a coalition government in 1974, before being outlawed in September 1980. Some former party members unsuccessfully sought to re-establish the MNP in 1976.

Both the MNP and the MSP used Arab phrases in their names, despite the fact that Turkish phrases for these concepts existed. Both parties, thus, evoke Ottoman-Islamic illusions, as opposed to the "pure Turkish" language stressed by secular Turkish nationalists. Both the MNP and the MSP successfully articulated the political issues of religiously motivated voters. On the issue of whether the caliphate should be restored, Erbakall said, "There could be great benefits if the Caliphate is restored, political benefits as well. I do not insist that it should come back, but if people want it to come back, it can" (Erken, 2013). Both the MNP and the MSP emphasized the concept of "order" as a major political theme. For example, Erbakan frequently invoked the term "Nizam" (order) implying that it sought to restore the Islamic "order" of the Ottoman caliphate. The MNPs founding document proclaimed: "Our nation, as the greatest nation of history, saw itself responsible for bringing order to the world."

See also: Adalet ve Kalimnma Partisi (AKP) (volume 1).

FURTHER READING

Arjomand, Said Amir. *From Nationalism to Revolutionary Islam*. Albany: State University of New York Press, 1984.

Erken, A.H.M. "Re-Imagining the Ottoman Past in Turkish Politics: Past and Present," *Insight Turkey* 15 no. 3 (June 22, 2013).

Heper, Metin. "Islam, Conservatism, and Democracy in Turkey: Comparing Turgut Ozal and Recep Tayyip Erdogan." *Insight Turkey* 15 no. 2 (March 22, 2013).

Landau, Jacob M. *The National Salvation Party in Turkey*. Jerusalem: Academic Press, 1976.

Stowasser, Barbara Freyer. *The Islamic Impulse*. London: Croom Helm, 1986.

Chapter 56

MUJAHEDEEN-E-KHALQ ORGANIZATION (MEK)/MUJAHEDIN-E KHALQ ORGANIZATION (MEK OR MKO) NATIONAL LIBERATION ARMY OF IRAN (NLA)/PEOPLE'S MOJAHEDIN OF IRAN (PMOI)/NATIONAL COUNCIL OF RESISTANCE (NCR)/NATIONAL COUNCIL OF RESISTANCE OF IRAN (NCRI)/MUSLIM IRANIAN STUDENT'S SOCIETY

OVERVIEW

The People's Mujahedeen of Iran (Mujahedeen-e-Khalq, or MEK), the Iranian resistance organization, that the US government once considered a foreign terrorist organization for killing American citizens in Iran in the 1970s, and for collaborating with Saddam Hussein, then President of Iraq. Acknowledging that MEK had rejected violent tactics to achieve its goals, the US Government officially no longer considered the MEK as a terrorist group in late 2012. Nonetheless, US authorities expressed concerns over reports that the group had allegedly mistreated many of its members.

EMERGENCE OF THE MEK

In 1965, college-educated leftist Iranian students established the MEK. Initially, the MEK fought against the government of Shah Mohammad Reza Pahlavi and the western governments who supported him (including the United States). The group originally claimed to be Marxist and promoted moderate view of Islam. The group believed that the Shah's government was corrupt and was virtually a puppet of the West. During the 1970s, the Shah imprisoned many early MEK leaders such as Massoud Rajavi. The Shah's government also executed several others.

The MEK and the Iranian Revolution

During the 1970s, the MEK attacked Iranian government sites, and killed several Iranian citizens, including military personnel and civilian contractors, employed by the Shah's government. Many of these individuals worked on military-related projects. The MEK struck against these targets because the U.S. government supported the Shah. In 1978, Americans numbered 45,000 of the 60,000 foreign nationals doing work in Iran.

Some commentators argue that a Maoist faction of MEK was responsible for the attacks. In November 1979, the MEK supported the assault and seizure of the US Embassy in Teheran. In that attack, 52 US diplomats and embassy workers were held captive for over a year. While the group was involved in the Iranian revolution, the MEK denied that it participated in the embassy seizure or the taking of hostages. Despite MEK denials, evidence emerged to indicate MEK involvement both in the 1979 attack and that the group later opposed an early release of the US hostages.

The MEK insisted, however, that Peykar, a separatist Marxist-Leninist faction, seized control of the group and participated in the embassy siege, following Rajavi's arrest. Rajavi reportedly, after his release, sought to rebuild the MEK, which Peykar control had damaged.

The MEK Breaks with the Regime

While MEK participated in the Iranian Revolution, it violently severed ties with Iran's clerical hardliners following Ayatollah Khomeini's seizure of power. Favoring secular government in Iran, the MEK combined Marxist, feminist, and Islamist ideologies. The MEK immediately clashed with Khomeini's regime, which brutally repressed what it perceived as a likely political rival. The new Iranian government later executed several MEK leaders.

The Role of the Rajavis

The MEK was long considered the largest militant Iranian opposition group attempting to depose the Iranian regime. It also has a military leadership that is female dominated. Massoud and Maryam Rajavi are the long-time husband and wife leaders of MEK. Maryam Rajavi joined the resistance against the Shah while studying in Tehran during the early 1970s. At her husband's request, Maryam became a co-leader of MEK in 1985. The MEK ideology was originally based on Islam, Marxism, and Feminism. Soon allegiance to the Rajavi family became part of the group's ideology, and the group became less Marxist-oriented over time.

Maryam Rajavi also emerged as MEK's most important leader. While active, Massoud Rajavi, commanded the MEK's armed wing. Maryam Rajavi (1953 -) was from a well to family in Iran. After moving with MEK to Paris France in 1981 and later becoming co-leader of MEK, Rajavi was named second in command of its armed wing. Massoud Rajavi vanished after the Iraq War began in 2003. It is not known whether he is alive, and if so, his whereabouts.

Some commentators criticize MEK for being a cult, because of its intense loyalty to its co-founders. Married female members were forced to leave their husbands in the late 1980s, and unmarried women were forbidden to enter into marriage or bear offspring.

In 1993, the NCRI named Maryam Rajavi as "Iran's future president". It also stated plans for a six-month democratic interim period in Iran after the current regime is overthrown. Based in Paris, she is the face of the group to the international community. NCRI claims to respect religious freedom, the rights of ethnic and religious minorities, human rights, and the rights of women. MEK also said it favored capitalism and Iran rejoining the broader world community.

The MEK has always claimed to be a legitimate peaceful Iranian resistance group. While MEK asserts that it does not attack noncombatants on purpose, the group has often carried out attacks that carried the high risk of death and injuries to noncombatants. For example, the MEK regularly attacked government buildings in crowded cities. The MEK also attacked Iranian regime officials and sites in Iran and overseas. Iran's government arrested and executed large numbers of MEK operatives. The MEK, then, retaliated by killing several key government officials. During the Iraq-Iran War (1980-1988), the MEK supported and fought for Iraq.

THE MEK AND SADAAM HUSSEIN

While he ruled Iraq, Saddam Hussein was MEK's primary financial supporter. MEK also formed front groups including the Muslim Iranian Student's Society, which received funds from expatriate Iranians living abroad. Iraq also gave bases, weapons, and sanctuary to the group.

The MEK Iranians who opposed Saddam. MEK's increasingly attacked Iran as Iranian-Iraqi relations worsened. Sadaam's regime facilitated or restricted the group's operations, based solely on the regime's wishes. After Sadaam was overthrown well-to-do Iranians abroad who opposed Iran's government funding the MEK.

In 1981, MEK members bombed several important Iranian buildings, including the headquarters of the ruling party and the office of Mohammad-Javad Bahonar, Iran's Prime Minister. Approximately 70 major Iranian politicians, including Mohammad-Ali Rajaei, Iran's President, and Bahonar.

In July 1981, the National Council of Resistance of Iran (NCRI), which its supporters refer to as a "parliament in exile," was first based in Teheran, before being forced to Paris. The Iranian regime forced the MEK from its bases near Iran's border with Iraq, and the group relocated to Paris in 1981.

In 1986, the French government ordered Rajavi and several MEK militants in an agreement with the Iranian government to free French citizens kidnaped by groups allied with Iran in Lebanon. Saddam Hussein and the Iraqi government then funded the group and provided it refuge. Armed by the Iraqi government, the group helped Saddam's government by attacking opponents of the Iraqi government and providing security for the regime. In 1986, the Iraqi government based MEK in eastern Iraq.

After the First Gulf War, MEK assisted the Iraqi military defeat the Kurdish revolt in the northern Iraq and the Shia uprising in southern Iraq in 1991. The MEK later denied involvement.

Late in the Iran-Iraq war, Saddam armed the MEK and sent waves of MEK fighters in a large-scale suicide attack against Iran's military. The Iranian military killed about 2000 MEK fighters in a failed attack referred to as "Operation Eternal Light".

Even after the end of the Iran-Iraq War, the MEK posed a major security threat to the Iranian government, and the group continued to attack Iranian targets. In the Spring of 1992, the MEK made coordinated attacks on Iranian targets in over a dozen nations, such as Iran's UN Mission.

The MEK attacked several leading government officials from the 1990s through the early 2000s. These included the assassination of Asadollah Lajevardi, who directed the penal system in Iran 1998, and Ali Sayyad Shirazi, a high ranking Iranian military official in 1999. In 2000, the MEK attacked the offices of Iran's Supreme Leader and the residence of Mohammad Khatami, Iran's President. In February 2000, MEK through "Operation Great Bahman," conducted multiple military strikes against Iran. From 2000 through 2001, MEK conducted several attacks and raids against regime facilities, including on that killed Iran's chief of staff. The MEK claimed the assaults were intended to retaliate for Iran's aerial bombardment on MEK bases. The Iranian government reported that the MEK had killed more than 12,000 Iranians over three decades.

The response of the global community and the United States government to the MEK has been unclear and a matter of considerable controversy. Madeleine Albright, US Secretary of State, named the MEK as a foreign terrorist organization in the fall of 1997 as a means intended to facilitate dialogue with Iranian moderates. President Bill Clinton believed that listing the MEK as a terrorist organization would be viewed as a friendly overture by Iran's incoming moderate president, Mohammad Khatami. The US government also named the NCRI as a terror group organization and ordered NCRI to close its Washington office in 2003.

Alleged MEK terrorist activities have significantly declined since late 2001. Police in France, in 2003, apprehended over 150 MEK operatives on terrorism charges. This reversed longstanding French policy of granting asylum to MEK. The European Union named the MEK as a terror group in 2002 and removed that designation in 2009.

THE MEK SINCE THE FALL OF SADDAM HUSSEIN

During the 2003 invasion of Iraq, the U.S. and coalition attacked the MEK in Iraq in spite of the MEK's assertions that it was not involved in that conflict. Both MEK and the United States entered into a cease-fire in which MEK militants laid down their arms and detained at Camp Ashraf, in northeastern Iraq. In 2004, Donald Rumsfeld, then the U.S. Defense Secretary, named MEK members as protected civilian as recognized by the Geneva Convention. This action, however, were contrary to the actions recommended by the UN High Commissioner for Refugees, the International Committee of the Red Cross, and the U.S. Department of State.

Several commentators criticized Rumsfeld's decision because it gave the appearance that the US Government arbitrarily applied protected civilian status to an organization engaged in terrorism. This protected status terminated after Iraq became completely sovereign in early 2009.

In 2011, MEK had between 5,000 10,000 members, with several of its members residing throughout Europe. The MEK has also developed a well-financed and sophisticated network of American supporters, and was assisted by several prominent US politicians, such as former Governors Howard Dean of Vermont and Edward Rendell of Pennsylvania, and, and Rudolph Giuliani, the former Mayor of New York City. Some of MEK's Western supporters assert that MEK helps to provide strategic balance to the Iranian regime in the region. They argue that MEK dissidents have long-standing connections in the Middle East that could help shifting the balance against extremist Sunnis and counter the radical Shiite regimes in Iran and Syria.

The MEK focused on efforts to delist it as a terrorist group. In September 2012, Hillary Clinton, the US Secretary of State formally delisted the MEK, which released the MEK's assets in the United States and permitted the group to do business with American firms.

MEK critics challenge the group's motivations and whether it was indeed committed to nonviolence and human rights. The US government articulated some of these doubts when it formally delisted the group. While overlooking MEK's terrorist attacks in the past, the Department also expressed serious concerns about alleged MEK mistreatment of its members. In April 2013, the NCRI re-opened an office in Washington, DC.

In June 2014, the government of France strongly criticized the MEK for its violent and anti-democratic record, for being cult-like in its operations, and for disseminating disinformation. Other critics of delisting argued that MEK may obstruct the efforts of moderate Iranian opposition organizations, including as the peaceful and increasingly popular "Green Movement", which was particularly active after the controversial Iranian presidential election in 2009.

Nouri al-Maliki, then Iraq's Prime Minister, sought to relocate MEK members out of Iraq. The MEK members were concerned about their fate after the Iraqi government gained control of Ashraf. After the U.S. military withdrawal from the camp in the Spring of 2011, Iraqi security forces and the detainees began clashing with each other, which resulted in the deaths of. 35 MEK detainees. Following this violence, Iraq reiterated its intention to close Ashraf and the US fully withdrew its troops in December 2011.

The Iraq government, the MEK, and the UN agreed in December 2011 to move the internees to Camp Liberty near Baghdad, temporarily until the relocation of the detainees. The United States government sought to safely and humanely resolve the situation of the detainees and support UN initiatives to resettle Ashraf residents. In 2014, nearly 3,000 MEK detainees lived at Camp Hurriya (Liberty) waiting to be resettled to other nations as refugees. In 2014, the UN appointed a special representative to facilitate the relocation of the detainees.

FURTHER READING

A bid to foment democracy in Iran; The Bush team unveils a plan to push for Iranian-led reform. Can it really yield 'regime change'? (USA). (2006, February 17). *The Christian Science Monitor.*

"*A Terrorist Group with Different Faces: Exposing the Terrorist Nature of the National Council of Resistance of Iran (NCRI/NCR) aka PMOI, NLA, MKO and MEK.*" London: MKO Watch, 2007.

Bloomfield, Lincoln P. & Sheehan, Ivan Sascha. *The Mujahedin-e-Khalq (MEK): Shackled by a Twisted History*. Baltimore, MD: University of Baltimore College of Public Affairs, 2013.

Camp Ashraf: Iraqi Obligations and State Department Accountability: Joint Hearing Before the Subcommittee on Oversight and Investigations and the Subcommittee on the Middle East and South Asia of the Committee on Foreign Affairs, House of Representatives. Washington: U.S. G.P.O, 2011.

LaFranchi, H. "Iranian Group MEK Coming off US Terror List: Unrelenting Campaign Pays Off," *The Christian Science Monitor,* Sep. 21, 2012.

Mausner, Adam. *The Outcome of Invasion US and Iranian Strategic Competition in Iraq*. Washington, D.C.: Center for Strategic and International Studies, 2012.

NEHRI Deplores the Execution of Ali Saremi, MEK Member Associated with Camp Ashraf. *Psychology & Psychiatry Journal,* Jan. 15, 2011.

Norris, C. *Mujahedeen-e-Khalq (MEK)*. Ft. Huachuca: University of Military Intelligence, 2008.

Peterson, S. "Iran Sees Less Threat in Exiled MKO Militants." *The Christian Science Monitor,* Feb. 11, 2008.

Peterson, S. "With Deadline Looming to Close MEK's Camp Ashraf in Iraq, What Next?" *The Christian Science Monitor,* Dec. 20, 2011.

"Thousands Demonstrate Outside the State Department, Calling For Delisting Iran's Main Opposition Movement, the MEK and Protection of Camp Ashraf." *Politics & Government Week, Sep. 15, 2011.*

"USCCAR: Secretary Clinton Must Delist MEK; Ensure Safety, Security, and Dignity of Iranian Dissidents in Iraq." *Defense & Aerospace Week,* March 21, 2012.

"Unshackle Iran's Main Opposition; Refusal to Remove MEK's Terrorist Designation Betrays Democracy." *The Washington Times,* Aug 26, 2011.

Chapter 57

Mujahidin Shura Council in the Environs of Jerusalem (MSC)

The Mujahidin Shura Council in the Environs of the Jerusalem (MSC) is a Gaza-based coordinating body that includes several Salafi jihadist groups operating in Gaza including, but not limited to: Tawhid and Jihad Group in Jerusalem, and Ansar al Sunnah. The goal major goal of the group is to fight the Jews for Islamist control of Palestine and entire world.

The MSC has a similar name but is related only in ideology to the Mujahidin Shura Council by Al Qaeda of Iraq. An increase of jihadist activity began in Sinai since the Egyptian Revolution began, which was sparked by the Arab Spring in 2011. The MSC is not the only Sinai-based jihadist group to claim ideological affinity with, if not organizational connections to, Al-Qaeda. There have been several other jihadist organizations, including others possibly connected to Al- Qaeda, that are supposedly active in that area.

The MSC has claimed responsibility for several attacks on Israel since the group was formed in 2012. These attacks included rocket attacks against Sderot Israel on March 21, 2013 and the southern Israel city of Eliat, Israel on April 17, 2013. The group also conducted a cross-border Gaza-Israel IED attack against an Israeli construction site on June 18, 2013 in which one civilian died. MSC dedicated this attack to al Qaeda and its leader, Ayman Zawahiri, as well as saying it was in retaliation for the killing of Osama bin Laden. In July 2013, Hamas (which effectively controls the Gaza strip launched a clamp down on MSC activities in Gaza and arrested several MSC militants. MSC also launched a rocket attack on Eliat in August 13, 2013. On February 2014, the MSC declared its support for ISIS. The US State Department placed the MSC on its list of terrorist organizations on August 2014. This action helps reduce the MSC's access to resources, interferes with its capacity to conduct its operations, and makes it more difficult for its operatives to conduct deadly acts. It does this in part by preventing them from using the international banking system, and interferes with their ability to transfer money to vendors and to receive money from donors; it freezes any funds held in banking system; and deters legitimate commercial entities from conducting business transactions with them. The MSC responded by stating that this designation was of little value or importance.

The Ibn Taymiyya Media Center (ITMC) is the propaganda agency for MSC and has provides covers the deaths of Al-Qaeda militants it refers to as "martyrs", who were killed while fighting the Assad government in Syria The MSC also disseminates propaganda for the jihadist group, Ansar Jerusalem, (Ansar Bayt al Maqdis), the main al Qaeda-linked group operating in the Sinai. Despite MSC links to Al-Qaeda, ITMC also posts positive references to ISIS.

The ITMC has also called for jihadist attacks against Egyptian security forces and has disseminated videos denouncing Egyptian operations in the Sinai. The MSC, however, has not said it conducted any attacks in Egypt and denied it was responsible for an August 5, 2012 attack on an Egyptian military base in Rafah in which sixteen Egyptian soldiers were killed.

See also: Ansar Bayt al Maqdis (ABM) (volume 1); Islamic State of Iraq and Syria (volume 1); State of Sinai (volume 1).

FURTHER READING

Armajani, Jon. *Modern Islamist Movements: History, Religion, and Politics*. Chichester, West Sussex, UK: Wiley-Blackwell, 2012.

Lingenfelder, Christian J. *The Elephant in the Room: Religious Extremism in the Israeli-Palestinian Conflict*. Monterey, CA: Naval Postgraduate School, 2006.

Rekhess, Eli. *Islamism Across the Green Line: Relations Among Islamist Movements in Israel, the West Bank and Gaza*. Washington, D.C.: Washington Institute, 1997.

Roy, Sara M. *Hamas and Civil Society in Gaza: Engaging the Islamist Social Sector*. Princeton, NJ: Princeton University Press, 2011, 2014.

Tamimi, Azzam. *Hamas: A History from Within*. Northampton, MA: Olive Branch, 2011.

The 2014 Gaza Conflict: 7 July - 26 August 2014: Factual and Legal Aspects, [Jerusalem]: State of Israel, 2015.

'Amr, Ziad Abū. *Islamic Fundamentalism in the West Bank and Gaza: Muslim Brotherhood and Islamic Jihad*. Bloomington: Indiana University Press, 1994, 2002

Chapter 58

MUSLIM BROTHERHOOD

OVERVIEW

The Muslim Brotherhood (al-Ikhwan al-Muslimeen) is the first and most prominent Islamist organization in the world. It is also the largest Islamist group in Egypt and has inspired Sunni Islamist groups worldwide. The group seeks to make the Quran and Sunnah the sole guide to govern the lives of the Muslim family, community, and government, as well as individual Muslims. For most of its history, the Brotherhood has formally renounced violence as a means to reach its objectives, except for situations such as clashes over Palestine and efforts depose the Assad regime in Syria.

FORMATION OF THE MUSLIM BROTHERHOOD

In 1928, a cleric and former school teacher Hasan al-Banna formed the group in Ismailia, Egypt. The group would eventually become the world's first modern Islamist movement. Banna opposed Western concepts of governance based on democratic and secular principles as antithetical to the ideal of worldwide Islamic governance. He sought to transform the society into a powerful political party to make Egypt independent of Western and non-Islamic governance. Islamic leaders glorified Arab history and the military accomplishments of Muslims. Mosques also often provide comfort and guidance for the impoverished and the powerless. The imams (prayer leaders) also condemned political corruption and oppression in secular Arab nations as evils caused by Westernization. They also denounced foreign influence in their nation's affairs.

While the Brotherhood originally sought to Islamize society by promoting Islamic law and morality, it has also consistently connected preaching with social welfare and political involvement. The group's asserted that its mission was to proselytize through both preaching and providing social services. The Muslim Brotherhood grew from Egypt to several other Middle Eastern nations including Syria, Jordan, Sudan Palestine, Yemen, Kuwait, Kuwait, and Tunisia. As the group spread throughout the Middle East, remained largely ethnically Arab organization. The Muslim Brotherhood branches in these nations also remained subordinate to the Egyptian Brotherhood and looked to the Egyptian group for leadership.

In addition to supporting its branches, the Muslim Brotherhood also supports Islamist groups such as Hamas in Algeria, the Islamic Tendency in Tunisia, the Movement of Islamic Youth, in Malaysia, and Justice and Charity in Morocco.

THE BROTHERHOOD AND EGYPT'S FIGHT FOR INDEPENDENCE

Egypt's lower-middle class became a key source of support for the Muslim Brotherhood, which because the Brotherhood was so effective in organizing opposition to British control of Egypt (which lasted from 1882 through 1952). When the Muslim Brotherhood sought to participate in Egypt's parliamentary elections in 1942, the Egyptian government, pressured by Britain, compelled the Brotherhood to withdraw from the race.

As the Muslim Brotherhood became stronger, some of its more radical members began attacking British troops based in Egypt. The Brotherhood's goal was to establish an Egyptian Islamic state that would inspire other Arab nations to overthrow their westernized regimes and replace them with Islamist governments.

The Muslim Brotherhood increasingly relied on violent tactics after Israel became a nation in 1948. Following Israel's victory in the Arab-Israeli War, Egyptian Muslims felt betrayed and bitterly humiliated. Brotherhood members blamed Egypt's King Farouk and his pro-Western orientation for the Arab defeat. They openly advocated for a revolution to establish an Islamic government in Egypt. On December 28, 1948, Brotherhood assassins killed Egypt's Prime Minister, Mahmud Fahmi Nokrashi. The secret police, the Mukhabarat retaliated by assassinating al-Banna in Cairo in 1949.

Devastated by al-Banna's death, the Muslim Brotherhood transformed itself into more of a religious and a less of a political-oriented group. In 1951, Hasan al-Hudayabi, a moderate fundamentalist, became the leader of the Muslim Brotherhood. Political turmoil, however, continued to grow.

REPRESSION OF THE BROTHERHOOD UNDER NASSER

Collaborating with Egypt's Free Officers (nationalist-oriented military officers), the Muslim Brotherhood sought to overthrow the Egyptian monarchy, which was supported by the British. After King Farouk was forced to relinquish the throne in 1952, the military officers and the Brotherhood began clashing with each other. Colonel Gamal Abdel Nasser led a military junta to seize control of the country. The military wanted Egypt to lead a socialist, secular, pan-Arab movement while the Muslim Brotherhood opposed egalitarianism and nationalism as un-Islamic and demanded that Islamic law (Sharia) be implemented.

Perceiving the powerful Brotherhood as a potential threat, Nasser outlawed the group in 1954 and arrested its members. The Muslim Brotherhood responded with several failed assassination attempts against Nasser. Nasser retaliated by seeking to destroy the movement, and did so by eliminating its leadership.

Sayyid Cutb was one of Egypt's most prominent Islamist theorist. Cutb's writings, especially *Milestones* (1964), established the ideological theological justifications that several Islamist Sunni Islamist groups, such as Al-Qaeda and Hamas cited ideologues such as Cutb to stress that government must be formed on Sharia (Islamic Law). If a government is not based on Sharia, it is an apostate regime that may be legitimately opposed through jihad. Cutb opposed the concept of man-made legislation, believing that Muslim-led governments that enacted their own law, as opposed to adopting Sharia, were not genuinely Muslim. Cutb argued that devout Muslims must oppose these types of governments.

Purusant to his ideas on jihad, Cutb pursued his doctrine of armed struggle in opposition to Nasser government and other similar regimes. In 1966, Nasser ordered Cutb to be executed for involvement in an attempted assassination and Cutb was hanged.

REVIVAL OF THE BROTHERHOOD

In May 1967, seeking to destroy Israel, Nasser deployed his military in the Sinai Peninsula, along with Syria and Jordan. On June 5, 1967, the Israeli Defense Forces (IDF) launched preemptive air strikes that destroyed Arab air forces before they became airborne. After six days of conflict, Israel captured significant territory from Egypt, Syria, and Jordan. This defeat was devastating for the Arabs. In its analysis of the debacle, the Egyptian Muslim Brotherhood asserted that a lack of Muslim spirituality caused Egypt's defeat.

Prohibited from political involvement because of its efforts to depose the Egyptian government, the Brotherhood formally denounced violence to achieve its aims in the 1970s. The group became very popular among Egypt's lower classes because it provided various types of social services including pharmacies, hospitals, and schools. While the Egyptian government allowed the group to function on a limited basis beginning in the 1970s, it circumscribed group activities with periodic arrests and crackdowns.

The Brotherhood disavowed the use of violent tactics, in an agreement with Egyptian President Anwar al-Sadat, permitted the group to preach and organize. In return for Brotherhood support against Nasser supporters, Communists and Socialists. Sadat freed Islamist prisoners but gave only perfunctory adherence to Sharia. In 1981, Sadat was killed by jihadists associated with Egyptian al-Jihad (EJ). EJ members defected from the Brotherhood in anger against Sadat both for failing to implement Sharia and agreeing to the 1979 peace accord with Israel (the Camp David Agreements).

The Brotherhood chafed under the government of Hosni Mubarak, Sadat's successor, which the group found was stultifying, corrupt, and oppressive. The Brotherhood reconciled its continuing commitment to Cutb's principles while abstaining from violent political activities asnd focused on the idea of a "vanguard", as expressed by Cutb. By serving as the vanguard, the Brotherhood would be as effective Islamizing society through a political elite as much as it does through mass organizing and connecting with less privileged Egyptians.

Candidates affiliated with the Brotherhood first competed in local and parliamentary elections as independents in 1984. Brotherhood (Islamists differ in how they perceive Islam, and whether they follow an ideological or pragmatic approach. Nonetheless, the conservative older faction of the group has largely prevailed in recent history.

Domestic and international pressure resulted in Egypt's open political environment in 2005. Egypt's government allowed the Brotherhood greater political freedom to campaign in the parliamentary elections in 2010. While the Brotherhood's 150 candidates nominally appeared on the ballot as independents, they clearly stated that they were affiliated with the

Brotherhood. Office-seekers openly campaigned, and use the Brotherhood's moniker along with its rallying cry, "Islam is the Solution."

THE RISE AND FALL OF MOHAMMED MORSI

The Brotherhood did not directly participate in the January-February 2011 "Arab Spring" uprising in Egypt. Social media and civil society, instead, led the effort for political change. The dramatically changed environment challenged both the Brotherhood and Al-Qaeda – because the popular demand for democracy and human rights rather than Sharia was considered a rejection of both Al-Qaeda and the argument that Egyptians sought to base their society on Sharia. At first, it appeared that the results of the Arab Spring in Jordan, Tunisia, and Bahrain, signaled that the Brotherhood and Al-Qaeda's demands for Sharia had been rejected in those nations as well.

Shortly after President Hosni Mubarak was ousted during the Arab Spring protests in 2011, the Freedom and Justice Party (FJP) (the political wing of the Brotherhood) prevailed in both the presidential and parliamentary elections. During the parliamentary elections in the winter of 2011-2012, the FJP gained close to half the seats in the lower house (People's Assembly). The Islamists also won 84 percent of the seats in the upper house (Shura Council). Concerned with the Brotherhood's increasing power, in June 2012 the Supreme Constitutional Court (with Mubarak-era appointed judges) dissolved the People's Assembly. The Court also revoked a law intended to prevent former Mubarak government officials from holding office, allowing Mubarak's prime minister Ahmed Shafiq to campaign for the presidency.

Following the first round of voting in May 2012, FJP candidate Mohammed Morsi received a slim majority (51.7 percent) of the vote in a June runoff election against Shafiq and was elected as Egypt's president. The Brotherhood's political successes were due largely its excellent organization. Further, Brotherhood had long built up a reservoir of good will with constituencies. Although forming an Islamic state (a caliphate) based on Sharia was a key goal of the Brotherhood, the group was also especially popular among the disadvantaged because it effectively provided social services, which that the Egyptian government had consistently failed to do. Issues arose after as to whether the Brotherhood would strictly retain its Islamist ideology or whether this would be downplayed by the realities of practical governance.

Upon taking office, Morsi demanded that the military, which had served as an interim government, remain in its barracks. Many army officers approved this decision, aware of growing public dissatisfaction with nearly one-and-a-half years of military rule.

The Brotherhood's political success, however, soon became adversely affected by the struggle for power between the judiciary and the military, including the divisive controversies over the creation of a new constitution for Egypt. The Morsi administration was also buffeted by large-scale discontent with economic mismanagement and ineffective public administration.

After dissolving the lower house of parliament, Morsi controlled both executive and legislative branches of the government. In late November 2012, Morsi asserted that he, the Shura Council (which had been a consultative body that did not have legislative authority), and the constituent assembly were immune from judicial review. This strategy was strongly opposed. Several protesters denounced the move as a usurpation of power. Morsi argued that the "feloul" (Mubarak supporters) controlled the judiciary and much of the government administration, and that these individuals sought to block implementation of the revolution's objectives. Morsi yielded to the intense popular opposition and rescinded the decree.

Although 64 percent of Egyptian voters approved the constitution in a national referendum in December 2012, only a third of eligible voters participated. Opponents were anxious Egyptian law based on Islam would not adequately protect the rrights, basic freedoms such as the freedom of speech, freedom of association, and freedom of religion. They also opposed the broad power that would be granted to the president under the constitution.

Morsi continue to clash with the Egyptian judiciary. In the Spring of 2013, Egypt's Supreme Administrative Court invalidated Morsi's order setting April elections for parliament as as violative of the Egyptian constitution. The secular opposition had earlier asked its supporters to boycott the elections.

Many commentators widely criticized Morsi's governing style as authoritarian, "majoritarianism," or "autocratic rule by the largest party." Morsi's rule faced increasing opposition in June 2013 when he appointed seventeen Brotherhood-affiliated provincial governors. Morsi's appointee as governor of Luxor was a member of the extremist group Gamaa Islamiya (GI), which killed several tourists in Luxor in 1997.

Morsi's government emphasized maintaining regional stability in foreign policy. Despite Morsi's often inflammatory rhetoric, Israeli concerns about conflicts with Egypt did not materialize. Morsi retained existing security and intelligence agreements, and the 1979 Camp David peace treaty between Egypt and Israel. He also helped negotiate a new truce between Hamas and Israel.

Following massive demonstrations, General Abdel Fattah al-Sisi led the Egyptian Army to depose Morsi on July 3, 2013, and abrogated the newly-drafted constitution. Several Brotherhood leaders, and thousands of members were arrested, and over one thousand supporters died. The military-supported government reinstated its ban on the Brotherhood by the end of 2013, prohibiting it from lawful political participation.

There were only two Islamists on the fifty-member committee tasked with deliberating amendments the Constitution. Neither of the Islamist representatives were affiliated with the Brotherhood. Egyptian voters approved a new constitution in January 2014.

While the revised constitution retained much of the 2012 text, but tempered provisions establishing Islam as the legal foundation in Egypt. The law also enhanced the power and freedom of action of both the judiciary and the military. The Committee also restored the 1971 constitutional prohibition on religiously affiliated political parties, which had effectively prohibited the FJP from partisan politics.

Immediately following Morsi's removal, the Brotherhood stated it would not cooperate with those that it believes assumed power illegally. Answering their leaders' demands to confront those who had stolen their revolution "with tanks and massacres," Brotherhood supporters conducted large protests against the provisional government. The military responded by arresting thousands of Brotherhood supports in a harsh clampdown.

The new Egyptian government accused Morsi of treason, encouraging violence, and cooperating with Iran, Hezbollah, and Hamas. Opponents of the military government claimed that political considerations motivated these charges and that they lacked credibility. In his initial trial in November 2013, Morsi challenged the court's authority and declared himself to be Egypt's true head of state. The judges hearing the case of Mohamed Badie, the Brotherhood's leader and Supreme Guide, and Khairat al-Shater, Badie's deputy, were among the judges who recused themselves from further participation to object to what they considered an unlawful trial. Egyptian authorities also refused to allow the accused to attend their trials.

The Egyptian provisional government officially listed the Brotherhood as a terrorist organization and accused the group of orchestrating a car bombing in late December 2013 at a military base in the Nile Delta. The authorities, however, did not prove Brotherhood involvement. The Brotherhood denounced the attack, and the Ansar Beit al-Maqdis (ABM), a jihadist group operating in the Sinai Peninsula, said it was the group that conducted this operation. The declaration followed a September ruling that prohibited Brotherhood activities and confiscated its funds, and the adoption of an anti-demonstration statute that authorized the government to restrict public meetings. Critics argued that government actions however, may greatly impede political reconciliation.

With Morsi's ouster from power, Egypt's "Deep State" regained much of its former power (the Deep State encompasses the conventional military, internal security and police persionnel, and the intelligence services) and restricted many of the personal and political freedoms Egyptians won after the 2011 revolution. Some commentators believe that many Egyptians have supported the actions of the security forces because of the chaos and lawlessness that followed Mubarak's downfall. When offered the choice of a democratic system with no guarantee of stability in the short or medium term as a strong military, many Egyptians seemed to have to supported the latter.

Egyptian authorities also sought to suppress dissent by non-Islamists. In November 2013, the government replaced the state of emergency then in effect with an anti-demonstration statute, which prohibits over 10 individuals from gathering together in public without prior approval by the police. The statute also allows the government to prohibit any protest they deem to threaten "public order." Many of those who led the anti-Mubarak protest movement in 2011 publicly denounced the statute. In December 2013, a court found three leading activists guilty of violating the anti-demonstration statute and remain incarcerated. They are appealing their convictions.

Since July 2013, Egypt's government has completely undermined the organizational effectiveness of the Muslim Brotherhood. Many observers were concerned with how the Islamists would respond. Nearly twenty percent of young Brotherhood members believed that anti-government violence may be the sole means to achieve political change.

Many Brotherhood members use social media to conduct campaigns of minor violent actions against the government using flaming aerosol cans and Molotov cocktails. Still, Muslim Brotherhood leaders who remain free or live abroad Egypt assert that the Brotherhood remains committed to nonviolent actions to oppose an "illegitimate" government. As the political process evolves in Egypt, it is unclear whether the Brotherhood has received increased popular support among Egypt's people although Brotherhood leaders claim that over time, they will prevail in the court of public opinion. In addition to the Brotherhood, the other major Islamist political actors include the Salafist parties, most notably the Nour Party, which discreetly gave its support to the interim government.

Several Middle Eastern nations (including The United Arab Emirates (UAE), Saudi Arabia, and Egypt) designate the Brotherhood as a terrorist group, along with several other Egyptian Islamist organizations. While the United States has not formally designated the

Brotherhood as a terrorist organization, the Obama Administration remains unconvinced that the Muslim Brotherhood has genuinely renounced its longstanding view that violence is sometime allowable to further certain political goals under certain circumstances.

Both the Muslim Brotherhood and Al-Qaeda frequently justify jihadism because they view political Islamism as ineffective in creating an Islamic government. Significant differences exists in approaches between the two groups. The Muslim Brotherhood has supported various militant groups including Palestinian Hamas (a splinter group of the Palestinian Muslim Brotherhood), Hezbollah in Lebanon, and various Jihadi groups in Iraq. It also backed efforts to participate in the political lives of their respective nations. Al-Qaeda, however, supports only violent Islamism. Al-Qaeda rejects the efforts of Islamist groups to achieve their goals through political means or peaceful means, as capitulation to the enemies of Islam.

See also: Al-Qaeda (volume 1); Ansar Bayt al Maqdis (ABM) (volume 1); Egyptian Islamist Political Parties (volume 1); Freedom and Justice Party (FJP) (volume 1).

FURTHER READING

Al-Awadi, Hesham. "A Struggle for Legitimacy: The Muslim Brotherhood and Mubarak, 1982–2009." *Contemporary Arab Affairs 2,* no. 2 (2009): 214-228.

Bakker, Edwin & Meijer, Roel. *The Muslim Brotherhood in Europe.* New York: Columbia University Press, 2012, 2014

Caromba, Laurence & Solomon, Hussein. "Understanding Egypt's Muslim Brotherhood." *African Security Review* 17, no. 3 (2008): 117-124

Ehrenfeld, Rachel. "The Muslim Brotherhood Evolution: An Overview." *American Foreign Policy Interests* 33, no. 2 (2011): 69-85.

"Islam as the State Religion a Muslim Brotherhood View in Syria." *The Muslim World* 44 no. 3-4 (1954): 215-217.

Lefevre, Raphael. *Ashes of Hama: The Muslim Brotherhood in Syria.* Cary: Oxford University Press, 2014

Martini, Jeffrey & Kaye, Dalia Dassa. *The Muslim Brotherhood, Its Youth, and Implications for U.S. Engagement.* Santa Monica, CA: Rand, 2012.

Ronen, Yehudit "Between the Mahdiyya and the Muslim Brotherhood: Continuity and Change in Islamic Radicalism in Sudan," *The Journal of North African Studies* 12, no. 1 (2007): 1-18.

Rubin, Barry. *The Muslim Brotherhood: The Organization and Policies of a Global Islamist Movement.* New York, NY: Palgrave Macmillan, 2010.

Starkman, Ruth. The Concept of Brotherhood: Beyond Arendt and the Muslim Brotherhood. *Critical Review of International Social and Political Philosophy* 16, no. 5 (2013): 595-613.

Vidino, Lorenzo. *The New Muslim Brotherhood in the West.* New York: Columbia University Press, 2010.

Wickham, Carrie Rosefsky. *The Muslim Brotherhood: Evolution of an Islamist Movement.* Princeton University Press, 2015.

Zahid, Mohammed. *The Muslim Brotherhood and Egypt's Succession Crisis the Politics of Liberalisation and Reform in the Middle East.* London: I.B. Tauris, 2010.

Chapter 59

MUSLIM BROTHERHOOD IN JORDAN/ JORDANIAN MUSLIM BROTHERHOOD

Jordan's first Muslim Brotherhood was licensed as a charity in 1945/46. In 1953, the government recognized the group as an "Islamic society" and a branch of the Egyptian Muslim Brotherhood

Many observers describe the relationship between Jordan's Hashemite monarchy and the Jordanian Muslim Brotherhood as "symbiotic" and relatively non-confrontational, especially considering the history of the Brotherhood in other Middle Eastern nations.

Unlike other Middle Eastern nations, the Jordanian Muslim Brotherhood was never forced underground, and its leaders were never imprisoned en masse. Jordan's Brotherhood organizations survived the prohibition of political parties ordered under martial law in 1957. After martial law, the Jordanian Muslim Brotherhood openly functioned as a registered charitable society. In 1992, the group formed a political party, known as the Islamic Action Front Party.

The Government allowed and encouraged Brotherhood expansion throughout Jordan, perceiving it (and political Islamism generally) to be a less threatening alternative to pan-Arab and leftist movements. The Brotherhood reciprocated by never challenged the legitimacy of the Jordanian monarchy, including during the 1970-971 Jordanian civil war and after the government signed the Israel-Jordan Peace Treaty of 1994.

The relationship between the government and the Jordanian Muslim Brotherhood is in marked contrast from Brotherhood affiliates elsewhere in the region, where government persecution and suppression directly impacted Brotherhood organization, leadership, strategy, thinking, and action.

The Jordanian Muslim Brotherhood developed a reform program and sought to gradually reestablish the Islamic lifestyle in the nation. The group has actively participated in elections after the parliamentary government in Jordan was reinstated in 1989. Beginning with the election of 1993, the government and the Muslim Brotherhood have engaged in a pattern of strategic interaction. Prior to each scheduled election, 1) the Muslim Brotherhood demanded certain election reforms such how many votes each voter is allowed cast, apportionment, and redistricting, 2) the government responded with incremental electoral reforms, and 3) then the Muslim Brotherhood then determines whether to participate or abstain from competing in the forthcoming election. The Muslim Brotherhood believes that its boycotts effectively questions the legitimacy of the election and the new parliament both by the Jordanian public and international public opinion.

This three-part process has played out before the 1997, 2003, 2007, and 2010 parliamentary elections. The Muslim Brotherhood along with its affiliated party, the Islamic Action Front Party, boycotted in 1997 and 2010 but participated in the 2003 and 2007 elections.

In addition to the Muslim Brotherhood, other Islamist groups operate in Jordan such as the Hizb-al-Tahir and various Salafi groups. The emergence of ISIS has had no significant effect on the Muslim Brotherhood. Between several hundred and a few thousand Jordanians are estimated to have fought in Syria since the Syrian uprising began. Most of these fighters joined with Jabhat al Nusra (the al Nusra Front). Many fewer Jordanians (from dozens to hundreds) have joined ISIS. ISIS has also received little support in Jordan. The February 2015 video depicting the horrific killing of Jordanian Air Force pilot Muath al-Kasasbeh dispelled much of the criticism directed at Jordan's role in fighting ISIS and shifted public opinion to strongly oppose ISIS.

See also: Al-Qaeda (volume 1); Islamic State of Iraq and Syria (volume 1); Jabhat Fateh Al-Sham (volume 1); Muslim Brotherhood (volume 1).

FURTHER READING

Boulby, Marion & Voll, John Obert. *The Muslim Brotherhood and the Kings of Jordan, 1945-1993*. Atlanta, GA: Scholars Press, 1999.

El-Said, Sabah. *Between Pragmatism and Ideology: The Muslim Brotherhood in Jordan, 1989-1994*. Washington, D.C.: Washington Institute for Near East Policy, 1995.

Sarah, Salwen F. *Inside the Brotherhood: Explaining the Strategic Choices of the Muslim Brothers in Egypt and Jordan and the Islamic movement in Israel*. 2012 (thesis)

Tal, Nahman. *Radical Islam in Egypt and Jordan*. Brighton: Sussex Academic Press/Jaffee Center for Strategic Studies, 2005.

Tamimi, Azzam. *Islam and Democracy: Jordan and the Muslim Brotherhood*. Tokyo: Islamic Area Studies Project, 2000.

Wickham, Carrie Rosefsky. The Muslim Brotherhood: Evolution of an Islamist Movement. Princeton University Press, 2015.

Wiktorowicz, Quintan. *The Management of Islamic Activism: Salafis, the Muslim Brotherhood, and State Power in Jordan*. Albany, NY: State University of New York Press, 2002.

Chapter 60

MUSLIM BROTHERHOOD IN SYRIA

While the Syrian Branch of the Muslim Brotherhood developed based on Syria's unique political realities, the Egyptian Brotherhood greatly influenced the Syrian Branch. The group originated in the many jam'iyyat (associations, or societies that first emerged in the late nineteenth century. They were largely organizations that served the material and spiritual needs of poor and dispossessed. They were followed by jam'iyyat that were politically-oriented, which would be the forerunners of today's political parties (hizb) in majority-Islam nations. The elites would dominate these parties. Being more Islamic-oriented, the Islamic jam'iyyat particularly attracted Syrians from the middle and lower-middle classes during the 1920s and 1930s. The many Syrian political jam'iyyat sought to revive Islam and eradicate Western cultural incursions, including movie theaters and what they perceived as immodest women's dress. The Egyptian Brotherhood in the late 1930s and 1940s provided the models for the ideology and organization for their Syrian counterparts.

The several Islamic jam'iyyat coalesced to form the Syrian branch in 1945. Syrian students, who attended the University of Cairo and participated in Egyptian Muslim Brotherhood activities and events, first brought the group to Syria. In returning to Syria, these students often established jam'iyyats under several different monikers, but often referred to each other as "Shabaab Muhammad" (the Youths of Muhammad). Shabaab Muhammad was later renamed Syrian Muslim Brotherhood. A common ideology and political viewpoints provide the cohesion that united these organizations.

The Syrian group became part of the legal opposition after Syria won independence from France. After independence, Syria experienced rapid and disruptive social and political change. Some of the factors destabilizing Syria were the termination of French colonial rule, the Second World War, and the issues related to independence and self-rule. By 1958, Syria came close to becoming a failed state with the collapse of the government led by Syria's traditional Sunni elite. Egypt assumed control of the government and joined Syria to the United Arab Republic (UAR). Along with religious voters, the Brotherhood also won significant support in the urban lower and middle-classes.

The Brotherhood resumed its political activities after Syria seceded from the UAR in 1961. In the 1961 elections, the Brotherhood won ten seats in the Syrian Parliament. The Brotherhood was outlawed in 1963 after the Secular Baath (Baathist) Party came to power after the military overthrew the government on March 8, 1963. This coup would marginalize Syria's Sunni community. The Muslim Brotherhood rejected the secular nature of the government's reforms, which it believed would harm the interests of its constituency. After the Baathists had suppressed the Brotherhood, the Brothers helped lead the Sunni opposition against the Baathists.

The Baathists staged another coup in February 1966, which enhanced the power of the Alawite Shiite faction of the Baath party. The Alawites have controlled the party ever since. There has long been friction between the Sunnis and Shiites in Syria, with mainstream Sunni Muslims traditionally viewing the Alawites as heretics. Because the Alawites monopolized political power in Syria, the Brotherhood began an openly sectarian anti-Alawite campaign, protesting what it claimed to be the Alawite majority's persecution of the Sunni majority.

The Brotherhood's campaign contributed to the violent clashes between the Sunnis and Shiites during the 1970s. During the Lebanese Civil War in 1975, Hafez al-Assad's Syrian government intervened to technically support Israel, leading to unrest within Syria. This led to the assassination of many prominent government officials, for which the Syrian Muslim Brotherhood claimed responsibility. In 1979, the Brotherhood killed a large number of Alawite artillery cadets in Aleppo.

On July 7, 1980, Syrian Emergency Law 49 decreed that Muslim Brotherhood membership was a capital offense. This law remains in force. Following this law, thousands of Brotherhood members surrendered hoping to avoid execution. Among these were professors, engineers, and mostly young students from Damascus.

Brotherhood opposition, nonetheless, continued to smolder until February 1982, when the Muslim Brotherhood seized control of the central Syrian city of Hama. The Syrian army responded by heavily bombing the city. This attack killed 10,000 to 30,000 people. Known as the "Hama massacre", many observers believed that this incident would end the Brotherhood's influence in Syria.

The Syrian Muslim Brotherhood's political activity in Syria has since significantly declined. It also relocated to London and Cyprus.

In the 1990s, the Brotherhood had somewhat of a revival in Syria. Both the Assad regime and the Brotherhood sought to peacefully resolve their differences. Assad wanted to revive Syria's declining economy and ensure a smooth succession for his son. The Brotherhood agreed to recognize the Assad regime if Brotherhood leaders were free to return to Syria. Most imprisoned Brotherhood leaders were freed from jail, many exiled members were allowed to come back to the country, and Assad permitted several Brotherhood members to campaign as independent candidates in the elections to the People's Assembly in 1990, 1994, and 1998. After Assad had died in June 2000, the Muslim Brotherhood reached out to his son, Bashar al-Assad, who would become Syria's new president. Bashar reciprocated in freeing incarcerated group members from prison. In negotiations with the Syrian government, the Brothers offered to end its operations against the Assad government. The Arab Spring, which began in January 2011, dramatically changed things in that country.

Bashar had failed to implement real change in Syria, which fueled the growth of militant Islamism, which had long festered in a repressive society, where the government had forbidden both free expression and association. The regime had damaged the relationship between government and its people. The stifling of Syrian political life and widespread repudiation of the Assad government created a promising environment for Islamist extremists to exploit.

The Syrian Muslim Brotherhood called for reforming the Assad regime in early 2011 and participated in the popular demonstrations that occurred in Syria connected with the Arab

Spring. While growing religiosity and a weak liberal movement in Syria could have helped the Muslim Brotherhood gain considerable political strength if it could freely mobilize, the Brotherhood would have been opposed by most of the nearly 30 percent of Syrians who were Kurds, Christians, or Alawis, any many upper–middle-class Syrians concerned about the emergence of a regime based on political Islamism. Prominent Syrian opposition leaders criticized the Islamist agenda, including the Muslim Brotherhood's, as being authoritarian. Some opposition activists were also concerned that the Brotherhood would dangerously exacerbate the situation into a large-scale sectarian conflict.

Early Brotherhood thought was influenced by reformist and moderate Salafi scholars. Reformist religious reasoning (ijtihad), is central to traditional Salafism. However, the Brotherhood has been criticized for using it to manipulate religious texts rather than using it to develop an interpretation of Islamic Sharia that corresponds to the moderation that the group is preaching in public.

The Muslim Brotherhood was dilatory in the Syrian uprising and did not publicly support "revolution" until late April 2011, well after the protests began. Unlike Tunisia and Egypt, the Syrian Muslim Brotherhood lacked a large popular organization in the country. The Brotherhood was also supported by the various Syrian minority groups.

Before 2011, Bashar Assad's regime had successfully suppressed internal challenges in the country. Even following the Arab Spring uprisings in Tunisia and Egypt's, the Syrian government appeared resilient and able to retain power. Despite the fact that Assad was a brutal dictator, some Syrians perceived Assad was a benevolent tyrant, who was responsible for at least some beneficial reforms in Syria. Further, the Syrian opposition was organizationally anemic, weakened by decades of severe authoritarian repression. Eventually, however, Syria was not spared from the Arab Spring, the Syrian Civil War, or ISIS.

Large protests began in Syria after March 2011. The demonstrators voiced intense rage that were intensified by the regime's harsh measures to suppress dissent. Unlike the 1970s and 1980s, when it emphasized sectarianism, the Muslim Brotherhood avoided interpreting the unrest in 2011 as a sectarian conflict.

Ali Sadreddine Bayanouni, who currently resides in London, is the current leader (Controller-General) of Syria's Muslim Brotherhood.

See also: Al-Qaeda (volume 1); Islamic State of Iraq and Syria (volume 1); Muslim Brotherhood (volume 1).

FURTHER READING

"How Syria's Brutal Past Colors Its Future: Yesterday in a Sign of Smooth Transition of Power, Bashar al-Assad Got a Key Post," *The Christian Science Monitor,* June 20, 2000.

"Islam as the State Religion a Muslim Brotherhood View in Syria." *The Muslim World* 44 no. 3-4 (1954): 215-217.

Khatib, Line & Lefevre, Raphael. *State and Islam in Baathist Syria: Confrontation or cooptation?* Fife, Scotland: University of St Andrews Centre for Syrian Studies, 2012.

Lefevre, Raphael. *Ashes of Hama: The Muslim Brotherhood in Syria.* Cary: Oxford University Press, 2014

Linjakumpu, Aini. *Political Islam in the Global World*. Reading, UK: Ithaca Press, 2008.

Rubin, Barry. *The Muslim Brotherhood: The Organization and Policies of a Global Islamist Movement*. New York, NY: Palgrave Macmillan, 2010.

"Syria's Secular and Islamist Opposition Unite Against Baathists; The Country's Ruling Baath Party Congress Concluded Thursday Without the Reforms Many Syrians Anticipated, " *The Christian Science Monitor,* June 10, 2005.

Talhamy, Y. "The Muslim Brotherhood Reborn." *Middle East Quarterly* 19, no. 2, (2012): 33-40.

Teitelbaum, Joshua. "The Muslim Brotherhood and the 'Struggle for Syria', 1947–1958 between Accommodation and Ideology," *Middle Eastern Studies,* 40, no. 3 (2004): 134-158

Teitelbaum, Joshua. "The Muslim Brotherhood in Syria, 1945–1958: Founding, Social Origins, Ideology." *The Middle East Journal* 65, no. 2 (2011): 213-233

Von Dam, Nikolaos. *The Struggle for Power in Syria Politics and Society under Assad and the Ba'th Party.* London: I.B. Tauris, 2011.

Ziyādah, Raḍwān, *Power and Policy in Syria: The Intelligence Services, Foreign Relations and Democracy in the Modern Middle East*. London: I.B. Tauris, 2011.

Chapter 61

NATIONAL TURKISH STUDENT UNION (MTTB)

Formed in 1948, the National Turkish Students Union (Milli Turk Tarikat Birligi, MTTB) was one of three major national youth movement coordinating bodies. The other two bodies were the National Turkish Students Federation (TMTF, formed in 1948), and the National Organization of Turkish Youth (TMT, formed in 1953). Because the government funded these groups, they were legally required to remain politically neutral. Nevertheless, the TMTF sympathized with leftist political parties, while the MTTB and TMT generally favored the more conservative political parties. In the 1970s, the MTTB became affiliated with the National Salvation Party (MSP). The MSP was an Islamist party formed in October 1972 and led by Necmettin Erbakan. The Turkish judiciary abolished all three organizations, as well as all youth movements affiliated to any political party following a military coup in September 1980. Several extremist former MTTB members, including Huseyin Velioglu, Burhan Basci, Isa Altsoy, Edip Gumus, Mehmet Emin Tekin, Suleyman Urek and Abdulaziz Tunc, opened the Ilim bookshop in Diyarbakir. This group later closed the bookshop and went into hiding to establish the Turkish Hezbollah organization. The government named Turkish Hezbollah as the 'Number One Enemy' of the Turkish state, a recognition formerly given the Kurdistan Workers Party (PKK). By that point the government had been fighting the PKK for over three decades. In January 2000, Turkish Hezbollah leader Huseyin Velioglu was killed in a police action. Following Velioglu's death, Isa Altsoy became Hezbollah's new leader.

Although the MTTB began as a secularist national student body which advocated Kemalist reform policies, the organization went through an ideological transformation as its leadership changed in the late 1960s under the leadership of Raisim Cinisli and Ismail Kahraman. The MTTB adopted its own type of Islamo-Turkish nationalism as ideological outlook along with its own interpretation of Ottoman history as the basis of Turkish identity.

Especially between 1965 and 1980, when military government suppressed the group, the MTTB operated as the youth auxiliary for Turkish political Islam. Current Turkish President Recep Tayyip Erdogan, former president Abdullah Gul, and several leading members of the Adalet ve Kalimnma Partisi (Justice and Development Party, AKP) (including several cabinet ministers) were all MTTB members.

President Tayyip Erdogan and the governing AKP (which he formed) are political Islamists, and have sought to restore religion as a major part of the public sphere. They have expanded religious education and allowed the head scarf, once banned from state offices, to be worn in state institutions such as public colleges and in the Turkish parliament.

The current speaker of the Turkish Parliament Ismail Kahraman advanced through the ranks of the MTTB in late 1960s and early 1970s, including serving as the group's president. In 1969, Kahraman publicly opposed against funeral services for Imran Oktem, then president of the Court of Appeals and a well-known anti-Islamist judge. When, a mufti agreed that the service should proceed, MTTB militants staged an attack against the funeral. In 1969, MTTB members also attacked a left-wing protest rally and stabbed two students to death.

In April 2016, Secularist commentators criticized Kahraman when he called for a new Turkish constitution that would omit references to secularisms, because this would contradict the modern republic's founding principles. Kahraman, in defending himself, claimed that these were his "personal views" and that any new constitution should guarantee religious freedoms.

See also: Adalet ve Kalimnma Partisi (AKP) (volume 1).

FURTHER READING

Casier, Marlies & Jongerden, Joost. *Nationalisms and Politics in Turkey: Political Islam, Kemalism, and the Kurdish Issue*. Milton Park, Abingdon, Oxon: Routledge, 2011.

Eligür, Banu. *The Mobilization of Political Islam in Turkey*. New York: Cambridge University Press, 2010.

Findley, Carter Vaughn. *Turkey, Islam, Nationalism, and Modernity: A History, 1789-2007*. New Haven, CT: Yale University Press, 2010.

Rabasa, Angel & Larrabee, F. Stephen. *The Rise of Political Islam in Turkey*. Santa Monica, CA: RAND, 2008.

Yavuz, M. Hakan. *Islamic Political Identity in Turkey*. Oxford: Oxford University Press, 2003.

Chapter 62

Palestinian Islamic Jihad (PIJ)/Harakat al-Jihad al-Islami fi Filastin/Islamic Jihad/Islamic Jihad Palestine (IJP)/Islamic Jihad – Palestine Faction and Islamic Holy War

Overview

A Sunni fundamentalist group formed by Jihadists such as Abd al-Aziz al-Awda and Fathi Shiqaqi, in the Gaza in 1979-1980. Various groups referred to themselves as Islamic Jihad, such as the Usrat al-Jihad (which was formed in 1948); the Detachment of Islamic Jihad, often associated with the Abu Jihad group of al-Fatah; the Islamic Jihad Organization al-Aqsa Battalions, formed by Sheikh Asad Bayyud al-Tamimi in Jordan in 1982; Tanzim al-Jihad al-Islami, under Ahmad Muhanna; and many non-Palestinian groups. The use of these various names led to considerable uncertainty as to which group is which.

The Emergence of PIJ

The PIJ, however, claimed to be one facet of a broad jihadi movement as opposed to a discrete organization. Palestinian students attending Egyptian universities formed PIJ in 1979. Although PIJ founders, Bashir Musa, Abd al-Azziz Odah, and Fathi Shiqaqi once had belonged to the Muslim Brotherhood, they eventually rejected the non-violence strategy of the Brotherhood, believing that the organization was ineffective because it was too moderate and not sufficiently focused on issues related to Palestine. The Iranian revolution inspired many of the members, who called for a rising of the masses to "liberate" Palestine by force. The al-Quds Brigade is PIJ's armed faction, which conducts all PIJ attacks.

PIJ WAGES JIHAD

After Shiqaqi returned to Israel, the PIJ announced its intent to wage jihad (holy war) against that country. PIJ's sole purpose is to eliminate Israel and it views violence as a legitimate means to achieve its aims. By 1985, The PIJ formed a known as the Jerusalem Brigades (Saraya al-Quds). The Brigades attacked Israeli military personnel, at a military ceremony in 1986. In summer of 1988, the Israeli government expelled two leading PIJ leaders, Shaqaqi and Odah to Lebanon, where Shaqai reorganized the PIJ and fostered closer ties with the Iranian Islamic Revolutionary Guard Corps and Hezbollah in Lebanon.

The PIJ attacked several targets in Gaza, Israel, and the West Bank. The PLJ also operated in Beirut, Lebanon, Teheran, Iran, and Khartoum, Sudan, where it raises its funds.

The PIJ also took responsibility for a suicide attack in Beit Led, near Netanya, Israel, on January 22, 1994. Nineteen Israelis were killed and 60 were injured in that attack. PIJ jihadists have conducted several suicide attacks against Israeli civilians and military personnel throughout Israel and the disputed territories. During the Second Intifada (which began in the Fall of 2000) PIJ attacks killed over one hundred people in over a year of violence. On June 29, 2003, the PIJ entered into ceasefire, at the request of Mahmoud Abbas, the Prime Minister of Palestine. Breaking the cease-fire soon thereafter, the PIJ claimed that Israel had not fully complied with its commitments such as releasing incarcerated PIJ fighters.

In the early 1980s, Shiqaqi was incarcerated. In 1986, Shiqaqi's sentence was extended for two more years. Both al-Awda and Shiqaqi deported to Lebanon in April 1988. The PIJ opened a headquarters in Syria, and was active in Lebanese Palestinian refugee camps.

Shallah had received a Ph.D. at the University of Durham, England, and was an editor of a publication entitled "World and Islam Studies Enterprise". He taught for a brief time at Florida University. When Israeli Defense Forces killed Shiqaqi in 1994, Shallah succeeded him as the PIJ's leader. He was associated with jihadists such as Imam Fawaz Damra and Sami al-Arian and who were prosecuted for assisting the PIJ on US territory.

Beginning in 1994, both PIJ and Hamas collaborated and coordinated bombings. In 2000, Iran attempted to have persuade both Hamas and PIJ to disrupt the Israeli-Palestinian peace process. Hezbollah, a group with close ties to Iran, served as the intermediary between the two groups. In June 2003, PIJ and Hamas announced a cease-fire and temporarily halted attacks on Israelis and Israeli interests.

PIJ and Hamas were rivals despite their similar viewpoints on most key issues. Hamas, however, emerged as more popular of the two groups. Nonetheless, many students at several institutions of higher education, Including Gaza's Islamic University, were PIJ members. The group also was actively involved in the Second Intifada (also known as the al-Aqsa Intifada) (September 2000 - February 8, 2005).

In Lebanon, the PIJ clashes with al-Fatah, the most prominent political faction, in the Palestine Liberation Organization (PLO). Similar to Hamas and secular organizations such as the Palestinian National Alliance (PNA), the PIJ opposed the 1993 Oslo peace agreement and seeks full Israeli withdrawal from the disputed territories.

Many Palestinian refugees support the PIJ. In Ain Hilweh and other refugee camps, however, the divided Palestinian and Islamist movements obstructed the PIJ in carrying out its objectives.

The Palestinian Authority (PA) has suppressed publications supporting the PIJ cause. The PA, however, later allowed it to resume operations. In June 2003, being pressured by the international community, the Syrian government terminated PIJ and Hamas activities in that nation. Shallah went to Lebanon, and Khaled Meshaal (the chairman of Hamas's Political Bureau) relocated to Qatar. Both then travelled to Syria to resume Jihadist activity.

PIJ's Differences with Other Palestinian Groups

In the Palestinian territories, the PIJ actively clashes with Hamas. Hamas ceased attacks against Israel beginning in 2004. The group won a majority of the votes in the Palestinian elections in early 2006. Moderates within Hamas seemed to be open to recognizing the state of Israel and seemed agreeable to a two-state solution. The PIJ, however, asked Palestinians not to participate in elections held in 2006 and to oppose any diplomatic accommodation with Israel.

After Hamas won the 2006 elections for the Palestinian Legislative Council, the PIJ condemned the deals offered to Israel by Hamas and Fatah. While PIJ backed Hamas in the election, it refused to join the any Hamas-led government.

PIJ has conducted suicide attacks after 2004. This was as revenge for Israeli armed incursions and deadly attacks on PIJ leaders, such as Louay Saadi in October 2005. The PIJ also said it was responsible for two suicide attacks in 2005.

The Israeli government has long stressed the PIJ's relationship with Iran, based on Shiqaqi's works supporting Ayatollah Ruhollah Khomeini and Iran's Islamic Revolution in 1979. Shiqaqi sought a Palestinian government based on Sharia (Islamic law) and praised Khomeini's support of the Jihadist cause in Palestine. The Israeli government has long asserted that the PIJ is heavily dependent on support from both Iran and Syria.

Despite the Shia/Sunni sectarian divide, the PIJ cooperates with receives much support from Hezbollah. The PIJ is affiliated with Hamas and militant groups like it. PIJ has also carried out joint attacks with jihadist groups such as al-Asqa Martyrs Brigades and Hamas. The PIJ has conducted operations only in the Middle East and has not deliberately attacked Western Interests.

See also: Al-Asqa Martyrs Brigades (volume 1), Hamas (volume 1); Hezbollah (volume 1); Palestine Liberation Organization – General Command (volume 1).

Further Reading

Abu-Amr, Ziad. *Islamic Fundamentalism in the West Bank and Gaza: Muslim Brotherhood and Islamic Jihad.* Bloomington: Indiana University Press, 1994.
"Al-Arian deal: He admits ties to terror group: The federal plea agreement links him to the Palestinian Islamic Jihad," *The Orlando Sentinel,* Apr. 18, 2006.
Alexander, Yonah. *Palestinian Religious Terrorism: Hamas and Islamic Jihad.* Ardsley, N.Y.: Transnational, 2002.
Amr, Ziad Abū'. *Islamic Fundamentalism in the West Bank and Gaza: Muslim Brotherhood*

and Islamic Jihad. Bloomington Indiana Univ. Press 2002.

Budeiri, Musa. "The Nationalist Dimension of Islamic Movements In Palestinian Politics: Hamas, From Religious Salvation To Political Transformation: The Rise of Hamas in Palestinian Society. H. H. Ahmad; Islamic Fundamentalism in the West Bank and Gaza: Muslim Brotherhood. *Journal of Palestine Studies* 24, no. 3 (1995): 89-95.

Cook, David. *Understanding Jihad.* Berkeley: University of California Press, 2005, 2015.

DeAtkine, N. "The Palestinian Islamic Jihad U.S. Cell [1988-95]." *American Diplomacy.*

Hatina, Meir. *Iran and the Palestinian Islamic movement.* Orient, 38, no. 1(1997): 107-120.

Hatina, Meir. *Islam and salvation in Palestine: The Islamic Jihad movement.* Tel Aviv: Moshe Dayan Center for Middle Eastern and African studies, Tel Aviv University, 2001.

Husain, Mir Zohair. *Global Islamic Politics* (2nd ed.). New York: Longman, 2003.

"Islam versus Israel." (Hamas, Islamic Jihad activists deported), *The Economist, Dec. 19, 1992.*

"Israeli Blast Shakes Political Landscape; Islamic Jihad Attacked a Busy Mall in Israel Monday, Killing at Least Five People, Ahead of Israeli and Palestinian Polls." T*he Christian Science Monitor, Dec. 6, 2005.*

Knudsen, Are. "Islamism in the Diaspora: Palestinian Refugees in Lebanon." *Journal of Refugee Studies* 18, no. 2 (2005): 216–34.

Milton-Edwards, Beverley. "The Concept of and the Palestinian Islamic Movement: A Comparison of Ideas and Techniques." *British Journal of Middle Eastern Studies* 19, no. 1 (1992): 48-53.

Scoggins, David. *International Islamic Da'Wah and Jihad a Qualitative and Quantitative Assessment* (thesis) (2005).

Seper, J.). "Eight Accused of Giving Aid to Terrorism; Four U.S. Residents Held as Suspected Members of Palestinian Islamic Jihad." *The Washington Times, Feb. 21 2003.*

"Sudanese President Receives Head of Palestinian Islamic Jihad." *Sudan Tribune,* Feb. 4, 2013.

"The Movement of Islamic Jihad and the Oslo Process: An Interview with Ramadan Abdullah Shallah." *Journal of Palestine Studies* 28 (1999): 61–73.

Chapter 63

POPULAR FRONT FOR THE LIBERATION OF PALESTINE – GENERAL COMMAND (PFLP-GC)

The PFLP-GC has an ideology that combines Marxist-Leninist and Islamism. It seeks to destroy Israel and replace that nation with an Islamist government for Palestine based on Sharia (Islamic Law). The PFLP-GC rejects any negotiated peace and asserts that violence is the only way to resolve the Israeli-Palestinian conflict.

In 1959, Ahmed Jibirl, a veteran Syrian army captain, helped form the Palestine Liberation Front (PLF). The PLF merged with Popular Front for the Liberation of Palestine (PFLP), led by George Habash, in 1967. In the following year, Jibirl, unlike Habash, refused to enter into peace talks with Israel. This, along with reduced Syrian support, led Jibril to defect from the PFLP to establish the PFLP-GC, based in Damascus, Syria in 1968 (the group remains based in Damascus. Jibril claimed he formed the new group because he wanted to focus more on fighting and less on achieving a political solution for Palestine. Jibril continues to lead the PFLP-GC. His son, Jihad, died in a car bomb attack in May 2002.

The PFLP-GC conducted a large number of attacks in Europe and the Middle East during the 1970s and 1980s. The group developed novel and unusual tactics to attack Israel, including using hot-air balloons and motorized hang gliders.

During the 1970s, the PFLP-GC served as a proxy military force for Syria more than a genuinely Palestinian militant nationalist group. The group also supported Syria against opposing Palestinian factions in the civil war in Lebanon in 1976. During this conflict, Abu Abbas defected from the PFLP-GC and established the Palestine Liberation Front (PLF) in 1977. The PFLP-GC, in 1983, joined Syria and allied itself with a Fatah faction to oust Yasser Arafat from Tunisia.

After Lebanese Prime Minister Rafiq al Hariri was assassinated, a United Nations inquiry was created to investigate the attack. Despite accusations against him and his group, Jibril denied that either he or PFLP-GC were involved in the attack.

The PFLP-GC was closely connected to the Soviet Union and Iraq, and remains closely connected to both Syria and Iran. Syria provides logistical and military support, while Iran provides funding for the PFLP-GC. During the 1990s, after the Soviet Union had collapsed and the Syrian economy deteriorated, the PFLP-GC restricted its activities to training and equipping other Palestinian groups such as Hamas and the Palestinian Islamic Jihad (PIJ). In May 2001, the PFLP-GC claimed it had sought to supply 40-tons of weapons to Palestinian jihadists. The Israeli navy seized the contraband. The group also said it had killed two Israeli soldiers in the West Bank on November 18, 2003.

The PFLP-GC conducts its activities in in Lebanon, Israel, and the disputed territories. The group currently focuses its attacks in southern Lebanon, training other Palestinian militant groups, and small – scale attacks in Israel, the West bank, and Gaza. The PLLP-GC is more allied with the Alliance of Palestinian Forces (APF) and jihadist groups such as the Palestinian Islamic Jihad (PIJ) and Hamas than secular nationalist extremist organizations. This arrangement facilities PFLP-GC's efforts to serve as an intermediary between jihadist and radical secular groups that wish to coordinate their attacks The Syrian government is the main supporter and director of The PFLP-GC.

See also: Hamas (volume 1); Palestinian Islamic Jihad (volume 1).

FURTHER READING

Baracskay, Daniel. *The Palestine Liberation Organization: Terrorism and prospects for peace in the Holy Land*. Santa Barbara, CA: Praeger, (2011).

Dunning, Tristan. *Hamas, Jihad and Popular Legitimacy: Reinterpreting Resistance in Palestine*. Routledge, 2017.

Ėmanuilov, R IA & IAshlavskiĭ, Andrei, A *Terror in the name of faith: Religion and political violence*. Boston: Academic Studies Press, 2011.

Ḥabash, Jūrj. *The Popular Front for the Liberation of Palestine*. [Place of publication not identified]: [publisher not identified], [197-?]

Nassar, Jamal Raji. *The Palestine Liberation Organization: From Armed Struggle to the Declaration of Independence*. New York: Praeger, 1991.

Norton, Augustus R. *The International Relations of the Palestine Liberation Organization*. Carbondale IL.: Southern Illinois Univ. Press, 1989

"Popular Front for the Liberation of Palestine: General Command (PFLP-GC), in, Adam Dolnik, *Understanding Terrorist Innovation Contemporary Terrorism Studies Technology, Tactics and Global Trends*. London: Routledge, 2007, at 81-103.

Quandt, William B. *The Middle East: Ten Years After Camp David*. Washington, D.C.: Brookings Institution, 1988.

The Popular Front for the Liberation of Palestine: General Command (PFLP-GC). Washington, D.C.: The Office, 1988.

Singh, Manvendra. *Popular Front for the Liberation of Palestine* (1987) (thesis).

Chapter 64

STATE OF SINAI/SINAI PROVINCE OF THE ISLAMIC STATE/WILAYAT SINAI

OVERVIEW

The Sinai Peninsula is a geographic area with its northern boundary formed by the Mediterranean Sea, its eastern border adjoins Israel and Gaza on the east, and its southern border adjoins the Red Sea.

THE EMERGENCE OF "SINAI STATE"

Formerly known as "Ansar Bait El-Maqdis", the State of Sinai is currently affiliated with ISIS. ISIS recognizes the group as an "ISIS wilaya", or as "province of the Islamic State." Ansar originated in the Egyptian jihadi tradition that began with Takfir wal-Hijra (ATWH) in the late 1970s. The jihadi group, Ansar Beit al-Maqdis, planned a 2012 attack on then-Egyptian President Mohamed Morsi. After several raids in Cairo and Alexandria following the discovery of a conspiracy, Egyptian authorities believed that they had destroyed Ansar. The group, however, proved to be surprisingly resilient. The Sinai experienced and widespread jihadi violence after the uprising in 2011. Some of the militants had previously affiliated themselves with Hamas or other Palestinian jihadi organizations, which often used the area to launch various rocket and other terror against Israel. Hezbollah was one of larger outside jihadi groups that collaborated with Ansar.

Through a "baya", Ansar swore its allegiance and loyalty ISIS and its ISIS leader, Abu Bakr al-Baghdadi. However, Ansar was not necessarily a fledgling organization that needed resources to resist government attacks. Ansar is the largest jihadi group in Egypt and has proven itself resilient in the face of government attacks. Some commentators believe that this may mean that the ISIS concept of a centralized caliphate has become increasingly popular with various radical jihadi groups throughout the world

In 2014, Baghdadi claimed the "wilaya" of Sinai to be territory under his control. At the time, Baghdadi claimed that his caliphate included Saudi Arabia, Yemen, Egypt, Libya, and Algeria, because he had accepted the allegiance of ISIS followers in those area, which he claimed as new provinces of ISIS.

SECURITY CRISIS ON THE SINAI

Even prior to 2011, the Egyptian military did not fully control security in the Sinai. To accommodate for this, Egyptian authorities made various ad hoc agreements with tribal leaders to better ensure security. These authorities, however, ignored the smuggling that had sustained the area's economy. The Egyptian Revolution in 2011 hampered efforts of both the security forces and the military. This distraction helped facilitate the movement of criminals and militants into the Sinai.

Prior to January 2015, Egyptian media reported military successes against jihadists in Sinai. The jihadists, however, still frequently attacked gas pipelines serving Israel and Jordan.

The government initially sent tanks into the area as a show of force, but soon encountered difficulties with the UN Multinational Force and Observers (MFO) stationed in the area. Due to an international agreement between Israel and Egypt, Egyptian armored units were not allowed to operate in certain areas of the Sinai. Furthermore, these armored units would not be that effective in contending with the problem at hand. Local jihadists are very familiar with the area and the movements of the military in the area. For example, the Egyptian army searches towns in the early day for jihadists, who depart to avoid capture night to reassert control. The Egyptian government also lacks Intelligence-gathering capacity in the Sinai.

On January 28, 2015, the "State of Sinai" conducted several, simultaneous attacks against the Egyptian military and police targets near places such as Rafah, El Arish, and Sheikh Zuweid. The militants struck several checkpoints, a police club, and security installations with several weapons such as mortars. They also claimed responsibility for a major suicide car bombing that killed sixty persons and maimed several more. The group used three explosive-laden vehicles to attack El Arish, justifying them as vengeance for the female prisoners incarcerated by the Egyptian government. These attacks were conducted shortly after Egyptian President Abdul-Fattah el-Sisi vowed to defeat terrorism in the Sinai. Vowing that Egypt would never abandon the area, Sisi added that, "Sinai will not separate from Egypt unless all of us are killed."

The "State of Sinai" claimed responsibility for a missile assault against an Egyptian navy ship patrolling for terrorists in the Mediterranean Sea, on July 20, 2015. The group said it employed a "guided missile" to attack the vessel ship near the city of Rafah.

The Egyptian army reported that a fire broke out on the ship after a clash between the military and attacking jihadists, and that no one was killed or injured in the incident.

Several Egyptian members of the military or security services have been killed in the Sinai from 2013 through 2016. The Egyptian military reported that more than 100 insurgents and 17 of its soldiers were killed in the July 2015 attacks. Israel accused Hamas of supporting ISIS attacks in the Sinai to facilitate arms smuggling to Gaza and provide training and medical treatment for the militants.

After the attacks, Sisi deployed additional troops reinforce military units already stationed there to fight the jihadists. The Egyptian military continues to need improvements in its operational and counterinsurgency strategy and capacities, along with additional troops to defeat the militants. On one level, the Egyptian intelligence agencies must improve human intelligence in important areas of northern Sinai. On another level, the government must find the resources necessary to implement a counterinsurgency strategy that includes measures to address local employment, social services, education, and infrastructure needs.

President Sisi has reinforced Egypt's military in the Sinai and has launched attacks that have reportedly killed hundreds of Ansar fighters. In addition to its attacks in the Sinai Peninsula, the "Sinai State" has launched attacks in Egypt's western desert, with the goal of uniting the Libyan wilaya (province), an affiliate of ISIS. Egypt's anarchic frontier with Libya is another serious challenge for Sisi's government.

THE ONGOING BATTLE AGAINST SINAI STATE

The Egyptian government has only limited options in its campaign against ISIS affiliates. An air campaign would be difficult to maintain and would be dependent on good intelligence. A combination of endurance, real time data, and the ability to use against targets are crucial for success. The Egyptian government has indicated that it needs long-range drones and border-monitoring equipment better be able to detect intrusions. It would also be challenging to maintain ground forces in Libya, as strong long logistics support would be necessary and this may be difficult for the Egyptians, for several reasons including the fact that the Egyptian military is organized to operate in and near the Nile Delta. Appropriate security for Egyptian-Libyan border is both a long-term and very expensive proposition requiring sophisticated systems of surveillance and monitoring.

The domestic situation is made more complicated in view of how polarized Egyptian politics became in the aftermath of the government's suppression of the Muslim Brotherhood and the fact that ISIS is seeking to conduct attacks within the country. Although widespread popular dissatisfaction with the Brotherhood's governance followed by the chain of events that installed Sisi as president appears appear to have led to a stable government, the large-scale suppression of Brotherhood may have encouraged some individuals to become jihadists, including becoming ISIS members.

See also: Al-Qaeda (volume 1); Islamic State of Iraq and Syria (volume 1); Muslim Brotherhood (volume 1); Takfir wal-Hijra (ATWH) (volume 1).

FURTHER READING

Aftandilian, Gregory L. *Assessing Egyptian Public Support for Security Crackdowns in the Sinai*. Carlisle, PA: Strategic Studies Institute and U.S. Army War College Press, 2015.

Egypt's Sinai Question. Brussels, Cairo: International Crisis Group, 2007.

Gold, Zack "Security in the Sinai: Present and Future." *Terrorism and Counter-Terrorism Studies ICCT Research Papers* (2014).

Gold, Zack. "Salafi Jihadist Violence in Egypt's North Sinai: From Local Insurgency to Islamic State Province." *Terrorism and Counter-Terrorism Studies ICCT Research Papers,* (2016).

Ronen, Yehudit. "The Effects of the 'Arab Spring' on Israel's Geostrategic and Security Environment: The Escalating Jihadist Terror in the Sinai Peninsula." *Israel Affairs,* 20, no. 3 (2014): 302-317.

Rougier, Bernard; Lacroix, Stéphane; & Schoch, Cynthia. *Egypt's Revolutions: Politics, Religion, and Social Movements*. Houndmills, Basingstoke, Hampshire; New York City: Palgrave Macmillan, 2016.

Stern, Jessica; & Berger, J. M. *ISIS: The State of Terror*. New York, N.Y.: Ecco Press, an imprint of Harper Collins Publishers, [2015]

Tal, Nahman. *Radical Islam in Egypt and Jordan*. Brighton: Sussex Academic Press/Jaffee Center for Strategic Studies, 2005.

Chapter 65

SUPREME COUNCIL FOR ISLAMIC REVOLUTION IN IRAQ

SCIRI, Supreme Islamic Iraqi Council (SIIC), Islamic Supreme Council of Iraq (ISCI), Supreme Assembly for the Islamic Revolution in Iraq.

OVERVIEW

Formed in 1982, The Supreme Council for Islamic Revolution in Iraq (SCIRI) is one of the most powerful Shiite political parties in Iraq. SCIR was formed by Abdul-Aziz al-Hakim and hid older brother Muhammad Baqer al-Hakim, when they were in exile in Iran, with the support of the Iranian government.

SCIRI advocates for the creation of a separate Shiite controlled region in southern Iraq as well as political control in Iraq's government. The Badr Brigade (SCIRI's military wing) had tens of thousands of men trained in Iran and fought alongside Iranian troops during the Iraq-Iran war (1980 and 1988). In 1991, thousands of troops in the Badr Brigade went to Iraq to support the Shiite rebellion in the south.

In 2002, Abdul Aziz al hakim led a SCIRI delegation to the United States to deliberate with the Bush administration, although public opposed a foreign invasion in Iraq. In 2003, the Badr Brigades transformed itself into a civilian unit. In September wood, the Badr Brigade changed its name to the Badr organization of Reconstruction and Development. In 2003, Abdul Aziz al Hakim became the President of the United States led Governing Council of Iraq.

After this, the SCIRI transformed from a militant insurgent group to an Iraqi political party seeking to encompass all Shiite political groups. In the 2005 elections, the first since Saddam Hussein was deposed, several SCIRI leaders were elected to seats in government after Abdul-al-Hakim hard formed an alliance of Shiite parties.

In 2007, SCIRI changed its name to the Supreme Islamic Iraqi Council. The group removed the word revolution from their name to win greater political appeal from Iraqi Nationalists and the US officials. Since 2008, SCIRI has had its primary political base in Southern Iraq where its members control most of the provincial governments. As of 2014, Hadi al-Ameri is the leader of the reformed Badr organization.

POLITICAL ACTIVITIES

SCIRI is the largest Shiite political party in Iraq. It is a Shiite alliance forged by Abdul Aziz al-Hakim for the January 2005 elections won the most seats in both the January and December 2005 elections.

By 2008, the ISCI became one of the power powerful parties in Iraq. It has the largest political bloc in Iraq's Council of representatives.

In 2014, SCIRI controlled 11 percent of seats in Parliament, down from 25 percent in 2007.

SPECIFIC GOALS

The SCIRI seeks to: 1) bring together different Shiite opposition groups for the purpose of creating an Islamic republic in Iraq and an autonomous Shiite federal region in southern Iraq and 2) Seek to gain political control in Iraq and appoint a government modeled after Iran's Islamic Revolution.

FINANCING

State sponsorship. SCIRI was established by the Hakim family, with direct support from Iran's government. In the years prior to SCIRI became a political party, their military wing (the Badr Brigade) received funding from Iran.

LEADERSHIP AND STRUCTURE

SCIRI is a militant wing was known as the Badr Brigade. In 2003, it changed its name to the Badr Brigade of Reconstruction and Development, while allegedly breaking direct ties to SCIRI

From 1982 through 2003, Muhammad Baquer al-Hakim was the leader of SCIRI until his death in 2003 due to a car bombing assassination by Al-Qaeda jihadists. He was succeeded after which his brother Abdul Azia al-Hakim, who won gained control. From 2003, Abdul ak-0Hakim was diagnosed with lung cancer and died on August 26, 2009.

From 2009 to the present, Ammar al-Hakim, Abdul Aziz's son, became SCIRI's new leader following his father's footsteps.

FURTHER READING

Al-Jabbār, Fāliḥ 'Abd'. *The Shī'ite Movement in Iraq*. London: Saqi, 2003.
Bayātī, Hamid. *From Dictatorship to Democracy: An Insider's Account of the Iraqi Opposition to Saddam*. Philadelphia: University of Pennsylvania Press, 2011.

Cole, Juan Ricardo. *The Ayatollahs and Democracy in Iraq*. Amsterdam: Amsterdam University Press, 2006.

Ganji, Babak. *A Shi'i enclave?: Iranian policy towards Iraq*. Camberley, Surrey: Defence Academy of the United Kingdom, Conflict Studies Research Centre, 2006.

Nakash, Yitzhak. *The Shi'is of Iraq*. Princeton, NJ: Princeton University Press, 1994.

Reda, Fouad Mustapha. *The Supreme Council of Islamic Revolution in Iraq: Structure and Political Role, 2005* (thesis).

Chapter 66

TAKFIRI GROUPS

OVERVIEW

Takfirism (Sunni Extremism) is based on medieval Islamic doctrine that Egyptian jihadists had been invoked after Israel defeated Egypt in the Six-day War in 1967. Takfirism holds that deviant and corrupt practices within Islam have weakened the Muslim ummah (the body of believers). Takfirism denounces all non-practicing Muslims as kafirs (infidels or unbelievers). Takfiri leaders teach their adherents to abandon existing Muslim societies, live in isolated communities and attack infidels.

The indiscriminate violence launched by Takfiri groups targeting members of other sects including other Muslims is the result of the Takfiri belief system adopted by extremist Sunni groups. In applying the Takfir, these radical groups automatically assume the authority to declare anyone to be a kafir or an apostate. In following this doctrine, the militants feel justified in persecuting non-Muslim groups, as well as committing atrocities against fellow Muslims and destroying mosques and shrines.

TAKFIRI FIGHTERS: WHERE THEY WERE AND WHERE THEY FIGHT

During the 1970s, small isolated cells of Takfirist militants lived throughout the Middle East in the 1970s. They fought in support of the mujahedeen in the Afghan-Soviet War, from 1979 through 1989. Ayman al-Zawahiri, from Egypt, Tahir Yuldash, from Uzbekistan, and Sheikh Essa, were leading Takfiris during this active time for their movement. All of them eventually became leaders of Al-Qaeda. Following the US-led incursion of Iraq, Takfirism became increasingly popular in many Middle Eastern nations. Some of the Arab nations in the Person Gulf area and in the Middle East have long been accused of arming, financing, money laundering and even providing ideological guidelines for the takfir groups, including ISIS, Al-Qaeda, and Boko Haram. Abu Musab Al-Zarqawi, who led Al-Qaeda in Iraq (AQI) strongly supported Takfirism until his death in 2006.

After 2003 many Al-Qaeda's leaders and members strongly supported Takfirism at a time when Takfirism began growing by more than just merely hatred of the West. Takfirism began to stress the belief that infidels in Muslim nations empowered their enemies and must be destroyed. They believed that infidel Muslim leaders should be removed from power before they could lead more Muslims away from what they perceived as genuine Islam. The Takfirists viewed all non-practicing Muslims as the enemy. They also made the rugged, isolated, and primitive terrain of North and South Waziristan in Afghanistan their new sanctuary during the US-led incursion.

THE GOALS OF TAKFIRIS

While Al-Qaeda, in the 1990s, focused on expelling western military forces from Muslim-majority nations, the Takfirists focused on attacking the enemy within Muslim-majority nations. Because they believed they were fighting Pakistani infidels (believing that the Pakistani government was an "apostate regime" as Western unbelievers, they believed that it was crucial to defeat the internal enemy prior to engaging with any external forces. An example of this concept in action was several assassination attempts against President Perez Musharraf during his tenure in office as Pakistani President.

Takfirist jihadists, whether al-Qaeda members or operatives of other jihadist groups, share these two objectives. They seek to fight Western militaries, while forming the framework of a repressive Islamic government to intimidate and control other Muslims. In addition to attacking various Muslim-led governments, the Takfiris have launched attacks against moderate Muslim reformists associated with various moderate organizations in Waziristan. Takfiris reject Shia Islam as a heretical deviation from Islam. Takfiris engage in both sectarian warfare and jihad. Takfirism promotes a messianic vision, in the sense that it is the sole legitimate voice of Islam and leader of the world's Muslims, in the struggle against Muslims that they view as apostates and West they views as the infidel enemy.

THE IRANIAN GOVERNMENT'S VIEW OF TAKFIR GROUPS

The Iranian government has warned nations that support Sunni jihadist groups in the Middle East will pay a heavy price for this support in the near future as this support would backfire on the hosts. The Iranian government argues that these jihadi groups operating in Muslim-majority nations such as Syria undermine the unity of the Islamic Ummah (nation). The Iranian government and Shias refer to ISIS and Al-Qaeda as takfir groups, and use the term in a derogatory fashion.

See also: Al-Qaeda (volume 1); Al-Qaeda in Iraq (AQI) (volume 1); Taliban (volume 2).

FURTHER READING

Alshech, Eli. "The Doctrinal Crisis within the Salafi-Jihadi Ranks and the Emergence of Neo-Takfirism." *Islamic Law and Society* 21 no. 4 (2014): 419-452.
Blanford, N. "Emboldened by Military Gains, Assad Regime Shows Resilience." *The Christian Science Monitor,* May 2, 2013.

Britain's National Security Challenges: Extremism, Cyber Terrorism, Sectarianism and Takfiri Jihadism. London: Afghan Academy International, 2010.

"Can Islam's Leaders Reach Its Radicals? Hard-Line Islamists are Increasingly Isolated from Mainstream Muslims." *The Christian Science Monitor,* July 14, 2005.

Eatwell, Roger & Goodwin, Matthew. *The New Extremism in 21st Century Britain*. Hoboken: Taylor and Francis, 2012.

"Hezbollah Chief to Supporters: Takfiris Have No Future," *Al-Arab (London, United Kingdom),* Nov. 4, 2014.

"Iraq's Deepening Religious Fissures; After the Largest Death Toll from a Single Attack since Hussein's Fall, Sectarian Bloodletting Seems Likely To Escalate." *The Christian Science Monitor,* Nov. 28, 2006.

Newell, Steven W. *Global Takfiri Radicalization: A Center of Gravity Deconstruction*. Ft. Belvoir: Defense Technical Information Center, 2010.

Paz, Re'uven. *Tangled Web: International Networking of the Islamist Struggle*. Washington, DC: Washington Institute for Near East Policy, 2002.

Spalek, Basia. "Community Engagement for Counterterrorism in Britain: An Exploration of the Role of "Connectors" in Countering Takfiri Jihadist Terrorism." *Studies in Conflict & Terrorism* 37, no. 10 (2014): 825-841.

"The Bloody Stalemate Persists; Iraq (Iraq's wobbly coalition government)," *The Economist,* Jul. 14, 2007.

"Why the Salafist-Takfiris Should Worry Us," *Al-Arab (London, United Kingdom)*, Feb. 16, 2014.

Chapter 67

TAWHID AND JIHAD/MONOTHEISM AND JIHAD

A group of jihadists who had defected from Jamaat al-Tawhid wal-Jihad, which had been formed by Aba Musab al-Zarqawi in the early 2000s, when he began training jihadist militants. Zarqawi was a Jordanian-born jihadist leader who began his radicalization process an s young man imprisoned for drug and sex crimes. He went to Afghanistan with the intention of joining the fight against the Soviet occupation of that nation. During the 1990s, Zarqawi adopted a Salafi ideology and was arrested for criticizing and for engaging in conspiracy against the royal family of Jordan. Zarqawi met with Osama bin Laden. Bin Laden invited Zarqawi to join Al-Qaeda despite ideological differences between the two. For example, Zarqawi preferred to target the "near enemies" such as Israel and the Jordanian government, while the Al Qaeda leadership chose to focus on the "far enemy", the United States. Zarqawi also had a deep hatred of the Shiites that bin Laden did not agree with.

While Zarqawi militants formed groups under different names, they became collectively known under the name of the most prominent Zarqawi group, Jamaat al-Tawhid wa-al-Jihad (JTJ). JTJ's first attack was in Jordan, when it organized the murder of Unsaid officer Laurence Foley in 2002. The force had a large number of foreign fighters, especially from Jordan, Syria, Afghanistan, Pakistan, and Kurdish areas. Some jihadist joined from the Kurdistan-based Jihadi group, Ansar Al-Islam, which been operating in Iraq before Zarqawi's group became organized and JTJ began to actively recruit other Iraqis.

In Iraq, JTJ became active after the US-led invasion of Iraq in 2003. JTJ was one of the factions that sought to force the US and other coalition forces out of the nation and disrupt the government transition. As part of its insurgency, JJTJ became known for its violent tactics and for targeting non-combatants, such as aid workers and native Iraqis (particularly those that JTJ believed were collaborating with the government). JTJ, for example, would conduct suicide bombings that killed civilians while other insurgent groups focused their attacks on US and coalition forces. The international community condemned the group for its killings and videos depicting beheadings that it released after kidnapping and killing non-Arabs in Iraq. JTJ also often conducted attacks on Shiite targets to incite sectarian conflicts and complicate the work of the Coalition Provisional Authority (CPA) and the government transition. Both JTJ and Zarqawi quickly became the best known entities associated with the insurgency in Iraq.

In October 2004, Zarqawi came to an agreement with bin Laden and formally joined with Al Qaeda. He renamed his organization "Tanzim Qaidat al-Jihad fi Bilad al-Rafidayn

Zarqawi, more commonly known as Al Qaeda in Iraq. Despite the official pledge of loyalty to bin Laden, Zarqawi and the Al Qaeda leadership still disagreed on key issues, such as Al Qaeda's willingness to cooperate with other groups against their various enemies and its focus on the United States and the West rather than "near enemies". These differences persisted through

Some members formed Tawhid and Jihad in Syria because they had attracted many Syrian nationalists as members. Several groups use the term "Tawhid and Jihad" to express their objectives. When Jamaat al-Tawhid wa al-Jihad became part of al-Qaeda in September 2004, many of its Syrian members returned to Syria. They sought to depose against Syria's secular government and impose Islamic state (a caliphate) based on Sharia (Islamic law). Tawhid and Jihad Syria also has more militant faction -- "Jund Al·Sham".

The group became widely known in November 2006, when its leader, Abu Jandal al-Dimashqi attacked Syrian security forces on the Syrian-Lebanese border and detonated a bomb that was attached to him. The group claimed that all Arab nations have "jalil" (infidel) governments because they are allegedly not based on Islamic law (Sharia). Therefore, he claims, they must be overthrown and replaced with Islamic governments. Currently, the group also has some militants in Lebanon. They, however, have not claimed responsibility for any attacks in that country.

See also: Al-Qaeda (volume 1); Islamic State of Iraq and Syria (volume 1).

FURTHER READING

"A Suspect Emerges as Key Link in Terror Chain." *Christian Science Monitor,* Jan. 23, 2004.
Blanford, Nicholas. "Is Al-Qaeda Actually Involved in the Syria Uprising?" *Christian Science Monitor,* Jan. 16, 2012.
Brisard, Jean and Damien Martinez. *Zarqawi: The New Face of Al-Qaeda.* New York: Other, 2005.
"Brotherhood, ISIS among 83 Terror Organisations Named by UAE." *Khaleej Times (Dubai, United Arab Emirates),* Nov. 15, 2014.
Debat, Alexis. "Vivisecting the Jihad." *National Interest,* June 22, 2004.
"ISIL Executes Tawhid Battalion Commander in Southern Syria." *FARS News Agency,* Jan. 5, 2014.
"Jail, Jihad and Exploding Kittens; Extremist Ideology." *Economist,* Nov.1, 2014. .
Khashan, Hilal. "Dateline: Arab Uprisings May Doom Middle East Christians." *Middle East Quarterly,* Sep. 22, 2014. .
"Militants in Iraq Release Video of U.S. Captive's Beheading." *The Washington Post,* Sep. 22, 2004.
Scarborough, Rowan. "Secretive Zarqawi Stays under Radar, on the Lam." *The Washington Times,* June 8, 2004.
"Syria's Salafist Foreign Legions." *The Daily Star (Beirut, Lebanon),* Mar. 5, 2013.
"U.S. Forces Battle Iraqi Insurgents." *The Cincinnati Post,* Oct. 23, 2004.

Chapter 68

TURKISH ISLAMIC JIHAD (TIJ)

The rise of militant Islam has created a crisis of identity in Turkey. The nation was formed in 1923, from the remnants of the defeated Ottoman Empire by Mustafa Kemal Ataturk, who sought to establish a secular and westernized republic. In later decades, Turkey became the only Muslim-majority nation with a democratic government, although the nation has lacked a strong record on human rights, press freedom, and the women's rights.

By the 1990s, Turkey was confronted with a growing Islamist militancy. Even individuals from the educated middle class became involved in Islamic extremism. This phenomenon was exacerbated by the Iraq War, which began in 2003. Often these Islamists focused on the Turkish Republic itself. Until the late 1990s, the Turkish government had tacitly nurtured Hezbollah, the violent Sunni jihadist group that operated in the restive southeastern Anatolia area of Turkey. One should note that the Turkish Hezbollah had no connection to the Shia group using the same name in Lebanon. In Bingol and other towns, men were recruited for a group that became a convenient government proxy to fight Kurdish guerillas. By 1998, the Turkish army was ordered to check Hezbollah activities, as the group had begun engaging in extremely brutal attacks. For example, Hizbullah has killed four journalists working for *Cumhuriyet*, one of Turkey's leading secularist newspaper. Turkey began a series of arrests and killings of group members. Some Hezbollah members went underground or went into exile outside of Turkey.

The quality and scope of Hezbollah and Salafist Islamism extremism in Turkey differed significantly. While most Hezbollah and Great Eastern Raider (IBDA-C) jihadists were poorly educated, with many members having criminal records, and largely restricted to one area of Turkey, many of the nation's Salafists were young, middle class, well-educated and reside in Turkey's urban areas. The scope of the two groups also differ. While Hezbollah's outlook is regional, the Turkish Salafists have a much more worldwide outlook.

Beginning in the 1980s, hundreds of Turks trained or fought in Afghanistan, Bosnia, Chechnya, and Pakistan and then returning to Turkey as battle-tested jihadists. Many Turkish fighters began fighting the jihadist struggle in Afghanistan. Over a hundred Turkish nationals received training at Al-Qaeda camps before the Taliban were deposed in Afghanistan. Hundreds more may remain unknown. Some of these Turks went to Iraq to join the insurgency in that nation, following the engagement of US troops in Iraq in 2003. Many Salafists believed that the "Iraqi jihad" is a Salafi jihad, a "pure jihad" that most closely resembles the concept of jihad envisioned by the prophet Muhammad.

In 2003, El Kaide Turka (Turkish Al-Qaeda) attacked Istanbul with four suicide bombings that killed more than 60 people. Four of the attackers came from Bingol, an impoverished and isolated area in southeastern Anatolia, in Turkey.

Formed ca. 1991, the Turkish Islamic Jihad (TIJ) is a Jihadist group that accused the US and Egyptian governments of conspiring to divide the Middle East between them. TIJ is an Islamist group is also linked closely to Iran. Radical Iranian elements were blamed for financing these jihadists.

The TIJ sought to undermine a Mideast peace conference then being held between Israel and the Palestinians in Madrid. The conference was to consider major issues such as a freeze on Jewish settlements in the disputed West Bank and Gaza Strip, a suspension of the Arab boycott against Israel, and Arab support that would repeal the UN resolution equating Zionism with racism. The TIJ staged jihadist attacks to prevent these negotiations in the name of the fight against imperialism and injustice. In 1991, TIJ bombed the car of an Iraqi diplomat in Ankara. In 1992, TIJ also bombed an Israeli diplomat and a synagogue in Istanbul after Israeli forces killed Hezbollah leader, Musawi in Lebanon. Also in 1992, TIJ said it a fire at the Tozbey Hotel in Istanbul that killed 17 Ukrainians and injured more than 40 persons. The Turkish Government reported that the fire was caused by faulty wiring and careless behavior by hotel guests. The TIJ is virulently anti-American and killed two US servicemen stationed in Turkey on October 28, 1991. The TIJ said that the attacks were in protest against the peace talks. At the same time, there were deadly attacks on Israeli residents in the disputed territories of the West Bank, including an attack on a bus that killed five Israelis. The West Bank was one of the areas Israel seized in the 1967 Mideast War. The attacks in 1991 and 1992 occurred at a time when foreign businesses had already significantly reduced their staffs in Turkey. These attacks effectively led to the collapse of the peace talks.

See also: Adalet ve Kalimnma Partisi (AKP) (volume 1); Al-Qaeda (volume 1); Hezbollah (volume 1); Islamic State of Iraq and Syria (volume 1).

FURTHER READING

Al-Dawoody, Ahmed. "Armed Jihad in the Islamic Legal Tradition." *Religion Compass* 7 no. 11 (Nov. 2013): 476-484.

Berger, Maurits S. "Jihad and Counter-Jihad: Western European Legal Responses to Islamic Militancy," in, M Cherif Bassiouni and Amna Guellali; *Jihad and Its Challenges to International and Domestic Law*. The Hague: Hague Academic Press, 2010, *at* 229-247.

"Blasts in Turkey Kill American, Injure Egyptian." *Boston Globe, Oct. 29, 1991.*

"Car Bomb Kills Israeli Diplomat." *Washington Post, Mar. 8, 1992.*

"Colonial Empire, Modern State, New Jihad," in, Bonner, Michael, *Doctrines and Practice Jihad in Islamic History.* Princeton: Princeton University Press, 2008.

Fadil, M. "Terrorism: Threat from the Shadows." *The Middle East* Nov. 1, 1993.

Fraser, A. "Turkish suicide bombers carried out synagogue attacks, Jewish victims buried." *Christian Science Monitor*, Nov. 18, 2003.

Karabell, Zachary. "Fundamental Misconceptions: Islamic Foreign Policy." *Foreign Policy,* No. 105 (Winter 1996/97): 77-90.

Khan, L. Ali. "Phenomenology of Jihad." In, L. Ali Khan, *A Theory of International Terrorism Understanding Islamic Militancy,* Leiden: Brill, 2006 at 170-205.

Soguel, D. "Turkey Shifts Tone on Islamic State. Will It Join US-Led Coalition?" *The Christian Science Monitor,* Sep. 29, 2014.

Stenhouse, Paul. "Islam's Trojan Horse? Turkish Nationalism and the Nakshibendi Sufi Order." *Quadrant* 51, no. 12 (Dec. 2007): 11-18.

"What's the Turkish for Struggle? (Secularism in political environment of Turkey). *The Economist,* Nov. 22, 1997.

Chapter 69

WALIY AL-FAQIH/THE JURIST'S GUARDIAN

Wilayat al-faqih, or the rule by jurisconsults, which Shi'as are required to obey, is a contemporary Iranian idea, despites its long historical pedigree. This concept applies only to the governance of Iran, and does not apply to Shias who do not live in Iran. Al-Sayyid Khamene'i is the current waliy al-faqih in Iran. Shia religious leaders, including Al-Sayyid Al-Sistani in Al- Najaf and Muhammad Husayn Fadlallah in Lebanon, are connected to wilayat al-faqih through a "religious authority", which differs from how wilayat al-faqih functions in Iran.

Because the theory of Waliy-al-Faqih emerged from the Immate (the political status of imams), which is crucial concept in Shiism, this political doctrine is crucial to understanding the Shia view of leadership. It is comparable to the traditional political theory of Sunni jurists regarding the doctrine of the caliphate.

In Iran's government, the Waliy-al-Faqih is the supreme authority in the Murshid-al-Thawra (Revolution's Guide) and the first guide of all authorities in Iran's Islamic Republic except for the Mahdi (a Muslim savior who will lead a worldwide revolution and establish a global Islamic empire). The Waliy-al-Faqih also leads Iran's military (including both Iran's regular security forces and the Iranian Revolutionary Guards). He is authorized to declare war, appoint the highest clerics on the constitutional council, approve presidential elections, call for elections, and supervise elections. In this "Twelvers' structure" (involving the Twelve Imams who Shia Muslims believe are Muhammad's spiritual and political successors), the Council of Experts chooses the guardian through a secret ballot. The council may also remove guardians who become unable to conduct their responsibilities. The first Waliy al-Faqih was Ayatollah Ruhollah al-Musawi Khomeini, who came to power in 1979. He was succeeded by Ayatollah Ali Khamenei, the present Waliy al-Faqih, in 1989.

Wilayat al-faqih, according to Ayatollah Khomeini, grants absolute authority to the jurist, in the executive, legislative, and the judiciary. The Iranian Revolution of 1979 made Iran's religious leadership also Iran's political governing elite, based on Khomeini's theory of "the guardianship of the jurisconsult" (vilayat al-faqih). The Shiite ulama (scholars) launched into a prolonged deliberation of the merits of this doctrine. Before this time, the Shia ulama (Islamic scholars) were largely perceived as jurists with no political authority or power.

In Shia Islam, Wilayat al-Faqih is a vital part of the sect's political thought. It maintains that Islamic doctrine grants a faqīh (Islamic jurist) a special type of guardianship over the people. While agreeing with the theory, the Ulama have various different ideas over how comprehensive this guardianship should properly be. One view accepts a limited view of the faqih's authority, i.e., that the guardianship should be limited to non-litigious issues (al-omour al-hesbiah) (matters not ajudicatabile by lawsuits) such as religious endowments (Waqf) judicial issues, and disposition of property without an owner. An alternative theory, "Absolute Guardianship of the Jurist", insists that the Guardianship of the faqih encompasses every matter that the Prophet of Islam and Shi'a Imam deals with in governing Iran. Khomeini first articulated the concept of guardianship as governance in 1970, which became the foundation of the Iranian Constitution. Iran's constitution requires that a faqih, or Vali-ye faqih (Guardian Jurist), serve as the Supreme Leader of Iran's Governing structure.

See also: Islamic Revolutionary Guard Corps (IRGC) (volume 1).

FURTHER READING

Badareen, Nayel A. *Identity and Authority: Changes in the Process of Debates over the Islamic Marriage Contract among Contemporary Muslim Arab Intellectuals*. (Thesis -- University of Arizona, 2014).

Grote, Rainer and Tilmann J Röder. *Constitutionalism in Islamic Countries: Between Upheaval and Continuity*. Oxford: Oxford University Press, 2012, 2016.

Karpat, Kemal H. *Political and Social Thought in the Contemporary Middle East,*. New York: Praeger, 1968, 1982

Sanei, Faraz and Sarah Leah Whitson. *Codifying Repression an Assessment of Iran's New Penal Code*. New York, N.Y.: Human Rights Watch, 2012.

Chapter 70

WORLD ISLAMIC FRONT FOR JIHAD AGAINST JEWS AND CRUSADERS

During the 1990s, Osama bin Laden, a fundamentalist militant and leader of Al-Qaeda, issued several fatwas (legal edicts) opposed to the stationing of US troops in Saudi Arabia. By the middle of 1996, Al-Qaeda was barely functioning as a terrorist organization, and had only thirty members. Facing irrelevance and anxious that he was losing his leadership role over Islamist militants worldwide, bin Laden, announced a "blessed jihad" to oppose the United States and its Western allies on August 23, 1996 (Bruce, et al., 2005). As part of this jihad, bin Laden declared war on the United States, which he intended to recruit new members for Al-Qaeda. This effort failed.

In February 1998, Bin Laden formed the "World Islamic Front for Jihad Against Jews and Crusaders" to persuade other Islamist groups to join him in jihad. The declaration said:

The ruling to kill the Americans and their allies – civilians and military – is an

Individual duty for every Muslim who can do it in any country in which it is possible to do it, in order to liberate the al-Asqa Mosque and the holy mosque (Meccas) from their grip (Hashim, 2001).

Along with Osama bin Laden, the following also signed the charter: Ayman al-Zawahiri for Egyptian Islamic Jihad; Ahmed Taha, for Islamic Group's Rifai, and several leading jihadists from Pakistan and Bangladesh. The group threatened attacks against the United States. In the end, however, this effort did not generate significant Islamist support. Al-Qaeda, however, at this time was well funded, technologically sophisticated and had a fairly large following of loyal militants.

Before the U.S. Embassy attacks in 1998, Taha began distancing himself from the coalition. Bin Laden threatened the United States, stating that, "The coming days will guarantee ... that America will face a black fate. Strikes will continue from everywhere, and Islamic groups will appear one after the other to fight American interests." He further said, "we do not differentiate between those [Americans] dressed in military uniforms and civilians. They're all targets... You will leave when the bodies of Americans soldiers and civilians are sent in the wooden boxes and coffins" (Vick, 1998).

Later in 1998, Al-Qaeda launched its first major attack: the bombings of the U.S. embassies in Kenya and Tanzania, hoping to garner notoriety and followers for his cause. These efforts, however, did not attract new Islamists to rally to his side. Some of these

Islamist groups criticized Al-Qaeda for conducting the attacks and lacking an appropriate manhaj (correct understanding of the Koran).

From an Islamic legal standpoint: 1) Bin laden was not authorized to issue a fatwa, or declare a jihad, as he was not an Islamic jurist and he never represented a recognized government (the only body that is allowed to issue a call for a holy war (in cases when a Muslim community is threatened on religious grounds; 2) bin Laden was also not authorized to change existing Islamic law because he was not an Islamist jurist; and 3) even if bin Laden was authorized to change existing Islamic law, he still needed to provide the rationale justifying the new decree.

See also: Al-Qaeda (volume 1); Islamic State of Iraq and Syria (volume 1).

FURTHER READING

Aboul-Enein, Youssef H. *Ayman Al-Zawahiri the Ideologue of Modern Islamic Militancy.* Maxwell Air Force Base, Ala.: USAF Counterproliferation Center, Air University, 2004.

Bartlett W. B. *Islam's War against the Crusaders.* New York: The History Press, 2013.

Bonner, Michael. *Jihad in Islamic History.* Princeton: Princeton University Press 2008.

Copinger-Symes, T. (n.d.). Is Osama Bin Laden's 'Fatwa urging Jihad against Americans' dated February 23, 1998 justified by Islamic law? *Defence Studies,* 3, no. 1 (2003): 44-65. .

Hashim, Ahmed S. "The World According to Usama bin Laden." *Naval College Review,* 54 no. 4 (2001): 11-34.

"Jihad: From the Qur'an to the Islamic State," in, Gabriele Marranci, *Jihad Beyond Islam.* Bloomsbury Academic 2006.

Khashan, Hilal. The New World Order and the Tempo of Militant Islam. *British Journal of Middle Eastern Studies* 24, no. 1(1997): 5-24.

Lacey, Jim. *The Canons of Jihad: Terrorist's Strategy for Defeating America.* Annapolis, Md.: Naval Institute Press, 2008.

Laden, Osama Bin, in Lawrence, Bruce. *Messages to the World: The Statements of Osama Bin Laden.* London: Verso, 2005.

McFarland, M. & Whitman, J. *Rethinking Secular and Sacred on the Role of Secular Thought in Religious Conflicts.* University of Bradford, 2005.

Pike, J. & Aftergood, S. *Al-Qa'ida (the base): Islamic Army for the Liberation of the Holy Places: World Islamic Front for Jihad Against Jews and Crusaders: Islamic Salvation Foundation: Usama bin Laden Network.* Washington, D.C.: Congressional Research Service, 2000.

Vick, K. "FBI, Police Search Hotel for Clues in Kenya Blast." *Washington Post*, Aug. 20, 1998.

Chapter 71

YEMENI ASSOCIATION FOR REFORM/AL-TAJAMMU' AL-YEMENI LI AL-ISLAH/TAJAMMU' AL-YAMANI LI'L-ISLAH

Contemporary Islamist politics in Yemen began in the 1960s when a chapter of the Muslim Brotherhood was formed in that nation. Another Islamist movement was active in the 1970s when the nation was still the nations of North and South Yemen. In North Yemen, both Muslim leaders and secularists allied with the West, believed they were threatened by South Yemen, and its Soviet backed Communist and nontheist government. Abdul Majid al Zindani, the main leader of Muslim clerics, helped form systems in North Yemen (including religiously-affiliated schools) to oppose anti-Islam groups and secular initiatives backed by South Yemen.

Held out as "scientific institutes," these religious schools functioned similar to the madrassas (religious schools) that educated young people based on religious works in Afghanistan and Pakistan and. The institutes offered accommodations and schooling for young Yemenis, who came to these madrassas without any previous education. The schools taught a curriculum that was pervasively Salafi or Wahhabist. The institutes eventually paralleled Yemen's government-operated education system, with several activities for youth. Similar to what occurred in Pakistan, many graduates from these schools fought in the Afghan-Soviet War (1979-1989).

The Islah Party was formed after North Yemen and South Yemen merged to form a united Yemen in May 1990. Formed as a result of an alliance between several tribal leaders in northern Yemen, the Yemeni Association for Reform (the Islah Party) became one of the most powerful Islamic political parties of the early 1990s.

Islah merged three influential groups in Yemen: influential tribes that held sway in rural parts of the country; 2) the Muslim Brotherhood, which was particularly politically powerful in the cities; and 3) Salafi sheiks, who operated several religious schools. The Islah party attracted a mix of supporters such as: the traditionally-minded, conservatives who were more pragmatic in their outlook, and intolerant ultraconservatives. The Islamist-oriented ruling General People's Congress (GPC) supported Islah.

Sheikhal-Ahmar Abd Allah, leader of the Rashid tribal confederation, led the party until 2007. Islah focused on constitutional reform and promoted Islamic ideology. When formed, the party also opposed radical leftist factions, which were becoming more powerful in Yemen. Eventually, the Muslim Brotherhood aligned itself with Islah and became active in Yemen's socio-political affairs. 'Abd al-Majid al-Zandani, leader of the Brotherhood faction, sought to reform Yemen's education system. A large number of Brotherhood members eventually joined the Islamic Renaissance Movement (Enhahda).

Throughout its history, Islah has practiced a relatively pragmatic approach to political Islam. The group claims itself to be a popular party "that seeks reform of all aspects of life on the basis of Islamic principles and teachings." This, the party adds, must be balanced by the requirement that policy choices are required to be "centered on the realities and events of their [people's] experiences" as well as "appreciating the network of external and internal factors that influence the running of … [Yemen's] affairs."

Islah's platform is not as ideological as in similar parties in many Muslim-majority nations. The document stresses that the party favors gradual reform. Islah's public rhetoric also emphasizes pragmatic issues of governance over theological issues. Islah is distinguished from other Islamist political parties because it stresses its beliefs in liberty and democracy, in addition to Islamic-based policy initiatives.

Islah has some divisions. Even 20 years after Islah was formed, the party remains seriously factionalized, which have resulted in serious internal disagreements on Islah's place in Yemen, how it should work with the government, and its positions relative to the rights of women. To hold the party together despite its ideological diversity, the party regularly issues opaque, unclear, and contradictory policy statements.

President Saleh, who came to power despite receiving only an elementary school education, developed Islah solely for his personal political ambitions. Saleh first rose through the ranks in army, before becoming North Yemen's leader from 1978 until 1990. In 1990, became leader of a united Yemen as provided in a merger agreement between the two nations. This Unification both strengthened Yemen, and made it a more diverse political nation.

Saleh hoped Islamism would assist his political party, the General People's Congress (GPC) keep his political competition at bay. Specifically, he intended that Islah's positions on religious and social issues would check the Yemeni Socialist Party (YSP), which had formerly governed South Yemen.

In forming Islah, Saleh recruited Zindani and Abdullah al Ahmar, leader of the northern Hashid Tribal Confederation, where Saleh's clan came from. The Hashid was had the largest population of Yemen's numerous tribes. Zindani recruited the Salafis for the new party. Islah gave Sindani legitimacy and a larger platform to promote his policies. Ahmar found that Islah provided the formal means to exert institutional power to accompany his well-respected but non-official role of a tribal elder. Ahmar also recruited his tribal and business colleagues, which helped increase the party's size.

Because the Muslim Brotherhood was not connected to any other Yemeni political group, it developed into another faction of Islah and the faction with the largest membership. This was true even though the Muslim Brothers took significantly different positions than either Zindani or Ahmar. Yemen's Brothers neither followed Zindani nor adhered to his strict Wahhabism. The Brothers also lacked tribal connections with Ahmar.

Islah has always been a hetereeogeneous group of educators, clerics, businesspeople, and tribal elders that had distinctive objectives that often clashed with each other. When they coalesced, however, these various groups allied themselves with the technocratically-oriented General People's Congress (GPC) that governed the country from 1990 to 1997. When it ran its initial list of candidates in 1993, Islah candidates prevailed in 62 of the 301 parliamentary contests. In 1997, it prevailed in 57 contests. After the elections in both years, Ahmar became the parliamentary speaker. From 1997 through 2011, Islah was either the largest party in opposition or joined the government to enact policy. At times, Islah played both roles at the same time.

From 1990 through 1996, tribal and Salafi factions controlled Islah. The Muslim Brotherhood faction captured control after a party meeting, when it gained control of the general secretariat. Four Brotherhood gained the most powerful posts within Islah secretary-general, assistants to the secretary-general, and chair of the Executive Council. These Brotherhood officers led the party and benefitted from Ahmar's support, while not necessarily ingratiating themselves to the tribal leaders.

As the Muslim Brotherhood became more powerful within the party, they became less cooperative with the governing GPC. In 1997, Islah officially became part of the opposition.

As an influential tribal chief, Ahmar remained as speaker of parliament and retained his connections to Yemen's president. The net result was that party of Islah was the opposition party, while much of its leadership was in collaboration with the ruling party. Ahmar collaborated with Saleh while the Islah rank and file was evolving into typical Muslim Brotherhood partisan organization,

Islah's internal divisions became clear in the Yemen's election for President in 1999. Islah founders, Ahmar and Zindani, continued to support Saleh, while Brotherhood leaders bulked at this arrangement. Because they knew that Saleh would be elected no matter what action they took, the Brotherhood opted to wait for a more opportune time and then work with opposition groups at that time.

In the elections for local offices in 2001, Islah challenged the governing GPC, and did not negotiate over apportioning the seats. In an unusual cooperative agreement between the Islamists and Communists, Islah's Brotherhood faction negotiated a power arrangement with the left-wing Yemeni Socialist Party (YSP).

Through these actions, the Brotherhood surprised observers with its willingness to engage in pragmatic politics. Despite its avowed Islamist program, Islah's Brotherhood faction demonstrated its willingness to negotiate pragmatically with parties diametrically opposed to its avowed political beliefs. Further, it is remarkable Islah was a party dominated by northerners was willing to cooperate with party dominated by southern Yemenis to prevail.

Islah's initiative came as the socialist party had been dramatically losing popular support. The YSP and other small left-wing parties chose not to field candidates in the 1997 elections. By 2000, they seemed to be heading towards political non-viability. Saleh claimed that they wanted to secede from the country and would use violence if necessary. Saleh sought to forbid funding for the YSP and seized its facilities in the Southern part of Yemen.

The YSP, however, still was widely perceived as the recognized voice for Southern Yemenis. The YSP was also the largest secular and left-wing party in Yemen. Islah's leaders who claimed to sympathize with the socially dispossessed.

Both the secular socialists and the Islamists claimed that they were seeking greater freedom of speech and association and fairer elections. In 2003, both of these groups along with three small parties formed a novel political alliance called the "Joint Meeting Parties" to confront the GCP. In 2006, the new party nominated a socialist candidate as its presidential pick. Faisal bin Shamlan captured nearly a quarter of the vote, a responsible performance in a race with the entrenched and well-financed incumbent party (the GCP).

Islah also grew more pragmatic on various matters under consideration by Parliament, and opposed reactionary legislation. It focused usually on secular issues such as laws involving elections, the economy, oversight by parliament, and the constitutional allocation of power. Islah supported the principle of separation of religion and government. Although Islah opposed imposing a Caliphate (Islamic state) or any type of theocracy, it still advocated its own brand of political Islamism.

Islah parliamentarians introduced few bills on religious issues. Less than half of the legislation Islah Members of Parliament introduced were religiously-motivated, i.e., outlawing alcoholic beverages. Islah's most significant legislation largely dealt with issues important to the party since it was originally formed, such as religiously-based education, health, and welfare.

Two key developments helped enhance Islah independence and power. One was Ahmar's death in 2007. He was a very influential public figure as well as being an Islah co-founder. Ahmar's death contributed to reduced tribal control of the party. This was followed by "Arab Spring" uprisings in 2011, when Islah had a crticial role in agreements that led to Saleh stepping down from power.

These two events also heralded Yemen's descent into political chaos and widespread violence. For decades, Ahmar was able to unite Islah's various groups and he supported Saleh. Ahmar's influence also ensured tribal support. All of these factors helped ensure political support for the country.

As a major tribal leader, Ahmar exercised significant power. He chaired Islah and was the speaker of parliament. Having these three roles combined made Ahmar the second most powerful public official in Yemen. Only Saleh was more powerful at the time. Indeed, because government actions often reflected the preferences of the tribes, Saleh needed Ahmar's approval for major government decisions. Saleh lacked the power to defeat Islah as long as Ahmar was on the scene. Saleh required Ahmar's ongoing backing, despite the opposition of various Islah factions.

Because Ahmar commanded the respect of Islah's various groups, he effectively mediated between the party's religious and tribal factions and thus ensured a sense of working order. He maintained a tenuous political truce by his authority, status, and personality. Ahmar and his armed tribesmen were also able to contain the increasing influence of the Salafists. The Islah technocratic wing, which supported the Muslim Brotherhood, sought to maintain an orderly and contemporary-oriented political party than one with a political paradigm focused on the tribe. They also deferred to Ahmar.

Shortly after Ahmar had died, Islah and other opposition parties in the "Joint Meeting of Parties" took action to seize power. In 2009, these groups developed a "national salvation" strategy to challenge Saleh and the GCP. Islah then held meetings throughout Yemen to promote the plan. Islah also asked that the parliamentary elections scheduled in 2009 be postponed. It sought and amendment to the national election laws that would compel Saleh to comply with terms of an agreement made in 2006, in which the incumbent government would step down by 2012.

Saleh had accepted reforms to Yemen's political process. He, however, requested that elections to parliament be postoned until 2011. The Islah Party agreed to Saleh's request for a delay, but declined to further maintain the status quo of the Yemeni government indefinitely. Saleh then went on the offensive to denounce the country's opposition parties as dangerous extremists.

The Islah initiative was accompanied by two major security challenges. The Shiite "Houthis" had launched a revolt in northern Yemen and the "Hirak" were demanding greater autonomy in South Yemen. Saleh responded by denouncing the Houthis as "Iranians," the Hirak as a "secessionist" movement and Islah as a branch of "Al-Qaeda." In contrast, Saleh sought to present himself as the moderate and the force for stability for his nation.

In January 2011, the upheaval of the Arab Spring spread throughout the Middle East and began to impact Yemen. Students joined large protests in Saana's "University Square", which the demonstrators began to refer to as "Change Square." At first, the demonstrators debated issues relating to economic difficulties, social inequalities, and whether the constitution should be amended to Saleh to remain as president. As unrest escalated, protestors soon demanded that Saleh resign from office.

Similar to other Islamist movements in the Middle East, Islah leaders were dilatory in recognizing the protests and were reluctant to join in the Yemeni Arab awakening. When they eventually participated, Islah sought to offer Saleh a negotiated relinquishment of power rather than a forced ouster that deposed the leaders of Tunisia, Egypt, and Libya.

As street protests worsened, Islah began talks with Saleh and GCP officials to prevent further unrest. The president proceeded to delay. Saleh's regime also forcefully responded against the protestors. On March 18, 2011, at least fifty demonstrators died in clashes with police, which marked a dangerous escalation of hostilities. In response to the violence, a high-ranking general and his entire brigade defected to the opposition. As elements of the military defected to opposition, a large number of Islah members (including formerly neutral members) began to support the uprising.

With the worsening crisis and increasing number of people killed throughout Yemen, Islah, the YSP, and the governing GCF formed a committee to defuse the crisis and restore order. The committee worked for several months to secure Saleh's resignation and prevent the collapse of the country. The Gulf Cooperation Council (consisting of Saudi Arabia, Qatar, the UAE, Oman, Bahrain, and Kuwait) also helped negotiate the agreement. On November 23, 2011, Saleh agreed to resign, He was succeeded by his vice president Abdrabuh Mansur Hadi. Saleh's resignation seemed to present Yemen's political opposition much greater opportunities to win political power.

While Islah greatly helped in facilitating Saleh's resignation, Islah had several defeats since the Arab Spring began. In 2012, newly installed President Hadi dismissed General Ali Muhsin Al Ahmar, who was a major supporter of Islah, from his military command. The ministers Islah chose to join Hadi's administration were ineffective or largely disliked. By mid-2014, Islah militants were fighting in several battles with Houthi fighters. Islah was decisively defeated in Amran, the de-facto capital of Islah and the stronghold of the Hashids and the prominent Al Ahmar clan. Suffering from devastating military and political setbacks, Islah received a new blow when Prime Minister Mohammed Salem Bassendwah, Islah's leader who government and, resigned in September 2014.

The Houthis and the Islah Party entered into peace accords in July 2014 in Amran, and in Al-Jawf in August, 2014. The first agreement collapsed after the Houthis ignored their promises and seized control of the whole governorate in July 2014. In the second case, the Houthis broke the terms of accord within 24 hours of the accords being signed. Eight other subsequent peace agreements were be signed and violated before a reasonably reliable peace was restored in the governorate.

The agreement was preceded by a long period of turmoil and fighting between Houthis and Islah. After the Houthi seized much of Sanaa on September, 21, 2014, they seized some Islah Party facilities owned by its members.

Islah Representatives met with Houthi leader Abd-al-Malik Al-Houthi in Saada city on November 27, 2014. The two sides agreed to cease hostilities. The two sides agreed to implement the agreements of the National Dialogue Conference (NDC), and the Peace and National Partnership Agreement, as well as agreeing to live peacefully in accord with the teachings of "orthodox Islam."

Abdu al-Ganadi, speaking for the GPC on November 29, 2014 said that that "The GPC supports national reconciliation between all of Yemen's various political parties. We consider this a step in the right direction."

See also: Al-Qaeda (volume 1); Al-Qaeda in the Arabian Peninsula (volume 1); Houthis (volume 1); Muslim Brotherhood (volume 1).

FURTHER READING

Chaudhry, Kiren Aziz. *The Price of Wealth: Economies and Institutions in the Middle East.* Ithaca, N.Y.: Cornell University Press, 1997, 2015.

Clark, Janine A. *Islam, Charity, and Activism Middle-Class Networks and Social Welfare in Egypt, Jordan, and Yemen*. Bloomington, Ind.: Indiana University Press, 2004.

"Experimental: Yemen. (5,000 candidates to compete for 301 parliament seats in first democratically held election)." *The Economist, Apr. 24, 1993.*

"Houthis Takeover; Yemen's Violent Politics." *The Economist, Sep 27, 2014.*

Islam, Charity, and Activism Middle-Class Networks and Social Welfare in Egypt, Jordan, and Yemen. Indiana Series in Middle East Studies. Indiana University Press, 2003.

Kasinof, L. "Yemen Students to Politicians: Don't Hijack our Revolution. *The Christian Science Monitor,* March 1, 2011.

"No Proper End; Yemen's Conference." *The Economist,* Jan. 25, 2014.

Phillips, Sarah Phillips & Tajammuʿ al-Yamanī lil-Iṣlāḥ. *Yemen's Democratic Experiment in Regional Perspective Patronage and Pluralized Authoritarianism*. New York, NY: Palgrave Macmillan, 2008.

"Reforming Yemen's Military." *Yemen Times (Sana'a, Yemen),* April 16, 2012.

Scott, R. "In Sanaa: Arms and the Man." *The Middle East, Jul. 1, 1995*.

Sharqieh, Ibrahim. *A Lasting Peace?: Yemen's Long Journey to National Reconciliation*. Washington, D.C.: The Brookings Institution, 2013. ©2013

"Tribes at War; The Battle for Yemen," *The Economist,* June 4, 2011.

Yadav, Stacey Philbrick *Islamists and the State: Legitimacy and Institutions in Yemen and Lebanon*. London: I B Tauris, 2013.

"Zaid Al-Shami, the Head of the Islah Party in Parliament, to the Yemen Times," *Yemen Times (Sana'a, Yemen)*, June 3, 2013.

GLOSSARY

- **A:** From
- **Abu:** Father (of) Mala: Justice
- **Adl:** Equity
- **Adhan:** Call to prayer.
- **Aql:** Reason
- **Al-Buchary:** Considered the most authentic Hadith (sayings of the Prophet Mohamed) in Sunni Islam.
- **All:** Family (of)
- **Allah:** The term for God in Arabic. The equivalent of "God" as used it in English. Christians and Muslim Arabic speakers use the term to refer to the monotheistic Supreme Being. Muslims believe that they, along with Christians, and Jews all believe in the same God that the Muslims call Allah. Muslims prefer Allah in referring to God. Allah refers to a strictly singular being and never refers to plural being. The term, Allah, is gender neutral. Descriptions referring to gender characteristics such as masculine, feminine or neuter attributes are not applicable to Allah.
- **Alami:** Global
- **Alawite:** A sect within Shia Islam, which many Sunnis consider to heretical. The Alawites live located primarily in Syria, where they compose approximately twelve percent of the population.
- **Amir/Emir:** Commander
- **Ansar:** Supporter. Often refers the Muslims of Medina, who assisted and supported the persecuted Muslims who came from Mecca.
- **Arabiya:** Arabian
- **Asala:** Authenticity
- **Aswad:** Black
- **At-Targheeb Wat-Tarheeb:** Targheeb encourages Muslims to apply Islamic law, while Tarheeb threatens them with eternal damnation if they fail to do so.
- **Baralevis:** Sunni Muslims who follow Sufi traditions.
- **Bay'a:** Oath of fealty.

- **Burka:** Clothing that many Muslim women wear to cover their full body and face, leaving only holes to allow the woman to see. They do so to comply with various injunctions of the Koran that require Muslim women to dress modestly.
- **Caliph:** Leader of an Islamic government or Muslim community, with both religious and civil authority. His followers view him as Allah's (God's) representative on earth. Upon Muhammad's death, he was succeeded by the four "Rightly-Guided Caliphs" who governed the Muslim community. These four caliphs are the most influential caliphs in Islamic history,
- **Caliphate:** (Arabic: khalifa). Kingdom. It also refers to a worldwide Islamic empire that implements Islamic Law (Sharia). A political and religious government that ruled the Muslim community and the territory and peoples under its dominion following the death (632 CE) of the Prophet Muhammad The caliph, or successor the Prophet Mohammed and its first leader) governs the caliphate. The Ottoman Empire was the last Islamic caliphate and it ended in 1924.
- **Csuliya:** Fundamentalism
- **Dar:** Abode
- **Dar-al-Islam:** The House or the abode of Islam, meaning the territory governed by Islamic Law (Sharia) in religious and social matters.
- **Da'wa (Da'wah):** Arabic for "making an invitation" or "to summon". The invitation of non-Muslims to Islam. It signifies the preaching of Islam since it is understood as the calling people to Islam. The process of calling individuals to Islam, by direct personal invitation, preaching, or by through the example of good deeds
    o Truth also means that Islam opposes disbelief in society, which Islamic fundamentalists believe caused by the West. Islamic fundamentalists believe that da'wa must first be used at the personal level and gradually rise to the international level, where the true power of Islam will be made clear. Through da 'wa, Islamic fundamentalists believe, the" jahili" society ceases to exist since its corruption will be removed by the da'i (caller or preacher). Da 'wa may be a spiritual exercise because it encourages people to participate in Islamic prayer, veneration, and piety. Da 'wa is emphasized as the complete effort of applying Islam to all aspects of life. Thus, da'wa is at the center of the faith life of Islamic fundamentalists.
- **Deobandi:** A sect of Sunni Islam that follows Wahhabism.
- **Dimucratiyya:** Democracy
- **Din:** Religion
- **Ennahda:** Renaissance
- **Falsafa:** Philosophy
- **Fard:** Actions that a Muslim must perform. These include fasting and praying five times a day.
- **Fatwa, or fetwa:** Legal edict or opinion of a Muslim scholar and jurist, that should be based on the Koran, Sunnah, and Islamic Sharia. A formal non-binding legal pronouncement made by a recognized expert in Islamic legal law (a mufti). Fatwas most frequently address issues in applying religious law in everyday life, including diet, gender relations, or the use of new technologies. To be authoritative, a fatwa must be accepted by the community of scholars. Their consensus on a legal opinion

makes that fatwa binding on the community. Islam does not have a final or ultimate authority, which results in a diversity of opinion, although major scholars agree on core issues.

- **Faqih:** Jurist
- **FGM (Female Genital Mutilation):** Partial or complete removal of the external female genitalia for non-medical reasons. This procedure is usually performed on girls from a few days old to puberty. Some Islamic authorities considered FGM to be a religious obligation to control the sexual desires of women. Over 125 young females currently alive have undergone FGM in the 29 countries in Africa and the Middle East where this procedure mostly practiced. FGM is recognized internationally as a violation of the human rights of girls and women.
- **Fedayeen:** Resistors
- **Fi:** In
- **Fiah:** Section
- **Filastin:** Palestine
- **Fiqh:** Jurisprudence, or interpretation of religious law (sharia). Along with Sharia, one of the two components of Islamic law. Fiqh is often referred to as the science of the Sharia.
- **Filra:** Intuition
- **Five Pillars:** (Arabic Arkan al-Islam, "pillars of Islam" or Arkan ud-Din, "pillars of the faith"). Every Muslim must perform the following five acts: profession of faith (shahada), ritual prayer (salat), fasting during Ramadan (sawm), pilgrimage to Mecca (hajj) and charity (zakat). Fulfillment of these duties brings rewards on earth and in the afterlife.
- **Furqan:** Proof
- **Gama'a:** Group
- **Gradualism:** An Islamist approach that the Muslim Brotherhood often takes, which calls for incremental and pragmatic social change towards adopting Islamic law (Sharia).
- **Hadatha:** Modernity
- **Hadith:** Saying; report; account. The traditional compilation of teachings and works of the Prophet Muhammad, which were recorded by his family, and companions. These are an important source of Islamic law and theology. The Hadith known as Hadith Qudsi (sacred Hadith) are said to have been divine messages given to the Prophet Muhammad.
- **Hajj:** Pilgrimage of Muslims from throughout the world to Mecca, Islam's holiest city. As a religious duty, all adult Muslims must make this religious pilgrimage to Mecca at least once in their lifetimes if healthy enough and has the monetary means to do so. It is considered one of Islam's "five pillars" of the faith The term Hajj is a Muslim man who made the Hajj, while a Hajjah is a Muslim woman who had done the same.
- **Hakimiyya:** Divine governance
- **Halal:** An action or object that is allowable or lawful for Muslims according to Islamic law (Sharia). It is food or drink that Muslims may consume under Islamic dietary laws.

- **Hanafi School of Islamic Law:** the oldest and regarded as the most progressive. The Ottoman Empire adopted it in the sixteenth century. Abu Hanifa (699-767) established the school, which is characterized by legal reasoning through analogy (qiyas); a type of personal reasoning must connect analogy, and judicial preference (isithsan), in which one rule is preferred over another. This is the practice in Afghanistan, Jordan, Lebanon, Pakistan and Turkey. This school makes distinctions between the concepts of wajib and fard. The wajib is viewed as a legal duty or requirement. Because it is not a divinely imposed duty, however, failing to comply with this duty is not considered sinful.
- **Hanbalism:** As the most conservative type of Islamic law, it is based only on what has been adopted by the Koran and the Hadith. Analogy to derive law is only acceptable if Scripture or tradition are silent on the issue. Hanbalist jurisprudence is prevalent in Saudi Arabia, Qatar, and Oman.
- **Harakat:** Governments
- **Harak-iyya:** Activism
- **Haram:** Acts that are unlawful or not permitted of Muslims, such as murder, adultery, or usury (riba).
- **Hashashin:** Assassin
- **Hawari:** Disciples
- **Hifadh:** Protection
- **Hijab:** (Arabic for "Cover"), also known as a khimar, an Islamic veil, Islamic head scarf that Muslim women wear to conceal their head and chest, but still reveals the face, to comply with Koranic commands to dress modestly. Along with the hijab, Muslim women will often where loose-fitting, non-revealing clothing. They Muslim females over the age of puberty wear the hijab when adult males outside their close family are present. Some Women follow this practice to demonstrate their faith and to visibly display their Muslim identity, while other Muslim females do not believe that the hijab is necessary to show that they are a good Muslim.
- **Hijra (**or Hijrah): (flight or departure) the Prophet Muhammad's flight from unbelief. It refers to travels of Muhammad and those who followed him from Mecca to Medina (in present day Saudi Arabia) in 622, which Muslims believe is the beginning of the Islamic era. The Islamic calendar commences from this event.
- **Hilffiyat:** Liberty
- **Hind:** India
- Hiwar: Dialog
- **Hizb:** Party
- **Honor Killing:** The traditional practice of killing a family member for allegedly "shaming" or dishonoring the family for engaging in behavior contrary to Islamic teachings. Often, victims of honor killings have either rejected an arranged marriage, or committed sexually acts viewed as illict by Islam.
- **Hudna:** Temporary truce or armistice. It is sometimes mistranslated as "cease-fire". While the term may refer to temporary halt in hostilities, but it does not necessarily entail that the conflict has ended. The nearly decade long truce between the Muhammad and the Quraish tribe, beginning in 628, is frequently invoked as a hudna.

- **Hudud:** Deterrents, Limits, or prohibition; pl. hudud. Punishments under Islamic Law (Sharia) and promulgated in the Koran and Hadiths for "crimes against God". It is uncodified. Hudud law is divine law because Allah prescribes it and it is unchangeable. The term describes the most severe punishments that can be meted out. The six crimes with prescribed punishments are: theft (Sariqah) (requiring the amputation of the hand), unlawful sexual encounters (Zina) (reqquiring killing of the offender by stoning or 100 lashes), making false accusations of sexual misconduct (eighty lashes), consuming alcohol (Khamar) (eighty lashes), apostasy (Irtidad) (death or banishment), and highway robbery (death). Evidentiary rules such as requiring witnesses limit use of these punishments in some cases. The courts have the discretion to determine punishment (tazir) for other crimes. Except for Saudi Arabia, hudud is very uncommon. Many extreme fundamentalists, however, currently seek the re-imposition of hudud in nations such as Afghanistan, Iran, and Sudan.
- **Hukuma:** Government
- **Huquq:** Rights
- **Hurriyya:** Freedom
- **Ihan(e):** Beneficence
- **Ijma:** Consensus. The consensus of scholars, whether expressed or implied, regarding law and practice.
- **Ikhwan:** (Brotherhood or Brethren) often used in referring to the Muslim Brotherhood. The Ikhwan also refers to an Islamic militia in Saudi Arabia; Muslims belonging to a Wahhabi sect in Saudi Arabia, or a separatist militia in Kashmir.
- **ImamInul:** Science
- **Imam:** Islamic prayer or worship leader, a recognized theologian, or community leader. Refers to the person who leads the prayer of worshippers in a mosque, or who founded an Islamic school of jurisprudence. For Shiites, the term refers to a number of Muslim leaders, especially those who one succeeded Muhammad as the Shiite leader. In "Twelver Shia" belief, the term refers to any of Muhammad's twelve descendants, who are considered divinely appointed spiritual and temporal leaders. Shiites confer the title of "Imam" to Ali and those who succeeded him.
- **Insan:** Human
- **Intifada:** "Shaking, uprising, insurrection." The term is often used to describe the uprising of Palestinian militants to Israeli control of the Gaza Strip and the West Bank in Palestine.
- **Islab:** Reform
- **Islah:** Reform, or to improve, to better, or to place something into a better position.
- **Islam:** (Arabic for "to surrender"). To surrender or submit to Allah's (God) will and the divine peace received by a person through obedience to Allah. The religious faith formed by Muhammad. Islam is a monotheistic religion, stressing a belief in one God. It also stresses its roots back to Abraham. Islam is based on Muhammad's writings as recorded in the Koran, a religious work, that Muslims believes is Allah's whole and inerrant word.
- **Islami:** Islamic.
- **Islamism:** An interpretation of Islam as a system of government that strictly interprets Islamic law (Sharia). This term is synonymous with Political Islam. As an

ideology, Islamism stresses that Islam must guide social and political as well as personal life. Today, there are two main types of Islamists. The first are political parties competing for political power within existing systems. The second group are extremists using violence to change the system from outside. Some political Islamist groups have attempted to be both. Today, political groups and extremist militias have also become rivals for influence, and sometimes even enemies.

- **Islamiyya:** Muslim
- **Islamiyyum:** Islamists.
- **Istihhad:** Martyrdom
- **Itishhad:** Martyrdom seeker
- **Iiihad:** union
- **Ijitihad:** legal reasoning.
- **Irfan:** Mystical Islam
- **Ittijah:** Tendency
- **Jabha:** Front
- **Jabhat** Fronts
- **Jafaria:** Shiite
- **Jaluli:** Pagan
- **Jilliyya:** paganism
- **Jaish:** Army
- **Jamaat:** Group
- **Jamal:** Beauty
- **Jam'iyyat:** Associations
- **Jazira:** Island
- **Jebheye:** Front
- **Jemaah:** Community
- **Jihad:** To struggle or strive. The Greater Jihad refers to the internal spiritual struggle, as a religious duty, to live one's life according to God's will, as much as possible. The Lesser Jihad, as a religious duty, is the external struggle that could include (but does not necessarily) include war, to defend Islam against unbelievers. As originally used, unbelievers only referred to other monotheists (such as Christians and Jews). The Lesser Jihad was only contemplated in contexts where Islam was threatened. A third meaning of Jihad is the struggle to develop a good Muslim society.
- **Jihadist International:** describes fighters ready to move from one conflict to antoher in the name of jihad, whether they have any personal connection to the specific conflict.
- **Jizia (Jizya):** A special tax imposed on Christian and Jews (referred to the "People of the Book") who are subject to an Islamic government
- **Kaff:** Stopping
- **Kafrr:** Infidel
- **Kalam:** Islamic theology
- **Katibat:** Brigade
- **Khairiyya:** Beneficence

- **Khalq:** People
- **Khatm:** Closing
- **Khilafat:** Caliphate
- **Kingdom:** Kirdas: Company
- **Koran:** Islam's holy book, which Muslims believe is Alllah's (God) word and will, which the angel Gabriel is said to have revealed to the Prophet Muhammad. Muslims believe the Koran to be Allah's final revelation to mankind. These divine messages were later compiled in a single volume that was first written in Arabic. For Muslims, this work forms the foundation of Islamic law, religion, culture, and politics.
- **Kufr:** Unbelief
- **Kurdiyya:** Kurdish
- **Lashkar:** Army
- **Madhahib:** the five distinct schools of Islamic law. The Sunni Schools are: Malikite, Hanafite, Shafi'ite, and Hanbalite. The Shi'ite school was formed by Imam Ja'far al-Sadiq. These schools were all formed by the ninth century. Each one developed their own specific approach to theological issues. The differences between them were based on the interpretative approaches allowed to the respective jurists, which determine their level of strict reliance on Koran and the Tradition (i.e., the Prophet's Sunna). All of the five legal schools rely on the Koran and scholarly consensus (ijma) as their primary sources of law governing religious matters and the everyday lives of Muslims (such as required ritual acts).
- **Madi:** The past
- **Madrasa (Madrassah):** (school), an Islamic school with a curriculum that focuses on Islamic belief and law. Several Taliban members attended Saudi-financed madrassas in Pakistan, which teach Wahhabism, a harsh, austere and rigid version of Islam that fist arose in Saudi Arabia. Madrassas also refer to Islamic institutions of higher education that arose in the tenth century. By the twelfth century, they were in the large cities Muslim-majority areas in the Middle East andNorth Africa.
- **Mahdi, al-Muntazar:** The "rightly-guided" savior, who pious Muslims expect to appear at the end-times to lead the Ummah (the Muslim Community) and bring justice to the world.
- **Mahdi:** The Mahdi is the savior that many Muslims believe the entire world to Islam after defeating a fraudulent religious leader. Shiites often describe the Mahdi as the "Hidden Imam."
- **Majlis:** Assembly
- **Malahim:** Battles
- **Manhaj:** Method
- **Mantiqi:** Region
- **Ma'rifa**: Knowledge
- **Marji:** Guide
- **Masjid:** Arabic for "place of prostration" (in prayer). The term refers to a mosque, which is an Islamic place of worship.
- **Mecca:** The holiest city in Islam
- **Menbar:** Pulpit

- **The Middle East:** a geographic and political term that usually refers to nations in eastern North Africa and southwestern Asia.
- **Millat:** Tenet
- **Milli:** Adherent
- **Minhaj Al-Muslim:** a leading treatise on Islamic jurisprudence
- **Mosharekate:** Participation
- **Mosque:** A place of prayer and worship Muslims.
- **Moulathaluotln:** Turbaned
- **Mubah:** Acts which Islamic Law (Sharia) view as morally neutral and thus, acts that Muslims are permitted to engage in, such as earning profit in commercial transactions.
- **Mubuyna:** Prophethood
- **Muhammad (570-632):** The Arab religious leader, who established the religion of Islam. He was born in 570 in Mecca, Saudi Arabia. Muslims believe that Muhammad was Allah's last messenger, who received a divine revelation at age 40, when God commanded him through Gabriel, the archangel, to deliver God's message to humankind. In Muhammad's time, most people living in Arabia worshiped several gods, and most of these gods were in the form of inanimate objects.
- **Mujahid/Mujahideen:** Struggler or striver for Islam, or Holy fighters. The term also refers to religiously-motivated fighters that fight Jihad against Islam's enemies. This term commonly refers to Afghan guerrillas who fought against the Soviet occupation in the Afghan-Soviet War, from 1979 and 1989. Most Mujahedeen consider themselves devout Muslims.
- **Mujrama:** Society
- **Mulla:** Islamic scholar or leader
- **Munazzama:** Organization
- **Muqatila:** fighting
- **Muqawama:** Resistance
- **Murtadd:** Apostate. A Muslim individual who joins another faith or rejected one of the fundamentals of Islam.
- **Musawar:** Equality
- **Muslim:** Arabic for "one who submits (to God)). A person who believes in, follows, or practices the religion of Islam. One who accepts Islam through the Shahadah.
- **Muslimin:** Muslims
- **Mustahabb (or Mandub):** While mandatory under Islam, these actions are morally preferred actions Muslims. Examples include: freeing slaves from captivity.
- **Muttahida:** Unified, united.
- **Nahda:** (Arabic for "Revival" or "Renaissance"), a cultural and intellectual modernizing movement in the Arab East. The Nahda entailed rationalism, the dominance of secularism, nationalism, scientism, urbanism and individualism. It occurred in both Lebanon and Egypt at the same time. In Lebanon, the Nahda was characterized efforts to modernize Arab culture through new types of writing reviving use of the Arabic language. Egyptian followers of the movement focused on the reform of Islamic religious organizations and aligning them to modern situations.

- **Nikah Mut'ah:** A temporary marriage contract of a limited duration, for monetary consideration. While Shiites regard accept these unions as valid marriages, Sunnis prohibit them. While Sunni prohibit mutʻah, they allow several other kinds of temporary nuptial unions, such misyar (itinerant marriage) and ʻurfi (marriage according to the customs of the place where the marriage occurs).
- **Niqab:** An Islamic veil, some Muslim women wear in public, that covers all or most of the face except for the eyes, and covers the hair and goes down to the shoulders. The Niqab is worn to comply with the Koranic injunction to wear modest clothing. It is part of a full-body covering that is especially common in the Middle Eastern nations, where fundamentalist Islam, or Salafism, is the strongest.
- **Niizam:** System
- **Niyyah:** Intention. A statement of intent, required by Islamic law, made before any devotional act, including, Hajj or sawm.
- **Partisi:** Party
- **Political Islam:** A view of Islam as system of government and politics. It is synonymous with Islamism. Political Islam is frequently used to describe Islam's involvement in secular politics. Political Islam differs from personal piety, belief, and ritual, in theat political Islam uses Islam for political purposes. Believers of political Islam argue that Islam should determine political and social issues in a nation, and that the government should implement and enforce Islamic law. Political Islam is also the means by which individuals, groups and organizations pursue political objectives said to be inspired by Islamic law. It provides political responses to contemporary societal challenges through a vision of a future, the foundations for which are based on reappropriated, reinvented concepts borrowed from Islamic tradition.
- **Qadar:** Allah's absolute control over fulfilling events. It is also known as destiny.
- **Quran:** see, Koran.
- **Ramadan:** The holiest time of the Muslim year. It is the ninth month of Islam's Calendar, in which a fast (sawm) is observed for thirty days. During this time, Muslims observe a strict fast from sunrise to sunset. During the fast, Muslims must avoid consuming food, drinking liquids, smoking, and sexual relations. Ramadan commemorates the revelation of the Koran by the archangel Gabriel to Muhammad.
- **Re-Islamization:** a tenet of Islamic fundamentalist thought. Supporters of re-Islamization believe that the problems in Muslim-majority nations are caused by Western influences that caused a departure from traditional Islamic ideals and that the solution to these problems is to return to a strict adherence to Islam.
- **Riba:** Profit made lending of capital (or Interest on money), which the Koran forbids. Some scholars interpret usury as "unjustified enrichment".
- **Ridda:** Apostasy
- **Sada:** Echo
- **Sahaba:** Companions
- **Salafi/Salafist:** In classical Arabic, this term refers to a person who is in the vanguard and the rearguard. A member of a reform movement that seeks to reform a corrupted Islam, by returning it back to its original ideals. Salafi movements include a nineteenth-century Egyptian reform movement, and the Salafi movement in Saudi

Arabia common referred to as Wahhabism. Salafi movements originated to reform practices in Islam that they believe deviated from true Islam. Some Salafists, but not all, are vehemently anti-Western. The term, Salafist, also commonly refers to revolutionary Islamists. Generally, Salafism is divided into four subgroups: 1) status-quo/authoritarian Salafism, 2) apolitical/scholarly Salafism, 3) political/reformist Salafism, and 4) armed or militant Salafism.

- **Salafism:** a branch of Sunni Islam whose followers believe in following a strict interpretation of Islamic law (Sharia) and a strict adherence social structures existing in Islam's earliest days. Salafis believe that Islam, as founded by Muhammad and his companions, was perfect when it was formed, and thus, Muslims must live according to the example of Mohammed and early Muslim leaders. Salafism developed in the early 20th century. It teaches that Muslims must reject materialism, rationalism, and innovations. Salafis also blame imperialism and Western culture for corrupting and contaminating society in the Muslim world. They consider moderate Muslims to be infidels Salafism is often used synonymously with Wahhabism.
- **Salafiyya:** Revivalist
- **Salafiyys:** A return to ancestors.
- **Salam:** Peace
- **Salat:** Prayer. Observant Muslims pray five a day at specified times. Salat is the second pillar of Islam.
- **Sariyah:** Group
- **Sawm:** Fasting. As one of the five pillars of faith, it requires the Muslim believer to totally abstaining from drink, food, tobacco products, and sexual intercourse during the daytime during the lunar month of Ramadan.
- **Secularization:** a process by which people abandon spiritual concerns and focus on present concerns of everyday life in the world.
- **Shabaab:** Youth
- **Shabiba:** Young people.
- **Shafi'i School Of Jurisprudence:** Founded by Abu Abdullah Muhammad ibn Idris al-Shafi'i. This school accepts analogical reasoning in interpreting as valid under certain circumstances, followed in places such as East Africa, Indonesia, Southern Egypt, Malaysiam and the countries in the Arabian Peninsula.
- **Shahada:** One of Islam's five pillars of faith, which is a creed, or statement of one's belief, required by Islamic law, articulating that Allah is the one God and that Mohammed is Allah's prophet or messenger.
- **Shahid:** Martyr
- **Sharia (Shari'ah):** Islamic law derived from the Koran and Sunnah. Muslims consider it to be idealized, sacred, or supra-temporal law. Sharia is Islamic canonical law, as derived from the Koran (Islam's holy book), other writings, and from Muhammed's words and deeds, which govern the spiritual and temporal behavior of Muslims. Rules based on Islamic scripture. Sharia law largely consists of Koranic injunctions. Various Muslim sects and governments, however, interpret and apply Sharia law in different ways most observant Muslims living in Islamic societies believe that Sharia and secular laws are compatible with each other. Militant

- fundamentalist groups and governments, including the Taliban, have used Sharia law to justify their harsh authoritarian rule.
- **Sharia Finance:** Investments that Islamic scholars ascertain as being Sharia-compliant. This is also called "Islamic banking." It is how corporations in the Muslim-majority nations, including banks and other lending institutions, raise capital to comply with Sharia (Islamic law). It also entails the types of investments that Islamic Law approves. As Islam does not distinguish between the spiritual and the secular spheres, Sharia governs financial issues. The Sharia forbids interest because the Koran states "Those who consume interest cannot stand except as one stands who is being beaten by Satan into insanity."
- **Shar'iyya:** Legitimacy
- **Shaytan:** Rebellious, proud. The devil.
- **Sheikh:** Leader, Scholar, specifically an Islamic Scholar. Usually refers to an Arab ruler or chief. It is also a title for prominent Islamic leaders or clerics.
- **Shia (Shi'ah):** Islam's second largest branch following the branch of Islam known as Sunni Islam. They believe in a strict interpretation of the Koran and to its teachings. They believe in twelve heavenly Imams (perfect teachers) who led the Shiites each succeeding each other. They believe that the Mahdi (guided one), also known as the Twelfth Imam", did not have an earthly death, but instead concealed himself from the world. The Mahdi will return at the best time to do so, and at that time, lead mankind into a realm of peace and justice. Shia Muslims believe that Ali, Mohammad's son-in-law, was the Prophet's legitimate successor, after the death of Mohammad and eleven of his "most pious, knowledgeable descendants." (a belief called "Imamah). Shia Islam has incorporated some Sufi practices. Shiism is practiced throughout the world. Shiites are most numerous in Iraq, Iran and areas of the Arab Peninsula.
- **Shirk:** Arabic term for Association. For observant Muslims, Shirk is regarding anything as equal to Allah. Islam forbids shirk. The term also refers to a sharing of Allah's divinity, which Islamic Law (Sharia) forbids.
- **Shura:** Consultation. Consultation of the leader with the people he governs to manage religious and temporal business. The Koran requires this duty of all those with any kind of authority, from the familal unit to those who lead a nation.
- **Sirah:** Written works discussing Muhammad's words and actions.
- **SufiToifah:** Group
- **Sufi:** A mystical sect within Islam focusing on the denial of self to achieve communion with Allah. It is a non-literal and mystical approach to Islam. Only some Sufi groups adhere to the ultimate Sufi beliefs.
- **Sufism:** Sufism arose in the Middle East during the twelfth century as a mystical movement in contrast to the heavy legalistic orientation of orthodox Islam. Sufi Brotherhoods that follow a particular spiritual leader or sheik. Sufism involves the veneration of local saints and by brotherhoods that practice unique rituals. Sufis organize themselves into Tariqas (or "orders" or groups). A Sheik, or group leader, is often considered the most spiritual man in the community, and the largest number of Taqwa in a specific Sufi community.

- o Sufism claims to offer its adherents a closer personal relationship with Allah through special spiritual rituals, including reciting prayers and Koranic passages and repeating the names or attributes, of Allah while performing physical movements sanctioned by the order.
  - o There are no Islamic nations that officially designate themselves as Sufi states.
- **Sunnah:** A compilation of Muhammad's teachings and accomplishments. Appropriate behavior as exemplified by Mohammed's life and compiled in the Hadith. This term is often used synonymously with ahadith.
- **Sunni:** Islam's largest denomination. Nearly 90% of all Muslims follow Sunnism. According to Sunni belief, the first four successors to the Prophet Muhammad were the legitimate leaders of Islam as opposed to Ali, his son-in-law. Sunnis are required to adhere to the sources of the law: the Koran and the Hadith.
- **Sura:** A chapter of the Koran. By tradition, sections of the Koran that are arranged from longest to shortest in length. The Koran contains 114 Sura(s). The chapters are then divided into verses
- **Ta'addudiyya:** Pluralism
- **Tabari:** a biography of prophet Mohamed
- **Tablighi:** Missionary
- **Tafsir:** Arabic term for exegesis or commentary. Interpretations of the Koran by Islamic theologians.
- **Takfir:** Accusing another Muslim of being an unbeliever. The punishment for one traditionally found to be an unbeliever is death. An Islamic Court is the only body empowered to pronounce this sentence. In one example, Ayatollah Khomeini declared Salman Rushdie to be a kafir and sentenced him to death by because of the latter's book, *The Satanic Verses*. While Takfir is traditionally defined as a Muslim who abandons Islam, Jihadists interpret the term as a Muslim who refuses to participate in the global jihad
- **Taghut:** Tyranny
- **Tahrir:** Liberation
- **Tajammu:** Assembly
- **Tajdeef:** Blasphemy
- **Tajdid:** Renewal
- **Takafui:** Solidarity
- **Takti:** Accusing of apostasy
- **Talai:** Vanguard
- **Tanmia:** Development
- **Tanzeem:** Organization
- **Taqiyya/Taqqiya:** "Deceit" or "dissimulation." Some Muslim teachings permit disseminating falsehoods to deceive the foe, especially infidels.
- **Taqlid:** Traditionalism, imitator
- **Tarikh:** History
- **Tashri':** Legislation
- **Tatarruf:** Extremism, radicalism
- **Tawazun:** Balance

Glossary

- **Tawhid:** Monotheism. A belief in Allah's oneness. Devout Muslims believe that Allah, and only Allah, is God. The term stresses the unity of God.
- **Tehrik:** Movement
- **Thawriyya:** Revolutionary
- **Tijaniyya:**
- **Twelver Shiism:** a branch of Shiism that is the largest Islamic sect in Iran and Lebanon. One distinctive belief of this sect is that Allah (God) has concealed the twelfth imam, Muhammad al-Mahdi, however, Allah will reveal him as the savior of the world.
- **Ukhuwwa:** Brotherhood
- **Ulema:** Arabic for Scholars. A group of legal scholars of the Sharia and Islamic jurisprudence (singular: Alim). Their level of organization and influence vary considerably among the various Muslim communities throughout the world.
- **Ulh:** Truce
- **Umma (Ummah):** Islamic nation of all Muslims in the world, e.g., the worldwide community of Muslims. Many fundamental Muslims believe this to be the universal ideal state. Muslims believe that the Prophet Mohammed established the ummah in the seventh century
- **Va:** And
- **Wahdat:** Union Wakalah: District
- **Waliy:** Governor
- **Wefaq:** Harmony
- **Wahhabism:** A strict and puritanical version of Islam that developed in present day Saudi Arabia, based on Mohammed al-Wahhab's teachings. Wahhabism became a powerful influence on Islam in Saudi Arabia. This sect seeks to promulgate and enforce Sharia law in nations where Sunnism is the predominant type of Islam.
- **The West:** a geographic and political term that usually refers to the United States and Western Europe.
- **Westernization:** a process favored by some Islamic politicians and leaders, of seeking the quality of the Islamic world with the Western world. "Westerners" generally believe that Islamic nations should be open to the political, economic and cultural practices of the West.
- **Zakat:** Obligatory donation of income in Islam. As one of Islam's five pillars, it is the view that a charitable contribution is a type of worship and obedience to Allah. This donation is customarilly about 2.5 percent of an individual's yearly income. These funds are usually intended to help the poor and the needy.

ABOUT THE AUTHOR

Professor Christopher T. Anglim is affiliated with both the University of the District of Columbia and American University. His degrees include a JD, MBA, MA in History, and a Masters in Library Science. A prolific author, in addition to being a long-time academic, Dr. Anglim has written several books, articles, and papers over the past 30 years on issues on law, political science, government, religion, and the Middle East. Dr. Anglim has written and researched intensively into issues relating to the modern Middle East such as the Iraq War. Dr. Anglim is originally from Minnesota and now lives in Silver Spring, Maryland.

INDEX

#

1920 Revolution Brigade, 3, 4, 149
20th century, xviii, xxii, xlviii, 296
21st century, 90
9/11, xl, lii, lxxxix, 50, 52, 54, 55, 70, 96, 221

A

Abis Brigade, 9
abolition, xliii
Abu Bakr al-Siddiq Fundamentalist Brigade, 13
Abu Hafs al-Masri Brigade (AHMB), 11, 12
accountability, 25, 99
activism, xxxi, xxxviii, xliv, liii, 35, 100, 108, 143
activists, 106, 154
Adalet ve Kalinma Partisi (AKP) (Justice and Development Party), xi, xiv, 17, 251
Aden-Abyan Islamic Army, 29
administrators, 172
adverse conditions, liii
advisory body, lxvii
advocacy, xliv
Afghanistan, xiii, xiv, xx, xxiii, li, lvi, lix, lxiii, lxv, lxvi, lxvii, lxviii, lxx, lxxi, lxxii, lxxiii, lxxiv, lxxvi, lxxx, lxxxi, lxxxii, lxxxiii, xc, xci, xciv, xcv, 7, 11, 46, 48, 49, 50, 52, 54, 55, 61, 62, 69, 85, 95, 96, 101, 116, 136, 190, 191, 221, 268, 271, 273, 281, 290, 291
Africa, xxxv, xlvii, lxi, xci, 21, 31, 51, 52, 54, 70, 116, 125, 199, 207, 289, 293, 296
age, xxxv, liii, 144, 290, 294
agencies, xlix, lxxi, 45, 172, 199, 260
aggression, 44, 196
Air Force, lxxviii, xcvi, 23, 246, 280

Al Qaeda, lxvii, lxviii, lxxxvii, 3, 4, 12, 30, 46, 52, 54, 59, 91, 157, 165, 202, 205, 207, 208, 213, 235, 271
Al-Aqsa Martyrs' Brigades, 134
Al-Asalah, 35
al-Awlaki, Anwar, lxvii, 65, 101
Al-Baghdadi, Abu Bakr, 207
Al-Fatah, 37, 133, 211
Algeria, xi, xii, xiv, xxiii, xxxviii, xlix, l, lvi, lvii, lviii, lix, lxi, lxii, lxiv, lxv, 46, 69, 72, 199, 238, 259
Al-Jihad, lxii, lxv, 115, 116
Al-Nusra Front, 92, 221, 222
Al-Qaeda, ix, xi, xxx, xxxiii, xxxv, xxxvii, lxiv, lxv, lxvi, lxvii, lxviii, lxxv, lxxvii, xc, xci, xcii, xcvi, 3, 4, 5, 7, 8, 11, 14, 29, 30, 43, 44, 45, 46, 47, 50, 51, 52, 53, 54, 55, 57, 58, 59, 61, 62, 63, 64, 65, 67, 69, 70, 71, 85, 86, 87, 89, 91, 92, 95, 96, 101, 115, 116, 117, 127, 130, 133, 134, 136, 142, 149, 151, 157, 169, 170, 175, 189, 190, 191, 192, 193, 196, 197, 202, 203, 205, 206, 207, 208, 209, 211, 218, 221, 222, 235, 238, 240, 243, 264, 267, 268, 271, 272, 273, 274, 279, 285
al-Shabaab, xii, lv, 52, 209
al-Turabi, Hassan, lxiv, 47
ancestors, xlv, 296
anger, xxx, 239
Ansar Allah, 169
Ansar Bayt al Maqdis, 53, 89, 236
anxiety, xlix, 24
apathy, 114
Arab countries, xcii, 29
Arab world, liii
Arabian Peninsula, xi, xviii, xxv, xxxv, xlix, lviii, lxxv, 30, 52, 53, 54, 64, 65, 101, 169, 175, 202, 205, 206, 221, 296
armed forces, 21, 22
arrests, xliv, lxxiii, lxxvii, 3, 14, 26, 58, 68, 70, 71, 162, 172, 174, 219, 230, 239, 273

Asia, xxxv, xlvi, xlvii, 54, 147, 155, 294
Asian countries, lxxxiii
assassination, xxxi, lxi, lxv, 4, 8, 34, 47, 68, 69, 70, 115, 116, 122, 125, 185, 215, 232, 238, 239, 248, 264, 268
assault, xvii, lxxxi, lxxxviii, 69, 92, 166, 192, 195, 230, 260
assets, xix, lxix, 97, 111, 139, 233
assimilation, 71
Association of Muslim Scholars, lxvi, 93
asylum, 47, 107, 232
atheists, xxv
atmosphere, xlviii, 76, 224
atrocities, lxviii, lxxv, 214, 267
attacker, lxxi, xc, xci, xcii
authoritarianism, xlv, li, 25, 181
authorities, lxxxiii, xc, 20, 30, 47, 48, 49, 51, 62, 63, 75, 76, 96, 100, 125, 135, 166, 172, 187, 188, 229, 242, 259, 260, 277, 278, 284, 288, 289, 297
autonomy, 22, 23, 130, 169, 170, 216, 285
awareness, 102, 153
Azerbaijan, xx, 95
Azzam, Abdullah Yusuf, lxiii

B

Badr Brigade (Badr Organization), 93, 263, 264
Bahrain, xix, lii, lxvi, xc, xci, xcii, 9, 10, 35, 36, 75, 76, 77, 81, 82, 83, 153, 154, 155, 163, 185, 240, 285
Balkans, 46
ballistic missiles, 187
Bangladesh, xiii, xciv, 48, 95, 129, 130, 202, 279
banking, 235, 297
banks, 136, 194, 297
basic needs, 99
Belgium, 71, 202
belief systems, xxi, 19
beneficiaries, 102
benefits, 86, 102, 200, 227
Benevolence International Foundation (BIF), xi, 95, 96
Bible, xxi, xxii
Bin Laden, Osama, xxxiii, xlix, lxiii, lxv, lxvii, xcii, 7, 11, 29, 43, 45, 46, 55, 56, 58, 61, 69, 70, 95, 96, 101, 115, 116, 126, 191, 221, 235, 271, 279, 280
blame, 154, 296
board members, 36
bomb attack, lxix, lxxv, lxxvi, lxxxi, xc, 76, 257
border crossing, lxxiv, xcii, 182
Bosnia, xlix, lvii, 48, 69, 95, 273
Britain, xiv, xviii, lxxi, lxxxvii, 12, 238, 269

brutality, liii, 53, 86, 194, 195, 201
budget deficit, 21
Bulgaria, lvii
bureaucracy, 17, 100
Burkina Faso, lxxxvii, 54
Burma, xiv, 48
businesses, 145, 193, 274

C

Cabinet, 127
Cairo, xxxv, lxiii, lxxxvi, 69, 89, 90, 115, 140, 146, 147, 238, 247, 259, 261
Cameroon, lxxii, lxxiii, lxxiv, lxxvii, lxxxii, lxxxiii
Camp David, lxiii, 239, 241, 258
campaigns, 3, 122, 200, 242
candidates, l, lxx, lxxi, lxxxvii, 24, 34, 75, 81, 100, 122, 177, 178, 181, 182, 224, 239, 248, 283, 286
capitalism, xxviii, 18, 20, 231
Catholics, lviii
Caucasus, 199
ceasefire, lxxi, xc, xcv, 37, 38, 40, 170, 172, 254
Center Party, 99, 100
Central Asia, xx, 21, 221
Chad, lxx, lxxii, lxxiii, lxxiv, lxxv, lxxxii, xciv, 4, 199
chaos, lxviii, 25, 38, 41, 52, 54, 170, 172, 173, 242, 284
charitable organizations, 157
Charitable Society for Social Welfare (CSSW), xii, 101, 102
checks and balances, 25
Chicago, lv, 63, 73, 95, 96, 106
child labor, 101
children, lxxiv, lxxvii, lxxviii, lxxix, lxxxiv, 95, 102, 111, 144, 175, 195
China, xlvi, xciii, 95, 178, 221
Christianity, xxi, xxxix, 215
Christians, xx, xxi, xxxi, l, lxx, xcii, 33, 43, 48, 91, 126, 144, 145, 195, 214, 249, 272, 287, 292
cities, lxxxi, 30, 35, 75, 107, 113, 130, 135, 172, 173, 192, 193, 194, 201, 231, 281, 293
citizens, liii, lix, lxxv, 13, 83, 106, 130, 197, 216, 217, 219, 229, 230, 231
citizenship, 46, 76, 77, 83, 95, 119, 153
civil law, xxxi
civil servants, xlvii
civil society, xxxii, liv, 22, 26, 77, 99, 157, 240
civil war, xxiii, lxvii, lxix, lxxxi, lxxxvii, lxxxviii, 23, 24, 25, 27, 30, 38, 54, 55, 57, 58, 64, 70, 71, 80, 101, 133, 135, 160, 163, 165, 166, 174, 185, 188, 191, 197, 245, 257
civilization, 99

classes, 239, 247
clothing, xxviii, xxix, xxxiii, 19, 21, 71, 221, 290, 295
coalition troops, 13
Coast Guard, 173
Cold War, xxiii, 18
collaboration, xxiii, 134, 283
college students, 114
colonial rule, 247
colonization, xliv
Committee for Solidarity with Arab and Middle Eastern Political Prisoners, xii, 105
Communist Party, xxxviii, 178
community service, 125
conflict, xvii, xxxiii, xlvi, lii, lxii, lxiv, lxvi, lxvii, lxix, lxx, lxxi, lxxii, lxxv, lxxx, lxxxi, lxxxii, lxxxiii, lxxxviii, xc, xcii, 8, 18, 37, 38, 46, 50, 52, 62, 64, 80, 85, 125, 133, 135, 144, 159, 161, 163, 165, 170, 174, 175, 191, 196, 202, 205, 208, 232, 239, 249, 257, 290, 292
confrontation, 64, 105, 136, 162
conspiracy, xciii, 21, 49, 71, 95, 105, 106, 133, 154, 163, 259, 271
constituent groups, 211
constitutional amendment, 30
construction, 13, 29, 235
controversial, xvii, xx, xxvi, xxxvi, xlvii, lii, 19, 33, 64, 139, 233
corruption, xxxix, liii, lxxvi, 26, 58, 102, 103, 136, 145, 169, 170, 172, 174, 194, 237, 288
cost, lxiv, lxxx, 49, 170
counterterrorism, lxxi, lxxvii, 54, 174, 191, 197
Coup, 26
Court of Appeals, 252
crimes, xxv, lxxv, lxxviii, 49, 195, 271, 291
criminal behavior, 72
criminals, 10, 72, 260
criticism, liv, lxxxvi, 246
cruise missiles, 49
cultural practices, xxviii, 299
cultural tradition, 169
culture, xxv, xxvii, liii, 17, 53, 82, 178, 293, 294, 296

D

Daesh, see Islamic State of Iraq and Syria (ISIS), ix, xx, xxx, xxxiii, xxxv, xxxvii, xlii, li, lii, liii, liv, lv, lxvii, lxviii, lxix, lxx, lxxi, lxxii, lxxiii, lxxiv, lxxv, lxxvi, lxxvii, lxxviii, lxxix, lxxx, lxxxi, lxxxii, lxxxiii, lxxxiv, lxxxv, lxxxvi, lxxxvii, lxxxviii, lxxxix, xc, xci, xcii, xciii, xciv, xcv, xcvi, 3, 4, 14, 23, 24, 51, 53, 54, 57, 58, 62, 63, 64, 67, 86, 90, 91, 92, 94, 129, 130, 131, 150, 151, 157, 189, 190, 191, 192, 193, 194, 195, 196, 197, 198, 199, 200, 201, 202, 203, 205, 206, 207, 208, 211, 213, 214, 216, 218, 219, 221, 222, 235, 236, 246, 249, 259, 260, 261, 262, 267, 268, 272
Darfur, lxvi
death penalty, 27, 142
deaths, lxiii, 10, 52, 70, 213, 219, 233, 235
democracy, xxvii, xxxii, xxxiv, xxxvii, xxxix, xlvi, liv, 18, 20, 22, 24, 25, 27, 30, 45, 76, 120, 121, 122, 146, 170, 177, 181, 233, 240, 282
Democratic Front for the Liberation of Palestine, xii, 111, 112
Democratic Party, xiv, 24, 25, 120, 121, 140
democratization, 22
demonstrations, lxvii, 80, 82, 93, 120, 141, 166, 173, 241, 248
Department of the Treasury, 96, 215
destruction, xix, xxvi, xxxiv, lxiii, lxxvi, lxxxvii, 23, 45, 144, 160, 190
detainees, xcii, 26, 233
Developers Coalition, 113
discrimination, xxxvi, 83, 153
dissatisfaction, 240, 261
diversity, 282, 289
domestic issues, xxxi, 8
draft, lxxii, 93, 140, 171
dream, xlvi, liii, liv, 201
drug trafficking, xciv, 69, 71, 72
drugs, 71, 72, 145

E

early retirement, 22
eavesdropping, 26
economic change, 182
economic crisis, 21, 27
economic downturn, 24
economic growth, 83
economic ideology, 111
economic indicator, 83
economic policy, 114
economic problem, xxxii, 23, 25
economic reform, 177, 224
education, xxvii, xlvii, lxxxii, 17, 21, 26, 71, 95, 174, 199, 227, 251, 260, 281, 282, 284
educational attainment, 130
educational institutions, xxxi
educators, 282
egalitarianism, 238
Egypt, xiv, xxiii, xxiv, xxxi, xxxviii, xlii, xliv, xlv, xlvi, xlvii, xlix, l, li, lv, lvi, lviii, lix, lx, lxi, lxii, lxiii, lxv, lxvi, lxviii, lxxxiv, lxxxvi, xciii, 7, 46,

50, 51, 55, 58, 67, 68, 70, 89, 90, 92, 99, 100, 103, 115, 116, 119, 120, 121, 122, 123, 125, 126, 127, 135, 139, 140, 154, 163, 182, 183, 191, 199, 202, 215, 236, 237, 238, 239, 240, 241, 242, 243, 244, 246, 247, 249, 259, 260, 261, 262, 267, 285, 286, 294, 296
Egyptian Islamic Jihad, xii, xlix, 11, 115, 117, 279
Egyptian Salafist Movement, 125
El Kaide Turka, 274
election, l, lxvi, lxvii, lxix, lxx, lxxi, lxxiii, lxxvi, 10, 21, 23, 24, 25, 34, 77, 81, 82, 108, 113, 114, 122, 139, 140, 141, 153, 178, 181, 182, 198, 224, 233, 240, 245, 255, 283, 284, 286
embargo, xxviii, xci
embassy, lxiv, lxix, lxxxvii, 13, 30, 47, 49, 105, 115, 160, 223, 230
employees, lxxxii, 3, 13, 102, 145, 174
employment, liii, 260
endowments, 69, 278
enemies, xvii, xxv, xlvi, 26, 46, 51, 143, 185, 186, 193, 219, 243, 267, 271, 272, 292, 294
energy, 99, 174, 200
England, xli, lxv, 92, 201, 209, 254
environment, xxxiii, liii, 18, 25, 33, 76, 239, 240, 248, 275
equality, xxxii, liii, 121, 122, 200
equipment, lxx, lxxxiv, 86, 194, 261
ethnic groups, 22, 215
ethnic minority, 120
ethnicity, liv, 53, 82, 216, 219
ethnocentrism, liii
Europe, xviii, lii, liv, lvi, lxviii, lxxx, lxxxiii, 11, 20, 49, 67, 69, 70, 71, 102, 130, 214, 233, 243, 257
European Union, liv, lxviii, 20, 27, 102, 142, 159, 232
evidence, lxxxv, 90, 96, 140, 162, 217, 218, 230
evil, xxv, xxxv, 35, 52
evolution, ix, xvii, xx, xxxix, 20, 144
execution, lxxxiii, lxxxvi, lxxxvii, xc, 30, 69, 213, 215, 248
executive branch, 99
executive power, lxvi, 23
exile, lxv, 9, 26, 68, 108, 135, 165, 202, 231, 263, 273
explosives, lxv, lxxviii, xciv, 30, 106, 142, 173, 191, 208, 221
expulsion, 3, 160, 214
extremists, xxi, xxiv, xxxiv, xxxvi, xlvi, lxiii, lxiv, lxviii, lxxvii, lxxix, lxxx, lxxxiii, lxxxvii, 18, 30, 50, 52, 58, 70, 116, 133, 197, 248, 284, 292

F

failed states, liii
faith, xviii, xxi, xxiv, xxvi, xli, xlii, 48, 258, 288, 289, 290, 291, 294, 296
families, lxix, 93, 102, 195, 201
family life, xxix
family members, xxix, 171
fanaticism, 186
fasting, xviii, xxiv, 288, 289
fatwa, lxiv, 48, 280, 288
fear, xvii, xxi, xxii, 25, 26, 139, 219
federal government, 96
federalism, 93
financial, xxxiii, lxxxiv, 21, 35, 50, 80, 86, 92, 101, 105, 111, 141, 145, 173, 193, 197, 199, 200, 221, 231, 297
financial crisis, 21
financial institutions, 141
financial resources, 50, 197, 199
financial support, 80, 86, 92, 111, 231
firearms, 202
flight, 23, 63, 290
food, xxxiii, lxxvi, 13, 20, 95, 170, 175, 201, 289, 295, 296
foreign affairs, 90
foreign assistance, xxxvii
foreign companies, 114
foreign direct investment, 20
foreign investment, 114
foreign nationals, 13, 14, 29, 230
foreign policy, xx, xxxiv, lxvii, 25, 44, 100, 105, 114, 159, 224, 241
France, xviii, lx, lxi, lxii, lxv, lxviii, lxx, lxxi, lxxv, lxxix, lxxxiv, lxxxv, lxxxvii, lxxxix, xci, xciii, 63, 71, 72, 105, 106, 129, 160, 173, 202, 230, 232, 233, 247
franchise, 54, 58, 221
fraud, lxvii, lxx, 75
free choice, xxiv
freedom, xxiv, xxix, xxxiv, xxxvi, xli, 20, 22, 25, 40, 76, 77, 119, 122, 139, 231, 239, 241, 273, 283
Freedom and Justice Party, 119, 122, 139, 240
funding, xxiii, 33, 39, 86, 150, 159, 185, 191, 201, 216, 231, 257, 264, 283
fundraising, xci, 49, 71, 72, 101
funds, xxiii, 49, 71, 76, 85, 96, 145, 192, 193, 199, 231, 235, 242, 254, 299

G

Gaza Strip, 37, 38, 111, 274, 291

gender equality, xxxiv, xlv
general election, 23
Geneva Convention, 232
genocide, 195
geography, 53
Germany, lx, lxxxiii, xc, xciii, xcv, 71, 129, 202
global economy, xxiv
globalization, xxxix
God, x, xiv, xxiii, xxiv, xxv, xxvi, xxviii, xxxi, xxxiii, xxxv, xxxix, xlii, xlvii, lvii, 9, 45, 48, 51, 68, 108, 159, 163, 169, 170, 186, 196, 200, 213, 225, 287, 288, 291, 292, 293, 294, 296, 299
governance, xix, xxiv, xxxii, xxxiii, xxxv, xlvii, liii, liv, 17, 18, 20, 22, 25, 41, 58, 69, 75, 108, 119, 120, 139, 157, 158, 160, 170, 175, 178, 200, 237, 240, 261, 277, 278, 282, 289
government policy, xxxi, 173
government repression, xlv, 136
governments, xix, xxiii, xxx, xxxi, xxxii, xxxvi, xxxviii, xxxix, xl, xli, xlii, xliii, xliv, xlv, xlix, l, li, lx, lxxxii, lxxxiii, 7, 11, 19, 25, 26, 45, 47, 49, 54, 58, 71, 159, 173, 174, 189, 190, 191, 193, 194, 198, 229, 238, 239, 263, 268, 272, 274, 296
governor, lxxxvi, 214, 241
gradualist approach, xliv
grants, 102, 174, 277
Great Britain, xi, xliv, lix, lx, lxi, xciii, 13, 90, 95, 175, 202
Great Eastern Islamic Raiders' Front, 141
group activities, 239
growth, xx, xxiii, xxvi, xliii, 54, 79, 99, 205, 248
growth rate, 99
guidance, xxxii, xli, 93, 123, 139, 187, 213, 237
guidelines, 52, 186, 267
guilty, 34, 63, 96, 223, 242

H

Hamas, xii, xlix, l, li, lxv, lxvii, lxxx, xciii, 3, 37, 38, 89, 91, 103, 108, 112, 143, 144, 145, 146, 147, 149, 150, 151, 163, 181, 182, 185, 188, 217, 218, 235, 236, 238, 241, 243, 254, 255, 256, 257, 258, 259, 260
Hamas in Iraq, 149, 150
Haq Movement for Liberty and Democracy, 153
harassment, xc, 182
health, xxxix, 20, 21, 99, 199, 284
health care, 20
health insurance, 99
health services, xxxix
hegemony, xxviii
Hezbollah, ix, x, xix, xxxv, xxxvii, l, li, lii, lxiii, lxiv, lxviii, lxix, lxxii, lxxiii, lxxvii, lxxxi, xciii, 8, 34, 39, 40, 41, 47, 67, 79, 80, 91, 105, 106, 108, 116, 134, 147, 151, 159, 160, 161, 162, 163, 164, 185, 187, 188, 241, 243, 251, 254, 255, 259, 269, 273, 274
higher education, 21, 254, 293
history, xviii, xix, xx, xxi, xxvi, xxxv, xli, xliii, xliv, lix, lxxiii, lxxxiv, xciii, 10, 17, 22, 34, 54, 68, 100, 159, 161, 189, 203, 227, 237, 239, 245, 251, 282, 288
Hizb-i-Wahdat/Unity Party, xiii
homeland security, 54
homes, lxxv, lxxvi, 39, 72, 102, 200
homogeneity, xxxvi
hostage taking, xlvii
hostilities, xxvii, lxvi, 41, 285, 286, 290
House of Representatives, 188, 202, 209, 234
Houthi Movement, 165, 205
human, xxiii, xxiv, xxviii, xxxiv, liv, lxxiv, xcii, xcvi, 20, 23, 45, 76, 77, 160, 185, 195, 231, 233, 240, 260, 273, 289
human activity, xxiii
human rights, xxiv, xxxiv, liv, xcii, xcvi, 20, 23, 76, 77, 195, 231, 233, 240, 273, 289
humanitarian aid, lxxvi, 174
humanitarian crises, 175

I

ideals, xxviii, xxxiv, xl, xli, xlvii, lii, liii, 92, 123, 178, 185, 186, 237, 295, 299
identity, liii, 18, 19, 33, 35, 157, 166, 251, 273, 290
ideology, xviii, xix, xx, xxii, xxiv, xxv, xxvi, xxxvii, xl, xli, xlii, xliv, xlv, xlvi, xlix, l, lii, liv, 19, 33, 45, 62, 64, 67, 68, 69, 70, 71, 89, 99, 108, 121, 136, 139, 146, 149, 157, 159, 161, 166, 185, 186, 203, 207, 208, 213, 215, 219, 227, 230, 235, 240, 247, 257, 271, 281, 292
imperialism, xxv, xxvii, xxxiii, 274, 296
imprisonment, 106, 142
incarceration, 105
income, xxiv, 7, 93, 102, 119, 145, 199, 299
income distribution, 119
income inequality, xxiv
independence, xxix, xxxii, xlv, lix, lx, lxi, lxii, xcii, 27, 114, 153, 172, 186, 214, 238, 247, 258, 284
India, xiv, xxv, xxxvii, xlvii, lviii, lix, lx, lxi, 290
Indians, 47
individuals, xxviii, xxxvi, xlii, xlvi, lxxxvi, 26, 71, 101, 113, 120, 125, 130, 187, 188, 190, 193, 200, 201, 216, 230, 241, 242, 261, 273, 288, 295
indoctrination, xliv, 43
Indonesia, xi, xii, xiii, xiv, xxxv, xxxviii, xlvii, liv, lvi, lxi, lxxxvii, 100, 129, 130, 202, 296

industry, xix, 89
inequality, 200
inflation, 20, 178
infrastructure, xxxvi, 9, 13, 47, 123, 170, 190, 199, 260
injuries, lxviii, lxxxvi, 47, 49, 70, 173, 231
insanity, 297
insecurity, 37, 170
institutions, xxiv, xxxix, xliii, xlvi, xciii, 20, 25, 26, 99, 100, 125, 136, 143, 150, 187, 251, 254, 293, 297
insurgency, 4, 7, 13, 14, 15, 39, 51, 61, 62, 86, 90, 125, 131, 150, 159, 175, 189, 190, 194, 209, 261, 271, 273
intelligence, xlix, lxix, 8, 34, 45, 46, 47, 48, 49, 54, 71, 129, 134, 173, 197, 200, 213, 216, 218, 241, 242, 260, 261
intelligence gathering, 200
interest rates, 20
interference, 76, 77, 82
International Monetary Fund, 10, 20
international relations, xxx
intervention, xx, xxxii, lxxiv, lxxx, lxxxii, lxxxiv
intimidation, 4, 126, 145, 195
investment, 24, 62, 99, 297
Iraq War, lxiii, lxiv, 3, 50, 59, 85, 108, 187, 190, 230, 232, 273
Islamabad, 115
Islamic Action Front, lxiv, 181, 183, 245, 246
Islamic Army of Aden, 29
Islamic Iran Development and Justice Party, 178
Islamic law, xix, xxiii, xxviii, xxix, xxxii, xxxiii, xxxiv, xxxv, xxxvi, xliv, 18, 44, 64, 68, 85, 93, 99, 123, 126, 133, 140, 142, 145, 160, 200, 237, 238, 255, 272, 280, 287, 289, 290, 291, 293, 295, 296, 297
Islamic Revolutionary Guards, 113, 114, 185
Islamic society, xxvii, xxix, xxxii, 67, 75, 245
Islamic state, xxiii, xxxii, xxxiii, xxxiv, xxxv, xxxvi, xli, xliii, xliv, li, liii, liv, lviii, lxvi, lxviii, lxx, 44, 50, 53, 68, 79, 89, 121, 135, 145, 159, 160, 162, 181, 189, 238, 240, 272, 284
Islamic State in Yemen, 205, 206
Islamic State of Iraq, xii, xiii, lxvii, lxviii, 3, 57, 189, 191, 192, 203
Islamic State of Iraq and Syria (ISIS, IS), xii, xlii, 189, 203
Islamic world, xviii, xli, 50, 299
Islamism, 1, iii, ix, xvii, xviii, xxiv, xxvi, xxvii, xxviii, xxix, xxx, xxxi, xxxiii, xxxiv, xxxvii, xxxix, xl, xli, xlii, xliii, xliv, xlv, xlvi, xlvii, xlviii, xlix, li, lii, liv, lv, lvi, 1, 17, 18, 19, 20, 26, 27, 33, 35, 45, 100, 111, 120, 123, 136, 139, 236, 243, 245, 248, 249, 255, 257, 273, 282, 284, 291, 295
Islamophobia, xvii
Israel, xxviii, xxxiv, xlviii, lxi, lxii, lxiii, lxv, lxvii, lxxii, lxxiii, xciii, 4, 8, 37, 44, 48, 52, 79, 80, 89, 91, 92, 111, 112, 133, 143, 144, 145, 147, 159, 160, 161, 162, 163, 164, 170, 182, 190, 201, 208, 235, 236, 238, 239, 241, 245, 246, 248, 254, 255, 256, 257, 258, 259, 260, 261, 267, 271, 274
issues, xvii, xviii, xix, xx, xxxi, xxxvi, xxxix, xl, xli, xliii, xlv, xlvii, l, liv, lxxxiv, xc, xcv, 18, 20, 24, 33, 36, 45, 52, 58, 62, 75, 80, 94, 99, 111, 119, 139, 198, 227, 247, 253, 254, 272, 278, 282, 284, 285, 288, 293, 295, 297

J

Jamestown, 203, 220
Jews, xx, xlvi, lviii, lxv, 43, 48, 69, 116, 141, 144, 145, 235, 279, 280, 287, 292
jihad, xx, xxv, xxx, xxxi, xxxv, xlvi, xlvii, li, lx, lxv, 3, 7, 9, 11, 29, 43, 46, 48, 52, 57, 68, 69, 71, 72, 107, 125, 126, 135, 143, 144, 159, 160, 161, 172, 189, 193, 200, 221, 239, 254, 268, 273, 279, 280, 292, 298
jihadist, xix, xxx, xxxiii, xlvii, xlviii, xlix, liv, lxiv, lxvi, lxviii, lxx, lxxxiv, lxxxv, xcii, xcvi, 7, 9, 11, 13, 35, 39, 40, 43, 44, 46, 49, 51, 52, 53, 54, 57, 58, 64, 67, 68, 70, 71, 85, 90, 91, 92, 95, 129, 133, 135, 136, 141, 143, 146, 149, 150, 159, 161, 173, 185, 186, 187, 195, 196, 197, 199, 201, 205, 207, 221, 222, 235, 236, 242, 255, 258, 268, 271, 273, 274
Jordan, xiii, xxxviii, lx, lxi, lxiv, lxv, lxvi, lxvii, xcii, 7, 49, 73, 85, 95, 103, 133, 135, 145, 181, 182, 183, 190, 193, 201, 202, 216, 237, 239, 240, 245, 246, 253, 260, 262, 271, 286, 290
Jordanian Muslim Brotherhood, 245
journalists, lxix, 69, 102, 141, 182, 196, 273
judiciary, lix, 20, 22, 24, 26, 92, 240, 241, 251, 277
just society, xxxv
justification, xxiv, 186
juvenile delinquents, 72

K

Kenya, lxvi, lxxii, 48, 115, 116, 199, 202, 279, 280
Khomeini, Ruhollah, xix, xxxvii, xxxix, 160, 177, 186, 224, 255
Khorasan Group, xiii, 208, 221, 222
kidnapping, lxxix, lxxxv, lxxxvii, 9, 13, 14, 29, 68, 111, 145, 271

kill, lxxv, xcii, xciii, 4, 8, 13, 14, 48, 70, 92, 106, 145, 195, 219, 279
Kosovo, lvii, lxxxii
Kurd, lxxxiii, 198
Kurdish Islamic Movement (KIM), 85
Kurdistan Workers Party, 251
Kurds, lxxi, lxxiv, lxxxii, lxxxiii, lxxxiv, 17, 18, 20, 23, 24, 26, 86, 195, 196, 208, 249
Kuwait, xlix, lv, lxiv, lxvi, lxxiii, lxxiv, lxxv, lxxxix, 45, 48, 147, 200, 221, 237, 285

L

law enforcement, 13, 70, 96, 157
laws, xxiii, xxxvi, 68, 99, 114, 150, 160, 284, 289, 296
lawyers, 102, 145
leadership, xix, xliii, xlv, lxviii, lxxv, 8, 22, 25, 40, 44, 52, 53, 63, 71, 76, 80, 91, 99, 125, 146, 150, 154, 165, 187, 191, 202, 205, 207, 213, 214, 219, 223, 230, 237, 238, 245, 251, 271, 272, 277, 279, 283
Lebanon, xii, xix, xxxv, xxxvii, xlii, xlvii, xlix, l, li, lx, lxi, lxii, lxiii, lxiv, lxvi, lxviii, lxix, lxx, lxxi, lxxii, lxxxix, 7, 8, 33, 34, 39, 69, 70, 72, 79, 80, 91, 92, 105, 106, 108, 116, 129, 133, 134, 144, 154, 155, 159, 160, 161, 162, 163, 164, 190, 192, 205, 231, 243, 254, 255, 257, 258, 272, 273, 274, 277, 286, 290, 294, 299
legal protection, 102, 140
legislation, xxxix, lxiii, 75, 139, 140, 181, 239, 284
legislative authority, 240
liberation, xlviii, 103, 145
loans, 102, 106, 200
local authorities, 62
local community, 52
local government, lxx, 199
logistics, 71, 216, 218, 261
loyalty, 36, 123, 125, 160, 170, 186, 187, 193, 207, 231, 259, 272

M

major decisions, 45
major issues, lxxxvi, 23, 274
Malaysia, xi, xiv, xv, xlvi, 129, 130, 238
marginalization, lxxxiv
marketplace, xxxii, xxxix, lxxvi, lxxxvi
marriage, xxxiii, 102, 199, 231, 290, 295
martial law, 245
Mauritania, lxix, lxx, lxxii, 199

media, ix, xxi, xxvi, xxxix, liv, lxxxii, lxxxiii, 22, 24, 50, 68, 69, 70, 99, 119, 186, 190, 201, 214, 215, 240, 242, 260
medical, 30, 145, 216, 260, 289
Mediterranean, lviii, 57, 145, 164, 259, 260
Middle East, xii, xviii, xxiii, xxviii, xxx, xxxi, xxxii, xxxiii, xxxvii, xl, xlvii, xlix, liii, liv, lvi, lx, lxvi, lxviii, lxxviii, lxxxvi, lxxxvii, xciii, 1, 4, 5, 10, 21, 22, 24, 31, 34, 36, 37, 38, 45, 48, 49, 51, 52, 53, 54, 71, 72, 77, 86, 100, 105, 117, 131, 133, 140, 142, 147, 151, 159, 163, 164, 173, 187, 188, 191, 197, 200, 202, 207, 208, 214, 225, 233, 234, 237, 242, 244, 245, 250, 255, 256, 257, 258, 267, 268, 272, 274, 278, 280, 285, 286, 289, 293, 294, 295, 297
migrants, lxxxiii, xciii, 82
migration, lxxx, lxxxiii
militancy, xx, xxii, xxxi, lxxxiii, 23, 115, 125, 144, 194, 273
military, xxiii, xxv, xxxii, xxxiv, xxxviii, xlix, liii, lix, lxi, lxiii, lxiv, lxv, lxvii, lxviii, lxix, lxx, lxxi, lxxiii, lxxiv, lxxv, lxxvi, lxxviii, lxxix, lxxx, lxxxi, lxxxii, lxxxiii, lxxxiv, lxxxv, lxxxvi, lxxxvii, lxxxviii, xc, xci, xcii, xciii, xciv, xcv, 3, 9, 10, 13, 17, 18, 19, 20, 21, 22, 23, 25, 26, 37, 40, 44, 45, 46, 47, 48, 49, 50, 51, 52, 53, 54, 58, 62, 63, 64, 69, 85, 86, 90, 93, 94, 100, 105, 114, 115, 116, 122, 126, 133, 134, 135, 136, 139, 143, 145, 149, 150, 159, 160, 161, 163, 165, 166, 170, 171, 172, 173, 174, 175, 178, 185, 186, 187, 191, 192, 193, 194, 195, 196, 197, 198, 200, 201, 202, 208, 211, 214, 216, 219, 222, 230, 232, 233, 236, 237, 238, 239, 240, 241, 242, 247, 251, 254, 257, 260, 261, 263, 264, 268, 277, 279, 285
military aid, lxxxii
military government, 122, 126, 139, 241, 251
military junta, 238
Milli Nizam Party (MNP), 18, 227
minorities, 20, 107, 195, 208, 231
minority groups, 140, 249
modernity, xxi, xxx, xxxviii, xl, xlviii, 35, 71
modernization, xix, xxxi, xl, lix, 17, 35, 36
money laundering, xci, 76, 267
Morocco, xiv, xlv, lix, lxi, lxii, lxvi, lxvii, 67, 70, 72, 199, 238
Morsi, Mohammed, 89, 139, 240
Mujahideen Shura Council (Shura Council of the Mujahideen of Iraq), lxvii
Mujahideen-e-Khalq Organization (MEK), 229, 230, 231, 232, 233, 234
murder, xxxvi, lxxxiii, 34, 70, 71, 115, 145, 162, 195, 271, 290

Muslim Brotherhood, ix, x, xiv, xxii, xxvii, xxxi, xxxiii, xxxv, xxxvii, xxxviii, xl, xliii, xliv, xlv, l, lii, lv, lx, lxi, lxii, lxiii, lxv, lxvi, lxvii, lxviii, 3, 19, 33, 46, 47, 53, 64, 67, 68, 72, 90, 92, 99, 115, 116, 119, 120, 121, 122, 123, 125, 126, 135, 136, 137,139, 140, 143, 144, 145, 146, 147, 154, 181, 182, 183, 236, 237, 238, 239, 242, 243, 244, 245, 246, 247, 248, 249, 250, 253, 255, 256, 261, 281, 282, 283, 284, 289, 291

Muslim Brotherhood in Jordan, 245, 246

Muslim Brotherhood in Syria, 136, 243, 247, 249, 250

Muslim extremists, 71

Muslims, xii, xvii, xviii, xix, xxi, xxii, xxiii, xxiv, xxv, xxvi, xxvii, xxviii, xxx, xxxi, xxxii, xxxiii, xxxiv, xxxv, xxxvi, xxxvii, xxxviii, xxxix, xli, xlii, xliii, xlv, xlvi, xlvii, xlviii, xlix, lii, liii, liv, lviii, lix, lxv, lxx, lxxiv, xciii, xciv, 7, 11, 17, 20, 33, 37, 43, 44, 45, 48, 50, 51, 55, 58, 64, 67, 68, 69, 70, 71, 72, 79, 89, 94, 97, 103, 105, 107, 117, 125, 126, 129, 141, 144, 159, 160, 190, 191, 193, 205, 219, 237, 238, 239, 248, 267, 268, 269, 277, 287, 288, 289, 290, 291, 293, 294, 295, 296, 297, 298, 299

N

national identity, xxxii, 82

national origin, 129

national security, lxxviii, lxxxviii, 24, 49, 58, 113, 114, 187

National Security Agency, xcii

National Security Council, 187

National Turkish Student Union, 251

nationalism, xx, xxxvii, xxxviii, liii, 17, 19, 146, 153, 238, 251, 294

nationalists, 227, 272

news coverage, ix

Nigeria, xlvii, lvi, lxix, lxx, lxxii, lxxiii, lxxiv, lxxv, lxxvi, lxxviii, lxxxi, lxxxiii, lxxxv, lxxxviii, lxxxix, xciii, xciv, xcv, xcvi, 63, 199, 201

Nile, 100, 242, 261

North Africa, 51, 55, 69, 214, 243, 294

North America, 11, 67, 71

North Atlantic Treaty Organization, 18

Northwest Airlines, 63

nuclear weapons, lxxvii

O

Obama Administration, 243

obedience, xlv, 35, 51, 187, 192, 291, 299

occupied territories, 200, 216

officials, xlvii, li, lxv, lxx, lxxxi, lxxxii, lxxxv, lxxxvi, lxxxvii, lxxxviii, xc, 11, 64, 70, 76, 89, 90, 105, 106, 139, 161, 162, 171, 173, 182, 197, 215, 231, 232, 240, 248, 263, 285

oil, xix, xxiii, xxviii, xxxii, xliv, lxx, lxxv, lxxxiv, lxxxv, lxxxvi, xc, 8, 30, 36, 45, 170, 173, 192, 195, 196, 199, 200, 201, 214, 218, 219

oil production, xliv, 196

online media, 218

operations, lxv, lxxi, xciii, 11, 13, 35, 40, 47, 49, 50, 51, 63, 64, 71, 90, 92, 95, 116, 129, 130, 142, 150, 161, 170, 173, 174, 192, 197, 199, 201, 207, 208, 216, 221, 222, 231, 233, 235, 236, 248, 255

opportunities, 51, 52, 58, 102, 191, 197, 285

opposition parties, 140, 182, 284

oppression, xxxv, xxxix, liv, 7, 48, 141, 237

oversight, 35, 122, 172, 187, 284

P

Pakistan, xiii, xiv, xxxvii, xli, xlviii, lxi, lxvi, lxvii, lxxv, xciv, 7, 8, 46, 47, 48, 50, 51, 52, 53, 95, 96, 109, 115, 154, 191, 201, 221, 271, 273, 279, 281, 290, 293

Palestinian Authority, xciii, 112, 255

Palestinian Islamic Jihad, xiv, lxv, 37, 253, 256, 257, 258

Palestinian uprising, 144

Parliament, lxxxv, xci, 19, 24, 35, 40, 75, 80, 100, 154, 181, 224, 247, 252, 264, 284, 286

peace, xxii, xxiv, xxxv, xli, liv, lxii, lxiii, lxv, lxviii, lxxi, lxxiv, lxxv, lxxxi, lxxxiv, lxxxviii, lxxxix, xc, xcv, 24, 26, 37, 51, 76, 111, 112, 144, 160, 161, 172, 178, 181, 239, 241, 254, 257, 258, 274, 285, 291, 297

peace accord, lxiii, lxv, 239, 285

peace process, 24, 26, 37, 111, 254

peacekeepers, 161

peacekeeping, 160

Pentagon, lxvi, lxxix, 50, 116, 209

Persian Gulf, xlviii, 36, 59, 145

personal benefit, 103

personal hygiene, xxxiii

personal life, xxxiii, 292

personal relations, 298

personal relationship, 298

personal views, 252

petroleum, 45, 174, 199

Philadelphia, lv, lvi, lxxxvi, 264

Philippines, xi, xiv, lxxxii, 49, 95

pluralism, xxiv, li, lxxviii, 33

police, liii, lxx, lxxiii, lxxv, lxxvii, lxxxiii, lxxxvi, xc, xci, xcv, 9, 11, 23, 26, 70, 90, 93, 105, 129, 154, 173, 194, 199, 238, 242, 251, 260, 285
policy, xix, xxxii, xxxvi, 120, 214, 216, 232, 265, 282, 283
policy choice, 282
policy initiative, 282
political instability, 174
political leaders, 58, 69, 198, 201
political opposition, 21, 22, 24, 285
political participation, 100, 241
political pluralism, xlv, li, 122
political power, xxxi, xxxii, xxxvi, xlviii, lii, 19, 23, 53, 146, 161, 248, 285, 292
political system, xxx, xxxi, xxxiii, li, 39, 52, 82, 99, 125, 140, 165, 224
politics, xxiv, xxvi, xxviii, xxxi, xxxii, xli, 15, 18, 19, 22, 25, 35, 52, 57, 62, 100, 103, 112, 140, 154, 161, 177, 178, 187, 223, 224, 241, 261, 281, 283, 293, 295
polling, 182
Popular Front, xiv, 82, 111, 112, 257, 258
Popular Front for the Liberation of Palestine, xiv, 111, 112, 257, 258
Popular Front for the Liberation of Palestine-General Command, 112
popular support, xxxix, l, 24, 50, 51, 54, 81, 120, 140, 143, 185, 242, 283
popular vote, 23, 25
population, xx, xxv, xxxviii, xlix, 62, 75, 79, 83, 108, 153, 157, 158, 169, 170, 175, 194, 200, 219, 282, 287
poverty, xxxi, xxxix, 7, 99, 102, 125, 170, 201
poverty reduction, 102
prayer, xxiv, xxix, xli, 136, 237, 287, 288, 289, 291, 293, 294
prejudice, xvii, liv
presidency, lxvi, 21, 99, 126, 172, 174, 240
prisoners, lxiv, lxvii, lxxvi, lxxviii, lxxxiii, lxxxvi, 68, 76, 111, 145, 162, 192, 194, 239
prisoners of war, 192
prisons, 72, 161
private sector, 35, 99
propaganda, xlvi, 52, 62, 63, 90, 129, 130, 136, 144, 160, 196, 197, 200, 215, 217, 219, 235
public administration, 240
public education, xxxix
public life, xxviii, xxxiii
public officials, xxxix, 57
public opinion, 223, 242, 246
public policy, xxiv, xxxii
public service, 170, 200
public support, 166

punishment, xxxiii, 291, 298

Q

Qutb, Sayyid, xxxvii, xl, xliv, lii, lv, lxii, 33

R

race, 99, 238, 283
racism, liii, 274
racketeering, 96
radicalism, xviii, 298
radicalization, 271
radicals, xxv
Ramadan, lxxv, lxxvi, 255, 289, 295, 296
rebel groups, lxix, 157, 193, 211
recruiting, 39, 63, 64, 116, 130, 185, 188, 215
refugee camps, lxiii, 91, 175, 254
refugees, lxix, lxx, lxxi, lxxii, lxxx, lxxxiii, lxxxix, 24, 79, 91, 95, 182, 195, 233, 254
relief, 47, 95, 157, 158, 192, 207, 224
religion, xvii, xviii, xx, xxi, xxiv, xxvi, xxviii, xxxi, xxxiii, xxxiv, xli, xlii, liv, lviii, lxi, 17, 18, 43, 45, 99, 100, 107, 121, 136, 139, 144, 166, 177, 195, 216, 241, 251, 284, 291, 293, 294
religiosity, xxvi, 43, 146, 249
religious beliefs, xlii, 215
religious observances, 205
repression, liii, 25, 170, 186, 187, 249
Republican Party, 17
resistance, lxxxvi, xciii, 7, 9, 21, 51, 94, 143, 160, 166, 173, 177, 193, 229, 230, 231
resources, xxxvi, 11, 43, 46, 52, 79, 85, 158, 163, 170, 201, 211, 214, 235, 259, 260
response, xviii, xxviii, 40, 50, 54, 76, 90, 102, 105, 153, 166, 197, 198, 207, 213, 232, 285
retaliation, lxxxiv, lxxxv, 29, 63, 89, 107, 235
revenue, xxviii, xxxii, lxxxvii, 170, 192, 193, 199, 200, 216
Revolutionary Guard, lxxxviii, 41, 113, 114, 178, 185, 186, 188, 198, 217, 254, 277
rhetoric, ix, xx, xxx, xli, xlv, xlvi, xlix, li, lii, lv, 9, 11, 20, 44, 144, 162, 207, 215, 219, 241, 282
rights, iv, xx, xxv, xxix, xxxiii, xxxvi, liv, lxxxii, 20, 22, 23, 35, 76, 77, 79, 82, 99, 102, 111, 120, 139, 160, 231, 273, 282
rule of law, liii, 20, 24, 27, 76, 119
Russia, xx, xxxviii, lx, lxxvii, lxxx, lxxxi, lxxxiv, lxxxvi, lxxxviii, xciii, 21, 25, 92, 95, 200, 202

S

safe haven, 52, 211, 216
safe havens, 216
Salafiyya, xxviii, 70, 121, 122, 126, 296
Salvation Army, lxv
sanctions, xix, xxiv, xxxii, lxxxvi, 25, 163
Saudi Arabia, xiv, xviii, xix, xx, xxiii, xxxiv, xxxvii, xxxviii, xlii, xliii, xliv, xlv, xlix, li, lii, lviii, lix, lx, lxi, lxiv, lxv, lxxiv, lxxvi, lxxvii, lxxviii, lxxix, lxxxiv, lxxxvi, lxxxvii, lxxxviii, lxxxix, xci, xcii, xciii, xciv, 7, 8, 35, 36, 45, 46, 47, 48, 58, 61, 64, 70, 82, 95, 96, 134, 145, 154, 162, 163, 169, 170, 173, 174, 175, 185, 193, 199, 202, 205, 216, 242, 259, 279, 285, 290, 291, 293, 294, 296, 299
school, xix, xxiii, xxviii, xxxvii, xli, xliv, xlvii, lvii, lviii, lxxix, xc, xcv, 26, 29, 33, 54, 105, 111, 188, 199, 237, 239, 281, 290, 291, 293, 296
schooling, 281
science, xxvii, xxviii, 289
scientific knowledge, xviii
sectarianism, 62, 76, 80, 249
secularism, xxiv, xxviii, xxxiv, 17, 19, 20, 21, 26, 29, 108, 141, 227, 294
security, xxxvi, liii, lxiii, lxxii, lxxvii, lxxviii, lxxxiv, lxxxvii, lxxxix, xcv, 3, 9, 13, 24, 25, 27, 29, 30, 40, 41, 51, 53, 58, 64, 68, 70, 76, 86, 89, 90, 93, 111, 114, 116, 125, 126, 130, 133, 136, 153, 154, 162, 165, 170, 172, 178, 190, 191, 193, 194, 195, 196, 198, 200, 201, 207, 208, 215, 231, 232, 233, 236, 241, 242, 260, 261, 272, 277, 285
security assistance, 170, 193
security forces, xxxvi, lxiii, lxxii, lxxvii, lxxxix, xcv, 3, 9, 29, 30, 53, 58, 68, 70, 76, 86, 89, 111, 125, 126, 133, 136, 153, 194, 195, 201, 207, 215, 233, 236, 242, 260, 272, 277
security services, 70, 190, 260
seizure, lxxxii, 214, 230
semantics, xx, 217
service provider, 41
services, iv, xxxix, lxix, 8, 34, 52, 126, 134, 193, 199, 242, 252
sexual behavior, xxi, xxix
sexual desire, 289
sexual intercourse, 296
sexual orientation, liv
Sharia, xxiv, xxv, xxviii, xxxii, xxxiii, xxxiv, xli, xlvi, xlviii, xlix, li, liii, lxii, lxiii, xcii, 18, 35, 44, 45, 51, 52, 53, 61, 62, 64, 69, 86, 91, 93, 107, 120, 121, 122, 123, 126, 133, 139, 140, 142, 145, 146, 150, 160, 174, 181, 189, 194, 200, 208, 238, 239, 240, 249, 255, 257, 272, 288, 289, 291, 294, 296, 297, 299

Shiite factions, 8
Shiites, xiv, xix, xx, xxxvii, xliv, xlv, lxxxii, lxxxv, lxxxvi, 3, 4, 8, 79, 81, 82, 83, 155, 159, 191, 193, 194, 196, 248, 271, 291, 293, 295, 297
Sinai, lxii, lxxxiv, lxxxvi, xciii, xcvi, 7, 89, 90, 199, 200, 235, 236, 239, 242, 259, 260, 261
slavery, lxxii, lxxiv
slaves, lxxi, 294
smuggling, lxxxv, 71, 90, 170, 173, 193, 199, 260
social activities, 93
social behavior, xli
social change, xxi, 289
social control, 193
social inequalities, 285
social interaction, xxix
social justice, xxxv, 114, 227
social network, 54
social norms, xxvii, xlvi
social order, 227
social organization, xxxiii
social problems, 170, 178
social programs, 121
social services, 20, 21, 122, 140, 170, 237, 239, 240, 260
social structure, 107, 296
social welfare, xxxix, 143, 237
socialism, xxviii, xxxviii
society, xxi, xxiii, xxiv, xxviii, xxix, xxxi, xxxiii, xxxiv, xxxv, xxxvii, xxxviii, xliv, xlvi, l, li, lxxxiii, 18, 20, 24, 68, 71, 72, 76, 81, 82, 102, 107, 136, 140, 143, 157, 160, 165, 177, 200, 237, 239, 240, 245, 248, 288, 292, 296
Society of Combatant Clergy, 178
Somalia, xi, xii, xxxviii, xlix, lv, lxii, lxxiv, xci, 46, 47, 48, 52, 55, 70, 199, 201
Sons of Iraq, 3, 57, 149
South Asia, xiii, xviii, xxiii, 52, 207, 234
South Korea, 89
Southeast Asia, xiii, lx
sovereign state, 192
sovereignty, 153, 186
Soviet Union, xxv, xxxi, lxiii, 257
Spain, xviii, lviii, 44, 71, 72, 129, 160, 202
Spring, xxxv, liii, lxi, xcii, 9, 22, 40, 51, 52, 61, 75, 77, 82, 100, 119, 126, 130, 139, 154, 163, 166, 194, 232, 233, 235, 240, 241, 248, 249, 261, 284, 285
St. Petersburg, lxxxiv, xci
state of emergency, 242
State of Sinai, 259, 260
Strait of Hormuz, 8
stress, xxiv, 80, 170, 239, 267

structure, lxxxvii, 24, 37, 40, 67, 79, 135, 153, 187, 217, 277, 278
Sudan, xiii, xlvi, xlix, l, li, lviii, lix, lxii, lxiv, lxv, lxvi, 46, 47, 48, 49, 69, 70, 95, 100, 116, 199, 237, 243, 254, 256, 291
suicide, xlvii, xlix, lxiv, lxvi, lxix, lxxiii, lxxiv, lxxv, lxxvi, lxxvii, lxxxi, lxxxii, lxxxiv, lxxxv, lxxxvii, lxxxviii, lxxxix, xci, xcii, xciii, xciv, xcv, 3, 4, 8, 30, 37, 64, 70, 85, 89, 116, 130, 142, 144, 159, 160, 181, 185, 194, 198, 202, 207, 221, 232, 254, 255, 260, 271, 274
suicide attacks, 64, 160, 194, 254, 255
suicide bombers, lxxv, lxxxiv, lxxxv, lxxxviii, 198, 274
Sunnis, xix, xxxvii, xliv, lxxi, 4, 8, 54, 58, 83, 86, 92, 136, 163, 190, 193, 194, 198, 233, 248, 287, 295, 298
suppression, lxxviii, 245, 261
Supreme Council, xiii, 94, 108, 263, 265
Supreme Council for Islamic Revolution in Iraq (SCRI), 263
Supreme Court, lxxii
Syria, xii, xiii, xx, xxxv, xxxvii, xxxviii, xlvii, li, lii, liii, lvii, lviii, lix, lx, lxi, lxvi, lxvii, lxviii, lxix, lxx, lxxi, lxxii, lxxiv, lxxvi, lxxvii, lxxviii, lxxix, lxxx, lxxxi, lxxxii, lxxxiii, lxxxiv, lxxxv, lxxxvi, lxxxvii, lxxxviii, lxxxix, xc, xcii, xciii, xciv, xcv, 7, 9, 14, 23, 26, 33, 34, 36, 52, 54, 55, 57, 58, 62, 80, 90, 91, 92, 111, 129, 130, 131, 133, 134, 135, 136, 137, 147, 151, 157, 158, 162, 163, 173, 174, 182, 183, 185, 189, 190, 191, 192, 193, 194, 196, 197, 198, 199, 200, 201, 202, 203, 207, 208, 209, 211, 216, 221, 222, 233, 235, 237, 239, 243, 246, 247, 248, 249, 250, 254, 255, 257, 268, 271, 272, 287

T

Tajikistan, xiii, xv, 48, 95
Taliban, lxv, lxvi, lxviii, lxxiv, lxxv, lxxvi, lxxviii, lxxx, lxxxi, lxxxii, lxxxiii, xciv, xcv, 48, 49, 50, 52, 61, 69, 71, 85, 221, 222, 273, 293, 297
Tanzania, lxvi, 48, 115, 116, 279
territory, xxxii, xxxv, xlvii, li, lix, lx, lxviii, lxix, lxx, lxxxi, lxxxii, lxxxv, lxxxvii, lxxxviii, xci, xcii, xciii, 13, 34, 38, 44, 50, 51, 53, 54, 58, 62, 64, 85, 130, 143, 157, 158, 160, 166, 189, 192, 195, 196, 197, 198, 199, 200, 201, 202, 239, 254, 259, 288
terrorism, xvii, xxi, xxii, xxxiv, xxxvi, xlii, xlviii, lxvi, lxxii, lxxxvi, xcii, xciv, xcvi, 7, 22, 23, 30, 37, 49, 51, 63, 71, 72, 76, 89, 96, 101, 126, 129, 159, 170, 174, 181, 186, 232, 233, 260
terrorist activities, lxv, 86, 105, 116, 133, 135, 232
terrorist acts, xlix, lxvi
terrorist attack, xlix, lxxiii, lxxiv, lxxxv, lxxxix, xciii, 11, 37, 43, 53, 61, 70, 71, 85, 90, 126, 129, 130, 143, 194, 221, 233
terrorist groups, xxxvi, xxxvii, 70
terrorist organization, xlii, lii, lxviii, lxxii, xcv, 26, 37, 111, 142, 189, 190, 194, 201, 215, 229, 232, 235, 242, 243, 279
terrorists, xxi, xxxvi, lxvi, lxxv, lxxviii, lxxxi, lxxxii, xc, 10, 58, 70, 96, 105, 161, 190, 260
Third World, 52, 109, 147
threats, lxxxiii, 11, 22, 186, 195, 197
torture, lxxv, lxxxiii, 3, 26
trade, 26, 224
trading partners, 26
traditions, xviii, xx, xxii, xlii, 161, 169, 205, 287
trafficking, 71, 72, 101
training, xxiii, lxxii, lxxix, xcii, xcv, 11, 39, 43, 46, 47, 48, 49, 70, 85, 86, 89, 95, 102, 116, 130, 133, 166, 170, 185, 187, 188, 257, 258, 260, 271, 273
transformation, xxxvii, xxxix, 22, 171, 251
treatment, lxxiii, lxxxvi, 94, 165, 216, 260
trial, 106, 142, 241
tribal rights, 94
tribesmen, 57, 192, 214, 284
Turkey, xi, xlvi, l, lv, lvii, lix, lx, lxii, lxv, lxvii, lxxxi, lxxxiii, lxxxvii, 12, 17, 18, 19, 20, 21, 22, 23, 24, 25, 26, 27, 44, 49, 100, 114, 141, 142, 183, 201, 202, 227, 228, 252, 273, 274, 275, 290
Turkish Hezbollah, 251, 273
Turkish Islamic Jihad, 273, 274
Turks, lvii, 20, 21, 23, 24, 25, 273

U

U.S. Department of Labor, 101
U.S. District Judge, 96
U.S. history, lxxxix
Ukraine, 92
United Kingdom, lx, 41, 95, 265, 269
United Nations, lxi, lxix, lxxxvi, lxxxvii, lxxxviii, xciv, 8, 95, 96, 153, 172, 174, 190, 195, 257
United States, xii, xxi, xxiii, xxxiii, xxxiv, xlix, lii, liv, lxvi, lxviii, lxxi, lxxvi, lxxxiv, lxxxvi, lxxxviii, xciii, xciv, xcv, 13, 18, 23, 26, 44, 48, 49, 50, 51, 52, 53, 54, 57, 58, 61, 63, 65, 71, 90, 94, 95, 126, 133, 142, 149, 151, 159, 160, 162, 170, 171, 173, 174, 175, 185, 190, 193, 194, 196, 197, 198, 200, 202, 203, 208, 214, 215, 221, 222, 223, 224, 229, 232, 233, 242, 263, 271, 272, 279, 299
Universal Declaration of Human Rights, xxxiv
universities, 19, 26, 102, 253

urban, xxxii, lxxi, 17, 20, 37, 62, 157, 201, 247, 273
urban areas, lxxi, 20, 37, 62, 157, 201, 273
USS Cole, lxvi, 30, 116
Uzbekistan, xiii, liv, xciii, 86, 267

V

veneration, xlvii, 35, 288, 297
victims, lxxv, lxxvii, lxxxvii, 72, 95, 177, 274, 290
videos, lxxxix, 214, 219, 236, 271
violence, xviii, xxii, xxiv, xxv, xxx, xxxi, xxxiii, xxxiv, xxxv, xlvii, xlviii, xlix, li, liii, liv, lxxi, lxxvi, lxxix, lxxxii, lxxxiv, lxxxviii, 20, 23, 24, 25, 30, 33, 37, 44, 50, 58, 68, 70, 76, 77, 83, 93, 100, 107, 111, 120, 122, 125, 126, 133, 135, 149, 150, 153, 162, 170, 173, 182, 185, 190, 191, 201, 233, 237, 239, 241, 242, 243, 253, 254, 257, 258, 259, 267, 283, 284, 285, 292
violent extremist, xxxiv
vision, xxxv, xliv, lii, liii, liv, 19, 26, 52, 53, 100, 149, 162, 201, 219, 268, 295
vote, l, lxvii, xcv, 21, 22, 24, 25, 114, 119, 122, 162, 178, 181, 182, 240, 283
voters, lxvii, xcii, 19, 21, 23, 24, 25, 75, 114, 153, 227, 241, 247
voting, xcv, 36, 119, 240

W

Wahhabism, xx, xxiii, xxviii, xxx, xliv, lviii, 282, 288, 293, 296, 299
Waliy-al-Faqih, 277
war, xix, xxiii, xxviii, xxxv, xxxvii, xlii, lx, lxviii, lxx, lxxii, lxxv, lxxvi, lxxxiv, lxxxv, lxxxviii, xc, xci, 8, 13, 27, 29, 46, 48, 50, 54, 68, 80, 89, 160, 161, 162, 163, 175, 177, 185, 186, 193, 195, 196, 202, 219, 232, 254, 263, 277, 279, 280, 292
war crimes, lxxv, xci, 195
War on Terror, lxvi, 106
Washington, liv, lvi, lxvi, 4, 10, 12, 36, 50, 55, 59, 64, 65, 77, 80, 94, 96, 103, 106, 114, 116, 137, 147, 175, 182, 188, 202, 203, 209, 220, 222, 232, 233, 234, 236, 246, 256, 258, 269, 272, 274, 280, 286
Waziristan, 268

wealth, xviii, xxiii, xliv, 99, 188
weapons, xx, xlvi, lxxi, lxxvi, lxxviii, lxxix, lxxxi, lxxxviii, 39, 49, 71, 106, 116, 145, 160, 162, 173, 185, 218, 221, 231, 257, 260
weapons of mass destruction, xlvi
Wefaq, 36, 75, 76, 81, 82, 83, 153, 154, 299
West Africa, xcvi
West Bank, lxii, 37, 38, 111, 147, 236, 254, 255, 256, 258, 274, 291
Western Europe, xviii, 17, 18, 274, 299
Western orientation, 238
White House, lxxvi, 10
withdrawal, xlvii, lxxiii, lxxx, lxxxiii, lxxxiv, 50, 71, 94, 150, 161, 191, 214, 219, 233, 254
workers, 14, 191, 199, 230, 271
working class, xxxii, 111
World Islamic Front for Jihad Against Jews and Crusaders, 43, 48, 279, 280
world order, xl
World Trade Center, lxv, lxvi, xciii, 47, 49, 50, 116
World War I, xxvii, xxxi, xxxviii, lx, 17, 18
worldview, xlvii, 193
worldwide, ix, xviii, xix, xxii, xxiv, xxvi, xxviii, xxx, xxxix, xl, xlvi, xlvii, liii, lxv, lxix, lxxxv, 11, 24, 43, 44, 46, 47, 49, 50, 52, 54, 64, 67, 69, 71, 86, 96, 129, 159, 185, 191, 193, 200, 201, 208, 237, 273, 277, 279, 288, 299

Y

Yale University, lvi, 108, 140, 147, 151, 179, 209, 252
Yassin, Ahmed, 143, 144
Yemen, xi, xxxviii, xlix, lii, lxvi, lxvii, lxix, lxx, lxxi, lxxii, lxxiii, lxxiv, lxxv, lxxvi, lxxvii, lxxx, lxxxi, lxxxvii, lxxxviii, xc, xci, xcii, xciii, xciv, xcv, 29, 30, 31, 46, 52, 54, 55, 61, 62, 63, 64, 65, 92, 95, 101, 102, 103, 111, 116, 165, 166, 169, 170, 171, 172, 173, 174, 175, 176, 183, 199, 202, 205, 206, 208, 216, 221, 237, 259, 281, 282, 283, 284, 285, 286
Yemeni Association for Reform, 281
young people, xlvii, liii, 170, 281
Yousef, Ramzi Ahmed, 47, 49